See also: "HOW LEE LOST THE
CIVIL WAR."
Author: ?
also: GRANT by Jean Edward Smith
He was a great man, General and
President

Lee's Cavalrymen

A History of the Mounted Forces
of the Army of Northern Virginia,
1861–1865

Edward G. Longacre

Troop Strength - U.S.
Company: 100 men
Regiment: 1000
Brigade: 4000
Division: 12,000
Corps: 24,000

STACKPOLE
BOOKS

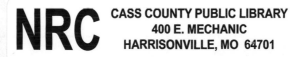

Published by
STACKPOLE BOOKS
5067 Ritter Road
Mechanicsburg, PA 17055
www.stackpolebooks.com

Printed in the United States of America

10 9 8 7 6 5 4 3 2 1

FIRST EDITION

Library of Congress Cataloging-in-Publication Data

Longacre, Edward G., 1946–
    Lee's cavalrymen : a history of the mounted forces of the Army of Northern
Virginia / Edward G. Longacre
      p. cm.
    ISBN 0-8117-0898-5
    1. Confederate States of America. Army of Northern Virginia—Cavalry.
  2. United States—History—Civil War, 1861–1865—Cavalry operations. I. Title

    E470.2.L66 2002
    973.7'455—dc21
2001055046

To my ancestors in the mounted ranks of the Confederacy:

Harris M. Flanagin, 2nd Arkansas Mounted Rifles
Franklin Hackney, 8th Missouri Cavalry
Isaac Hackney, 8th Missouri Cavalry
Benjamin F. Longacre, 11th Virginia Cavalry
Calvin J. Longacre, 11th Virginia Cavalry
David M. Longacre, 3rd and 10th Missouri Cavalry
Martin V. Longacre, 10th Missouri Cavalry

CONTENTS

ACKNOWLEDGMENTS

Dozens of people and institutions helped me research this study. The list of those to whom I am indebted begins with my highly productive team of research assistants: Charles Bowery, Raleigh, N.C.; Andre Fleche, Charlottesville, Va.; Linda Sellars, Chapel Hill, N.C.; and Bryce Suderow, Washington, D.C. I owe almost as large a debt to those Confederate historians who took the time to criticize and improve this book in draft form: Scott Mauger, Hopewell, Va.; Horace Mewborn, Springfield, Va.; Tom Perry, Ararat, Va.; and Bob Trout, Myerstown, Pa.

Others whose assistance proved vital, and in many cases critical, to my research include Rufus Barringer, Rocky Mount, N.C.; Patricia G. Bennett, Charleston Library Society, Charleston, S.C.; Joe Bilby, Wall Township, N.J.; DeAnn Blanton and Mike Musick, Military Reference Branch, National Archives, Washington, D.C.; Mary Boccaccio and Martha G. Elmore, J. Y. Joyner Library, East Carolina University, Greenville, N.C.; Andy Boisseau and E. Lee Shepard, Virginia Historical Society, Richmond; Patrick A. Bowmaster, West Roxbury, Mass.; Karen Cooper, Shenandoah County Library, Woodstock, Va.; Susan Cornett and Will Sibayan, Herbert Bateman Memorial Library, Langley Air Force Base, Va.; John and Ruth Coski, Eleanor S. Brockenbrough Library, Museum of the Confederacy, Richmond; Rebecca Ebert, Handley Regional Library, Winchester, Va.; Leslie Fields, Gilder Lehrman Collection, New York; Sam Fore, South Caroliniana Library, University of South Carolina, Columbia; Bill Godfrey, Hampton, Va.; John Heiser, Gettysburg National Military Park, Gettysburg, Pa.; Kenneth W. Holt, Media, Pa.; Margaret Hrabe, Alderman Library, University of Virginia, Charlottesville; Perry D. Jamieson, Crofton, Md.; Gary K. Leak, Omaha, Neb.; Betty B. Low, History Museum of Western Virginia, Roanoke; Al Mackey, Las Vegas, Nev.; Lisa McCown, James Graham Leyburn Library, Washington and Lee University, Lexington, Va.; Mary Molineux, Earl Gregg Swem Library, College of William and Mary, Williamsburg, Va.; Janet Ness, University of Washington Libraries, Seattle; Andy Phrydas, Georgia Department of Archives and History, Atlanta; John Rhodehamel,

Henry E. Huntington Library, San Marino, Calif.; Richard J. Sommers, U.S. Army Military History Institute, Carlisle Barracks, Pa.; Bob Spore, Lexington, Va.; Kathy Stewart and Patricia Watkinson, Library of Virginia, Richmond; Eric J. Wittenberg, Columbus, Ohio; and John W. Woodard, Z. Smith Reynolds Library, Wake Forest University, Winston-Salem, N.C.

As before, I am indebted to my editors, Jack Davis and Leigh Ann Berry of Stackpole Books; to my cartographer, Paul Dangel; to my indexer, Lanice Peach; and to my wife, Melody Ann Longacre.

PREFACE

This book is a companion volume to *Lincoln's Cavalrymen: A History of the Mounted Forces of the Army of the Potomac, 1861–1865,* published in 2000. Like the earlier work, *Lee's Cavalrymen* chronicles the operational, organizational, and administrative history of its subject—in this case, the mounted forces of the Army of Northern Virginia, the preeminent fighting force of the Confederacy. Because the troopers of "Jeb" Stuart, Wade Hampton, and Fitzhugh Lee have received proportionally greater historical coverage than their less flamboyant and less successful opponents, it is hard to believe that the present volume is the first of its kind. Numerous biographies, battle and campaign studies, and regimental histories have covered, and often romanticized, the horse soldiers who served in Robert E. Lee's army. Yet only a few magazine and journal articles have attempted an overview of the Cavalry Division (and, later, the Cavalry Corps), A.N.V.

This lapse is especially curious given the many hardships and deficiencies that Lee's cavalrymen and horse artillerymen experienced from April 1861 to April 1865, a dramatic story that cries cry out for a chronicler. Although the Confederate horsemen entered the war with a firmer grasp of horsemanship and weaponry than their adversaries, and although their advantages in experience, leadership, and tactical expertise served them well in 1861–62, thereafter they had to battle the kind of adversity their enemy never knew: shortages—both acute and chronic—of weapons, ammunition, equipment, and horseflesh. The Southern horsemen may not have prevailed in the long run, but the fact that they fought through to Appomattox in the face of such disadvantages speaks volumes about their tenacity and fortitude, a fact that makes their story too important to ignore any longer.

Like *Lincoln's Cavalrymen,* this book treats of every major campaign in which its subject served, although the reader may perceive a few exceptions. Only passing reference is made to Stonewall Jackson's Shenandoah Valley campaign of April–June 1862 and to the winter campaigns of 1863–64 and 1864–65 in the Valley and in neighboring West Virginia. The first omission is a matter of proportion: Jackson's Valley campaign, while a major operation with repercussions for the fighting farther east, involved only two regiments then a part of what became known as the Army of Northern Virginia. The other campaigns, in which larger detachments of the army participated, were sideshows to, and had a limited effect on, the war in the main theater of operations; moreover, in those operations, Lee's horsemen did not engage their natural opponents, the troopers of the Union Army of the Potomac. On the other hand, the fighting in the Shenandoah Valley between August 1864 and February 1865 is examined at length. Substantial portions of the cavalry, Army of Northern Virginia, took part, and they maintained essentially the same organizational structure as when serving in eastern Virginia; they opposed thousands of cavalrymen temporarily detached from the Army of the Potomac; and their service was critical to the outcome of the larger war effort.

While primarily an operational history, *Lee's Cavalrymen* is also concerned with tactics and leadership. I attempt to place the cavalry and horse artillery of Lee's army in a tactical context, and examine and evaluate not only Stuart and his successors in corps command, but also influential subordinates such as M. Calbraith Butler, James B. Gordon, William E. Jones, W. H. F. ("Rooney") Lee, Lunsford L. Lomax, Thomas T. Munford, John Pelham, Beverly H. Robertson, Thomas L. Rosser, and Williams C. Wickham. Furthermore, through my research of more than 400 collections of unpublished letters, diaries, and memoirs, as well as scores of published first-person sources, I attempt to form a mosaic portrait of the common soldiers of Lee's cavalry—the officers and enlisted men who experienced four years of adversity, glory, triumph, and defeat, never acknowledging, much less bowing to, the odds against them.

An editorial note: Unless otherwise indicated, all regimental references are to cavalry outfits. For convenience's sake, the "Comanches" of the 35th Virginia Battalion and the "Laurel Brigade" of Virginia cavalry are identified throughout the text by those nicknames, although the units did not receive their appellations until December 1863 and early 1864, respectively.

Chapter One

"Look Out for the Damned Virginia Horsemen!"

Peering through his field glasses, the long-legged man with the cinnamon-colored beard waited silently for dawn to break. Slowly, almost imperceptibly, the mist that hugged the floor of the valley began to dissipate. It released the landscape piece by piece—a stand of trees, a barn and some outbuildings, a line of fencing. Shadows lifted; plowed fields and pastureland swam into view. Toward the northeast, on the outskirts of Smithfield, Virginia, a ridgeline became visible; atop it, human shapes were dimly discernible, their blue uniforms indistinguishable in the murk. Some of the shapes were in motion—horses and riders—but standing figures predominated.

The riders were too few to be cavalry. The bearded man saw that he was facing an outpost manned by Yankee infantry, a few of whose officers were mounted. A smile played at the corners of his mouth. The troops of Maj. Gen. Robert Patterson were standing about, as if they intended to go nowhere any time soon—as if their position within hailing distance of Winchester would hold their opponents in place. This, the observer reflected, was wishful thinking of the highest order.

Lt. Col. James Ewell Brown Stuart of the 1st Virginia Cavalry turned to a staff officer, snapped off some instructions, and sent the man pounding southward. After taking additional sightings, Stuart mounted and rode along the length of his perimeter, stopping at several points to confer with his subordinates. At his order, groups of riders trotted forward to make their presence known. In a matter of minutes, pistol and rifle fire was rattling across the valley, as the gray riders struck at the outposts opposite them. As the racket grew with the sunlight, Stuart nodded in approval. Pressure exerted continuously along Patterson's picket line would ensure that his troops remained rooted to their ground. Their immobility would be critical to the strategy that Stuart's superior, Gen. Joseph E. Johnston, commander of the Army of the Shenandoah, hoped to put into effect this day.

The picket skirmishing—most of it conducted at long range and productive of few casualties on either side—continued well into the morning. By 9:00 A.M.

Stuart was sufficiently convinced of the enemy's intentions to convey his impression to Winchester. The Yankees could be expected to remain and in around Smithfield indefinitely; Johnston need not factor them into any planning he did this day.[1]

Stuart's 9:00 report, combined with earlier communiqués of similar nature from the picket line, persuaded Johnston of the viability of a decision he had tentatively reached hours before: to abandon Winchester and the Valley itself. He would lead his eleven thousand-man command more than seventy miles eastward to link with the larger army of Brig. Gen. Pierre G. T. Beauregard. That army had gathered around Manassas Junction, Virginia, twenty-two miles below Washington, D.C., where it hugged the banks of a stream known as Bull Run. Patterson's army of the Department of Pennsylvania, fourteen thousand strong, had been sent to the Valley to hold Johnston's troops in place. But the aged, slow-moving Patterson had shown himself too cautious, too fearful of confronting his opponent, to carry out the mission assigned him.

Three days earlier—Monday, July 15, 1861—the Union leader had appeared on the verge of attacking Winchester. Patterson had moved south from the Martinsburg vicinity as though to force a fight, but almost at the last minute, he veered east to Smithfield. At first Johnston suspected that his opponent was preparing a flank attack aimed at cutting his lines of communication. Stuart's morning report, however, revealed that Patterson had surrendered the initiative, allowing the Army of the Shenandoah to make the next move.

Johnston believed he knew the source of his adversary's timidity. Patterson lacked the mobile reconnaissance forces he needed to determine Rebel numbers and dispositions. While Johnston's army included several companies of Virginians skilled in scouting operations, Patterson's command was supported by a minuscule force of raw and inexperienced troopers. They had proven no match for the seasoned cavaliers under Stuart. Adept at defensive operations, the Confederate horsemen had encircled Winchester with an impenetrable counterreconnaissance screen, ensuring that Patterson knew little about Johnston's movements, and nothing at all of his plans.[2]

Those plans were ambitious and carried risks, but they were the product of dire necessity. On July 16, as Patterson advanced from Martinsburg, thirty-six thousand Federals had left the Washington suburbs heading for Richmond, the newly established capital of the Confederate States of America. The green but enthusiastic army of Brig. Gen. Irvin McDowell was on a collision course with the equally untutored defenders of the Manassas–Bull Run line. Since McDowell's force outnumbered Beauregard's almost two to one, the outcome of the pending clash seemed preordained.

Any hope the Confederacy had of staving off disaster rested on a swift concentration of forces. Should Johnston and Beauregard link before McDowell could strike, the numerical odds would draw even. The tactical situation would then favor the Confederates, for when green troops fought, the defender had the advantage. For days, Johnston had been seeking a way to disengage from his enemy and join Beauregard. Now, thanks to his cavalry's intelligence gathering and screening, he had his opportunity. As Johnston noted, by marking time well to the northeast, the Yankees were "certainly too far from our road, therefore, to be able to prevent or delay our march. His [Stuart's] information left no doubt of the expediency of moving as soon as possible."

The intelligence had not come an hour too soon. At 1:00 on the morning of the eighteenth, an urgent telegram from the Adjutant and Inspector General's Office in Richmond had reached Winchester, warning Johnston that the Federals were advancing on Manasses: "General Beauregard is attacked," it read. "To strike the enemy a decisive blow, a junction of all your effective force will be needed. If practicable, make the movement." A half hour later, Johnston received a wire from Beauregard himself—one penned much earlier but whose transmission had been delayed—calling his situation critical and reminding Johnston of his earlier promises of assistance.[3]

Minutes after Johnston received Stuart's morning report, he issued the necessary orders. He detailed two brigades of militia to hold Winchester and its environs, although he thought it unlikely that Patterson would attack even so small a force. Then he mustered the four infantry brigades that composed his main body and started them southeastward toward Ashby's Gap in the Blue Ridge. After debouching from the mountains, the troops would turn south toward the Manassas Gap Railroad. Passenger coaches, flatcars, and boxcars would be waiting near Piedmont Station to carry the foot soldiers eastward. Speed was of the essence. Though the recent attack of the eighteenth had been of limited size, McDowell might strike in force at any moment in hopes of overwhelming Beauregard. Should Johnston's men reach Bull Run even a little late, the result might be the death of their new nation.

While the infantry marched, cannons, limbers, caissons, and battery wagons trundled along parallel roads. The five batteries of light artillery in Johnston's army would march overland all the way to Manassas Junction. The guns' departure left only Stuart's troopers in place outside Winchester. In accordance with his orders, the lieutenant colonel stretched his picket lines as far east as Berryville, directly below Smithfield. All along this perimeter, parties of horsemen advanced across farm fields and meadows, firearms ablaze. Just as Johnston had hoped, the commotion held the attention of Patterson's foot soldiers and, by making them believe that a full-scale attack was imminent, kept them stationary.

Not a single reconnaissance party penetrated the screen erected by Stuart's men. Yankees peering south saw only lines of horsemen; none ventured close enough to observe the clouds of dust advancing toward the mountains. Even the militia Johnston had left behind was blocked from view. The exodus from Winchester went unheeded and unchallenged.

The result was everything that the Confederate high command could have hoped for. By the time Stuart's people ended their demonstration, broke contact, and passed gingerly to the rear, the head of Johnston's column was halfway to Piedmont Station. There, at about 7:00 A.M. on the nineteenth, the

advance echelon boarded the cars that would carry them eastward. By midafternoon, soldiers were chugging into Manassas Junction, an easy march from the
Bull Run defenses.

They arrived to find that McDowell's army had not followed up the strike
it had made near Blackburn's Ford on Bull Run. The action had inflicted little
damage but had alerted Beauregard to the vulnerability of his right flank.
Throughout the nineteenth, the Yankees remained quiescent, although the inactivity only increased Beauregard's suspicion that a new and heavier blow was
soon to fall.

Every hour that McDowell delayed was a gift to his opponent. It became
clear that time remained for most, if not all, of Johnston's troops to reach the
field in time to meet a new attack. Thus it appeared increasingly likely that the
most critical confrontation of this brief war was going to be fought by opponents
of approximately equal size. For this, the Confederates could thank not only
McDowell's hesitation, but also the screening skills of Stuart's highly mobile,
admirably aggressive troopers—a critical resource lacking to their enemy.[4]

>—◦—◦—◦—◦—◦—<

Perhaps it should come as no surprise that at war's outset the Confederate
troopers outnumbered and outperformed their counterparts in blue. In many
respects, the Southern nation enjoyed early advantages in cavalry material. For
one thing, it had placed many of its sons in the mounted arm of the prewar U.S.
Army. While historians and sociologists debate the existence of a Southern
military tradition, there is no doubt that in the 1840s and 1850s, Southerners
dominated the dragoon and cavalry regiments of the Regular establishment.[5]

Then, too, though the region could draw upon less than one-third the white
population of the states warring against it, it boasted a proportionally larger
number of active militia outfits. While it cannot be determined precisely, the
proportion of mounted to foot units of militia appears to have been larger in the
South. Many of these units sprang up in the year and a half preceding the war's
opening shots, delivered by South Carolina batteries against the U.S. Army garrison inside Fort Sumter, Charleston Harbor, on April 12, 1861. John Brown's
October 1859 raid on the government armory and arsenal at Harpers Ferry, Virginia, aimed at igniting a slave insurrection, had been a catalyst in recruiting
mounted militiamen throughout the South, especially in the state whose soil
"Old Osawatomie" had violated. Other units of horsemen evolved from the
patrols that had been formed to locate runaway slaves and prevent an uprising
by the chattels themselves.

These militia companies—the pride of their local communities, their men
garbed in fanciful uniforms, riding good horses, but toting obsolete weaponry—
formed the nucleus of the Confederate cavalry in the eastern theater of the war.
Their numbers ensured that by some point in 1861, mounted units overflowed
with recruits. The first regiment to take the field, the 1st Virginia, organized in

early May 1861 at Harpers Ferry, eventually grew to include fourteen companies, in contrast to the ten-company structure that later prevailed in the Confederate cavalry service. All but one of the colorfully named units were converted militia companies: the Newtown Troop, the Berkeley Troop, the 1st Rockbridge Dragoons, the Clarke Cavalry, the Valley Rangers, the Shepherdstown Troop, the Amelia Dragoons (or Amelia Troop), the Loudoun Light Horse, the Harrisonburg Cavalry, the Rockingham Cavalry, the Gloucester Cavalry (also known as the Gloucester Light Dragoons), the Adams Troop, and the Sumter Mounted Guards. In the fall of 1861, the last two companies were transferred to the Jeff Davis Legion, a combination infantry-cavalry-artillery organization whose mounted contingent was also recruited in Alabama, Georgia, and Mississippi.[6]

Despite the regiment's large size on paper, it took much time for the 1st Virginia to be recruited to full strength. For the first six weeks of its field service, Stuart could call on only six companies of indifferently armed troopers, no more than 350 officers and men present for duty. Until the regiment consisted of at least ten companies, Stuart would be denied the full colonelcy he desired.

Many, perhaps most, of the militiamen of Virginia and her sister states had joined their units for social or political reasons. Until the spring of 1861, their troops often seemed to be playing at the business of soldiering. Even so, the men had absorbed at least some of the lessons of military life. They had followed superiors' orders; had roughed it in the field; had taken part in musters, reviews and parades; and, it is presumed, had learned some semblance of discipline. Briefly, perhaps, they had even spent time on a drill field under the watchful eye of a tactician. As the war clouds gathered, some felt a heightened sense of urgency to assimilate the basics of the military art and did so energetically and thoroughly. By professional standards, their training was woefully inadequate, but the fact that they had any tutoring at all gave them a leg up in a war fought primarily by amateur soldiers.

Militiamen predominated not only in Stuart's regiment but also in a mounted outfit organized a few days before the 1st Virginia began to assemble at Harpers Ferry. The 30th Regiment, Virginia Volunteers, most of whose ten companies were mustered into service at Lynchburg on May 8, was commanded by Col. Richard C. W. Radford, like Stuart, a West Pointer and an "old army" veteran. Originally the 30th was to have been an infantry outfit, but Radford's prewar service had been as a dragoon, a soldier armed, equipped, and trained to fight mounted and afoot with equal effectiveness, the product of an economy-minded Congress. Through officials in Lynchburg, Radford appealed successfully to Maj. Gen. Robert E. Lee, commanding the military forces of Virginia, to allow the 30th to be recruited, instead, as cavalry.

Radford's command boasted two dozen graduates of Virginia's military academy, including its lieutenant colonel and co-organizer, Thomas Taylor Munford. Described early on as "a fine body of men," the 30th was among the first mounted units to join the defenders of the Bull Run line. There, throughout June and for most of July 1861, the regiment performed the same reconnaissance and counterreconnaissance duties that Stuart's men shouldered in the Shenandoah Valley.[7]

Soon after Stuart's and Radford's outfits entered active service, additional organizations of horse soldiers—many of them transformed militia units, others raised in the wake of the Fort Sumter crisis—made their services available to the Virginia authorities. Some reported for duty in the Valley; others joined the 30th Virginia inside the fortifications along and north of Bull Run; still others were earmarked for service on the Virginia Peninsula, sixty-some miles below Richmond, where Union troops menaced southeastern Virginia from Fort Monroe.

In the Shenandoah, the 1st Virginia was joined by several independent companies of horsemen. Many eventually formed the 7th Virginia Cavalry, led by an elderly West Pointer with political influence, Col. Angus W. McDonald. One of these companies was commanded by Capt. Turner Ashby, a gentleman farmer and militia officer from Fauquier County who quickly became the heir apparent to the soldier-politician.

Although he lacked a military education, Ashby was a born leader as well as an expert horseman, a dead shot, and an enterprising scout. His courage and daring became the stuff of legend in the Valley, as did his ability to slip undetected inside Yankee lines, gather critical intelligence, and place it in the hands of superiors while still warm. Ashby was dashing and colorful in the manner of J. E. B. Stuart, although he eschewed the gaudier trappings that Stuart affected, including ostrich-plumed hats, golden spurs, and crimson-lined capes.[8]

Perhaps not surprisingly, when Ashby and Stuart came into close association—shortly before McDonald's regiment was transferred from state service into the Provisional Army of the Confederacy—their relationship was marred by friction, mistrust, and jealousy. At this time, Ashby was on detached duty, scouting enemy-infested territory well in advance of Harpers Ferry. Although the captain considered himself an integral member of McDonald's outfit, Stuart did not; thus, on May 27, he ordered Ashby to report to him for duty. Fearful of losing the independence he had enjoyed as McDonald's subordinate, Ashby appealed for redress to Joe Johnston, reminding the army leader he had decreed that Ashby "was to receive all orders from you direct, and was to make reports to you direct." While Ashby's contention appeared to invalidate his claim to being a member of the 7th Virginia, he asked to be permitted to rejoin McDonald's outfit. A matter of pride was at the heart of the dispute. Ashby was older than Stuart, and although he lacked Stuart's professional credentials, he had already made a reputation in the Valley that not even a West Pointer could match.

The Ashby-Stuart clash vexed their common superior, who appreciated the value of a smoothly functioning mounted arm ("I become more convinced daily," he informed Richmond, "of the great value of cavalry, compared with infantry, for service on this frontier"). At first he pleaded an inability to countermand an order from Stuart, who had titular command of all the horsemen in the Valley. But on June 15, after Ashby lodged a second protest, along with a thinly veiled threat to resign his commission if forced to serve under Stuart, Johnston relented and permitted the captain to return to McDonald. In doing so, the army leader assured Ashby that "the knowledge that you were between us and the enemy made me sleep very soundly last night; and that your presence among the troops, under my command, would always have such an effect."[9]

Restored to what he considered his rightful position, Ashby quickly became the motive force behind the 7th Virginia. Late in June he was promoted to lieutenant colonel, and nine months later he won a colonel's stars. In regimental command, as he had in partisan service, Ashby continued to shine as the brightest light in the Confederate firmament during this early morning of the war—"the idol of all the troopers in the field," as one colleague put it. No one expected Ashby's star to wink out little more than a year after he took the field.[10]

>—⊹ ⟨⟩ O ⟨⟩ ⊹—⊰

Given its proximity to Washington, D.C., it seemed logical that the northern extremities of the Manassas–Bull Run line should witness the first clash of mounted units in this war. The encounter, which amounted to no more than a brief skirmish, took place on June 1 at Fairfax Court House, almost within sight of the fortifications that surrounded the federal capital. The outpost that the Confederates had set up in the village was designed to provide the defenders farther south with an early-warning capability. While of no strategic consequence, the action produced the first casualties on either side, presaged a larger confrontation between McDowell and Beauregard, and demonstrated that not every Southern trooper was combat-ready.

Beauregard exercised not the remotest of control over the fight. The Louisiana Creole had been assigned to command at Manassas only one day before; he was en route to relieve his predecessor, Brig. Gen. Milledge L. Bonham, when the shooting started. Upon arriving at his new station, he learned the basic facts behind the engagement; other elements of the story he pieced together from later accounts by the participants.[11]

It had all begun on May thirty-first, when Col. David Hunter, a native Virginian who had remained in the U.S. Army and now led a brigade of Union volunteers, sent one of his units, Company B of the 2nd United States Cavalry, under Lieutenant Charles H. Tompkins, from recently occupied Alexandria, Virginia, to probe the defenses at Fairfax. The horsemen struck under cover of night, clattering into the courthouse town at 3:00 A.M. on June 1. They found the place garrisoned by perhaps 250 militia under Lt. Col. Richard S. Ewell of the provisional Confederate army, formerly an officer of United States dragoons. Two-thirds of Ewell's force consisted of horsemen, the Prince Edward Dragoons of Capt. John T. Thornton and Capt. John Shackleford Green's Rappahannock Cavalry, also known as the "Old Guard." According to Ewell, both units were so poorly armed and so low on ammunition that neither offered much resistance.[12]

It did not help that the Yankees had snatched up most of the pickets Ewell had stationed on the road from Falls Church, ensuring that the attack achieved complete surprise. When Tompkins's seventy-five men charged through the streets, firing pistols and carbines, several of Thornton's and Green's sleep-fogged troopers were captured. Most, however, had time to flee—and flee they did. A few others, although lacking adequate weaponry (some had no firearms at all), refused to leave. One who remained later insisted that "the Imperial guard of Napoleon himself would not have stood as long as some twenty of us did, exposed to a dreadful fire, having nothing [with which] to return the fire, deserted by our own officers and half the company." Whether he ran or remained, every Confederate experienced a nightmarish introduction to war.[13]

Only when a nightshirt-clad Ewell rushed to the scene and deployed Capt. John Quincy Marr's infantry company did the defenders make an effective stand. Marr's hastily assembled troops raked the Yankees as they charged past. Ragged but repeated volleys caused the horsemen to halt, mill about, then speed out the Little River Turnpike toward Germantown and Chantilly. In that area, Tompkins re-formed Company B for a second strike on Ewell's headquarters. A half hour after exiting Fairfax, he and his men returned, shooting up the town as before.

Having anticipated a repeat performance, Ewell had formed Marr's rifle-men behind good cover, bolstered by the few troopers who had not run off. By now, too, the lieutenant colonel had sent couriers to alert General Bonham to the attack and to seek his assistance. Although Bonham did not order the 30th Virginia to Fairfax Court House, he did dispatch Maj. Julien Harrison with one of the four companies of horsemen that had recently reached Manassas Junction from Richmond.

Ewell had also appealed to a troop of horsemen based not far from Fairfax, Capt. Williams C. Wickham's Hanover Dragoons. Like Tompkins's entrance into the town, Ewell's cry for help "created much confusion, and some trepidation." The result was so chaotic as to be laughable. One of Wickham's men observed a fellow trooper "weighing over 200 pounds attempting to get into the pants of another weighing about 110, while another mistakenly put . . . on the boots of a comrade."[14]

As Ewell probably foresaw, no reinforcements reached him in time to oppose Tompkins's second assault, although local civilians helped out by firing on the Yankees through first- and second-story windows. Makeshift as it was, the opposition took a toll: One Federal fell wounded, and nine of Tompkins's horses were disabled. Fearing that Ewell had supports close at hand, and having already formed a good idea of the size and composition of the local force, Tompkins led his band out of town in the direction of Falls Church. The lieutenant believed, as he later told General Hunter, that he had killed twenty-five defenders. In fact, Ewell's only casualty had been Captain Marr, shot through the heart late in the fight, the first fatality of this young conflict.

For his part, Dick Ewell won a brigadier's star by playing up the skirmish as a glorious victory. He attempted to enlarge his success by ordering Harrison's and Wickham's troopers, upon their arrival at Fairfax, to overtake the Yankees short of their lines. The belated pursuit, however, proved barren of results.[15]

For a month after the fracas on the doorstep of Washington, the lines along Bull Run, on the Peninsula, and in the Valley of Virginia remained largely quiescent. The only action of any consequence during this period occurred on June 17, one day after an expeditionary force under Col. Maxcy Gregg of the 1st South Carolina Infantry left Fairfax Court House—where it had gone to prevent a recurrence of Tompkins's raid—to reconnoiter the approaches to the Potomac River. The expedition consisted of 575 members of Gregg's regiment, two artillery pieces, and an unusually large body of mounted men: Capt. William Ball's Chesterfield Cavalry, a detachment of Wickham's company, and a squadron of the 30th Virginia under Capt. William R. Terry and Capt. John S. Langhorne.[16]

Near day's end, having scouted the countryside around the hamlet of Vienna, five miles north of Fairfax, the expedition turned back toward home base when Gregg detected the approach of a train on the Loudoun & Hampshire Railroad. In his after-action report, the colonel claimed to have heard the train approaching; more likely, his mounted scouts gave first warning of its coming and noted that it carried Yankee troops out of Alexandria.

Concealing his force around a bend in the track, Gregg planned a surprise for the enemy. He emplaced his cannons on a hillock, from which they opened without warning on the approaching cars. Shells killed eight members of the 1st Ohio Volunteers and wounded four others. Panicked comrades scrambled from the derailed train and raced up the track until beyond artillery range, pursued briefly by Terry's horsemen. Though none of the fugitives was overtaken, Gregg later praised the conduct of his troopers, declaring they all "commanded my entire confidence by their bearing, and only needed [an] opportunity for more effective action."[17]

Prior to the clashes at Fairfax Court House and Vienna, troops had been trickling into all three theaters of operations in Virginia. In later weeks, as though inspired by Ewell's and Gregg's success, recruits entered the field in impressive numbers. A certain percentage of the newcomers—but not necessarily a desirable percentage—were horsemen. Leading military theorists of the day posited that for an army to achieve proper balance 10 to 15 percent of its total strength should be in mounted troops. At this stage of the conflict, however, the ratio of cavalry to army on both sides was much lower. In Washington, bureaucrats feared that volunteer cavalry, each regiment of which would require upward of $500,000 a year to maintain, would prove an extravagant and wasteful expense. For this reason, they considered the few thousand Regular horsemen in existence at war's start sufficient for the nation's needs. Not till late summer did the government appreciate its shortsightedness and scramble to make amends.[18]

In the South, so rich in mounted experience, the cavalry picture was somewhat brighter. By early June 1861, although Joe Johnston's army, still ensconced at Harpers Ferry, had added thousands of infantry and several artillery batteries, the 1st and 7th Virginia continued to bear the burden of mounted operations. A few independent companies of horsemen had reported to Johnston for duty, but few were effectively mounted, armed, or equipped; most were useful only as scouts and partisan rangers.

The commanders at Manassas and on the Peninsula seemed to have fared better. Beauregard's growing army was supported not only by Radford's regiment and Green's, Thornton's, and Wickham's companies, but also by several other units of mounted militia and home guards. Three of the militia units would later be combined with Wickham's and Ball's companies to form the nucleus of the 4th Virginia Cavalry: Capt. Robert E. Utterback's Little Fork Rangers (also known as the Culpeper Troop), Capt. John F. Lay's Powhatan Cavalry, and Capt. William H. F. Payne's Black Horse Cavalry. Also available to Beauregard was Capt. E. B. Powell's Washington Home Guard of Cavalry.[19]

While each of these units was well known in its native region, only one had acquired a national reputation. The Black Horse Cavalry had been formed by Payne, Maj. John Moore, and Capt. D. H. Jones four months before John Brown's raid on Harpers Ferry. Throughout Brown's trial, as well as at his December 1859 execution at Charles Town, Virginia, the company guarded the prisoner, forestalling attempts to lynch him. Reportedly, Brown had been surprised by the consideration shown him by the Black Horse, given the enormity of his crime in the eyes of Virginians. After the firing on Fort Sumter, a great deal of newspaper attention was given the unit with the color-coordinated mounts. Despite its humane treatment of Brown, Northern tabloids characterized the typical Black Horseman as a savage fighter, a combination of Cossack and Comanche—a description at variance with the prevailing view of the Southern trooper as chivalrous cavalier.[20]

It was uncertain how effective Beauregard's heterogeneous assortment of horse soldiers would prove to be. As the senior cavalry officer on the Bull Run line, Colonel Radford theoretically commanded every mounted unit in the so-called Army of the Potomac. In the best traditions of states' rights, however, the commanders of some of the independent companies believed they answered neither to Radford nor to Beauregard, but to Virginia governor John Letcher, who had authorized their formation and in a few cases had appointed their officers (although most had been elected by the rank and file). Moreover, Radford's ability to get the most out of the units assigned to him appeared to be compromised by his general lack of familiarity with the personnel, arms, equipment, and tactical proficiency of the militiamen and home guards. It remained to be seen whether Beauregard's horsemen could be fashioned into an effective weapon by the time McDowell left Washington for points south.

The situation on the Virginia Peninsula, the domain of Col. (later Maj. Gen.) John Bankhead Magruder, seemed less uncertain. When he arrived at his

*Appt'd comm. of West Point, but resigned. He had foogt in Mexican War with Grant, Lee, J. Davis, etc

Yorktown headquarters on May 21, Magruder found that the few thousand troops in his Army of the Peninsula included no horsemen. The new arrival, who had been known in the prewar U.S. Army as "Prince John" for his pomposity and showmanship, seemed to regard the lack of a mounted arm as a personal affront. A few days after taking command, he importuned Robert E. Lee to send him as many cavalry companies as could be spared.[21]

As a former cavalryman, Lee was sympathetic to Magruder's request and worked hard to fulfill it. Over a several-week period beginning May 29, he supplied Prince John with Capt. Robert Douthat's Charles City Cavalry, Capt. Thomas F. Goode's Boydton Cavalry (also known as the Mecklenburg Cavalry, or Mecklenburg Dragoons), Capt. John E. Jones's Nottoway Troop, the Old Dominion Dragoons (a.k.a. the Elizabeth City Company) of Capt. Jefferson C. Phillips, Capt. William H. Easley's Black Walnut Dragoons, Capt. Henry R. Johnson's Cumberland Light Dragoons, the Catawba Troop (sometimes known as the Halifax Troop) under Capt. William Collins, Jr., and Capt. William A. Adams's Dinwiddie Cavalry. The combined force probably enjoyed a greater degree of cohesion than Beauregard's cavalry, because several of its components had common roots, having been recruited on or adjacent to the Peninsula. Later, the seven companies joined with three others to form the 2nd Virginia Cavalry, soon afterward redesignated the 3rd Cavalry, with Robert Johnston (no relation to the army leader) as its first colonel.[22]

The troopers saw action within days of their assignment to Magruder. Their baptism of fire was a success. In fact, they acquitted themselves so well they earned a memorable sobriquet from their enemy.

On June 7, one of Magruder's most trusted subordinates, Capt. W. H. Werth, led a twenty-man detachment of the Old Dominion Dragoons, Captain Phillips commanding, toward Union-held Newport News, a fortified camp at the southwestern tip of the Peninsula. Bypassing the lowermost of Magruder's outposts, Big Bethel Church, astride the road to Hampton about eight miles from their destination, Werth and Phillips penetrated within several hundred yards of the enemy position before being detected. Because they had failed to cut off an enemy detachment along the James River, the fortified camp received a last-minute warning of their approach.

Before a party of Massachusetts infantry that had been on fatigue duty outside the camp could react to the alarm, Werth and Phillips attacked, causing many of the Bay Staters, who lacked readily available weapons, to run for their lives. The Confederates had the satisfaction of hearing one Yankee shout to his comrades, "Look out for the damned Virginia horsemen; they are down upon us!"

When other Federals heard the cry, the stampede became general. Werth and Phillips spurred forward, riding down the slowest-footed in the group. Werth, who imagined himself an Indian in war paint, shot down a Yankee officer, plunged into the enemy "at full speed (giving at the same time a loud walla-walla war-whoop), and then delivered [his] second shot, which brought another man (a private) dead to the ground." He bragged, "I shot the first man through the heart, and the last one under the right shoulder-blade."

In response to the carnage, the fugitives increased their race for the works, hollering "Virginia horsemen! Virginia horsemen!" They scampered out of the attackers' reach so quickly that Werth and Phillips had plenty of time to study the works behind which the survivors huddled. The defenders were so traumatized they delivered a scattered, inaccurate fire from their recently retrieved rifles. Their work well done, the Confederates slowly retired.[23]

They rode off in lofty spirits, impressed by the terror they had inflicted on the foe. It was true that the Yankees had cursed them, but they had done so in a way that paid tribute to the ferocity of the Old Dominion Dragoons. Everyone involved agreed that however the utterance had been intended, "damned Virginia horsemen" had a nice ring to it.

⊱⊶⬥⊶◯⊷⬦⊷⊰

The reconnaissance of June 7 dismayed and annoyed Benjamin F. Butler, commanding at Fort Monroe. It may also have prompted Butler to order an advance of his own. Just after midnight, June 9–10, the politician-general sent a column about forty-four hundred strong under a brigadier in the Massachusetts militia, Ebenezer W. Pierce, to flank the outpost on the Hampton Road, interposing between Big Bethel and a more southerly position, Little Bethel. If all went as planned, Pierce's force, which contained infantry and artillery but no horsemen, would cut off the fourteen hundred troops Magruder had placed at Big Bethel a few days before: Col. D. H. Hill's 1st North Carolina Infantry, supported by some companies of the 3rd Virginia Infantry, a howitzer battalion, and the troopers of Phillips, Douthat, and Jones.[24]

Butler's plan of attack may have looked promising on paper, but the tactics that underlay it were too complicated for raw troops to execute, especially in the murk of early morning. Pierce advanced in three columns, two of which he directed to rendezvous at a road junction a mile or more below Little Bethel. This was a mistake because, lacking cavalry to screen their advance, the columns collided in the dark and fired into each other in the belief that each had encountered the enemy. The friendly fire claimed twenty-three casualties, disarranged Pierce's timetable, and cost him the element of surprise.

The Yankees finally sorted themselves out and blundered ahead. When they attacked Big Bethel shortly after 9:00 A.M., Hill and his supports met them from behind well-constructed works. For twenty minutes, fighting coursed along the banks of a Chesapeake Bay tributary known as Back River. During this time, Pierce's hapless troops were shot up, repulsed, and sent reeling in the direction of Ben Butler's fortress.

Magruder's troopers did their part in the brief battle, most of them fighting afoot, spelling their infantry comrades inside the works at Big Bethel. One hundred others were held in the rear as a mounted reserve. When the Federals gave way, Hill tried to make things worse for them by sending all one hundred, under

Captain Douthat, in pursuit. As in the aftermath of the fighting at Fairfax Court House, Vienna, and Newport News, the cavalry gobbled up no more than a few stragglers. They did, however, hasten the foe on its way. "The pursuit soon became a chase," Hill exulted, adding that "the enemy in his haste threw away hundreds of canteens, haversacks, overcoats, &c.; even the dead were thrown out of the wagons." Once again, retreating Federals hollered that the Virginia horsemen were about to trample them or cut them down. Some did not stop shouting till within the protective embrace of Fort Monroe. There they and their comrades would quietly remain for the next nine months.[25]

Chapter Two

Stirring Events

As early as mid-June 1861, Joe Johnston demonstrated that he cared little for holding territory, regardless of its strategic value, especially if he considered it vulnerable to an attack or a turning movement. When the timid Patterson finally nerved himself—after repeated prompting by his superior, General in Chief Winfield Scott—to invade the Shenandoah Valley, and after other generals began to threaten Confederate defenses in western Virginia, Johnston decided to evacuate Harpers Ferry. Weeks earlier, he had proclaimed the garrison too small to fend off an army the size of Patterson's or to prevent a flank movement by the Potomac River crossings. Johnston publicized his view in an apparent attempt to forestall the criticism of military and political superiors, including President Jefferson Davis, to whom every square foot of Confederate soil was holy ground.[1]

Without waiting for formal permission from Richmond, on the fifteenth Johnston made preparations to depart John Brown's old haunt. After destroying the local railroad bridge, dismantling cannon emplacements, and torching those rations and supplies that could not be carted off, he fell back toward Winchester, Martinsburg, and Bunker Hill. The withdrawal was screened, front and rear, by the three hundred-some members of Stuart's regiment. Despite its incomplete organization and imperfect equipping—most of the regiment continued to lack serviceable carbines and, as Stuart informed President Davis, a full complement of Colt revolvers—the 1st Virginia did a thorough, effective job. Johnston's chief engineer, Capt. William H. C. Whiting, noted that "under that very active and vigilant officer," Stuart's regiment held the line of the Potomac against mounting pressure, while providing "almost hourly information of every movement of the enemy." Meanwhile, Turner Ashby, with detachments of the 7th Virginia, guarded strategic points on the river, including bridges that remained intact.

As Whiting observed, Johnston's eight thousand evacuees halted their southwestward march at 4:00 in the afternoon, having reached a defensible point three miles beyond Charles Town. "At 5 P.M.," he added, "a courier arrived

from Richmond directing Harper's Ferry to be evacuated and the public buildings destroyed."[2]

Crossing the Potomac at Williamsport, Maryland, Patterson's Federals
sauntered into Harpers Ferry a few hours after the Confederates left. There they
appeared content to remain, but Stuart could not be certain they would. That
night he kept his men awake and under arms lest the Yankees push ahead—
something his more combative troopers hoped would occur. Trooper John
Ervine of Company I wrote that on the road to Charles Town, he and his comrades had been "kept waiting for 7 or 8 hours dismounted with our guns in hand
ready to mount at the [word] & two companys sent out to meet the northern
men & get them to advance on us but they had not the spunk."[3]

The stationary posture of Patterson's army was consistent with its commander's piecemeal approach to warfare and his reluctance to force any issue.
So timorous was the aged general that on the seventeenth, when he received a
false report that Johnston, with no fewer than fifteen thousand troops, was
advancing to interpose between Harpers Ferry and Williamsport, he withdrew
his entire force to the north bank of the Potomac. There he waited, all aquiver,
for an attack that never came.

Johnston, believing that his opponent would eventually recover his nerve,
refused to retrace his path to Harpers Ferry. He continued on to Winchester,
while establishing outposts north and northeast of the town. In obedience to
orders, Stuart sprinkled his troopers along a fifty-mile front from Shepherdstown to Leesburg, eyeing the principal crossing points on the upper Potomac.
Every day his pickets clashed with bluecoats on the far shore, doing their best
with their inadequate weaponry to keep Patterson in a state of anxiety. The
work took a toll; as one of Stuart's biographers puts it, "little clashes and affairs
at arms, that keep you interested, and occasionally kill a man . . . are very hard
on men and horses."[4]

For two weeks the armies remained on opposite sides of the stream, each
waiting for the other to make a move. Patterson finally did so on the humid
morning of July 1, this time as part of a larger Federal strategy. While the troops
in Washington marched on Richmond via Bull Run, Patterson was to keep Johnston in the Valley, preventing him from augmenting Beauregard. The only way
to do this was to take a deep breath and go forward. By the second, Patterson's
advance echelon was wading the Potomac downstream from Williamsport, in
the vicinity of the Rebel outpost at Falling Waters.

Stuart's troopers resisted the fording operation to the utmost of their
resources, fighting and falling back, buying time for reinforcements to arrive.
They came in the guise of an infantry force under the officer whom Johnston, in
late May, had succeeded in command of Harpers Ferry: Brig. Gen. Thomas
Jonathan Jackson. The arrival from Martinsburg of one regiment and one battery under the former V.M.I. professor forced Patterson's troops to recoil, but
they recovered and again advanced. They threatened, and eventually turned, the
right flank of Jackson's command, forcing his grudging withdrawal toward
Martinsburg.[5]

Neither additional reinforcements from Johnston nor Stuart's own attempt
at a flanking maneuver saved the day at Falling Waters. The cavalry was forced
to return to Jackson's side, but only after its devil-may-care commander, riding
alone in the advance, came within an eyelash of being captured by a company
of Pennsylvania foot soldiers. Thereafter, in the words of Captain Whiting, Stuart covered Jackson's pullback, "detecting every movement [of the enemy] and
harassing their pickets by continual activity." The retrograde ended after dawn
on the third, when Johnston's main body hustled up to keep Patterson in the
vicinity of Martinsburg.[6]

Stuart immediately placed his regiment between the armies, the better to
keep his superior supplied with intelligence. On the Union's Independence Day
he wrote his "Darling Wife" from a position "before the enemy," informing
Flora Cooke Stuart: "I am occupying the advance post of Johnston's army only
2 miles from the enemy's lines. Johnston is $3\frac{1}{2}$ miles behind me. . . . Look out
for stirring events here."[7]

For the next two weeks, his warning had a hollow ring. On the seventh,
Johnston withdrew everyone else to Winchester, far enough from Patterson to
make a sudden engagement unlikely. Two days later, Stuart reported signs of an
advance from Martinsburg, but Patterson had second thoughts and stayed put.
Fear of the consequences restrained him from moving farther south as both Stuart and Johnston had anticipated.

During the following week, the stalemate held; Union detachments marched
hither and yon, but none struck out for Winchester. When Patterson finally
lunged forward on July 15, he stopped five miles short of Winchester before
veering eastward to Smithfield. It seemed clear to his enemy that the commander of the Army of Pennsylvania could not commit himself to a decisive push.
Stuart continued to keep a close watch over the Smithfield region in the unlikely
event Patterson had a sudden change of heart. By the eighteenth, the cavalry
leader could tell his superior with a degree of certitude that Patterson would not
interfere if Johnston had ideas of hitting the road to Bull Run. "Stirring events"
were indeed about to take place, but they would occur well to the east of the
Blue Ridge.[8]

>-+-‹•›-O-‹•›-+-‹

On the afternoon of July 16, McDowell's raw recruits marched out of Washington in three columns, heading for Richmond and confrontation. Two days'
march to the southwest, Beauregard's Army of the Potomac—seven brigades of
infantry, with artillery and cavalry attached, plus miscellaneous reserves—held
an eight-mile cordon of breastworks along the south bank of Bull Run. The
army's southeastward-running line stretched from Stone Bridge, where the
Warrenton Turnpike crossed the run, to Union Mills Ford, below the trestle that
carried the Orange & Alexandria Railroad over the water. Army scouts and
civilian spies brought Beauregard timely word of the enemy's advance, ensuring that the defenders were as ready for a fight as pea green soldiers could be.

As the blue ranks came on, Beauregard's forwardmost pickets scurried out
of their path, but only after dosing the head of each column with rifle fire. First
to encounter the Yankees were members of Bonham's South Carolina brigade,
including several companies of horsemen under overall command of Colonel
Radford. Some unbrigaded units, including Ball's Chesterfield Cavalry, met the
Yankees well in advance of Bonham's outposts. Meanwhile, a squadron consisting of Wickham's company and Capt. Joel W. Flood's Company H, 30th
Virginia, had attached themselves to Bonham's rear guard, led by Col. Joseph
B. Kershaw of the 2nd South Carolina Infantry. An additional five companies
from the 30th Virginia—three under Radford's direct supervision, the others
under Lieutenant Colonel Munford—temporarily served with the 8th and 7th
South Carolina, respectively.

By all accounts, the inexperienced troopers won their spurs as they retired
grudgingly from Fairfax Court House to Centreville and then to the Bull Run
defenses. At various points, they stood their ground long after prudence dictated retreat, pulling back only when the buildup of Federals in their front
became irresistible. Despite tempting fate so egregiously, only two of Radford's
troopers were captured, none killed or wounded.[9]

Once he came within striking distance of Beauregard's line, McDowell
aimed a blow at it. Shortly before noon on the eighteenth, he sent a division of
infantry, supported by cannons, on a reconnaissance in force against the Confederate right in the vicinity of Mitchell's and Blackburn's Fords. Infantry and
artillery under Brig. Gen. James Longstreet guarded Blackburn's Ford.
Upstream at Mitchell's, four infantry regiments and two batteries of Bonham's
brigade had been augmented by six mounted companies under the overall command of Radford: Company G of the 30th Virginia, led by the regimental commander's brother, Capt. E. Winston Radford, plus Wickham's, Payne's, Ball's,
and Flood's militia and Powell's home guards.

For five hours, fighting raged in front of both positions. Bonham's force
was large enough and its people sufficiently combative that the Union division
was prevented from fording. After McDowell's infantry gave up the effort, the
opposing sides commenced what Beauregard called a "remarkable artillery
duel." Reduced to serving as battery supports, Radford's troopers endured two
hours of shot and shell but suffered few casualties. Finally the enemy pulled
back, then withdrew a safe distance from Mitchell's Ford. By then the fighting
on Longstreet's front had ceased as well, allowing the defenders to claim victory in what they regarded as a full-fledged battle.[10]

Thus far, the cavalry had contributed relatively little to the defense of the
Bull Run line, but things were about to change. No matter what the Confederates thought, the action of the eighteenth was merely a tune-up to the main
event. Believing correctly that his probe had driven Beauregard to shore up his
south flank, McDowell laid plans for a heavy assault on the Rebel left. Early on
the twenty-first, while a portion of his army feigned a crossing near Stone
Bridge, a turning column would cross the run near Sudley Springs Ford. The

flank drive was to be spearheaded by a division under David Hunter (recently promoted to brigadier general), backed by the division of Brig. Gen. Samuel P. Heintzelman. Launched in morning darkness, the attack would take the Rebels by surprise, rolling up their line from west to east, achieving victory before the sun was high in the sky.

The plan appeared well conceived, especially in its use of deception tactics. It called, however, for a forced march too long for green troops to make in the interval allotted them, and it was predicated on opposing only Beauregard's men. While it was rumored that a part of Johnston's army had slipped Patterson's trap and was now at Bull Run, McDowell had no means of confirming the story.

In fact, by the morning of the twenty-first, more than half of the Army of the Shenandoah—large portions of three of Johnston's infantry brigades, plus Stuart's hard-marching troopers—was in position to oppose McDowell, with additional troops en route. Johnston himself was on the scene, but although he outranked Beauregard, he permitted the hero of Fort Sumter, who had made the dispositions and had a better knowledge of the terrain, to manage the tactics of opposing McDowell. Johnston also approved the plan of operations Beauregard had developed prior to the Army of the Shenandoah's arrival at Manassas Junction—a plan that called for a strike at the enemy's left.

As McDowell had foreseen, Beauregard had taken steps to build up his right flank, but not for defensive purposes. Ever fond of the offensive, on the twentieth the Creole had drawn up a special order detailing the composition of an assault column. Cavalry units played a prominent role in his strategy. Stuart and the 1st Virginia, along with two infantry brigades and a battery, would form a reserve force. Meanwhile, at least nine, and perhaps a dozen, companies of mounted men, including Radford's regiment, had been attached to infantry units along the army's right and right center. When the order to advance was given on the morning of the twenty-first, the assault forces would cross the river, dislodge the enemy, and drive them toward Centreville and Fairfax Court House. As befit Beauregard's style, it was an ambitious plan, and fully as complex as his opponent's. If both plans were put into operation simultaneously, the armies would cartwheel in a gigantic circle. Chance and circumstance would decide how that strange movement ended.[11]

⊱—⊹—◯—⊹—⊰

In the predawn darkness of July 21, Beauregard's troops held their positions on the south bank of the run, anxiously awaiting the call to action. Infantry and artillery were in heavy force all along that line, while the cavalry was posted in irregularly spaced pockets. The heaviest concentration of horsemen was at and near Mitchell's Ford, where Bonham retained the troopers who had supported him on the eighteenth. The next largest body guarded the far right at and near Union Mills Ford. There the newly minted Brigadier General Ewell enjoyed the support of Green's Rappahannock Cavalry, which had been with him at Fairfax Court House, along with companies under Julien Harrison and Capt. John G.

Cabell. In later months, Green's and Harrison's units joined the 6th Virginia Cavalry, while Cabell's became Company I of the 4th Virginia.[12]

Those elements of the Army of the Shenandoah that had reached Beauregard's side were likewise positioned along the right and right center. Jackson's brigade was situated in rear of both Bonham and Longstreet, the latter still at Blackburn's Ford, while the brigades of Brig. Gen. Barnard Bee and Col. Francis S. Bartow were stationed even farther to the right. Of the newcomers, only the 1st Virginia Cavalry, four companies strong, lay near the center of the defensive line, filling the gap between Mitchell's Ford and the Stone Bridge.

Fewer than one hundred horsemen—two companies of Radford's regiment—patrolled Beauregard's left, where the battle of First Manassas (or First Bull Run) began. They appear to have done a poor job, for the army's signal corps, not the cavalry, alerted the commander in that sector, Col. Nathan G. Evans, to McDowell's turning movement. The warning meant that McDowell's attack would rule the day and that his opponent would merely react to it.

Fortunately for Beauregard's peace of mind, Evans moved to the threatened point quickly enough to blunt some of Hunter's momentum. As a muggy dawn broke, Bee's and Bartow's men moved to within supporting distance of Evans along the south side of a Bull Run tributary, Young's Branch. Even so, the heavier Union column muscled its way into Beauregard's midst, eventually forcing its opponents onto the crest of high ground known as Henry Hill. There, late in the morning, the defenders dug in for a desperate stand against the larger columns of Hunter and Heintzelman. Despite the disparity of numbers, Jackson's brigade held its ground so stubbornly that command and commander won the enduring nickname "Stonewall."[13]

For a time it appeared that the concentration of defensive power could not prevent the left flank from going under. By early afternoon, Hunter's men were giving the holders of Henry Hill all they could handle, while to their right, Heintzelman's fresher ranks were moving up the Sudley Springs Road. The new arrivals included a pair of well-appointed batteries of Regular artillery, supported by a couple regiments of New York volunteers, including the "Fire Zouaves" of the 11th Infantry, garbed in drill-team attire: Fezzes, short jackets, baggy pants, and white gaiters. While the cannons began to pound Jackson's front, the Zouaves moved into position to sweep around his left flank into his rear, a potentially devastating maneuver.

The lodgment was never made, thanks to the timely intervention of Stuart and his riders. Since the battle's opening shots, the plumed officer had waited nervously for orders to commit his regiment en masse. Until afternoon, he had been confined to leading small detachments across Bull Run to scout the Union buildup opposite Sudley Springs Ford. Returning to the south bank, he had idled for hours in rear of Bonham's lightly engaged infantry, his view of the fighting to the north and west blocked by trees and hillocks.[14]

One of Stuart's officers, Capt. W. W. Blackford, described his commander as "striding backwards and forwards in great impatience." At intervals the lieutenant colonel would leave his assigned post and ride off to confer with superiors, whom he importuned for orders to engage the enemy. He began to fear that the call would never come; apparently Beauregard considered his regiment a rear guard rather than a front-line force. Stuart's anxiety peaked when, sometime in afternoon, he observed demoralized South Carolina infantrymen fleeing the embattled left. After a few minutes, however, the flow of fugitives—members of a multiarm organization known as the Hampton Legion—ceased. He later learned that the legion, galvanized by the courage of its wounded leader, Col. Wade Hampton, rallied on Jackson's right and gave a strong account of itself through the rest of the fight.[15]

At about 2:00 P.M., with the fighting on Henry Hill at the critical stage, and just as Stuart despaired of seeing action, an aide from army headquarters rode up, saluted, and shouted to make himself heard above the din: "Colonel Stuart,   *P. G. T.* General Beauregard directs that you bring your command into action at once and that you attack where the firing is hottest!" Almost before the officer finished speaking, Stuart was leading two squadrons of grim-faced troopers through the trees, out the Sudley Spring Road, and toward the place of greatest need.[16]

At first Stuart sought to circumvent the enemy's flank along the Sudley Spring Road, turning the tables on Irvin McDowell. Failing to locate a byroad to his objective, he headed for Jackson's position on the high ground below Young's Branch. Noting the cavalry's approach, Jackson, who had been slightly wounded, informed Stuart that his command was within minutes of being forced to the rear. Stuart saluted and went to work. Leaving a squadron under his second-in-command, Maj. Robert Swan, to guard Jackson's right, Stuart made for the other end of the brigade line with his two remaining companies, perhaps 150 officers and troopers.

An extended gallop brought the head of the column to within seventy yards of the 11th New York, whose men were poised to strike Jackson's left. After a moment's hesitation—aware that Beauregard's army also included Zouaves, and unsure whether he was facing friend or foe—Stuart led his regiment forward at a gallop. "At them we went," wrote one of his men, "like an arrow from a bow."[17]

As the Virginians thundered toward the New Yorkers, they attracted the notice of numerous Zouaves, who treated them to a fusillade originally intended for Jackson's infantry. Nineteen-year-old Bushrod Lynn, who rode at the head of the charging column, recalled that "the deadly fire emptied many a saddle before we reached their line; but after they had delivered their fire, those of us who had remained in our saddles had little difficulty in riding through their ranks and scattering them." Flailing about with pistols and sabers, the Virginians quickly lined the ground with recumbent figures in gaily colored uniforms. Within minutes, the infantry's formation had been broken beyond hope of quick repair.[18]

Once they recovered from the shock of the attack, unhurt Zouaves strove to hold their ground. Some unfastened their bayonets and thrust them at the passing riders, inflicting severe wounds on men and mounts. When the Virginians turned about and spurred back toward them, however, most of the Zouaves took off running, some of them screaming bloody murder. Few stopped short of the stream they had forded with hope and confidence short hours before. Captain Blackford observed with satisfaction that the enemy had been "completely paralyzed by this charge, and though their actual loss in killed and wounded was not very great, their demoralization was complete." Looking back years later, he decided that had the 1st Virginia not come on the scene when it did, the enemy would have uprooted Jackson's brigade: "The arrest of their dangerous move upon the exposed flank of our main line of battle . . . saved the day."[19]

The 1st Virginia initiated a pursuit, but Stuart recalled his troopers and returned them, by a roundabout route, to the starting point of their attack. The roads leading to Bull Run remained clogged with the enemy, and to challenge so many adversaries—even when in retreat—posed risks. Besides, as the lieutenant colonel knew, his hard-fighting squadron had already accomplished its mission, and in fine style.[20]

>─┤─◆>─O─<◆─┤─<

The Zouaves' retreat left Hunter's and Heintzelman's batteries vulnerable to assault by Jackson and his supports. The subsequent capture of all but one cannon ensured that the newly christened Stonewall Brigade would hold its ground. Then, too, the arrival of supports from less-threatened portions of the line, as well as from Manassas Junction, where transferees from the Valley continued to disembark, meant that the Confederate left, once given up for dead, would survive the afternoon.

For two hours following the 1st Virginia's attack, fighting swept over the high ground below Young's Branch, until the steady increase of troops opposite the Union right enabled Johnston and Beauregard to counterattack. By now McDowell's exhausted troops had been fighting for ten hours under a merciless sun, sustained by the prospect of a glorious victory. When the recruits found themselves pressed backward, their resolve and their formations suddenly crumbled. Small groups, then whole regiments and brigades, began to stream across Bull Run in retreat. At first the withdrawal proceeded in good order, but when shells from a Confederate battery destroyed the bridge over Cub Run, the main retreat route to Centreville, panic seized the Federals and a rout ensued.[21]

Although gratified and relieved by his opponent's flight, Beauregard was unwilling to let it proceed under its own power. At his order, Stuart's and Radford's troopers took up a pursuit along divergent lines, in some places accompanied by infantry and artillery. Having moved farther to the left following the rout of the 11th New York, Stuart hurled the two companies in his charge against the western end of the retreat column. They pressed the Yankees hard, but so many prisoners fell into their hands, requiring the detaching of an ever-increasing number of guards, that eventually Stuart "had not a squad left" to continue the harassment.

By then, he had inflicted severe blows on the Union rear, some delivered with the help of a talented young artillerist, Lt. Robert F. Beckham. To Stuart's delight, Beckham placed two guns atop a hill just off the Sudley Springs Road and was soon creating "great havoc in the enemy's ranks." Once the Yankees outdistanced his men, Stuart guided his tired but invigorated squadron to a farm near Sudley Springs Ford, where it went into bivouac.[22]

There Stuart was joined by the two companies under Swan, which, by remaining on Jackson's flank in support of some artillery, had taken no part in the pursuit. Given the patent need for its services elsewhere, the detachment's idleness distressed many of its men. One of these, John Singleton Mosby, a young lawyer from Bristol destined to become the war's most famous partisan leader, observed sarcastically that "Swan did not get a man or a horse scratched. He did a life insurance business that day. Instead of Swan supporting the battery, the battery supported Swan." An unenterprising officer could not hope to remain in the ranks of the 1st Virginia. Nine months later, when the regiment was reorganized and new officers were elected, Swan found himself out of a job.[23]

Elsewhere on the field of victory, Confederate cavalrymen pursued the foe with devastating effect. Two columns crossed Bull Run well downstream of Stuart's sector. Spurring hard to overtake the beaten enemy, they put the final touches to the rout of McDowell's army.

These were the troopers that had been covering Beauregard's right and right center. Most had spent the early hours of the battle as couriers, scouts, and artillery supports; after Jackson's advance to Henry Hill, many had guarded the brigadier's right flank in concert with Swan's squadron. Now, however, the troopers under Colonel Radford and Lieutenant Colonel Munford were going to see more active—and more gratifying—service.

Shortly before 5:00 P.M., responding to an order from one of General Bonham's staff officers, Radford splashed across the stream just south of the Stone Bridge at the head of four companies of his own regiment—Terry's, Winston Radford's, Capt. Andrew L. Pitzer's, and Capt. John D. Alexander's—plus the militia under Wickham and the home guards of Powell. When he reached the far side of the stream, Radford planned to march well to the west of the Cub Run bridge. When an aide from Johnston rushed up to redirect him, Radford was incensed; he told the staff officer he could "go to the Devil—that he was acting under Beauregard's orders." Only when Johnston himself came up from the rear did Radford comply with his order to make for the strategic bridge.[24]

A few minutes after Radford's men took off, Col. Alexander R. Chisholm of Beauregard's staff also ordered Munford's detachment to make for the Cub Run span. Munford crossed Bull Run at Ball's Ford, followed by the 30th Virginia companies of Langhorne and Capt. Giles W. B. Hale, backed by the troopers of Ball and Payne. As the paths of the columns began to converge, both forces rode down the enemy, laying low dozens of hapless Yankees and capturing scores of others, including Col. Michael Corcoran of the 69th New York Militia. Some of the prisoners were philosophical about their fate. Once told his captors he was not surprised the Southern horsemen had carried the day. In contrast to their large numbers, his army had "no cavalry that was worth a damn." Indeed, the six companies of Regular horsemen McDowell had led out of Washington offered little resistance to their counterparts under Stuart, Radford, and Munford.[25]

The Rebel troopers gathered up not only demoralized fugitives, but also baggage wagons, caissons, limbers, discarded weapons of all types, equipment ranging from cartridge boxes to cooking utensils, and from ten to twenty-four artillery pieces. Several guns were found in a giant tangle on the Cub Run bridge; Payne's men spent most of the evening disentangling them. As soon as he could gather up these prizes, Munford conveyed them to the rear, where he proudly presented them to a battlefield visitor, Jefferson Davis.[26]

The trophies were not seized without cost. As their pursuers closed in, they heard the same anguished clamor that had greeted Werth's and Phillips's assault on Newport News. Today's warning of choice was: "The Black Horse! The Black Horse!" Lieutenant Blackford, who heard the same cry on Stuart's part of the battlefield, surmised that the reputation Payne's troopers had gained via the Northern press now extended to every horse soldier in Virginia.[27]

While the warning cries spurred many fugitives to a faster pace, they galvanized some into halting and resisting. At some point, the leading ranks of Radford's and Munford's columns were met by a "scattering fire" that emptied some saddles. Then two cannons on a hill beyond the run opened on the riders, killing Captain Radford, another officer, and five enlisted men. The captain's brother admitted that for a time both columns were thrown "into some confusion," but they rallied quickly enough. A phalanx of dismounted men was soon advancing on the guns. Before they could be shot or captured, the Federals abandoned their suddenly precarious position.[28]

Although most of the fugitives were soon beyond capture, a number of horsemen forded Cub Run as if unwilling to desist until every Yankee was locked inside the Washington defenses. For the most part, however, the cavalry's pursuit ended at the clogged bridge. The troopers halted there to re-form, tend to their casualties, gather up their prisoners and spoils, and contemplate the meaning of their achievement. One of Radford's subordinates called July 21 "a day long to be remembered, and such a Sunday as men seldom spend." To a member of the Black Horse, the battle as a whole, and especially its frenetic denouement, ranked as "the most brilliant victory ever achieved by arms in America."[29]

Many horsemen, in common with comrades in the infantry and artillery, pronounced the outcome decisive, professing to believe the war over and Southern independence assured. Troopers given to more sober reflection saw the battle just ended as a prologue, not a finale. Even with the day's events as a guide, it might not be possible to predict the final result of this conflict. And yet one thing seemed certain: Horse soldiers would play a major, perhaps a pivotal, role in the outcome.

Chapter Three

If You Want to Smell Hell

The Confederate horsemen in the eastern theater entered the war with great advantages and severe disadvantages. How well they balanced these factors—how successfully they exploited the former and minimized the latter—would determine whether they prevailed against an enemy that shared some of the same strengths and weaknesses.

At the outset, assets appeared to outweigh liabilities by a comfortable margin. As one of Stuart's veterans observed, "probably no nation ever went to war richer in resource as to its cavalry material." For one thing, perhaps more so than comrades in the other arms of the service, the average trooper was enthusiastic about taking the field. He was motivated not only by a desire to protect hearth and home, but by an urge to demonstrate the moral fiber and combat prowess of the Southern patriot.[1]

For many years prior to 1861, Virginians, South Carolinians, Georgians, and their brethren had been convinced of the military superiority of their region—now was the time to prove it. More than they feared death or disabling, most recruits worried that the conflict would prove too short to showcase their martial abilities. After the war, William Blackford remembered that when the men of the 1st Virginia assembled at Richmond in early May 1861, "the only care we felt was the dread that the war would be over before we got there. It is amusing now to recall how general this feeling was—every one seemed to think one battle would settle it," and the thought that he might miss that opportunity was unbearable.[2]

While this enthusiasm to show one's mettle motivated the young men of every Southern state, it seemed especially strong among Virginians. The military history and traditions of the Old Dominion, as well as her status as the region's center of commerce and industry, assured the state of a critical role in the war and in the army that bore her name. The majority of those who went into the cavalry from Virginia were members of the lower and middle classes; most entertained no delusions of physical or moral superiority, and almost none made any claim to it. Still, the "Virginia mystique" motivated the dirt farmer just as strongly as it did the son of the landed gentry. It fostered in him a sense of inherent strength and skill, which gave him a leg up on his adversary in terms of morale and self-confidence.

By precipitating the breakup of the Union, South Carolina fire-eaters may have brought on the war, but Virginians believed it was they who would have to win it. One who reflected deeply on his motivations for entering military service, George Cary Eggleston of J. E. B. Stuart's regiment, declared that "Virginians understood what secession implied much more perfectly than did the rest of the Southern people." It meant revolution, death, destruction, and perhaps economic, political, and social chaos, but whatever its effects, it could not be ignored or wished away. The conflict that lay ahead had to be prosecuted with maximum effort and in a spirit of wholehearted commitment.

Many Virginians viewed war as an essential experience for a young man, one that validated his honor and furthered his social aspirations. As Eggleston noted, in the aftermath of Fort Sumter, leaving the comforts of home for the dangers of the battlefield "became absolutely essential to the maintenance of one's reputation as a gentleman." Those who tried to evade the responsibility risked being shunned, if not ostracized, by friends, neighbors, even relatives.[3]

Not every Virginian, or every Southerner, was a hostage to the martial impulse or the male ethos. Many who entered the field in 1861 had a firm grasp on reality and tended to sober reflection. These men saw soldiering as a responsibility, not a proving ground for masculinity. A member of the 13th Virginia Cavalry called joining the army "my most solemn duty" and pledged "to add what little may lay in my power to the support of my countries rights. . . . So long as I am able I expect to fight when my country calls." Those for whom soldiering was a regrettable necessity blamed the situation on a power-mad, conquest-driven North. "It is the duty of every man," a North Carolina trooper declared, "to turn out and show them that we are determined to resist every effort made by them for our subjugation."[4]

The desire to defend home, state, and way of life was the only motivation of some cavalrymen. "I have no thirst for military fame," wrote a field officer in the 3rd Virginia, "for I know it is won through blood and tears and suffering. But I do desire to aid in driving the base invader from Virginia's soil." Those who violated Southern sovereignty deserved little mercy. A member of the 6th Virginia put it succinctly: "Every northern soldier who puts his foot on our soil justly forfeits his life." And if the confrontation ended with the defender, not the invader, being struck down, so be it. "If a Yankey don't kill me," declared one member of the 2nd Virginia, "I will fite them as long as I have a drop of blod."[5]

If a Southerner had to become a soldier in order to defend his rights and his region, he could do worse than join the cavalry. Mounted service conjured up images from an age when knighthood flourished and gave life to the literary images of Thomas Mallory, Sir Walter Scott, and Charles O'Malley, the cavalry's poet laureate. Riding to war seemed a genteel and sublime way of serving one's region. It also answered a call to an adventurous life, a theme played up by numerous early-war stories and songs, including a favorite ditty of Stuart himself, "Jine the Cavalry," which described the cavalry as the branch to join "if you want to have a high time" and "if you want to smell hell."[6]

Many youngsters who answered the call were not disappointed—at least, not at first. One who enlisted in the 2nd Virginia in 1861 acknowledged that "there is certainly something in the perilous excitement of war which serves to enliven & revive the health of mind & body. Especially is this the case in the cavalry."

Mounted duty appeared even more attractive in comparison to treading rough or muddy roads in the infantry or bouncing along atop an artillery caisson. An enlisted man in the 1st North Carolina informed his wife that though he regretted being unable to secure a commission in his regiment, "my position in [the] Cavalry is preferable to a Lieutenancy in Infantry." A comrade from Virginia claimed that "the privileges of the foot companies are as nothing compared to ours." Those who had bypassed the cavalry for the infantryman's life tended to regret their decision. One advised his parents to tell a younger brother desirous of enlisting "by all means to Join the Cavalry—and bear in mind that a private in The Infantry is the worse place he can possibly be put into in this war."[7]

Trapped in such an undesirable branch, many foot soldiers developed a bitter resentment toward their mounted comrades, to which they gave voice at the first opportunity. The adjutant of the 3rd Virginia recalled that infantrymen would loudly refer to passing horsemen as "calvery," while gesturing obscenely or shouting epithets, the least objectionable being, "Here's your mule!" At first the officer wondered why the foot troops "were all very spiteful towards us." Then one day his black servant told him, "Dey jes do so cause dey down in de mud while you on good horse."[8]

For some enlistees, the lure of the trooper's life had an enduring quality. As late as September 1862, a North Carolinian in the Jeff Davis Legion continued to be "delighted with the Cavalry service." Yet this man appears to have been the exception, not the rule, for horse soldiers performed duty more arduous and more frequent than most infantrymen or artillerists. In battle, they fought alongside their less mobile comrades, often on foot but without a foot soldier's weaponry and training. They also risked their lives by guarding the flanks and rear of the main army, by spearheading attacks and pursuits, and, when serving as skirmishers, by drawing hostile fire in an attempt to pinpoint the enemy's location and numbers.[9]

Horsemen worked as hard off the battlefield as on it. During so-called inactive campaigning, while the other branches remained snug in their tents or lolled about camp, exerting themselves only for roll call or target practice, horsemen were constantly in motion, serving as pickets (mounted sentinels), garrison and train guards, scouts, couriers, orderlies, and escort troops. The grueling pace was not slowed by the darkness of night or inclement weather. Moreover, while the foot soldier or the cannoneer had only himself to care for, the trooper had to water, feed, groom, exercise, and stable his mount on a daily basis. No matter how weary or ill he might be after a day's service, a cavalry-man realized that his continued survival depended on tending to his horse's needs before his own.

The daily routine, especially when a unit was confined to a fixed camp, was so crowded and so repetitive as to be stultifying. Writing home in May 1861, a private in the 3rd Virginia described the program that prevailed in the camp of instruction at Ashland, Hanover County, twelve miles north of Richmond:

> The bugle calls us up at 4½ in the morning, at 6 every trooper is required to answer to his name (unless on guard or in the hospital) and get feed for his horse, at 6½ breakfast call, 7 water horses, 8 Mounted Drill when all the Troops in the Regiment are marched out to the field and drilled for two hours. At 12 water and feed again, 12½ Dinner, 2 PM foot drill, 5 inspection of arms. Sundown Dress-parade when the whole Regiment is marched to a beautiful grove where the officers of the different companies report their number of men on drill. . . . Stand-ing guard is the hardest duty we are required to perform. Each man has to stand eight hours in twenty-four, alternating however, standing two hours and resting four. We are detailed alphabetically and the time comes 'round once in four or five days. I stood one night when it rained in torrents all the time.[10]

The frequency and duration of the hardships a trooper was exposed to, especially when on picket duty in the face of the enemy, could play hob with his physical and mental stamina. Some men took the assignment philosophi-cally, such as the 9th Virginia trooper who reflected that "the snow and rain beat upon every man in the Division, Generals, Colonels, all the officers," as well as the "wearied, dusty, and worn out" enlisted men. Yet the misery-loves-company school of thought did little to comfort troopers forced to stand picket for long periods. More than a few comrades must have shared the sentiment of one anonymous trooper who called outpost duty "the most disagreeable life I ever led." A veteran of the cavalry portion of Cobb's (Georgia) Legion complained that a civilian had not the faintest idea "of what constitutes comfort" until he had "experience[d] the hardships of War," and especially those of picket duty.[11]

In addition to fatigue, a picket had to ward off the sense of isolation and vulnerability the duty invited. A member of the 2nd Virginia dreaded the prospect of having "to sit on your horse at midnight in a lonely road a couple of miles from camp, in bitter weather, with the possibility, sometimes probability, of being rushed upon and captured or quietly shot by the enemy." An enlisted man in the Jeff Davis Legion was never happier than when relieved on picket, fearing that had he stood guard even a few minutes longer, "a Yankee might have slipped up and put a knife in my back."[12]

The cavalryman's life included little that compensated him for his onerous burdens. What free time he could squeeze out of his day was filled with such simple forms of relaxation as reading books, writing letters home, visiting comrades, gambling (betting on card games, wrestling matches, horse races, and every other form of human or animal competition), and the like. When the regimental chaplain performed services, the pious and the curious joined their infantry and artillery friends in attendance. Even nonbelievers were likely to attend, if only to escape duty for an hour or two.

Troopers could not even count on a regular issuance of rations. When available, army food was often of limited variety or poor quality, or was prepared haphazardly. As John Ervine of the 1st Virginia told his wife:

> If you was to see the beef strewn about on the ground & men cooking off it you would think we did not care for dirt. Our fare is naught nothing but beef or bacon & wheat bread. The bread is baked. Coffee we have to toast & grind ourselves. We have had sugar all the time until a few days ago the supply gave out.

Even if rations could be had, cooking utensils were not always available. A member of the 4th Virginia complained that he and his messmates subsisted on "nothing but bread and meat all the time," even though "we have nothing to cook in, only one frying pan amongst us.[13]

Unlike their usually well-fed enemy, Confederate horsemen might go without rations for long periods. A South Carolina veteran explained that the troopers' peripatetic existence, with "their numerous and unexpected movements," ensured that they were "more irregularly supplied than the other branches of the service." More often than their infantry or artillery friends, they were forced to live off the land not only for their own sustenance, but also for that of their horses. While their mobility helped troopers to forage effectively, the practice became less and less remunerative as the war dragged on and the armies denuded the farmlands of Virginia.[14]

All things considered, the cavalryman's life usually fell short of the gallant and glorious exploits that storybook horsemen enjoyed. In making this point, the South Carolinian offered an anecdote about a young trooper he had come to know. On one occasion, soon after the youth joined the cavalry, he found himself "tired, hungry, dirty, and generally miserable and disgusted," the result of a long night of picket duty along the marshy banks of a river within carbine shot of the enemy:

> There had been enough fighting to give everyone a stomachful. . . . The malaria seemed visible in the misty exhalations rising from the swamp and the swarms of mosquitoes were certainly of thoroughbred stock, with whom it was impossible to arrange a *modus vivendi*. To

make things more comfortable, two bodies—whether of friend or foe no one knew—had been buried close at hand in such shallow holes as to be partly visible. All night long, from time to time, two dogs, though driven off again and again, would come back and try to scratch away the earth from the corpses, either from affection for the dead or in order to devour them. At length, after a long, gloomy silence, the new recruit said to a comrade:

"Did you ever read Charles O'Malley? It is a blanketty, blanketty, blank pack of lies from beginning to end!"[15]

>–+–<>–-O–-<+–+–<

The typical Confederate cavalryman enjoyed a material advantage over his opponent in the experience he had acquired in the basics of soldiering. George Eggleston believed that the young men of the South "were more universally accustomed to field sports and the use of arms than were those of the North." Thomas Lafayette Rosser, one of the Confederacy's most celebrated mounted leaders, recalled that the cavalry of the Army of Northern Virginia "was composed almost entirely of young men, who were perfectly at home in the saddle and accustomed to the independent life of gentlemen."[16]

Contemporary observations of a similar nature were made not only by the Confederates themselves, but also by more objective spectators. Lord Wolsley, a British military observer, commented that every Southern trooper who came to his notice "rode well, in which particular they present a striking contrast to the Northern cavalry, who can scarcely sit their horses, even when trotting. . . . Every man in the South rides from childhood. . . . In the North thousands keep horses," but as a means of powering carriages and wagons.[17]

Early familiarity with horsemanship turned many young Southerners to cavalry service. "My love of horses," wrote an enlistee in the 3rd Virginia, "would, of course, permit me to join no other branch of the service." A grasp of equestrianism also instilled in recruits a sense of superiority that fortified morale. Lt. (later Brig. Gen.) Richard L. T. Beale recalled the formation of his 9th Virginia: "Relying upon our perfect familiarity with firearms from boyhood and our horsemanship, we feared not the disparity of numbers, and though without an officer who had ever seen service, or studied tactics, we felt confident of our ability to cope successfully with thrice our numbers."[18]

Just as the dearth of good roads in the region forced Southerners to ride early and often, the sparsely settled territory below the Mason-Dixon line spawned the development of a generation of scouts that gave the Confederate cavalry another inherent advantage over its opponent. From the earliest days of the conflict, the armies operated in territory with which the Southern horseman was intimately familiar. Within that area, he maneuvered freely along woods, trails, and backroads with which his enemy was unacquainted.

Not surprisingly, some of the war's most effective scouts populated the cavalry of the Army of Northern Virginia. Scouting expertise was resident in many regiments, but especially so in the ranks of the 1st and 4th Virginia. The 1st supplied the superb partisan leader Mosby and provided him with the nucleus of his 43rd Virginia Battalion; it also furnished Stuart with his favorite scout, Robert W. Goode. The 4th Virginia gave rise to the celebrated scout and spy B. Franklin Stringfellow, who operated within Union lines with impunity, clad sometimes in gray, sometimes in blue, sometimes in mufti. A master of disguise, on at least one occasion this beardless youth gained critical intelligence by wiggling into a hoopskirt and impersonating a young woman so convincingly that Yankee officers flirted with him.[19]

From the 4th Virginia also came Rob Towles, a teenage daredevil who never achieved Stringfellow's celebrity but whose adventures in Yankeedom matched the older man's, hairbreadth escape for hairbreadth escape. Then there was the South Carolinian known throughout the army as "Farley, the Scout." This was Capt. William D. Farley, a chivalrous volunteer on Stuart's staff whom one colleague described as "a man so notable for daring, skill, and efficiency as a partisan, that all who valued those great qualities honoured him as their chiefest exemplar."[20]

A cavalryman is only as effective as his horse, and the Confederacy benefited greatly from its early-war monopoly on quality horseflesh. Virginia was especially blessed in the quality and quantity of its blooded stock, numerous specimens of which found their way into cavalry service. "From the foundation of the colony," wrote William L. Royall of the 9th Virginia, "Virginians have been devoted to fine horses, and in 1861 the State was as well supplied with thoroughbred and partially thoroughbred horses as with sheep and cattle. . . . The young men in Virginia were all perfect horsemen, and mounted on their thoroughbred or half-breed horses they made a magnificent spectacle in regimental formation."[21]

Equine bloodlines were true titles to Virginia nobility. As Maj. Henry Brainard McClellan, J. E. B. Stuart's adjutant, put it, "The descendants of such racers as Sir Archy, Boston, Eclipse, Timoleon, Exchequer, Red-Eye, and many others more or less famous on the turf, were scattered over the State. Gentlemen fond of following the hounds had raised these horses for their own use." The fine qualities of these studs' offspring, "their speed, endurance, and surefootedness," were prevalent in the ranks of Stuart's cavalry. When mounts such as these maneuvered against Yankee horses only weeks removed from the cart or the plow, small wonder that their riders emerged victorious.[22]

Another critical early advantage enjoyed by Stuart's cavalry was its broad and deep leadership base. By virtue of their prewar cavalry experience, a plethora of high-ranking commanders, including Lee and Johnston, knew instinctively the best way to support, promote, and utilize their horsemen. They ensured that the mounted arm was commanded by the most talented young officers the South could furnish.

The man at the top was a case in point. J. E. B. Stuart was a native of Patrick County, Virginia, a West Pointer, and a leading light in the dragoon service of the Old Army. Twenty-eight at war's start, with unusually long legs and an impressive growth of cinnamon-colored beard that supposedly hid a weak chin, Stuart was already a learned member of his profession when his state left the Union. He had won his spurs in a series of engagements against the Plains Indians, during one of which he received a near-fatal wound. In many respects, he was also the embodiment of the Virginia cavalier, imbued as he was with courtly manners and a respect for the chivalric code of an earlier era.[23]

To observers who focused only on external qualities, Stuart was as much a performer as a soldier. His aide, John Esten Cooke, a talented novelist and essayist, believed that "everything stirring, brilliant, and picturesque, seemed to centre in him." Cooke's most enduring image of his boss had Stuart

> wearing a uniform brilliant with gold braid, golden spurs, and a hat looped up with a golden star and decorated with a black plume; going on marches at the head of his cavalry column with his banjo-player gayly thrumming behind him; leading his troops to battle with a camp song on his lips; here to-day and away to-morrow, riding, fighting, laughing, dancing.[24]

Yet Stuart was no fugitive from some *opera bouffe*. The "Knight of the Golden Spurs" may have been flashy, and he was ever image-conscious, but he was neither pompous nor arrogant. He had an open, frank manner and a guileless simplicity that won the trust and affection of associates and subordinates. A strong sense of humor prevented him from taking himself too seriously. He loved to play jokes on those close to him, but when the joke was on him, he laughed just as heartily at his own expense. Through such traits, he became immensely popular among his troopers, who regarded him with genuine devotion. Having won their loyalty, Stuart had little trouble convincing them that when they followed him, they need fear no foe, not even a better armed and equipped one. It helped immensely that time after time he proved as much against forces of equal or larger size. There was no more effective motivator, no greater spur to corporate morale, in any branch of the Army of Northern Virginia.

Stuart had his complexities, his contradictions, his flaws. Modern-day psychologists describe him as an extrovert with a strong need for power, autonomy, and achievement. Relatively few contemporaries were openly critical of him, although even his friends would occasionally fault his susceptibility to the flattery of powerful men and the attentions of attractive women. As Esten Cooke liked to point out, behind Stuart's back some sneered "at his splendid costume, his careless laughter, his 'love of ladies,' at his banjo-player, his flower wreathed horses, and his gay verses." Occasionally someone would make a careless accusation that reeked of jealousy, pique, or malice. One disgruntled subordinate went so far as to claim, without producing evidence to sustain his contention, that the general had been "as false to me as he has ever been to his Country and to his Wife."[25]

Even those well disposed toward Stuart could be critical not only of his personality, but of his leadership as well. Virtually everyone who attempted to get to the core of this soldier—and many did, during his lifetime and after—described him as a man-child of war, a curious mix of savvy veteran and wide-eyed recruit. It is true that Stuart accepted war's brutality and wastage while savoring its beguiling appeal, but so did countless colleagues. He was an incurable romantic with the ability—and the need—to believe that beauty could not only coexist with brutality, but transcend it. More than a few of his contemporaries, comrades and enemies alike, depended on that same faculty for self-deception to make it through the day.

The only problem with Stuart's immaturity was that it occasionally overrode his better judgment. The boy in him loved risk-taking, the thrill of slipping into and out of dangerous situations with a minimum of assistance. To Stuart, victory was never sweeter than when achieved against daunting odds, and the way he went about proving the point sometimes placed his people unnecessarily in harm's way.[26]

If, by naming Stuart their leading horseman, Lee and Johnston demonstrated their sagacity, Stuart displayed similar gifts when selecting his own subordinates. In the early going, he attached to his side kindred spirits, hard fighters who thoroughly enjoyed the lighter moments that war could produce. While it took several months for him to acquire every subordinate whose services he coveted, several were in the fold before the end of 1861. Most would continue to serve him for the next two years, their fortunes, their reputations, inextricably linked with his.

Stuart's most trusted lieutenant was Fitzhugh Lee, nephew of Robert E. Lee, and Stuart's successor as lieutenant colonel of the 1st Virginia. Fitz was a small-scale version of his friend and superior: jovial, convivial, a born romantic, the man Douglas Southall Freeman christened the "Laughing Cavalier." Unlike the married teetotaler Stuart, however, Fitz was a bachelor with the palate of an epicure and a fondness for alcoholic spirits, although he drank to excess rarely, if ever. While no intellectual (he graduated forty-fifth in the forty-nine-man West Point Class of 1856), he had gifts that transcended book learning, for he had the instincts, the reflexes, of a born cavalryman.[27]

Other skillful subordinates assigned to Stuart before or shortly after the close of 1861 included Robert E. Lee's second son, William Henry Fitzhugh ("Rooney") Lee, a Harvard man rather than a West Pointer, the first field commander of the 9th Virginia, on whose solid good sense and unflappable demeanor Stuart learned to depend; the quietly capable Tom Munford, who early in 1862 succeeded Colonel Radford in command of the 30th Virginia (by then redesignated the 2nd Virginia Cavalry); two combat-proven veterans of First Manassas, Williams Wickham and William Payne, the original lieutenant colonel and major, respectively, of the 4th Virginia; William Thompson Martin, a native Kentuckian who became, in succession, major, lieutenant colonel, and colonel of the Jeff Davis Legion and who won more early-war distinction than any other subordinate born outside the Old Dominion; and two North Carolinians, Laurence Simmons Baker and James Byron Gordon of the state's 9th Volunteers (1st North Carolina Cavalry), both of whom rose to prominence through fearlessness and a determination to lead from the front—traits that played hob with their physical health.[28]

An early-war lieutenant of another stripe was William Edmondson Jones, who became colonel of the 1st Virginia after Stuart won his first star, relinquishing the command to Fitz Lee six months later. A cantankerous malcontent who came to despise Stuart and was eventually forced into exile, Jones nevertheless won the respect of his men through his lack of ego and the firm yet fair hand with which he ruled them. Yet another subordinate who made an early mark was not a cavalryman at all: Lt. (later Maj.) John Pelham, an Alabamian with pretty-boy looks whose intelligence, courage, and tactical gifts made him the war's most famous artillery officer. Although not an administrative genius, by sheer force of will Pelham transformed Stuart's horse artillery from an impotent clutter of guns, men, and horses into a major force in battle, one he maneuvered with dash, imagination, and on occasion, audacity.[29]

With the exception of Pelham, who fell mortally wounded halfway through the war, each of these subordinates—even the crotchety Jones—became general officers. Thanks to the rank and authority they attained, their leadership styles had a major impact on the operational record and corporate image of the cavalry of the Army of Northern Virginia. Other, equally talented officers, who for the first year of the war held positions lower than they deserved—men such as M. Calbraith Butler of the mounted contingent of the Hampton Legion (later the 2nd South Carolina Cavalry) and Pierce M. B. Young of the Cobb's Legion cavalry—won promotion and made their reputations in later months. They were joined in Stuart's inner circle by officers who had begun the war in other branches of the service but who possessed the versatility to make a successful transition to the cavalry, of whom the best known were Wade Hampton and Lunsford L. Lomax of the infantry and Thomas Rosser of the mounted artillery.[30]

One final advantage enjoyed by the cavalry of the main Confederate army in the East was a staff system—one of the largest in Confederate service—that operated with wondrous efficiency behind the lines as well as on the field of combat. No one's staff had more talented personnel than Stuart's. In addition to Blackford (his chief engineer), Cooke (his ordnance officer), and McClellan (his fourth and last adjutant general), the cavalry leader was blessed with such talented aides as Dabney Ball (commissary officer and later the semiofficial chaplain of Stuart's command), Heros von Borcke, late of the Prussian Army (inspector of cavalry), Alexander R. Boteler (volunteer aide-de-camp), L. Tiernan Brien (Stuart's first adjutant general), Chiswell Dabney (aide-de-camp),

Norman R. FitzHugh (second adjutant general of Stuart's command), Theodore S. Garnett, Jr. (aide-de-camp), Peter W. Hairston, Stuart's brother-in-law (aide-de-camp), Philip Henry Powers (chief quartermaster), R. Channing Price (Stuart's third adjutant general), Francis Smith Robertson (assistant engineer), James Hardeman Stuart, a cousin of the general's (aide-de-camp), and Andrew Reid Venable (adjutant and inspector general).

Stuart's military family accompanied him into the thick of battle, where two of them, Channing Price and Hardeman Stuart, lost their lives. Other aides incurred severe and, in the case of the towering von Borcke, disabling wounds. The blood they shed indicates how closely they all stuck to their commander, no matter the risk, so intent were they on discerning Stuart's intentions and on communicating them as clearly and as precisely as possible.

Every subordinate to whom they conveyed Stuart's orders trusted the staff as implicitly as they did the general himself. This was a tribute not every staff officer in the Army of Northern Virginia could expect. Stuart felt truly blessed with his military family, some members of which he treated like sons, others as brothers. Upon occasion he poured out his emotion to his wife, glorying in the fact that the staff "are so devoted to me—isn't it gratifying?"[31]

Chapter Four

An Uneven Fight

If the advantages enjoyed by Stuart's cavalrymen were many and formidable, so were the challenges they faced on a daily basis. Even in the early days of the war, the debit side of the ledger was a cause for concern. In the last two years of the conflict, the troopers of the Army of Northern Virginia spent as much time fighting resource shortages as they did the horsemen in blue.

The most obvious disadvantage the troopers faced was one that bedeviled its army, and its nation, as a whole: the small population base from which it drew its manpower. According to the census of 1860, the states that fought for the Union had a total white population of almost nineteen million, as against perhaps six million in the seceding states and in those border-state areas sympathetic to the Confederate cause. The draft-age population in both regions roughly matched this ratio. The manpower disparity mirrored the contrast between the wide and deep industrial foundation of the North, which provided critical support to the Union effort, and the industry-poor Confederacy.[1]

The South attempted to solve its manpower problem by passing and rigidly enforcing a conscription law more than a year before its opponent went to the draft, but the results were disappointing. The region sought to overcome its industrial weakness by importing large quantities of war goods from Britain and France, yet the supply dried up fairly quickly thanks to the U.S. Navy. The resource imbalance between North and South became permanent.

In the Confederate cavalry, the imbalance was reflected in the smaller size of its regiments and the widespread shortage of appropriate weapons. Until mid-1862, most Union cavalry outfits consisted of ten companies, upward of one thousand officers and men; thereafter, however, virtually all were increased to twelve companies, a paper strength of twelve hundred. The expansion was complete by the Gettysburg campaign of June and July 1863. In contrast, the ten-company standard for Confederate regiments remained in effect throughout the war. For the first two years, when Union regiments were fragmented for service on and off the battlefield, the difference was not so acute. But after early 1863, when the Union horsemen in the East were grouped into a corps, they began to be used in large, powerful combinations, ensuring that in combat their opponents were outnumbered and outgunned.[2]

Its disadvantage in weaponry was one of the most formidable obstacles that Stuart's cavalry faced. Types and numbers of weapons varied from regiment to regiment and even from company to company, but the average trooper could not match his Union counterpart in the quality and quantity of his arms and ammunition.

Especially at war's outset, Confederate troopers were poorly armed, some abysmally so. Members of the 10th Virginia went to war toting "horse pistols" dating from the 1840s and muskets with barrels "cut off about midway for cavalry use." A veteran of the 3rd Virginia recalled that "some of us were equipped with old sabres that had done service in the Revolutionary War, the War of 1812, or the war with Mexico. Some of the troop had derringers, others had revolvers of ancient vintage, while only a few had modern weapons." Other regiments, such as the 7th Virginia, wielded only pistols and shotguns.[3]

More than a few units had makeshift weapons, or none at all—and not only during the first weeks of the war. The Little Fork Rangers (later Company D of the 4th Virginia) started out with nothing but dirks, handmade by a local blacksmith. Its men believed these would be quickly replaced with real cavalry arms, but "the condition of the company in regard to weapons was poor for some time to come. In fact, at no time during the war was the entire company well armed." The unit's historian recalled the plaintive comment of one comrade: "We might have fought, if we had had something to fight with."[4]

It appears axiomatic that the Confederate government should have concentrated its efforts on supplying its mounted forces with large numbers of carbines. That short-barreled rifle, capable of effective use at distances of up to five hundred yards from the target and light enough to permit its use in the saddle or on foot, was the trooper's primary shoulder arm. At the start of the war, the Union cavalry received carbines with a breechloading capability, something lacking in the longer, heavier rifles of the infantry. The ability to reload a carbine through its breech greatly increased a trooper's rate of fire. By 1862, repeating rifles became available to the Union horsemen, and in the autumn of 1863, carbines capable of firing seven rounds without reloading entered their arsenal as well. While repeaters facilitated massed firepower, the greatest asset of the carbine provided to the Federals was the ease with which it could be loaded in any tactical situation.[5]

Since it was not a direct beneficiary of the North's extensive network of arms manufactories, Stuart's cavalry never enjoyed widespread use of breechloaders, either single-shot models or repeaters. In fact, carbines of any sort were relatively rare in the Confederate mounted ranks, especially early in the fight. The typical regiment consisted of one squadron—at the most, two squadrons—of "sharpshooters," its remaining companies being armed with sabers and pistols.[6]

The primary reason for this deficiency was that the few government-run armories in the Confederacy—only one was in existence at war's start, five at its end, supplemented by an unknown number of smaller, state and privately owned arms plants—could not meet the demand for cavalry arms. The quality of the few thousand muzzle-loading carbines the Confederacy did turn out, including the Maynard/Perry and the Tarpley, was inferior to that of their Northern-made counterparts. On numerous occasions, field commanders complained about the performance of these weapons to officials of the understaffed and overworked Confederate Ordnance Department. General Lee himself criticized the breechloading version of the Northern-made Sharps single-shot carbine, about five thousand copies of which were turned out by the armory in Richmond. Of those that did not break, Lee reported, many "were so defective as to be demoralizing to the men."[7]

The Confederacy and its soldiers exploited, with mixed success, other outlets for securing the shoulder arms they needed. In the months before the bombardment of Sumter, many Southern states had purchased in the North large quantities of carbines and other weapons. Once the shooting started, however, most of the shipments were seized by Union officials. In the war's early months, European manufacturers delivered thousands of cavalry arms to Southern ports, but by mid-1862 the Union shipping blockade stanched the flow.

That left the Confederacy with one effective means of securing carbines and other arms and equipment—capture. Especially in 1861–62, when their enemy seemed to run at first contact, Stuart's troopers procured good weaponry on a regular basis. They came to prefer this practice to waiting for their own army to supply them with inferior materiel. It reached the point where whole brigades were said to carry Northern-made weapons. Thomas Rosser noted that by mid-1864, "nearly all my men were armed with captured arms," the use of which the Confederacy promoted by manufacturing ammunition for them.[8]

This method of supply had its limitations. Some of the seized breechloaders fired newly developed metallic ammunition; they could be used only as long as the cartridges captured with them held out. Southern arms makers easily copied the paper and linen cartridges used by many Federal carbines, but methods of duplicating metal cartridges were devised too late in the war to supply more than a few regiments. Some Virginia outfits appear to have used captured breechloaders for weeks or even months. According to one source, in August 1864 all were confiscated "because the impossibility of procuring fresh supplies of cartridges would make them useless at critical moments." This statement is contradicted, however, by a report issued three months later to the effect that every brigade save one in the Cavalry Corps, A.N.V., had Spencer breechloaders in service.[9]

If most of Rosser's men armed themselves with captured carbines, they were exceptionally fortunate. The South Carolina officer who contributed the anecdote about the disillusioned picket suspected that Rosser's men acquired their weapons during long service in the Shenandoah Valley. Most of the horse-men in the Army of Northern Virginia were denied the privilege of extended duty in that haven of second-rank Union armies, which "had been throughout the war in a measure an adjunct to the Confederate Ordnance Department." Carbine-toting Confederates in the main theater of operations were mostly armed with muzzle-loaders, which left them at a distinct disadvantage when opposed by breechloaders in the hands of the enemy.

When Confederate regiments could not procure carbines of any type, they resorted to inadequate substitutes. Most often, they armed themselves with rifles, which were useful mainly in dismounted fighting, a tactic Southern horse-men practiced only upon occasion. Before the blockade clamped down, many troopers were issued rifles such as the British-made Enfield, which could be fired accurately nearly one thousand yards from the target but whose reloading process was described as "slow work at best." All too often, Southern troopers carried less reliable rifles; large numbers made do with muskets and shotguns.[10]

At least one commander actually championed the use of these and other, even less effective, expedients. Early in the war, John Magruder recommended that his cavalry be armed with shotguns and lances. There is no evidence that the Ordnance Department agreed with this strange request, the most curious aspect of which was Magruder's preference for the lance, an antiquated weapon of virtually no use on a Virginia battlefield. The weapon was, however, rela-tively simple to produce (it could "be made by any carpenter and ordinary blacksmith," Magruder believed), and it struck terror in the hearts of the enemy, as did every edged weapon. In June 1862, when the second incarnation of the 5th Virginia Cavalry was organized (the first outfit with that number, a Provi-sional Army unit, was disbanded earlier that same month), some of its compa-nies were armed with handmade lances. As was true of the 6th Pennsylvania Cavalry, the only lancer unit in Federal service, the 5th Virginia discarded its unwieldy "poles" after a brief tryout.[11]

Problems that stemmed from a lack of quality shoulder arms were aggra-vated by the mixture of weapons found in many companies and regiments, which led to inconsistent battlefield performances. As late as mid-1863, one company of the 10th Virginia was issued nine sabers, eight "Mississippi rifles," two double-barrel shotguns, three Enfields (in two different sizes), six "Harpers Ferry rifles," one Derringer rifle, three Connecticut-made rifles, and one Spring-field rifle-musket. The ordnance officer who had to supply these weapons with ammunition was to be pitied.[12]

When it came to supplying the Confederate cavalry in the East with sabers and pistols, the picture was much the same as it was for carbines. At war's start, the South contained few plants capable of producing swords (and only one large manufactory, in Columbus, Georgia), none for making revolvers. The greater portion of both weapons came from abroad—the sabers from Austria, Germany, and England, the pistols from England and France—but they, too, became scarce once the blockade took hold.

Early on, Southern armories began to turn out copies of foreign-made sabers, along with .36-caliber Navy and .44-caliber Army Colts, and revolvers based on English patterns such as the Adams and the Kerr. While these copies proved more durable than the Sharps carbines produced in Richmond, they became harder and harder to procure as the fighting went on, forcing Confederates to look to their enemy for sidearms as well as for carbines.

The Confederate trooper came to rely more heavily on his pistol than on his single- or double-bladed sword. Brig. Gen. Rufus Barringer, who began the war as a captain of the 1st North Carolina, noticed that as the war progressed, "the sabre grew into less and less favor." According to a nineteenth-century chronicler of Confederate soldier life, because the saber became "very tiresome when swung to the belt," it was steadily discarded in favor of other weapons.

The necessity of keeping blades sharp through the use of grindstones also proved wearisome; occasionally, the practice ruined instead of improved the weapons. William Royall of the 9th Virginia may have damaged his saber in this way, for the first time he used it—to chop off a tree limb—the blade broke off at the hilt. Thereafter, he wondered, "What I should have done, armed with that saber hilt, if I had met a Yankee armed with a Springfield musket."[13]

The saber fell into disfavor not merely because it was a cumbersome appendage. Many troopers viewed it as a terror weapon no gentleman would use. Others considered it valuable in a mounted charge but not in the close-quarters fighting that often followed. As John Mosby put it, "The sabre is of no use against gunpowder." A "pair of Navy sixes" served much more effectively in hand-to-hand combat because six-shooters required less mobility to wield; with his pistol, a trooper could dispatch a victim at once, whereas with a saber, it was usually necessary to deliver multiple blows. Stuart and many of his commanders felt differently; they considered the saber, which had proven itself in battle over the centuries, the preeminent offensive weapon. But they could not overcome the prejudices of their men, many of whom, upon entering battle, shouted to their opponents: "Put up your sabers, and fight like gentlemen!"[14]

Deficiencies of cavalry equipment paralleled those that limited the effectiveness of cavalry weapons. Southern-made saddles, bridles, halters, and other items of tack were always in short supply and generally inferior to the enemy's. Other shortages abounded; as William Blackford pointed out, "Horseshoes, nails, and forges were procured with difficulty, and it was not an uncommon occurrence to see a cavalryman leading his limping horse along the road, while from his saddle dangled the hoofs of a dead horse, which he had cut off for the sake of the sound shoes nailed to them."[15]

Southern-made saddles, the most prevalent being of a design by Walter Jenifer of Maryland and Virginia, were considered to be especially poor. Many troopers undoubtedly shared the belief of the 2nd Virginia veteran who considered his "wretched Confederate-made saddle" the bane of his existence. Not only was this English roundtree-pattern saddle uncomfortable for extended riding, it also produced sorebacked horses. Rebels learned to exchange their

Jenifer saddles for the more comfortable and more durable McClellan pattern, favored by their adversaries. One historian notes that by the time of the Chancellorsville campaign of spring 1863, "Confederate cavalry generally had a complete outfit of saddles, bridle, blankets, and weapons, all imported . . . or, more generally, taken from the enemy."[16]

>--+--<>--O--<>--+--<

The South in general, and Virginia in particular, may have been a fertile source of horseflesh, but the supply of animals fit for military service was not inexhaustible. Throughout the fighting, however, the demand for fresh steeds constantly increased. As the war ground on, more and more horses fell victim to bullets and disease or broke down through overwork and had to be replaced.

Because the Union armies had a much wider territory from which to draw, they had little difficulty, even late in the conflict, gathering the remounts they needed. Only in the Confederacy's homeland did diminishing returns set in. Probably by late 1862, certainly by mid-1863, the armies had begun to strip the war zone of available horses, clouding the future of Stuart's command.

Unlike other resource deficiencies, a scarcity of remounts could not be remedied by alternative sources of supply. Southerners found it difficult to supply themselves from the enemy, because when the Yankees abandoned a position, they usually took their mounts with them. Moreover, captured animals were, by law, the property of the Confederate government, which controlled their disposition (although it was noted that "after a time, unwritten law largely overrode this red tape, and captured mounts would be retained by their captors in lieu of their own dead or unserviceable animals"). While they occasionally became available in battle, horses proved a great deal more difficult to seize than carbines, sabers, and pistols. One result was that increasing numbers of gray troopers were mounted on the kind of plugs their opponents would have discarded without a second thought.[17]

Union troopers could be profligate because they were not penalized for the loss of their animals. A ready supply of remounts was always available, thanks not only to the vast resources of the North, but also to its superior distribution facilities, even though these facilities did not achieve efficiency until the second year of fighting. In contrast to his opponent, the Confederate horseman had to provide his own mount. As a result, when he needed a replacement, both he and his army were liable to suffer.

While the Confederacy established a number of "recruiting camps" in which sick or worn horses were slowly restored to health, it never developed a system of remount depots. In most cases the horseless soldier had to secure a furlough during which to return home and raid the family herd. This process took several days in the case of most Virginians; it could take weeks for natives of the Carolinas, Georgia, and Mississippi to reach home, remount, and return to the front. While the trooper was away, his unit did without him. The steady egress of horse hunters ensured that Stuart's command was never at peak strength.

A temporary absence was bad enough, but a trooper's services could be lost forever. Should he fail to locate a remount, he was liable to be transferred to the infantry or the artillery—a fate worse than death for any self-respecting horseman. Often an unhorsed trooper preferred to join the ranks of "Company Q," keeping pace with his regiment on foot, sometimes while carrying his saddle, in the hope of securing a remount during or following a battle.[18]

Because the cavalryman's horse and tack were his personal property, the Confederate government reimbursed him for their use at a rate of 40 cents per day, while also providing forage, shoes, and the services of a blacksmith. When a horse was killed in action, the government supposedly paid the man a predetermined sum. The amount was set during or shortly after the muster-in of his regiment, when a board of inspectors assessed the value of every mount in the outfit. Yet, as one veteran noted, if an unhorsed trooper "ever received the money at all, it would be at a fixed valuation . . . in depreciated currency equivalent to only a small fraction of the actual value of the animal." And if a horse died in service from any cause other than battle wounds—even if through no fault of his rider—no compensation was paid.

By compelling each rider to furnish his own mount, the Confederacy was able to put a full-size cavalry force into the field much earlier than the Union. In theory, it also provided an incentive for a trooper to ensure that his mount received proper care. In actuality, as one of Stuart's veterans explained, it induced some horsemen to be "*too* regardful when the needs of the service demanded that he should not spare his steed, while the temptation of a furlough—'horse details' we called them—led many to purposely neglect the proper care of their horses."[19]

The remount practice had other defects. As the fighting continued and quality horseflesh grew scarce, soldiers became unwilling to furnish good remounts from their home stock, while the rising cost of available animals made it prohibitively expensive to purchase one. Then, too, a regiment's best animals were liable to be ridden by its least experienced soldiers, its raw recruits. The veterans, of greater value to the outfit, if not absent, hunting up remounts, were stuck on worn-out, battle-scarred animals. Yet another flaw of the system was that it promoted a dangerous sense of independence and autonomy. Many who rode into the army considered themselves free agents, able to come and go as they pleased—which they did.[20]

Factors besides battle wounds and overwork compromised the health of cavalry mounts; some had the potential to alter the way in which Stuart employed his command. Poor-quality saddles and equipment could prematurely end an animal's service life, but an even greater danger to equine health was the continuous shortage of hay, oats, corn, and other forage stock in the Virginia theater. This was one problem that could not be solved by resorting to expedients. Riders might be able to make do on less than full rations, but a horse could not go for long without adequate forage before breaking down. As an officer put it, "A man can usually do some foraging on his own account apart from commissariat supply, or at a pinch can take up successive holes in his waist belt, to the point where the belt-buckle begins to grate against his vertebra, but the principle does not apply to a saddle-cinch somehow."[21]

The lack of quality forage quickly assumed serious proportions. The per diem ration for Confederate cavalry mounts was originally set at ten pounds (almost six quarts) of corn and ten pounds of "long" forage, or grain. As early as the spring of 1862, however, fodder became so scarce in Virginia that the daily subsistence dropped to four or five pounds of corn per day, and occasionally to two and a half pounds; often, no long forage was issued. "Sometimes there would be no corn at all," an officer said, "and merely scant rations of hay, or even straw. Not infrequently the only subsistence would be unthreshed wheat." The results could be devastating:

> The unsatisfied craving for long forage produces a morbid appetite, and the horse will then greedily seize and swallow almost anything to distend the stomach. Where a camp had been located for a few days one would notice the trees to which the horses had been fastened stripped of bark from the ground to as high up as the animals could reach, and where the place was occupied for a week or two many of the smaller trees would be eaten entirely away. Empty bags, scraps of paper, and similar things would often be voraciously devoured. . . . All of this was lamentable in a humane point of view and extremely painful to those fond of their horses, but it was also an immense injury to the efficiency of the cavalry.[22]

One recourse was to step up the frequency and duration of foraging expeditions. This practice, however, could not expand the available forage. Early in 1862, surplus fodder in North Carolina, a state that had seen far less fighting than Virginia, was earmarked for Lee's army, but the supply did not outlast the following winter.

Eventually, Stuart and his subordinates resorted to sending large portions of their commands from the fighting front to less fought-over areas where hay and grain was still available. This practice, of course, prevented a concentration of force in those areas where cavalry strength was most needed. In time, even this proved insufficient. By the winter of 1863-64, the scarcity of forage in the main theater of operations had grown to alarming proportions. Stuart was forced to grant wholesale furloughs so that his men could subsist their horses at home. The result was the virtual disbanding of the cavalry, Army of Northern Virginia.[23]

>─┼─◆>─○─<◆┼─<

Confederate horsemen in the East shared two related disadvantages with their opponents: a lack of adequate training and an inconsistent, inchoate approach to tactical instruction. During the war's early weeks, training camps were set up not only at Ashland (where a local racecourse provided a drill ground of sorts), but also at various rendezvous across Virginia and elsewhere in the South. Though details of their training programs have not been uncovered, it seems clear that these camps failed to prepare the average recruit for the arduous, multifaceted service he assumed in the field.

One reason for the difficulties the Federal cavalry experienced in the early going was that so many of its enlistees lacked an equestrian background. Especially in those regiments that drew from the large cities of the East, a large percentage of recruits had never sat a horse before joining the army. It appears, in fact, that many Northerners joined up to take advantage of the opportunities to ride and shoot that had long been denied them. Unsurprisingly, these untutored horsemen suffered through a training period so long and difficult that few ever forgot the experience. When they wrote of their war service in after years, they devoted a great deal of attention to their early instruction, ensuring that this stage of a cavalryman's life was thoroughly documented.[24]

Their opponents' writings offer a sharp contrast. While Confederate cavalry memoirs abound, few provide a detailed view of training methods at any point in the conflict. One reason may be that the Southern recruit was so conversant with horses and firearms, he needed relatively little teaching, and this little he considered not worthy of comment. On the other hand, he may have kept silent from a reluctance to admit that any Southern boy should have required more than a modicum of schooling.

A modicum may be all he got. Indications are that Rebel horse soldiers did not receive a great deal of parade-ground training, certainly nothing approaching what their blue-clad counterparts received. Nor was consistency of drill-field performance strictly enforced. Trooper Eggleston described his regiment's training sessions as "irregular, disorderly affairs, over which no rod of discipline could very well be held." He complained:

> Maneuvers of the most utterly impossible sort were carefully taught to the men. Every amateur officer had his own pet system of tactics, and the effect of the incongruous teachings, when brought out in battalion drill, closely resembled that of the music at Mr. Bob Sawyer's party, where each guest sang the chorus to the tune he knew best.[25]

It appears that Confederates received instruction mainly in small-unit tactics (the so-called "School of the Trooper") and drilled most often in company-size formations, rarely in regimental-size, and almost never at the brigade level. This program contrasted with the training given to Confederate infantry and Union cavalry, some of whose men trained in brigade strength. Apparently, too, the gray troopers practiced mostly in the saddle with pistols and sabers, much less often on foot with their shoulder arms.[26]

In contrast to the many drill manuals available to the Northern trooper, Confederate units had few instructional books tailored to their resources. For the most part, they learned from texts published by the U.S. War Department, the earliest of which, a three-volume work with the simple title *Cavalry Tactics,* had been published in 1841 through the efforts of Secretary of War Joel Poinsett. Two-volume editions of this manual were published in 1855, 1856, and 1861, and three-volume editions reemerged in 1862–64. A later work that also provided a model for Confederate instruction was basically a rehash of Poinsett: *Cavalry Tactics or Regulations for the Instruction, Formations, and Movements of the Cavalry of the Army and Volunteers of the United States.* This two-volume treatise was the work of one of the best-known officers in the prewar army, Col. (later Brig. Gen.) Philip St. George Cooke of the 2nd U.S. Dragoons, a native Virginian who happened to be J. E. B. Stuart's father-in-law.

A Confederate-specific manual published in Richmond in 1861 and again the following year was the primary source of instruction for Stuart's cavalry: *The Trooper's Manual; or, Tactics for Light Dragoons and Mounted Riflemen,* compiled by Col. J. Lucius Davis of the 10th Virginia. Davis emphasized the tactics that predominated in Virginia, fighting in the saddle with rifles and pistols, instead of both mounted and on foot with sabers and carbines.

Davis's tome, as well as the work from which it borrowed—and, for that matter, every instructional book available in 1861, including Cooke's—defined cavalry primarily as an offensive weapon. All paid appropriate attention to the arm's reconnaissance, screening, and outpost capabilities, but they emphasized the value of shock tactics. Based on the achievements of cavalry in the Mexican-American War, when mounted charges by the U.S. dragoons appeared to carry the day on several occasions, expectations for Civil War-era cavalry in combat were quite high. While sometimes cautious in making pronouncements on the subject, some textbooks suggested that charging troopers could even overthrow infantry, especially when the latter had been demoralized by rifle balls or shot and shell. Stuart's men had proven as much on the plains of Manassas. Even without prior softening up, the 11th New York had virtually dissolved under the pounding hooves of the 1st Virginia.[27]

The mounted charge had an unmistakable allure: It caused the spirits of the rider to rise, his pulse to quicken, his adrenaline to pump. Crossing open ground at an extended gallop, hurling oneself at a mass of horsemen coming the other way at the same breakneck pace, could be the experience of a lifetime. It was also an exercise in pure terror, for in making such a charge, both horse and horseman risked great physical harm. To an enlisted member of the 5th Virginia, the charge was "an awful thing."

> Almost before you could think, the shock of horse against horse, the clash of steel against steel, crack of pistols, yells of some poor lost one, as he lost his seat and went down under those iron shod hoofs that knew no mercy, or the shriek of some horse overturned and cut to pieces by his own kind. It is Hell while it lasts.[28]

Mounted attacks may have been the stuff of cavalry lore, but they seemed to be headed for extinction. No prewar manual, not even the more recent ones like Cooke's, took fully into account the fact that cavalry tactics—and the tactics of every other combat arm—had undergone a fundamental change since the war in Mexico, especially in the last six years. The widespread adoption, both in the United States and Europe, of the rifle and the minié ball—a hollow-based bullet that expanded upon firing to fit grooves inside the barrel of the weapon—made small-arms fire effective at three times the range of the smoothbore musket. The revolutionary capabilities of the new weapons—by 1861, many cannons were rifled too—were simply lost on tacticians and theorists. The result was that troopers who dared charge riflemen, whether they did so in mass or in small detachments, were likely to suffer unacceptable losses. It had became equally perilous for cavalry to charge other cavalry when the latter wielded breechloading carbines. Saddles could be emptied well before pounding horses and undulating riders came within saber and pistol range of their target.[29]

Ignorance of the power of the rifle was not exclusive to the Southern cavalry; at war's start, Federal troopers also suffered for this lack of knowledge. The difference was that the Yankees learned from bitter experience, while their opponents either did not or, having learned, refused to change. The high-quality firearms issued to the Union cavalry enabled its men to dismount and fight on foot, behind cover, with growing effectiveness. In time—by early 1863, at the latest—they appeared to have learned the rules of dragoon warfare, fighting mounted or on foot as conditions dictated. This tactical versatility proved to be one of the keys to final victory.

By contrast, Confederate troopers could not, or would not, fight on foot with regularity. One reason was that, unless armed with captured breechloaders, they lacked weapons easy to reload, a prequisite for staying power afoot. Long-barreled rifles, shotguns, and muskets were no match for carbines in the hands of troopers who knew how to use them to advantage. Another reason Rebels rejected dismounted fighting was their cavalier mentality. As one admitted, "Dismounted fighting was never with the spirit of the Southern trooper, who felt that he was only half a man when separated from his horse."

This veteran offered an anecdote to illustrate his point. On one occasion—perhaps in 1862, perhaps much later in the war—the men of a Virginia company were ordered to fight as dismounted skirmishers. The commander of the brigade to which the unit was attached happened by as the troopers sullenly swung down from their saddles. As was customary, they began "counting fours" to determine who would go to the rear with his own mount and those of three comrades. The brigade leader winced when every fourth man, the designated horse holder, shouted "Bully!" instead of his number, thus displaying his pleasure at not being forced to fight on foot. The brigadier reined in, called for the company commander, and spat out an order: "Captain, when you dismount your men, you will detail number *one* to hold horses, and deploy numbers two, three, and 'bully' to the front as skirmishers!"[30]

The man at the top understood the reluctance of his men to fight on terra firma. In July 1857, Lt. J. E. B. Stuart of the 1st U.S. Cavalry had taken part in an attack upon a band of Cheyenne warriors along the Kansas River, not far from Fort Riley. While dismounted fighting was a major element of Plains Indian fighting, on this occasion Stuart's commander, Col. Edwin Vose Sumner, ordered a mounted attack with sabers alone, which utterly routed the tribesmen. Sumner's tactic, though later criticized by some of his senior subordinates, impressed Stuart no end. One cavalry historian notes that "the part this experience . . . had, in the later development of the brilliant cavalry of the South, is apparent in the fact that the Confederate cavalry under Stuart always or almost always fought cavalry mounted."[31]

Given the predilections of Stuart and his troopers, and the limitations imposed on them by their weapons and equipment, it is difficult to classify the Confederate horsemen in the eastern theater according to a distinct tactical model. While they always did a certain amount of fighting on foot, and especially so after spring 1864, they were at philosophical odds with the concept; thus they cannot be classified as dragoons. Nor were they cavalry in the true sense, for a majority eschewed the traditional cavalry weapon, the saber, in favor of the arms and tactics of mounted riflemen. Yet the latter designation cannot be bestowed on them either, for too many preferred to fight in the saddle with six-shooters, muskets, and shotguns. In actuality, the typical horseman in the Army of Northern Virginia was a hybrid, a soldier who fought according to no particular mode of tactics. Rather, by defying all labels, he created for himself a role unique in the annals of mounted warfare.

>-+-<+>-o-<+-+-<

One final disadvantage under which Stuart's command labored concerned regimental organization. While the ten-company standard prevailed for most of the cavalry regiments that served in the eastern theater (exceptions included not only the 1st Virginia, but also the eleven-company 8th Virginia and the twelve-company 14th Virginia), every Southern state also fielded independent battalions of horsemen. The average size seems to have been six companies per battalion. These figures appear to apply also to the cavalry contingents of the various legions that entered the Confederate ranks in 1861–62.[32]

Whether regiment or battalion, a Confederate unit contrasted rather sharply with the typical Union outfit. The difference was more than a matter of manpower. Its twelve-company standard permitted a Federal regiment to maintain three battalions of two squadrons (four companies) each. The battalion structure gave the regiment five field-grade officers: a colonel, a lieutenant colonel, and three majors, one to command each battalion. All but a handful of Confederate regiments had three field officers, including a single major. A Rebel battalion had even fewer field officers, in almost every case one lieutenant colonel and one major.[33]

For the Confederacy, the shortage of field-grade officers translated into decentralized authority, with power shifting from the top of a unit to the company level, each company being commanded by a captain, assisted by one, two, or in some cases, three lieutenants. This arrangement was perfectly in keeping with the loose central authority of the Confederate government, based as it was on the hallowed principle of states' rights. Yet it also meant that when a regiment or battalion experienced attrition, the broad authority of a colonel, lieutenant colonel, and major could erode very quickly. In that case, control of the entire unit gravitated to officers who may have had the interests of their own companies, not of the unit as a whole, at heart.

⋗⋅⊢⋖⋗⋅⊸⊙⊸⋗⋖⋅⊣⋉

These, then, were some of the major obstacles faced by the Confederate horsemen as they sought a fair fight with opponents more bountifully endowed with the tools of their trade. The disparity of resources was so great that an objective observer would be forgiven for concluding that Stuart's people had no chance of prevailing. Too much can be made, however, of material disadvantages, as attested to by the Confederates' record of repeated victories in the field, beginning with Big Bethel and First Manassas and continuing almost to Appomattox.

In the final analysis, the defects and the limitations were not as critical to success as the belief of the cavalrymen of the Army of Northern Virginia that these things could be surmounted. As a trooper in the 3rd Virginia put it, though his training might have been inadequate, his equipment shoddy and in short supply, and "though we had everything from shotguns to sporting rifles, we were not daunted, knowing that we could shoot accurately with what we had, and when it came to horses, we had steeds that could overtake . . . anything the Yankees had."[34]

Chapter Five

Holding the Alexandria Line

The struggle on Bull Run left the victors almost as disorganized as the vanquished. The Yankees failed to halt and rally, as their officers had hoped, at Centreville; instead, they rushed on to Washington. Their flight left the road north open to a Confederate advance. But while hundreds of Beauregard's and Johnston's troops had seen combat this day, they were still tinged with green. The suddenness of the enemy's retreat took them by surprise, leaving them unprepared to pursue. Meanwhile, the approach of evening inhibited offensive thinking. *J.E.B's Cavalry had followed Feds up the road*

Then came an erroneous report that a large force in blue was marching on Union Mills Ford, threatening the Confederate right. The upshot was that a single brigade started north in hopes of overtaking a demoralized foe, only to be recalled and held stationary. No further efforts were made to press the foe, although a visitor to the battlefield, Jefferson Davis, tried to persuade his generals to follow up on their success. The next morning, a division headed north on a reconnaissance-in-force, but a heavy rain impeded its progress, ensuring that no pursuit worthy of the name would be made.[1]

When elements of Johnston's Army of the Potomac, as his and Beauregard's forces were now known, finally hit the road in strength, they failed to display the confidence of victors. Gingerly, they reoccupied familiar places—Centreville, Fairfax Court House, Vienna, Germantown. Even more tentatively, they probed toward Washington until they established a presence a few miles from the nearest Yankee outpost, at Annandale on the Little River Turnpike. At this point began what became known as the Alexandria Line, a cordon of outposts and picket stations stretching almost thirty miles to the north and west, ending at Leesburg on the upper Potomac The distended perimeter was noticeably thin at many points. Still, the fact that it existed at all—and that it included posts almost within sight of the White House and the Capitol—enabled its builders to proclaim that the "siege of Washington" had begun.

Stuart's and Radford's cavalrymen played a prominent role in maintaining the Alexandria Line; in many places they were its only defenders. They were responsible for those outposts closest to the Washington defenses, the theory being that if attacked—even if taken by surprise—they could clear harm's way more quickly than infantry or artillery units. To keep in close contact with his pickets, Stuart set up headquarters along the road from Centreville to Fairfax Court House. As if to emphasize the vigilance required of every picket and patrol member, he named the place "Camp Qui Vive" ("Who Goes There?")[2]

At first Stuart commanded only his own regiment, now nine companies strong, to which had been attached some of the independent companies that had served under Radford before and during the battle. Because the line to be protected was so elongated, small detachments held widely spaced points. Occasionally Stuart's units shared territory assigned to Radford's regiment, a circumstance that generated friction between their commanders, both of whom had healthy egos. The situation was reminiscent of the coolness that had existed between Stuart and Ashby in the Valley.

For a brief period, in fact, it appeared that the Stuart-Ashby relationship might resume in eastern Virginia. Ashby's regiment had not accompanied the Army of the Shenandoah from Winchester to Bull Run. When Johnston left the Valley for Manassas Junction, the 7th Virginia was fifty miles to the west, near the town of Romney (later a part of West Virginia), trying to destroy a strategic stretch of the Baltimore & Ohio Railroad. Not until July 19, two days after it received Johnston's hasty order to report to Winchester, did the 7th arrive there, to find the Army of the Shenandoah gone. On the day of the battle along Bull Run, Ashby and his men were crossing the Blue Ridge. Next day they bivouacked on the edge of the battlefield, having arrived twenty-four hours too late to see action.

At this point it might seem logical that Johnston should assign the 7th Virginia to the Army of the Potomac, but he decided otherwise. Perhaps mindful of their earlier difficulties, the army leader ensured that Stuart and Ashby served far apart from each other. On the twenty-fourth, he ordered the 7th Virginia back to the Valley. There it would remain for almost two years.[3]

Johnston's action effectively confined Ashby to a secondary theater of operations, where he served out of sight of the politicians who advanced soldiers' careers and the editors who made their reputations. Ashby eventually won promotion, but only a tithe of the fame that would have been bestowed on him had he campaigned in eastern Virginia. Some historians believe that Ashby matched Stuart in daring, resourcefulness, and leadership (with the exception that he was neither the tactician nor the disciplinarian Stuart was). Yet he never garnered the publicity and acclaim that were lavished on the Knight of the Golden Spurs. His death in battle at Harrisonburg, Virginia, in June 1862, further prevented him from becoming the household name, in North as well as in South, that he might have become in a different theater of operations.[4]

With Ashby out of the picture, Stuart quickly became the preeminent horseman on the Alexandria Line. The outcome was largely the result of the power wielded by Stuart's patron, Joe Johnston. Although Beauregard was appointed a full general a few days after the fight at Manassas—a victory the popular press ascribed to him, rather than to the late-arriving Johnston—the Creole remained second in command to the Virginian, who outranked him by virtue of seniority. Because he was Johnston's cavalry leader, and although junior to Colonel Radford, Stuart stood to gain command of every mounted man on duty opposite the Washington defenses.

Johnston was not hesitant to advance Stuart's case. On August 10, in a communiqué to Jefferson Davis, the army commander praised his cavalry chief as "a rare man, wonderfully endowed by nature with the qualities necessary for an officer of light cavalry. Cool, firm, acute, active, and enterprising, I know no one more competent than he to estimate the occurrences before him at their true value." Such a man deserved higher rank and authority; thus Johnston asked that the various companies of cavalry that had joined the army before and since the battle be formed into regiments and the regiments into a brigade under Stuart's command.[5]

Johnston's seniority was sufficient to carry the argument. On September 24, Stuart was promoted from colonel (which he had become only recently when the 1st Virginia added a tenth company) to brigadier general. Four days later, he was succeeded as commander of the 1st Virginia by Grumble Jones. The Confederate Senate acted swiftly to please and reward Johnston; it confirmed Stuart's appointment early in December.[6]

Not surprisingly, the promotion rankled Colonel Radford, over whose head Stuart had been jumped and whose regiment had been operating apart from Stuart, attached to Bonham's infantry. Although he had served competently enough at Manassas to win Beauregard's confidence, Radford was a stranger to Johnston and would never enjoy his patronage.

Stuart's rise to command all the horsemen on the Alexandria Line was greeted by a certain amount of grumbling, and not merely from Radford's outfit. Some officers believed the brigadier had prevailed on the basis of army connections, rather than through merit (he and Johnston had served together in the 1st U.S. Cavalry). They pointed out that while Radford's men had staged an energetic and successful pursuit on July 21, Stuart's had done little beyond dispersing a single infantry regiment—a feat that any cavalry force advancing at an extended gallop and with the advantage of surprise would have accomplished. These critics downplayed the critical importance of Stuart's contribution to the battle, especially considering the small size of his force and its relegation to the rear for much of that day.[7]

For a short time after Stuart made brigadier, it appeared that his authority would be circumscribed by transfer from Johnston's direct command. In mid-October, at Jefferson Davis's behest, Maj. Gen. Earl Van Dorn was transferred from Texas to Virginia. Van Dorn, once a field officer in the 2nd U.S. Cavalry, had become something of a celebrity in the Trans-Mississippi theater. When word of his coming east made the rounds, it was generally supposed that he would join the recently created Department of Northern Virginia, commanded by Johnston. This organization included not only Johnston's army (still known as the Army of the Potomac), but three subsidiary elements as well: the Potomac District, under General Beauregard; the Shenandoah Valley District, under now–Maj. Gen. Stonewall Jackson; and Maj. Gen. Theophilus H. Holmes's Aquia District, headquartered near Fredericksburg. Instead, Davis assigned the newcomer to lead a division in Beauregard's command, composed of two brigades from Van Dorn's native Mississippi. To this force, the president later added the Hampton Legion as well as all the cavalry in the Department of Northern Virginia.

The arrangement infuriated Stuart and dismayed Johnston. One day after the assignment was announced, the latter wrote Davis, perhaps at Stuart's behest, opposing it. Johnston argued that placing every trooper in the department in a single division weakened the arm and ensured that it would be out of position "either for its daily service of observing the enemy or to play its part in battle." He added that while grouping the cavalry into a single, unified force was a good idea, the arm should be removed from Van Dorn's control and replaced by an equal force of foot soldiers. When Van Dorn himself endorsed Johnston's proposal, Davis accepted the verdict and reassigned the Mississippian accordingly. Stuart was at once restored to Johnston's jurisdiction and to command of the horsemen in the Department of Northern Virginia. As it turned out, Van Dorn would serve in the East for less than three months before being returned to the western theater of operations.[8]

Stuart's brush with an undesirable assignment worked to his advantage. It resulted in the creation of a full-fledged brigade of horsemen under his command. To man it, state and Confederate authorities were forced to group the various companies of horsemen serving in Stuart's bailiwick into regiments. By the start of September, the 1st, 6th, and 30th Virginia Cavalries had been fully organized. A bit later in the month, the 4th Virginia officially came into being, although not till October did the outfit reach its full size, ten companies.

Beverly H. Robertson, a subaltern in the celebrated 2nd U.S. Dragoons until accused of "having given proof of his disloyalty" to the Federal government, became the 4th Virginia's first commander. The assignment of Robertson, who had not been present at Manassas, prompted several of the captains who had distinguished themselves in the battle, including Williams Wickham, to consider resigning their commissions. In the end, however, all stayed on to support the new colonel, who appears to have been something of a prima donna. Within a few weeks of Robertson's assuming command, Stuart was calling him "by far the most troublesome man I have to deal with."[9]

By October, Stuart commanded about two hundred officers and twenty-four hundred troopers. Over the next seven months, thousands of others joined him as regiments were created or re-created and assigned to Stuart. In late October the 2nd Virginia, which continued to serve with Magruder's forces on the Peninsula, was redesignated the 3rd Virginia Cavalry, at which point Radford's outfit assumed the vacated designation. Meanwhile, the 9th Virginia Cavalry came into existence in mid-December, although it required several months to complete its organization. Finally, the cavalry of the Wise Legion (later the 10th Virginia) had seen early-war service in western Virginia, but only in battalion strength. It would not become a full-size regiment until May 1862. Despite their growing pains, the 9th and 10th were led by talented commanders: respectively, Lt. Col. (later Col.) Rooney Lee and Col. J. Lucius Davis, the well-known tactician.[10]

By October 1861, in addition to the 1st, 2nd, 4th, and 6th Virginia, Stuart commanded two out-of-state units. In the middle of that month, Col. Robert Ransom, Jr.'s 1st North Carolina, ten companies strong, arrived from the Old North State to augment Johnston's cavalry arm. Later that same month, William Martin and the 2nd Mississippi Cavalry Battalion, made up of three companies raised in Mississippi and one in Alabama, also reached Virginia. In November, Martin's fifth company, also from Alabama, and a sixth, formed in Georgia, joined the organization, which Martin renamed the Jeff Davis Legion. Later still, the cavalry portion of the Hampton Legion—four companies under Maj. M. Calbraith Butler—would break off from its parent command to form the nucleus of the 2nd South Carolina Cavalry.

While pleased with the quantity and quality of the units in his brigade, Stuart feared that something was lacking. If he had his way, he would command not only horsemen, but also horse artillerymen. To supply the long-range power that carbines and even rifles lacked, the brigadier wished to augment his command with at least two lightweight artillery pieces served by cannoneers who rode horses, enabling them to keep pace with the troopers they supported. Dating from his assignment to brigade command, Stuart tried to interest the War Department in a proposal to transform two troopers from each company under his command into cannoneers. Although Stuart thought it likely that Governor Letcher would supply the guns, Jefferson Davis was not receptive to the idea of a horse artillery unit. Nor did he think much of Stuart's plan to place John Esten Cooke, who before the war had served as a sergeant in the celebrated Richmond Howitzers, in command of the unit.[11]

Davis's opposition ensured that Stuart had to wait for almost two months to add an artillery unit to his brigade. Late in November John Pelham—until then a little-known lieutenant in the 1st Virginia Artillery, mainly confined to inspecting and mustering duties—took command of what quickly became known as the "Stuart Horse Artillery." The battery would not see action until the following spring, and not for another month would it expand into the de facto battalion it would remain for the rest of the war. Even so, Pelham and his new unit were on the road to fame and glory. Eventually the youngster would command a battalion consisting of three, and later five, batteries.[12]

The delay in gaining Pelham's services ensured that another army gained the distinction of fielding the first Confederate horse artillery unit in Virginia. Early in September, Roger Preston Chew, a cadet at the Virginia Military Institute, had tried to interest the Adjutant and Inspector General's Office in Richmond in the formation of a horse battery. When the government showed the same indifference it displayed to Stuart the following month, Chew and a fellow cadet with artillery aspirations, Milton Rouss, returned to the Shenandoah Valley and presented their proposal to Turner Ashby and later to the new district commander, Stonewall Jackson.

Both officers believed Chew's and Rouss's idea had merit; the result was the Ashby Battery, formed on November 13, 1861. As originally constituted, the unit, which Chew had named for the commander who first showed an interest in it, mounted two guns and was staffed by thirty-three men and four officers, including Chew as captain and Rouss as first lieutenant. Although it served with Jackson during its first eight months of service, thereafter the battery supported Stuart, under whom it made a reputation second to none in the premier Confederate army in the East.[13]

>—<>—O—<>—<

The regiments assigned to Stuart were rarely available for service at anything approaching full strength. Even those that had completed their organization were broken into companies or smaller detachments for service as pickets, outpost troops, scouts, escorts, and couriers. While this practice prevented Stuart from bringing maximum weight to bear on any point at any one time, his enemy would be similarly handicapped. By early autumn, volunteer cavalry had reached Washington from New York, Pennsylvania, New Jersey, and every New England state, as well as from Illinois and Indiana. Most were retained inside the capital defenses, where McDowell's successor, Maj. Gen. George B. McClellan (the incompetent Patterson had been allowed to retire), seemed intent on drilling them until they achieved tactical perfection. Those few units he sent across the Potomac to serve under his cavalry chief, Brig. Gen. George Stoneman, were broken into platoons and companies for field service.

Since Stoneman's men were more numerous than Stuart's, their scattered, piecemeal deployment suggested that McClellan feared to use the pea green troopers in mass. In a sense, it was a matter of proportion. If a platoon retreated in haste after an encounter with Stuart's cavaliers, the Northern newspapers would characterize it as a setback; should a regiment be routed and put to flight, the result would be reported as a major disaster. McClellan did not want his cavalry to become demoralized by widespread, premature commitment against a more experienced foe. He wished to keep it well in hand, campaigning under controlled conditions, until his drill program had run its course.

Despite McClellan's attempts to minimize their incidence, several clashes between the opposing cavalries punctuated the period between early August and year's end. Some of these engagements involved other arms as well, raising the stakes involved. Predictably, Stuart's soldiers emerged victorious from almost every one, beginning with a series of small-scale, late-summer actions near Mason's, Munson's, and Upton's Hills, along the Columbia Turnpike west of Alexandria. James Longstreet, commanding Johnston's advance forces, reported that in each instance Stuart "has been entirely successful. Where he has lost a man, he has brought in at least two of the enemy, dead or alive."[14]

Rumors that large infantry forces were advancing on Stuart's outposts ran rife throughout this period. None, however, resulted in sightings of oncoming hordes. As an officer of cavalry in the Hampton Legion informed his wife, "both armies seem to know their respective places" and appeared reluctant to range beyond them except briefly.[15]

All that changed on the morning of September 11. Just after midnight, then-Colonel Stuart learned that a force of Yankee infantry, artillery, and horsemen, thought to total two thousand officers and men, had evicted his pickets from Lewinsville, four miles outside Washington, and had occupied the village. At Longstreet's order, Stuart left his temporary headquarters at Munson's Hill and advanced on Lewinsville at the head of a column consisting of one company of the 1st Virginia, some three hundred members of the 13th Virginia Infantry, and a two-gun section of the venerable Washington Artillery of New Orleans, under Capt. Thomas Rosser. Stuart's intent was to surprise the enemy force, cut it off from its nearest supports, and capture it whole.

Although his column was too bulky to achieve true stealth, it managed to reach the Lewinsville vicinity undetected, a tribute to Stuart's skill at reconnaissance. The colonel moved just as carefully toward the left flank of the Yankee force, which was found to be withdrawing from the village. In reply to Stuart's whispered instructions, the commander of the 13th Virginia took up a position from which not only to hit the flank, but to silence the single cannon supporting it. Then Rosser's guns ran into battery a quarter mile from the nearest body of troops and opened fire. Within minutes the Federals were accelerating their retreat, "exposing their entire column to flank fire." The fugitives included members of three infantry regiments, some horsemen, and several cannons.

Although a few Federals attempted to make a stand, Rosser's two pieces, a rifle and a howitzer, pounded away, "shells bursting directly over their heads, and creating the greatest havoc and confusion in their ranks." From his close-up position in the midst of the 1st Virginia, John Mosby observed, "I never enjoyed anything so much in my life as standing by the cannon and watching our shells when they burst over them." Apparently the contest was not completely one-sided: According to Mosby, "One of our men had his head shot off by a shell and another [was] wounded." His statement contradicts Stuart's claim that "our loss was not a scratch to man or horse." Whichever the case, Stuart's force killed or mortally wounded four Yankees and captured four others; an unknown number of wounded were carried off by comrades.

Not until its men had scampered more than a mile south of town did the enemy force seek to re-form as a group. It formed a defensive line blocking the road and discouraging pursuit. Stuart seemed not to mind; he was content to let them go. At a leisurely pace, he marched his force back home in triumphal procession. In his after-action report, he lauded everyone involved in the action, but he singled out Captain Rosser and his artillerists, whose performance this day "for accuracy and effect challenges comparison with any [other]."[16]

Stuart was impressed not only by the captain's leadership but also by his talent for public relations. For months after Lewinsville, Rosser and his fellow battery officers presented Stuart with a token of their esteem, a gilt-smothered kepi that the recipient considered a "beautiful" gift. By that point, if not before, the general had begun to consider offering Rosser a permanent position in his brigade.[17]

➤━◆━○━◆━◄

For six weeks after the affair at Lewinsville, as chill winds began to strip the trees of their foliage, quiet prevailed along the Alexandria Line, as though the Yankees had been chastised into inactivity. Then, in mid-October, the scene of action shifted to the upper Potomac, where a series of Union reconnaissances toward Leesburg culminated in a sharp encounter on the twenty-first. At nearby Balls Bluff, four companies of Virginia horsemen, led by Colonel Jenifer (inventor of the much-maligned saddle), supported seventeen hundred foot soldiers under Nathan Evans in blunting an attack by an equal number of Yankees and driving them back across the Potomac.[18]

To forestall another, more formidable, offensive in the same area, Stuart, who had recently replaced Longstreet in command of the "Advance Forces" of the Department of Northern Virginia, was compelled to augment his patrols on the upper Potomac. In mid-November, he dispatched four companies of the 2nd Virginia, under Lieutenant Colonel Munford, to the Leesburg area. The vigilant troopers gave Evans the most up-to-date intelligence on "the positions and probable intentions" of the Federals across the river from him.[19]

The next action of any consequence on the Alexandria Line occurred on November 16, when fifty Mississippi troopers under Major Martin reconnoitered a neighborhood southwest of Falls Church where Union foragers were believed to be at work. Approaching the position undetected, the 2nd Mississippi found perhaps seventy-five Yankees harvesting a cornfield on Frank Dulin's Farm. Without hesitation, Martin attacked the Northerners in the cornfield with the majority of his troopers, while the rest of his battalion charged an orchard adjacent to the Dulin house, which other Federals had occupied.

As at Lewinsville, the enemy elected not to stand and fight, but fled precipitately. Pursuing the fugitives through the corn, then across a boggy meadow, Martin and his subordinates rounded up thirty prisoners, including two officers, members of a New York infantry regiment, as well as a huge cache of arms and equipment, and five wagons filled with stolen corn. Martin commended his men for their gallant behavior "though most of them were for the first time under fire." In submitting Martin's report, Stuart praised the major himself, whose "gallantry and prowess" recommended him for advancement to lieutenant colonel. Although Stuart's superiors concurred, the promotion did not come through until the following February.[20]

Martin's triumph sparked a run of Confederate cavalry success that extended into December. Only two days after Dulin's Farm, a three-hundred-man detachment of the 1st Virginia under Fitzhugh Lee swept down on a picket post outside Falls Church. The attack, launched at Stuart's behest, achieved surprise thanks to the capture of a series of outposts along the muddy road from Fairfax Court House. This feat prevented a warning from reaching the main Union position, manned by a small detachment of the 14th New York State Militia (84th New York Infantry). The antagonists had met before: At Manassas, the New Yorkers had closely supported the Fire Zouaves. As a result, they had suffered several casualties during Stuart's dramatic charge.[21]

This day, as on the previous occasion, the 14th New York had no time to assume the defensive. Lee's riders galloped through the camp of the detachment, a cluster of tents, huts, and makeshift defenses bordering a deep swamp. Rushing from their shelters, the flabbergasted enemy responded with a ragged fire that drew little blood. Despite the odds against them, the Yankees fought to hold their ground with what Lee called "more bravery than the Federal troops usually exhibit." Their stubborn resistance compelled the colonel to adopt little-used tactics. He dismounted many of his men and led them afoot against all sides of the encampment. At that point surrender became a matter of time; presently the surviving New Yorkers—all nine of them—threw down their guns and raised their hands. By then eight of their comrades had been killed and several others wounded. The attackers had lost one trooper and a civilian guide, both killed.

Another casualty was Lee himself. At the height of the action, the lieutenant colonel was thrown from his wounded charger headfirst into the swamp. He rose a bit unsteadily, covered with mud from head to boot, to supervise the final stages of the attack. It was too late in the day to continue the reconnaissance toward Falls Church, so the soiled officer tended to his wounded, rounded up his prisoners, and slowly returned to camp.[22]

The series of outpost victories continued on the frosty afternoon of November 26, when a 140-man detachment of the 1st North Carolina under Colonel Ransom and Major Gordon saw combat for the first time. While on a scouting mission along the Loudoun & Hamphire Railroad near Vienna, the North Carolinians discovered they were trailing a much larger body of Yankees on the same errand. Although local civilians reported that the enemy force numbered in the thousands, retreat was not an option. Discovering that the enemy's rear guard had bogged down in the narrow, heavily rutted road to Vienna, Ransom moved within a few hundred yards of it, then charged across the rough ground in column of fours.

The suddenness and unexpectedness of the assault stunned Ransom's target, which, as it turned out, consisted of fewer than one hundred members of the 3rd Pennsylvania Cavalry. The Pennsylvanians retreated so swiftly that their ranks appeared to melt away. As Stuart later put it, the force of Ransom's attack "put to ignominious flight the entire column—the officers leading."

At Ransom's order, his second in command took up the pursuit. Although the enemy had a three hundred-yard headstart, Gordon, with the main body of the detachment, soon overtook them. Swarming over the fugitives, the pistol-wielding Tarheels killed one Yankee, wounded six, and took nearly thirty prisoners. When the rest of the Pennsylvanians galloped away, many spoils fell into the attackers' hands, including two dozen sabers and revolvers, and fifteen highly prized Sharps carbines.

The price paid for these gifts was not steep. "My men were soon assembled," Ransom reported, "and I am happy to state that not one was hurt by the enemy." He praised everyone involved in the charge, especially the intrepid Gordon. When endorsing the report, Stuart again drew attention to the ranking officer, commending Ransom's "untiring zeal and unceasing efforts."[23]

The run of success was not over. On December 2, a detachment of the 6th Virginia under Col. Charles W. Field made what Stuart called "a bold and successful dash" on a picket post outside Annandale. Before Federal supports could reach the scene, Field's riders shot up the post, killed four of its occupants—members of the 45th New York Infantry—and carried off fifteen other men along with their arms and equipment. Field's loss was two men missing in action. To cap his success, when he retired in the direction of Fairfax Court House and Centreville, the colonel easily outdistanced his pursuers—not only infantrymen, but also a large body of mounted riflemen.[24]

>–◄►–O–◄►–◄

Over a three-week period, the exploits of the Jeff Davis Legion, the 1st Virginia, the 1st North Carolina, and the 6th Virginia had raised the spirits of Stuart's men so high that some had begun to think of themselves as invincible in combat. Conversely, their exploits had visited gloom and frustration on the enemy, some of whom had begun to question the wisdom of holding positions so far from the defenses of Washington. The lopsided defeats they had suffered had drawn wrathful rebukes from superiors, including Irvin McDowell, now a division commander under McClellan, and Brig. Gen. Fitz John Porter, Little Mac's favorite lieutenant. Subsequent attempts to steal the Rebels' thunder, such as a series of attacks on picket posts at Dranesville by the 1st Pennsylvania Cavalry, and on Fairfax Court House by a squadron of the 1st New York ("Lincoln") Cavalry, failed to counter the prevailing belief that the Confederates were superior to their adversary in raiding, fighting, and intelligence gathering.[25]

Even so, the year closed on a low note not only for Stuart and his horsemen, but for the entire Confederate army, with an event that gave their opponents hope and cause for optimism. On December 20, in his capacity as commander of the Advance Forces, Stuart took charge of a sixteen hundred–man expeditionary force that included four infantry regiments, 150 troopers, and four artillery pieces. He was ordered to cover a foraging party operating in the vicinity of Dranesville, a settlement along the Alexandria-Leesburg Turnpike. The size of Stuart's command indicated the importance Confederate authorities attached to the job of finding rations and forage in the disputed territory between the armies.

Stuart started out enthusiastically, eager to prove himself worthy of handling a sizable body of combined arms. As a good cavalryman, he pushed his mounted men—a detachment of the 1st North Carolina under Major Gordon and Captain Pitzer's company of the 2nd Virginia—well in advance of the main body to scout the ground to be covered. The troopers had been instructed to pay special notice to the point, east of the village, where the turnpike met the Leesburg-Georgetown Pike, a portal to the Union sector of the Alexandria Line.

Approaching the road junction late in the morning, the mounted contingent discovered outside Dranesville the rear echelon of a large enemy force. For once the Confederates failed to gain basic intelligence: Although this contingent, thirty-five hundred troops of all arms under Brig. Gen. Edward O. C. Ord, was likewise protecting a foraging operation, Stuart believed it was marching on Leesburg and thus had to be stopped at all costs. While his mounted men attacked Ord's rear, Stuart sent back for the infantry. Ord quickly assumed a defensive posture, and the fight was on.[26]

Although Gordon's and Pitzer's troopers gave a strong account of themselves, Stuart's foot troops served him poorly. Upon reaching the scene, one regiment deployed so sloppily it had to be re-formed by Stuart. Two other outfits took positions in a thicket so dense they could see neither the enemy nor each other. Confusion led each to fire on the other in the mistaken belief they had encountered Ord's soldiers. In his report, Stuart admitted that "a few casualties" resulted from the friendly fire. At length, the expeditionary leader got his regiments sorted out and began to pound Ord's position with his cannons. Yet the artillery, although emplaced in a roadside woods, drew a heavy counterbattery fire, and Stuart could find no opportunity to advance.

For two hours, an indecisive duel raged on the outskirts of Dranesville, neither side gaining an advantage or taking the offensive. Then Stuart perceived that he was opposing a greatly reinforced opponent; additional batteries opened on him, forcing him to withdraw his own guns, then to disengage. With Federals pressing his rear guard with unaccustomed determination, Stuart led his men southwestward to a crossroads hamlet with the quaint name of Frying Pan, where they went into a bone-chilling bivouac.[27]

Having been forced to quit the fight after suffering substantial casualties—nearly two hundred killed, wounded, and missing, as against fewer than seventy, all told, for Ord—Stuart wished to resume the fight, and recoup lost pride, in the morning. His force augmented by the arrival of two more infantry regiments and a detachment of the 1st North Carolina under Lieutenant Colonel Baker, sometime after dawn on the twenty-first he retraced his path to the scene of the fighting—and found his adversary gone.

When scouting parties turned up no trace of Ord's column, Stuart sent burial parties to inter the dead he had left on the field the previous night. Then he returned to Camp Qui Vive to write a report, in which he needlessly inflated the numbers he had faced and argued unconvincingly that the fight had ended as a draw. Although he had not witnessed Ord's withdrawal, he also claimed that when the Yankees left the field, they had been accompanied by "twenty wagon loads of killed and wounded."

Downplaying the details of his tactical performance, Stuart lauded the skill and spirit of his troops, citing the good work of his infantry subordinates, as well as that of Gordon, Pitzer, and their officers and troopers. He closed by declaring that despite the "overwhelming odds against us . . . we saved the transportation, inflicted upon the enemy a loss severer than our own, rendering him unequal to the task of pursuit, [and] retired in perfect order . . . bringing with us nearly all our wounded." For these and other reasons, the fight at Dranesville could in a sense be regarded as a "glorious success."[28]

Stuart had a high regard for honesty, at least as an abstract principle. But while he would have hesitated to tell an outright lie, he was not above using guile to mask a less-than-sterling performance in the field. His report of the Dranesville fight stands as a model of evasion and special pleading, with inconsistencies and implausibilities cloaked in prose of the deepest purple.

Many of those who either took part in the fighting of December 20 or interviewed the participants took a different view of the outcome. When a trooper in Pitzer's company wrote his family of the fight, he stressed the high number of casualties Stuart had suffered and admitted to being outfought, adding, however, that the Confederates had withdrawn only because "ther [sic] forces was two [sic] large." Others involved in the fight called it a mismanaged botch from start to finish. Representative of the view of the civilian community was the comment of a Confederate War Department clerk, who called the engagement "the first serious wound inflicted on the country."[29]

In the immediate aftermath of the engagement, the Army of the Potomac settled down to its first Christmas in the field. Rather than the gay occasion it had been before the war, more than a few soldiers found the holiday "dull and gloomy." It was as if, by unfortunate timing, one less-than-satisfactory outing in the field had swept away the many successes that Stuart's command and its comrades in the other arms had experienced in the five months since Manassas. The only remedy was to start 1862 with a new series of victories that might combine to inflict overwhelming defeat on the invaders of Virginia.[30]

Chapter Six

Descent to the Peninsula (Jan. 1862)

If some of his men spent a gloomy Christmas, Stuart found the season full of the customary good cheer. Camp Qui Vive was the scene of holiday merriment, much of it served up by his musicians, who also performed at a round of parties hosted by local planters. At these galas, Stuart and his staff danced with neighboring damsels, sang holiday songs, and enjoyed choice victuals, including alcohol-laden eggnog.

Stuart did not partake of spirits, but he did indulge other tastes. It was at this time that he made the acquaintance of nineteen-year-old Laura Ratcliffe, whose mother owned several plantations in the vicinity of Frying Pan. Captivated by Laura's beauty, pleasant nature, and helpfulness (he had observed her nursing some of his wounded), the cavalry leader not only waltzed with the young woman, but accompanied her on horseback rides as well. When snow fell after the first of the year, the couple went sleighing. It would appear that Stuart was smitten. Even as he wrote letters home expressing his devotion to Flora, he composed moonstruck poetry to Laura Ratcliffe.[1]

Even in winter quarters, duty had a way of intruding on Stuart's private life. Every day he inspected his outposts, including those within rifle range of the enemy. To foster vigilance among his pickets, early in the new year he staged a mock attack on sections of the advance picket line. Sentinels sprang to arms and passed the alarm, returning to normal activity only when the playacting became evident. Ending the ruse, Stuart called together many of the pickets and addressed them in solemn tones. A member of the general's old regiment heard him explain that everyone had to be "on the alert all the time; that as cavalry, we were the eyes and ears of the army and that upon our vigilance depended the safety of the army."[2]

When not inspecting or instructing, Stuart reviewed his growing command. Soon after year's start, he was able to do so without having to ride long distances. By then, for the first time, he had gathered together the components of his brigade: four regiments, the greater part of a fifth (the newly renamed 2nd

63

Virginia), the legion sometimes known as the "Little Jeff," and, as Stuart proudly explained to his brother-in-law, Maj. (later Gen.) John Rogers Cooke, "1 Battery of Horse Artillery, composed of 4 12 pdr [twelve-pounder] Howitzers, 1 Blakely 12 pdr Rifle, 1 6 pdr and 2 Mountain Howitzers. It is called the Stuart Horse Artillery & is commanded by Capt Jno Pelham."

It was largely due to the addition of Pelham's battery, which had been organizing since early December and now numbered almost one hundred men and horses, that Stuart could describe his command as "flourishing." Since the affair at Lewinsville, Captain Rosser had been Stuart's ideal artillerymen—he must have regretted Rosser's unwillingness to transfer from the mounted artillery to the horse artillery—but Pelham, who had distinguished himself at Manassas, was a close second in the general's book.[3]

Stuart was impressed with the men Pelham had recruited for his unit, especially his ranking subordinates, 1st Lt. James Breathed and 2nd Lt. William McGregor. Both officers would later command batteries of their own and, before war's end, battalions of horse artillery. Equally impressive were the enlisted men who had flocked to Pelham's standard from his native Alabama, as well as from New Orleans and other cosmopolitan centers. A large number of Pelham's so-called Napoleon Detachment were immigrants from France and Italy who were fond of singing "La Marseillaise" as they ran their guns into battery on the drill field. A few of the Europeans had military experience; all were fiercely loyal to their adopted country and region.[4]

The brigade did not remain massed for long. At about the time Stuart wrote his brother-in-law, Colonel Radford led two companies of the 2nd Virginia to Leesburg, where they joined the four other companies of their regiment in supporting the local forces, now commanded by Brig. Gen. Daniel Harvey Hill. Six weeks later, Ransom's 1st North Carolina departed Virginia for its home state. In February, Federal forces under Maj. Gen. Ambrose E. Burnside had invaded the east coast of North Carolina. Early in February, the Yankees captured the garrison on Roanoke Island; afterward they moved against strategic New Bern, threatening Confederate fortunes in the East ("our cause looks dark now," wrote one North Carolinian in Stuart's brigade). One result was the transfer of Ransom's regiment, along with other North Carolina units in Johnston's army, to the state's defense forces.[5]

The 1st North Carolina would not return to Stuart until the latter half of June. Ransom would not come with it, in the interim having been promoted to brigadier general of infantry under Longstreet. Nor was Ransom the only high-ranking personnel loss Stuart would suffer. Before winter ended, he lacked the services of Colonel Field, who had left the 6th Virginia to take over a brigade in Maj. Gen. A. P. Hill's "Light Division."[6]

By the end of January, those troopers and horse artillerymen who remained with Stuart had begun to construct winter quarters. They added wooden flooring to their tents, erected log huts, and reinforced their units' stables against the elements. They snuggled into their new or improved lodgings just in time to

ward off what a trooper of the 1st Virginia called the "verry filthy wether" that
came calling in midwinter.[7]

Some soldiers found it easier than others to keep warm. One snowy
evening in early February, John Mosby arrived on foot at Stuart's temporary
headquarters between Centerville and Manassas, where he had been summoned
on routine business. The future raider met Stuart for the first time when the general unexpectedly interviewed him in person. He was further surprised when
Stuart, noting the falling snow, invited him to spend the night in the private
home he was occupying. Years later, Mosby recalled:

> I never dreamed . . . that I should ever rise to intimacy with him.
> There could have been nothing prepossessing in my general appear-
> ance to induce him to make an exception of me, for I was as roughly
> dressed as any common soldier. . . . Of course I obeyed and took my
> seat before a big, blazing fire.

A few minutes after entering the house, Mosby found himself sitting
between Stuart and another guest, Joseph E. Johnston. The dumbfounded private remained motionless, staring into the fire, while the generals carried on an
animated conversation. "I felt so small in their presence," he recalled. ". . . I
would have felt far more comfortable trudging back to camp through the snow."
Greater embarrassment followed. After perhaps a half hour of talk, supper
was announced, and the generals arose and went to the table. Mosby remained
by the fire until Stuart insisted that he take a seat beside him. As the three men
ate, Mosby writhed in discomfort. "I do not think I raised my eyes from my
plate," he remembered, although the others "chatted freely." When the meal was
over, Stuart spread some blankets on the floor of the parlor, and Mosby spent
the night there in fitful sleep—only to be summoned to the breakfast table, in
company with the generals, when dawn broke. The trooper felt every bit as
uncomfortable as he had the night before, although by now he had come to
appreciate his host's kindness: "So here began my friendship for Stuart which
lasted as long as he lived."
The memorable occasion had a surprise ending. After breakfast, Stuart sent
Mosby back to camp on a borrowed horse so he would not have to negotiate the
snow-covered roads on foot. As soon as he reached his tent, he was summoned
to regimental headquarters. Mosby probably assumed that the querulous Jones
intended to quiz him on his whereabouts. Thus he was shocked when Jones
offered him the position of regimental adjutant, with the rank of first lieutenant.
"Of course," he observed, "I was glad to accept it." But he never learned
whether his recent host had had a hand in the promotion.[8]

>─┤─◇─○─◇─┤─◁

For the Confederate Army of the Potomac, winter camp ended abruptly in the
first week of March 1862 with a general withdrawal below the Rappahannock

River to the Fredericksburg area. The fallback was another product of Joe John-ston's cautious, defense-oriented strategy. For weeks, the general had feared that in its present position, his army was vulnerable to a quick strike by the mas-sive horde McClellan had collected on both banks of the Potomac. As he had nine months earlier, when he mulled over leaving Harpers Ferry for Winchester, Johnston carefully laid out his objections to remaining on the Alexandria Line, objections he forcefully presented at a high-level conference of military and political leaders in Richmond late in February. Jefferson Davis and his cabinet reluctantly approved the withdrawal, and two weeks of planning began.[9]

Stuart and his men had a role to play in ensuring the success of the opera-tion: They would guard the army's flanks and rear as it lumbered south. They would also help set the departure time. On March 5, Stuart's forward scouts reported a Federal buildup in the Alexandria–Falls Church vicinity, which made Johnston believe that if he did not move, he would face a head-on assault or a flank envelopment. On the seventh, the army began to depart its winter camps with as much stealth as snow-covered roads of half-frozen mud would allow. While Johnston's main body abandoned the greater part of the Alexandria Line, D. H. Hill's command evacuated Leesburg and fell back in the same direction, its rear and flanks covered by Radford, Munford, and the 2nd Virginia.[10]

The cavalry found the going especially rough. Most of Stuart's men did not withdraw until their infantry comrades had taken the road. Some helped John-ston's quartermasters burn warehouses on the Orange & Alexandria, crammed with foodstuffs, weapons, equipment, and soldiers' baggage that could not be allowed to fall into enemy hands. A member of the 1st Virginia called the destruction "a terrible waste." Several of his comrades "remarked that we would see the day when we would regret it." Indeed, as this man later recalled, the army's provisions "became very scarce, and rations were cut down. Two years later our rations got down to one pint of corn meal and one-quarter pound of bacon per day."[11]

Those troopers assigned to lead the way to Fredericksburg had to keep ahead of the main body despite riding worn-out horses. Throughout the winter, Stuart had made strenuous efforts to ensure the care of his animals; even so, months of picket and patrol duty in rough weather had taken a toll. John Mosby claimed that "three-fourths of the horses had been broken down by the hard work of the winter" and that numerous men were apart from their regiments looking for remounts. While Mosby exaggerated the extent of the problem, his main point had validity: The cavalry had been overtaxed even before it assumed the stressful burden of covering the withdrawal.[12]

Within three days of leaving the Alexandria Line, most of Johnston's com-mand was ensconced in new positions below the Rappahannock, and its com-mander was mulling over a further withdrawal—perhaps as far as the south bank of the Rapidan River. He need not have concerned himself. By putting down roots on the outskirts of Fredericksburg, he appeared free from hindrance; his enemy followed him with such deliberation as to suggest it was content to let him go. Even so, over the next week and more, Stuart's cavalry remained in close touch with a small force of Yankee infantry, supported by a few mounted regiments under General Stoneman, who had followed their retreating opponents to the north bank of Cedar Run, about twelve miles above Johnston's new headquarters.

On the afternoon of March 14, Stoneman, accompanied by an infantry regiment, suddenly attacked about three hundred of Stuart's troopers, the rear guard of Johnston's army. A mounted detachment, a squadron of the 5th U.S. Cavalry under 2nd Lt. George Armstrong Custer, pushed the Confederates across the run but was prevented from reaching the other side. The rear guard, some of its men mounted, others on foot, offered so much resistance that Custer and his men beat a decidedly quick retreat.

For a time, the Federals remained on the north bank. Next morning, two companies of infantry made a demonstration as if to cross the stream. They fared no better than Custer's troopers, and before the day ended the entire pursuit force was in retreat to Union Mills. Although heavier forces later retraced Stoneman's path to Cedar Run, the effort of March 14–15 ended McClellan's belated attempt to punish Johnston for slipping a trap that had been set for him above the Rappahannock.[13]

⇒·◄◆·()·◆►·◄

Over the next two weeks, Stuart's horsemen settled into the routine of service along the Rappahannock. Their primary mission was to patrol both banks of the river, remaining in touch with the enemy and keeping Johnston informed of their movements. To fulfill that mission, Stuart established a discontinuous picket line stretching as far west as the foothills of the Blue Ridge. His men rarely remained stationary. Thanks to what Stuart called "the daring boldness of a few scouts," at several points they penetrated well inside the enemy's lines.[14]

Stuart and his men expected that sooner or later, the better part of McClellan's army would confront them. When the Federals failed to show themselves in force by late March, their opponents began to wonder if Little Mac had no stomach for a fight.

As it happened, the Union commander, at Lincoln's urging, was planning a movement into his enemy's rear. Only days before Johnston's pullback, he had put closing touches to a plan to ship his one hundred thousand-plus soldiers, along with a vast amount of materiel, down Chesapeake Bay and up the Rappahannock and York Rivers, thus taking the Alexandria Line from the rear. Johnston's withdrawal, however, had forced Little Mac to plan anew. Finally aware that time was slipping away, by mid-March he had determined to transport men and supplies to Fort Monroe, where he would begin an overland march on Richmond. The plan underscored one of McClellan's strategic philosophies: His primary target was not Johnston's army, but the capital of the Southern nation. To his mind, should Richmond fall to attack or siege, the Confederacy would wither and die.

While McClellan made ready to sail from Washington, Alexandria, and other points, Johnston's army enjoyed a respite from combat, during which it drilled, refitted, and reorganized behind the lines. Only Stuart's cavalry and supporting infantry, including the division of Maj. Gen. Richard S. Ewell, saw action during the last half of March, and that action was brief and productive of few casualties. On the twenty-sixth, McClellan launched a new probe of the Cedar Run line, finally pushing across the stream and heading for Warrenton Junction on the Orange & Alexandria. The cavalry advanced to meet the threat. At the junction, as well as at nearby Bealton Station, Stuart's troopers—principally members of the 1st, 4th, and 6th Virginia—slowed the advance by fighting furiously with pistols, rifles, and carbines.[15]

Stuart did not trust entirely to the defensive. Near Warrenton Junction on the twenty-seventh, Grumble Jones, with the main body of the 1st, assailed the right flank of a force reconnoitering toward the Rappahannock and came away with two dozen prisoners. The limited strike was the extent of Stuart's risk taking, for he "had no intention of offering him [the enemy] battle." He only wished to "threaten him with demonstrations toward his flanks and in front, and by every possible means delay his progress and secure accurate information of his strength and, if possible, his designs."

As Stuart's men retreated to the river, the reconnaissance force reached Rappahannock Bridge, which the Confederates had helped torch to prevent a crossing. Cavalrymen also carted off a supply cache that Johnston had positioned near the span, while a tiny band under Jones's supervision provided an effective covering fire. "Some half a dozen men," Stuart reported, "thus held the advance of the enemy, with infantry, cavalry, and artillery, at bay till all the stores were removed." The Federals, discovering no ford at which to cross, retired sullenly to Warrenton Junction.

As always, Stuart was generous in commending officers and troopers for a job well done. In reporting the sparring along the Rappahannock, he singled out the 1st Virginia, even as he stressed that other outfits under his command "shared cheerfully" in the dangers of combat. Despite his personal feelings toward Jones, he lauded the colonel's "excellent service" throughout the period, especially when attacking near Warrenton and defending the removal of supplies. (It seems doubtful that such praise reduced the animosity the prickly subordinate felt toward his superior.) Stuart also wrote glowingly of the service of his staff and of Captain Blackford of the 1st Virginia, who had distinguished himself while disputing the enemy's advance, "no less in the bush than in the saddle."[16]

Upon reaching the south bank of the Rappahannock, Stuart's command—which again included the 2nd Virginia—took up its picket and patrol responsibilities. Then, suddenly, the scene of action shifted to the Virginia Peninsula, where, before the close of March, McClellan's transfer operation became evident to local Confederates, then to the authorities in Richmond, and finally to the troops under Johnston.

John Magruder (now a major general) had been expecting to find Yankees on his doorstep for weeks. Originally he believed they would advance down the James River; to counter them, he had importuned Richmond for additional troops. By the twenty-fifth, Prince John was sufficiently aware of increased activity in Hampton Roads to suppose that the attack would come, instead, from the south. He doubted that his principal position, Yorktown, would withstand the blow unless at least twenty thousand reinforcements reached him without delay. As he informed the new secretary of war, George W. Randolph, the alternative was to lose the entire Peninsula, as well as Norfolk and the line of the York River.[17]

In dire need of reconnaissance units, Magruder was especially anxious that his cavalry be enlarged. It continued to consist primarily of the 3rd Virginia. Though the mounted portion of Cobb's (Georgia) Legion had been ordered to join the Army of the Peninsula, it had been shunted, instead, to North Carolina. To make good the loss, Magruder sought to regain some horsemen who had been sent across the water to Suffolk. He also petitioned for authority to add at least part of the 9th Virginia Cavalry, then serving near Fredericksburg, as well as several companies of horsemen stationed in Sussex and Mecklenburg Counties.

The hard-pressed officials did what they could for Magruder. They checked on the status of the independent companies, while ordering the horsemen attached to the Wise Legion, under J. Lucius Davis (later the 10th Virginia Cavalry), to hasten to Yorktown from their new camp in North Carolina. At the head of two squadrons of his battalion-size force, Davis reported to Magruder during the first week in April.[18]

Stuart did not learn of McClellan's embarkation for Fort Monroe until April 2, when he relayed to his immediate superior, Longstreet, a report from a civilian informant in Alexandria. The man testified to having seen transports carrying at least two Union corps put out into the Potomac, apparently southward bound. He also reported that the posts near Fairfax Court House and Centreville had been stripped of troops; their former occupants were thought to have gone to Alexandria preparatory to shipping out.

This was important news, to be sure, but it was also outdated. By the time Stuart relayed it to Johnston, McClellan himself was disembarking at Fort Monroe, joining several thousand of his men already on Old Point Comfort. By the following day, almost sixty thousand troops and one hundred cannons—fully half the Union army—were on dry ground in rear of the Confederates on the Rappahannock.[19]

McClellan's first objective should have been to march without delay on Richmond, some seventy miles to the northwest. Instead, he decided to move first against Yorktown, which commanded shipping in the York River. When McClellan was ready to advance on the enemy capital, he would supply his army via the York and the railroad that connected the head of the stream with Richmond.

For a time before leaving Alexandria, Little Mac had feared that his river-borne strategy had been compromised by the appearance in Hampton Roads of a revolutionary vessel, the Confederate ironclad *Virginia.* On March 8, this odd-looking warship attacked the fleet of wooden ships that lay off Fort Monroe, sinking one, running a second aground, and threatening to close both the York and the James to Union ships. Denied those sources of logistical support, McClellan could not have operated freely anywhere on the Peninsula, even with the support of the gunboat fleet that had accompanied his troopships.

His strategy—and his peace of mind—were restored only after an ironclad addition to the Union navy, *Monitor,* appeared off Fort Monroe one day after *Virginia*'s debut. On the ninth, the ungainly men-of-war fought to a draw, cannonballs bouncing harmlessly off the plated sides of each. The standoff meant that McClellan need not relinquish the water route to Richmond.[20]

Having reached dry ground, Little Mac could concentrate on neutralizing the land-based obstacles facing him: not only Magruder's stronghold, but the works the Virginian had erected across the Peninsula, below, above, and west of Yorktown. During the evening of April 3–4, he issued orders governing the march north, which would proceed by way of the roads to Warwick Court House and Yorktown. In the predawn hours of the fourth, the Union advance got under way.[21]

Forced to oppose the behemoth coming his way with about 13,500 men, Magruder did an exemplary job of slowing both Union columns, thanks mainly to the fight-and-fall-back tactics of the 3rd Virginia and the four independent companies of horsemen at his disposal. Also helpful was Magruder's theatrical bent, which had gained him his royal nickname. Along his median line of works, which ran from Yorktown to Lee's Mill on the James River, the general set in motion a carefully managed procession of troops, which the approaching Yankees could clearly discern. Once beyond the enemy's sight, Magruder's soldiers double-quicked to their starting point and countermarched over the same ground, thus giving the impression of a never-ending line of gray. The ruse made the commanders of each Union column advance slowly and warily. The delay bought Magruder the time he needed to reposition men and guns to meet the threat and (as he hoped) to stock his defenses with reinforcements.[22]

The additions came in slowly. On the fifth, Maj. Gen. Benjamin Huger at Norfolk dispatched a brigade to Yorktown. The following day, Magruder learned that Johnston's advance echelon was marching through the streets of Richmond to the cheers of local citizens. On the seventh, the advance passed Virginia's colonial capital, Williamsburg; a few hours later, it began to file inside the Yorktown works. In another four days, the port village would be held by more than thirty-four thousand troops, all under Johnston's command. While the garrison represented barely a third of McClellan's manpower, Yorktown was no longer Little Mac's for the taking.[23]

Although Johnston's infantry and artillery marched to Magruder's assistance almost as soon as McClellan left Fort Monroe, Stuart's brigade remained on the south side of the Rappahannock for several days longer. During that time, the cavalry leader appeared more concerned with logistical and administrative issues than anything else. He made efforts to secure horse equipment, commissary stores, and wheeled transport for his troopers and horse artillerymen. On the fourth, he wrote Jefferson Davis to seek promotion for Tom Rosser, whose "extra-ordinary merit, unsurpassed ability, and conspicuous gallantry, displayed in action," recommended him for high rank in the cavalry. All the while, his men kept a close watch over the Federals north of the river. As late as April 6, they were reporting a Yankee buildup between Manassas and Cedar Run.[24]

On the eighth, Stuart finally turned his attention, and his brigade, southward. He made a leisurely march of it; by the twelfth he had placed his troopers—who remained ignorant of their ultimate destination—in bivouac seven miles below Richmond. In reaching that point, the brigade had made a triumphal procession through the streets of the capital, basking in the adulation of the citizenry, just as their infantry and artillery comrades had a week ago. While the reception pleased the troopers, unanswered questions nagged them. Stuart's quartermaster, Philip Powers, spoke for many when he asked himself: "Where are we going? . . . We all supposed we were hurrying to the Peninsula, where the great battle of the War seems to be impending, but it is now intimated that our services are not needed there, that they have enough Cavalry." This was manifestly untrue, but Stuart's deliberate pace suggested otherwise.[25]

The brigade did not reach Yorktown until the morning of the eighteenth. It arrived to find a heavy siege well under way. At first deceived by Magruder's theatricals, and then made aware that the garrison had been, or would soon be, reinforced, McClellan decided to besiege Yorktown until he could pound the place into submission. On April 5, engineer teams and fatigue details began to construct earthworks, redoubts, redans, and heavy gun emplacements. Over the next four weeks, the siege lines were expanded south and west of Yorktown and anchored not only by cannons, but also by thirteen-inch seacoast mortars borrowed from the navy. The investment would not be complete until the first days of May, but the vision of raining fire, smoke, destruction, and panic on his enemy induced Little Mac and his army to keep digging.

Given the relatively static nature of siege warfare, Stuart suspected that his cavalry would see precious little action on the Yorktown front. He was correct: For more than two weeks, his men occupied themselves in picketing the rear and right flanks of the local forces, occasionally venturing into the ever-shrinking land between the armies. This was war at its most monotonous—certainly not the kind most cavalrymen had enlisted to fight. The relative inactivity depressed their commander; he blamed it on the local topography. As Stuart's most recent biographer observes, upon reaching Yorktown, he "determined that his cavalry would have to be content with a minor role on the peninsula because of the wooded ground and the deep ravines that intersected otherwise flat terrain. This was no country for the deployment of massed cavalry."[26]

Stuart was also chagrined to find his command considerably reduced as the result of operations well to the west and north. When Johnston reinforced Magruder, he left Ewell's division near Orange Court House to hold the line of the Rapidan against Union encroachment. To Stuart's dismay, the 2nd and 6th Virginia were attached to Ewell's eight thousand-man force and thus remained behind when the rest of the cavalry headed for the Peninsula. Farther to the east, along the Rappahannock, other mounted detachments that should have been assigned to Stuart were also serving apart from him. They included Rooney Lee's 9th Virginia, which had been observing and impeding enemy forces marching south on Fredericksburg. Despite Lee's efforts, on the day Stuart reached Yorktown, the advance of Irvin McDowell's forty thousand-man I Army Corps occupied Falmouth, opposite Fredericksburg, only fifty miles from Richmond.[27]

Having been withheld from McClellan to guard the approaches to Washington, McDowell's soldiers were now almost halfway to the Army of the Potomac. It appeared that Lincoln and his war secretary, Edwin Stanton, would soon release the I Corps to McClellan's custody. If they chose not to, McDowell could march on Richmond direct while McClellan occupied Johnston on the Peninsula. Either prospect made Confederate officials pale.

Grasping for a means of keeping McDowell far from Richmond and Yorktown, Jefferson Davis and his military advisor, Robert E. Lee, turned to Stonewall Jackson. Jackson's ten thousand troops had a precarious grip on the lower Shenandoah Valley, where they were opposed by almost twice as many Federals under Nathaniel Banks; the manpower disparity had helped Banks defeat Stonewall at Kernstown in late March. Now Davis and Lee asked Jackson to renew contact with Banks in such a dramatic fashion that Lincoln and Stanton would be compelled to reinforce the Valley troops with McDowell. Jackson promised to do what he could—which turned out to be quite a lot—and late in April, Ewell started west to assist him, with the 2nd and 6th Virginia leading the way.[28]

Happily, Stuart was compensated for the loss of these regiments. Upon reaching Yorktown, Johnston had absorbed the Army of the Peninsula (Magruder was given command of the "right wing" of the combined forces), and thus he assigned Stuart command of the mounted force that had served Prince John. The new additions, which had joined Stuart's brigade by early May, included not only the 3rd Virginia and a few independent companies, but also the new arrivals of the Wise Legion. In coming weeks, the 9th Virginia and one squadron of the Hampton Legion's cavalry would be assigned to Stuart as well.

In addition to growing, Stuart's brigade underwent changes in its officer ranks. The Confederate conscription law that went into effect in mid-April required all short-term regiments then in the field to reenlist for the duration of the war and to reelect their field and company officers. Though election day varied from outfit to outfit, most regiments cast their votes between April 16 and the first week in May. In almost every instance, the balloting was preceded by days of energetic and sometimes shameless politicking. Candidates for the same position vied with each other in making stump speeches. Often they promised their "constituents" considerate and even lenient treatment once they gained or regained their commissions.[29]

When "reorganizing for the war," only one of Stuart's subordinates, Lieutenant Colonel Martin of the Jeff Davis Legion, held on to his position. Despite potentially harmful effects on regimental morale, Stuart was pleased when the two subordinates he liked the least, Grumble Jones and Beverly Robertson, were voted out of office. The temperament and leadership style of each had alienated not only their common superior, but also the rank and file, most of whom resented the harsh discipline the colonels doled out. Jones later contested the results, claiming that ineligible voters had ousted him at Stuart's urging, but his protests fell on deaf ears. Replaced by Stuart's friend, the courtly and affable Fitz Lee, the man called Grumble was packed off to the Shenandoah Valley, where he later replaced Ashby in command of the 7th Virginia.

When Fitz Lee succeeded Jones, the post he vacated was filled by Stuart's former adjutant, L. Tiernan Brien. Robertson, meanwhile, lost his position to Williams Wickham, although the latter did not receive his promotion for four months, apparently because he was wounded soon afterward and subsequently captured. For his part, Robertson was without a command only briefly before being elevated—against Stuart's wishes—to brigadier general, to rank from June 9. Of those regiments and legions that had recently come under Stuart's authority, the only major change occurred in the ranks of the 3rd Virginia, where the dour old Regular Robert Johnston was defeated by the congenial volunteer Thomas Goode.[30]

>─┼─◄►─O─◄►─┼─◄

The horsemen Stuart had led down from the Rappahannock remained outside Yorktown for barely two weeks. With the arrival of May, McClellan's investment lines were all but complete, the last pieces of long-range ordnance being manhandled into position south of town. Once those guns opened, Johnston's hold on Yorktown would probably be reduced to a few hours.

The Confederate leader, who never occupied a position he could not retreat from, had been planning to evacuate for some time. Shortly after midnight on May 3–4, a day or so before McClellan opened fire, Johnston beat him to the punch. For hours he pounded the Union works with his own formidable array of artillery. Under cover of the bombardment, he began to evacuate. He placed a large segment of his army on the Yorktown-Williamsburg Road, the rest on a roughly parallel thoroughfare farther to the west, the Lee's Mill Road. By daybreak, as the guns finally fell silent, Magruder's old stronghold was empty except for stragglers, some artillerymen, and the few hardy civilians who had weathered the siege.[31]

This latest withdrawal kept Stuart and his troopers busy. While a few horsemen guarded the flanks of both retreat columns, most were massed to form the all-important rear guard. It was hard work from the start, made especially so by the boggy nature of the few roads between Yorktown and Williamsburg, the result of three weeks of intermittent rain. "Owing to the peculiar difficulties of the ground," Stuart originally established his base of operations on the James River side of the Peninsula along a tributary known as Skiff Creek, then carefully extended his lines to the north and east. The line parted where it crossed the roads the army was using, allowing infantry, artillery, and wagons to pass through during the night of May 3 and into the rainy morning of the fourth.[32]

, Aware that even the lackadaisical McClellan would muster the energy to follow, Stuart divided his main body to cover all avenues of pursuit. He left Martin's legion on Skiff Creek to defend and then destroy the bridge that carried the Lee's Mill Road over the stream. As soon as the left-hand column had crossed, Federals appeared in the distance, and Martin's men set the span on fire, then turned and headed for Williamsburg.

To guard the other flank, astride the direct road from Yorktown, Stuart posted Wickham's 4th Virginia. (Robertson, who had yet to surrender command of the regiment, was in Richmond on sick leave.) Stuart himself, along with much of the 3rd Virginia, established an outpost near Blow's Mill in the approximate middle of the Peninsula. This central position was further defended by two mountain howitzers of the Stuart Horse Artillery under 2nd Lt. James T. Shepherd. Stuart had dispatched John Pelham, with the rest of the battery, to Bigler's Wharf on the York River, northeast of Williamsburg, where Fitz Lee and the 1st Virginia held the cavalry's most advanced position. In that same general sector, but closer to Williamsburg, Stuart had also stationed Davis's Virginians and the two companies of South Carolinians attached to the Hampton Legion, under Calbraith Butler.[33]

By noon, with the rain still falling, Johnston's main body had cleared the Skiff Creek line. As if on cue, McClellan's cavalry, with artillery attached and infantry to the rear, approached the Rebels via both of the northward-leading roads. The force on the Lee's Mill road, which included the resourceful Lieutenant Custer, managed to extinguish the flames quickly enough to save the bridge Will Martin had tried to destroy. Custer's force then crossed Skiff Creek to menace Stuart's right and center.

Soon afterward, a much larger column under George Stoneman's leadership advanced on Wickham's position, which abutted the Halfway House, perhaps four miles from Williamsburg. Wickham sallied forth to meet the Yankees and a firefight broke out, one that expanded to fill the fields on either side of the Yorktown Road. The Virginians quickly found themselves outnumbered, outpositioned, and about to be surrounded. They were in especially dire straits after Stoneman sent up a battery to shell their front and flanks, inflicting several casualties. For a time, the 4th resisted, fighting savagely with sabers, pistols, and occasionally, shoulder arms. In the end, however, the regiment was forced to retreat—at first slowly and stubbornly, later with accelerating speed.

Late in the morning, Wickham regrouped in front of Fort Magruder. This formidable bastion crowned a line of earthworks on the southern outskirts of Williamsburg, the northernmost of the defensive perimeters with which Magruder had girdled the Peninsula. Near Fort Magruder the Virginians were joined not only by the horsemen of Davis and Butler, but also by the foot soldiers of Longstreet's division, the rear echelon of Johnston's main body.[34]

The 4th Virginia may have rallied, but it had withdrawn so swiftly that it uncovered Stuart's left flank. Early in the afternoon, after thrusting Wickham toward Williamsburg, Stoneman's troopers turned west and advanced on the rear of the 3rd Virginia. The unexpected move interposed them between Goode and his comrades near Williamsburg. Rather than give way to concern, Stuart met the challenge head-on. He considered turning the tables by cutting into Stoneman's rear, but the roads in that direction were too spongy to support an attempt. Instead, he faced Goode's men to the north and ordered them to break through the roadblock.

Goode led his men forward across what Pvt. Robert Hudgins called "a big field that had been previously sown to hay and . . . as pretty a place as one could ask for a fight." Lieutenant Shepherd's howitzers provided a brief but effective covering fire. Trooper Hudgins saw "horses and riders going down in the tangled Yankee ranks as Pelham's shells found their mark." When Stoneman's battery returned the fire, however, Shepherd was forced to withdraw after discharging a few rounds of shrapnel. "One shell landed to my right," Hudgins noted, "killing a man and mortally wounding his horse. This was the first time I had ever heard a horse squeal when wounded, and it was truly horrifying."[35]

Goode's "handsome charge," as Stuart called it, struck a portion of the Yankee force before it could properly form. The crunching impact sent a battalion of Illinois horsemen to the rear in hot haste, minus a captured guidon. Stuart was less pleased when a portion of the 3rd Virginia fled in turn after being blasted by dismounted carbineers hiding in a woods.

Stuart attempted to hold his ground, but luck and geography were against him. Goode's overthrow had weakened his position, and blue-jacketed reinforcements were coming up by the dozens. To save what remained of the 3rd Virginia, he broke off the fight and led everyone southeastward in the rain, looping around the enemy until he struck the James River. Turning abruptly north, he continued up the sandy bank until he cleared the roadblock. Before dark, he entered the streets of Williamsburg, where he linked with Wickham, Martin, Davis, and Butler.

Assessing the results of the day's action—the first fighting by his command in numbers that approached full strength—Stuart gave its performance mixed reviews. Although the brigade had helped make good Johnston's escape from Yorktown, it had taken hard knocks from the upstart Yankee cavalry. Wickham's wing had been severely handled, suffering several casualties, including the disabling of its leader, who had taken a saber thrust in the side. Goode's regiment

had suffered less severely, although many of its men had been cut off and captured before the balance of the 3rd could reach safety.[36]

In fairness to Stuart and his men, they had been opposed for most of the day
by heavier forces, including artillery whose firepower they could not match. And
yet the gray riders had shown a fighting spirit throughout the day; even after
Longstreet's infantry arrived to secure their flanks and rear, they continued to
lash out. Stuart was heartened to learn that a pair of spirited charges by the
horsemen of the Wise and Hampton Legions had driven back not only bodies of
Regular cavalry, but also some foot soldiers in Stoneman's rear, thereby preventing the capture of Fort Magruder. The general was especially pleased that the
opposition had included the brigade led by his father-in-law, the apostate Virginian Philip St. George Cooke. For Stuart, the day may have begun badly, but it
had ended on a high note, and he was certain that sweeter music would follow.

Chapter Seven

A Feather of the Tallest Sort *MAY 1862*

B ecause neither antagonist abandoned the field of battle, Stuart realized that fighting would resume on May 5. At daylight, after snatching an hour or two of sleep, he galloped forth in the rain in company with a party of his troopers to discover what had become of Stoneman and his infantry friends. To his surprise, for miles in front of Fort Magruder, the land was free of blue soldiers. Obviously the Yankees were a cautious lot, unwilling to venture within rifle range of the defenses that General Longstreet's men continued to occupy.

Just how far off were they? His view south blocked by woods, Stuart could not study the lower reaches of the Lee's Mill road, the most logical avenue of Union advance. Needing to know who lurked there, he dispatched a company of the 4th Virginia to reconnoiter the thoroughfare. Minutes after the little band started out, however, Stuart received a partial answer when his party was fired on by skirmishers concealed in a woods near the point to which the scouting party was heading. The concerned brigadier sent a volunteer aide, Capt. W. E. Towles, to extricate the Virginians from what looked like a trap. The aide not only accomplished his mission without loss, but also brought Stuart word that a sizable force of foot soldiers was advancing up the road. Stuart relayed the information to Longstreet, whose troops were soon moving south to counter the threat. As Stuart noted in his after-action report, "Thus began the battle of Williamsburg."[1]

The fighting this day did not heavily involve Stuart's horsemen. For the better part of the ten-hour struggle, much of it waged in a driving storm, Stuart took on the role of artillery commander, directing the fire of the cannons that defended the earthworks on either side of Fort Magruder. He also acted as a traffic cop, shuttling Longstreet's troops into sectors where they could effectively challenge the Federal divisions of Joseph Hooker, William Farrar Smith, and Philip Kearny—all under the command of McClellan's ranking subordinate (and Stuart's former commander in the 1st U.S. Cavalry), Maj. Gen. Edwin Sumner. By all accounts, Stuart did a masterful job of helping supervise the Confederate response to Sumner's advance.[2]

For most of the fight, the cavalry remained in column, mounted and ready for instant employment, in rear of the two redoubts just west of Fort Magruder. Longstreet, who commanded the rear guard while Johnston continued on to Richmond with the main body and supply wagons of the army, sought active employment for the horsemen, but the clotted woods and muddy roads worked against him. Stuart's subordinates nevertheless kept alert. Shortly after midday, Lieutenant Colonel Martin informed Stuart that a Union column (it turned out to be a brigade of Smith's division, under Brig. Gen. Winfield Scott Hancock) had taken position east of Fort Magruder as if to attack Longstreet's left. Thus forewarned, Stuart carefully monitored the brigade's movement. Although Hancock's role in the fight would win him the sobriquet "The Superb," Stuart was unimpressed by the officer's slow advance and the ragged volleys his command trained on Fort Magruder. At length, Stuart decided that "he was either weak, timid, or feigning, and in neither contingency to be feared."[3]

Early in the afternoon, as Longstreet's men began to get the upper hand, forcing Hooker, Smith, and Kearny backward, the Stuart Horse Artillery—three of its guns, at any rate, under Pelham—reached the field at a dead gallop, having charged down from Bigler's Wharf in response to Stuart's summons. The youthful captain halted just off the Yorktown Road, near the point at which a full-scale pursuit would soon commence. For a time, Pelham waited beside his two twelve-pounder "Napoleon" cannons and single twelve-pounder Blakely rifle while Stuart's horsemen pushed to the front of the pursuit column—only to be sent flying when volleys of rifle fire crashed out of adjacent trees. Surmising that a reserve force had come up to cover Sumner's withdrawal, Stuart rode to the position of the horse artillery, intent on having it open on the newcomers. Upon arriving, he found that "the gallant Pelham" had anticipated him. Having unlimbered in record time, the captain (as Stuart noted in characteristic prose) was already "speaking to the enemy in thunder tones of defiance." Pelham's first rounds slammed into the crowded woods, evicting its occupants. Then the artilleryman obeyed Stuart's order to reposition and sweep the Yorktown Road with a crossfire. Stuart observed that Pelham kept up a deadly fire "as long as the presence of the enemy warranted the expenditure of ammunition." At least in some sectors, Sumner must have held his ground with stubbornness, for by day's close the Stuart Horse Artillery had fired off 360 rounds of shot and shell.[4]

The enfilade of the Yankee-held road effectively closed out the fighting. By sundown, Longstreet had suffered nearly sixteen hundred casualties while inflicting almost twenty-three hundred on his enemy. His victory, so ably facilitated by Stuart, had enabled Johnston's army to make good its escape on the road to the Chickahominy River.[5]

The cavalry, by being held out of the fighting, suffered only four casualties. The most notable was the severe wounding of Major Payne, Wickham's successor in command of the 4th Virginia. Late in the afternoon, the cofounder of the Black Horse Cavalry had ventured down the Yorktown Road at the head of a reconnaissance detail, when ambushed by a detachment of Stoneman's Regulars. Struck in the face by a carbine ball, which shattered his jaw and severed arteries in his mouth, Payne had been left between the lines when his men retreated. Unconscious, drowning in his own blood, he was spared from death when one of his troopers returned to minister to him.

Captured along with his benefactor and treated by an enemy surgeon, Payne pulled through by the sheerest of margins. As he was expected to be *hors de combat* for many months, he was quickly paroled and allowed to recuperate at his home in Fauquier County. Defying the odds, he would return to duty the following September, wearing a rubber mask the Union doctor had made for him, which held the bones of his jaw together until they healed.[6]

><del>+</del><+>—O—<+>+<del>+</del>

Despite sloppy weather and ungovernable terrain, Stuart considered the two-day battle just ended "a glorious affair" for his army, and for his command in particular. "On the 4th," he informed Flora, "my Brigade distinguished itself, and on the 5th by its attitude and maneuvering, under constant fire prevented the enemy's leaving the woods for the open ground—thus narrowing his artillery scope of fire. *I* consider the most brilliant feat of the 5th to have been a dash of the *Stuart* Horse Artillery to the front. Coming suddenly under a galling fire from the woods, from a reinforcement of the enemy, they wheeled into action sustaining in the most brilliant manner the fortunes of the day till the Inf'y could come to their support." He could not refrain from adding a dose of self-praise: "If you had seen your husband you would have been proud of him." To be sure, he was proud of himself, but not without reason.

In contrast to his Dranesville report, Stuart did not resort to exaggeration or evasion when explaining his role in the fighting at Williamsburg. The only untruth he put on paper was that the Confederates had abandoned the field on May 5 because "we were without rations." In fact, the rear guard was just as interested in clearing the area as its comrades in Johnston's main body. Although evading a much larger enemy and seeking a more advantageous position carried no disgrace, Stuart was loath to admit that his army would quit any field, even the field of victory, for any reason, however defensible.[7]

The withdrawal to Richmond proceeded with frustrating slowness, the result of roads that were both few and poor. "The march up the Pensinsular [*sic*] like the one down," recalled a private in the 1st Virginia, "gave us a fair conception of how deep mud could get." Philip Powers of Stuart's staff told his wife that his horse "several times sunk so deep in the mud that with great difficulty I could get him out." The aide added an allusion that his boss would not have appreciated: "It reminded me of the Yankee retreat at Bull Run."[8]

Despite Johnston's glacial pace, McClellan failed to overtake the Rebel column, except intermittently. Little Mac concentrated, instead, on making an end run with the assistance of his naval comrades. Anticipating an enemy retreat, he had sent an infantry division by transport up the York River to its confluence with the Pamunkey, then up the Pamunkey to Eltham's Landing. So far, so good, but the promising operation soon bogged down. The troops debarked at the landing on May 7, moved cautiously inland, and made a feeble effort to intercept the Confederates in midretreat. Johnston responded by coolly detaching two infantry brigades from his right flank, which drove the newcomers back to the river and the protection of a gunboat fleet.[9]

Although the cavalry was not involved in the fight at Eltham's, the Stuart Horse Artillery saw action not far to the west, near Burnt Ordinary on the Richmond-Williamsburg Road. In opposing a pursuit by one of Stoneman's subordinates, Brig. Gen. William W. Averell, Lieutenant Breathed, commanding a rifle and a howitzer, shelled the 3rd Pennsylvania and 8th Illinois Cavalries into retreat. His work economically done (only five rounds had been expended), Breathed rejoined Pelham and resumed the withdrawal.

On the eighth, his army's retreat carried Stuart's horsemen and cannoneers through Slatersville and toward New Kent Court House, less than thirty miles from Richmond. Rushing ahead of Stoneman's main body, a detachment of Regulars chased Stuart's advance guard out of New Kent. The following day, Stuart took revenge on Federals who threatened his rear guard outside Slatersville. Yankee cavalry, with the support of some fast-marching foot regiments, struck boldly, interposing between the rear echelon and Stuart's main force. For a time, portions of the 1st, 3rd, and 4th Virginia were cut off; all but a half dozen men, however, escaped capture. The rest cut across fields, circumventing the enemy, and linked with their comrades on the outskirts of New Kent. There they formed a barrier across the narrow road to the courthouse.

The Federals advanced as if ready to launch a second attack, but this time Stuart struck first. A member of the 4th Virginia noted that the entire rear guard surged forward and thudded into the bluecoats before they could form to meet it. The result was the overthrow of Stoneman's troopers. As they hastened to the rear, the Virginian decided that "they could not do otherwise as they neither had room nor time to wheel."[10]

Stuart's command had demonstrated strength out of proportion to its numbers. As if unappreciative of the fact, five days later Johnston importuned Robert E. Lee for more manpower, insisting that "the cavalry force of the army is inadequate—entirely out of proportion to the other arms of the service." He might have added that had those other arms exhibited the same striking power, the army would not have had to evacuate the Peninsula.[11]

><del>+<>·O·<+<del>·<

The fighting of May 8–9 marked the last time the Confederate rear was seriously threatened short of the Richmond defenses. Danger signals, however, were going up in other quarters. On May 15, as Johnston's vanguard crossed the Chickahominy River to within three miles of the capital, Union gunboats, including the *Monitor*—freed for offensive operations by the scuttling of the *Virginia* off captured Norfolk—ran up the James in an unsuccessful attempt to blast the city into surrender. Two days later, Little Mac pursued another water route toward Richmond when he sent a small expedition up the Pamunkey River. This thrust missed its mark, but a more ominous threat materialized that same day, when McDowell's corps was authorized to depart the Rappahannock and join McClellan by an overland march.[12]

For a time unaware of McDowell's plans, the Confederates continued to devote their attention to McClellan's army. They were relieved to observe that the Federals continued to crawl up the Peninsula. Until mid-May, the greater part of Stuart's command retained its blocking position near New Kent, as if daring its enemy to close up and give battle.

When the cavalry finally turned north to join its comrades inside newly improved works along the Chickahominy, many looked forward to the change of scenery. The Peninsula had been a dreary collection of wretched roads and ramshackle dwellings. The streets of the nerve center of the Confederacy presented a much more attractive picture.

Even for a lifelong native of the Peninsula like Robert Hudgins, "the thought of being quartered in Richmond—the capital of the Confederacy—with its pretty girls brought possibilities" that warmed his imagination. Visions became reality a few days later, when the 3rd Virginia trooped through the city, in concert with the rest of Stuart's command, to take position on the northern outskirts. For the second time in less than a month, most of Stuart's riders basked in the applause of the citizenry. Men and women shouted and clapped, minute guns boomed, boys set off fireworks, and "pretty girls waved flags and strewed flowers" across the path of each regiment. Recalling the scene years later, Hudgins observed that as of May 1862, "the glamorous side of war had not yet succumbed to that of heavy casualties."[13]

Almost as soon as they bivouacked, Stuart's men were put in motion, patrolling the roads that led to the Chickahominy in the vicinity of the suburb of Mechanicsville. At first it was quiet, easy duty, but within a week the troopers were staring across the river at rank upon rank of blue-clad infantry, cavalry, and artillery—McClellan had finally moved within striking distance of the capital. A battle seemed imminent—one that would undoubtedly decide the outcome of this year-old experiment in rebellion.

As the Federals settled in, Joe Johnston and his military and political superiors weighed their options. Would it be easier to oppose a swift, powerful assault or to weather a long, debilitating siege? Time and the enemy furnished an answer. As McClellan continued to stock his lines with men and guns, Johnston became increasingly reluctant to wait for the blow to fall. At length, he resolved to strike first.

By the fourth week in May, an opportunity appeared to present itself. McClellan's dispositions were all but complete and, fortunately for his opponent, they were logistically faulty. The "Young Napoleon" had allowed the Chickahominy to split his army; three of his five corps were stationed north of

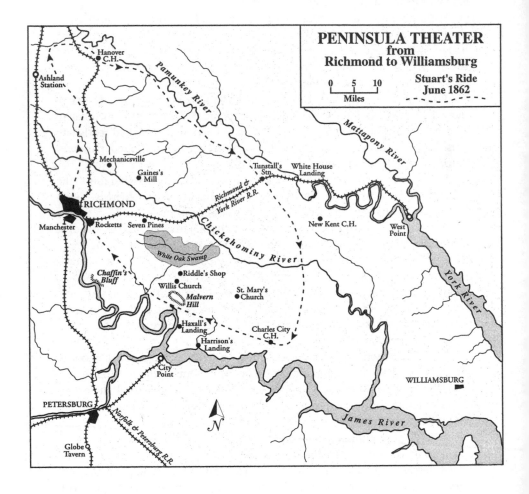

PENINSULA THEATER
from
Richmond to Williamsburg

0   5   10
Miles

Stuart's Ride
June 1862

where was R.E Lee?

the stream, the other two below it. An attack on either side of the river, therefore, would not bring the Confederates into contact with all one hundred thousand-plus soldiers facing them.

While the Yankees below the stream appeared the more inviting target, Johnston grudgingly decided he must strike on the north bank to prevent the imminent linkup of McClellan's right flank and McDowell's corps. By the afternoon of the twenty-seventh, the Confederate leader had drawn up plans to attack with the three divisions assigned to his ranking subordinate, Maj. Gen. Gustavus W. Smith. (Beauregard had been transferred to the western theater.) *Shiloh* At the last minute, however—thanks largely to Stonewall Jackson's genius on the offensive and J. E. B. Stuart's mastery of intelligence gathering—Johnston learned that he need not take such a gamble, after all.[14] *Stonewall*

While Johnston and Richmond dithered, Jackson's small but mighty command in the Valley began to fulfill the demands of its diversionary mission. On May 23, having advanced on the strategic outpost at Front Royal, Stonewall's men attacked and routed the Union garrison. They then occupied a position from which to cut off the larger command of Nathaniel Banks, at that moment falling back to the communications center of Winchester.[15]

The infantry portion of Jackson's force had moved so swiftly on Front Royal that it gained the enduring nickname "foot cavalry." His command also contained more traditional cavalry, including two regiments recently assigned to Stuart, the 2nd and 6th Virginia. For a time, both regiments were led by Tom Munford, who had become the senior officer in either outfit when, during the recent elections, he had outpolled Colonel Radford and the loser had quit the field. By the time Jackson moved against Winchester, however, both regiments had been assigned to Brig. Gen. George H. Steuart of Maryland, formerly an officer of U.S. dragoons. One more reorganization had yet to occur. Early in June, following the death of Turner Ashby, the outfits would pass into the hands of Beverly Robertson and be joined by Grumble Jones's 7th Virginia, the 12th Virginia Cavalry, the 17th Virginia Battalion (later the 11th Virginia Cavalry), and Chew's battery of horse artillery. The result was the basic configuration of what would become known as the "Laurel Brigade."[16]

Unwilling to rest with the future of the Confederacy at stake, two days after his success at Front Royal Jackson moved on Winchester and challenged Banks's army. Following a desperate, several-hour fight, the Federals were driven from the town and toward the crossings of the upper Potomac. The victory ✓ meant that all but a sliver of the Shenandoah was in Confederate hands.[17]

The officials in Washington, who in the best of times feared for the safety of the capital, were panicked by the news from Winchester. In the aftermath of the debacle, Lincoln canceled a planned transfer of troops from the Valley to McClellan's army. More important, on the twenty-eighth he ordered McDowell to halt his advance to the Peninsula, turn west, and hasten to the Valley, there to cooperate with Banks in defeating Jackson. Stuart's scouts detected McDowell's change of heading early on the twenty-eighth; Stuart informed Johnston only hours before he met with his generals to fix details of the coming offensive.[18]

The changed situation spawned a new plan. On the morning of the thirty-first, Johnston advanced along both sides of the Chickahominy; now, however, his primary objective was the enemy force below the river. The battle that ensued began badly enough. Thanks to garbled and misunderstood orders, the divisions of Longstreet, Huger, and D. H. Hill attempted to march over the same road at the same time to assault Maj. Gen. Erasmus D. Keyes's IV Army Corps. When the attackers finally sorted themselves out, they launched an attack that crushed Keyes's right flank near a landmark known as Seven Pines. After a failed counterattack, the Yankees pulled back to a new line near Fair Oaks Station on the Richmond & York River Railroad. Other Confederates battled Brig. Gen. Samuel P. Heintzelman's III Corps as well as elements of Sumner's II Corps, which late in the day crossed the rain-swollen river on a rickety bridge to reinforce Keyes. By early evening, the attack had stalled and the fighting sputtered out, but not before Johnston had suffered more than sixty-one hundred casualties to McClellan's five thousand.

Among the wounded was Johnston himself, struck by a shell fragment. On June 1, after the general had been invalided to Richmond, G. W. Smith took over and tried to mount a new offensive. For a number of reasons, the effort gained almost no ground; meanwhile, Smith fell apart under the weight of his new responsibilities. Early in the afternoon, Jefferson Davis sent his trusted advisor, Robert E. Lee, to relieve the unstrung subordinate. Sizing up the offensive as a lost cause, Lee withdrew the army to its old positions. He would never relinquish command of what he had already begun to call the "Army of Northern Virginia."[19]

As at Williamsburg, firm, open ground had been scarce in the vicinity of Seven Pines and Fair Oaks. In consequence, neither Stuart's horsemen nor their counterparts in blue saw much service on either day of the fighting. Attached to Longstreet's command throughout the battle, Stuart proved unable to rectify his superior's errant march on the thirty-first or extend the abortive assault Longstreet made the next morning under Smith's supervision. Stuart could provide only moral support, for which Longstreet was nevertheless grateful. "In the absence of any opportunity to use the cavalry," he wrote in his after-action report, Stuart had been "of material service by his presence with me on the field." Tribute was also paid to Stuart's old regiment: General Smith observed that a segment of the 1st Virginia attached to his headquarters lacked the opportunity "on May 31 of charging and driving a full regiment of infantry from the field as they did on the 21st of July last at Manassas, but . . . bearing important orders whenever called upon, they rendered very important service."[20]

One cheering aspect of the otherwise disappointing battle was the spoils that fell into Confederate hands over the two days of fighting. Returning to his regiment's position north of the capital, William Clark Corson of the 3rd Virginia informed his fiancée that Stuart's men alone had brought off five thousand captured firearms, "many of them splendid rifles." The battlefield also yielded nonmilitary gifts. On June 1, Corson's regiment had passed an abandoned campground, where he picked up "a number of trophies, among which I have saved a Yankee daguerotype [sic] and a lot of letters, envelopes etc. for you which I will send up by the first opportunity." He added matter-of-factly: "I tried to cut a ring off a dead Yankee's finger, but my knife was too dull. This may appear revolting to you but if you had seen as much of the scoundrels as I have you would think otherwise."[21]

Upon withdrawing to his capital's defenses, Stuart took on a variety of duties. On June 2, Longstreet, to whom he remained attached, tendered him command of Huger's division during its commander's unauthorized absence from head-quarters. When Huger reappeared next morning, Stuart returned to his brigade—not to ponder cavalry matters, but to plot grand strategy. On the fourth, in an apparent attempt to cast himself as a deep thinker, not merely a competent tactician, he sent his new superior a detailed plan for future opera-tions on the Chickahominy.[22]

In submitting his plan, Stuart hoped to forestall accusations that he was being presumptuous—only "the present imperiled condition of the Nation" had prompted him to write. Close observation of the enemy had shown him that to await attack invited peril, because when the Federals struck, they would do so in overwhelming strength. Better to attack south of the Chickahominy before McClellan, who was shifting resources in that direction, could advance en masse. "We have an army far better adapted to attack than defense," Stuart argued. "Let us fight at advantage before we are forced to fight at disadvan-tage."[23]

Another commander, especially one so new to his position, might not have accepted with good grace an unsolicited proposal such as Stuart's. Robert E. Lee, however, gave the plan a sympathetic review. He had known its author since West Point, when Stuart was a student during Lee's superintendency. They had served closely during John Brown's raid on Harpers Ferry; while Lee directed the opposition to the insurrectionists, Lieutenant Stuart of the 1st Cav-alry had served as his emissary to them. Lee regarded Stuart as flamboyant, impetuous, sometimes possessed of an overabundance of enthusiasm, but also a loyal subordinate, one with a gift for intuiting an enemy's intentions. Such a man was worth hearing out.

In the end, he dismissed Stuart's blueprint as impractical—in essence, it called for suicide attacks on defenses already reinforced to the point of impreg-nability—but he did not dismiss the suggester. On the rainy morning of June 10, two days after one of Stuart's men complained that "the two armies below Richmond are at a standstill," Lee moved to break the deadlock, with his cav-alry chief's assistance. The army leader had an imperfect understanding of the dispositions McClellan had made since the recent battle. He knew only that

troops were passing from one end of the Union line to the other, their movements facilitated by permanent and temporary bridges over the Chickahominy.

In particular, Lee wished to know how far above the river the enemy's right
flank extended, and where and how well it was protected. It was this sector, not
the flank below the river, that Lee was planning to assault. Thus he called Stuart
to army headquarters and explained how he could help dispel the cloud of ignorance.[24]

Although Lee's plan did not tally with Stuart's view of things, the cavalryman was immediately receptive to the mission his superior assigned him: An
expedition—not merely a scout or an armed reconnaissance—around the
enemy's right flank and into his rear. Stuart nodded in eager agreement; he even
suggested that his troopers might do more than size up the forces McClellan
had stationed between the Chickahominy and the Pamunkey. They might sweep
across the rear of the entire Army of the Potomac—around its lower flank, as
well. Such an act appealed to Stuart's sense of the dramatic, and he knew that if
accomplished without heavy loss, it would create a sensation throughout the
South.

Lee gently shook his head. While the basis of his objection remains
unknown, he undoubtedly regarded the encircling of the enemy as a stunt—
something one did simply to prove it could be done. And yet he appears not to
have quashed the idea so decisively that Stuart consigned it to oblivion.

Stuart's written instructions, which he received on the eleventh, stressed
speed of execution and caution—recent reports suggested that the strength of
the Federal right remained substantial and might even have increased—in addition to the importance of gaining precise information about McClellan's flank.
Stuart accepted Lee's suggestion that he select for the expedition "only such
men as can stand" the exertion involved—a reference to the condition of the
cavalry following weeks of almost constant service at the front.[25]

In building his raiding column, Stuart displayed a characteristic conser-
vatism. The force he led out of camp along the Richmond, Fredericksburg &
Potomac Railroad north of the Chickahominy in the predawn darkness of June
12 totaled barely twelve hundred officers and troopers. Not surprisingly, it
included Fitz Lee's 1st and Rooney Lee's 9th Virginia. Perhaps mindful of the
regiment's scouting abilities, Stuart had added the 4th Virginia, but because its
senior officers were out of action, he had attached four of its companies to Fitz
and four others to Rooney. Bringing up the rear of the raiding column were Will
Martin, 250 picked men of his legion, and a two-gun section of the Stuart Horse
Artillery under James Breathed.[26]

At the outset, few beyond Stuart himself were privy to the details of the
mission, the first large-scale independent operation of the cavalry, Army of
Northern Virginia. Lt. William T. Robins, adjutant of Rooney Lee's regiment,
observed that as soon as the raiders were in motion, "surmises and conjectures
as to our destination" traveled the length of the column. For most of the men,

the objective of the mission would not become clear for another twenty-four hours or more.

As dawn broke, the riders passed rain-drenched fields and a portentous landmark, Yellow Tavern. Just beyond the weatherbeaten hostelry, they veered left onto the Mountain Road. Guided by John Mosby, William Farley, and other scouts, the column crossed the tracks of the Richmond, Fredericksburg & Potomac and continued north for several miles before turning sharply eastward just shy of the South Anna River. The new direction quelled speculation, till then rife in the ranks, that they were bound for the Shenandoah Valley, where they would reinforce Stonewall Jackson.[27]

After again crossing the R, F & P, the column bivouacked for the night on the property of a farmer named Winston. Troopers and artillerists had come more than twenty miles since breaking camp. Stuart and Rooney Lee spent the night not with their troops, but five miles away at a plantation known as Hickory Hill. They had come to visit the owner of the estate, Williams Wickham, still convalescing from his Williamsburg wound.

When the horsemen retook the road on the bright, warm morning of June 13, they wended their way southeastward in the direction of Hanover Court House and Old Church. Troopers familiar with the neighborhood suddenly understood what was happening: They were skirting the right flank of McClellan's army and heading for its rear along the banks of the Pamunkey. This fact Stuart soon made clear to his ranking subordinates. None cheered the news, at least not loudly, for, as had been the case since journey's start, everyone remained under strict orders to maintain silence. The need for this precaution was evident: The Confederates might be traveling through rural Virginia, but this part of it was temporarily the enemy's homeland.

Stuart's scouts had reported the road as far as Hanover Court House free of enemy forces; still, the general proceeded gingerly, warily. His caution was validated when, at about 9:00 A.M., after crossing the line of yet another railroad, the Virginia Central, Robins's advance guard closed up on the courthouse town. Suddenly word came back that Yankee cavalry—a detachment of the 6th United States—occupied the town. Halting on the outskirts, Stuart laid plans to ensnare his opponents. While massing the 9th Virginia for a frontal attack on the town, he sent Fitz Lee's regiment around to the south to block the only route of escape. His strategy was spoiled, however, when the Regulars, catching wind of the raiders' presence, saddled up and galloped down the road to Old Church before the 1st Virginia could get into position. Stuart sent a detachment to pursue, but it overtook only one Yankee.[28]

Fearing the escapees would alert others in the Union rear, after departing Hanover Court House, Stuart turned off the direct road to Old Church and left the line of the Pamunkey. He marched his reunited force cross-country in the direction of Haw's Shop. Beyond the flour mill, his advance forded Totopotomoy Creek and swept toward Old Church from the northwest.

Stuart was not surprised to find the surrounding countryside in enemy hands. Yankees regularly patrolled the line between Hanover Court House and Old Church, a direct route to McClellan's supply hub at White House Landing. This day the region was occupied by two squadrons of the 5th U.S. Cavalry, based at Old Church under command of Capt. William B. Royall. A little after 11:00 A.M., one of Royall's subordinates, whose company was patrolling well up the road to Hanover Court House, spied the approaching raiders—he could not be certain of their strength—near Totopotomoy Creek, meanwhile sending couriers to apprise Royall of the situation. Early that afternoon Lieutenant Robins's advance encountered the Federal detachment along the creek. A brisk fight broke out; characteristically, most of the Confederates remained in the saddle, while the greater part of Royall's force fought dismounted.

Although Robins's men inflicted few casualties, they gained the advantage when Stuart and Rooney Lee reached the scene at the head of the 9th Virginia. The outnumbered Regulars remounted and took off, screaming Rebels at their heels. "You should have seen them Federals run for home and mother," one of Lee's troopers exulted. The Federals made a brief stand, but resumed their retreat when Rooney Lee's skirmishers waded Totopotomoy Creek, threatening their flanks and rear.[29]

The enemy did not halt until reaching a road junction at Linney's Corner, about a mile northwest of Old Church. There they linked with Royall to form a force three companies strong, a total of perhaps 150 officers and troopers in the aftermath of detachments Royall had made to run various errands. The captain was also missing several couriers, sent to bring word of Stuart's presence to his father-in-law, whose headquarters as commander, Reserve Cavalry Brigade, Army of the Potomac, stood about fourteen miles south of Royall's position.

By the time Stuart's column, with the 9th Virginia still in the vanguard, reached the crossroads, it found Royall's men drawn up in line of battle. At Lee's order, the squadron of Capt. William Latané (rhymes with matinée) charged them, sabers and pistols raised. The roadblock quickly disintegrated under the weight of galloping horses, and a confused, hand-to-hand melee erupted in the road, spilling over to the fields on either side.

As more and more Rebels reached the scene, Royall's troopers gave ground, then wheeled to the rear and galloped off. At their commander's urging, most of them halted, turned about, and attempted a second stand. Again, however, the Confederates put them to flight, this time for good. The disorganized force that raced off in the direction of Old Church had lost four men killed and nearly a dozen others wounded; its leader numbered among the casualties, having received several saber cuts about the head and shoulders.

Royall had made his assailants pay. Captain Latané lay dead in the dusty road, a pistol ball in his skull. The squadron leader was the only Rebel fatality, although almost twenty of his men had acquired saber wounds. "He died nobly," one of the captain's men noted, "& almost every one in the Reg. might envy him his fate."[30]

While the victors regrouped near the road junction, Stuart considered what he had accomplished thus far and pondered his next move. The few patrols he had encountered between Hanover Court House and Old Church suggested that he had already learned what Robert E. Lee needed to know: McClellan's flank above the Chickahominy was "in the air," neither held in force nor anchored to some natural barrier such as the unguarded Totopotomoy. At any time, Lee's cavalry chief could return to army headquarters to report his mission accomplished.[31]

But could he return safely by the way he had come? Stuart was certain that either Royall's men or the detachment of the 6th Cavalry he had encountered at Hanover Court House—probably both—had spread the word of his presence. Therefore, to double back was to invite interception by pursuit forces that probably included infantry as well as cavalry. If, instead, Stuart followed the plan he had proposed to General Lee, pushing on to encircle the Army of the Potomac, he not only would catch the enemy off-guard, but also could inflict critical damage on one of its supply bases, Tunstall's Station on the York River Railroad. From Tunstall's, Stuart could turn south, crossing the Chickahominy near Forge Bridge or some other point beyond the enemy's left flank—providing, of course, that flank was not well guarded. Stuart could not foresee the dangers that such a circuitous route entailed, but he was all too cognizant of the risks involved in retracing his path homeward.

In making his decision, he was animated by a desire to validate his men's faith in his tactical judgment. As he remarked in his mission report, "There was something of the sublime in the implicit confidence and unquestioning trust of the rank and file in a leader guiding them straight, apparently, into the very jaws of the enemy, every step appearing to them to diminish the faintest hope of extrication." He could not—he would not—betray that trust and that confidence.[32]

It did not take Stuart long to adopt the course he had favored all along. He seemed unfazed that none of his commanders voiced approval of the plan; he cared only that they pledged to support him in implementing it. By midafternoon on the thirteenth, the main body was heading southeastward, at a rapid clip, toward the railroad. With Stuart's consent, Fitz Lee and the 1st Virginia forged ahead of the rest to sack Royall's camp at Old Church. Afterward, Fitz would reunite with his superior.

The raiders moved on their objective so swiftly they easily outdistanced a growing mob of pursuers. These included portions of the 1st, 5th, and 6th United States plus the single volunteer regiment in Cooke's command, the lancers of the 6th Pennsylvania, as well as a brigade of foot soldiers, with artillery attached, under Col. G. K. Warren. The Yankees moved fitfully toward Old Church from divergent points on the Chickahominy, slowed by a lack of good intelligence, ambiguous orders, and logistical foul-ups.

Although General Cooke, who oversaw the pursuit, had been alerted to the raid in the middle of the afternoon on the thirteenth (his fifty-third brithday), his pursuit did not get under way in earnest until the following morning.

Consequently, when it reached Old Church, Cooke's advance found the Confederates long gone. By the time Cooke started for the York River Railroad and Stuart's rear, the raiders had gained a head start too formidable to be overcome by cavalry, let alone by Warren's foot troops.[33]

As his expedition neared its apogee, Stuart visited on the enemy a substantial amount of physical damage. En route to Tunstall's Station, the main column overtook unescorted supply wagons bound for the right flank of McClellan's army. Some carried rations, which the famished raiders wolfed down; one hauled a cache of Colt's revolvers, which they appropriated no less avidly.

Other targets cropped up short of Tunstall's. Early in the evening, two squadrons of Virginians—one each from Fitz and Rooney Lee's regiments—filed off to the left and made for the smaller supply depot at Garlick's Landing on the Pamunkey. The squadrons attacked and scattered the fifteen-man force that guarded the stores at the landing, most of which they plundered before torching the rest. Smoke from the burning contents of thirty supply wagons and two river schooners was soon spiraling into the darkening sky.[34]

While Garlick's underwent ruination, Stuart closed up on Tunstall's, whose garrison—thought to consist of two companies of infantry—appeared to have been forewarned of his approach. Although unable to support his advance with Breathed's artillery, which had sunk to its axles in the mud of the main road, Stuart moved boldly to the attack, his main body preceded by an advance echelon of thirty troopers under the combative Adjutant Robins.

Despite the column's confident air and speedy approach, its assault nearly collapsed when Robins unexpectedly encountered a detachment of Pennsylvania cavalry, on patrol from White House Landing. The meeting surprised both forces, whose men milled about in confusion, uncertain whether to attack or withdraw. The standoff ended when Stuart pounded up with the main body and put the interlopers to flight.

With Stuart right behind, Robins's men made straight for the depot, which they entered at an extended gallop, spreading consternation and panic. Confederate expectations notwithstanding, the garrison had not been apprised of their approach and thus was ripe for capture. Flabbergasted Yankees made little effort to resist; most surrendered without firing a shot. While Robins's men rounded up prisoners, comrades downed telegraph wires to prevent an alarm from being sent along the railroad, then felled trees to block the tracks to approaching trains. The barrier, however, failed to stop a locomotive hauling flatcars from barreling through to safety, despite losing one of its passengers to a carbine shot fired by "Farley the Scout."[35]

While his people busied themselves with torches, axes, and crowbars, Stuart considered continuing on to White House rather than swinging south to the Chickahominy. He finally decided that though destroying the supply depot on the Pamunkey would be a tremendous coup, one that would make a raiding leader's reputation, it would also subject his men to unacceptable risk while delaying Lee's receipt of intelligence critical to his planning. Before darkness fully descended and his pursuers closed in, he rode south from the blazing depot at the head of his column, which had expanded upon the return of the squadrons sent to Garlick's Landing and with the addition of dozens of prisoners who had been mounted on captured horses and mules. Near Talleysville, four miles from Tunstall's, Stuart allowed the troopers and their captives three hours' sleep before rousing them for the last leg of the journey to the Chickahominy.

Until now, the pursuit effort had been so feeble as to appear nonexistent. Some of those involved speculated that General Cooke was reluctant to press the raiders for fear of being set upon, throttled, and captured by his son-in-law. This being the case, the raiders should have been home free. Instead, many of them recalled the balance of the expedition as fraught with greater dangers and difficulties than the rest of the expedition put together. Despite their recent nap, many troopers suffered from insufficient sleep. One of Rooney Lee's men spoke for many comrades in observing, "I never experienced such a tiresome and sleepy march."[36]

There was a full moon, but it failed to light the way. On the road to Sycamore Springs on the Chickahominy, Fitz Lee's regiment unaccountably lost contact with his cousin's outfit. The process of finding and halting the 1st Virginia, piecing the column back together, and regaining the proper heading cost Stuart several hours he might have used to put more distance between himself and his relative's cavalry.

The error-prone march bothered Stuart, but when he reached the river early on the morning of June 14, he found that his troubles had just begun. Although one of his officers, a native of this region, had guaranteed that the river would be fordable at Sycamore Springs, Stuart found the river at that point a swollen, churning obstacle, courtesy of the recent rains.

Testing the water, Rooney Lee and a small escort managed to reach the south bank, but only with extreme difficulty. Doubting that the balance of the column, including Breathed's guns, could navigate the stream, Stuart put his men to work cutting down trees from which to fashion a makeshift bridge. But every trunk that was tossed into the water was swept downstream by the raging current.

Aware that the lethargic troopers in his rear would eventually show up, perhaps in company with infantry and artillery, Stuart turned philosophical. When Esten Cooke asked Rooney Lee what he made of the situation, Stuart spoke up: "Well, Lieutenant, I think we are caught." Yet he was far from resigned to failure. Surveying his options, he sent couriers to inform Robert E. Lee of his plight and to suggest that the army make a diversion in the raiders' behalf, keeping at bay opponents south of the river. Then he strode along the riverbank, studying the freshet and the surrounding terrain with the air of an engineer lost in theoretical calculations. Taking their cue from their unflappable leader, Stuart's men fell to the ground and slept as though none had a care in the world.[37]

A few stayed awake long enough to approach their commander with an idea. At their suggestion, Stuart mounted and rode a mile downstream to survey the charred remains of Forge Bridge, a recent casualty of war. The abutments remained standing, and the water ran shallower here than it did at Sycamore Springs. After some minutes lost in thought, Stuart awakened most of his men and set them to work constructing a temporary bridge to be placed upon the remains of the original span. Materials for the project came from abandoned farm buildings. An old skiff served as a pontoon; moored in the stream, it enabled construction to proceed at both ends of the bridge simultaneously. According to one account, Stuart joined in the work, stripping to his shirt-sleeves and humming merrily as he hammered planks into place.

Within three hours, troopers were crossing the emergency bridge to deposit their equipment on the far side. They then returned and crossed a second time, holding the reins of their horses, which swam the stream alongside them. After men and mounts had gotten safely over, the repair crews shored up the bridge with additional lumber, permitting the artillery to trundle across. By 1:00 P.M., the operation was complete; at that hour, Lieutenant Robins—now command-ing the rear guard—set fire to the makeshift span. By doing so, Stuart denied its use to the enemy, whose advance elements had finally begun to raise dust clouds in the near distance.[38]

Free at last of the possibility of being overtaken, the tired but invigorated raiders started homeward across territory guarded by Yankee units of all arms. Their scouts guided them safely through by way of Charles City Court House, then up the banks of the James River to Richmond. The column passed inside the capital defenses, via New Market Heights, early on June 15. There, at the end of the one hundred-mile circuit of McClellan's army, Stuart's men divested themselves of 164 prisoners and more than 250 captured animals. They had completed the mission of intelligence gathering and resource destruction at pal-try cost: one officer killed, several men wounded, and an artillery limber aban-doned in the swamps on the south side of the Chickahominy.[39]

Before his men could return to their old camps, Stuart left them to ride to army headquarters and report his recent accomplishments. Although the caval-ryman had exceeded his orders, Robert E. Lee greeted him cordially and offered heartfelt congratulations. While the generals conferred, the raiders paraded through Richmond's streets, where, for the third time in as many months, they were saluted by residents shouting, "Hurrah for Stuart's cavalry!" and "God bless you, boys, you have covered yourselves with glory!" A member of the 1st Virginia mused, "What soldier would regret a ride of fifty-odd hours, and dare to face most any danger, to receive such an ovation and the best dinner Richmond could afford from the ladies."[40]

The praise heaped on Stuart and his soldiers soon after their return paled in comparison to the outpouring of acclaim their exploits generated in later days. Once the full extent of its achievements became known, officers, politicians, and editors scaled rhetorical heights to proclaim the "Chickahominy Raid" a glorious success. Governor Letcher, to whom Stuart gave a personal account of the expedition, pronounced it "the most brilliant reconnaissance of the war" and called on Jefferson Davis to promote its leader in recognition of his "distin-guished energy—his efficient service—his personal bravery" and other traits displayed during the journey. The *Richmond Examiner* called the raid "one of the most brilliant affairs of the war, bold in its inception and most brilliant in its execution." It was clear to the editor of the *Richmond Dispatch* that "Stuart and his troopers are now forever in history." Even the Northern press chimed in, one of its leading journals declaring that the expedition rated "a feather of the very tallest sort in the rebel cap."[41]

Properly humble in the face of such praise, Stuart accepted it graciously, although perfectly content with the plume that now adorned his headgear on a daily basis.

Chapter Eight

Everywhere Victorious

Two days after Stuart's "very tired sore and hungry" men returned from their excursion into the Federal rear, their leader published an address lauding their energy, fortitude, and grace under pressure. The exertions they had undergone "history will record in imperishable characters and a grateful country will remember with gratitude." The same day, Stuart petitioned General Lee to award promotions to his own son and nephew, as well as sundry other deserving participants, including the steady-going Will Martin; the ever-vigilant W. T. Robins; Heros von Borcke, newest addition to Stuart's headquarters family, who had proved himself "a thorough soldier and a splendid officer"; and Captains Mosby and Farley, whose scouting expertise had been instrumental in bringing everyone home with minimal loss.[1]

Although their exploits would long remain a topic of conversation throughout the army, the raiders could not bask in the adulation for long. As Trooper Hudgins remembered, "We had very little leisure time after the raid. . . . All of a sudden we had no more time for drill, but it became obvious that the time we had spent drilling would [soon] be put to good use."[2]

The change in the daily routine portended a full-scale offensive. Armed with the vital intelligence Stuart had brought him, Lee firmed up plans for striking his enemy's right and gaining their rear, cutting them off from their bases of supply on the York and Pamunkey. To make all this a reality, the main army would be augmented by Stonewall Jackson, who on June 17 began to depart the scene of his recent triumphs for the Richmond front. Stonewall did so without most of his cavalry; Robertson and Jones, left behind to guard the rear, did not cross the Blue Ridge until the twenty-first. Two days later, Jackson, having ridden ahead of his troops, was at Lee's side for a war council along with other commanders.[3]

Each conferee was assigned a role in the coming offensive, the major weight of which would be directed north of the Chickahominy toward Mechanicsville and Beaver Dam Creek. That sector was now defended by the V Corps of Fitz John Porter, supported by Stoneman's horsemen. Both commands were poised to unite with McDowell's corps, which, freed of its obligations in the Shenandoah by Jackson's withdrawal, was again preparing to reinforce the Army of the Potomac. Porter's and Stoneman's presence on the north side meant that McClellan had shifted the rest of his army to the south bank of the river. Lee had his eye on this sector as well: While sixty-five thousand men under Longstreet, Jackson, A. P. Hill, and D. H. Hill struck northward, another twenty-five thousand under Magruder and Huger would launch diversionary attacks against McClellan's main body.[4]

Stuart knew he would play a role of some importance in Lee's plans. He would do so with a recently enlarged force, more than five thousand officers and men. While he had been raiding, three companies of the 1st North Carolina under the newly promoted Lieutenant Colonel Gordon had returned from the eastern part of their state for renewed service with Stuart; on June 27, they would be joined near Richmond by the remainder of the regiment under now-Colonel Baker. Stuart had also been assigned the mounted contingent of Cobb's Legion, led by a prominent citizen-soldier, Col. Thomas R. R. Cobb, and a talented West Pointer (ex-Class of 1861), Lt. Col. Pierce M. B. Young.[5]

Soon after returning from his expedition, Stuart had been further augmented by the second incarnation of the 5th Virginia Cavalry, an outfit with a troubled past and an uncertain future. The regiment had been built around an independent battalion organized and led by Lt. Col. Henry Clay Pate. A hard-fighting officer given to eccentric and sometimes erratic behavior, Pate had a faculty for antagonizing officers and men, some of whom had accused him of stealing their private possessions. Pate gave so little attention to drill and discipline that Stuart feared his outfit would fall apart before it took the field.

Desperate to remedy the problem, he procured a colonelcy for Tom Rosser, whom he continued to regard as excellent cavalry material despite the man's occasional bouts of intemperance. When informing Rosser of his promotion, Stuart assured him that he would "play an important part in the next battle" and told him to "Come a-runnin." To his surprise, Stuart got no response. Despite his unquenchable hunger for high rank, Rosser hesitated to accept the position. Recently he had been tendered a lieutenant colonel's rank in the artillery, with the promise of another promotion down the road. The prospect of having to make veterans of a gaggle of recruits armed with lances and pistols under an odd duck like Pate did not captivate him. Stuart was forced to use his persuasive powers to the fullest to secure Rosser's acceptance.[6]

A masterful organizer and disciplinarian, Rosser validated Stuart's confidence by placing the 5th in fighting trim in record time. His appointment, however, gave offense to some of Pate's officers, who considered the new man an interloper and believed that the lieutenant colonel, for all his faults, deserved the promotion. When Pate himself took up the fight, claiming foul on Stuart's part as well as Rosser's, he made himself so obnoxious that Rosser (perhaps at Stuart's urging) hauled him before a court-martial on charges of insubordination and conduct unbecoming an officer. Pate claimed his only offense had been an attempt to bring Rosser up on charges for drunkenness on duty. The tribunal, which met intermittently for eight months, made jurors and witnesses of several officers whose services were thereby lost to Stuart for an extended period. In the end, the accused was acquitted on all charges, but the bad blood arising from the trial affected Pate's relations with his superiors for months afterward.[7]

>─┼◆>─○─<◆┼─<

In the manner of a spoilsport, McClellan landed a blow hours before Lee could deliver his. On the twenty-fifth, the Union commander unexpectedly advanced part of the III Corps from the Seven Pines vicinity toward Huger's outposts near Oak Grove and King's School House. A division under the energetic Joseph Hooker drove in Rebel pickets along the Williamsburg Road, occupied the ground thus abandoned, and acted as if it meant to hang on to its gains. Darkness intervened before damage could be done to the Confederate right, but the advance prompted Lee to defer his offensive no longer. He attacked McClellan the next day, and continued to attack every day for nearly a week.[8]

The result, the last six of the "Seven Days' Battles," provided many elements of the Army of Northern Virginia, including the additions under Jackson, with a showcase for their talents. Not so, however, for the cavalry, which, as at Williamsburg, lacked the wide, unobstructed ground required to support large-scale mounted operations. In consequence, while Stuart's horsemen provided close support to the army during the first two days of the fighting, a lack of viable objectives drove them to spend the next four days wandering over some of the same ground they had recently crossed, seeking the Union rear. The trip failed to enhance the reputation all had gained on their celebrated raid.

They started out in good style, breaking camp and moving out in concert with the main army late on the twenty-fifth. Accompanied by the 1st, 4th, and 9th Virginia, the troopers of the Cobb and Jeff Davis Legions, and Pelham's men and guns, Stuart led the way northeast of Richmond toward Ashland Station on the R, F & P. Troopers and horse artillerists moved out in light marching order, with no baggage wagons to slow them, each man carrying three days' rations in his haversack. Envious comrades watched them ride off. To support Huger and Magruder in their operation south of the Chickahominy, Stuart had left behind the 3rd, 5th, and 10th Virginia, plus the single squadron of the Hampton Legion. When the main body of the 1st North Carolina arrived to join this force, overall command would go to Laurence Baker.[9]

Stuart's primary mission was to cooperate with, and guard the flanks and rear of, Jackson's command as it came in from the Valley. Stuart looked forward to the assignment. The two men had been close since serving at Harpers Ferry in the early days of the war; their friendship had been cemented at Manassas, when Stuart so ably supported the newly christened Stonewall Brigade. Stuart made contact with Stonewall late in the afternoon of the twenty-sixth, when the head of Jackson's column reached a position north of the Chickahominy from which it could assail Porter's upper flank while the remainder of Lee's force hit the V Corps head-on.

Jackson had reached his assigned position later than Lee had anticipated, but in time to contribute to the army leader's strategy. He failed to put that time to good use. Although Stuart assured his friend that based on careful reconnaissance, no defensive works barred his path to Porter's flank, Jackson elected not to attack. When he failed to open the contest, other elements of the army went ahead without him—only to be halted by well-manned defenses along Beaver Dam Creek, which prebattle reconnaissance had failed to discern. Stuart spent the day faithfully guarding Jackson's rear. If he wondered about Stonewall's inactivity, he made no mention of it in his campaign report.[10]

Next morning, the battered Confederates prepared a new effort against Porter's lines. When they went forward, however, they found the enemy's works vacant, their occupants having retreated toward the James River via Gaines's Mill. Stuart pursued with commendable dispatch but gained little to show for it. He spent morning and afternoon, as he said, "skirmishing with, killing and capturing, small detachments of the enemy's cavalry" that protected Porter's retreat. His opponents appeared so anxious to put space between them and their pursuers that Stuart referred to them derisively as "flying cavalry."[11]

When Stuart reached Porter's new position near Gaines's Mill, he was frustrated to find that, given "the nature of the ground, [and] the position of the enemy in a wood . . . the cavalry proper had no hand-to-hand conflict with the enemy." After the main army arrived and began to assault the Federals' swamp-bound defenses, Stuart's men found themselves reduced to spectators. This was bad enough, but lacking adequate cover, the cavalry, which had massed on Jackson's left near a crossroads called Cold Harbor, was "subject to the severe ordeal of a raking artillery fire from guns beyond its reach."

The only portion of Stuart's command to enjoy maneuver room was the horse artillery. The fight had begun badly for Pelham's battery, whose Blakely rifle was put out of commission by a Yankee shell minutes after it reached the front. Undaunted, Pelham set one of his Napoleons on top of a tree-shrouded ridge from which it dueled with two Union batteries. The cannon drew a heavy return fire, but the captain refused to shift it to a less vulnerable position. Eventually, he hit his opponents so accurately and so often that they limbered up and withdrew. Stuart, who observed "the noble captain" throughout the fight, described his performance as "one of the most gallant and heroic feats of the war."[12]

Although Porter's men held their position at Gaines's Mill through most of the fight, waves of attack breached their left flank late in the day, causing them to pull out and head for the crossings of the Chickahominy. Stuart pursued them with speed and determination, covering three miles in the general direction of White House and rounding up scores of stragglers. After nightfall, he returned to Cold Harbor to find that a squadron left there had collected an even greater number of prisoners.

Robert E. Lee's field headquarters were also near Cold Harbor; Stuart reported there on the morning of the twenty-eighth. Since the enemy's ultimate destination was unknown, he was ordered to move along the Richmond & York River Railroad until able to assail their rear and menace their communications. Happy to be assigned such an important mission, the cavalry chief saluted and rejoined his command. Less than an hour later, they were heading for the York and the Pamunkey in two columns, he riding with the main body while Rooney Lee's regiment took a parallel road, followed by Ewell's infantry and Munford's horsemen.[13]

Because his column did not have to conform its movements to those of foot soldiers, Stuart forged ahead of Lee and Ewell on the road to Dispatch Station. En route, Cobb's Legion routed a squadron-size force of Yankee cavalry, which fled toward the Chickahominy. At Dispatch Station, the column halted to destroy several hundred yards of track and telegraph wire. After Ewell reached the depot, the infantry remained there, along with Munford, to await further orders. The energetic Stuart "determined to push boldly down the White House road . . . to find what force was in that direction and, if possible, rout it." He took along Rooney Lee, whose spacious home—which his wife and children had tearfully evacuated—sat adjacent to the supply depot on the Pamunkey. A sign over the front door begged the occupation troops not to harm the dwelling, the first home of George and Martha Washington following their marriage in 1759.[14]

Traversing familiar ground, Stuart's column headed for the landing by way of Tunstall's Station. On the trip, it overtook and confiscated forage and sutler's wagons and captured the cavalry detail guarding them. To this haul, Stuart added sentinels he found posted at various points on the river road. Other items worth appropriating awaited him at White House, but long before he reached the valley of the Pamunkey, he and his men saw black clouds rising skyward in the distance. McClellan's quartermasters, assisted by Stoneman's troopers, had set fire to the stores at the landing. Stuart immediately perceived that Little Mac, his hold on the Chickahominy irretrievably broken, was transferring his base of supply to the James River. This was a good sign, for it offered hope that McClellan's drive on Richmond would be deferred, if not canceled outright.[15]

By the time Stuart reached the landing early on June 29, quartermasters and cavalrymen were gone, having left behind acres of charred ruins. And yet a welcoming party of sorts was on hand. On nearing the place, Stuart's scouts spotted a gunboat, the *Marblehead,* which had anchored in the river within gunnery range of the depot. Leaving the main body two miles from White House, Stuart proceeded cautiously with a seventy-five-man escort, supported by one of Pelham's howitzers. To counter their arrival, the skipper of the "Yankee bugaboo" put ashore a party of sailors armed with rifles and, as Stuart reported, "quite a determined engagement of skirmishers ensued." It ended when the howitzer began to lob shells at the ship. The accurate fire persuaded the shore party to return to the vessel, and prompted her to get under way in a hurry. As the *Marblehead* steamed off, the howitzer limbered up and "gave chase at a gallop," its crew shouting in triumph.[16]

Receiving the "all clear," the raiders entered the ruined depot. The extent of the damage was depressing, but Rooney Lee was truly heartsick to discover that his "once beautiful estate" had been reduced to "ashes and desolation." The conflagration had been set so hastily, however, that numerous stores, including barrels of rations and bags of forage, had escaped the flames. "With all these supplies," one of Lee's troopers exulted, "we plan to eat right well for a while to come."

While this man and his comrades fed, others drank, having discovered a case of whiskey that had escaped the flames. Most imbibed on the sly; fearing to do so in front of their officers, they hid bottles on their persons for future consumption. Concerned that the alcohol would cause trouble, Colonel Lee started a rumor that the Yankees had poisoned the stock and that one trooper had already died in agony from drinking it. For an hour or so thereafter, the shattering of glass could be heard throughout Lee's column as his men tossed bottles to the ground in disgust.[17]

While his main body picked through the debris, salvaging what it could, Stuart received instructions by courier to scout the area for signs of the retreating foe. He did so but reported finding few bluecoats in the area beyond the inevitable stragglers, which seemed to indicate that no part of McClellan's army was fleeing down the Peninsula to Fort Monroe. This made sense: The only place where Little Mac would feel safe was on the James, where most of his gunboats lay at anchor.

Stuart spent the balance of that day feeding and equipping his brigade from what John Esten Cooke called "the wild, tragic, loathsome Chaos of Sutler's houses, tents, hospital tents, cars, [and] stores burning and smelling an awful stench." Next morning, he faced southward and started for the Chickahominy. Before long, the greater part of the command was back at Forge Bridge, where only days before they had crossed the river to safety. Meanwhile, Fitz Lee's regiment trotted upriver to Long Bridge, which had also been dismantled. At both locales, enemy forces, including artillery, could be seen on the opposite bank. Pelham opened on some of them, but after one shot, the Napoleon that had accompanied the 1st Virginia was put out of action when its trail broke under the impact of recoil. Pelham kept up the fire with his only serviceable pieces—two howitzers—until he succeeded in driving off a large group of Yankees.[18]

On the morning of July 1, Stuart was made uncomfortably aware of how distant he was from Lee's army, which was then engaged with the retreating Federals at Malvern Hill, just north of the James River. The last of the Seven Days was about to begin; it would feature an all-out attack on an enemy that Lee considered cornered and vulnerable to a parting, decisive blow. Stuart grew concerned that he should be on hand for the fight; others thought so, too. Before dawn, a messenger from army headquarters reached him with an order to cross the Chickahominy and rejoin Stonewall Jackson somewhere near Haxall's Landing on the James. Because Jackson's troops were continually in motion, their whereabouts could not be pinpointed.

Stuart was glad to oblige, though he objected to Lee's stipulation that he cross the river at Grapevine Bridge, several hours' march from his present position. He started off, instead, for Bottom's Bridge, only eleven miles distant. He was about to cross the column when he saw why Lee had not directed him there. The roads on the far side were clogged with Confederate infantry hastening to the James. Lacking the room to move inland, Stuart led the column back to Forge Bridge. The river had fallen considerably since his last visit; thus he had his riders ford the stream at that point. During the operation, he made contact with a party of Munford's regiment, which continued to be attached to Jackson's command. Its men informed Stuart of the route Stonewall had taken to Haxall's.

Once on the south bank, Stuart hastened toward the landing, in which direction he could hear the ominous thump of artillery. But the echoes had ceased by nightfall, when his men went into bivouac shy of their destination. They had no inkling that the day just ended had visited disaster upon a part of Lee's army, which had attacked impregnable positions atop Malvern Hill at tremendous cost—more than fifty-three hundred men killed, wounded, or missing as against approximately thirty-two hundred Union casualties. Even later, when Stuart learned the details, he refused to accept the magnitude of the defeat, insisting—to himself and to others—that the Yankees had been throttled. For evidence, he pointed to McClellan's continued retreat to the north bank of the James near Harrison's Landing.[19]

Concerned about his inability to locate Jackson's troops, Stuart dispatched William Blackford to the general's presumed location. The staff officer returned with a sheepish look: He had found Lee's army, but not Jackson. Stuart must have been embarrassed when, early on the second, Jackson sent for him by courier. He followed the messenger to Stonewall's field headquarters, where the generals had a hurried conference.

The meeting spurred Stuart into action. As soon as he learned that McClellan's rear guard had yet to reach the James, he galloped back to his main body and led it the rest of the way to the river via a road that skirted Turkey Creek. En route, his advance guard nabbed "scores of the discomfited and demoralized foe at every turn." Upon reaching the James, the Jeff Davis Legion added to the prisoner total by gobbling up a shore party from the famous *Monitor,* which lay at anchor in the James. Then, accompanied by one of Pelham's howitzers, Martin galloped upstream until he struck one of the enemy's columns. He attacked it, taking still more prisoners and "causing marked havoc and confusion in his ranks."[20]

That evening, after Stuart's command had closed up at river's edge, John Pelham advised his boss of another tactical opportunity for the artillery. Having reconnoitered toward Westover, the Byrd Family's historic plantation, which sprawled east of Harrison's Landing, Pelham had happened upon a large enemy encampment. Now he proposed to shell the lightly guarded position from atop a ridge, Evelington Heights, that commanded the camp. Stuart, who ever appreciated initiative and aggressiveness in his subordinates, approved the venture.

In the predawn darkness of July 3, Stuart led a detachment to the summit of the ridge, from which he chased a squadron of Union horsemen. Pelham duly occupied the crest, and shortly after 9:00 A.M. he opened on the enemy with a single howitzer. The effect was immediate: Pandemonium and panic swept the encampment. For five hours, the Yankees were subjected to a plunging fire that raked tents and huts, wrecked supply trains, and drove everyone to shelter. Troops who ran off blindly were snatched up by the cavalry. As Stuart observed happily, "We soon had prisoners from various corps and divisions."

Captives continued to fall into his hands until an enemy battery, hastily trundled into position, finally got Pelham's range, and a line of infantry began to advance under cover of its fire. Only when Pelham's howitzer fired its last round and the dismounted troopers supporting it began to run low on ammunition did Stuart haul everyone to safer ground—"not, however," said he, "without teaching many a foeman the bitter lesson of death."[21]

A controversy later arose as to the effectiveness of the shelling and whether it had been fatally premature. By late that evening, infantry under Longstreet would have occupied Evelington Heights, from which it could not easily have been driven. According to a theory popular among infantry and artillery officers, thousands of McClellan's soldiers would have surrendered had Pelham not flushed the game, alerting the Federals to the vulnerability of their position. Other critics of Stuart's operations in this campaign would fault him for penetrating too far into the enemy's rear when he should have been with the main army, screening its movement to the James.

Not surprisingly, Stuart saw things differently. In his view, he had followed his orders to the letter, and with conspicuous success. Summing up his participation in a July 5 letter to Flora, he exulted, "I have been marching and fighting for one solid week. Generally on my own hook, with the cavalry detached from the main body. . . . We have been everywhere victorious," even where comrades had feared to accompany him. "If the army had been up with me, we could have finished this business."[22]

>-+•>-O-<•+-<

If the Army of the Potomac had been permitted to escape destruction, at least it had been brought to bay, and it did not appear to be going anywhere very soon. But while the siege of Richmond had been lifted, elsewhere in the fractured Union Southern fortunes were under threat. The Confederacy's largest city, New Orleans, was in Yankee hands, as was the rail center of Corinth, Mississippi, while operations were afoot against Vicksburg, Mississippi, Chattanooga, Tennessee, and other strategic points the Confederacy could not afford to lose.

Closer to home, Virginia was suddenly the focus of a new Union army under Maj. Gen. John Pope. A transferee from the western theater, where he had won some small but highly publicized victories, Pope had been charged by Lincoln and Stanton to cooperate with McClellan against the Army of Northern Virginia, with special reference to cutting Lee's communication link to the middle of the state. By early July, Pope's fifty-thousand-man Army of Virginia, centered just east of the Blue Ridge Mountains, had been in existence for only a few weeks. The Illinois-born commander, however, had already been branded a swaggering blowhard not only by his opponents, but also by many of his own troops, whom he had antagonized by a series of addresses that reeked of arrogance and braggadocio. In time, even Robert E. Lee, who rarely vilified his enemies, came to regard his new opponent as "the miscreant Pope," a soldier that had to be "suppressed" by any available means.[23]

Within ten days of confirming McClellan's retreat to Harrison's Landing, Stuart, who had moved his headquarters to Atlee's Station on the Virginia Central Railroad, began to realize that he and his troopers would soon be up against a fresh team of Yankees. By July 13, Jackson's twelve thousand troops had left their most recent position north of Richmond on a fifty-mile northwestward journey to the rail junction at Gordonsville. The following day, Pope's Federals began to move toward that same point from the north. Before the month ended, A. P. Hill's division was also heading for Gordonsville; when it reported to Jackson, the latter's command—soon to be styled the left wing of the Army of Northern Virginia—would double in size. Still, the Confederates facing Pope would be handily outnumbered until Lee and Longstreet joined them, something Stuart anticipated, although he was unable to say when it would occur.[24]

While he awaited the word to head west, the cavalry leader tried to ready his command for what lay ahead. It was not a simple chore, for during the recent campaign the brigade had marched and countermarched hundreds of miles. The near-constant travel had worn down men and mounts, leaving the command in need of a refit, as most of the supplies confiscated at White House had long given out. Working diligently with the army's quartermaster and commissary officers, Stuart did what he could to rectify the situation during what he suspected would be a painfully brief period of inactivity.

At the same time, he tried to plug some manpower gaps. While the brigade as a whole had suffered lightly over the past month, heavy losses in one regiment had skewed the casualty count. While Stuart's main body had been campaigning above the Chickahominy, the troops he had left behind under Laurence Baker had reconnoitered obediently toward the crossings of the James. Their service had taken on heightened significance when McClellan's army began its retreat from Richmond to Harrison's Landing. While following up the withdrawal, Baker, at the head of the five available companies of the 1st North Carolina, backed by the entire 3rd Virginia, had encountered a small body of Yankee cavalry on the morning of June 29 near Willis Church, a few miles north of Malvern Hill.[25]

The Federals proved to be members of the 3rd Pennsylvania, the same regiment Baker had routed near Vienna the previous November. The Tarheels had visions of reprising that performance, but when chasing their adversaries northward from Willis Church toward the hamlet of Glendale, Baker failed to note the presence up ahead of six ten-pounder Parrott rifles, behind strong fieldworks. As the colonel and his riders impulsively shifted into a charge, the cannons opened on them, blowing gaping holes in their column-of-fours formation.[26]

Shouting to make himself heard over the barrage, Baker called for a left wheel, but too late—before his men could gain the shelter of roadside woods, three of them were dead and fourteen wounded, while a 3rd Virginia trooper who had been supporting them lay mortally wounded. After five minutes, the guns fell silent, whereupon the 3rd Pennsylvanians advanced to take almost fifty prisoners. Baker led the remainder of his command to safety, although one of his officers, Capt. (later Brig. Gen.) Rufus Barringer, admitted that the survivors rushed to the rear "in utter confusion." Although only a single regiment had suffered this afternoon, June 29 was the deadliest day in the brief history of the mounted arm of the A.N.V.[27]

><+>-O-<+<

While refitting, Stuart also reorganized. From his new headquarters at Hanover Court House, seven miles north of Atlee's Station, he oversaw the transformation of his brigade into a division. The event coincided with Stuart's attainment of a cherished goal: His promotion to major general, the traditional rank of a division commander.[28]

The expansion had been made possible by an influx of manpower throughout the recent campaign; Stuart now led more than fifty-two hundred officers and men. Enough hailed from outside Virginia that he could divide the whole along geographic lines, a structure in keeping with the political philosophy of his army and its nation.[29]

Stuart determined that all but one of the Virginia regiments would make up his 1st Brigade: Brien's 1st, Goode's 3rd, Wickham's 4th (for the most part led by the newly promoted Major Utterback while Wickham and Payne continued to recuperate, although for a time beginning in late July, an outsider, Col. Stephen D. Lee, was assigned to command), Rosser's 5th, and Rooney Lee's 9th Virginia. The 2nd Brigade would consist of Baker's 1st North Carolina; Cobb's Legion Cavalry, under Lieutenant Colonel Young; Martin's Jeff Davis Legion; Butler's Hampton Legion Cavalry; and a single Virginia outfit, the 10th, temporarily led by Lt. Col. Z. S. Magruder. The Stuart Horse Artillery was aligned under the division itself; guns and crews would be attached to regiments or brigades as conditions warranted.[30]

Stuart had limited control over the assignment of his ranking subordinates, but he made one preference known. As far as he was concerned, Fitz Lee alone had the qualifications to lead the 1st Brigade. In fact, as Stuart had written in the immediate aftermath of the Chickahominy Raid, "no one in the Confederacy possesses more of the elements of what a brigadier of cavalry ought to be than he." The man's uncle agreed, and Fitz received his wreathed stars and sleeve lace on July 26.[31]

The other brigade leader was an inspired selection, although not Stuart's. On the twenty-sixth, Brig. Gen. Wade Hampton of South Carolina, a veteran of fifteen months' infantry service, reported at Hanover Court House. Despite conspicuous service on several fields, and although wounded at both Manassas and Seven Pines, the tall, hulking aristocrat had found himself without a command at the end of the Peninsula Campaign. Jefferson Davis had suggested a transfer to the cavalry, which would allow him to keep the rank his battlefield prowess had won for him. After some deliberation, and perhaps with some misgivings as well, Hampton had accepted the position. He let it be known, however, that he did not consider the assignment a permanent one; his preference was to return to infantry service should a command become available to him.[32]

Stuart seems to have received him warily. He may have been influenced by rumors in some circles that Hampton had been at least partly to blame for the flight of a portion of his legion at Manassas, and for the precipitate withdrawal of a segment of his brigade at Seven Pines. More likely, he was concerned by Hampton's status as a nonprofessional (he was a graduate not of West Point, but of his state's university) and his complete lack of cavalry experience. For all that, Hampton was known as a highly competent field leader (he fairly oozed coolness and courage under fire); he was also an accomplished equestrian and swordsman. Even so, he was less known for his soldierly abilities than for being one of the wealthiest planters in the South as well as one of its largest slaveholders.[33]

What may have worked most against Hampton in the eyes of his new comrades was his age, forty-four. From the first, his maturity and conservative style of leadership contrasted markedly with the cavalier mentality of Stuart, Fitz Lee, and other younger colleagues. In time, however, his lack of flamboyance won Hampton the respect of his associates. John Esten Cooke, for one, appreciated that Hampton "fought from a sense of duty, and not from passion, or to win renown. The war was a gala-day, full of attraction and excitement to some; to him it was hard work, not sought but accepted." Above all else, Hampton was "an honest gentleman who disdained all pretense or artifice . . . he thought nothing of personal decorations or military show, and never dreamed of 'producing an impression' upon anyone."[34]

Although Stuart, too, came to value such traits, and to rely on the man's good judgment and quick thinking, Hampton would always be his subordinate, never his friend. Apparently, both wanted it that way. Hampton, in turn, grew to respect the quality of Stuart's leadership, his tactical acumen, his special talent at reconnaissance, and his ability to inspire his troops, but he never appreciated the flamboyance and foppery of the Knight of the Golden Spurs. For Hampton, war was a dirty business to be dispensed with as quickly and as successfully as possible; fancy hats and chivalric poses were gestures of fakery and deceit, beneath the dignity of a citizen-soldier.

While the Stuart-Hampton relationship would always have its rocky moments, at times it was strained needlessly. The pair got off to a rough start when Stuart, in drafting his table of organization for his commander's perusal, named Fitz Lee to lead the 1st Brigade, Hampton the 2nd. Perhaps responding to a complaint from Stuart's newest lieutenant, Robert E. Lee approved the composition of both brigades but not their numbering. At his insistence, Stuart reversed the numerical order, thereby acknowledging Hampton's seniority as brigadier.[35]

Stuart may also have antagonized Hampton by an early act that seemed to imply a lack of trust in him. To be sure, Hampton deserved as much time as possible in which to learn his new responsibilities. Perhaps with this end in mind, in early August, when Lee and Longstreet prepared to leave the Richmond front for the Gordonsville vicinity, Stuart decided to accompany them with Fitz Lee's brigade alone. To support a small infantry and artillery force to be left behind, Stuart opted to leave Hampton's command within observation range of Harrison's Landing in case McClellan recovered from his defeat-induced funk and threatened the Confederate capital.

Later Stuart explained that stationing Hampton in the vicinity of Charles City Court House was simply a reaction to "the enemy's demonstrations [which] left us in some doubt about his intentions." In fact, by that point, no one of standing in Lee's army expected McClellan to do anything more than reinforce Pope; it was common knowledge that Little Mac had already begun to do so in prelude to quitting the Peninsula. Thus, by leaving Hampton behind, Stuart gave the impression that he could not rely on him in a combat situation. Given Hampton's inexperience, Stuart's action was justifiable, but it was not a way to win the goodwill of a new lieutenant.[36]

>─┤─◆>─O─<◆─┤─◄

Before Stuart departed for points west, he headed north on a five-day mission to protect the railroads above Richmond—without Hampton. The mission was designed to put an end to threats by the Federals around Fredericksburg against the line of communications that linked Jackson at Gordonsville to Lee and Longstreet at Richmond. On July 19, a patrol of the 2nd New York Cavalry had broken the Virginia Central at Beaver Dam Station. Although Robert E. Lee noted that the Yankees "did no serious damage," he desired to forestall any recurrence. Stuart, with a few hundred men, was to ensure this.[37]

The blow dealt Beaver Dam may have been small, but the vandals had achieved more than either they or General Lee realized. When attacking the depot, the 2nd New York had captured some Confederates waiting for a coming train; they included John Mosby, then only a few months away from leaving Stuart's service to begin his career as a partisan leader. Mosby, in fact, had been about to embark on one of his last major missions as a member of the Army of Northern Virginia—one of his own devising.

His target was the rear of Pope's army, in the Manassas-Fairfax Court House vicinity, where he hoped to gather critical information on enemy activities. Armed with Stuart's permission to execute his plan, the captain had been carrying a note from the general to his friend Jackson, who stood to benefit most from any intelligence Mosby gathered. The note introduced Mosby to Jackson, apprised Stonewall of his intentions, and vouched for his effectiveness; Stuart described the scout as "bold, daring, intelligent, and discreet."[38]

Mosby looked so young and so frail, and he hid Stuart's note so deftly, that his captors never suspected they had nabbed one of the most dangerous scouts in Rebel service. Without fanfare, they sent him to Washington, where Mosby was furnished a room in the Old Capitol Prison. In those days—unlike the last year or so of the conflict—the prisoner exchange system worked quickly; within ten days the young lawyer was en route by ship to Fort Monroe and from there to the POW exchange site on the James River.

Even captivity could not prevent Mosby from spying on his enemy. During the brief stopover at Fort Monroe, his sharp eyes detected an unusual buildup of shipping in Hampton Roads. Surreptitious inquiries convinced him they were carrying thousands of Burnside's troops, fresh from North Carolina, on their way to reinforce Pope. As soon as he was released, Mosby walked a dozen miles to army headquarters outside Richmond, where, after some difficulty, he personally related his findings to Robert E. Lee. Within a few days, Lee was leading the remainder of the Army of Northern Virginia, including Stuart and Fitz Lee's brigade, to join Jackson. While the evidence is not conclusive, the fact that Lee waited no longer to reinforce the troops opposing Pope suggests that he was reacting to the intelligence Mosby had brought him.[39]

Unaware of Mosby's captivity or its beneficial repercussions, Stuart on August 4 started on his mission to Fredericksburg. It was his second attempt; the first, made in the wake of the damage to Beaver Dam, had been frustrated by bottomless roads and rain-swollen streams. This time his troops, culled from Lee's brigade, and supported by the Stuart Horse Artillery, followed dry roads that led them northwest to Bowling Green and then on to Port Royal on the Rappahannock. On the fifth, the column headed up the riverbank to Fredericksburg.

It halted abruptly when Stuart learned that Yankees intent on inflicting new damage to the Virginia Central had just left Fredericksburg for the railroad. By hard riding, the following day he closed in on a sizable force of all arms, the roads in whose rear he found clogged with "straggling infantry and wagons."[40]

At Fitz Lee's order, and with Stuart's approval, the advance guard charged, striking the enemy rear "like a thunderbolt . . . pursuing for miles and intercepting all wagons and fugitives but one courier, whose fright baffled pursuit." Other Yankees could not get away so quickly; Stuart rode them down as they pushed on to the line of the Ny River. His pursuit was spearheaded by the 3rd Virginia under Lt. Col. John T. Thornton; the 4th Virginia under its provisional commander, S. D. Lee; and some of Pelham's cannons. The combined force moved so relentlessly that scores of Federals fell into their clutches, along with supply vehicles and large quantities of miscellaneous materiel.

Eventually, the harassed enemy veered away from the railroad. No longer concerned with anything other than protecting itself, the column began a return march to Fredericksburg. For a time, the infantry portion of the rear guard, which took up sharpshooter positions in woods where mounted men could not venture, made a fight of it. They even compelled Stuart to cross to the north bank of the Ny. For a time, as a lieutenant in the 4th Virginia put it, the Confederates found themselves in "a pretty close place . . . though we did not loose anything by it." Since the withdrawal caused no harm, except perhaps to pride, a private in the 9th Virginia called the day's action "a grand little fight" that ended well for the Confederates. This man's outfit alone captured a dozen wagons loaded with grain and beef. After helping themselves, he and his comrades distributed the remainder to local citizens, "with the compliments of the Ninth."[41]

When he was certain that his opponents posed no further threat to the Virginia Central, Stuart was content to head south to Bowling Green. On the eighth, he returned to Hanover Court House, along with eighty-five prisoners and eleven of the captured wagons. The cavalry leader could afford to be pleased with what he had accomplished, even though he had failed to prevent another Federal column from wrecking a two-mile stretch of the railroad on the afternoon of August 6. Looking back on the operation almost five months later, Stuart observed that "this wholesome check to the enemy prevented any further raids upon the railroad, and kept him in a state of trepidation for fear of attack in the rear for the remainder of the summer."[42]

One threat neutralized, Stuart could return his attention to another. Within hours of returning to Hanover Court House, he was readying Lee's brigade for active service against John Pope. The road ahead promised to be as long and hard as it was uncertain, but with his newly enlarged command, led by talented subordinates, and with a series of victories, large and small, under his belt, Stuart could not bring himself to fear the future.

Chapter Nine

Making the Yankees Pay

Stuart traveled not once, but twice, to the new theater of operations, and on neither occasion was he accompanied by his command. He made the first trip at the behest of Robert E. Lee, and he went alone. He did so gladly, for it gave him the opportunity not only to preview a command about to be assigned to him, but to make a personnel change without which the acquisition would lose much of its attractiveness.

When Longstreet's wing joined Jackson's near Gordonsville, the army would be reunited under Lee. The cavalry would also become a single unit, meaning that Beverly Robertson's brigade, along with Chew's battery, would join Stuart's command. With any luck, the addition would not include Robertson. Almost from the day the Virginian had succeeded George Steuart in command of the brigade, Stonewall Jackson had been dissatisfied with Robertson's leadership and had sought his ouster. Although the source of Jackson's discontent was somewhat vague, and despite Robertson's reputation as an excellent administrator and disciplinarian, Robert E. Lee had decided to inquire into the competence of the man and the condition of his command. He chose Stuart for the task and sent him west on August 8.[1]

Stuart arrived at Jackson's headquarters near Orange Court House, seven miles above Gordonsville, on the tenth—one day after Stonewall's men had waged the opening struggle of the campaign against Pope. On the seventh, the braggart in blue had advanced one of his corps, under N. P. Banks, and two days later Banks attacked Jackson west of Cedar (or Slaughter) Mountain. By day's end the high ground had lived up to its name, twenty-three hundred Federals and thirteen hundred Confederates having become casualties. It ended in victory for Jackson, but only barely. Two-thirds of Stonewall's command had been thrust backward by the enemy's onslaught before A. P. Hill's division counterattacked, blunting the Union drive and shoving Banks to the north side of Cedar Run.[2]

When Stuart arrived the next day, Jackson's men were still skirmishing with the Yankees across Cedar Run. His attention thus diverted, Jackson nevertheless welcomed his friend warmly. At his request, Stuart placed himself at the head of Robertson's brigade and led it forward to monitor Banks's movements. By day's end, he could inform Jackson that the Yankees across the run were many and dangerous. Moreover, Pope's main army was within supporting distance of them. The timely intelligence persuaded Jackson to refrain from renewing the battle; instead, he made preparations to retire below the Rapidan and wait for Lee and Longstreet to join him.[3]

While conducting his reconnaissance, Stuart had the time to confer with Robertson and to examine his troops. In some ways, he liked what he saw. Whatever reservations he harbored about Robertson's fitness to command, Stuart had to admit that the man had whipped his brigade into fighting trim. Though indifferently armed and equipped, Robertson's units showed the effects of rigorous training and appeared well led at the regimental and company levels. Furthermore, Chew's was as efficient a horse artillery unit as Stuart had ever seen. He would welcome the command into his division.

But that did not change his mind about Robertson's leadership. Stuart concurred with Jackson's description of Robertson as incompetent. Further, the brigade leader appeared to lack the confidence of his own men. This was an especially serious flaw in a cavalry general, who was expected to lead in battle, not supervise from the rear. In sum, Robertson was unfit to continue in his present position.[4]

Stuart's assessment of the unwanted subordinate appears to have been rooted in preconceived opinion. The two had clashed from their first meeting, and time and distance had not improved the relationship. The source of their animosity remains obscure, but it cannot be attributed wholly to Robertson's incompetence. One possible factor was of a personal nature. In earlier years, Robertson had been a suitor of the future Mrs. Stuart, the "daughter" of his regiment, the 2nd Dragoons. It appears that if Robertson did not carry a torch for Flora Cooke Stuart, he remained cordial toward her, a situation that may have rankled her husband. Whatever lay at the heart of the rift, the two men could not interact without generating tension, disagreement, and resentment. It did not matter whether Stuart was correct in his belief that Robertson lacked the confidence of his men—he would never gain Stuart's. For that reason alone, he had to go.[5]

Events conspired to grant Robertson a reprieve. By the time Stuart returned to Richmond on the fifteenth, he found that Lee and Longstreet had entrained for Jackson's headquarters at Gordonsville. The news was most unwelcome, for it meant not only that Robertson's disposition would be delayed, but also that Stuart would have to return almost immediately to Jackson. In fact, Lee wanted to see him as quickly as possible.

Before he left, he had a hurried conference with his lieutenants. He briefed Hampton on his observation mission and instructed Fitz Lee to ready his brigade for an overland march to the Rapidan River. Stuart, after conferring with Fitz's uncle, would meet the 2nd Brigade on the evening of the seventeenth near Raccoon Ford. Stuart believed he had made clear that Fitz should lose no time in rejoining him, for timing would be a critical factor in the coming campaign. Preliminaries attended to, late on the sixteenth Stuart again took a seat on a westbound train, this time in company with several members of his staff. The journey to Gordonsville on the Virginia Central, then up the O & A to Lee's headquarters at Orange Court House, took all night. When Stuart and his aides alighted on the siding at Orange in the dim hours of the seventeenth, everyone was tired, rumpled, and sooty.[6]

As soon as he reported to General Lee, Stuart unburdened himself of his feelings toward Robertson. Lee filed away the information for later action; at present, he was more interested in outlining Stuart's role in what lay ahead. Lee planned to strike the east (left) flank of Pope's army near Culpeper Court House before Pope could escape north of the Rappahannock. Stuart, with Fitz Lee and Robertson, would spearhead the offensive by slipping around that flank and gaining Pope's rear near Rappahannock Station—much as Stuart had gotten behind McClellan after Gaines's Mill. By wrecking the railroad bridge near the depot, Stuart would trap the Federals between the Rapidan and the Rappahannock, ensuring that Pope would have to oppose Jackson and Longstreet sans reinforcements.[7]

Lee's plan appeared highly promising. As Stuart had predicted, however, it hinged on exact timing. It was to be put in motion on the eighteenth, and it had to be carried out swiftly and smoothly. If not, Pope would fall back above the Rappahannock, where he might be unassailable. This being the case, Stuart was deeply chagrined by what occurred at the outset of his role in the proceedings.

Late in the afternoon of August 17, along with John Mosby, Heros von Borcke, and Lt. St. Pierre Gibson of the 4th Virginia, Stuart left Orange Court House to meet Fitz Lee and his men. At New Verdiersville on the Orange Plank Road, the party found not the 2nd Brigade, but Stuart's aide Chiswell Dabney and the division adjutant, Norman FitzHugh. Aware that New Verdiersville sat along the route Fitz Lee would have to take to the Rapidan, Stuart planned to wait for him in the village. He decided, however, to send his adjutant, along with a courier, a mile farther in the direction Fitz would be coming from, to warn of his approach. Stuart professed to be untroubled by Fitz's absence; as he wrote, he "expected confidently to meet Lee's brigade that evening."[8]

But the troopers did not arrive that night, or the next morning. Later Stuart would learn that the brigade, which for some reason had run low on both rations and ammunition, had taken a roundabout route to its destination so that it might resupply at Louisa Court House on the Virginia Central. Unaccountably, Fitz Lee had received the impression that celerity was not a requirement of his mission. By adding twenty miles to the march, the stopover at Louisa would delay his arrival on the Rapidan by several hours, but he believed Stuart would understand and approve.

Fitz's superior spent that night stretched out on the porch of a house along the plank road, his only bed being his cloak, his only pillow his plumed hat. At dawn on the eighteenth he was awakened either by Captain Mosby or by the distant drumming of horses' hooves. Thinking that Fitz had finally arrived, he dispatched Mosby and Gibson to meet the head of the column. Stuart, however, was "not left long in this delusion," for when the horsemen came into view, they fired on Mosby and his colleague. The newcomers were not Virginians, but a patrol of Michiganders from the command of Brig. Gen. John Buford. They had crossed the Rapidan into Lee's rear undetected, through the blundering of one of Longstreet's subordinates, charged with blocking the local fords.[9]

Almost too late, Stuart realized he was in danger of death or capture. As the Yankees approached, he dashed bareheaded from the porch, leaving behind not only his hat, but also his crimson-lined cape, sash, gauntlets, and a knapsack filled with official papers. In his report of the affair, Stuart claimed that he and Dabney managed to mount and gallop to safety, but an officer in the party that nearly captured them claimed that both men escaped on foot. Whichever the case, Stuart and Dabney were grateful that their would-be captors, ignorant of the identities of the men they chased, pursued only briefly before giving up the effort.

Of the others in Stuart's party, Mosby and Gibson evaded capture by hard, and at times wild, riding, as did von Borcke. Major FitzHugh was neither so agile nor so lucky. He was taken into custody, along with the possessions Stuart had left behind. The Yankees were jubilant over their good fortune: A staff officer of the celebrated J. E. B. Stuart was a major catch, although some thought Stuart's plumed hat a greater prize. Everyone revised his estimate, however, when the staff officer was found to be carrying a letter from Lee to his cavalry chief discussing the linkup of Jackson and Longstreet and detailing the turning movement against Pope. The information was deemed so valuable that the patrol abruptly left Verdiersville for home base, FitzHugh in tow.[10]

Stuart and Dabney remained in the woods only long enough to confirm the enemy's departure. Then they emerged and, on foot or on horseback, hastened out of harm's way. In later weeks, Stuart's undignified flight was the source of numerous jokes, all of which he took good-naturedly. "I am greeted on all sides," he observed, "with congratulations and 'Where's your hat?' I intend to make the Yankees pay for the price of that hat." The near future would reveal him to be as good as his word.[11]

Although Stuart bore his humiliation well, he could not contain his anger over the compromise of Lee's plans. As soon as Pope saw the captured documents, he ordered his army across the Rappahannock, foiling Lee's plans to trap him on the shore below. Lee would not learn of Pope's reaction, however, until midday on the nineteenth. When the withdrawal became known, Stuart laid all the blame on Fitz Lee. Not only had the brigade commander been unconscionably late, not rejoining Stuart until the evening of the eighteenth, he also had overtaxed his troopers and their mounts. When army headquarters learned of the brigade's fatigue—the direct result of its unexpectedly long march—Stuart was advised to defer his operations against Pope's flank.[12]

Stuart considered himself stigmatized by the outcome; he feared others would conclude that the cavalry had cost the army a priceless opportunity. This was not the case, and Stuart was overreacting. Even if Fitz had arrived when expected, events beyond Stuart's control would have prevented R. E. Lee from implementing his plan, which was predicated on an unrealistic timetable. Had the cavalry been ready to move on the eighteenth, Lee's commissary and some of his foot units would not have been—the operation would have been postponed anyway, if not canceled outright.

Upon Fitz Lee's arrival, Stuart was not in possession of these facts, but even if he had been, his temper might have gotten the best of him. While ever ready to praise subordinates whose performance reflected well on the Cavalry Division and its leader, Stuart could be rough on those whose blundering made him and the command look bad. When Fitz tried to justify his late arrival, his superior cut him short and dressed him down. In his official report of the campaign, he repeated some of his criticisms: "By this failure to comply with instructions not only the movement of the cavalry across the Rapidan was postponed a day, but a fine opportunity lost to overhaul a body of the enemy's cavalry on a predatory excursion far beyond their lines."[13]

Apparently Stuart's pointed (and in the view of some headquarters personnel, unjustified) criticism had no lasting effect on his personal and professional relationship with Fitz Lee. Afterward, Fitz said and wrote almost nothing about the matter. Yet it seemed clear that he was now the one who felt unfairly stigmatized.

>—⟨⟩—O—⟨⟩—⟨

A frustrated Stuart spent the nineteenth resting and preparing his command, which had gone into bivouac near Mitchell's Ford on the Rapidan. There Fitz Lee's troopers joined those under Robertson, while Pelham exchanged greetings with Chew. During the day, Stuart learned he should cross upriver at Morton's Ford come dawn. The infantry would ford the stream at other points, Jackson's wing on the left, Longstreet's farther eastward. Once on the upper bank, the cavalry was to head, via Stevensburg, for Rappahannock Station, an O & A depot on the river of the same name. The troopers were to destroy the railroad bridge adjacent to the station, then move into position on Longstreet's right.

Late in the afternoon, Stuart received a report that had the potential to revamp Lee's strategy. Army headquarters had learned that Pope was in retreat toward the Rappahannock; most of his army had already cleared the Stevensburg vicinity. Now Lee would have to race his opponent to the upper river. Stuart was warned to give the enemy a wide berth as his men moved in the same direction.[14]

In conformance with additional instructions from Lee, Stuart began to ford the Rapidan at 4:00 A.M. on the twentieth. Lee's brigade, accompanied by Pelham's battery, crossed at Raccoon Ford, while Robertson—whom Stuart accompanied, apparently to keep a close eye on him—did so farther west, at Tobacco Stick Ford. Both columns moved in a northeastward arc, Lee's toward Kelly's and Ellis's Fords on the Rappahannock, Robertson's toward the Orange & Alexandria Railroad depot of Brandy Station. To guard the Rapidan crossings, open a return route for Stuart, and provide distant support to Jackson's infantry, Tom Munford remained behind with his 2nd Virginia and Chew's battery.

Moving inland, Lee's and Robertson's brigades met the enemy almost simultaneously. Lee encountered the rear of Pope's main body, guarded by Buford's brigade, near Kelly's Ford. "By vigorous attack," Stuart wrote, Lee "secured several prisoners and a cavalry color." Robertson, meanwhile, overtook another rear guard—three regiments of horsemen from the brigade of George D. Bayard—between Stevensburg and Brandy Station. The clouds of dust Robertson's brigade kicked up prevented him from taking his adversary by surprise; forewarned, Bayard put up stiff resistance. For quite some time, he held at bay Grumble Jones, whose 7th Virginia led Robertson's advance. While he did, Bayard's comrades reached and crossed the river at Rappahannock Station.[15]

Looking on in frustration, Stuart ordered Jones to mass his regiment and charge the enemy. The order was conveyed by Major von Borcke, whose massive presence created quite an impression on one of Jones's troopers: "When this gallant officer came riding hastily up, his horse actually swayed with the weight it carried—the gigantic Prussian and his ponderous saber, the latter long and straight, and of a size no ordinary man could handle."[16]

Von Borcke delivered his message in heavily accented English, whereupon Jones formed his regiment for an attack and led it forward. The once-resolute Yankees gave way almost at first contact, pursued not only by the 7th Virginia, but by the rest of the brigade as well. When about midway between Brandy Station and the bridge, however, resistance again stiffened. The Federal horsemen took position on a long ridge in column of squadrons, a heavy line of skirmishers deployed in front, ready for a set-to.

Apparently Stuart accompanied Jones as the cantankerous subordinate maneuvered to confront the new position. Meanwhile, Robertson guided the better part of the brigade farther to the left in an attempt to flank the enemy. Stuart regretted the decision to take his attention from Robertson, for the latter made too wide a detour and failed to strike at the opportune time. Taking personal command of the remaining regiments, Stuart hurled them at the Yankees in rapid succession. To his gratification, Bayard's men gave way, falling back to the river. There they enjoyed the protection of several batteries that had unlimbered on the far shore. Stuart looked about and decided that "the ground was such that cavalry alone could not have attacked the enemy under such protection without sacrifice inadequate to the risk."

Stuart had been stymied, but he believed he could get moving again with a little help. He sent couriers to find Fitz Lee, who was less heavily engaged. Fitz dispatched the 1st and 5th Virginia, but again he responded too slowly to please his boss. By the time the regiments reached Stuart and Robertson, their opponents had crossed the river under cover of shell and shrapnel.

There was nothing for Stuart to do but pull back from the stream and wait for the infantry to come up. He massed the majority of both brigades near Brandy Station, while skirmishers kept up an intermittent fire and Pelham traded rounds with his counterpart across the water. For the balance of the command, "the remainder of the day was devoted to rest."[17]

Rest his men could always use, but given their inability to inflict more than modest injury on Bayard, Stuart was not certain they had earned it. He admitted that in general his officers and men had comported themselves ably, especially after first contact with the foe, but he had the nagging suspicion that more should have been accomplished.

In his official report, he was more conservative than usual in commending his lieutenants. He failed to mention Fitz Lee beyond a brief recitation of his brigade's participation. Apparently he was reluctant to heap praise on a commander who had not come under his personal observation this day, although Stuart's reticence may also reflect lingering resentment over Fitz's performance on the seventeenth. Instead, he lauded his most peevish subordinate, noting that Grumble Jones and his men had behaved throughout the fight with "marked courage and determination."

He even found a way to say something nice about Robertson, although it must have been an effort. While not overlooking his errant flank march, Stuart lauded the "superior discipline, organization, and drill" Robertson had imparted to his brigade, by which it had acquired "the stability of veterans." Considering the effusive praise of which Stuart was capable, this was a paltry tribute, but it was probably the best he could do.[18]

>-+<>-O-<>+-<

The head of Jackson's column reached Brandy Station in early evening. By then Stuart and Robertson had tended to their casualties, burying the three dead and ministering to the dozen wounded the day's action had cost them. Apparently they paid little attention to the enemy's casualties, at least those who littered the fringes of the battlefield. A trooper in the 9th Virginia "laid at night in the woods, 'mong the dead and dying." For much of the night he and his comrades "succored . . . wounded, dying Yankees, wrapping our blankets around them," until they fell to sleep "in spite of groans and cold."[19]

The following day, the Confederates took the time to clean the field of its human and equine debris. Pope having crossed the river without material damage, Robert E. Lee gave his army a respite while he pondered his next move. But Stuart did not permit his regiments to wile the day away. He clung to visions of turning the enemy's flank and getting into their rear, as Lee had originally intended, although now Stuart's attention focused on the Union right. His rumination was based on the supposition that the flank extended no farther upriver than Rappahannock Bridge. Stuart could skirt that area by sending Rosser's 5th Virginia across Beverly Ford, two miles upstream. In fact, Union infantry and artillery guarded that site; if he sought to cross there, Rosser would have a fight on his hands.

Ignorant of the risks, Stuart went ahead with his plan. At daylight, he dispatched Rosser to Beverly while also positioning Robertson's brigade to cross even farther upstream. The plan was that Robertson would sweep along the river, link with Rosser, and guard the ford while Jackson's men waded across. Of course, as soon as Rosser's men splashed over the stream, the Yankees on the far shore offered resistance. Rosser replied with a section of field artillery borrowed from the head of Jackson's column. Under the shelling, many Federals took off running, leaving behind at least fifty rifles, which Rosser happily possessed. The colonel then ranged inland until, as Stuart wrote, the 5th Virginia "held enough of the bank beyond to make a crossing by our infantry practicable."[20]

Rosser's grip was broken upon the approach of two brigades of Union infantry and another battery. At first Rosser did not perceive the danger, but Robertson, whose brigade had crossed on the colonel's left at Freeman's Ford, detected the advance and warned Stuart. The major general immediately withdrew the 5th Virginia, along with its spoils—including several prisoners—to the near bank. In the face of the expanding opposition, Jackson, looking on from the rear, decided to forgo his crossing. In his report of the affair, Stuart, who saw the day as another opportunity lost, wondered why the infantry had failed to expand Rosser's foothold.

Robert E. Lee was equally chagrined that a way had not been found to strike Pope before he could be reinforced by McClellan or Burnside. But the Confederate leader had not run out of ideas. His plan to outflank Pope having fallen short, he would try again, by a more roundabout route. On the rainy morning of the twenty-second, he sent Stuart, followed by Ewell's division of Jackson's wing, as far out as Freeman's Ford—only to find that point, too, blocked by Pope's infantry. Although reluctant to force a crossing, Stuart engaged the enemy with his sharpshooters, as well as with the guns of Pelham and Chew. The results were indecisive. Although Stuart believed, and Jackson agreed, that Ewell could force his way over at Freeman's, Lee feared the cost would prove too steep. He resolved to try yet another tack, and to carry it out, he turned to his cavalry leader.[21]

The new idea had originated with Stuart himself, who the previous evening had suggested that his horsemen slip around Pope's right, curve into his rear, and destroy substantial stretches of his main supply line, the Orange & Alexandria. At first Lee failed to discern strategic value in the undertaking, but he had been mulling it over ever since. Now, in view of the difficulty of outflanking Pope with infantry alone, he saw a cavalry raid as a means of distracting, and perhaps moving, Pope. If Stuart could inflict substantial damage in the rear, the Union leader might turn about to confront him, in the process loosening his grip on the Rappahannock. In the end, Lee decided the project was worth the gamble. He told Stuart so shortly before 10:00 A.M. on the twenty-second.[22]

The cavalry commander was ecstatic. He saw in the raid a chance not only to dislodge the enemy, but also to repay them for the embarrassment of his near capture. No time was to be lost to preparation. Within half an hour after receiving Lee's approval—by then Jackson's foot soldiers had replaced their cavalry comrades opposite Freeman's Ford—Stuart was leading most of Lee's and Robertson's men (all but one regiment of each brigade), plus two guns of Chew's battery, upriver toward Waterloo Bridge and Hart's Mill. The combined force of fifteen hundred forded the stream near those landmarks, well beyond the Union right flank, then proceeded east in the direction of Union-held Warrenton.

The Yankees who occupied that town fled on Stuart's approach. When the raiders entered the village late that afternoon, they were greeted as deliverers, the townspeople turning out in droves to welcome them with food, drink, and shouted greetings. Stuart lingered long enough to absorb the adulation and to quiz the locals about the rail line that lay eight miles to the east. From scouts including Frank Stringfellow, he had been briefed on the most strategic points along the road and the positions of at least some of its guards; the good folk of Warrenton confirmed the intelligence. After digesting whatever additional facts he could glean, Stuart determined to strike the bridge near Catlett's Station, which carried the O & A over Cedar Run. By all indications, that span was critical to the operation of Pope's supply system; moreover, from what Stuart could learn, it was vulnerable to attack.[23]

By the time the column left town, heading southeast toward Catlett's, Captain Blackford was memorizing the name of Maj. Charles Goulding, one of Pope's quartermaster officers. Until recently a member of the occupation force in Warrenton, Goulding had made a friendly wager with a local woman, Annie Lucas, that he (in other words, Pope's army) would be in Richmond within thirty days. The young woman had agreed that, should Goulding's prediction come true, she would present him with a bottle of wine. Aware that Stuart was heading for the major's present location, she asked the general to look for him at Catlett's. If taken prisoner, Goulding would soon be on his way to an officer's prison in the capital—in which case Miss Lucas would gladly pay off. The idea so tickled Stuart that he had ordered his engineer to hunt up the major.[24]

From Warrenton, the rain-lashed trail led to Auburn, which the raiders reached after dark. Following a brief layover, Stuart decided to push on to Catlett's minus his artillery—the steady rain had left the roads too soggy to support the weight of guns, caissons, and limbers. When the head of the lighter-weight column approached the depot at about 7:30, Stuart sent Blackford on ahead to scout the environs, mainly to determine the size of the guard. Perhaps an hour later, the aide reported back: He had observed a vast array of wagons, tents, and supplies of all kinds, including an immense stockpile of rations, but few defenders. By this time, Stuart had learned from a free African-American whom his men had taken into custody—and who claimed a past acquaintance with Stuart—that Pope's headquarters baggage was also stored at the depot. The man not only knew where the tempting prize could be found, but he also offered to guide Stuart to it. Stuart's response was concise: Lead on!

As he neared the depot, Stuart assigned Rooney Lee and the 9th Virginia to attack that part of the supply base that lay north of the O & A, while Rosser's 5th

Virginia and another regiment would head for the garrison encampment south of the tracks. Another detail would make for the railroad bridge over Cedar Run, whose destruction Stuart considered his primary objective. Told off for the bridge assault was the 4th Virginia under now-Colonel Wickham, back in the field after his release from captivity and the healing of his Williamsburg wound. Backing Wickham was another recent returnee, Major Payne, his fractured jaw encased in the rubber mask the Yankee surgeon had fashioned for him.[25]

Once the various forces had gone into their assigned positions, Stuart made a final survey of the depot, where everyone but a few lonesome pickets appeared to be asleep. Then he had his bugler blow the charge. The notes were barely audible over the sounds of rain, wind, and thunder, but they reached the ears of hundreds of men, who answered in unison. Captain Blackford was enthralled by the response: "From two thousand throats came the dreaded yell, and at full gallop two thousand horsemen came thundering on."[26]

A minute later, bedlam reigned. Rooney Lee's men charged through the streets of the depot, cheering, shooting, and flailing about with cold steel. The commotion roused startled quartermasters and guards, who rushed from their tents to find themselves quickly surrounded. Most surrendered without a fight—a reprise of the June assault on Tunstall's Station. A few defenders grabbed their rifles and dove for cover. Members of the 13th Pennsylvania Reserves ("The Bucktail Regiment") took position behind a row of warehouses, from which they emptied a few saddles with a hasty volley. Soon, however, the Bucktails were flushed from cover, ridden down, knocked to the earth, and trampled on, or chased into nearby woods.[27]

The balance of the 9th Virginia, supported by other units of Lee's brigade, made a shambles of the neatly stacked rows of supplies they encountered. They helped themselves to everything of conceivable use, including weapons, ammunition, horse equipment, clothing of all types and sizes, tents and bedding materials, items of furniture, and edibles ranging from boxes of hardtack and salted beef to delicacies such as canned fruits and bottles of wine and liquor. Joining the men in their merry work, Stuart located Pope's baggage wagons and came away with one of the general's dress uniforms, splendidly accoutered and spanking new. Later he wrote to its owner, offering to trade the uniform for the hat Stuart had left behind on that porch. As expected, he received no reply. He was not surprised to learn that Pope had no sense of humor (even if his strategy suggested otherwise).

At Verdiersville, the enemy had also captured documents from which they had profited strategically. For a time it appeared that Stuart had evened the score on that count as well. Among the treasures extracted from Pope's baggage was a collection of official papers, signed by the general. They contained information on the size and composition of his army, as well as on its imminent reinforcement by McClellan. Ironically, they also revealed Pope's anxiety over the security of his supply lines, especially the O & A, which he feared was vulnerable to just such a strike as Stuart's. In fact, Pope had recently ordered that additional guards be sent to Catlett's—they were en route when the raiders attacked.

Some who examined the papers declared them to be of great significance to Robert E. Lee. More than a few historians have adopted this view, declaring that their discovery influenced the way Lee conducted the balance of the campaign. Yet the army leader never claimed as much. It is true the documents disclosed some facts previously unknown to him, such as Pope's concern that his hold on the Rappahannock was too precarious to be maintained for long. For the most part, however, the papers merely confirmed Lee's suppositions about his opponent's intentions, while reinforcing his desire to land a decisive blow before Pope's army could double or treble in size.[28]

If Stuart's rifling of Pope's possessions failed to yield important results, so did Rosser's attack on the camp south of the O & A. Impeded by the rain, the darkness of night, and water-filled ditches, the two regiments under the colonel's direction failed to reach their objective and aborted the attack. One reason for Rosser's failure was the large number of prisoners he had gathered en route, which overtaxed his resources. When their guards complained that the captives were becoming unmanageable, an angry and frustrated Rosser gave an order that the POWs interpreted as authority to execute them. Rosser later claimed his words had been misinterpreted; regardless, the terrified prisoners began to fight for their lives. "With the fury of demons," he wrote, "they seized fence rails and stones, and attacked the guard like wild beasts, and many of them lost their lives before they could be reassured that they would be treated as prisoners of war." One Yankee attacked the colonel himself with a concealed bayonet, wounding him and his horse and forcing one of Rosser's lieutenants to shoot him.[29]

If Rosser came up empty-handed, so did Wickham, Payne, and the troopers sent to wreck the bridge over Cedar Run. The pouring rain frustrated every attempt to burn the trestle, while axes and hatchets merely dented the superstructure. In the end, the demolition team gave up the effort, costing the raid its only chance to attain strategic value.

Stuart contented himself by reflecting on the most visible results of the operation—the prizes that had fallen into his hands, which had been acquired at a relatively small loss of life. In addition to material goods—including a paymaster's safe containing a half million dollars in greenbacks and twenty thousand dollars in gold—the raiders had captured more than three hundred prisoners and almost twice as many horses and mules. Surely, they had also put a crimp in the enemy's supply system, the effects of which would not, however, be felt for some time.

High on Stuart's list of prizes was Major Goulding. Captain Blackford—fresh from a losing battle with a Newfoundland, who had prevented the looting of his master's tent—had called the major out of the column of prisoners, much to his surprise and concern. Next morning, when the Confederates marched back to Warrenton, dozens of burning storehouses in their wake, Stuart saw to it that Goulding had an awkward reunion with Miss Lucas, from whom he accepted the bottle of wine. It was the only luxury he could expect to enjoy in Libby Prison.[30]

>–+‹›–O–‹›+–‹

Once he saw how easily Stuart had slipped into the Federal rear and how vulnerable were Pope's communications, the commander of the Army of Northern Virginia decided that a repeat performance, in heavier force, would yield even greater returns. By the twenty-fifth Lee had determined to send Jackson's wing along the same route the cavalry had taken. Once Jackson had gained Pope's rear, Lee would duplicate Stonewall's envelopment using the rest of the army. If Jackson moved with enough speed and stealth, Pope would not turn to strike him until he was caught between two wings of the A.N.V. It was, by any standard of measure, a risky maneuver; disaster loomed if everything did not go precisely as envisioned. But with reinforcements only days away from joining Pope, Lee had no alternative to rolling the dice of war.[31]

As usual, the cavalry would have an early involvement in the undertaking. It had returned from Catlett's Station early on the twenty-fourth, having spent the previous night on the enemy's side of the river, but beyond its right flank. After fording the stream, the erstwhile raiders took position in the open country between Jeffersonton and Amissville. For the rest of that day they engaged pickets who had sidled down the riverbank toward Waterloo Bridge. The span, the last one standing on that stretch of the river, Lee wished to remain intact. To see to it, one hundred sharpshooters under Rosser laid a continual fire along the upper shore. They made a success of the mission, keeping back parties of bridge burners until relieved by Jackson's infantry. If Rosser had disappointed Stuart at Catlett's Station, he regained his superior's confidence by this hours-long display of power and determination.[32]

On the evening of the twenty-fifth, Stuart was called to army headquarters, where he received final instructions for the coming offensive. At 2:00 the next morning, following a night without an hour's sleep, the cavalry commander put in motion both of his brigades, all of his artillery, and a column of supply wagons and ambulances. Jackson's men had already begun to play their role in this plan, moving toward crossing sites beyond Pope's line of vision. The horsemen promptly fell in on Jackson's flanks and in his rear. They waded the river near Henson's Mill and on the far bank headed north through the towns of Orleans and Salem. Aware that Jackson himself was riding in the advance, Stuart, accompanied by a few aides, rode hard to overtake him, leaving the main body behind. The route carried him through the Bull Run Mountains via Thoroughfare Gap to Gainesville. Reporting to Jackson outside that village, Stuart was instructed to guard both of the infantry's flanks.

The assignment smacked of mundane activity, but Stuart managed to break the monotony by sending detachments on auxiliary missions. On the twenty-sixth, Fitz Lee left the column near Haymarket to seize a forage train bound for the rear of Pope's army. Later that day, as the cavalry on Jackson's right, which Stuart was accompanying, crossed Broad Run a few miles above Bristoe Station, the Confederates poised to make their first strike at Pope's railroad. At Stuart's order, Munford led the 2nd Virginia to Bristoe, which was known to be held by troops of all arms. Munford charged in at a full gallop, scattering Yankee cavalry but also losing a few men to infantry fire. Ewell's advance quickly joined him in securing the depot. Foot soldiers and horsemen, working in tandem, tore up track and piled obstructions on other, intact sections of the railroad. Their labor was rewarded when two trains on their way to pick up reinforcements for Pope barreled into the roadblock and derailed.[33]

Neither the trains nor the depot itself contained supplies that Jackson's or Stuart's soldiers could appropriate. Soon after arriving, however, Jackson learned that Manassas Junction, four miles up the tracks, housed the principal supply depot of Pope's army. Its coffers were reported to be bursting with enough rations and materiel to feed and equip every man in Jackson's wing. Incongruously, it was lightly guarded. By now it was nearly dark, but at the suggestion of Brig. Gen. Isaac Trimble, Jackson directed that officer, with five hundred men from his infantry brigade, to march at once on Manassas. A large number of troopers were also told off for the mission, which Stuart, as senior officer involved, would command. Apparently Jackson failed to inform Trimble of the fact, for the infantryman proceeded as if he were in charge.[34]

As he started north, Stuart was keenly aware that Jackson had gotten squarely behind Pope's army, which remained on the Rappahannock, unaware of the danger in its rear. Yet when that massive force finally sensed the threat and turned about, its opponents might be the ones in danger. Even so, Stuart leaped at the opportunity to visit the junction near which he had started on the road to promotion and prominence, if only to succor his hungry, ill-supplied troopers.

He marched well in advance of Trimble at the head of most of Robertson's brigade and a portion of Lee's. At the first crossroads he came to, he took the precaution of dispatching Wickham and the 4th Virginia to the rear of the depot, while the main body continued along the road from Bristoe. After a little more than an hour on the march, the cavalry's advance encountered a brace of sentinels, backed by artillery, suggesting that the approaches to Manassas, unlike the junction itself, were well guarded. A few rounds of shrapnel and canister persuaded Stuart to back off and await Trimble's arrival.

According to Stuart, the infantry reached him after sunset, moved forward as if to attack, then suddenly halted. Its commander announced that it was too dark to proceed with adequate care. Stuart agreed to defer the assault till daylight. When dawn came, "the place," as Stuart reported, "was taken without much difficulty" by Trimble's men but with cavalry support.[35]

In his report of the capture, Trimble told a different story. The attack was made not in daylight, but around midnight, and by his troops alone. The cavalry provided no assistance whatsoever; in fact, Stuart did not appear on the scene until the base was in the hands of the infantry. Stuart's partisans, as well as other, disinterested observers, branded Trimble's charges inaccurate, unjust, and mean-spirited. Showing commendable restraint, Stuart allowed the whole thing to blow over.[36]

High-level squabbling aside, the attack on Manassas Junction was a smashing success—literally. For hours, troopers and infantrymen ransacked storehouses that held an even greater abundance of food, clothing, and equipment than those at Catlett's Station. Jackson later enumerated the spoils at 200 new tents, 50,000 pounds of bacon, 1,000 barrels of corned beef, 2,000 barrels of salt pork, and 2,000 barrels of flour, as well as 175 horses and mules, 300 prisoners, and "200 negroes."[37]

As Robert E. Lee had hoped, his people had scored such a coup that John Pope could no longer ignore the threat to his rear. From reports, he suspected that Lee had split his army, a large portion of which remained below the Rappahannock. Early on the twenty-seventh, he began to pull back to the Manassas area, hopeful of running Jackson to earth and then turning on Longstreet.

Given Pope's three-to-one numerical advantage—he had already been augmented by portions of two of McClellan's corps, as well as by troops recently stationed in western Virginia—he considered Jackson's destruction a foregone conclusion. What he did not know was that as soon as he loosened his hold on the Rappahannock, Lee had placed Longstreet's soldiers on the same roads that Jackson had followed to Thoroughfare Gap. The Confederate commander was hoping against hope that he could reunite his widely separated wings before Pope landed a decisive blow.[38]

>-+‹•›-O-‹•›+-‹

Stuart spent the twenty-seventh "rationing the command" at Manassas, which the balance of Jackson's corps (minus Ewell's division) reached early that day. The newcomers arrived in time to fend off some outside interference. With the help of Stuart's resupplied command, they beat back a demonstration by a brigade of New Jersey troops along the north side of Bull Run, in which the enemy commander, Brig. Gen. George Taylor, was killed.

When the Federals fell back, Stuart sent Fitz Lee, with three of his regiments, around the bend to Fairfax Court House in an enterprising but unsuccessful attempt to cut off their retreat. Stuart had previously detached Munford and Rosser to support Ewell, who late in the day joined Jackson at Manassas after being forced out of Bristoe by Pope's advance echelon, the infantry division of Joseph Hooker.[39]

That evening, a few hours before Hooker and other Yankees could arrive, Jackson and Stuart departed Manassas, which, having been plundered of everything of value to infantry and cavalry, was a mass of smoking ruins. While the infantry marched north toward Groveton on the Warrenton Turnpike, Stuart, with the regiments that remained with him (Fitz Lee had not returned from Fairfax) retraced his route to Haymarket. He had learned from captured couriers that

Pope's cavalry was massing in that area. But when Stuart drew near the place that afternoon, he found it occupied by too many troopers to challenge in his reduced circumstances. He did ascertain, however, that farther west Lee and Longstreet were pushing their way through Thoroughfare Gap to join Jackson. Devout Christian Stuart prayed that the linkup would come off without a hitch.

Unable to establish communication with Longstreet's wing, and learning that Jackson had clashed with Pope's advance at Groveton, Stuart hastened there by early evening but arrived too late to take part in the fighting, which had been long, bloody, and inconclusive. He was proud to discover, however, that Rosser's troopers and Pelham's gunners had provided flank support to Jackson throughout the fight. While these units had not been major factors in the outcome, at least the Cavalry Division had been heard from.[40]

Stuart woke his still-weary men early the next morning, the twenty-ninth. At Jackson's behest, he retraced his path toward the Bull Run Mountains in a second attempt to communicate with Lee and Longstreet. Soon after starting out, his column was fired on by Federals hiding in the trees that lined the road from Groveton to Sudley Springs. At the latter place, Jackson had parked his supply wagons, which groaned under the weight of newly acquired treasures. Stuart attempted to flush out the enemy with salvos from Pelham's battery. At the same time, he warned Jackson of the danger to his train and alerted the six companies of the 17th Virginia Battalion that had been stationed near Sudley Springs to protect the wagons. When the Yankees attacked later in the day, the battalion's commander, Maj. William Patrick, engineered an effective defense, but at the cost of his life.[41]

Once roadside resistance abated, Stuart resumed his westward travel. Nearing Gainesville, he was relieved to meet the head of Longstreet's wing, which had forced its way through the mountains against stubborn resistance from a small portion of Pope's army, mostly cavalry. Here was another indication that Stuart's opponents were becoming skilled defenders, even if their offensive capabilities left much to be desired.

Stuart sent couriers to report Jackson's position to General Lee, then fell in on the right flank of Longstreet's column and followed it back toward Manassas. Upon reaching the Warrenton Pike, the foot soldiers veered left and headed north toward sounds indicating that Jackson and Pope were again joined in battle. The route would bring Longstreet in on Jackson's right, although he would not become fully engaged until the following day. The newcomers moved into position so stealthily that Pope failed to detect their arrival; he continued to concentrate his attention and his weight against Jackson. He would pay for his single-mindedness.

After Longstreet turned onto the pike, Stuart continued on to Manassas, where some Union detachments had gathered. Stuart engaged the Yankees with Rosser's regiment and portions of Robertson's brigade. Then his scouts reported the approach of other Federals—elements of Fitz John Porter's V Corps, Army of the Potomac—from the direction of Bristoe Station. Fearing

that Porter would detect Longstreet's presence on the Warrenton Pike, the cavalry leader devised a stratagem. He put whole companies of his troopers to
work dragging brush along the Gainesville Road, which intersected the road
from Bristoe. Stuart hoped the clouds of dust would make Porter believe a
heavy column was moving his way. Apparently the ruse worked: Porter's march
slowed, even as Stuart alerted Longstreet to his approach. Three infantry
brigades and some cannons were soon at Stuart's side; without tipping off the
enemy to Longstreet's presence, they persuaded Porter's troops to pull back,
mill about for a while, and then withdraw.[42]

On the critical morning of August 30, Stuart guided his command, including the recently returned men under Fitz Lee, up the road that ran along Longstreet's right flank. To Stuart's relief, his scouts reported that Pope's troops,
unaware of Longstreet's presence near the battlefield, continued to devote their
full attention to Jackson. Even better, the troops opposite Longstreet were shifting toward the other end of the Confederate line, leaving themselves open to a
flank attack. Stuart made sure Lee was aware of this glittering opportunity.

In fact, Lee already knew; he was waiting for just the right moment to
exploit it. Finally, at about 3:00 P.M., with Pope's army fully committed in
another direction, Lee unleashed Longstreet. Thousands of men keening the
Rebel yell fell on Pope's unguarded flank and flattened it. The attackers then
drove northward, rolling up the Union line like a frayed blue carpet.[43]

Soon after Longstreet started forward, Stuart went into action as well. With
Pelham's guns well to the rear, he directed Rosser, the ex-artilleryman, to take
charge of several batteries in Longstreet's rear. Rosser trundled the guns into
position to lace the shattered flank with a vicious enfilade. Then Stuart sent
Robertson into the fray against John Buford's brigade, which had been trying
desperately to cover Pope's left near Lewis Ford on Bull Run. To Stuart's pleasant surprise, Robertson's troopers, the 2nd Virginia in the lead, charged into the
blue ranks to begin what one of Munford's men called "a regular hand to hand
sabre fight."

Munford's outfit bowled over Buford's leading units, the 1st Michigan and
4th New York, killing and wounding several of their men and taking dozens of
prisoners. The Federals gamely regrouped and counterattacked with enough
force to knock Munford backward. At that point Robertson committed the 12th
and 7th Virginia, which sliced through the blue ranks and wounded Buford.
With its leader incapacitated, most of his men abruptly withdrew from the fight,
leaving the field, and the many casualties on it, to Robertson.[44]

Soon, in fact, the entire Union army in that sector was streaming toward
the rear, beaten, broken, utterly demoralized. Comrades farther north followed
suit as their once-formidable line steadily and irrecoverably unraveled. From
his vantage point opposite what had recently been Pope's left, Stuart could only
marvel at the completeness of his army's triumph and the ever-expanding magnitude of John Pope's defeat.

Chapter Ten

The Confederate
Rubicon Crossed

Reeling from Longstreet's attack, the demoralized forces of the Army of
Virginia headed for the rear by the hundreds. In full retreat, they streamed
across Stone Bridge and adjacent fords, heading for Centreville, Fairfax Court
House, and beyond. Their ultimate destination was Washington, where the bulk
of McClellan's army, just up from the Peninsula, provided support. It was First
Manassas all over again, with the exception that the victorious Confederates
were ready and willing to mount a hard-driving pursuit. But Pope's rear guard,
unlike McDowell's, put up a spirited defense so that their demoralized comrades might escape.

Stuart's job was to prevent that from happening. Yet, although he reported
himself "anxious to cut off that retreat," he found the roads to the north and east
so crowded with infantry, blue and gray, that he could make slow progress, if
any, toward Bull Run. He responded by halting and letting the army go on without him. Gathering up his scattered units, including Lee's brigade, which, since
returning from Fairfax, had been guarding Jackson's left flank, he put them in
bivouac for the night. Before daylight on the thirty-first, he had them back in
the saddle, heading to the enemy's rear via now-open roads. His men picked up
large numbers of that battlefield staple, the straggler, but for several hours they
encountered no solid, organized body of Yankees. Only when near Centreville
did they draw fire, and then it came from artillery, indicating a truly determined
rear-guard action.[1]

Against such opposition, Stuart made little headway. Detachments sent in
other directions fared better. Tom Rosser, with at least fifty men from Robertson's brigade and two guns, pursued Yankees whom he found heading southward to Manassas Junction. Rosser, who the previous day had commanded
several batteries massed in Stuart's sector, including his old unit, the Washington Artillery of New Orleans, found an additional four hundred stragglers at the
junction, whom he gathered up along with a cache of small arms and "five
elegant ambulances." With no other Federals in the vicinity worth fighting,

Rosser returned to Stuart with his captures, proud to have demonstrated his tactical versatility.[2]

Fitz Lee and Beverly Robertson met more substantial opposition than Rosser, and surmounted it. At the head of both brigades, Stuart left the Warrenton Pike about midday, circled north to the Little River Turnpike, and advanced toward Chantilly, behind Pope's rear guard. Entering the village, Stuart's advance met bodies of Yankee cavalry and immediately attacked. Robertson captured an entire company of New Yorkers, while Lee routed Robertson's old 2nd Dragoons (now known as the 2nd U.S. Cavalry). Both brigadiers then gained positions that commanded the pike between Centreville and Fairfax Court House; meanwhile, Pelham's guns swept the road with shell "as long as it seemed desirable." Eventually, as troops out of Washington flooded into the area, Stuart withdrew everyone into bivouacs north of Chantilly.[3]

For a time, a rumor circulated that Stuart had captured his prewar superior, Edwin Sumner, commander of the newly arrived reinforcements. The overthrow of the 2nd Cavalry had been a coup; Sumner's capture would have topped off Stuart's day in sublime fashion. In fact, however, Sumner remained at large. He not only fashioned his II Corps into a shield behind which Pope's fugitives might rally, he also kept McClellan in Washington apprised of the progress of the Confederate pursuit.

Sumner's reports only confirmed his superior's opinion of John Pope. An increasingly disgusted McClellan observed "a total absence of brains" on Pope's part, which made "the total destruction" of his army a real possibility. In ominous tones, Little Mac informed General in Chief Henry Wager Halleck that "the occasion is grave & demands grave measures. The question is the salvation of the country." McClellan would answer that question two days hence, by riding out of Washington and, without official sanction, reassuming command of his own army and adding to it what remained of Pope's.[4]

The final act in the drama that was the Second Manassas (or Second Bull Run) campaign was played out on September 1, when Lee poised to deliver a stunning blow before the Yankees could move beyond his reach. The result was a confused but bloody clash around Chantilly and nearby Ox Hill. Three divisions under Jackson followed Stuart's lead in reaching the Little River Turnpike, hoping to strike Pope's rear guard from the blind side. Instead, the Federals faced about, and in a driving rainstorm held their ground against repeated but poorly coordinated assaults before withdrawing to Washington under early darkness.

The cavalry saw relatively little action on this day of wretched weather and lost opportunities. At the height of the fighting between Jackson and his opponents (two of whom, Maj. Gens. Philip Kearney and Isaac I. Stevens, were killed in the fight), Stuart sent Lee's brigade around the Union right to Flint Hill, but the gummy roads made Fitz late getting into position; when he arrived, he found it occupied by blue infantry. For a brief period, Pelham's guns were engaged, but after dark Stuart declared the fight over. Recalling his detachments, he led them south to Germantown. There everyone suffered through a thoroughly miserable night.[5]

Next day, September 2, Pope's survivors completed their flight to the capital, where their leader—his arrogance a thing of the past—was relieved of command. Having squandered what many considered a fine opportunity to destroy its enemy, the Army of Northern Virginia pulled back to recruit its strength and review its options.

As always, while the main army rested, the cavalry labored. On September 2, Stuart advanced again to Flint Hill, this time to challenge an outpost Sumner had established before leaving the scene. This day, for the first time, the cavalry was at maximum strength, three brigades, Hampton having joined Lee and Robertson after a long march from Richmond. His men had spent the past fortnight in the difficult and unglamorous work of shadowing McClellan's main body.[6]

Stuart was glad to have his new subordinate by his side; he was especially pleased to find that Hampton had brought his own battery, the third horse artillery unit to be assigned to the cavalry. At Hampton's urging, Secretary of War Randolph had authorized the conversion of Capt. James F. Hart's Washington (South Carolina) Battery, the mounted artillery contingent of the Hampton Legion, to horse artillery, consisting of two 6-pounder and four 12-pounder howitzers.

Hart's coming meant that the Cavalry Division consisted of twenty cannons, eight of them in the Stuart Horse Artillery. As senior captain, Pelham exercised a loose authority over all three batteries. Although in essence a battalion, the units were not formally designated as such for another three weeks; at that time the boyish artillerist was promoted to major to command the entire force.[7]

Hart's guns went into action within minutes of reaching Stuart, joining Pelham's and Chew's guns in lacing the post at Flint Hill. When some of Stuart's carbineers advanced on the position under cover of the barrage, its occupants hastily decamped for Washington. Refusing to let them go, Pelham wheeled his guns into a position from which he shelled the moving troops "with telling effect," as Stuart wrote, "scattering them in every direction."[8]

Hampton's new arrivals prodded the foot soldiers on their way, taking some prisoners, before falling back and joining Stuart in bivouac near Fairfax Court House. The cavalry had done all it could to follow up the great victory of the thirtieth. The campaign to harm, harass, and humble John Pope was over.

>−◀▶−O−◀▶−◁

In later weeks, R. E. Lee explained his thinking at this critical point in the conflict. Pope having retreated behind an impregnable arc of fortifications, and McClellan having yet to emerge from it, Lee was temporarily without an opponent. Northeastern Virginia was now free from Yankee occupation, as was much of the Valley of Virginia, Union troops having withdrawn from Winchester to Harpers Ferry and other places at the bottom (i.e., the northern part) of the

Shenandoah. The situation pleased Lee immensely; he wished to do nothing to
jeopardize it. "To prolong a state of affairs in every way desirable," he
observed, "and not to permit the season for active operations to pass without
endeavoring to inflict further injury upon the enemy, the best course appeared
to be the transfer of the army into Maryland."

In so deciding, Lee was playing for time. He realized his army lacked
many of the resources required to operate above the Potomac for an extended
period, including adequate supplies of cold-weather clothing and wheeled
transport. Still, he hoped to remain in Maryland until winter, when the Yankees
might find it difficult to reestablish themselves in Virginia. Invading Maryland
might also cause Lincoln to husband his troops for the protection of the capital
rather than free them for field campaigning. Then, too, Lee hoped that the vast
numbers of Confederate sympathizers who supposedly resided in southern
Maryland would flock to his colors, while the citizenry succored his troops.
Already Maryland had provided much support to the Army of Northern Virginia, and Lee saw an extended stay in the state as a means of restoring freedom
to those suffering under Union occupation.[9]

For these and other reasons, one day after locking the last of Pope's survivors inside Washington, Lee began to move his army toward the Potomac
crossings near Leesburg. Stuart, always one to seize the strategic initiative,
thought the plan a good one and vowed to play his part in the proceedings to the
utmost of his abilities—this time, there would be no foul-ups of the
Verdiersville variety. On the third, as the army exited the Manassas-Centreville-
Fairfax area, the cavalry covered its withdrawal by demonstrating loudly and
conspicuously from Dranesville to Lewinsville, from Falls Church to George-
town. Once the screening ended, most of the cavalry turned toward the
Potomac, bringing up the rear of the army.

Given Lee's headstart, and the proverbial timidity of McClellan's cavalry,
Stuart's men were not hard-pressed on the road to Leesburg. They crossed the
Potomac in unhurried fashion on the afternoon and evening of the fifth. A member of the Jeff Davis Legion called the crossing "a beautiful sight on that clear
moonlight night. The water reached our saddles, & some small horses had to
swim. As Regt. after Regt. reached the Maryland side, the men cheered and the
bands played Maryland My Maryland."[10]

Virtually everyone involved saw the crossing as a momentous occasion,
one on which the course of the war might turn. After reaching the Maryland
side, Stuart's aide Channing Price wrote his mother that "the Rubicon has been
crossed . . . and glad am I of it." Everything around him—the fine weather, the
brisk marching pace, the high spirits of officers and men—told the staff officer
that the army was making the right move, both strategically and psychologi-
cally. The army's tide of success was carrying it into a region touched lightly, if
at all, by the armies. The air seemed fresher, the foliage greener, the pastures
lusher, the crops more bountiful in Maryland.[11]

Stuart himself was in high spirits as he navigated the stream that separated North and South. On the Maryland side he sat his horse and watched his men trot past. Fitz Lee, as usual, had the vanguard; behind him came the brigade of Hampton. Stuart's third brigade, which had remained in position near Flint Hill until the rest of the command cleared the area, was bringing up the rear; in a couple of days it would enter Maryland—under the command of Tom Munford. Stuart's old nemesis, Beverly Robertson, was miles away and headed in the opposite direction. On the fifth, he had been relieved from command with the Army of Northern Virginia and sent to North Carolina for reassignment.[12]

The order that had brought this about may have carried Robert E. Lee's signature, but it bore the fingerprints of J. E. B. Stuart. Despite competent— even commendable—performances at Second Manassas and on later, less sanguinary, fields, Robertson had never gained a modicum of Stuart's confidence. Up to the last, in fact, the man had blundered. On the evening of the second, Robertson, misinterpreting his orders, had withdrawn his troopers to Chantilly when they were supposed to be supporting Hampton at Flint Hill.[13]

If past performances had not already done so, that error had sealed the brigadier's fate. Whether Stuart had been forced to remind Lee of his subordinate's failings, or whether the army commander had acted without prompting, Robertson was on his way south to organize and recruit additional regiments of cavalry. With great feeling, if without outward demonstration, Stuart celebrated his absence—never suspecting that Robertson would return to him nine months hence to renew a relationship that gave him fits.

Stuart was buoyed up not only by the departure of an unwanted subordinate, but also by the reception his command received as it moved inland. On the road to Poolesville, the troopers were treated to "the greatest demonstrations of joy," which only strengthened their "hope of enabling the inhabitants to throw off the tyrant's yoke." An officer in Lee's brigade, however, took a more cynical view of their reception: "Here we . . . heard pretty general expressions of joy at our coming, as it suspended the operation of the Yankee Draft. I rather suppose their joy arises from the fact that they believe they will be left to do as they please & can stay at home unmolested by either party."[14]

Not even small-scale intrusions by the enemy dampened the general enthusiasm. Upon nearing Poolesville, Fitz Lee had to shoo some Yankees from his path, but the effort required little exertion. On the seventh, after a brief stopover in the Poolesville area, Stuart moved north to Urbana, where he pitched his headquarters. He and his staff remained there for several days while the main army pushed on to Frederick, seven miles to the northwest. During that time, however, the cavalry was far from idle. It scouted McClellan's approach on an hourly basis, enabling Stuart to chart the enemy's movements almost as confidently as his own.[15]

While the forward scouts might be kept busy, Stuart's staff observed a lighter duty schedule. Years later, Captain Blackford recalled, "Our life at headquarters was a delightful one, an oasis in the war-torn desert of our lives." For nearly a week, Stuart's aides, as well as most of the rank and file, lolled in their bivouacs waiting to be challenged by Pope, McClellan, or some other general just as unlikely to force them out of Maryland before they were ready to go.[16]

As usual, Stuart saw to it that his time was not consumed in dreary routine. The general, said Blackford, "knew how to improve the passing hour in the enjoyment of the charming society the country round offered." Although Stuart and his staff slept fully clothed beside their perpetually saddled horses, there was plenty of time for socializing. Despite the need to remain "ready of instant action," Blackford and the rest of the staff "enjoyed the society of the charming girls around [them] to the utmost."

On the evening of the eighth, Stuart hosted a ball for his officers and the local gentry, held in an abandoned female academy on the edge of town. Beneath ceilings festooned with regimental flags, as well as less warlike decorations, men and women dressed to the nines glided gaily about the dance floor to the music of a band from a Mississippi infantry regiment. Stuart spent much of the evening, on and off the dance floor, in the company of a pretty girl from the North who had been visiting friends in the area. Her Confederate sympathies, which she expressed vehemently and often, to her partner's delight, led Stuart to dub her the "New York Rebel."[17]

The "Maryland Ball" had been under way for only a few minutes when reality intruded. As Blackford recalled, without warning, "there came shivering through the night air the boom of artillery, followed by the angry rattle of musketry." Moments later, dancers were scrambling from the floor, officers snatching up the sabers they had laid neatly against the wall. Stuart and the other men dashed outside, threw themselves into the saddle, and galloped off, to return perhaps an hour later. "McClellan's advance guards had struck our outposts," wrote Blackford, "but after a sharp skirmish they withdrew for the night." Dancing resumed, but the festivities broke up for good when wounded troopers were carried in on stretchers, to be ministered to by surgeons in dress uniforms and nurses in ball gowns.[18]

Against this dramatic backdrop, Stuart and his men entered upon the main business of the campaign. Lee's infantry and artillery were ranging westward, via Frederick, toward the Blue Ridge chain known as South Mountain. While Longstreet moved in the direction of Hagerstown, six divisions under Jackson, having passed South Mountain, were heading back to the Potomac. According to plan, Stonewall's columns were converging on the Union garrison at Harpers Ferry, which Lee wished neutralized to protect his communications with Virginia. Stuart's multifaceted mission was to guard the eastern flank of the invasion force, keep Lee informed of the progress of McClellan's pursuit, and block both mountain ranges and thus prevent interference with Jackson's movement on Harpers Ferry.

While awaiting McClellan's pursuit, Stuart had been facing east. His right flank, anchored by Munford's brigade, had been located near Poolesville, his center (Hampton's brigade) outside Hyattstown, and his upper, or left, flank (Fitz Lee's brigade) at New Market on the Baltimore & Ohio Railroad. Hampton was the first to feel enemy pressure, and he withstood it gamely. Although engaged in several skirmishes over a week's time, his Georgians, Mississippians, and Carolinians held their ground, "driving the enemy back," as Stuart recorded, "on every occasion." Having served his apprenticeship, Stuart's newest lieutenant was improving steadily in his adopted arm.[19]

Munford was the next to become engaged. On the eighth, he drove three regiments of cavalry, with artillery support, out of Poolesville following spirited fighting that cost his brigade fifteen casualties but the opposition much more. Desultory skirmishing occupied Robertson's old command up to the eleventh, when the advancing Yankees persuaded Stuart to recall Munford to within a few miles of Frederick.

Mounting pressure forced Lee's brigade to fall back as well. To straighten his line and to conform its movements to those of the main army, whose rear he must protect at all hazards, Stuart pulled both Lee and Hampton back to Frederick. By the twelfth, he supposed that Jackson had captured Harpers Ferry—attackers could render the garrison helpless simply by occupying the mountains that surrounded it. But Stuart was wrong: The place would not surrender until early on the fifteenth. Fortunately, he considered it his duty to cover the mountain passes as long as he could do so without risk of being overwhelmed by the steadily arriving Federals.

On the twelfth, Stuart fell back west of Frederick to plug the gaps that must be denied to McClellan. He detached from Hampton's command Will Martin, who, with his Jeff Davis Legion and two guns, loaded up the pass that conveyed the National Road—the country's first major internal improvement—through the Catoctins from Frederick. Next day the rest of Hampton's brigade joined the lieutenant colonel in the gap. Farther south, Stuart had Munford—who commanded only two of his five regiments on this day, the others being on detached service block the Catoctin pass that led to Jefferson.[20]

Meanwhile, Stuart sent Fitz Lee, still holding the cavalry's left, to loop around McClellan's upper flank and ascertain the exact nature of the Union movement. Stuart was not sure whether Little Mac intended to burst through the passes and take on both Longstreet and Jackson, or to attempt some sort of end run. No doubt Stuart was surprised by the suddenly swift advance of the Union forces, especially given the lethargic pace they had adhered to while the cavalry camped near Urbana. Stuart did not yet know that on this day, the thirteenth, an errant copy of Lee's campaign orders, disclosing not only his intentions but also the location of each of his forces, had fallen into enemy hands. Henceforth, McClellan would push for the mountain passes with renewed vigor, hoping to clear them quickly, that he might fall on each of Lee's wings before they could reunite.[21]

If Stuart and his subordinates had their way, Little Mac would go nowhere very fast. Early on the thirteenth, the Yankees renewed the attack on Colonel

Martin that had begun the night before. With the support of other elements of Hampton's brigade, especially the 1st North Carolina, Martin thrust back the attackers, then settled down to an artillery duel. Stuart was pleased to observe that Hart's battery, despite its newness to mounted service, unleashed a fire "so effective that the enemy's battery was forced several times to change its position." Only after the Federals were substantially reinforced—Stuart believed they brought up two full brigades—did Martin, Hart, and their supports fall back into the valley beyond. Stuart duly informed his superiors of the withdrawal even as he prepared to defend the South Mountain gorges.[22]

The timely information allowed infantry to block the gaps as well. By the time Hampton's brigade reached South Mountain, the division of D. H. Hill had taken possession of Turner's Gap, which gave access to Boonsboro. On the fourteenth, heavy fighting swirled around and through that pass, as portions of McClellan's I and IX Corps attacked there, as well as at adjacent Fox's Gap. Eventually the Yankees bulled their way through, but Hill held on to the last, buying time for Lee to regroup farther west in the event he had to accept battle.[23]

Throughout his fight, Hill received little assistance from Stuart. Although he supplied the infantry commander with useful intelligence on the positions and movements of the approaching Federals, the cavalry leader decided to head south before the fight began to assist another infantry force in blocking Crampton's Gap, near Burkittsville.

Stuart's decision to abandon Turner's Gap would generate controversy among the officer corps of the A.N.V. His reasoning, however, is both understandable and defensible. Stuart had expected that Fitz Lee, via his reconnaissance into the rear of the Union army, would gain enough insight into McClellan's intentions to show the cavalry how best to respond. Instead, when he rejoined Stuart at Boonsboro, west of South Mountain, late on the fourteenth, Fitz reported his failure to make sense of McClellan's movements.

With only his instincts to guide him, Stuart decided that the narrow, rocky defile at Turner's was "no place for cavalry operations." On the other hand, Crampton's Gap, through which the enemy could move against Jackson at Harpers Ferry, was "now the weakest point" in the Confederate defense line. The cavalryman had come to regard protecting Jackson as his primary duty, at least at this juncture.[24]

Therefore, on the morning of the fourteenth, after leaving Martin's legion near Turner's Gap, he led the rest of Hampton's brigade and Pelham's guns to Crampton's Gap, "which I had reason to believe was as much threatened as any other." On his way to the lower pass, where Stuart had previously stationed Munford's demibrigade, Hampton met opposition from two regiments of Yankee horsemen. At the brigadier's order, Lieutenant Colonel Young, backed by Capt. Gilbert J. Wright, led Cobb's Legion in a charge that chased away the 8th Illinois and 3rd Indiana. Young inflicted more than thirty casualties but suffered some in turn; he himself fell wounded. Greater losses nearly befell Hampton's brigade soon afterward, when Munford, in advance of the gap, mistook the approaching Confederates for the enemy. Only a hastily fashioned truce flag enabled Hampton to approach without being fired on.[25]

When Stuart reached the defile, the Federals had yet to draw opposite in heavy force. Making another quick decision that would leave him open to second-guessing, he left Munford at Crampton's and rode south with Hampton, heading for the Potomac. He was acting now from a concern that McClellan might bypass the gaps altogether and move directly to the relief of Harpers Ferry.

Near the river, Stuart conferred with the area commander, Maj. Gen. Lafayette McLaws, whose division of Longstreet's wing was assisting Jackson by occupying strategic Maryland Heights. Stuart, who recalled the neighborhood from his 1859 service against John Brown, directed McLaws's attention to an unguarded road leading north from Harpers Ferry to the village of Sharpsburg. But the warning went unheeded, and a few hours later the cavalry portion of the doomed garrison—some thirteen hundred officers and troopers—used that byway to depart the area and escape Jackson's clutches.[26]

_ The instincts that led Stuart to the Potomac may have been sound, but his timing was off. He was still near Harpers Ferry when, late in the day, the advance of the VI Corps, Army of the Potomac, attacked Crampton's Gap. Colonel Munford, for a time the ranking defender, made maximum use of his minimal resources. At the outset, he held the pass with few troops besides his own 2nd and 12th Virginia, whose men Stuart praised for behaving under fire "with commendable coolness and gallantry." By creative scrambling, the colonel staved off disaster and purchased time for McLaws to rush forces to the scene from his own division and that of Maj. Gen. R. H. Anderson. Fighting occupied the balance of the day, with the Yankees eventually bursting through the gap, but too late to lift Jackson's siege.[27]

Stuart, with Hampton's brigade, was himself too late. Arriving just after dark, he found the battle over and McLaws and Anderson thrust into the valley to the west. The principal fighting along South Mountain had ended, having cost approximately eighteen hundred Union and twenty-seven hundred Confederate casualties. The disparity was a telling indication of the outcome. And yet Jackson had been given the time he needed to stamp out resistance at Harpers Ferry, and Lee the time he needed to assume a defensive position near Sharpsburg. "Marse Robert" was preparing for a confrontation that would determine how much longer his army would remain apart from Virginia.

>─┤◄►─O─◄►┤─◄

On the sixteenth, Stuart rode back to Harpers Ferry for a brief interview with Old Stonewall. Afterward, he headed north in a hurry. Leaving Hampton's men behind to assist McLaws, he led Lee's and Munford's brigades to join Lee and Longstreet outside Sharpsburg. Arriving late that morning on the field of imminent battle, the cavalryman found Longstreet's men drawn up east of the meandering Potomac and west of Antietam Creek. On the opposite side of the creek, they were confronted by a swiftly growing force of Yankees. Stuart observed that those forces on the right of McClellan's line were advancing against Longstreet's left. They were moving along a road that ran past a whitewashed building used as a church by members of a German sect known to native-born Americans as "Dunkers."

Reporting to Lee, Stuart informed him of Jackson's belated success at Harpers Ferry and disclosed that many of Stonewall's troops were already on the road to Sharpsburg. Then Stuart repaired to the front to monitor the progress of the fighting that had broken out around the Dunker Church. The tempo of combat alternately rose and fell before guttering out toward nightfall. Stuart correctly surmised that the action had been a prelude to what would occur once both armies reached the field in force.[28]

During and after the skirmishing, Stuart busied himself with reconnaissance and with shifting his troops into position along the Confederate left. Troopers and horse artillerymen moved farther and farther northward, as Longstreet's infantry, followed by Jackson's, filled in the gaps along the army's front. By daybreak on the seventeenth, Lee's line stretched for more than four miles. There were still spaces to be filled, however, and Lee was hopeful they would close up before his men became heavily engaged. With McLaws's and Anderson's infantry and Hampton's horsemen still somewhere in Pleasant Valley, and with the "Light Division" of A. P. Hill at Harpers Ferry taking the paroles of eleven thousand captured Yankees, only two-thirds of the Army of Northern Virginia was on the ground. By contrast, the Army of the Potomac appeared to be at full strength and eager for the fray.

When the fighting resumed early on the seventeenth, it quickly rose to white heat, and just as quickly expanded. It began opposite Lee's left, as Joseph Hooker's I Corps moved into attack positions north and east of Stuart's sector. Later, the locus of combat shifted south as other Federal units—committed piecemeal in furtherance of a confused, disjointed offensive—struck the center of the Rebel line and finally its right. This was the choreography of the bloodiest *danse macabre* in American history: By day's end, 12,400 attackers and 13,700 defenders would be dead, wounded, or missing.[29]

With the first hint of dawn on the seventeenth, Stuart was ready to do his part to throw back the aggressors. He would do so, however, with the support of few of his troopers. The greater portion of Fitz Lee's brigade had been placed near Stuart's field headquarters on the northern end of the battlefield, but it was not committed until late in the fighting. This was fortunate, for the command had recently experienced rough handling. On the morning of the fifteenth, as Longstreet's infantry passed through Boonsboro heading southwestward, Fitz's riders had guarded the army's rear en route to Sharpsburg. About noon, McClellan's advance reached the outskirts of Boonsboro and challenged Lee's brigade with troops of all arms. While most of its comrades continued on, Rooney Lee's 9th Virginia faced about and launched a preemptive attack.[30]

In the melee that ensued, Fitz's cousin was seriously injured when his mount stopped a minié ball and threw him; afterward, his men were pushed back steadily. As Capt. William Carter of the 3rd Virginia explained, "The enemy pressing, we charged him twice, but owing to . . . the advantage the enemy had gained by our too long delay in the town, and their introduction of Sharpshooters, we were repulsed & fell back with considerable loss to our Brigade." Despite the absence of Rooney Lee, who was now in the hands of the surgeons, the 9th managed to outdistance the Yankees and suffered no further molestation on the road to Sharpsburg.[31]

On the seventeenth, while Fitz Lee guarded the left, Stonewall Jackson's part of the line, Munford's abbreviated brigade, anchored the opposite end, below the town. There it helped protect Longstreet's flank against fitful, morning-long advances by Ambrose Burnside's IX Corps. With Hampton absent, no cavalry was available to shore up the center or rear of the line.

For the better part of the day, as wave after wave of blue-clad troops advanced in his general direction, Stuart served—as he had on other fields—as an artillery commander. Lee had entrusted to him control of fourteen cannons, including some mounted artillery pieces. Stuart had placed most of the guns atop a ridge known as Nicodemus Heights. The position was not as lofty as its name would suggest; still, it commanded a wide expanse of ground in its front. The ridge enabled Stuart to pour a vicious enfilade into the right of Brig. Gen. Abner Doubleday's division of Hooker's corps as it advanced down the Hagerstown Pike shortly after daybreak. The fire from the heights proved so destructive that Jackson sent a brigade of foot soldiers to provide Stuart close support. He wanted no one to force the fourteen guns to desist.[32]

Hooker, however, made a valiant attempt to do so. Ultimately, he assigned nearly half the guns attached to his corps the task of neutralizing Stuart. But whenever hard-pressed, the general simply hauled his guns—which, thanks to continual additions, eventually numbered nineteen—to less vulnerable but equally advantageous positions. The fire that Stuart drew wounded several of Fitz Lee's troopers. One of them, Lieutenant Colonel Thornton of the 3rd Virginia—a man of letters as well as of war, and one of the most devout soldiers in a heavily Christian army—had his arm shattered by a shell fragment, from the effects of which he died early the next day.[33]

Late in the morning, Stuart used his growing artillery force to cover a series of counterattacks. His guns lay down a barrage that helped force into retreat not only elements of Hooker's command, but also II and XII Corps units in and near the so-called West Woods. By the time Stuart was through, so was the assault on the Confederate left. His shelling had likewise taken a heavy toll farther south, one result being that McClellan's offensive against Lee's center had begun to falter.[34]

Sometime after noon, Stuart's immediate superior, Jackson, devised a counterattack that would return Stuart to cavalry command. Stonewall envisioned a sweeping movement by Lee's horsemen around the Union right, while farther to the south, infantry advanced against some battered but still-dangerous Yankees who held a key part of the field. The intent was to squeeze the enemy in a pincerlike grip. At Jackson's order, Stuart collected seven mounted regiments, including the few under Munford. Jackson added to the column a regiment of infantry, and R. E. Lee supplied it with additional cannons, giving Stuart a grand total of twenty-one. With this mixed force, he was to move north and then east around McClellan's right, held by the all-but-fought-out soldiers of the I Corps—now led by Brig. Gen. George Gordon Meade, Hooker having been wounded.

If Stuart anticipated capping off the day by strong-arming Meade's men into oblivion, penetrating to McClellan's rear, and stampeding his reserves, he was doomed to disappointment. No sooner had he started forward, about 2:00 P.M., than he found his way blocked by hastily constructed breastworks on fields owned by a farmer named Poffenberger. These defenses not only were manned by vigilant troops, but also were supported in rear by thirty-four artillery pieces on a ridge more elevated than Nicodemus Heights. Hoping against hope, Stuart laid down another barrage, but it was not enough: Most of his guns were silenced in less than a half an hour. Throughout that period, the infantry continued to hammer away, too; one volley struck Stuart's horse, just missing its rider. Eventually, to the chagrin of Jackson and the infantry subordinate who was to cooperate with Stuart, the cavalry leader called off the advance and returned his column to its former position.[35]

While Stuart's decision disappointed everyone involved, it did not mean that the day was lost. Less than an hour after his column returned from the Poffenberger farm, McClellan began his final offensive, hurling Burnside's troops against the Confederate right. After a series of costly delays, the IX Corps crossed the Antietam under fire at Rohrbach Bridge, then drove toward the thinnest, most vulnerable sector of Lee's line. The time lost to getting over the stream proved fatal when most of A. P. Hill's division, just up from Harpers Ferry after a killing march, arrived at the critical moment to nail down the flank. When Hill forced the IX Corps back across the stream, McClellan called it a day. His vacillation and irresolution had combined with a murky plan of battle to grant his enemy a strategic draw, one secured at a truly horrific cost in human suffering.[36]

>━◀▸━○━◀▸━◄

Robert E. Lee could console himself that, tactically at least, he had won a victory along Antietam Creek. On the other hand, with his army on unfamiliar soil and with a major river at its back, he could not afford to stay in Maryland much longer. He remained on the field for most of the eighteenth, wondering if he could afford to renew the fight. His men appreciated the show of spirit and believed the enemy quailed before it. As one of Fitz Lee's officers put it, "Day breaks, the Sun rises. Here stands the Army of Northern Va.—defiant. There stands the Army of the Potomac irresolute."[37]

In the end, defiance gave way to sober reflection; by midday Lee had come to admit that the risks he would incur by shifting to the offensive outweighed the potential benefits. Another day of bloodletting, even if the enemy got much the worst of it, would end as it had begun—with a massive army in his front and a water barrier in his rear. That evening he began to withdraw, crossing into Virginia at and near Shepherdstown. His first attempt to give the citizens of the North a close-up view of war was over.[38]

Many of his officers and men were quite willing to leave. They had entered Maryland to the cheers and well wishes of the populace, but no one mourned their departure. While some sections had provided the army with foodstuffs, remounts, and a few recruits, the state as a whole had turned out to be an inhospitable place. This was hard enough to take, but the obvious fact that the army was going home earlier than expected made for unhappy memories and bitter feelings. One of Munford's troopers summed up the sentiments of many comrades when he wrote his sister from Shepherdstown: "I never want to go back again. I would like to go through into Pennsylvania but I don't want to stop in Maryland five minutes longer than I can help."[39]

As the outset of the retreat, Stuart bore up better than most. He carried the vivid memory of a performance that had won him the plaudits of superiors and colleagues alike. Additionally, he was kept busy throughout the operation, leaving him little or no time to brood over lost opportunities or ponder the might-have-beens.

Ensuring the success of the withdrawal was a variegated operation. While Fitz Lee's men guarded the army's fording sites, Stuart, with Munford's regiments and Hampton's recently returned brigade, crossed at another ford, rode downstream, and splashed back to the Maryland side, thus creating a diversion in favor of the main army. Stuart carried out the majority of his assignment after dark, which made both fording operations difficult, as well as more than a little risky. Yet the only danger occurred when some of Hampton's riders wandered into high water and had to swim for their lives.[40]

The recrossing, near Williamsport, was accomplished in two columns, Hampton fording above the town and a portion of Munford's command trooping through its streets. With the assistance of two infantry regiments and some light artillery loaned him for the occasion, Stuart took position on high ground beyond Williamsport and dared the enemy to make him leave. No one did; he remained along the river, making "active demonstrations" in the enemy's direction, until the evening of the twentieth. That night, after dark, the rest of the army having made good its escape into the lower Shenandoah Valley, Stuart leapfrogged his troops to and across the river.

Looking back on the campaign just ended, the cavalry could be proud of the work it had accomplished under almost uniformly adverse conditions. As Colonel Munford put it in his postaction report, "In Maryland we lived on green corn, principally, for both men and horses, and our [Catoctin] valley campaign

was one of constant toil." Stuart summed it up in greater detail and more elo-
quent prose:

> My command did not suffer on any one day as much as their com-
> rades of other arms, but theirs was the sleepless watch and the harass-
> ing daily *petit guerre*. . . . There was not a single day, from the time
> my command crossed the Potomac until it recrossed that it was not
> engaged with the enemy, and at Sharpsburg was several times sub-
> jected to severe shelling. Their services were indispensable to every
> success attained.

In brief, if the campaign had fallen short of hopes and expectations, it was
not the fault of the officers and troopers of the Cavalry Division, A.N.V.[41]

Chapter Eleven

Romance and Real Life

L ee may have wanted out of Maryland, but his opponent saw no reason to
go. For the next six weeks, McClellan remained above the Potomac, resting and refitting his command and busying himself with the myriad things a
man attends to when he wishes to put off something more disagreeable. To Lee,
of course, the respite was providential. The battle of the seventeenth had taken a
fearful toll, and he needed time to attempt a restoration. He spent the rest of
September and most of October reorganizing, tending to personnel losses, and
securing rations and forage in the Valley, while countering the advances of
those few elements of McClellan's command that displayed any desire to return
to Virginia.

Throughout that period, Stuart's men, when not resupplying, devoted
themselves to picket duty and reconnaissance. The cavalry's line of operations
ran south from Martinsburg to the area around Charles Town, where John
Brown was hanged, a distance of almost ten miles. Stuart made his headquarters on the southern end of the line, he and his staff residing at the Bower, the
spacious plantation of the Dandridge family. The Dandridges, being gracious
hosts, supplied their guests with every creature comfort: platters of veal and
capon, trays of mint juleps, and the company of attractive daughters, sons,
nieces, and nephews. They made some of the area's finest blooded stock available for Stuart's riding pleasure, and a hunting range furnished Wade Hampton,
Heros von Borcke, and other outdoorsmen with hours of diversion. At times,
Stuart felt he was vacationing rather than waging cruel war. Blackford considered the month he spent at the Bower "the most remarkable combination of
romance and real life that it had ever been my fortune to encounter."[1]

Growing concerned that he was hoarding all the merriment, Stuart decided
to share, sending his newly acquired banjoist Sam Sweeney and the other musicians to army headquarters to serenade General Lee. Stuart, who accompanied
the pipers and fiddlers, joined the commander's staff in a songfest around their
campfire. For a time, Lee remained in his tent, although it was evident he appreciated the music. In his absence, one of his officers produced a jug of "fine old

rye" and passed it around. Everyone but Stuart partook of the refreshment, which at some point was offered to the players as well. Thereafter their music took on a peculiar tone, whereupon Lee joined the party. With a curious smile he surveyed the scene, then asked: "Gentlemen, am I to thank General Stuart or the jug for this fine music?"[2]

On other occasions, Stuart visited Bunker Hill, headquarters of Stonewall Jackson. Their many differences of style and personality made the two men the oddest of couples, but they seemed happy in each other's company. Stuart, and no one else, was able to make the dour Calvinist smile, whether by presenting him with a spanking new uniform to replace his worn, rumpled suit of cadet gray or by making Jackson the butt of practical jokes.

One example of Stuart's humor made the rounds of his command, to everyone's glee. Early one evening, the cavalryman arrived at Jackson's tent to find his friend fast asleep. Without removing his boots, Stuart crawled into bed with his unwitting host and fought him for the covers until dawn. Upon waking, he stole out of the tent while Jackson continued to snooze. Later Stonewall awoke to find his visitor seated around the headquarters' fire. Stuart, who supposed that his friend had been dead to the world throughout the night, inquired with a grin if he had slept well. Jackson paused a minute, as if trying to recall, before declaring that he had. Seating himself beside the fire, he allowed that he was always glad to see Stuart, even though the cavalryman kept strange hours. With a twinkle in his tiny blue eyes, Jackson added: "But General, you must not get into my bed with your boots and spurs on and ride me around like a cavalry horse all night."[3]

The good times at the Bower included amateur theatricals performed by an officer with some comedic talent, Tiernan Brien of the 1st Virginia, and the sometimes outrageous Major von Borcke. The "amusing series of scenes" the pair enacted in the Dandridges' parlor for the entertainment of Stuart, his staff, their hosts, and family friends never failed to amuse the audience and sometimes sent it into hysterics. On one occasion Brien, decked out in spectacles, swallowtail coat, and stovepipe hat, portrayed a physician, while von Borcke, his considerable girth enlarged with the aid of several pillows stuffed inside his tunic, played a patient sickened by overeating. After the sufferer enumerated, in his thick accent, what he had consumed ("beef, venison, oysters, cabbage, etc."), the doctor appeared to thrust his hand down the man's throat.

Blackford described what followed: "With great effort of muscular power expended in jerks and tugs, [Brien] pulls out in succession, and holds up for inspection, a pair of deer's horns, some beef's horns, cabbages, stalks and all, quantities of oyster shells, etc., etc., and finally a pair of boots." Suddenly relieved of his suffering, the epicure springs from his couch and grabs his healer in a bear hug. The performance "closes in an uproarious dance of doctor and patient." Years later, the tableau still coaxed a chuckle from Blackford, who recalled that "its effect on the audience was convulsive."[4]

On another occasion when the Dandridges entertained, the same actors performed, this time in even more outlandish attire. Brien appeared before the audience as an Irishman in sporting clothes, with billycock hat, pipe, and walking stick. On his arm was a vision of loveliness standing six feet, two and a half inches tall and weighing 250 pounds. With the aid of Mrs. Dandridge and her daughters, von Borcke had been transformed into "a blushing maiden," who smiled coquettishly at the man she adored. A floor-length hoop skirt concealed knee-top cavalry boots, while pillows expanded von Borcke's "naturally ample bosom." His arms fairly dripped with Dandridge family jewelry, his face was hidden beneath layers of powder and rouge, and his hair hung in braids from beneath a fetching "love bonnet." Again Blackford narrated: "Paddy entertained the fair girl on his arm with loud and humorous remarks as they sauntered about the room, to which she replied with a simpering affectation that was irresistibly ludicrous."

On cue, the musicians launched into a waltz, "and round and round the couple went, faster and faster went the music, and faster and faster flew the strangers." According to Stuart's engineer, von Borcke's disguise was so complete that not until he whirled about, "with hoop skirts flying horizontally" did his well-known boots give away his identity. Then, as suddenly as the couple had appeared, "they vanished, waltzing out through the open door and followed by convulsive roars of laughter from the delighted audience." Stuart was positively overcome; hugging the massive Prussian, he declared that von Borcke's "appearance as a woman would never fade from [his] memory."[5]

>-+-<>-O-<>-+-<

When October arrived, life at the Bower lost some of its jollity, at least for a time. Late on the afternoon of the first, about seven hundred Yankee cavalrymen under Brig. Gen. Alfred Pleasonton crossed the Potomac opposite Shepherdstown and attacked the nearest outposts. Showing their growing aggressiveness, the Yankees penetrated deep inside Fitz Lee's sector near Martinsburg—temporarily under the control of Rooney Lee, Fitz having been disabled by a mule kick. Of necessity, Stuart and his staff departed their little paradise and hastened to the front. Blackford observed that their hostesses gave way to "consternation and tears, but we assured them it would soon be over and that we would not all be killed."[6]

He was right on both counts. Stuart, fire in his eyes, pounded off for Martinsburg but got there too late. Arriving early in the evening, he discovered, as a member of the 1st Virginia put it, "the enemy leaving on one side as we entered on the other." Soon afterward, Pleasonton's men began to recross the river. The Confederates hastened them along, killing a few and taking several prisoners, Stuart "leading his men with great gallantry and inspiring confidence and enthusiasm wherever he went." Another unpleasant but necessary job attended to, he returned to the Dandridge estate for a new round of balls, parties, and parlor games.[7]

The return of happy hours lasted only a week. On the sixth, General Lee called his Beau Sabreur to army headquarters for a consultation, and on the

PP
raid

eighth, he approved a plan proposed by Stuart for a raid designed to damage McClellan's communications. Little Mac's principal supply line reached into south-central Pennsylvania via a railroad bridge outside the town of Chambersburg. If Stuart thought it practicable, he should head in that direction. Beyond inflicting what damage he could in Little Mac's rear, he was to supply Lee with as much intelligence as possible on the strength and dispositions of McClellan's outposts. He was also to procure cavalry horses and draft animals, shortages of which were becoming epidemic in Virginia. Already elements of Hampton's brigade were serving apart from the main body, hunting for remounts in the countryside above Richmond. As always, troopers from each brigade in Stuart's command were away from the army, seeking to replace injured or worn-out steeds from their family stables. Finally, Stuart should take hostages—Pennsylvania officials to be used as barter for the release of Confederate sympathizers jailed in the North.[8]

By the time Stuart returned from his second meeting with Lee, his camps were abuzz with rumors of a raid—somewhere. The grapevine went into high gear after Stuart called together his ranking subordinates for a briefing. Attendees included Hampton and Rooney Lee; other invitations may have gone to Tom Rosser, M. C. Butler, Williams Wickham, and Grumble Jones, who had temporarily replaced Munford at the head of the Laurel Brigade. For some reason, Munford was on detached duty at Leesburg with his 2nd Virginia. One month hence, Jones would be promoted to brigadier general and as such would assume permanent command of the brigade. The situation pleased neither Stuart, who was finding it increasingly difficult to remain on civil terms with the man, nor Munford, who, having been senior to Jones when both were colonels, resented being passed over by him. Robert E. Lee, however, had confidence in Jones as an administrator and a field leader and believed that his problems with Stuart would work themselves out. Lee also believed that in due course, Munford's abilities would win him the wreathed stars he coveted. The army leader was wrong on both counts.[9]

It is not known how much of Lee's plan Stuart imparted to his lieutenants. It is unlikely that he publicized every restraint his superior had placed on the expedition, including this one: "It is not intended or desired that you should jeopardize the safety of your command, or go farther than your good judgment and prudence may dictate." Stuart's superior recalled how he had exceeded his orders on the Chickahominy Raid, in the process risking the lives of twelve hundred men. Of course, that expedition had ended in spectacular success, but Lee believed this had been achieved in spite of, rather than because of, Stuart's daring.[10]

Another restriction Lee had imposed was that Stuart take with him no more than fifteen hundred officers and men, fearing that a larger force would not only impede his progress, but also deprive the army of too many pickets and scouts. Stuart, however, did not agree. In contrast to his usual tendency to take the minimum number needed for a job, he selected for the expedition three brigades, plus four guns under Pelham and Hart, a total of eighteen hundred troopers and artillerymen.

While his subordinates rounded up men and horses, Stuart repaired to his tent to finish some paperwork. Even so, he found time to make merry—twice. As Channing Price noted, "We had a pleasant time, music and dancing, until 11 o'clock, then returned to our tents, the General finished up all his business, and about one o'clock we got the music (violin, banjo, and bones) and gave a farewell serenade to the ladies of the Bower."[11]

Due to the lateness of the evening's entertainment, Stuart and his staff slept in the next morning. They could afford to, for this day would be devoted to moving into position to cross the Potomac. Close to noon, Stuart, accompanied by some of his staff, trotted north to Darkesville, where he picked up Jones's brigade. From there he rode to Hedgesville, where Hampton's men were in camp; en route he picked up Fitz Lee's troopers, still commanded by Cousin Rooney.

Arriving at the rendezvous at Hedgesville, not far from McCoy's Ferry, where he planned to cross the Potomac, Stuart had everyone, including Pelham's crews, gather round as his aides read copies of an address he had composed. They were all about to embark on a momentous enterprise that required the utmost "coolness, decision and bravery; implicit obedience to orders without question or cavil, and the strictest order and sobriety on the march and in bivouac." The objective of the mission "had better be kept to myself than known to you," a precaution that started the rumor mill churning once more. One trooper reported that "1001 conjectures were made as to what was the object of the scout, and where we were going to turn up. Some said one thing, and some said another until in the confusion of opinions and ideas the mystery was made deeper and deeper and the excitement grew higher."

A clue to their destination was offered by a list of prohibitions that staff officers also read to the assembled: Officers and men were at all times "to respect public and private property not earmarked for destruction." To the more discerning listeners, that sounded as if they were bound for enemy territory— Maryland, to be sure, and probably the country beyond. The announcements done, the men were released and permitted to bed down. Stuart and the staff roughed it along with the rank and file, sleeping on a straw rick fully exposed to the autumn weather.[12]

Before dawn the next morning, they were in the saddle, marching north through a dense fog that had drifted in over the river. When they neared McCoy's Ferry, an advance guard splashed across the stream and attacked the nearest Yankees, members of an Illinois cavalry regiment. To the accompaniment of carbine and pistol fire, the main body forded the Potomac. Upon reaching the Maryland side, it turned left toward the Pennsylvania line, eight miles off.

As they rode, Illinoisans who had escaped the clutches of the advance guard were heading inland with breathless and exaggerated word of the enemy's breakout. They inflated the size of the raiding column to twenty-five

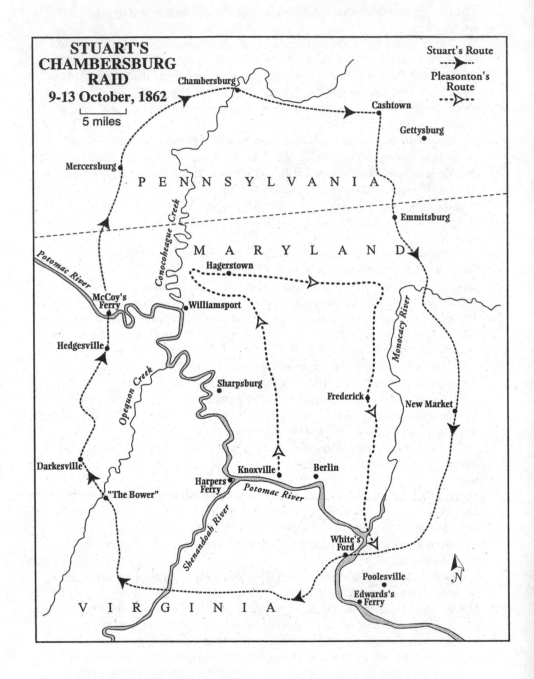

STUART'S CHAMBERSBURG RAID
9-13 October, 1862
5 miles

hundred men and eight guns, and reported it as moving toward Mercersburg, Pennsylvania. Had he known, Stuart would have smiled at the size of the force attributed to him, a product of the fog and fear-induced imagination. He would not, however, have been happy with the prediction about his heading, which was accurate. On the other hand, the direction taken by such a conspicuous body of riders could hardly be kept under wraps.[13]

About 8:00 A.M., west of Clear Spring, Maryland, the raiders crossed a familiar byway, the National Road, along which they surrounded and captured a signal station. From the prisoners taken there, Stuart learned that several regiments of Union infantry, along with two batteries, had passed through the area less than an hour before, heading west toward Hancock. Stuart was glad he had not encountered them, not because he could not have dealt with them effectively, but because he would have lost precious time. He calculated that within a few hours, McClellan would have initiated a full-scale pursuit; thereafter, troops of all arms would converge against him from a dozen or more widely separated points. The only way to avoid being overtaken by heavier numbers was to stay alert and keep moving.[14]

Two hours beyond Clear Spring, the column surged across the Pennsylvania border. Cheers and shouts greeted the momentous event and spread the news to the surrounding countryside. Staff officers took the opportunity to range along the line, reading additional orders aloud. The new announcements rang with some memorable phrases: "We are now in enemy country. Hold yourselves ready for attack or defense, and behave with no other thought than victory. If any man cannot abide cheerfully by the order and spirit of these instructions, he will be returned to Virginia with a guard of honor." But no one availed himself of the opportunity.[15]

Mercersburg, the first sizable village on the raiders' route, came into view at around noon. Members of the advance tore through its streets, putting the fear of God and J. E. B. Stuart into the residents but inflicting little physical damage. They did, however, use all available means to procure remounts. Before the raid ended, six hundred raiders were scouring lower Pennsylvania for animals that, if unsuited to cavalry service, could at least haul cannons or supply wagons. "It was really diverting," wrote Trooper Corson of the 3rd Virginia, "to see our fellows chasing the flying and frightened animals over the fields in every direction. We took them out of the stable, wagon, plough, threshing-machine and wherever we found them." Every plea to spare a favorite horse or team was rejected. When one farmer lodged an especially anguished protest, Stuart's aide Chiswell Dabney told him that "this was what we called making the solid [Union] men feel the war."[16]

When not securing remounts, the raiders papered local stores with Confederate currency in exchange for articles of equipment and clothing, especially boots and brogans. "Thousands of dollars worth of goods," Corson added, "were taken in the way of hats, boots, cloth &&. One man in the 3d regiment sold a piece of broadcloth after he got back for $155.00. . . . I took nothing but horses for I did not think it right, although the Yankees have treated our people much worse." Most looters met no resistance from the frightened townspeople. "The citizens stood by looking on without saying a word," recalled a member of the 9th Virginia, "and if ever I saw wonder & surprise mingled with fear depicted upon the countenances of any one I certainly saw it upon . . . the citizens of Pa."[17]

While at Mercersburg, Stuart, concerned that the local telegraph had already spread word of his coming, briefly considered aborting the raid. After conferring with his subordinates, he chided himself for his temporary weakness and led onward toward Chambersburg. En route he was relieved to observe that no roadblocks, human or inanimate, slowed his pace. Evidently, not even the telegraph could keep pace with his column.

Shortly after 7:00 P.M., the vanguard of the raiding force neared Chambersburg. The night was pitch dark as well as wet, the result of a moonless sky and a sudden shower. The point riders approached with understandable wariness. Wade Hampton, whose brigade had the advance, feared that the locals were expecting them and perhaps had set a trap. To find out, he sent his most trusted subordinate, now-Col. M. C. Butler, with a detail of twenty-five men from a recent addition to the brigade, the 2nd South Carolina, under a truce flag to demand the town's surrender. Hampton and Butler breathed more easily when a delegation of terrified citizens came forth to ask the terms being proposed. "Unconditional surrender," replied Hampton, who promised that the residents' possessions—excepting, of course, those items of military utility—would be protected. The city fathers acceded—they had no choice—and by 8:00 the main body of the 1st Brigade was safely ensconced in Chambersburg, where it had established a "rigid provost guard."[18]

Soon after, Stuart rode into town to inspect Hampton's dispositions and anoint his subordinate "military governor" for the duration of their stay. Then he sent every available member of the brigade to search for provender. Hampton's men responding by cleaning out dozens of mercantile establishments and opening bank vaults and drawers. The latter effort fell short of expectations; in anticipation of the raiders' arrival, local bankers had spirited away those assets that were truly mobile. Stuart and Hampton fared only slightly better in their search for potential hostages. For a time, they were frustrated to find that "no one would admit he held office in the place." In the end, through careful interviewing, Stuart identified a few minor officials, whom he placed in the custody of Butler's provost guards, to the consternation of the citizens and their families.[19]

The main portion of the raiding force, which had bivouacked on the edge of town, was kept just as busy. Details of ten to twenty men visited outlying farms, where they gathered up horses and mules, as well as wagonloads of foodstuffs and forage. Stuart assigned Jones's brigade an even more vital task, the demolition of the railroad bridge over Conococheague Creek. The raiding leader was deeply chagrined when his subordinate returned late in the day to report his mission unaccomplished. Jones had not even reached the bridge, which he mistakenly believed had been constructed almost wholly of wrought iron and thus impervious to matches, axes, and other agents of destruction.[20]

Stuart assuaged his disappointment by ransacking some government warehouses at the edge of town. These provided his ill-clad troopers with huge quantities of hats and caps, overcoats, tunics, trousers, boots, and shoes, as well as five thousand rifles and almost as many sabers and pistols, none of which had seen service. Glad to gain additional protection against the October winds, the Confederates hardly minded that their new attire came in a single color—blue.[21]

So clothed, the raiders may have slept more comfortably than usual on that raw, rainy evening. Yet not even new clothing could ensure everyone of a good night's sleep. "We were soaked to the skin," wrote a sergeant in the 10th Virginia, whose company had bivouacked in a farmer's field, "& had to lie down in puddles of water." Stuart at least kept dry, stretching out on the floor of a highway tollhouse surrounded by his staff.[22]

Hours later, he awoke stiff and sore, but he felt better after a hasty breakfast and a return to the saddle. Placing himself at the head of the reassembled column, he led the way out of town under the continuing rain. The citizenry watched him go with almost audible relief. The gray line headed east toward Cashtown and, eight miles beyond, Gettysburg. The choice of direction surprised most of the raiders. It had become apparent to all that Chambersburg had been their destination all along; now, their business in the town done, they had expected to head home the way they had come. Few had suspected that for the second time in four months, Stuart was about to encircle the Army of the Potomac.

The general had his reasons. As he explained to William Blackford shortly after leaving Chambersburg, the regiments they had evaded on the National Road probably had countermarched to block the return route. By now, too, other forces, including McClellan's ever-improving cavalry, undoubtedly were in the hunt; if the raiders backtracked, there would be a collision. Even the detail at McCoy's Ferry would have been strengthened, perhaps substantially, by this time. Conversely, by marching south from Cashtown, they would cross territory where no one would know to look for them. They could return to the Potomac well downriver from McCoy's Ferry, where a large selection of fords—too many to be guarded individually—would be available to them. Blackford wholeheartedly concurred with his superior's reasoning; moreover, he felt privileged that Stuart had explained it to him personally.[23]

As the main body of the column cleared Chambersburg, the rear guard put an exclamation point to the sojourn in Pennsylvania. Lieutenant Price watched as parties of picked men set fire to "all the public property (machine shops, depots, 5 or 6,000 stand of arms, etc.)," goods Stuart lacked the time to carry off but which he was determined to deny to the enemy.

The first leg of the homeward march passed smoothly. Debouching from the South Mountain Gaps, the raiders reached Cashtown without difficulty.

There they veered sharply south, via Fairfield, toward the Maryland border. As they neared the presumed location of McClellan's rear echelon, Stuart grew more cautious and security tightened up. Once in Maryland, his point riders took into custody every traveler they met on the road, lest he be a Union sympathizer intent on sounding an alarm or, worse, a spy.[24]

Before night came on, the column reached Emmitsburg. There Stuart stopped over for a while to partake of the local hospitality, which was abundant. In this pro-Confederate enclave, townspeople offered him and his staff food and drink, watered and fed their horses, even stole buttons off their blouses for souvenirs.

When he finally pried himself away, Stuart angled toward the southwest, as though heading for Frederick. His outriders had captured a Yankee courier whose documents indicated that troops under Burnside had recently moved in that direction. At a certain point, having thrown off any pursuers, Stuart returned to his original route, which ran through Rocky Ridge, Woodsboro, Liberty, New London, and New Market, each being well east of Frederick. The itinerary had been compiled by some of the same scouts who had guided Stuart on his first trip across the enemy's rear; a couple were natives of this very region.[25]

That evening, the column passed through Hyattstown, only a few miles south of Urbana, which had hosted pleasant times not so long ago. Recalling them, Stuart was suddenly overcome by the urge to visit a nearby friend. When nearly opposite Urbana, he hunted up Blackford and inquired: "How would you like to see the 'New York rebel' tonight?" At first a bit taken aback, the engineer officer replied that he would be delighted to renew acquaintances with the young woman and the family with whom she was staying.

While the column continued south toward the Potomac, Stuart, Blackford, and other aides left the column and galloped west. Sometime after midnight, they were knocking on a familiar door and equally familiar voices—those of Stuart's dance partner and several female friends—were making nervous inquiries from an upstairs bedroom. As soon as their visitors identified themselves, there came "a rush down stairs," Blackford recalled, "bolts and bars rattled and our lovely friends appeared in the moonlight, their kind faces beaming with pleasure." Stuart's party spent a half hour or so with the hostesses before tearing themselves away and returning to the column.[26]

Regaining his place in the marching order, Stuart saw that everyone was fighting fatigue, the inevitable result of hours of travel in the anticlimactic aftermath of Chambersburg. The corporate weariness only added to the dangers that lurked in the night. Confederate sympathizers along the route had alerted Stuart that nearly five thousand Yankees, mostly infantry under General Stoneman, were guarding the Potomac fords toward which the raiders were heading. Stuart had also heard that an unknown number of horsemen under Alfred Pleasonton were hot on his trail, although they had yet to put in an appearance.

As he covered the last dozen miles to the Potomac, Stuart reviewed his options for crossing. He considered, but rejected as too predictable, using the nearest ford, near the mouth of the Monocacy River. The enemy might also be watching the ford at Edwards's Ferry, eight miles farther south, expecting the raiders to give Stoneman's troops at the Monocacy a wide berth. After discarding that possibility as well, he decided to try to cross at some point in between, hoping to split the defense forces.

One of the scouts, a native of the area, suggested they make for little-used White's Ford. Stuart liked the idea and allowed the man to guide him toward that point, four miles above Edwards's Ferry. The raiders rode on, fighting to remain awake in the saddle, their nearly exhausted mounts straining to keep moving. Stuart, apparently tireless, kept glancing toward the flanks and rear, alert to signs of trouble.[27]

Those signs began to appear at about 8:00 A.M. on the twelfth. With White's Ford nearly in view, a small body of Pleasonton's cavalry appeared along a byroad from the northwest. Having followed Stuart's trail to and from Chambersburg, failing to overtake him by a few hours, the Yankees had redoubled their pace until within striking distance of the Confederate advance. Pleasonton commanded at least as many men as Stuart; if he could trap the raiders between his force and Stoneman's at the river, the odds would be heavily in the pursuers' favor.[28]

Pleasonton's only liability was his belief that his quarry was heading for a ford adjacent to the mouth of the Monocacy; thus he had positioned his main force in that area. Only a fraction of Pleasonton's command was near enough to challenge Stuart's, and it approached the Rebel column warily, tentatively—having flushed the game, the Federals were uncertain how to bag it.[29]

Stuart was aided not only by Pleasonton's timidity, but also by two almost simultaneous strokes of good fortune. When nearly to the head of the column, the Federals stopped short at the sight of the blue overcoats the raiders had donned. Wondering if they had contacted friend, not foe, the cavalry gave way to uncertainty and doubt. Other members of Pleasonton's force, who had wandered south toward the hamlet of Beallsville, encountered at some distance the head of an infantry column—one of Stoneman's brigades, under Brig. Gen. W. H. H. Ward. At first the cavalry took the foot soldiers—whom they had not known to be in the area—for Confederates attached to Stuart's column. In turn, the infantry stood staring at Pleasonton's horsemen, uncertain of their identity.[30]

While his opponents dithered, Stuart sent a squadron of the 1st Virginia under Capt. Charles Irving to charge Pleasonton's detachment. The bluecoats retreated before Irving could engage them, whereupon Stuart recalled the squadron and used it to build a defensive perimeter, which he bolstered with Pelham and two of his guns. Meanwhile, Stuart made for the river with the main body—everyone but the rear guard, under Colonel Butler, which, with the help of a single cannon, was fending off miscellaneous pursuers. By marching almost directly west to White's Ford, Stuart neatly interposed between Pleasonton on the Monocacy and Ward near Beallsville.

Rooney Lee, with six hundred picked men, rode ahead to the ford. He discovered that the opposite bank was patrolled by a thin cordon of pickets. Before Stuart and the main body could reach the river, however, several companies of a Pennsylvania infantry regiment of Stoneman's command materialized on a bluff across the Chesapeake and Ohio Canal from White's Ford. With time running out and the enemy closing in, Lee attempted to bluff his way across to safety. Under flag of truce, he send a harshly worded surrender demand to the infantry commander: Unless his men laid down their arms in fifteen minutes they would be attacked and overrun by thousands of Confederates who would give no quarter. When the time was up, Lee formed an assault column, but before he could lead it forward, his advance guard reported the opposite bluff suddenly free of enemy troops.[31]

With the way clear, the advance began to ford at White's. "We all made a rush for the river," wrote a member of Lee's regiment, "yet in regular order, the Regts. in front first . . . and succeeded in getting every one and every thing over." While the 9th Virginia crossed, Stuart drew in his flankers, including Pelham's cannons. Then the main body splashed across the stream: Jones's brigade, followed by Hampton's—all of it except the rear guard. Butler's band was extricated through the daring of Captain Blackford, who dashed between the enemy forces to the north and south, located the guard, and led it to the river only minutes before the defense forces converged across the road.

Blackford had told Butler: "When you reach the ford, hit the water at the gallop." The South Carolinian did, his men and their gun sending up an immense spray as they charged into and through the stream. Pelham's last piece, which against daunting odds had kept open the approach to the ford, swung into the water behind the rear guard, bullets from Yankee cavalry and infantry passing above the heads of its crew. On the far shore, the other members of the Stuart Horse Artillery covered the swimmers with a cannonade that, according to Blackford, "mitigated" the Yankee's barrage "considerably."[32]

Looking on from the Virginia side, Stuart, in unison with his troopers, cheered the rear guard's passage. The hairbreadth escape provided a perfect ending to a dashing enterprise conducted by daring men—during which not a single life had been lost, although great things had been accomplished every step of the way. It was, thought Stuart, one of those rare events that not only gave a boost to morale, but also helped raise warfare above the mud and the blood, the misery and the suffering, the horror and the violence.

Chapter Twelve

Unquiet on
the Rappahannock

L ike the Chickahominy Raid, Stuart's second circuit of the Army of the
Potomac caused a sensation in and outside the army. The participants were
virtually unanimous in declaring it, as a trooper in the 10th Virginia expressed
it, "one of the greatest raids on record." It had also been a feat of almost super-
human endurance: Stuart's men had marched more than 120 miles in three
days, the last eighty in a little over twenty-four hours.[1]

For most of the raiders, the expedition's accomplishments made their
recent ordeal worthwhile. Channing Price enumerated them in this way:

> 1000 or 1200 Horses (mostly suitable for Artillery), 30 or 40 Civil
> prisoners, about the same number of Soldiers & 300 or more Sick
> paroled in Chambersburg, the immense amount of property brought
> from Chambersburg in Clothing &c, & 1 million Dollars worth
> destroyed, and the moral effects which are great teaching the Pennsyl-
> vanians something of war, & showing how J. E. B. Stuart can make
> McClellan's circuit at [his] pleasure.

Stuart himself took pride in the combination of physical and psychological
effects. As he claimed in his after-action report, "The results of this expedition,
in a moral and political point of view, can barely be estimated, and the consternation among property holders in Pennsylvania beggars description."[2]

As they had been when commenting on his first raid, Stuart's enemies were
gracious in their assessment of the second. The editor and politician Alexander
K. McClure, who resided in Chambersburg—and barely escaped becoming a
hostage—admitted, "Our people were confounded with astonishment at the
brilliant audacity of the rebels penetrating twenty miles in Gen. McClellan's
rear." Although Northern newspapers devoted most of their coverage to the lax-
ity of the Army of the Potomac and the inertia of its leader, they could not
refrain from playing up the dash and nerve of the raiders.[3]

One of the few critical comments came from within Stuart's division. The adjutant of the 3rd Virginia, who had not taken part in it, called the undertaking another of Stuart's "foolish raids," in the course of which the general "broke down more [horses] than he secured." Another comment that can be construed as criticism came from a lieutenant in the 10th Virginia, who admitted that raids furnished "some excitement" to the parties involved but added, "I am getting a little tired of [them] . . . and prefer repose and quiet."[4]

Other participants may have felt as this man did but refrained from putting their comments on record. Wade Hampton, for one, probably agreed with the adjutant's assessment of raids as foolishness. The South Carolinian considered the great majority of expeditions to be glorified horse rides of little or no strategic importance. One cannot imagine him reasoning that the goods secured during the expedition, or the fear it had instilled in the hearts of Pennsylvanians, compensated for the fatigue, wear and tear, and danger Stuart's people had endured over a three-day period.

>-+◆>-O-<+-+-<

Upon returning from his latest foray into the enemy's heartland, Stuart, his staff, and many of his subordinates repaired to the Bower, where they collaborated with the Dandridges in a new round of merrymaking. Newcomers joined in the festivities; they included two gentlemen of the British press, observers at army headquarters: Francis Lawley, reporter for the august *Times* of London, and Frank Vizetelly, artist-correspondent of the *Illustrated London News*. Stuart and his staff found the visitors "intelligent and refined" conversationalists and "fascinating" raconteurs. Stuart treated them royally, and they repaid him by publishing flattering portraits of the South's premier cavalryman. To facilitate their access to him while on the move, Stuart furnished them with a buggy and team confiscated in Pennsylvania.[5]

The happy times on the Dandridge estate survived the Pennsylvania excursion by a little more than two weeks. On the twenty-ninth, the Army of Northern Virginia began its return to middle Virginia. In ordering the movement, Robert E. Lee was reacting to news that McClellan had finally bestirred himself; all signs pointed to his imminent crossing of the Potomac. This time Stuart's parting from the Bower smacked of permanence. On the twenty-ninth, tents, camp equipage, and personal baggage were packed into wagons and carted away. "We all rode down to the house," recalled Blackford, "to take a last, sad farewell of our kind host and his charming family, whose tears fell fast as they bade us good-bye."[6]

McClellan had begun his crossing on the twenty-sixth; his last corps reached Virginia on the thirtieth. Anticipating that the Yankees would reoccupy the Rappahannock-Rapidan basin, Lee sent Longstreet to get ahead of them. Before month's end, Longstreet's wing—soon to be designated the First Corps, Army of Northern Virginia—was moving through the Blue Ridge toward Culpeper Court House. Most of Jackson's command—days away from being styled the Second Corps, A.N.V.—remained in the lower Valley to block McClellan should he choose to head south that way.

In fact, Little Mac had no intention of challenging Jackson. After crossing the river, he moved into the Loudoun Valley, the fertile country east of the Blue Ridge and west of the Bull Run Mountains. His cavalry, supported by Bayard's brigade from the Washington defenses, rode well in advance of the main body to remove any roadblocks toward Warrenton, the army's initial destination.

Stuart's primary task was to keep back the Federal army—infantry and artillery, as well as horsemen—until Longstreet could complete his withdrawal below the Rappahannock. The First Corps had to settle firmly into place before the Second Corps could join it, restoring the army to full strength.[7]

As soon as Stuart left the Bower, he moved to engage McClellan, not only to keep him from bothering Longstreet, but also to locate the major components of his army and, if possible, determine their destination. He began by leading Fitz Lee's horsemen (now under Williams Wickham) and six of Pelham's guns through the mountains via Snicker's Gap. He had left Hampton at Martinsburg until he could draw in his foraging parties; the 1st Brigade was to rejoin Stuart at Upperville, about twenty-two miles north of Warrenton, on November 3. Jones's brigade, with its long history of supporting Jackson, was left behind to guard Stonewall's flank and rear and to cover his withdrawal once he moved to join Longstreet. Although Stuart could not know, the Laurel Brigade would remain in the Valley long after Jackson left it; Stuart would not see it again for seven months. Its loss left him with mixed feelings. He regretted that one-third of his division was beyond his reach for an indefinite period, but he rejoiced at Grumble Jones's estrangement from him.[8]

If he lacked cavalry, Stuart looked forward to an imminent increase in horse artillery. Already Pelham's command sported a new look. It had been divided into two batteries of four guns each, the first under now-Captain Breathed, the second led by Capt. Mathis W. Henry. The battalion—for such it was, although not officially known by that name—would soon add another member. Early in November, the mounted artillery unit originally known as the Beauregard Rifles would be converted to horse artillery. Renamed the Lynchburg Battery and commanded by Capt. Marcellus N. Moorman, the unit would combine with the 1st and 2nd Stuart Horse Artillery and Chew's and Hart's batteries to give Pelham a total of twenty guns. The blond Alabamian would make the most of his new additions.[9]

Stuart's prompt execution of his orders put his command on a collision course with McClellan's horsemen. The initial clash occurred on the last day of October, and the antagonists maintained violent contact for the next week. Most of the fighting took place in the wedge of land between the Snickersville and the Ashby's Gap Turnpikes. As John Esten Cooke remarked, throughout that week "the order of the day was 'Draw sabre! charge!'—and every species of 'projectile' got after us: rifle[d] cannon, carbines, musket and pistol."[10]

The Confederates got off to a rousing start on the morning of the thirty-first as Stuart, with the 3rd and 9th Virginia, ranged east from Snickersville along the pike of the same name, heading for the most exposed of McClellan's outposts. He found it at Mountsville, where the pike crossed Goose Creek. By a little-used road, Stuart sneaked up on a hundred man-man detachment of the 1st Rhode Island Cavalry, a regiment attached to Stoneman's infantry division. "When the Yanks saw us coming," observed an officer in the 9th, "they attempted to mount and form ranks, but as their first notification of our coming was the sound of our horses' feet and the dust they raised, of course, we were upon them before they could prepare to resist us. Many of them surrendered without attempting to run."[11]

While Stuart rounded up his prisoners, Wickham's 4th Virginia, along with Pelham and the guns of his old battery, ranged up the pike to Aldie, where they met a large detachment of Bayard's command, including artillery support. Following a round of heavy skirmishing, Wickham drove the Yankees two miles. For a time, however, the more numerous Federals had made conditions so hot for their adversaries that Esten Cooke called Aldie "the hornets' hive."

Cooke believed Pelham had made the difference in the fight. The Yankee batteries seemed to change position as soon as they came under his fire: "I always thought they must have known when Pelham was opposed to them. In the Southern army there was no greater artillerist than this boy." All in all, it had been a good day for Stuart's command. Even the officer who had criticized the general's raiding mentality admitted that on this day, "Stuart acquitted himself with real credit."[12]

The first day of November was not as hectic as the last of October. That morning, Stuart rushed north to the support of a detachment whose pickets had been driven in by Pleasonton's cavalry at Philomont, northwest of Aldie. Upon Stuart's arrival, Pleasonton declined to follow up his partial success and let the fighting die out. Stuart spent most of the day on the Ashby's Gap Turnpike between Paris and Upperville, covering the front of D. H. Hill's division, which Jackson had sent into the Loudoun Valley via Ashby's Gap.

Action heated up early on November 2, when Pleasonton, backed by an infantry brigade and two batteries, advanced on Stuart from the northeast. The Confederate leader met the enemy in prepared positions near Unison, between the road and the turnpike. For most of the day, the two sides fought across farm fields broken up by stone fences. At one point, "the incomparable Pelham" advanced one of his howitzers beyond effective support of Stuart's sharpshooters. From his exposed position, the major poured a devastating fire into a large body of horsemen, "putting them to flight," as Stuart wrote, while "capturing their flag and various articles—their arms, equipment, and horses, as well as some prisoners—sustaining in this extraordinary feat no loss whatever." By day's end, the Confederates were falling back to Upperville in the face of superior numbers, "but every hill-top and every foot of ground was disputed, so that the enemy made progress of less than a mile during the day."[13]

By early on the third, reconnaissance missions by scouts and members of his staff had convinced Stuart that McClellan's main body was moving toward the mountains via the Unison-Philomont area. Despite being in overwhelming strength, the Federals were unable to counter effectively Stuart's fight-and-fall-back tactics. By this method—which required his men to fight dismounted for a change—he "obstinately and successfully" resisted Pleasonton's reinforced command through most of the day. Late in the afternoon, the Federals seized Upperville but made no further progress toward Ashby's Gap. Via that pass, Pleasonton might have attacked part of Hill's division and perhaps cut off one part of Jackson's column from another. But Stuart's success came at the cost of several casualties, including the loss of Wickham, who had been wounded in the neck by a shell fragment. He was succeeded by Tom Rosser, who eagerly embarked on his first stint in brigade command.[14]

Late on the third, Stuart heard that Jackson's column was _not_ in motion southward, as he had been led to believe. He sent Rosser, with the 3rd and 9th Virginia, to Piedmont Station on the railroad from Manassas Gap, to monitor any movement by Pleasonton toward that defile. Then Stuart himself, with a small escort, galloped to Paris, adjacent to Ashby's Gap, for a hurried conference with Jackson. He learned that the wing commander was going to remain for the present in the Valley, keeping an eye on McClellan's forces and threatening their flank. Stuart thereby discarded a plan to make a last-ditch stand at Ashby's until Jackson cleared the gap.

Instead, early on the fourth, he headed south to Linden Station on the Manassas Gap Railroad, where, one day late, he met Hampton's column. He led his subordinate's brigade south to Barbee's Cross Roads, where they went into bivouac. That night, they were joined by Rosser, whose two regiments had been forced out of the Piedmont Station area by a much heavier force under Brig. Gen. William Woods Averell, which had reinforced Pleasonton on November 2. Rosser had retreated, however, only after a sharp fight in which the Yankees appeared to have gotten the worst of it.

On the fifth, Stuart expected to renew battle at Barbee's Cross Roads, and he was not disappointed. At 9:00 A.M. the enemy advanced from the north to initiate several hours of skirmishing. At first Stuart had the advantage, mainly because the enlarged Stuart Horse Artillery commanded every spoke of the crossroads. But the situation changed without warning: Around noon, he heard that McClellan's advance had slipped past him to occupy Warrenton, a dozen miles behind his line. When the fire in his front appeared to slacken, Stuart feared that the skirmishing had been designed to distract him from an attack from the rear.

At his order, his brigades quickly departed Barbee's, Hampton's by a south-westward-leading road, Rosser's by the direct route south. To cover the withdrawal, Hampton had Gordon's 1st North Carolina deliver a saber charge by squadron front at a body of pursuing Yankees. The charge drove Gordon's opponents into retreat, but he pursued them too far and received too little support from Hampton. Suddenly, his right flank drew a blistering fire from dismounted cavalry and an artillery piece ensconced behind one of those ubiquitous stone fences. Several horses went down, throwing their riders and blocking any further advance. Before more carnage could occur, Gordon called a left-about wheel and led the survivors back to their point of advance, pursued briefly by the victors. In this action, painfully reminiscent of the regiment's ambush at Willis Church, the 1st suffered twenty-one casualties.[15]

Stuart's scattered forces regrouped at Orleans, where they learned that the report of Warrenton's occupation had been false. Next morning the Beau Sabreur sent part of Rosser's brigade to hold that place while he and Hampton moved southwestward to Waterloo Bridge, a site familiar from the campaign against Pope. There they crossed the Rappahannock without difficulty.

On the south bank, they were joined a few hours later by Rosser, who again had been forced from a position by a larger force of Union cavalry. One of Rosser's officers complained that the colonel "did not handle the brigade very well," undoubtedly because he lacked "the directing hand of Stuart." If true, Rosser's debut in brigade command left much to be desired.[16]

Once on the lower shore, Stuart had Hampton throw out a picket line that stretched as far west as Sperryville. After positioning Rosser's men to patrol the river, the major general led the balance of the 2nd Brigade south to Jeffersonton, where he established another picket line. This position was quickly challenged by Yankee troopers, but Stuart did not have to resist them by himself. At Jeffersonton he was only a few miles from Longstreet's new bailiwick at Culpeper Court House; soon he had all the infantry and mounted artillery support he could have desired.

As on-scene commander, Stuart employed the foot soldiers in close cooperation with his cavalry to resist a series of limited advances by Pleasonton, sometimes with infantry support of his own. Over the next several days, as cold winds began to lash the region south of the Rappahannock, the skirmishing assumed a quality of permanence, suggesting that the antagonists would confront each other along this line indefinitely. The recent spate of marching, maneuvering, feinting, and limited attacks had ended; by November 7 the armies—including Jackson's corps, which remained beyond the Blue Ridge—appeared stalemated.

But while immobile armies glowered at each other across the river, the complexion of the war in the East underwent a fundamental change. On the seventh, McClellan was notified by the War Department that he had been replaced as commander of the Army of the Potomac by Burnside. Many factors had contributed to this outcome, an event that surprised McClellan's opponents but confirmed the suspicions of many of his own troops. One factor in particular was in the mind of everyone who ruminated on the general's downfall: Stuart's expedition to Chambersburg, his second circuit of the Federal army in less than four months. The first had made McClellan look inept or at least careless; the second had made him look expendable.[17]

>-⋅+⋅⟩-⋅O⋅-⟨⋅+⋅-<

The close of that violent week in the Loudoun Valley left Stuart tired and dispirited. He had successfully shouldered the primary burden given him by Lee, having prevented McClellan's advance from observing—let alone interfering with—Longstreet's passage to Culpeper. Even so, the several-day stint of combat had followed a disquieting pattern: A proud and polished but outnumbered cavalry knocked about and forced into retreat by an upstart enemy. One of Stuart's missions had been to scout McClellan's dispositions, but he had been unable to penetrate the screen Pleasonton had thrown around his army. The troopers of the Army of the Potomac—with the highly competent John Buford supervising them in his new role of chief of cavalry—were coming on too fast and too strong for Stuart's peace of mind.

What bothered him most was that the Yankees were drawing on a seemingly inexhaustible supply of horses, weapons, and equipment. Meanwhile, incessant marching and hard fighting had begun to drag down the Confederate cavalry. Given the growing scarcity of remounts and forage, many of Stuart's regiments were finding it difficult to field a full complement of men—hence, perhaps, the ease with which the Yankees had pushed them around at various points in the recent fighting.

The problem was not simply a lack of resources, but the condition of those on hand. On November 7, when Robert E. Lee reported on his army's well-being to Secretary of War Randolph, he stressed the troubles with his horsemen. He noted how large and efficient the enemy's mounted arm appeared, and lamented, "Our cavalry, diminished by the casualties of battle and hard service, is now reduced by disease among the horses, sore tongue and soft hoof." Equine maladies were not a new problem, and the enemy suffered from them too—especially the "hoof rot" that Lee mentioned—but the Federals had a vast quantity of horseflesh at their disposal, provided by a large and efficient government. Proportionally, therefore, Stuart's troopers were more seriously stricken by the cold-weather sicknesses that ravaged their stables and picket lines.[18]

For Stuart, the gloomiest fact was that the situation could only get worse. If shortages of manpower and mounts were plaguing the division now, what would be its condition next summer—or, for that matter, in the coming winter? He did not care to answer the question.

Events of a personal nature were also lowering his spirits. When embarking on the recent fighting, he had gotten word from home that his five-year-old daughter, Flora, was ill; just as the campaign ended, he learned that the child had died. Heartbroken, and regretting his inability to be with his daughter in her last days, he mourned her deeply and continuously. "I will never get over it—never," he told John Esten Cooke, tears streaking his face.[19]

Fortunately, war intrudes on a soldier's sorrow as it does on his hopes and dreams. As soon as he settled down on the Rappahannock, Stuart threw himself into reorganizing his division to incorporate a fourth brigade. The new command would be assigned to W. H. F. Lee, who, over the past several months, had proved himself time and again worthy of promotion and additional responsibility. On the tenth, Robert E. Lee's son—still feeling the aftereffects of his fall at Boonsboro—was appointed a brigadier and assigned five regiments. Two of them, Davis's 10th Virginia and Col. Solomon Williams's 2nd North Carolina, had previously served under Hampton. A third outfit, Rooney's own 9th Virginia, came over from the brigade of Cousin Fitz, who was ready to retake the field after recovering from his recent disability. The brigade was rounded out by two new regiments, the 13th Virginia of Col. John R. Chambliss, Jr., and Col. William B. Ball's 15th Virginia.

Despite giving up some units to Rooney Lee, Hampton's and Fitz Lee's brigades remained strong, at least in the number of their components. Hampton's now consisted of the 1st North Carolina, the 1st and 2nd South Carolina, and two legions from Georgia, Cobb's and Phillips's. The last-named unit, commanded by Lt. Col. W. W. Rich, was a newcomer, having recently been relieved of a long-term attachment to one of Longstreet's brigades.[20]

The transfer helped compensate Hampton for the temporary loss of the Jeff Davis Legion, which shortly before the reorganization had been attached to Longstreet; soon afterward, it would transition to Jackson's corps. The Davis Legion would return to Hampton's brigade late in November, but the tenure of its leader was almost up. On November 30, Will Martin would receive a deserved promotion to brigadier general. Because no vacancies existed in Stuart's command, he would go west to take a position in the Army of Tennessee. Hampton deeply regretted his loss, although he was consoled by the succession of Lt. Col. J. Frederick Waring, an officer whose abilities compared favorably with Martin's.[21]

Meanwhile, the 2nd Brigade retained its all-Virginia coloration, consisting of the 1st, 2nd, 3rd, 4th, and 5th Regiments. The loss of the 9th Virginia had been made good by the transfer from Jones's brigade of Munford's 2nd. The balance of the Laurel Brigade—which would remain in the Valley after Stonewall joined Longstreet on the Rappahannock—was nominally under Stuart's command. It now embraced three regiments, the 6th, 7th, and 12th Virginia, as well as two Virginia battalions, the 17th and the 35th. The last-named unit, commanded by Maj. (later Lt. Col.) Elijah V. White, was later better known by its colorful nickname, "The Comanches." Finally, Pelham's artillery continued to embrace the batteries of Breathed, Henry, Chew, Hart, and Moorman.[22]

Stuart had barely finished putting the new table of organization on paper, securing R. E. Lee's approval of it, and overseeing the physical adjustments it necessitated, when he was pressed into field service. On November 6, hours after he learned that the rumor about the occupation of Warrenton had been untrue, the Yankees took and held the place, less than twenty miles from Longstreet's headquarters at Culpeper. Nine days later, Robert E. Lee heard that the Yankees were already leaving Warrenton. The report was duly confirmed, and on the eighteenth, Lee's cavalry leader, with most of Hampton's and Fitz Lee's men, was sent to find out where Burnside was heading, and why.[23]

Shortly after fording the Rappahannock near Jeffersonton, Stuart ran into cavalry screening Burnside's pullout. His men swiftly drove the Federals away, in the process clearing an unhappy memory from Stuart's mind. Ten days earlier, his plan for a two-pronged attack on Warrenton had miscarried when orders failed to reach Hampton in time. Lee's brigade, still under Rosser, had gone ahead on its own. Although initially successful, the colonel had been forced to withdraw for lack of support.[24] *FREDERICKSBURG*

The reconnaissance of November 18–19 revealed that McClellan's successor was moving toward the lower Rappahannock. The shift of position had begun on the fifteenth with a degree of speed and stealth uncharacteristic of the Army of the Potomac. Stuart subsequently learned that "Old Burn" had hoped to march on Richmond by crossing the river opposite Fredericksburg. In fact, Lee and Stuart had already anticipated such a movement; on the twelfth, the 9th Virginia had been ordered to Fredericksburg in advance of a move in that direction by two of Longstreet's divisions. At Fredericksburg, the 9th, now under Col. Richard L. T. Beale, joined the 15th Virginia, which had been patrolling the area since its formation.[25]

Armed with Stuart's report, Lee committed the army to a march down the Rappahannock. The balance of Longstreet's corps started for Fredericksburg on the morning of the nineteenth; at about the same time, Jackson was ordered to leave the Valley for the Rappahannock. Due to a number of delays, he would not reach Fredericksburg until December 2.

Even then, Jackson would not be too late to block Burnside's march on Richmond. The new leader had stolen a march on his enemy, having reached Falmouth, across the bridgeless river from Fredericksburg, before Lee could block his crossing. At the last minute, however, everything went wrong for the Army of the Potomac, not the least of which was the late arrival from Washington of its pontoon train. An apoplectic Burnside found himself stranded on the upper shore until the portable bridge arrived on the evening of the twenty-fifth. By then Longstreet's corps was well established below Fredericksburg, and Burnside considered himself stymied. "It became necessary," he wrote, "to make arrangements to cross in the face of a vigilant and formidable foe. These arrangements were not completed until about December 10."[26]

By that date, thanks to the addition of Jackson's command, Lee's defensive line extended along the river for six and a half miles. The time granted him had permitted his army to perfect its works by stocking them with rank upon rank of riflemen and dozens of artillery pieces. The guns commanded an expanse of open ground that sloped gradually to the water. This plain—Burnside's only avenue of advance, when and if he bridged the Rappahannock—could not be crossed without subjecting everyone on it to rifle- and cannon fire.

In the weeks before Burnside broke the inactivity on the Rappahannock, Stuart's horsemen were kept busy with a variety of missions: guarding their main army's flanks and rear, picketing the river above and below Fredericksburg, scouting the enemy's side, and seeking to harass, and if possible sever, Burnside's communications. When an opportunity for more active service presented itself, they seized it.

One opportunity was so inviting it persuaded Wade Hampton to revise his low opinion of raiding. On November 28, he led two hundred of his men (enemy accounts quadrupled the number) across the river at Kelly's Ford and into the Union rear. The next day, having ranged behind Burnside's lines at will, Hampton returned to the river near Hartwood Church, about eight miles above Falmouth, and attacked a picket line manned by members of Averell's division. The weather was frigid, the stream looked too cold to cross, and the pickets had lapsed into complacency. When Hampton struck, he wounded several of them and captured eighty-two others, including five officers, before heading home at his leisure. Averell and Burnside were furious over the coup; Stuart and Robert E. Lee rejoiced, lauding Hampton's daring, stealth, and enterprise.[27]

Hampton's success inspired a similar attack a few days later at the other end of Stuart's line, patrolled by Rooney Lee's brigade. On the evening of December 1, a ninety-man party of the 9th Virginia crossed the lower Rappahannock on flatboats near Port Royal, almost twenty miles south of Fredericksburg. On the far shore, they crept up on a large detachment of Pennsylvania cavalry, surrounded its camp, called on its men to surrender, and when they reached for their arms instead, sprayed them with carbine fire. From the opposite shore, Colonel Beale and the rest of the 9th "could hear the shouts and firing, and knew all was well." The result was the death of several Pennsylvanians and the capture of sixty others. The victors transported the captives to the south bank in their boats and forced many of their horses to swim the frigid stream— all at the cost of one Virginian wounded and one captured.[28]

A few days later the waters off Port Royal became the scene of the first cavalry-versus-warship encounter since the attack on the *Marblehead* the previous June. On December 4, artillery attached to D. H. Hill's division, which included an English-made, long-range Whitworth rifle, was sent to chastise four gunboats that had turned their guns on the homes of local residents. Trundled down to the river by Captains R. A. Hardaway and T. H. Carter, the cannons unlimbered with a minimum of noise, trained their sights on the anchored vessels, and blasted away. Hill, who witnessed the contest, rejoiced that "these piratical cruisers, which have bombarded so many peaceful homes, shrank from the wager of battle and kept close under the shelter of town, [then] . . . fled down the river."[29]

When the vessels steamed off, they came abreast of W. H. F. Lee's stretch of the riverbank. The brigadier decided to join in the action with Moorman's battery, which had been temporarily attached to his brigade. John Pelham happened to be on hand; he personally directed the fire of two of Moorman's rifles. Their aim proved true, the guns "putting shot through and through one of the boats" until it limped out of range. Afterward Stuart commended Pelham and his gunners to Robert E. Lee's notice, not failing to laud the army leader's son as well.

Rooney Lee's new brigade was doing "gallant service on the Lower Rappahannock, and no opportunity to strike the enemy will be allowed to pass."[30]

Another such opportunity came one week later, after Burnside steeled himself to cross the river and engage his enemy. The crossing took place on December 11 via the long-delayed pontoons. They had been laid with difficulty, thanks to the fire of Rebel sharpshooters in Fredericksburg. After the snipers had been neutralized, Burnside put part of his army over that day, the rest on the twelfth, and on the raw, blustery morning of the thirteenth, he led all of it to the slaughter.

12-11-62

Stuart was on hand for the bloodletting, as were Fitz and Rooney Lee, although Hampton was not, his brigade having been left to picket the upper Rappahannock. For much of the day, those troopers on the scene, positioned on the far right of the army, observed rather than fought. They stood "to horse" throughout the afternoon and into the evening under an intermittent artillery fire. Late in the battle, when Burnside's survivors turned to the rear in a body, Stuart apparently ordered Fitz Lee to charge the retreating troops, only to have the order countermanded by Jackson, who commanded on the right. At day's end, Stuart's casualty total stood at thirteen wounded, all in Rooney Lee's brigade.[31]

A section of Pelham's battalion was the only element of the division that saw much service on the thirteenth. For the first few hours of the battle, Pelham waited patiently beside his guns, caissons, and limbers in a field near Hamilton's Crossing, looking for an opportunity to join in. At about 9:00 on that fog-shrouded morning, Stuart ordered him to advance up the Massaponax Road and, from a close-in position, try to determine how the battle was progressing. Pelham went forward in company with Captain Henry, one Blakely rifle, one 12-pounder Napoleon, and their crews.

The pair found a good position behind a stand of cedars at the junction of the Massaponax Road and the Old Richmond Stage Road. Unlimbering at a right angle to the Confederate line, Pelham and Henry swung their guns in the general direction of Federals obliquing past them to the left. At first the fog precluded a clear view, but when it began to lift, it revealed an irresistible target: the open flank of a full division of Burnside's infantry.[32]

At Pelham's signal, both guns opened fire. Their first shots were slightly off-mark, but later rounds bowled over rows of men in dark blue overcoats. Troops from George Meade's division of the I Army Corps whirled to face the unexpected threat, only to crumple under Pelham's barrage. In minutes, confusion and panic were rippling through the blue ranks. The Napoleon and the Blakely continued to fling shells as quickly as they could be loaded, taking a fearful toll not only of Meade's command, but of supporting units as well, including Abner Doubleday's division.

The fire was so devastating that Meade directed three of his batteries to beat it down. Later two batteries under Doubleday also trained their guns on Pelham's position. Their shells plowed up the earth around Pelham and Henry, but the officers moved their pieces about so nimbly that neither made a good target.

After several minutes, a fortunate shot struck close enough to put the Blakely out of commission. Pelham continued to rake the Union line with the Napoleon, oblivious to the counterbattery fire coming at him with increasing severity.

He remained in his exposed position for close to two hours, withdrawing only when his ammunition chest ran dry. Even then he was not finished. After a respite, he returned to the attack by contributing fresh guns and crews to a barrage by Jackson's artillery, which ended Burnside's effort against the south end of Lee's line. Thanks largely to Pelham's enfilade, hundreds of Meade's men raced back across the Stage Road, while many of Doubleday's regiments remained well to the rear, unwilling to share the fate of their comrades.[33]

Having observed Pelham at various times during the day, Stuart and R. E. Lee were greatly impressed by his daring, his coolness under fire, and the effectiveness of his gunnery. Stuart, who had witnessed so many outstanding performances by his young artillerist, expressed quiet pride. His superior responded more effusively, exclaiming to his subordinates, "It is glorious to see such courage in one so young!" In his report of the battle, Lee echoed a sobriquet favored by his cavalry commander when he praised the performance of "the gallant Pelham."[34]

Although his soldiers went down in droves not only in Pelham's sector, but all along the line, Burnside kept attacking well into the evening. In the darkness, the fighting finally tapered off and the carnage ceased. Only then did the Union leader appreciate what his enemy, and most of his own men, had grasped hours earlier: The futility of attacking across hundreds of yards of open ground against well-prepared defenses crammed with heavy ordnance. It had taken more than thirteen thousand casualties to drive home the point. A large percentage of those poor souls—the dead, the dying, the wounded, and the unhurt who found it impossible to either advance or withdraw without risking their lives—remained on the frozen ground through the night. By morning, there were fewer wounded, more dead.

Burnside's army remained on the enemy shore until the evening of the fourteenth, when, having done what it could to succor fallen comrades, it began a slow, painful withdrawal. As the vanquished departed, the victors advanced to survey the littered field. Stuart rode over it in the company of foreign observers. Later he wrote a West Point classmate that his companions, "who surveyed Solferino and all the battlefields of Italy say that the pile of dead on the plains of Fredericksburg exceeds anything of the sort ever seen by them."

The Confederates buried the dead their enemy had left behind and ministered to the few Yankees who remained alive, having survived wounds and plunging temperatures. Within a few days, convinced that Burnside would not renew the fight except at long range, Lee placed his army in winter quarters on the edge of the battlefield.[35]

Perhaps chafing at the inactivity his troopers had experienced on the thirteenth, Stuart sought an opportunity for active service before operations shut
down for the season. Wade Hampton had provided him with an idea. Shortly
before and just after the great battle, the South Carolinian had led large detachments against Burnside's principal supply link to Washington, the historic Telegraph Road. On the first raid, December 10–12, Hampton hit the supply depot
at Dumfries; on the second, December 17–19, he ranged farther north to attack
the warehouses at Occoquan.[36]

Although the eight-mile stretch of highway between those villages was
patrolled regularly by Burnside's cavalry, both expeditions had been gloriously
successful. In addition to capturing pickets, sacking commissary stores, and
severing telegraph lines, Hampton had waylaid supply trains and sutlers' shops.
He had returned to the Rappahannock with a truly immense haul of plunder,
everything from footwear to cigars and champagne—"all the good things you
could think of," one raider informed his wife. A comrade wrote, "We had a fine
but cold time of it. We captured one hundred and fifty Yankees, about three
hundred mules and horses and thirty two wagons . . . [and] did not lose a single
man on the whole scout."[37]

Stuart secured Lee's permission for a third strike on the Telegraph Road,
then spent several days working out the logistics. On December 26, following a
happy holiday spent in the company of his visiting wife, Stuart, accompanied
by his aides, rode to Kelly's Ford. Nearby, Hampton and the Lees had massed
eighteen hundred riders, culled from each of their brigades. Along for the ride
were Pelham, fresh from his recent heroics, and four cannons.

That afternoon, after the pickets opposite the ford had been attacked and
either captured or dispersed, Stuart led the two-mile-long column across the
river and on to Morrisville, then to Bristersburg, nine miles farther north, where
they spent the balance of the day in bivouac. Stuart was not especially concerned that in response to Hampton's forays, the Yankees might have increased
their presence in the area. One of his objectives was to deplete Burnside's army
by forcing it to detach forces to run him down. Based on recent history, Stuart
anticipated little difficulty in giving any number of pursuers the slip, unless he
chose to turn about and pummel them into retreat.[38]

Leaving Bristersburg in the small hours of the twenty-seventh, Stuart split
his column into three detachments to strike the Telegraph Road in as many
places. Hampton's men took the most northerly route, toward Occoquan, while
Fitz Lee pounded almost directly east, expecting to strike the road just below
Dumfries. Riding with Rooney Lee's troopers, Stuart took a median position,
angling northeastward under a steel gray sky, heading for the valley of Quantico
Creek. There he planned to join Fitz for a two-pronged attack on the outpost.

First contact with the enemy occurred late that day. Soon after Fitz Lee
reached the Telegraph Road and turned north, his advance overtook a long column of sutlers' wagons. Every vehicle was captured but none looted—at the
time. An officer in the 3rd Virginia recalled that some time later, "after our four

days rations had given out . . . the men broke in the captured wagons and had nothing else to eat than the notions they got therefrom."[39]

Fitz Lee encountered no opposition on the way to Yankee-held Dumfries, and when Stuart and Rooney Lee emerged onto the road farther north, enemy cavalry fled before them. Stuart linked with Fitz at the appointed place, then split up again in preparation for attacking the town with the Scottish name. Then, at the last minute, trouble cropped up. The plan of assault, which had been carefully devised, fell apart minutes before it could be executed when Stuart learned from his scouts that the local garrison was larger than expected—in fact, it outnumbered his command. Worse, perhaps, was the news that in response to warnings of the raiders' approach, the most valuable stores had been removed from Dumfries to points unknown.

After fruitlessly shelling the place with Pelham's guns—two of which quickly used up their ammunition and had to return home prematurely—a disappointed Stuart canceled the attack. He was willing to expend shot and shell in dubious battle, but not the lives of his men. Hoping to achieve more after linking with Hampton, after nightfall he led his reunited force north along a route that bypassed Dumfries.[40]

Hampton's experience at Occoquan had been almost as frustrating as Stuart's farther south. The prize he discovered upon reaching the village was not the depot itself, which had not been fully restocked since his earlier raid, but a pea green Yankee regiment, the 17th Pennsylvania Cavalry, stationed outside the village. Hampton decided to strike the Pennsylvanians simultaneously from two sides and capture them as a body. After he moved off with the main force to gain the Yankees' rear south of town, Colonel Butler charged his 2nd South Carolina into and through their bivouac, where a post-Christmas turkey dinner was cooking. John Mosby, who had accompanied Butler—Mosby's last outing with the Army of Northern Virginia before embarking on his career as a partisan leader—recalled that "the combat was short and sharp, and soon became a rout; the federal cavalry ran right through their camp, and gave a last look at their turkeys as they passed."[41]

Panic-stricken troopers fled in every direction, although most circled southward, just as Hampton had anticipated. Unfortunately, Butler had attacked a few minutes too soon; not yet in position to cut off their retreat, Hampton looked on in frustration as the Pennsylvanians raced past him to safety. Glumly, he reunited his column, mounted a brief pursuit, then headed south for a prearranged junction with Stuart along the Occoquan River.

The meeting of the raiding leaders was a depressing affair. So little of consequence having been achieved, and having attracted no sizable pursuit force, Stuart determined to abort the expedition and head back to the Rappahannock in company with Pelham's useless guns, several prisoners, and supply wagons pulled by some of the sorriest-looking mules he had ever seen. But as he looped north and west on the road to Brentsville, Stuart learned from a traveler that a large body of Union horsemen was galloping toward him from the north.

The news seemed to give the raid new purpose and its leader new resolve. Stuart had forced Burnside to tail him, after all. The pursuit gave him an opportunity to salvage pride and strategic purpose by meeting and throttling his opponents. Once they had been disposed of, he would cross the Occoquan and raid northward. In fact, he would keep riding until someone stopped him.[42]

Turning the column about and countermarching, he reached the road on which the Yankees were approaching and advanced to meet them. En route, he set a trap; in response to his order, Hampton sent Butler's regiment off to the west, near Bacon Race Church, there to launch a flank attack at an opportune time.

Not long after Butler moved out, Fitz Lee spied the Yankees—some three hundred dismounted troopers deployed across the road ahead as well as in nearby trees. At a signal from Stuart, Lee's leading ranks rushed forward, mixed with the Yankees, overwhelmed them after a few minutes' fighting, and sent them into headlong retreat. A trooper in the 5th Virginia used an overworked metaphor to describe the result: "The Yankees ran like sheep," leaving "dead men, wounded men, & dead horses . . . strewn on the road." A member of the 3rd Virginia recalled that "we did considerable execution, killing about 20 and taking some forty prisoners" before reaching the Occoquan River.

At that point, the pursuit should have halted, but Stuart's fighting blood was up. He sent Rosser's 5th Virginia across the river via a rocky, shallow ford that should have been too dangerous to use. Behind Rosser came the rest of Fitz Lee's brigade, followed, impossibly, by John Pelham and his two remaining guns. Stuart stared in amazement at the artillerist's feat.[43]

Though impressive, the crossing availed Stuart nothing. It took so long that by the time his men reached dry ground, their opponents had spurred beyond range of pursuit. Stuart turned his attention to ransacking the camps they had left standing along the river. After gathering up everything of value and burning what could not be carried off, the raiders proceeded north. On the way, they were overtaken by Colonel Butler, who had been unable to join in the attack as planned, having happened upon another, larger pursuit force that had yet to pick up Stuart's trail. His regiment had avoided its clutches by the narrowest of margins.

By Butler's account, the newcomers had interposed between the raiders and the Rappahannock. Unconcerned about the repercussions, Stuart had part of Hampton's command demonstrate toward the east, to throw off the as-yet-unseen pursuers. With the rest of the column, he continued north into the teeth of an icy wind. He had decided to keep going until he struck the tracks of the Orange & Alexandria. Cutting the railroad would give the expedition a degree of strategic importance it had yet to achieve.

Late in the afternoon of the twenty-eighth, having met no impediments thus far, Stuart's vanguard approached the O & A at Burke's Station, ten miles north of Occoquan and about as far west of Union-held Alexandria. The depot and its guards were surrounded so quickly that the local telegrapher, then in touch with officials in Alexandria, had no time to tap out an alarm. Rather than cut the wire immediately, Stuart had one of his troopers, a prewar "brass pounder," take over the instrument. For several minutes, the man monitored local dispatches while Stuart's staff jotted down information, including the dispositions of forces out of Washington. Much of the message traffic concerned the raiders—it was music to Stuart's ears. Lieutenant Price reported gleefully that the local authorities "were in great alarm, and orders were telegraphed to destroy everything in case of our attacking them." Thus the expedition had dealt the enemy psychological as well as physical blows. Stuart was immensely pleased, as he had a right to be.

His spirits entirely restored, he decided to cap the expedition with a flourish. Before the cable was cut, he had his telegrapher send out a message of his own. In an act of remarkable audacity, even by Stuart's standards, he complained to the U.S. Army's quartermaster general, Montgomery C. Meigs, about "the bad quality of the mules lately furnished, which interfered seriously with our moving the captured wagons." With that, he remounted and started for home. By now his men had not only downed telegraph wire, but had also torn up track and burned rolling stock.[44]

Except for a violent brush with an infantry picket east of Fairfax Court House, the return trip proved to be a joyride, if not in joyride weather. The pursuers Butler had encountered near Bacon Race Church never materialized; farmers provided the raiders with food and drink at many points on their route; and Stuart took the time to stop off at Frying Pan and visit the family of his lady friend Laura Ratcliffe.

By New Year's Day, Stuart, his men, and their immense haul of booty were back in camp below the Rappahannock. On their five-day journey, the raiders had lost a single man killed and a dozen wounded. Although begun in adverse conditions, and for a time regarded as a failure, the expedition had added laurels to the Cavalry Division, A.N.V.—a belated Christmas gift that put good cheer in the hearts of Stuart and every other raider.[45]

Chapter Thirteen

Wilderness Outing

Taking into account only prisoners and plunder, the raid to Dumfries and Occoquan was a smashing success. Once again, however, days of almost uninterrupted travel—and hours at a rapid gait—had ruined too many horses. Those seized on the expedition did not approach the number that had broken down.

The dearth of serviceable horseflesh, plus the acute shortage of forage available along the Rappahannock, prompted Stuart to order, and R. E. Lee to approve, rotating forces out of the immediate war zone in order to recruit their strength. In early January, Fitz Lee's brigade left the Rappahannock for King William County, northeast of Richmond, where provender was more abundant. There its horses fared, as one officer noted, "tolerably well getting sometimes 5 or 6 lbs. of corn and same amount of wheat straw, sometimes nothing but top fodder." Two weeks later, Rooney Lee's men were relieved from duty on the lower end of the river to spend a few weeks in Essex County, on Virginia's Middle Peninsula.[1]

Early in February, Fitz Lee's men and horses—their health presumably restored—returned to their post near Fredericksburg. Only two weeks later, however, they were sent upriver to assume the workload formerly borne by Hampton's brigade. As soon as his units were relieved, Hampton led them into Page County, in the midsection of the Shenandoah Valley. Even more so than Essex and King William Counties, this area, having thus far escaped the hard hand of war, overflowed with hay, oats, wheat, and corn. Yet it was two days' ride from the scene of Hampton's most recent posting. His command would be hard-pressed to rejoin Stuart in time to oppose a sudden attack.[2]

Whereas Stuart appears to have authorized Rooney and Fitz Lee to quarter their troops far from the Rappahannock, Hampton's transfer was the work of Robert E. Lee. Evidently it was a response to recent complaints by the South Carolinian that his men were being overworked and neglected. He may have had reason to feel this way, given the army's chronic favoritism toward its Virginia units. Then, too, during the previous six weeks or so, his brigade had seen more service than the others under Stuart, having gone on three raids prior to the post-Christmas expedition. Hampton, never one to be taken advantage of, expressed his frustration in a letter to his sister in South Carolina:

> All my time and correspondence of late have been taken up in quarreling with Stuart, who keeps me here doing all the hard work, while the Va. Brigades are quietly doing nothing. His partiality toward these Brigades is as marked, as it is disgusting and it constantly makes me indignant. I do not object to work, but I do object to seeing my command broken down by positive starvation. We cannot get forage, and in the course of a few weeks, my Brigade will be totally unfit for service. This is a hard case, but unless Genl. Lee, to whom I have appealed, interferes, Stuart will certainly have my Brigade out of the field before very long.[3]

Hampton expressed his dissatisfaction so loudly and so often that in April army headquarters granted him leave to go home to South Carolina, where he sought the help of state authorities in raising additional units for his brigade. One hundred of its troopers, former members of Company Q, were permitted to accompany him in a search for remounts.[4]

The constant absence of at least one-third of its strength played hob with the cavalry's readiness. Should Burnside's troopers advance against any part of the army, especially if it returned recent favors by raiding behind Confederate lines, would Stuart have the manpower to make them cease and desist? Yet it was Robert E. Lee's "great desire to recuperate the Cavy" by any acceptable expedient. Fortunately, Ambrose Burnside had gone sullenly into winter quarters around Falmouth. He appeared in no mood to launch another offensive, and his cavalry seemed content to watch their side of the river.[5]

Lee's peace of mind was threatened briefly late in January, when Burnside confounded everyone, his own troops included, by putting the entire army in motion. On the nineteenth, he advanced to Banks's Ford, where he planned to cross beyond Lee's left rear. For about twenty-four hours, the strategy looked promising, but then a devilish mix of snow, sleet, and freezing rain immobilized everyone—men, horses, wagons, artillery teams. Four days after the luckless commander marched (or slid) back to Falmouth, he was relieved of command and replaced by "Fighting Joe" Hooker. Burnside had learned, to his acute regret, that though he might steal a march on Robert E. Lee, he could not steal a march on winter.[6]

>‑!‑<>‑O‑<>‑!‑<

For weeks after returning from his latest raid, Stuart spent his time attacking paperwork and devising ways to keep his command active and alert in winter quarters. On the administrative front, he strove to hold on to Williams Wickham, who submitted his resignation in mid-January. Although he gave no reason for his action, the colonel was depressed by the effects of his wounds and disgruntled over his inability to secure the promotion he felt he deserved. Unwilling "to lose so valuable an officer as Col Wickham from the army," Stuart fought the petition. In the end, he persuaded the new secretary of war, James A. Seddon, to disapprove it.[7]

Stuart then sought a brigadier's appointment for Wickham, as also for Rosser, whom he later praised as "an officer of superior ability" with "the talent to command and the skill to lead with coolness and decision." He also recommended Pelham, in the strongest terms, for promotion to lieutenant colonel, while deploring the unavailability of higher rank in the major's branch of the service.[8]

As for active operations, for some weeks Stuart was unable to occupy his men beyond picket duty and the snowball fights they waged to occupy their hours in winter camp. Then, in mid-February, it suddenly looked as if Stuart, with a portion of Fitz Lee's brigade, would follow Hampton to the Valley. Fitz's uncle was anxious to strike a blow against Brig. Gen. Robert H. Milroy, whose garrison at Winchester had been oppressing local residents. Lee went so far as to arrange cooperation from Grumble Jones, the recently appointed commander of the Valley District, but he gave Stuart discretion to launch or withhold the operation. In the end, Stuart begged off, probably fearful of the effects of a winter campaign on his ailing mounts. The prospect of being reunited with Jones may also have played a role in his decision.[9]

Spared a long march in bad weather, Fitz Lee took it on himself to secure useful work closer to home. Recalling the success of Hampton's attack on Hartwood Church, and certain that Averell had not tightened up his picket lines in the interim, Lee decided to see if the trick would work a second time. With Stuart's approval, on the morning of the twenty-fourth he crossed at Kelly's Ford with four hundred members of the 1st, 2nd, and 3rd Virginia and started inland across snow-covered earth.

As he had hoped, his column slipped past the nearest vedettes with almost laughable ease. The Virginians encamped that night at Morrisville and spent the following morning getting into the rear of the picket force still stationed near Hartwood. At 2:00 P.M., Lee's men swept down on the guard, composed of members of several regiments in Averell's division. When the shooting and swordplay ended, a few Yankees had been killed or wounded and 150 others were in Confederate hands. Fitz Lee found the number of captives most pleasing. Though he admired Hampton's abilities, he was no friend of the South Carolinian—now he had outdone him.[10]

Leaving Hartwood Church, the raiders were occasionally hard-pressed by members of the picket reserve, but never seriously threatened. Whenever the Yankees closed in, the rear guard whirled about and attacked, sending horses and riders running for cover through the snow. At one point, the pursuers became the pursued, Lee's men following them to within five miles of Falmouth, where Union infantry put an end to the chase. By then the raiders had created such a fuss that reports doubling or trebling their numbers were crackling over Hooker's telegraph lines. When he heard the news, Averell formed a huge pursuit force, as did Alfred Pleasonton. The two, however, failed to coordinate movements, ensuring that neither came close to bagging the Rebels.

Shortly before crossing, unmolested, to his side of the river, Fitz crowned his triumph with a gesture almost as outrageous—and every bit as insulting— as his superior's telegram to General Meigs. When Averell, at the head of hundreds of troopers, belatedly reached Kelly's Ford, he found a note his old West Point friend had left for him. In it, Fitz Lee chided him for his lax security, derided his troops' lack of vigilance and tenacity, and called on him to leave Virginia and go home; failing that, he should bring Fitz a gift—a bag of coffee.

The injury and insult Fitz thus inflicted had long-term effects not only on Lee's enemy, but on his own brigade as well. In January the new Union leader, Hooker, had formed his underachieving cavalry into a separate corps and removed it from the control of infantry commanders. Fighting Joe believed that organizational reforms, as well as the improvements he had instituted in the procurement and distribution of arms, equipment, and remounts, should have produced a stronger, more cohesive, more highly motivated cavalry. He was incensed that his pet command should have been so thoroughly humiliated. Hooker demanded retaliation, and he ordered Averell to administer it.[11]

Averell spent the next three weeks alternately brooding over his shabby treatment at the hands of an old friend and trying to determine when, where, and how to get even. Finally, on the evening of March 16, one day after a hailstorm buffeted the Rappahannock shore, he marched up the river toward Kelly's Ford at the point of a column almost four thousand strong, including six pieces of horse artillery. Even after dropping off two regiments to guard his rear near Brentsville, Averell had more than enough manpower to overwhelm Lee, whose brigade, minus its normal complement of men on detached duty and horse-hunting expeditions, numbered fewer than two thousand and lacked artillery support. Averell cared not at all that the upcoming fight might be viewed as unfair. He may have outnumbered the enemy two to one, but he would not have considered twenty-to-one odds overkill.

Averell believed he had chosen an opportune time to strike, for he doubted that the Rebels expected him. Although winter had begun to loosen its grip on middle Virginia, the weather was foul enough to discourage thoughts of active operations. Furthermore, even if the day had been warm and sunny, the Confederates would not have anticipated an assault by their unassertive opponents.

Unknown to Averell, another factor appeared to favor his chances. Although Fitz Lee was with his troops, Stuart was not. Along with Tom Rosser and other witnesses, he was at Culpeper Court House, a dozen miles west of Kelly's Ford, appearing before the seemingly never-ending court-martial of Henry Clay Pate. In his absence, cavalry headquarters was a "very dull" place, and the listlessness seems to have spread to the rest of the command. For instance, the Stuart Horse Artillery was in camp well back from the river, and its leader, John Pelham, had gone to Culpeper to visit some friends, including a pretty girl or two in whom the flirtatious major had a personal interest. Once Averell came calling, however, Stuart, Rosser, and Pelham cut short their other pursuits and rushed to the scene of action.[12]

Sometime after 5:00 A.M. on the seventeenth, the head of Averell's column forced its way across at Kelly's Ford. As it happened, the Yankees were not entirely unexpected. Fitz Lee had been warned of their advance by army headquarters, as well as by his own scouts, although where they were heading was anybody's guess. Just in case, Fitz had dug rifle pits and erected obstructions opposite Kelly's, while augmenting the normal twenty-man picket guard with a reserve made up of forty members of the 2nd Virginia. The forty, however, were stationed so far back from the river that they could not reach it in time to prevent the Federals from crossing. Even so, Averell launched four attacks before he broke through the barriers. He suffered several casualties in doing so, but captured twenty-five Virginians.[13]

It took Averell more than two hours to pass his entire force over the river; until the last man crossed, he remained in place, as if fearful of what he might encounter inland. While he massed, Fitz galloped up from his headquarters at Culpeper, gathered up his two thousand troopers, and led them to Brandy Station on the Orange & Alexandria Railroad. He expected to meet Averell's attack at that point, but when his Academy friend did not appear, he proceeded south, by a diagonal road, to the river.

Averell had advanced less than half a mile from Kelly's when Fitz made contact with him at about noon. "We met them in ful[l] force," wrote a member of the 5th Virginia, "drawn up in line of battle across an opening of several hundred yards. They had an entire division of cavalry, to oppose Fitzhugh Lee's one brigade."[14]

Lee (and Stuart, who had arrived on the scene but at first only to advise) found that Averell's right still rested on the river, while his left lay on open farmland. Both flanks, however, were anchored by artillery; moreover, they were connected by a line of stone fencing that sheltered numerous sharpshooters. A large reserve was stationed in the rear, ready for use wherever needed.

The dispositions appeared formidable, and Averell certainly had an edge in numbers, but neither Stuart nor Lee believed him capable of withstanding a well-mounted saber charge. They launched several of these, but only after softening up Averell's position with rifle fire from dismounted skirmishers of the 3rd Virginia. When the troopers on Averell's left appeared to waver under this fusillade, Lee ordered the 2nd Virginia, led this day by Maj. Cary Breckinridge, to strike the flank in column of fours.

At a distance of six hundred yards from its target, the 2nd bounded forward, to be met halfway by counterattacking members of the 1st Rhode Island, one of the regiments Lee had routed on February 25. To Stuart's and Lee's amazement, most of the 2nd Virginia turned and fled even before the Rhode Islanders thudded into them. A concerned Stuart stepped in to order up the 1st

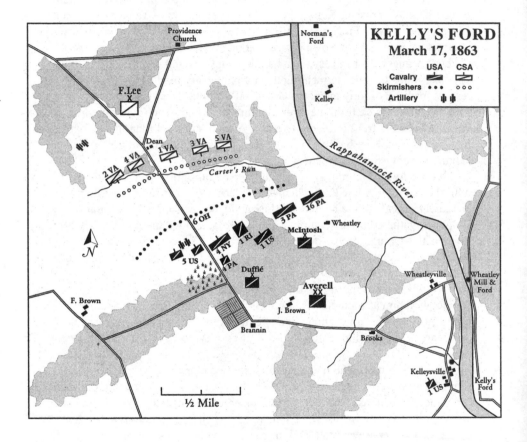

KELLY'S FORD
March 17, 1863

and 4th Virginia. Galloping south, they broke the Rhode Islanders' formation and hustled them to the rear.[15]

During Breckinridge's abortive assault, the 3rd Virginia of Col. Thomas Owen had advanced against the other end of Averell's line, which intersected pastureland owned by a farmer named Wheatley. "Here we were met by Gen. Lee," wrote Captain Carter of the 3rd, "who ordered Col. Owen to charge the enemy. This was done in gallant style, [the] Regiment sweeping down the fence along the road & passing through an opening between the rail fences running at right angles across the field."

Having cleared one barrier, the 3rd ran aground against the next:

> We found it impossible to get through the stone fence . . . & so the Regiment turned across the field to our left to some straw stacks & wheeled down toward Wheatleys ice house hoping to be able to get at their right flank. But observing this, the enemy's sharpshooters, who had fled from the approach of the column, returned to their posts & opened a hot fire into it as it passed.

Several of Carter's comrades, including a few officers, went down with wounds. Eventually the regiment, having lost its momentum, turned to the rear to avoid further damage. So did Rosser's 5th Virginia, which had charged to the left of the 3rd, only to be stymied by the same obstructions. In addition to defeat, Rosser suffered a painful wound in the foot.[16]

The two regiments had been turned back not only by farm barriers, but also by the sharpshooters of the 16th Pennsylvania. The Pennsylvanians had something to prove; the majority of the captives taken at Hartwood Church had come from their regiment. Effective, too, were the volleys delivered by the artillery defending that flank. Among those who fell to cannon fire was John Pelham, who, upon arriving from Culpeper with the Stuart Horse Artillery, had impulsively joined the 3rd Virginia in its charge. Struck in the skull by a shell fragment, Pelham was led to the rear, his unconscious body draped over his saddle. The artillerist succumbed to his wound just after midnight, mourned by everyone who knew him. Receiving the news of his death, both Stuart and von Borcke broke down and wept. Stuart saw to it that the fallen officer received a posthumous promotion to lieutenant colonel. He considered the gesture the least he could do for the "gallant Pelham."[17]

Once Owen's and Rosser's outfits withdrew, Stuart, who had assumed command on the left, personally rallied the 2nd Virginia and positioned it for another charge, this time flanked by the 1st and 4th Virginia. As bugles shrilled, all went forward, the Rebel yell on their lips. In minutes, however, the war cry had been drowned out by Averell's artillery, which broke the attackers' columns well short of their objective. As soon as the guns fell silent, Federal troopers countercharged in such numbers as to put all three regiments to flight.

Now Stuart and Lee were beside themselves with anxiety, anger, and disbelief. How could well-aligned ranks of charging Virginians be so quickly scattered and driven back? Soon afterward, in fact, everyone fell back to the protection of the Stuart Horse Artillery, now under Captain Breathed. After retreating about a mile, the Confederate leaders again wheeled their lines about to oppose the enemy. Their men had too much fight in them to concede defeat just yet.[18]

As if reluctant to jeopardize the success he had gained thus far, Averell did not follow for almost an hour, and when he did, he refused to attack. At Stuart's urging, Fitz Lee returned to the offensive, this time leading the able-bodied men of each of his regiments forward en masse. The adjutant of the 3rd Virginia described the moment Lee committed his regiment to battle: "About 3 P.M. our signal guns now fired, then we heard the loud voice . . . commanding 'Forward gallop March'—saw the gleam of his battle blade and dashed onward to the charge. It was a . . . splendid charge, the prettiest I ever witnessed."[19]

Pleasing to the eye it might have been, but it achieved nothing of lasting importance. Perhaps the most successful participant was the 4th Virginia, under now-Lieutenant Colonel Payne, still recuperating from his Williamsburg wound but unwilling to remain inactive. Thanks to an effective covering fire from Breathed's guns, Payne and some of his troopers penetrated Averell's left and ranged along the Union line, shooting and slashing, until counterattacks thrust them back decisively, along with every other regiment involved in the assault. By the time the cannon smoke wafted away, Averell's gunners and carbineers had littered the field with almost fifty horses and riders. Hundreds of other Virginians had been persuaded to return to their preattack positions.

Stuart and Lee now feared for the safety of the entire command, especially for its least mobile component, the horse artillery. The guns might be lost should Averell advance and follow up his gains. Lee's regiments were fought out, and no reserves were on hand. Rooney Lee had been sent for, but his men were too far off to be of assistance. Summoning Hampton's brigade was out of the question.[20]

Instead of exploiting his gains, the Union commander elected to withdraw. With the afternoon nearly spent, darkness was fast approaching; this worried him, as did the evident weariness of many of his troops. By 5:30, Averell was guiding everyone across Kelly's Ford, leaving the debris-strewn field to his opponents. Also left behind was a sack of roasting beans, with a note attached. Taunt for taunt, the note answered the one Lee had written to him: "Dear Fitz: Here's your coffee. Here's your visit. How did you like it?"[21]

>─┤◇>──O──<◇>─┤─<

The aftermath of the fighting at Kelly's Ford included a division-wide effort at mind control and self-delusion. Averell's retreat gave Stuart grounds, however shaky, for declaring that Lee's men had emerged the victors. This symbol of success, and the supreme difficulty of accepting the premise that on every part

of the field they had been driven into headlong—even frenzied—retreat, prevented the cavalry of the Army of Northern Virginia from admitting defeat.
Those few participants willing to grant the enemy some small tactical advantage stressed Averell's great numerical superiority—overlooking the fact that
the forces actually engaged were of approximately equal size.

For their part, the Yankees regarded the fight as an unambiguous victory,
proof that two arduous years of training and field experience—replete with miscues, defeats, and disasters—had paid off in combat. Although less than one-
third of Hooker's cavalry had taken part, everyone wearing a blue jacket with
yellow trim professed to be heartened and uplifted by the success Averell's
troopers and gunners had achieved. They vowed never again to fear matching
swords with Stuart's cavaliers.[22]

If the outcome gave the Yankees a heaping dose of self-confidence, Stuart
and Lee could not allow it to cost their men the sense of superiority they had
been cultivating since First Manassas. Therefore, in the days following the
engagement, they published a series of congratulatory addresses calculated to
sweep away the least hint of doubt that their men had prevailed over Averell.

To Stuart, the performance of Lee's brigade reflected "the highest credit on
its commander, its officers, and its men. On no occasion have I seen more
instances of individual prowess—never such heroic firmness in the presence of
danger." This steadfastness had produced "the serious disaster inflicted upon
this insolent foe, in which he was driven, broken and discomfited, across the
Rappahannock—leaving many of his dead and wounded on the field." Triumph,
however, had not come without cost: "The gallant Pelham—so noble, so true—
will be mourned by the nation."

For his part, Fitz Lee applauded the "heroic achievements" of his men,
who "confronted and hurled back" an enemy whose intent had been "to penetrate the interior, to destroy our railroads, to burn, rob, and devastate, and to
commit their customary depredations upon the property of our peaceful citizens." In addition to validating the Confederates' skill and steadfastness, the
results "have confirmed Abolition cavalry in their notions of running."[23]

This was so much stuff and nonsense, and most of Stuart's men knew it.
All the celebratory rhetoric at the command of the Confederate cavalry hierar-
chy could not disguise the fact that someone had blundered, and badly. Even
the high command came to see things this way. One indication was a military
court, convened three weeks after the battle, to evaluate the conduct of the officers on duty at Kelly's Ford when Averell fought his way across the river.
Inquiries of this sort do not follow a decisive, glorious victory.[24]

>—◆—O—◆—<

In later days, Stuart was forced to make staff changes, one of which was partic-
ularly painful. On the twenty-first, he replaced his former adjutant general, Maj.
J. T. W. Hairston, who had quit the staff, with Channing Price. It was an
inspired move; William Blackford later described the twenty-year-old—whose

near-photographic memory enabled him to transcribe verbatim lengthy orders hours after Stuart imparted them—as the finest adjutant he had ever seen.[25]

Five days later, Stuart tended to a much sadder chore, asking the Adjutant and Inspector General's Office in Richmond to approve the assignment of Maj. Robert F. Beckham to command the Stuart Horse Artillery in Pelham's stead. To obtain Beckham's services, Stuart had gone outside the command—for that matter, outside the horse artillery—to the infantry-affiliated mounted artillery. He might have selected a subordinate who had proven his worth under Pelham, such as Breathed, Chew, Hart, or Moorman. (To gain promotion, Henry had recently transferred to the mounted artillery, being replaced by Captain William M. McGregor.)[26]

Whatever Stuart's reasons for not promoting from within, he had chosen well. He had been familiar with Beckham's record since First Manassas, when the officer's two-gun section had helped Stuart harass McDowell's fugitives. While Beckham—to no one's surprise—would not match his lamented predecessor as a combat leader, he was a more effective organizer and administrator than Pelham had ever been. Perhaps in recognition of these talents, as soon as Beckham's appointment was confirmed, Stuart announced that the horse artillery would henceforth be a "separate corps," its batteries no longer attached to individual brigades. Beckham, therefore, would exercise centralized control over the battalion, authority that had not been granted to his predecessor.[27]

Beckham would soon be able to prove to skeptical comrades, and to himself, whether he could fill Pelham's boots. Late on April 13, six days after he was announced as commander of the Stuart Horse Artillery Battalion, a long line of Yankee cavalry, accompanied by batteries, pack mules, and led horses, wended its way up the Rappahannock from Falmouth. Stuart's scouts scrutinized the movement, which their leader at first supposed was a diversion to cover a change of base by Hooker "or some other operation of the grand army."[28]

Stuart was half right, but he would not know it for some time. This advance by ten thousand troopers under George Stoneman—who had returned to cavalry command after his brief, checkered stint with the infantry—was the opening gambit in Joe Hooker's effort to outmaneuver, entrap, and destroy the Army of Northern Virginia. With winter over, Fighting Joe had revived Burnside's weather-plagued strategy of sweeping around the Rebel left. This he planned to accomplish with approximately half of his 125,000-man army, while the remainder attacked Lee's front to hold his attention. Stoneman and his troopers were to deliver the first blows against Lee's rear, while positioning themselves to harass his troops as they fell back on Richmond under the pounding of Hooker's infantry. The plan of campaign would give the rejuvenated Federal horse the chance to do some raiding of its own after chasing down so many Confederate expeditions. Stoneman's objectives included strategic stretches of the Virginia Central and the Richmond, Fredericksburg & Potomac Railroads, Lee's lifelines of supply.[29]

But Hooker put his plan in motion too early in the season. It was Hooker's and Stoneman's misfortune—as it had been Burnside's—to run afoul of winter-like weather. Late on the fourteenth, despite opposition from Fitz Lee's men on the lower shore, Stoneman began crossing at Beverly Ford, seven miles upriver from Kelly's. Only one brigade had gotten over when rain began to fall, followed by hail. One Federal called it "the most dreadful storm I ever saw." With difficulty, Stoneman recalled the unit that had crossed, then waited for the weather to clear. While he pondered the vagaries of nature, Stuart's scouts fixed a close eye on him and kept their superior abreast of his progress, or lack thereof. From Stuart's point of view, the news was good, and it kept getting better. By the next morning, he could inform R. E. Lee that the continuing rain and swollen rivers had "entirely arrested military operations on the upper Rappahannock."[30]

The skies did not clear for days, and the freshet did not recede for two weeks. During that time, as Stoneman paced the upper bank, his enemy tried to determine his reason for being there. Stuart and other commanders began to suspect that a full-scale turning movement was in the works, not merely a change of position. Hooker himself, concerned that he had lost the advantage of surprise, reluctantly revamped his strategy. By the twenty-ninth, when the river had fallen to the point where Stoneman could cross, Hooker put into operation a new plan to strike Lee from the blind side. The main effort would now be made by the infantry and artillery. Stoneman's raiders would head south as before, but in detachments that Hooker hoped would "dash off to right and left, and inflict a vast deal of mischief," thus keeping the enemy off balance and ignorant of the intentions of the main body.[31]

Even before Stoneman could cross, Hooker started for Kelly's Ford with three of his corps. The foot soldiers marched far enough back from the river to escape the notice of Stuart's pickets and scouts; the Confederates' attention was also diverted by noisy demonstrations downstream. The corps crossed on the evening of the twenty-eighth and the following morning. On the lower bank, they marched through heavy forest cover toward two fords on the Rapidan River, below which they would find a direct route to the rear of Lee's troops at Fredericksburg, ten miles away.

By the evening of April 30, the Federals had rendezvoused at Chancellorsville, a crossroads clearing in the midst of a three hundred-square-mile tangle of scrub oak and second-growth pine known as the Wilderness. Meanwhile, Lee was held in place by the nearly sixty thousand troops Hooker had left behind, who had bridged the river opposite Fredericksburg much as Burnside had four months earlier. Stoneman's riders were now well on their way to the rail lines in Lee's rear. Thus far Hooker's plan had progressed without a noticeable hitch. Should his luck hold for a few hours more, the Army of Northern Virginia would find itself in the jaws of a murderous vise.[32]

By now, Lee was aware that something was going on behind his back. The previous morning, he had begun to suspect that the attacks from Falmouth were a feint and that "the principal effort of the enemy would be made in some other quarter." Almost simultaneously, Stuart informed him that large bodies of Yankees were crossing the Rappahannock on pontoons at Kelly's, having thrust aside the guard there. Later in the day, Hooker's soldiers were seen heading for the Rapidan fords via roads that converged at Chancellorsville. The eyes and ears of the army had done their job, if a trifle belatedly.[33]

As soon as they received word of Hooker's coming, Stuart's troopers—the only part of the army in position to disrupt the enemy's march to the Rapidan— went into action. Following Stoneman's mid-April advance, Stuart had concentrated Fitz and Rooney's Lee's brigades in the Brandy Station area. Sometime before 9:00 A.M. on the twenty-ninth, Rooney Lee, who was stationed closest to the river with two regiments—his other outfits having been detached to forage— sent Colonel Chambliss's 13th Virginia to meet the head of the infantry column.

According to Stuart, Chambliss "checked" the foot soldiers—undoubtedly by fighting, falling back, and fighting again—at a point about a mile inland. Apparently Chambliss maintained contact with his opponents throughout the morning, doing his utmost to impede their advance. With the rest of his brigade, R. E. Lee's son dug in about midway between the disputed ford and Brandy Station, with his cousin's troopers right behind him.

About 1:00 P.M., Stuart learned that another, larger body of infantry was moving east of him near a farmstead called Madden's. Leaving Chambliss to hold the first column in check, he led the balance of his force, Fitz Lee's men in advance, toward the point in question. But by the time he neared Madden's, most of the foot soldiers had already passed through the area, heading south.

In a bold move, bands of troopers attacked and cut off a portion of the column, taking prisoners from all three of its corps. The captives revealed that their comrades were heading for Germanna Ford on the Rapidan. Stuart began to understand what Hooker was up to; he relayed his findings to Lee's headquarters via the field telegraph. At this point, more than ever, Stuart must have wished that Hampton's brigade had not been sent so far from the Rappahannock as to be beyond quick recall.[34]

The Beau Sabreur saw he must get in front of the blue column and halt, or at least slow, its progress toward Lee's rear. He accompanied Fitz Lee as the latter's brigade, despite its "hungry and jaded condition," galloped off to Raccoon Ford, upstream from Germanna. At the same time, Rooney Lee, with Beale's 9th Virginia (Chambliss's regiment would join him at Culpeper Court House that evening) and four artillery pieces, was ordered to a more westerly point on the Rapidan, where he might observe events in the direction of Gordonsville. From that quarter, Stuart had received a report that Stoneman's raiders were advancing on the Virginia Central.

With two regiments, Rooney Lee could hardly have expected to turn back Stoneman's corps. He could, however, harass and impede the raiders and perhaps limit the damage they inflicted on his father's supply lines. For the next week, he did just that, winning Stuart's praise for his "sagacity" and "good conduct," as well as for "the great efficiency on the part of his command."[35]

The period began quietly enough. On the thirtieth, Chambliss, in advance of Lee's main force, encountered one of Stoneman's columns under Averell, above and, later, at Brandy Station. At both points, the colonel slowed his enemy substantially before rejoining his brigade leader. The following day, Rooney Lee, with the larger part of both regiments, occupied Rapidan Station on the Orange & Alexandria Railroad as Averell approached from the north side of the river. Lee maneuvered so nimbly and used his guns to such good effect that his adversary, who commanded thirty-four hundred men, feared he was outnumbered. Averell spent most of May 1 trying to force his way over the stream, a feat that became an impossibility after Lee's troopers burned the only bridge in the area.

With Averell stymied—he would lose his command as a result— Lee traveled down the O & A to Gordonsville. At the junction, he turned east, having learned that another raiding party, under John Buford, with General Stoneman in accompaniment, had struck the Virginia Central at Trevilian Station and Louisa Court House. Meeting Buford's vedettes west of Trevilian, the 9th Virginia drove them back upon the main force, taking more than thirty prisoners at a cost of four men wounded. After reinforcing Beale's regiment with Chambliss's, Rooney Lee advanced boldly, although believing his opposition to consist of at least three regiments. When the Yankees shied from him, turning south toward the James, Lee, his "men and horses being worried out by four days' fighting and marching," retired to Gordonsville.[36]

Next day, after a brief rest, Lee made for the confluence of the James and Rivanna Rivers, where the village of Columbia was under attack by still another of Stoneman's detachments. The Confederates arrived too late on May 3 to prevent the leader of the party, Col. Sir Percy Wyndham, English-born commander of the 1st New Jersey Cavalry, from burning bridges, supply houses, and river barges. Even so, their approach deterred the Briton from destroying the canal and aqueduct at Columbia and torching the Richmond & Danville Railroad bridge at Ashland Station.[37]

On its tired animals, Lee's half brigade failed to overtake the departing raiders. It made amends after locating Stoneman's temporary headquarters at Thompson's Cross Roads on the South Anna River, midway between Columbia and Louisa Court House. In the pre-dawn darkness of the fourth, it surprised and routed a reconnoitering party from the 5th U.S. Cavalry, wounding four Regulars and capturing thirty-two. When his opponents broke contact and fled, Lee's men, who had marched more than seventy miles in the past two days and more than twice that distance since leaving Stuart, were in no condition to pursue.

But they were not done with Stoneman. After resting for a day, they followed his reunited command on its way back to Hooker's army. As the raiders crossed the North Anna River, Rooney Lee struck again; as a result, another eighteen prisoners fell into his hands. On the evening of the sixth, Lee finally ended his attacks and stepped back to admire his accomplishments. He was generally pleased by what he saw. While Stoneman had inflicted much miscellaneous damage to the railroads, bridges, and canals of south-central Virginia, he had achieved nothing of enduring importance. On the other hand, had Lee and his hard-marching pursuers not dogged his heels, harassing him at many turns, Stoneman might have put a critical segment of the Confederate transportation system out of commission for weeks or even months.[38]

>-+-◊>-+-◊--◊-+-◊-+-<

As Fitz Lee and he hurried to the Rapidan on the afternoon of April 29, Stuart sent couriers to warn the few guards patrolling that stream of Hooker's approach. He later learned that every messenger was captured before reaching his destination. Fortunately, a local resident carried the news to a small body of troops at Germanna Ford, including Maj. Charles R. Collins of the 15th Virginia and two of Stuart's staff officers, Lt. Frank Robertson and Lt. Thomas R. Price, brother of Channing Price. The trio had been supervising an eighty-man engineer party in rebuilding a bridge near the crossing site. The warning came too late to permit them to escape, but it gave them time to prepare a defense. Upon arriving, Lt. Col. Duncan McVicar's 6th New York Cavalry, leading the Union column, made prisoners of about half the party. The rest, however, put up such a spirited fight that they delayed the crossing of two army corps for something over an hour before finally being forced to surrender.

Collins, Robertson, and Price all managed to escape, but not without difficulty—or, in Price's case, without embarrassment. The aide had been forced to leave behind his personal diary, which contained several unflattering references to Stuart, whom he had found to be pompous, garrulous, and egotistical. The book fell into Union hands, military and civilian. When excerpts were later published in the *New York Times,* Price quit the division staff in disgrace.[39]

Early that evening, Stuart and Lee reached and crossed the Rapidan at Raccoon Ford. While the main body grabbed a few hours' sleep, Owen's 3rd Virginia was sent, by way of the road from Germanna Ford to Fredericksburg, to get in front of Hooker's foot soldiers. Waking the balance of Lee's brigade early on the thirtieth, Stuart led its men through the trees toward Wilderness Tavern, on the turnpike to Fredericksburg. By that route, he could keep on Hooker's right flank, monitoring and perhaps hindering his progress.

In the light of early morning, the head of Fitz Lee's command made contact with the Federals near the tavern, where a sharp fight broke out. Stuart claimed that by forcing Hooker to deploy several regiments in lines of battle, Fitz delayed his march until noon. But at some point during the clash, Stuart heard from roving scouts that he was engaging only a part of the force involved in Hooker's turning movement. Another large body—which turned out to be Meade's V Army Corps—had crossed the river several miles closer to Fredericksburg and had already reached Chancellorsville, cutting Stuart off from the larger portion of his army.

To get around this body and join Robert E. Lee, he would have to make a wide circuit to the south and east. Breaking contact with the enemy, he left the turnpike for Todd's Tavern, along the southern edge of the Wilderness. From there he hoped to reach Spotsylvania Court House, at which point he could turn north to Fredericksburg.

A rainy night came on before Fitz Lee's men could pass Todd's Tavern. Stuart placed them in bivouac near the hostelry and then, "anxious to know what the commanding general desired me to do," rode on ahead to Fredericksburg, accompanied by his staff and a small escort. He had not gone far before he encountered in the darkness a party from McVicar's 6th New York. This unit, one of only three cavalry regiments that had not accompanied Stoneman on his expedition, had already seen much action in the unfolding campaign. Early that morning, hours after capturing half the engineer party at Germanna Ford, it had wrested control of a bridge over Wilderness Run from the 3rd Virginia. In fulfillment of its orders from Stuart, Owen's regiment, by taking possession of the span, had interposed between the oncoming Federals and Fredericksburg. But Owen was not at full strength, several of his companies having become detached after losing their way in the dark woods. The fragment that remained put up a "splendid fight," but in the end the New Yorkers forced it into retreat.[40]

McVicar could not, however, prevent Owen from spreading word of the Federal advance on Fredericksburg. As what was left of the 3rd Virginia circled back toward Fitz Lee's main body, it halted briefly in the forest. While a courier stood by, Owen's adjutant, Lt. Robert Hubard, scribbled a message to Robert E. Lee "on a miserable bit of paper, upon [his] knee and while it was dripping rain." Years later, Hubard claimed that the dispatch "carried to General Lee his first positive knowledge that a flanking column was moving upon him! For Stuart's [earlier] dispatch was uncertain and gave no definite information as to whether this was a heavy flank movement or some little feint." Upon receiving the intelligence, Lee supposedly ordered Jackson's corps to march at once for Chancellorsville. Correctly or not, Hubard always believed his message prompted his army's commander to face about and confront Hooker, one of the turning points of the campaign.[41]

As the 3rd Virginia groped its way back to Todd's Tavern, McVicar's Federals beat it there. Impulsively they attacked, taking on the better part of a brigade. At first Fitz Lee's men were stunned. Two of their regiments fell back under the onslaught, but Rosser's 5th Virginia counterattacked with great verve, scattering the New Yorkers and killing McVicar.

McVicar's attack—which Stuart called "by no means an insignificant affair," since the Federals had penetrated almost to some roads filled with wagon trains and artillery teams—made Stuart fear that at Todd's Tavern, Fitz Lee's men were isolated and vulnerable. Thus, when he resumed his trek to army headquarters, he took the entire brigade along. Without waiting for rations and forage, the troopers pushed on through the night. Early on May 1—thanks to the efficiency of their guides—they made contact with Jackson's corps on the Orange Plank Road southeast of Chancellorsville.[42]

Jackson held the left flank of the line that Robert E. Lee had built after leaving Fredericksburg to accept Hooker's challenge. The previous day, Fighting Joe had pushed almost two miles closer to the Confederate rear at Fredericksburg before pulling back to fortify the crossroads his advance had secured hours before. It appeared that he was passing the initiative to his opponent. If so, Stuart had no doubt it would prove a fatal mistake.

Soon after joining Jackson, Fitz Lee's horsemen took position on his left, west of the plank road near a forest ironworks known as Catharine Furnace. While the main armies fought that day, the cavalry had little to do, especially given Stoneman's absence from the front. Late in the afternoon, Stuart advanced Beckham, with guns from Breathed's and McGregor's batteries, to clear Yankee infantry from a ridge in front of Brig. Gen. Ambrose R. Wright's brigade of Jackson's corps. The movement, and the shelling Beckham unleashed, drew a heated response from eight or ten Union batteries, well masked by the high ground. The exchange of fire lasted nearly an hour, after which Beckham was withdrawn. By then, however, the major believed he had silenced at least some of the enemy cannons.[43]

By then, too, the enemy had taken a toll not only of Beckham's gunners but also of spectators, including Channing Price, who had been struck in the leg by a shell fragment. A few hours later, even as he appeared to be recovering from the wound, the youngster succumbed to blood loss. As Stuart assured Price's mother, his passing was "deeply felt by the Cavalry Division (of which he was a bright ornament) and unanimously mourned." With a heavy heart, Stuart replaced his adjutant with Maj. Henry Brainard McClellan of the 3rd Virginia, a cousin of the deposed commander of the Army of the Potomac.[44]

While Channing Price lay dying, Robert E. Lee made a limited reconnaissance of Hooker's fortified line and reached the unsettling conclusion that every part of it was strongly held. Even so, that afternoon a few of Fitz Lee's more enterprising scouts ventured west, emerged from the trees on the far end of the Union battle line, and discovered that Hooker's right flank, held by the XI Corps of Maj. Gen. Oliver Otis Howard, was "in the air" and vulnerable to assault. Stuart relayed the news to Lee that evening as the army leader conferred with Jackson about the possibility of taking the offensive. Lee incorporated the intelligence into his planning, which was predicated on shoving Hooker out of the woods and across the Rappahannock.

After intense discussion, Lee decided that Jackson would take his entire corps, twenty-eight thousand strong, on a march across the front of Hooker's seventy-three thousand troops to attack the far end of the XI Corps. Lee would remain in front of his enemy with two divisions of infantry, supported by the 3rd and 4th Virginia of his nephew's brigade—the remainder of which would screen Jackson's advance. The army leader appreciated the magnitude of the risk he was taking: Should Hooker attack him in his weakened condition, he would have to retreat south, abandoning Fredericksburg. But Lee believed the gamble had been forced on him by events and could not be avoided.

The flank march, via a little-used woodcutter's road, began at 7:30 on the morning of the second. Fitz Lee's cavalry not only led the way but, along with several guns of the Stuart Horse Artillery Battalion, also guarded Jackson's right, the flank most exposed to enemy view. The march proceeded smoothly, punctuated by only a few clashes with cavalry patrols. Every thrust was parried by Fitz Lee's troopers; no Yankees penetrated far enough to spy Jackson's column, which Stuart was accompanying. Meanwhile, the strangely quiescent Hooker made no attempt to overwhelm the small force in front of him.[45]

Late in the day, the cavalry scouts led Jackson to the turnpike beyond Hooker's right. At one point, the column halted. As Col. E. P. Alexander of Jackson's artillery recalled:

> Fitz took Gen. Jackson forward to a point where, without being himself seen, he could overlook quite a portion of the enemy's position. When he [Jackson] came back from the view there was a perceptible increase of eagerness in his air, & he hurried the head of the column over to a cross road we had to follow.[46]

A little after 6:00 P.M., after massing his men in the woods just beyond the open flank, Jackson passed the word to advance. Covered by artillery, including two cannons under Beckham—whose work this day won plaudits from Old Stonewall himself—thousands of Confederates, shouting and cheering, sprang forward to the attack. They caught Howard's troops at supper, their arms stacked beside their campfires. The Union line promptly went under in the manner of Pope's left flank when Longstreet struck at Second Manassas. Consternation and panic swept along the line, as terror-stricken Federals fled through the trees. Only after dark did the tide of defeat reach the works at Chancellorsville, where it began to recede.

Soon after the attack rolled forward, Jackson detached an infantry regiment and sent it north to secure Ely's Ford, a possible avenue of enemy escape. Stuart, who had been left with little to do once the shooting started, asked his friend if some of his men should accompany the foot soldiers. Jackson assented, and Stuart rode off with a sizable detachment of Lee's brigade. Sometime after dark, having gained the heights overlooking the ford, he was sought out by a courier, who announced that Stuart had been summoned to Jackson's headquarters. Upon arriving, Stuart learned that Stonewall had been wounded—as it turned out, by his own men, firing blindly in the dark—and that his ranking subordinate, A. P. Hill, was also incapacitated. While they were out of action, Stuart had been assigned to command the Second Corps.[47]

The following day, May 3, Fitz Lee's horsemen returned to their customary mission of guarding the flanks and rear of the infantry. It was important work, but for strategic significance, it paled in comparison to the effort Stuart turned in as Jackson's temporary successor. Although he had occasionally commanded forces of combined arms, Stuart was largely unfamiliar with infantry operations. Nevertheless, he engineered an attack along the pike that shattered the now-compacted Union line and forced its defenders to take refuge behind a hastily constructed and less defensible position north of Chancellorsville.

With the Confederates in possession of the field at day's end, Hooker had no option but to recross the rivers in his rear and head home in defeat. His well-crafted campaign to take the Army of Northern Virginia unawares had been reduced to rubble. Stuart and his horsemen could reflect with pride that from start to finish, they had been an integral part of the wrecking crew.[48]

Chapter Fourteen

From the Heights
to the Valley

Stuart's performance in corps command won the praise of many observers, including veteran infantry officers. After Hooker withdrew from Chancellorsville and returned to Falmouth, a rumor circulated through the army's grapevine that Stuart would receive permanent command of the corps. Another rumor had it that on his deathbed Jackson had asked that Stuart be named his successor. The speculation ceased when army headquarters announced Stuart's 5-10-63 return to the cavalry on May 6, four days before Jackson died of complications from his wounds. Two weeks later, as the army continued to mourn Stonewall's loss, Robert E. Lee elevated Ewell to the command of Jackson's old corps, while forming a Third Corps, which he assigned to A. P. Hill.[1]

When Stuart reassumed command of his division, he found it reunited for the first time in three months. Soon after Hooker crossed the Rappahannock, Hampton's brigade had been recalled from its winter camp. Butler, along with those men who rode the best mounts, galloped on ahead of the main body. Hampton himself, recently returned from South Carolina with his horse hunters, followed. Neither force arrived in time to evict Hooker from the Wilderness. Along with elements of Fitz and Rooney Lee's brigades, however, they crossed the Rappahannock to ensure that the Yankees returned to their camps opposite Fredericksburg.[2]

On May 11, Stuart recalled his far-flung detachments and, in accordance with Robert E. Lee's wishes, grouped them near Culpeper Court House. Lee had directed Stuart: "Get your cavalry together and give them breathing time, so that, when you strike, Stoneman may feel you." In fact, George Stoneman was on inactive service and would not be heard from again in the main theater of operations. Like Averell, he had fallen victim to the perceived failure of his excursion into the Confederate rear.

His replacement, the energetic but erratic and impetuous Alfred Pleasonton, took careful note of Stuart's concentration in Culpeper County. Pleasonton may also have learned of Lee's injunction that Stuart recruit his strength before striking. Although less excitable subordinates such as John Buford believed that

Stuart was going nowhere on his own, Pleasonton got the impression that Stuart was preparing to raid behind Union lines, and soon. He took pains to communicate his opinion to Hooker.[3]

In fact, neither Lee nor Stuart was contemplating a cavalry expedition. Stuart had been sent to Culpeper to take advantage of the area's good grazing land, which compensated to some extent for the scarcity of forage, and to guard the army's rear against a repetition of Stoneman's Raid. Additionally, Stuart was preparing his soon-to-be-reinforced command for participation in a major campaign that was already well formed in Robert E. Lee's mind.[4]

With the enemy across from him chastised, quiet, and immobile, Lee was feeling confident enough to lay the groundwork for another invasion of the North. In midmonth, he revealed his vision to President Davis and Secretary of War Seddon. Their meetings focused on the theme that Lee would achieve several objectives by invading Maryland and Pennsylvania. These included relieving Virginia, at least temporarily, of the ravages of war; subsisting the army on the rich farmlands of the enemy; and giving aid and comfort to allies of the Confederacy, including "peace party" politicians in the North.

Another objective was to force Federal troops to be withdrawn from Maj. Gen. Ulysses S. Grant's Army of the Tennessee, thereby preventing it from attacking or besieging Vicksburg. This end was not realized; before May ended, Grant had begun to invest the Mississippi River stronghold. Therefore, Lee, in later meetings with government officials, began to portray the invasion as a lever for lifting the siege Grant had imposed on the garrison of Lt. Gen. John C. Pemberton. In the end, the general's persuasiveness won out. He was pleased by the authority given him, but he was also aware that yet again he was going to gamble with the limited resources of his nation. Even so, based on the heroic performances his army had turned in throughout his tenure, Lee had every right to believe that a second campaign above the Potomac would prove more successful than the first.[5]

Recalling how the Yankees had treated his nephew's brigade at Kelly's Ford, Lee took pains to ensure that the cavalry was strong enough to support the invasion fully. He spent weeks seeking a way to augment it. One place he looked for reinforcements was Maj. Gen. Samuel Jones's Department of Western Virginia. At first Jones tried to beg off, but by mid-May he agreed to loan Lee the Virginia brigade of Brig. Gen. Albert G. Jenkins, then concentrating at Staunton. Jones also permitted Lee to recall the Laurel Brigade from the Valley. Finally, Lee got the commander of the Department of North Carolina, D. H. Hill, to send him two state regiments under Beverly Robertson.[6]

Though happy to see his division increased, Stuart blanched at the thought of renewing acquaintances with Grumble Jones and Robertson. He was also troubled by the quality of some of the additions. Jones's command, which now included Capt. Wiley H. Griffin's Baltimore Light Artillery, was experienced and savvy, but the regiments Robertson would lead north were raw and untried. Stuart did not know enough about the quality of Jenkins's brigade—which consisted of three regiments and two battalions of horsemen, as well as Capt. Thomas E. Jackson's Charlottesville Battery—to form an early opinion, but he was aware that its leader was not a professional soldier. In the end, Stuart's men came to view their temporary comrades from western Virginia as "essentially mounted infantry and only effective as such" and as "a species of irregular auxiliaries."[7]

That description also fit yet another mounted force that, theoretically at least, would assist the A.N.V. on the road north. This was the brigade of Brig. Gen. John D. Imboden, which most recently had been campaigning in northwestern Virginia. In time, even Lee would come to regard Imboden's command—one regiment of cavalry, one of mounted infantry, a company of partisan rangers, and a horse artillery unit (Capt. John H. McClanahan's Staunton Battery)—as unsteady and therefore unreliable. But it was available for service, and the army could use the extra manpower.

At least at the outset of the campaign, Imboden would enjoy a semi-independent status. Rather than serving under Stuart, his men would advance well to the west of the army, guarding its left flank. Imboden would also be expected to cut the supply lines of the forces opposing Lee, including the mighty Baltimore & Ohio, and to gather remounts, rations, and forage that Lee might use upon returning to Virginia. Imboden, who had to collect his scattered troops, would be unable to join Lee at the outset of the invasion, but he would move north as soon as possible. If he did a thorough job on the enemy's supply lines, Lee would know Imboden was in place, protecting his western flank.[8]

If Lee's overriding purpose was to secure warm bodies for his cavalry, he had succeeded. Even without Imboden, Stuart would have a present-for-duty strength of 756 officers and 9,536 troopers, the largest number the Army of Northern Virginia's cavalry would ever field.[9]

While awaiting the newcomers' arrival, Stuart spent weeks resupplying his own units, remounting as many as possible, and drilling and inspecting them. He considered it especially important that instruction be given to the many recruits who had joined the division upon the return of spring. Throughout this period of preparation, the enemy caused no trouble beyond the usual probing of Stuart's picket lines. Yet the Yankees continued to keep close watch on the goings-on near Culpeper. Their observations only confirmed their commander's suspicion that the Beau Sabreur of the Confederacy was about to go raiding once again, perhaps bound for Ohio, western Pennsylvania, or even Washington, D.C.[10]

Toward the end of May, Stuart's camps took on a festive air, as if a holiday picnic, not a major campaign, were in the offing. On the twenty-second, the general reviewed the brigades of Hampton and the Lees, as well as Beckham's horse artillery. Lieutenant Robertson of Stuart's staff called the proceedings "one of the most imposing scenes I ever witnessed." At a certain point, Beckham's guns unleashed a mock barrage, "the Cavalry Division at the same time moving up at a brisk trot and each Squadron as it reached a certain spot, charging with a yell that almost drowned the roar of the opposite batteries." The spectacle "produced a very pleasant excitement and somehow inspired me with a confidence in our cause and an assurance of eventual success."[11]

The festive season continued the following week. On Thursday, the twenty-eighth, Stuart, his wife, his staff, and subordinates including Fitzhugh Lee, Butler, and Young attended a wedding reception for Tom Rosser and his bride, the former Elizabeth Winston, at her family's estate in eastern Hanover County. Rosser's best man was his West Point friend and former colleague in the Washington Artillery, Maj. James Dearing. Still an artilleryman, Dearing would later gravitate, with Rosser's assistance, to a command in the cavalry of the A.N.V.

The following day, as bride and groom started on a brief honeymoon, Fitz Lee and his staff hosted a picnic in Culpeper at which, according to one guest, "all the young ladies from the neighborhood . . . were present. Music and refreshments were on hand and all went off very merrily." Perhaps the bachelor Fitz, having observed Colonel Rosser's marital bliss, hoped to attract a prospective mate.[12]

The holiday season was just getting started. Stuart proposed another review for the first week in June. This would incorporate Robertson's regiments, which had reached Culpeper from Richmond on May 25, and the Laurel Brigade, which Grumble Jones led into camp on June 4, three days after leaving the Valley. General and Mrs. Rosser returned from their wedding trip that same day, and Stuart saw to it that other civilian spectators were on hand for the gala event, as well as for a preview ball at the local courthouse.[13]

Both events passed off in lavish style. At the ball, dancers, musicians, and conversationalists—including many dignitaries from Richmond—combined to present a "gay and dazzling scene" such as the French aristocracy would have applauded. The following day, the troopers and horse artillerymen put on another pageant that enthused participants and spectators alike. A gala review, conducted on the open fields outside Culpeper by Stuart in his finest toggery—golden spurs, ostrich plume, the works—was followed by another sham battle, the work of four and a half brigades of horsemen and no fewer than sixteen cannons. As if the sounds of simulated combat were insufficient to inspire the spectators, three bands provided a tuneful accompaniment. When it ended, the onlookers agreed it had been a memorable event, worth getting the seat of one's pants dirty from sitting on a farmer's hilltop to watch. Yet some of the participants—notably the hard realist Hampton and the curmudgeon Jones—expressed dislike, even distaste, at having participated in such military make-believe.[14]

Stuart had hoped the review would have as its guest of honor the army commander himself. Lee had expressed an interest in attending, but that morning, Joe Hooker, concerned that at least some Confederates had left his front for parts unknown, probed across the Rappahannock near Hamilton's Crossing. The reconnaissance, which failed to give him a definitive answer, forced Lee to remain at Fredericksburg and miss Stuart's show.[15]

Unknown to his opponent, Lee had already begun to shift his army away from the river. On the third, Longstreet's corps had taken up the march toward the Shenandoah, the main corridor of invasion, via Culpeper. Ewell started from Fredericksburg the following day, although A. P. Hill did not pull out until mid-month. By remaining in place, Hill kept Hooker in the dark as to the movements of the rest of the army. By the time Fighting Joe realized Lee was gone, it would be too late to stop him short of the Potomac.[16]

Lee's absence on June 5 prompted him to order another review. The army leader reached Culpeper, with a part of Ewell's column, on the seventh. The next day, Stuart again paraded his legions across open fields east of the courthouse. Because it was hastily put together, the event did not include a mock battle; it also lacked the audience of civilian dignitaries its predecessors had drawn. In their place were hundreds of foot soldiers from John Bell Hood's division of Longstreet's corps, whom Stuart had invited to attend—to his regret.

Although he was a former cavalryman, Hood figured his men would enjoy observing the antics of that part of the army they usually treated with derision, if not downright contempt. Not surprisingly, the spectators hooted, guffawed, and catcalled throughout the review, especially when the horses of raw recruits got out of step or a rider lost his hat trying to keep pace with his comrades. They were especially insulting toward their host, laughing and gesturing as Stuart, awash in gilt-spangled splendor, rode in front of his squadrons, trying to look soldierly in spite of everything.

The scornful noise subsided only after General Lee joined Stuart on the review plain and rode with him to the head of his column. Suddenly the crowd began to cheer, this time without sarcasm—a tribute to the revered army commander. Grudgingly, many of Hood's men extended the honor to Lee's companion as well. If Marse Robert thought highly enough of J. E. B. Stuart to ride beside him in full view of the army, perhaps those cavalry fellows weren't such worthless cusses, after all.[17]

> ⊱──◈──◦──◈──◃

When the day's events ended, Stuart conferred briefly with Lee, who praised the pageant that had been staged in his honor. Then Lee repaired to his headquarters at Culpeper, and Stuart rode east to join his brigades, which had already reached their new bivouacs around Brandy Station. At his headquarters atop Fleetwood Heights, a long, open ridge that overlooked the rail depot, Stuart held last-minute consultations with his staff and a few subordinates. Plans for the morrow were in place and ready to be implemented. At dawn, the division would cross the river to begin screening the army's movement north and west toward the Valley of Virginia. The only component of Stuart's command not on the ground was Jenkins's brigade, which, by prearrangement, was at Front Royal, ready to fall in with the advance of Ewell's corps.

Three of Stuart's brigades spent the night north of the depot: Fitzhugh Lee's, under Tom Munford (Fitz had been laid up by a bout of inflammatory rheumatism) near Oak Shade Church above the Hazel River; Rooney Lee's, on the Welford farm; and Jones's, around a woods chapel known as St. James Church, near the park of Beckham's horse artillery. Hampton's and Robertson's commands had bivouacked below the station, between Fleetwood Heights and Stevensburg. Stuart had placed small bands of picket forces at the local crossing points, including Beverly Ford and, eight miles farther south, the much-fought-over Kelly's Ford. All told, Stuart's lines stretched for ten miles, an indication of the strength and power the cavalry would bring to the task of safeguarding the flanks and rear of the army as it carried the war to the enemy's country.[18]

Unknown to Stuart and his slumbering troopers, for several hours their side of the Rappahannock had been under the eyes of blue-clad cavalrymen. Alfred Pleasonton had convinced his commander that the best way to prevent Stuart from raiding into their rear was to pitch into him, disrupting his preparations and disarranging his regiments. With Hooker's approval, the cavalry leader had assembled his three divisions, some eight thousand strong; had formed them into two columns under Buford and Brig. Gen. David McMurtrie Gregg; and on the eighth had led them by a well-sheltered route to points opposite Beverly and Kelly's Fords. While Stuart's men snoozed, both columns prepared to cross at dawn. On the other side, they would converge on Brandy Station for a united advance against Culpeper Court House, where Pleasonton believed Stuart's troopers were still encamped. Although the Union leader thought of himself as sharp-eyed and perceptive, he was so poor at intelligence gathering that he did not know his enemy's whereabouts.[19]

At about 4:00 A.M., Buford's men crossed at Beverly Ford. They shoved in Jones's startled pickets, then poured inland and surged through the forests northeast of St. James Church. Their vanguard headed for a clearing where Beckham's cannons stood unlimbered and ripe for capture.

Awakened by the sound of pistol and carbine fire, Grumble Jones caught his bearings, then ordered the regiments nearest his headquarters—the 6th and 7th Virginia, under Maj. C. E. Flournoy and Lt. Col. Thomas Marshall—to oppose the newcomers. Half-dressed troopers, some riding bareback, raced past the chapel and, just beyond it, slammed into the head of Buford's column, briefly pushing it back. But as more and more Yankees crossed at Beverly, Jones's men were thrust toward the rear. Even when withdrawing, however, they threw a protective cover around the horse artillery, whose gunners were frantically hitching up the battery teams in the hope of hauling the guns to safety. Even so, they were nearly captured; Yankees were within a few hundred feet of the guns when Jones arrived with the balance of his brigade. By then a few attackers had managed to circle behind the guns, making the gunners believe they were trapped. "The battle raged in our rear," wrote George Neese of the Ashby Battery, "and we were surrounded. For a moment our condition was critical." One of Neese's comrades found himself thinking, "This is a wide contrast from yesterdays Sham Battle."[20]

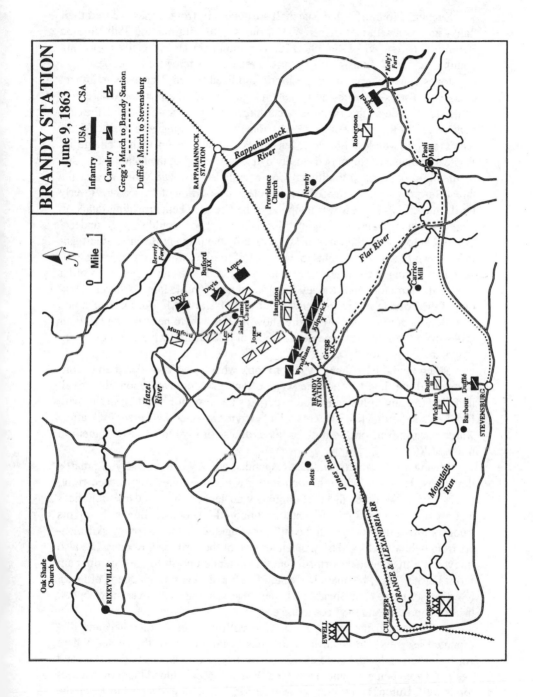

Keeping Flournoy's and Marshall's troopers in front, Jones secured their flanks and rear with Col. Asher W. Harman's 12th Virginia, the 35th Virginia Battalion of Lige White, and the 11th Virginia under an especially promising young officer, Col. Lunsford L. Lomax, a recent transferee from the West.

Jones's newly expanded position stabilized when Harman's regiment charged Buford's advance and Beckham's guns reached a position where they could safely open on the Yankees. According to one of Jones's troopers, the cannons' roar "in the woods at that early hour in the morning was terrific." Harman's assault was less effective, but Jones followed it up with a charge by White's Comanches, supported closely by Lomax, many of the men fighting dismounted, in contrast to traditional Confederate tactics. The series of assaults thrust Buford's leading brigade back and cleared a portion of the road to Beverly Ford. But Jones's success was temporary; the Federals kept crowding inland in large numbers, making it likely that the Laurel Brigade would soon go under.[21]

But help was on the way. Shaken awake by the firing at Beverly, Stuart galloped down Fleetwood Heights to the scene of trouble, wondering how the Yankees had managed to surprise his men. As he rode, he sent couriers to order Munford, Hampton, and Rooney Lee to converge on St. James Church. Only two of the brigade leaders responded in timely fashion. Munford later claimed that Stuart's courier rode off before showing him where he was wanted. Four miles from the fighting, the colonel could not determine what to do or where to march.

When he did head south, Munford took what Stuart considered an unconscionably long time to reach the scene of action. Moreover, upon his arrival, he failed to commit his entire force, perhaps because of his unfamiliarity with Fitz Lee's subordinates. The colonel's behavior affected his career ever afterward: Stuart never forgave him for his tardiness or his limited involvement in the fight.[22]

Meanwhile, Hampton and Lee responded quickly and precisely to Stuart's directions. Hampton's men hustled into position on Jones's embattled right, Lee's astride the other flank. Hampton, who lacked the standard prejudices against dismounted fighting, sent one hundred—later two hundred—of his troopers forward afoot against the still-growing enemy force, driving skirmishers from behind rocks and trees on either side of the ford road. Rooney Lee also threw out a dismounted skirmish line that extended north to the Cunningham farm. Farther back, his main body stood to horse, ready to charge if ordered. Even farther to the rear, Breathed's battery was sending shells over the troopers' heads to burst among the trees to the east.[23]

Buford tested the enemy's new line with a series of mounted and dismounted assaults. He could find no weak point except in the center, where Jones's troopers lacked good cover and were forced to shift position time and again to avoid being caught in the open. When success eluded them in that sector as well, Buford and his on-scene superior, Pleasonton, decided to go on the defensive. When they pulled back to higher ground, Hampton's skirmishers, seeing an opening, pressed forward opposite the Union left. Buford responded with a saber charge by one of his volunteer regiments, supported by a regiment of Regulars, but it failed to regain the initiative. Its repulse confirmed Buford's decision to hold the line until Gregg's column could cross the river at Kelly's and sweep north to join him.[24]

The lower wing, however, was having troubles of its own. When Gregg's delay-plagued column crossed the river sometime after 6:00, his progress was monitored, but not challenged, by Robertson's demibrigade. Unimpeded, the blue riders trotted west and then north toward Brandy Station, their rendezvous with Buford. Gregg's own command was preceded by a smaller division under French-born Col. Alfred N. Duffié, whose six regiments and two batteries continued west toward Stevensburg in order to clear the lower flank. Instead of trying to block one or both columns, or at least keep in touch with them, Robertson merely warned his comrades farther north of their approach. His inaction confirmed Stuart's worst suspicions of Robertson as a field leader.[25]

The news of Gregg's coming finally reached Stuart via relay from Grumble Jones. At first the Confederate leader did not believe—did not *want* to believe—his enemy could have gotten into his rear. His refusal to credit the report enraged Jones and nearly cost Stuart the battle. A trap failed to close on the Confederates at St. James Church only because the crew of a lone howitzer, which, low on ammunition, had drifted out of the fighting, reported to the division adjutant, Major McClellan, whom Stuart had left behind on Fleetwood Heights. As the Union column neared the high ground on its way to Brandy, the howitzer frightened the leader of Gregg's advance, Percy Wyndham, into halting and sending out skirmishers. The delay enabled McClellan to rush word to Stuart, who, finally aware of the threat at his back, sent part of Jones's brigade, followed by most of Hampton's, to the threatened point. McClellan prayed that the reinforcements would arrive before he and the howitzer crew were taken prisoner.[26]

Already McClellan had taken it upon himself to send Butler's 2nd South Carolina, which had been on station at Brandy, toward Stevensburg to guard the rear. The South Carolinian met Duffié east of the village and at first gave him all he could handle. Suddenly, however, Union resistance stiffened. A counterattack scattered the advance guard of the 2nd and killed its lieutenant colonel, Frank Hampton, Wade Hampton's younger brother. Then Duffié trained his troopers and a battery of horse artillery on a second regiment that had come down to oppose him, the 4th Virginia. Catching the new arrivals as they attempted to change position in a narrow, tree-lined road, charging Federals broke the regiment, scattered its pieces, and nearly captured a humiliated Williams Wickham. Before being recalled to Gregg's side at Brandy, Duffié also lobbed some rounds in Butler's direction. One shell nearly tore off the colonel's right foot, and amputated the right leg of the officer riding beside him, William Downs Farley. Butler survived his wound, although he would be out of action for almost a year, but the legendary scout died as he clutched his severed limb.[27]

When Duffié withdrew from Stevensburg, the battle reached its apogee near Brandy Station. No longer cowed by Major McClellan and his howitzer, Gregg's division advanced to and then across the ridge that held Stuart's headquarters. It was almost within striking distance of the Confederate rear at St. James Church when it was met by the advance echelon of the Laurel Brigade. Jones's troopers, accompanied by a section of McGregor's battery and followed by Hampton's brigade and three of Hart's guns, had covered the two miles to Fleetwood Heights in a furious, extended gallop.

Lacking time to form battle lines, the Laurel Brigade slammed into the head of Gregg's column. "Here we had a general fight," observed a trooper in the 12th Virginia, "all mixed up and every man for himself." The more numerous and better-aligned Federals put the first two regiments to flight before being taken in flank by the Deep South units under Hampton. Cobb's Legion, under the hard-driving Pierce Young, struck first, forcing many Yankees to abandon the heights. Simultaneously, Jones's rearmost outfits engaged the gunners of a New York battery that had unlimbered at the base of the ridge, preventing it from training its guns on Hampton's men.[28]

Despite their best efforts, Jones and Hampton were eventually forced off Fleetwood Heights by late-arriving brigades under Gregg. Yet the Federals' advantage could not be sustained. Rallying his displaced troopers and leading them back to the high ground, Hampton retook the ridge as much by force of will as by motive power, his men cutting a jagged swath through the enemy with saber and pistol. After several minutes of the most desperate mounted combat of the war, Hampton uprooted the Federals and flung them down the slope. Victory was secured when Lomax's 11th Virginia overran the battery below the heights, forcing its commander to spike and abandon his guns.[29]

While Gregg grappled desperately with Jones and Hampton, Buford attempted to regain the initiative near St. James Church. Every effort was repulsed by the mounted and dismounted troopers of Rooney Lee, supplemented now by a part of Munford's brigade. Before the fighting ceased, however, Solomon Williams of Lee's 2nd North Carolina ("a good officer much beloved by his men") fell from his horse, a bullet in his skull. Another talented and well-liked officer, Rooney Lee, went down with a disabling wound in the leg. He was fated to spend the next ten months on the sidelines, first as a convalescent, then as a prisoner of war. In the short term, he was succeeded by John Chambliss.[30]

By 5:00, Pleasonton had decided that none of his columns could make additional headway. With Stuart's troopers on the ropes (as he saw it), the Union commander considered his mission accomplished. Calling in Gregg and Duffié, he ordered them, along with Buford's men, back across the river. Their withdrawal via Beverly and Rappahannock Fords was aided by two brigades of infantry that Pleasonton had borrowed from the main army to guard his flanks and rear while his troopers and horse artillerymen concentrated on Stuart.

The foot soldiers' presence in Pleasonton's rear would provide their enemy with grounds for declaring Brandy Station an unfair fight. Yet the infantry had been so lightly engaged as to have been a negligible factor. The thirteen-hour battle had essentially been a cavalry contest, the largest of the war—almost 8,000 Federals had opposed more than 9,000 Confederates. It had resulted in heavy losses on both sides: initially, 866 for the attackers (including many men only temporarily missing from their outfits) and about 500 in the ranks of the defenders.[31]

Feeling every one of those casualties, J. E. B. Stuart was content to let his opponents go at afternoon's close. He was fully aware that his men were fought out and exhausted, their horses blown, disabled, or dead. He realized, too, just how close his division—as well as his own reputation and career—had come to meeting disaster this day. If this was an indication of what lay ahead, the path of invasion might not prove the route to victory that Stuart and many of his troopers had imagined it would be.

>—+—<>—O—<>—+—<

His opponent's opinion notwithstanding, Stuart did not consider his command battered or broken up. True, he had suffered considerably at Pleasonton's hands, but his casualty list amounted to only 5 percent of his total strength—necessary repairs could be made relatively quickly. Thus he was chagrined when Robert E. Lee, who reached the field a few hours after his son fell wounded, expressed concern at the condition of the command and decreed that Stuart remain on the Rappahannock to rest and recuperate while a part of the army went ahead without him. When the last injury had been attended to, the cavalry could rejoin the invasion column. Its advance echelon, Ewell's corps, would make do with Jenkins's brigade. On the way to the Valley, it would be escorted by Lige White, whose Comanches, despite having taken some hard knocks at Brandy Station, had regained their prebattle form in record time.[32]

Physical damage was bad enough—the horses lost in the battle alone posed major problems—but Stuart might find it even harder to repair the psyche of his command, which had received not so much a shock as a jolt of blue lightning. The realization of how roughly they had been treated on various parts of the field rankled and unsettled Stuart's men, whether or not they gave voice to their feelings. As he had after Kelly's Ford, their commander made a game effort at thought control: "Your saber blows, inflicted on that glorious day, have taught them again the weight of Southern vengeance . . ." But it is doubtful this latest round of motivational psychology achieved its purpose. The facts of the case were clear to everyone. As an officer in the 6th Virginia later expressed it, "At Brandy, for the first time, in . . . [a] fair fight, with anything like equality of numbers," the Federal cavalry had maintained themselves against "the superior dash and horsemanship of the Southrons."[33]

The Confederates' self-worth took additional blows in later days, when the public seemed to blame them for all the woes the Confederacy had experienced since its inception. Stuart bore the brunt of the condemnation. Editors and politicians who had once chuckled at his behavior even as they praised his martial prowess turned on him, accusing him of everything from incompetence to drunkenness on duty. The consensus was that the Knight of the Golden Spurs had been egregiously negligent in allowing Pleasonton (literally) to catch him napping and to cuff him about for much of the day.

Certain aspects of Stuart's personal behavior, including those that had endeared him to the public—his exaggerated courtliness, his flashy uniforms, his flirtatious ways—suddenly became character flaws. Perhaps the most vituperative comment on this score came from a Virginia matron who, in a letter to Jefferson Davis, characterized the cavalry leader as "one of those fops, devoting his whole time to his lady friends' company" while neglecting responsibilities that should have monopolized his attention.[34]

Some of Stuart's own men shared the reaction of the public. "It is the opinion of all," wrote a trooper of the 2nd Virginia, "that Genl. Stuart managed badly." Their officers were less vocal in their reactions—even Wade Hampton, whose brother had been killed, as it might have seemed, as a result of Stuart's lack of vigilance, kept silent about the near defeat. Officers and men realized, however, that their enemy would take heart from the events of June 9. As Major McClellan later put it, the battle "*made* the federal cavalry" by strengthening its faith in itself and in its leaders, a faith that had been wholly lacking for the first two years of the conflict.[35]

Most of Stuart's troopers refused to view the outcome as signaling a new, permanent state of affairs. Instead, they chose to regard Brandy Station as a fluke. A major campaign was just beginning; they would have all the opportunities they could want to prove that their spirit, skill, and dedication to cause and country had not been left on the battlefield amid the bodies and the carcasses of the slain.

>−+−◇>−○−<◇−+−<

Stuart's division did not join the march to the Potomac until June 16, six days after Ewell's corps crossed the Rappahannock and started for the Blue Ridge. Ewell, in fact, was the reason the cavalry finally hit the road. On the thirteenth and fourteenth, the Second Corps attacked and overwhelmed Milroy's garrison at Winchester. Until then, Hooker had remained at Falmouth, believing that no large portion of Lee's army had left his front—a fiction spread by the reconnaissance-challenged troopers under Pleasonton. The crisis at Winchester finally prompted him to draw his army toward Washington. His withdrawal told Lee it was time to add the infantry of Longstreet and Hill, and the cavalry of Stuart, to the movement north.[36]

By the time Stuart left Brandy Station to screen the right flank of Longstreet's column, which would bring up Lee's rear, most of the wounds his command had sustained there had been salved and patched. Literally and figuratively, however, angry scars remained. The only way the cavalry could assuage the pain was to locate the upstarts in blue, bring them to battle, and defeat them decisively. Aggressiveness in challenging the enemy and keeping them back from Lee's main body would be critical to the successful conclusion of an invasion already well under way. By the time Stuart joined the march, Ewell and Jenkins had crossed not only the Potomac, but also the Pennsylvania line, occupying some locales, such as Chambersburg, that were familiar with enemy occupation.[37]

The way north led Stuart's column—the troopers of Munford, Chambliss, and Robertson, with Hampton's and Jones's brigades to follow a few days later—to a venue in some ways reminiscent of lower Pennsylvania. This was the Loudoun Valley, amid whose lush pastures and undulating hills Stuart's men had spent the first frenetic days of November. Then, as now, their mission had been to screen Longstreet and Hill against enemy detection and interference. Now, as then, Stuart's men were in for a hectic week.

On the first full day of the march, June 17, Stuart accompanied Munford's brigade to picturesque Middleburg. On that warm but pleasant afternoon, he pitched his camp on the edge of a village that sat only a few miles from Longstreet's main body. Longstreet was moving along the east side of the Blue Ridge; he would not duck behind the mountains, lining up behind Ewell and Hill, for another two days.[38]

After establishing his headquarters, Stuart sent Munford through Aldie Gap in the Bull Run range to prevent a surprise attack by Pleasonton's cavalry, which was thought to be near Manassas. Stuart also dispatched Chambliss's brigade toward Thoroughfare Gap, farther south. At the same time, Robertson's brigade took up a median position near Rector's Cross Roads. These blocking forces would keep Longstreet safe from prying eyes until he could complete his journey through Loudoun.[39]

Stuart was correct in his assumption that the Yankees were not far off. Fighting began at about 4:00, when Munford neared Aldie Gap and the town of the same name via the Little River Turnpike and encountered the advance of David Gregg's division, a brigade from New York, Massachusetts, and Ohio under a Pleasonton clone, Col. H. Judson Kilpatrick. A party from Kilpatrick's old regiment, the 2nd New York, attacked, chasing Munford's skirmishes through the pass. Then Munford galloped up with his main body, Rosser's 5th Virginia in the forefront, and counterattacked. The opposing forces collided with a bone-jarring crunch along the Snickersville Pike. They shot and slashed at one another for several minutes, then drew apart as if by mutual consent.

To nail down his position on the contested road, Kilpatrick brought up his main body and a Regular battery. He then committed his 1st Massachusetts along the Snickersville Pike, which diverged from the Little River Turnpike and snaked northwestward toward Snicker's Gap in the Blue Ridge. Munford countered by committing Drake's 1st and Wickham's 4th Virginia—the latter seeking to atone for its failure of eight days ago—plus Breathed's battery. Under a covering fire from Breathed, Wickham rushed forward to meet the Bay Staters in a new round of hand-to-hand fighting. The contest ended when the 1st Massachusetts staggered to the rear, cut up and demoralized.[40]

Thereafter, action shifted south to the lower pike, where more New Yorkers advanced against Munford's right flank, only to see their formation broken by Rosser's sharpshooters and Breathed's gunners. Other Federals rushed up, hoping to succeed where the New York unit had failed, but they gained only a shaky foothold on the Rebel flank.

As afternoon merged into evening, Kilpatrick once again advanced along the Snickersville Pike, threatening Munford's exhausted command. However, the opportune—if belated—arrival of the 2nd and 3rd Virginia saved the Confederates. Both regiments charged the enemy, the 3rd straight up the road, part of the 2nd along the right shoulder (the larger part of the 2nd had dismounted behind a stone wall that ran along the pike and formed a natural fortification).

Most of the Federals fled before contact was made, but a single squadron of the 1st Massachusetts gamely, and tragically, held its ground. A trooper in the 2nd Virginia, St. George Brooke, recalled his thoughts and deeds at this juncture:

> It occurred to me we were to have a head-on collision between the too [sic] opposing bodies. . . . I was so close to these men as they charged by me, that I could see the dust fly from their blue jackets as the bullets from our revolvers would strike them. I was not fifteen feet from them. I saw at least one of their horses shot when running at full speed, throwing its rider over its head. Of course, the rider was run over by his comrades behind. Not a man of this squadron ever got back. Many were killed, the rest were captured.[41]

Those New Englanders not dispatched by the revolvers of the 2nd Virginia fell beneath the little-used swords of the 3rd. An officer in Owen's regiment declared that "I had never before so beautiful an opportunity to use my sabre." He employed his to good effect, while Colonel Owen, riding beside him, "cut down two men himself." All told, this day the 1st Massachusetts lost eighty men killed or wounded, the highest casualty total of any Union cavalry regiment in this campaign.[42]

Kilpatrick made a final effort to carry the upper road by committing his inexperienced 4th New York, then the veteran 1st Maine, the latter on loan from Col. John Irvin Gregg's brigade. When it drew a blistering fire from the newly arrived Virginians, the 4th raced to the rear as a body, leaving its colonel in enemy hands to face almost a year in Libby Prison. The men of Maine, however, restored the balance of battle by repulsing Owen and prying the marksmen of the 2nd Virginia from their stone wall.[43]

By this point, darkness was coming on, and both sides were bone-weary. Having kept the enemy away from Lee's main body, Munford considered his job done and withdrew his units. Kilpatrick, having experienced an exhausting maiden effort in brigade command, did not pursue. The Confederates departed in high spirits, especially the prideful Rosser, who wrote his bride: "I was first to begin [the fight], and last to retire from the field. Had it not been for me there would have been another surprise"—a jab at Stuart for Brandy Station.[44]

While Munford and Kilpatrick tilted outside Aldie, Stuart experienced yet another embarrassing surprise, this one at the hands of a single Yankee regiment; today, however, he retaliated quickly and successfully. Early that morning, Pleasonton had sent Colonel Duffié—who, in the aftermath of Brandy Station, had been demoted to the command of his old outfit, the 1st Rhode Island—on a scouting mission through Thoroughfare Gap to Middleburg. The fact that 275 Yankees had been set adrift in a valley teeming with Confederates suggested a suicide mission. Yet at first it was Stuart who suffered when, at about 4:00 P.M., Duffié's men arrived unannounced at Middleburg and drove him, his staff, and his escort from the village. The leave-taking was all the more embarrassing because minutes before, the Beau Sabreur had been the object of the affection of numerous local females, whose encircling of the general and his steed reminded Heros von Borcke of "a dance around a maypole."[45]

Now an enraged Stuart vowed revenge. He galloped west to Rector's Cross Roads, sending for Chambliss en route. Near the road junction, he rejoined Robertson's brigade and led it back to Middleburg, where Duffié had remained, in defiance of every self-protective instinct. Arriving in early evening, Stuart found that the Frenchman had barricaded the streets. The defenses were insufficient to stymie even Robertson's small command, which swarmed over them and slowly but surely evicted the Rhode Islanders.

Duffié's departure was hastened when Chambliss arrived from the south to add his weight to the effort. A surgeon in the 10th Virginia noted that upon arriving, the men were "ordered in low voices to [dis]mount, & we crept along for a mile. All at once there seemed [to be] a dash from every side & loud yells of 'surrender.' We had surrounded and captured the entire 1st R.I. Cavalry."[46]

The surgeon exaggerated Duffié's losses, but only slightly. Seventy-five Yankees were taken; the rest, including their colonel, got away. A few managed to reach Hooker's new headquarters at Fairfax Station, where Duffié found himself relieved of command—mainly, it would seem, for obeying his orders from Pleasonton. Meanwhile, Stuart and his aides returned to Middleburg, where they were again immersed in a sea of femininity. For the second time in eight days, the cavalry leader had been surprised and bedeviled by the Yankees. And yet, though defections had occurred, his hold on the hearts and minds of the female population evidently remained strong.[47]

━━•━0━•━•━

For the most part, Stuart spent the eighteenth resting and reconnoitering. He also met with John Mosby, who for the past five months had been scouting in, and harassing Federals passing through, Loudoun, Fairfax, and Fauquier Counties. The partisan leader's latest coup—the fruits of which he happily shared with his erstwhile superior and current patron—had been the capture of two of Hooker's staff officers. From papers captured with them, Mosby, and now Stuart, learned that Pleasonton's troopers enjoyed the close support of Meade's V Corps, which had encamped ten miles east of Aldie. In response, Stuart decided to forgo any attack on the Union horse. He would concentrate on his counterreconnaissance mission, keeping Pleasonton as far as possible from the Blue Ridge.[48]

Pleasonton, who was under no obligation to relinquish the offensive, sent David Gregg to attack Stuart at Middleburg shortly after 7:00 on the morning of the nineteenth. Advancing along the road from Upperville, Gregg's division found its path blocked by mounted and dismounted men from Chambliss's and Robertson's brigades, backed by the recently arrived battery of Moorman. Stuart's opponents continued their forward movement but more slowly and cautiously than before. Just as slowly, they positioned themselves for an attack. Perhaps due to the day's excessive heat, the assault did not come off until nearly 6:00 P.M., and when it did, it seemed to be made in slow motion, dismounted men creeping forward to draw Chambliss's fire, followed by a measured advance up the road by a mounted contingent of the 1st Maine.

Before the enemy came into carbine range, Hart's cannon raked them with case shot—canister and shrapnel—and inflicted many casualties. Then, however, a Union battery fixed on Hart's position and pounded it till he withdrew from the fight. Hart's exit enabled Gregg's dismounted men to rush up the road, carbines ablaze, although the mounted 1st Maine was blocked from advancing by Chambliss's men north of the road. Then Chambliss turned his attention to the troopers on foot. Mounted men who had been in the rear suddenly galloped up, overran the Union line, and chased the sharpshooters back to their starting point.[49]

At this point, Gregg threw in reserves of his own—mainly members of the 10th New York—who threatened to seize Chambliss's position. They never got close enough to do so, for at a critical moment, the 2nd North Carolina, under William Payne, temporary successor to Sol Williams, counterattacked along a wooded ridge and put most of the New Yorkers to flight. Still more Yankees rushed up, and there was a brief stalemate, broken by the timely advance of Robertson. The fighting continued to seesaw back and forth for several minutes, one wave of attack repulsing another before being repulsed in turn. "Such fighting I never before witnessed," one North Carolinian marveled.[50]

Believing the tide had turned in his favor, Stuart predicted to von Borcke that Gregg's command stood on the verge of extinction. But he misspoke; at the eleventh hour, an uncommitted segment of the 10th New York, backed by Kilpatrick's old 2nd, made a mounted charge that cleared the road of Confederates. This was no Herculean effort, for Chambliss, without orders, had begun to pull back to the high ground beyond Middleburg. At this point, a suddenly disconsolate Stuart relinquished all hope of routing his enemy and ordered his weary, sunburnt men to evacuate Middleburg.

He withdrew in a black mood that worsened when a Yankee drilled von Borcke through the neck with a minié ball. The Prussian nearly died of his wound before making a protracted recovery; his services, however, would be lost to the Confederacy. It seemed a sad but fitting end to a day that had turned from a Confederate victory into a disappointing stalemate.[51]

During the twentieth, the battered opponents recuperated beyond each other's sight, but the following morning, the Yankees broke the Sabbath peace by attacking with the close support of one of Meade's infantry brigades. Pleasonton's use of foot soldiers told Stuart that his counterpart was desperate to break into the Shenandoah Valley and study Robert E. Lee's dispositions.

Today the Yankees attempted simultaneous strikes against both ends of the Confederate line that protected Stuart's new headquarters before Upperville. Above a meandering stream, Goose Creek, Buford would seek to flank the north end of that line, defended by the troopers of Chambliss and those of the recently arrived Jones. Gregg would make a limited attack farther south, to hold in place troopers along the Rebel center and right. These sectors were defended not only by Robertson's brigade, but also by Hampton's, the latter also recently arrived from the Rappahannock (Munford's men had moved farther north to guard the road to Snicker's Gap and the pass itself). If Buford reached Stuart's rear, Gregg would convert his holding action into an attack, galloping past Upperville to Ashby's Gap and fighting his way into the valley beyond.[52]

When Stuart saw combinations of infantry and horsemen coming his way from two directions, he registered concern, but not panic. It was imperative that for at least a few hours longer he keep his antagonists from gaining access to the Shenandoah. Hill and Longstreet had yet to close up in Ewell's rear and so remained in danger of being cut off from the Potomac should Hooker rush west to challenge them. Thus Stuart was obliged to take on all comers one more time, keeping his adversaries at arm's length.

His day began badly. When David Gregg advanced on him via the pike at 8:00 A.M., Hart's battery showered it with shells. Artillery supporting Gregg replied, and a shell struck one of Hart's caissons. The unearthly detonation damaged a cannon that Stuart was forced to leave behind, all the horses having been shot down. It was the first artillery piece he had lost in combat, and the realization stung.[53]

Matters improved after the Confederates fell back through Upperville. Outdistancing his infantry support, Judson Kilpatrick pounded up to challenge Robertson's men in the streets and alleys of town. The little band of North Carolinians seemed on the verge of annihilation when Hampton led his brigade to the rescue. His counterattack was spearheaded by the Jeff Davis Legion under Lieutenant Colonel Waring, supported by Baker's 1st North Carolina and Cobb's Legion, under Pierce Young. After several minutes of shooting and stabbing, Kilpatrick broke off the attack and fled town—only to re-form after Gregg reinforced him. Late in the afternoon, he renewed his assault through the streets. The effort ended no more successfully than the first, although it did cause the mortal wounding of the 4th North Carolina's Col. Peter G. Evans. For his part, Kilpatrick was unhorsed in the melee and briefly held captive.[54]

Kilpatrick's failure pleased Stuart, but he was cheered even more by Buford's inability to make headway against the upper flank. Thanks to the poor intelligence work of Pleasonton, his subordinate was startled to find the road to the flank blocked by an impassable branch of Goose Creek. After hours of marching and countermarching under a torrid sun in a fruitless attempt to find a ford, Buford saw his quest as a lost cause.

His hopes were revived late in the day, when Jones and Chambliss relinquished their naturally strong position and fell back toward the mountains in accordance with Stuart's orders. The opportunistic Buford moved forward, angling toward Stuart's supply train, which had accompanied Jones's column. Before he could strike, however, his men were challenged by Jones's main body, backed by many of Chambliss's troopers, Chew's battery, and a section of Moorman's. The ensuing encounter was a desperate one. At one point, one of Chew's veterans said the battery was "firing faster than I ever saw artillery fire." Against such opposition, Buford could make little headway.[55]

His repulse did not end the day's fighting. Following closely on the heels of the retreating Confederates, Buford's men, as well as Gregg's, strove to overtake Stuart before he reached the mountain passes. Their pursuit was highly effective. A member of Moorman's battery, which had retreated to Snicker's Gap, recalled that "the enemy were pressing us so hard we could not take another position & had to fall back in disorder."[56]

Although most of Stuart's men eluded Buford, Yankee scouts clambered up the steep ridges on either side of Ashby's Gap. In the last of the afternoon sunlight, they reached the summit, faced west, and peered down on Longstreet's camps just inside the valley. Once Buford had made careful notes on the enemy dispositions, Pleasonton rushed the information—to gain which his corps had sustained almost nine hundred casualties over the past four days—to army headquarters.

Upon its receipt, Joe Hooker perused the intelligence report and filed it away, never to be acted upon.[57]

Chapter Fifteen

Sabers Dazzling in the Sun

"The improvised war"
Lee's loose command of his
excellent, improvising generals

Stuart's screening mission had been well and faithfully performed, but it had come at a steep price, nearly five hundred men killed, wounded, or missing. Manifestly, the Cavalry, A.N.V., needed a rest. Therefore, as soon as his scouts certified, early on the twenty-second, that Pleasonton and his legions had drawn off, Stuart withdrew everyone to Rector's Cross Roads and put them into bivouac. Then he rode northwest to Robert E. Lee's headquarters at Berryville for a conference. With the defensive portion of his responsibilities out of the way, Stuart hungered for more active service. He hoped his commander would see his way clear to oblige.

Stuart had in mind another of those long-distance raids behind enemy lines that gave his life purpose and pleasure. On the twentieth, he had suggested to army headquarters that he move north in advance of Longstreet and Hill to link with Ewell in Pennsylvania. By operating independently in the enemy's country, he could keep close tabs on Hooker, threaten his communications, and gather supplies the main army might use when it returned to its war-torn homeland. Stuart believed the reconnaissance aspect of his plan was its biggest selling point. What better way to monitor Hooker's movements and discern his intentions than to operate on the fringes of his army, looking over Fighting Joe's shoulder during the most critical hours of the invasion?

By the twenty-second, Lee had come to accept Stuart's reasoning. At their meeting, and again the next day, he gave his cavalry leader authorization to cross the Potomac east of the main army, advance into Pennsylvania, and fall in with the right flank of Ewell's corps at some undetermined point on the Susquehanna River. A member of Stuart's staff later declared that point to be the city of York, one of Ewell's destinations, but no source corroborates his statement.

Regardless of contrary claims by contemporary critics or latter-day historians, the junction between Stuart and Ewell was not governed by a timetable. Lee stipulated only that Stuart leave behind at least two brigades to guard the army's rear, that he attempt to encircle the Army of the Potomac only if he found it stationary in northern Virginia, and that he return at once to Lee's side if the enemy seriously impeded his progress. Virtually every other detail, including Stuart's route, was left to the cavalry leader's discretion.[1]

John Mosby, who joined Stuart at Rector's Cross Roads on the twenty-third, had suggested the route that Stuart adopted for the expedition. Fresh from a recent reconnaissance inside Hooker's lines, the partisan leader reported that the Yankees were lying idle along a twenty-five-mile line from Thoroughfare Gap north to Leesburg. This was what Stuart wanted to hear, as well as Mosby's belief that the enemy was stretched so thinly that they could be ridden through—Stuart need not go around them. Mosby recommended that his patron swing south and east through lightly guarded Hopewell Gap in the Bull Run Mountains. Then he could head north, crossing the Potomac at or near Seneca Ford, twenty miles upstream from Washington, D.C.

Stuart liked the plan so well that he had Mosby repeat the details while his staff put them on paper. Stuart the showed the plan to Wade Hampton and to the now-healthy Fitzhugh Lee; both appeared to favor the scheme. Stuart hoped R. E. Lee would also. He did. That night, while sleeping outdoors in the rain at Rector's, Stuart was shaken into consciousness by Adjutant McClellan. The groggy commander came fully awake as soon as he scanned a note that a courier from army headquarters had just delivered, conveying Lee's permission for Stuart to follow his chosen route. The recipient of Lee's approval was delighted, especially since the army leader had enclosed a favorable comment on the plan from Longstreet, who, as commander of the rear echelon, was Stuart's immediate superior.[2]

Without fanfare, Stuart began to assemble the troops. In doing so, he reverted to old habits, selecting a small force for a weighty job. He would take only 40 percent of his available horsemen, those under Hampton, Fitz Lee, and Chambliss, a total of about forty-two hundred officers and men. Those left behind included not only the cavalry's smallest component, Robertson's brigade, but also its largest, the Laurel Brigade of Grumble Jones. Although it would seem natural that Stuart should wish to rid himself of his least favorite subordinates, it also made sense to detach Jones, who was widely regarded as the best outpost commander in the army. By leaving more than five thousand troopers in Lee's rear, along with every cannon in Beckham's battalion except six, Stuart guaranteed that the army had enough cavalry and horse artillery to protect it in enemy territory. This was especially true given that Ewell was already supported not only by Jenkins's West Virginians, Jackson's battery, and Lige White's Comanches, but also by the 1st Maryland Cavalry Battalion of Maj. Ridgely Brown.

Through Robertson, Jones's senior, Stuart on the twenty-fourth issued orders governing the activities of both brigades in his absence. They were to cover Ashby's and Snicker's Gaps, observe the enemy's movements ("let nothing escape your observation"), and report anything of note to Longstreet, with whom they would keep in contact via courier relays through Charles Town, West Virginia. Robertson and Jones were also to harass Hooker once he retired.

Finally, the minute they found the enemy had left their front, they were to cross
the Potomac, attach themselves to Lee's right flank, and follow him north.[3]

⊱─⟡─◦─⟡─⊰

In the midst of his preparations to cast loose from the army, Stuart moved his
headquarters to Salem, on the Manassas Gap Railroad not far from Thoroughfare Gap in the Bull Run chain. There the brigades assembled, and from there
they shoved off at about 1:00 A.M. on the twenty-fifth. At the outset, the road
was smooth and clear, literally and figuratively. The rain that Stuart feared
would plague the march had stopped, but it had fallen recently enough that the
horses kicked up relatively little dust. And when the head of the column
reached Glascock's Gap, it encountered only a small guard. A few hours later,
however, substantial bodies of Union infantry—members of Winfield Scott
Hancock's II Corps, Army of the Potomac—appeared on the road ahead, just
short of Haymarket.[4]

Hancock's intervention—which would not have occurred had Stuart taken
Mosby's advice and used Hopewell Gap—forced the Confederate leader to
make his first major decision of the expedition. The Yankees were heading
north on roads that might bring them into contact with the rear of the main
army. According to Stuart's instructions, he should curtail the expedition and
return at once to Lee's side. But he decided that the issue was not so clear-cut
as that. Lee's stipulation that Stuart be governed by his judgment and discretion
appeared to outweigh the need to return in the event he found Hooker in
motion. He knew how time-consuming and difficult it would be to retrace his
steps and locate Longstreet's moving column. In the interim, he would be of no
use to his army, whereas if he kept riding, he might yet make the raid the effective campaign-within-a-campaign that he and Lee had envisioned. In the end,
he determined to march on, albeit by a more southerly route.[5]

To make the detour possible, Stuart engaged Hancock's men at long range
with his artillery, while his horsemen took another byway, probably Pilgrims
Rest Road, a shortcut to the commodious Warrenton Pike. Spurring to the new
front of the column, Stuart ordered Lee's brigade to Gainesville on the Manassas Gap Railroad, where it spent the night. The troopers of Hampton and
Chambliss, whom Stuart accompanied, bivouacked at nearby Buckland, on the
turnpike. The raiding leader slept soundly that night, unaware that the messengers he had sent to inform army headquarters of Hancock's approach were captured before they could reach their destination.

Stuart's detour was extended on the twenty-sixth. Instead of taking the
Alexandria Turnpike north from Gainesville and Buckland, as originally
planned, he cautiously continued southeast, crossing the Orange & Alexandria
Railroad at Bristoe Station and continuing on to Brentsville. Beyond Brentsville, he finally turned north, heading for Wolf Run Shoals on the Occoquan
River. When he halted his brigades for the night, he reckoned that on the new
route, they had covered fewer than forty miles since leaving Salem.

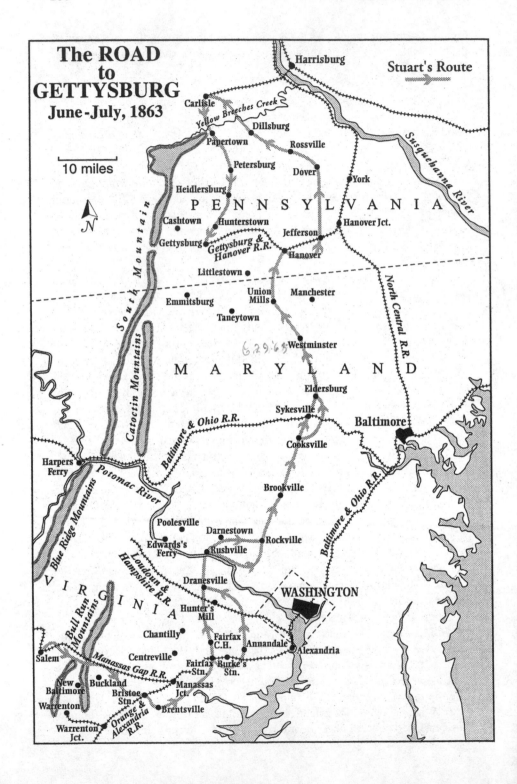

The ROAD to GETTYSBURG
June-July, 1863

Stuart's Route

10 miles

N

Harrisburg

Carlisle
Yellow Breeches Creek
Dillsburg
Papertown
Rossville
Petersburg
Dover
Heidlersburg
York

P E N N S Y L V A N I A

Cashtown
Hunterstown
Jefferson
Hanover Jct.
Gettysburg
Gettysburg & Hanover R.R.
Hanover
Littlestown
Manchester
Union Mills
Emmitsburg
Taneytown

South Mountain

6.29.63 Westminster

M A R Y L A N D

Eldersburg
Sykesville
Baltimore
Cooksville

North Central R.R.

Catoctin Mountains

Baltimore & Ohio R.R.

Harpers Ferry
Potomac River
Brookville

Poolesville
Darnestown
Rockville
Edwards's Ferry
Rushville

Baltimore & Ohio R.R.

Blue Ridge Mountains

Dranesville
WASHINGTON

Loudoun & Hampshire R.R.

V I R G I N I A
Hunter's Mill

Bull Run Mountains

Chantilly
Fairfax C.H.
Annandale
Alexandria
Salem
Centreville
Fairfax Stn.
Burke's Stn.
Manassas Gap R.R.
New Baltimore
Buckland
Bristoe Stn.
Manassas Jct.
Warrenton
Brentsville
Warrenton Jct.
Orange & Alexandria R.R.

Thus far, Stuart's itinerary had included sites familiar from the Second Manassas Campaign. On the twenty-seventh, recrossing the O & A west of Alexandria, he neared an old haunt from the Dumfries raid, Burke's Station. While Fitz Lee's brigade rode there to demolish track and cut telegraph wire for the second time in six months, Stuart accompanied Hampton and Chambliss to Fairfax Station, three and a half miles to the west. Nearing that depot—erstwhile headquarters of the Army of the Potomac—the head of the column was suddenly attacked by one hundred members of the 11th New York Cavalry, part of the XXII Army Corps, Defenses of Washington. The reckless New Yorkers waylaid a segment of Hampton's lead regiment, the 1st North Carolina, killing one of its field officers and several of its men, before being rocked backward by a counterattack. Twenty-six Yankees became prisoners; their comrades took refuge in nearby woods.[6]

Upon the enemy's departure, Stuart's men seized and plundered the depot of war goods and sutlers' stores, while Fitz Lee, having departed Burke's Station, did the same at Annandale, northeast of Stuart's location. The spoils included choice edibles reminiscent of those they had obtained on their visits to Catlett's Station, Manassas Junction, and Dumfries. Stuart let the men eat and rest for an hour or two before bugles called them to horse and the column got moving again.

After crossing the Loudoun & Hampshire Railroad at Hunter's Mill, the raiders headed for the Potomac. Their route led them downriver to Seneca or Rowzee's Mill Ford, directly above another of Stuart's old stamping grounds, Dranesville. In the darkness of evening, the riders crossed the moonlit stream. John Esten Cooke thought the scene picturesque, "the water washing to and fro across the backs of the horses, which kept their feet with difficulty." In fact, as another officer noted, the current was so strong that "a number of the weaker horses were washed down the river." Not till 3:00 A.M. on the twenty-eighth was the crossing complete, with Stuart's men on northern soil for the first time in nine months.[7]

Targets loomed up almost immediately. Stuart put many troopers to work destroying boats, locks, and miscellaneous property on the Chesapeake & Ohio Canal, a major avenue of barge traffic to the Federal capital and Hooker's army. There the raiders took numerous prisoners, three hundred of whom had been en route to Washington by canal boat from Ohio and the new state of West Virginia. The captives were added to those taken at Fairfax Station; the entire group was sent on ahead, under escort, to Rockville, Maryland.

A lieutenant in the 5th Virginia observed that spoils were to be had on the river as well: "We found one boat heavily loaded with whiskey and a goodly portion of that was . . . put away in a place of safety by the men." Other barges yielded up rations that were consumed with gusto by men whose haversacks were empty. As early as the second day of the march, a trooper in the 4th Virginia had noted in his diary: "Rations out. Nothing to eat for man or beast." The mounts had it worse than their riders. An officer in the 3rd Virginia complained that Stuart's route provided "very poor grazing for horses, this being a miserably poor country & the armies having entirely consumed it."[8]

Stuart started for his next port of call, Rockville, late in the morning. At this point, the marching pace picked up. Prisoners taken at the river had informed Stuart that the Army of the Potomac was fast approaching the river it had been named after, which it intended to cross. It appeared that Hooker had finally nerved himself to close with his enemy. Stuart wanted to be on hand for the confrontation.

His vow of speed was challenged when his advance reached Rockville, only eight miles from the Washington suburbs. First the column stopped to evict local defenders, mostly escapees from the 11th New York and other members of the XXII Corps. Then Stuart felt obliged to lay over long enough to chat, and flirt, with admirers from a local female academy. The young ladies surrounded Stuart and his staff, fed them sandwiches and cider, pinned ribbons on their tunics, even took locks of their hair as keepsakes.[9]

The longest delay at Rockville occurred when the point riders—some of Hampton's South Carolinians—spied a supply column, more than a hundred wagons long, moving along a road outside town. The train was carrying all manner of materiel from Washington to Hooker's headquarters. When the riders swooped down on the wagons, teamsters lashed mules and horses into a frenzy in a vain effort to escape. Whooping with delight, the Confederates spurred their mounts and pursued. Overtaking the rear of the column, they shot down the teams, causing several wagons to overturn and dump their contents into the dusty road. When pistol balls began to fly past their heads, the teamsters suddenly yanked on the reins, and the column shuddered to a halt.

Stuart was vastly pleased with this new prize. One of the purposes of this expedition was to gather provisions for the army. His men, who considered themselves the immediate beneficiaries of the captured goods, were beside themselves with delight. Colonel Beale of the 9th Virginia found some wagons loaded with oats and corn, others with "bakers' bread, crackers, whiskey in bottles of great variety, sugar, hams, with some tin and woodware, knives and forks. . . The bacon and crackers, as well as the whiskey, proved to our jaded and hungry troopers most acceptable."[10]

Stuart saw to it that the salvageable wagons—about 125, all told—accompanied the column north from Rockville. They would reduce its speed, but their inherent value outweighed this objection. Stuart's many critics in the army later faulted him for taking on the impedimenta, as did generations of historians. But, especially since his column was traveling without wagons of its own, its horses desperately needed the forage the wagons carried; so did the animals that supported the main army. And by appropriating it, Stuart was also denying the grain to the horses of the enemy.

Nevertheless, he grew concerned about his decelerating pace. Thus he marched the men through the night and into the early hours of the twenty-ninth. That morning, the column reached the Baltimore & Ohio ("the enemy's main war artery," Stuart called it) at Hood's Mill and Sykesville. At his command, detachments from all three brigades ranged along the right-of-way, stopping frequently to wreak havoc with axes and crowbars appropriated from trackside warehouses. Another body of raiders wrecked the railroad bridge at Sykesville, while still another chased off Yankee patrols farther south near Cookesville. In early afternoon, the column rode on, leaving in its wake derailed trains, charred depot buildings, and hundreds of yards of mangled track.[11]

The weight of the wagons exerted a steady drag. By 4:00 P.M., when the column approached Westminster, Maryland, the terminus of a branch line of the Northern Central Railroad, Stuart calculated that he should have been in Pennsylvania by now, helping Ewell carry the war into the bowels of Yankeedom. But if his lagging progress bothered him before he reached Westminster, it became a matter of grave concern once he entered town and encountered ninety-five determined troopers of the 1st Delaware Cavalry, members of the Baltimore-based VIII Army Corps. The small but plucky unit plowed into Stuart's advance guard and sent its surprised troopers reeling back on the main body. Then, when the head of Stuart's column hove into view, the Delawareans attacked again in defiance of fifty-to-one odds. Before they could be stopped, they killed two of the most popular officers in the 4th Virginia and wounded four enlisted men.

An enraged Stuart demanded a counterattack. A private in the 2nd Virginia watched as "Gen'l Fitz Lee came galloping up to the head of our regiment and led us in a charge entirely through the town. The enemy made no serious attempt to hold the town and fled before us." Most of the Yankees did not make it to safety; when the shooting and swordplay ended, sixty-seven of them had been killed, wounded, or taken prisoner.[12]

Opposition surmounted, Stuart took possession of the town, where he decided to spend the night. In the daylight that remained, he tended to his casualties, interrogated and paroled his prisoners, and sent scouts ranging toward the Pennsylvania line, only a few miles to the north. They picked up neither signs nor rumors of Ewell's presence between Westminster and Hunterstown, Pennsylvania, just above the Adams County seat of Gettysburg. The news troubled Stuart, whose calculations indicated that he should be almost within sight of friendly infantry. What would he do if he could not locate Dick Ewell?

>─┼─<>─O─<>─┼─<

At daylight on June 30, an achy Stuart—who had spent an uncomfortable night in town, seated in a chair propped against the wall of a private home—fired up the column and put it in motion. In midmorning, while the rest of the men continued north, he halted at Union Mills, a few miles from the Mason-Dixon line, to breakfast at the home of Confederate sympathizers. There he and his aides spent an hour chatting with their hosts, then crowding around the family Steinway, belting out chorus after chorus of "Jine the Cavalry" and other favorite songs. Amused that Stuart would enter so fully into the entertainment, one family member called him "the very personification of fun and spirit."[13]

Then the jollity was over, and it was back in the saddle for the ride into Pennsylvania. For this leg of the journey, Stuart had a new guide, the sixteen-year-old son of his hosts. Near Littlestown, Pennsylvania, seven miles north of Union Mills, Stuart's scouts had discovered a body of Yankee horsemen, an advance detachment of the Army of the Potomac, now under George Gordon Meade, Hooker having gone the way of George B. McClellan, John Pope, and Ambrose Burnside. The boy, who was intimately familiar with the area north of his home, had offered to lead Stuart around Littlestown by rarely used roads that snaked northeast to Hanover. Ordinarily Stuart would not have feared taking on enemy cavalry, no matter how many, but his goal was to reach the Susquehanna without further delay.

Thus he was upset and frustrated when his road intersected, near Hanover, the path of the eastward-moving Yankees. Stuart approached the lower end of town perhaps an hour after the enemy—the newly formed 3rd Cavalry Division, Army of the Potomac, under now-Brig. Gen. Judson Kilpatrick—had entered Hanover on its way north. From their advance position, Kilpatrick's troopers were covering the center of Meade's army as it prepared to enter Pennsylvania in pursuit of Lee. Gregg's division, guarding the right, was still in Maryland with the main army, while John Buford's men, on the left, had advanced to Gettysburg, twelve miles west of Hanover, where their leader had established an observation post.[14]

Lacking a road on which to turn about, Stuart had no choice but to push straight ahead and take on the Yankees. Upon his arrival, one of Kilpatrick's two brigades had already passed through the town, but the other remained strung out on the road from Pennville. When Chambliss's troopers, leading Stuart's column, approached from the south, the rear of this brigade fired into them. Chambliss's lead regiment, the 13th Virginia of Lt. Col. Jefferson C. Phillips, responded with an attack that broke an untried regiment of Pennsylvanians and sent its fragments fleeing through the streets of town. Then a New York regiment, followed by elements of two other outfits—all more experienced and better disciplined than the Pennsylvanians—raced out of Hanover, counterattacked, and sent Phillips's men back the way they had come.

Stuart, realizing that a full-scale encounter could not be avoided, rushed up and began to shout instructions. To prevent Chambliss from being swept off the field, he brought up two of his cannons and emplaced them on the left, along Plum Creek. The guns laid down an accurate fire that kept the counterattackers at bay while a flanking force—William Payne and his newly acquired 2nd North Carolina—charged up a parallel road farther west. Payne struck the only portion of the Pennsylvania regiment that had not retreated in panic; soon it too was careening through town, thoroughly demoralized.

Payne's men pursued up the street, hacking and shooting their way toward Centre Square. But before they reached that point, re-formed Pennsylvanians and New Yorkers began to press them on all sides, slowing their advance to a crawl. After several minutes of close-quarters fighting, the Tarheels gave ground, then turned to withdraw. Their antagonists pursued to the edge of town, where a tannery was in operation. There Payne's horse was shot from under him, and the lieutenant colonel was dumped into an open tanning vat. He emerged unhurt but covered from head to boot in brown dye. To cap his plight, he was taken prisoner.[15]

When the 2nd North Carolina fled town, Chambliss's entire line appeared ready to collapse. Stuart could not reinforce it from the rear, as Hampton's brigade was prevented from moving up quickly by the captured wagons it was escorting. Not until about 2:00 P.M. was the 1st Brigade at Stuart's side, along with the other four guns in Stuart's column. Forming on Chambliss's right near Mount Olivet Cemetery, Hampton trained the guns on a large detachment of Yankees who showed intentions of advancing. The shelling, and the presence beside the guns of Cobb's Legion—Pierce Young and his men on horseback, pistols drawn, ready to charge if needed—drove all thought of a flank attack from Kilpatrick's mind.

Soon after Hampton settled into position, however, Federals farther west began to threaten Stuart's line. From time to time they made abrupt advances, at one point nearly capturing the general himself. He was carried to safety when his warhorse, Virginia, leaped a fifteen-foot-wide ditch that his assailants could not clear.

Late in the afternoon, fighting heated up on the western end of the line. Early in the fight, Fitz Lee's brigade had taken position on Chambliss's left, where it was quickly pinned down by Michigan troopers advancing from Hanover's southwestern outskirts. These members of the so-called "Wolverine Brigade" were led in person by Brig. Gen. George Armstrong Custer, who, as a shavetail lieutenant, had pursued Stuart across Cedar Run during Joe Johnston's withdrawal from Manassas.

For a few hours, Lee kept the Wolverines back with sharpshooter fire and the rapid shelling of the two guns on his front. In late afternoon, however, the twenty-three-year-old Custer dismounted about six hundred members of his 6th Michigan and led them toward the rise that held Stuart's guns. To evade detection, the Yankees covered much of that distance on hands and knees. When about three hundred yards from the guns, they bobbed up and sprayed the top of the ridge with their Spencer repeating rifles.

A dozen or more cannoneers and some of the cavalrymen supporting them toppled over; many other Confederates ran to the rear, temporarily uncovering the guns. Before Custer's men could secure them as prizes of war, Stuart hustled up reinforcements from Chambliss's brigade, who stabilized the left. But it had been a close call, and for the rest of the fight, Stuart remained firmly on the defensive, biding his time until darkness permitted him to disengage, put his wagons on the road, and head north.[16]

>-+◦>-O-‹◦+-‹

Although Stuart's command was, in the words of one officer, "broken down & in no condition to fight," withdrawing from Hanover posed few problems after the sun went down. Stuart had Fitz Lee fall back, while Hampton extended his lines to cover the gap thus created. Once in the rear, Fitz took custody of the wagons, which he started off in the direction of Jefferson. The choice of destination, largely predicated on keeping the wheeled trophies well east of any pursuers, would add about ten miles to Stuart's route to the Susquehanna.

By the time Hampton and Chambliss pulled out of Hanover to follow the train, troopers exhausted from hours of combat under a torrid sun were suddenly returned to the weariness and monotony of travel. But because Stuart was now truly worried that he might have missed his rendezvous with Ewell—whether at York or somewhere else in lower Pennsylvania—he again asked his men and animals to pick up the pace. The column responded by making twenty-three grueling miles before sunup on July 1.[17]

Numerous men covered all or part of that distance while asleep in the saddle. A few were so overcome by fatigue that they fell unconscious to the ground; comrades had to haul them off the road before they were trampled to death. Many animals were also at the end of their endurance; several went lame on this leg of the trip. Those that did were shot by their riders, who thereafter accompanied the column on foot, lugging their saddles on their backs. For days afterward, the roads north of Hanover were littered with the carcasses of mounts that had played out en route to Jefferson.

Stuart's proverbial endurance enabled him to stay awake and alert as his men penetrated ever deeper into enemy territory. As he rode, he was driven less by worry and more by hope of finding a safe haven at the end of his ride. Newspapers he confiscated near Jefferson overflowed with accounts of Rebel infantry running wild in the vicinity of York.

Soon after sunrise, however, his mood plummeted. Striking the turnpike that led east to York, his scouts reported no signs of Ewell's troops anywhere in the area. Detachments sent toward the city returned with word that Early had left the area, but when and in what direction they could not say. Citizens had provided contradictory information, perhaps deliberately. The newspapers merely repeated old rumors that Ewell's objective, as Robert E. Lee's, was Shippensburg, forty miles to the west. Stuart discounted the report but had no theories of his own.[18]

In frustration, he ordered the column to continue north. Near the village of Dover, he sent one of his staff officers, Major Venable, with a small escort, to scour the countryside for signs of Ewell's column. Until the aide reported back, Stuart decided to angle westward in the direction of Carlisle. He had heard that a substantial portion of the Second Corps had recently occupied that area—perhaps stragglers or townspeople knew where it had gone.

Much later, Stuart would learn it had gone south. On the twenty-ninth, Robert E. Lee, from his headquarters at Chambersburg, beyond South Mountain, had issued orders grouping his far-flung army—including the forces under

Gen. J. E. B. Stuart
LIBRARY OF CONGRESS

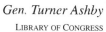

Gen. Turner Ashby
LIBRARY OF CONGRESS

Gen. Joseph E. Johnston

bi-racial?

Gen. Robert E. Lee

Gen. "Stonewall" Jackson
BATTLES AND LEADERS OF THE CIVIL WAR

"OLD BLUE LIGHT"

Gen. Wade Hampton
LIBRARY OF CONGRESS

Gen. Fitzhugh Lee
LIBRARY OF CONGRESS

Gen. W. H. F. "Rooney" Lee
LIBRARY OF CONGRESS

Gen. Williams C. Wickham
LIBRARY OF CONGRESS

Gen. Thomas L. Rosser
PHOTOGRAPHIC HISTORY OF THE CIVIL WAR

PHOTOGRAPHIC HISTORY OF THE CIVIL WAR

Gen. William E. Jones

Gen. Beverly H. Robertson

Gen. John R. Chambliss, Jr.

Gen. John D. Imboden
LIBRARY OF CONGRESS

Gen. M. Calbraith Butler
LIBRARY OF CONGRESS

Gen. Laurence S. Baker

Gen. James B. Gordon

Gen. Pierce M. B. Young

Gen. James Dearing
LIBRARY OF CONGRESS

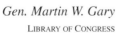

Gen. Martin W. Gary
LIBRARY OF CONGRESS

Gen. Thomas T. Munford
LIBRARY OF CONGRESS

Col. John S. Mosby
LIBRARY OF CONGRESS

Col. J. Frederick Waring
GEORGIA HISTORICAL SOCIETY

Col. Gilbert J. Wright
GEORGIA HISTORICAL SOCIETY

Lt. Col. Elijah V. White
LIBRARY OF CONGRESS

bi-racial?

Col. Jefferson C. Phillips
HAMPTON, VA., CITY MUSEUMS

Maj. John Pelham
LIBRARY OF CONGRESS

Maj. R. Preston Chew
V. M. I. ARCHIVES

Maj. James Breathed
NATIONAL ARCHIVES

Maj. Robert F. Beckham
U.S. ARMY MILITARY HISTORY
RESEARCH INSTITUTE

Gen. Alfred Pleasonton, U.S.A.
LIBRARY OF CONGRESS

Gen. Philip H. Sheridan, U.S.A. (standing), and his subordinates, 1864. From left: Gen. Wesley Merritt, Gen. David McMurtrie Gregg, Gen. Henry E. Davies, Gen. James H. Wilson, Gen. Alfred T. A. Torbert. LIBRARY OF CONGRESS

Stuart's Cavalry on the march. AUTHOR'S COLLECTION

Stuart's Chambersburg Raid. HARPER'S WEEKLY

Battle of Brandy Station, June 9, 1863. LIBRARY OF CONGRESS

Ewell that had gone to Carlisle and York—before it could be overtaken by Meade's dogged pursuit. Most of the roads in that section converged toward Gettysburg, the seat of Adams County. Largely as a result, early on July 1, fighting broke out on the outskirts of that village between the advance of A. P. Hill's corps, moving east from Chambersburg, and Buford's division of cavalry. The battle was in progress as Stuart headed from Hanover to York. Being more than twenty miles east of the battlefield, he failed to heed the boom of artillery or the rattle of musketry.[19]

When his troopers entered Carlisle on the afternoon of the first, they found no one in town wearing gray. The place was occupied, however, by a division of Union militia, with some artillery, sent to defend the area against invasion and led by a veteran of the Army of the Potomac, Brig. Gen. William Farrar Smith. Stuart's command was hardly in condition to fight even second-string warriors, "the mules, horses & men being much jaded," as one officer admitted. The twenty-four-mile journey from Dover—the last point at which his column had rested—through Rossville and Dillsburg and across the northernmost spur of South Mountain, had almost done in riders and horses alike. A lieutenant in the 9th Virginia informed loved ones at home that "from our great exertion, constant mental excitement, want of sleep and food, the men were overcome and so tired and stupid as almost to be ignorant of what was taking place around them."[20]

In addition to lacking the strength for a prolonged struggle, Stuart "disliked to subject the town to the consequence of attack." Yet it was obvious that with Smith now on hand, Carlisle was not going to surrender to him as it had, days before, to Ewell. Stuart had to oppose the militia if only to gain access to local supplies of rations and forage, commodities his command desperately needed. After some deliberation, he sent a delegation of citizens to hand Smith a surrender demand. When Smith rejected it, Stuart placed his artillery on high ground surrounding the town, "took possession of the main avenues to the place," and sent in a second demand. This gesture was also spurned, whereupon Stuart's batteries sent shells screaming over the trees and into the streets of Carlisle. At the same time, a detachment of Lee's brigade set fire to the barracks of the U.S. Cavalry School of Instruction, on the town's outskirts. If Stuart felt uneasy about vandalizing one of the landmarks of his arm, he told no one.[21]

The shelling continued intermittently until 1:00 A.M. on the second. By then several parts of town were ablaze, the result of the "hot shot" that some of Stuart's gunners had fired, although the militia had suffered only a dozen casualties. In turn, Smith had inflicted no casualties on Stuart—nor could he have expected to, given his feeble response to the cavalry's shelling. Suddenly, however, Stuart lost interest in the uneven contest. "At this time," an officer wrote, "a courier was seen to approach General Stuart and we learned, that it was an order from General Lee to advance as rapidly as possible to his relief at Gettysburg." Major Venable had chanced upon a courier from army headquarters, who, having accompanied the aide to Carlisle, informed Stuart that the army had been engaged at Gettysburg for the past eighteen hours. At once the general called everyone—those awake and those half asleep—into line, and by 2:00 they were following him and the messenger south.[22]

The road to Gettysburg followed a straight line to Papertown, curved to the east en route to Petersburg, then southwestward through Heidlersburg to Hunterstown, which Stuart and the vanguard reached just after noon. By this time the sounds of gunfire, especially the reverberating thump of artillery, assailed the ears of everyone in the column. The contending armies were in full force south and west of Gettysburg, and the battle hung in the balance.

While Stuart rode on to Gettysburg, the rest of the column, with the wagon train to its rear, entered Hunterstown. By 2:00 P.M., Hampton's brigade, bringing up the rear, had passed through the village. The brigade line extended all the way to Brinkerhoff's Ridge, which overlooked Ewell's position north of Gettysburg.[23]

At that hour, outlying detachments of Yankee cavalry were prowling about the Hunterstown area. A party of Custer's 6th Michigan suddenly appeared north of the village, charged through its only street, and attacked the end of the Confederate line. Two of its members made an assault on Wade Hampton himself. A private who dismounted among trees south of town began taking potshots at the towering patrician—who made a large target even on horseback—with his Spencer repeater. The brigadier returned the fire with his pistol, then, seeing his disadvantage, charged his antagonist and managed to put a pistol ball in his wrist, ending the duel.

Minutes later, an officer in the trooper's regiment bolted out of the same woods, closed on Hampton from the blind side, and landed a saber blow on the back of his skull. An enraged Hampton turned about to confront his assailant, who immediately fled. Blood streaming down his face from a several-inch gash, Hampton pursued, shouting imprecations and snapping his pistol impotently— a defective cartridge prevented it from firing. By desperate riding, the unchivalrous Yankee eluded his pursuer, whereupon a still-sputtering Hampton rode off to seek medical attention.[24]

He was being ministered to when, shortly before 4:00, outriders galloped up to report that a larger party of cavalry had occupied Hunterstown, evicting Hampton's rear guard. After ordering some of the regiments that had moved toward Gettysburg to countermarch, Hampton formed a defensive perimeter along the fence-lined road to town. When the rear element joined him, he positioned Cobb's Legion in the road itself, with the Phillips Legion on its right and the 1st South Carolina to its left.

Almost as soon as the men had taken position, they were challenged by a detachment of the enemy that advanced four abreast, all the narrow road could accommodate. Dismounted Yankees took cover on its flanks, and batteries wheeled into line in the fields farther back, their muzzles facing south. Hampton waited patiently for the mounted men to come into carbine and rifle range; only then would his sharpshooters open fire. Suddenly the riders—they appeared to be no more than a squadron, perhaps a hundred men—spurred forward.

It was a foolish thing to do. Before halfway to the Rebel line, almost every Yankee went down—felled by the Confederates in front, and caught in a cross-fire from their own poorly positioned flankers. In less than ten minutes, thirty-two men and as many horses were lying in the road, thrashing about. At that distance, Hampton could not see that the fallen included a general officer—the daredevil Custer, who had gone in with his men only to be shot off his horse and dazed by the fall. The boy general was saved from death or serious injury by a daring trooper who took him up on his horse and carried him to safety under a torrent of bullets.[25]

As if he had not appreciated the enormity of Custer's folly, Hampton ordered Young's Georgians to counterattack up the road. Like its enemy, Cobb's Legion had barely gotten up a head of steam before absorbing blasts from several angles. Unlike Custer's men, Young's were subjected to horse artillery shelling as well as small-arms fire. Young himself was unhorsed, as were several of his officers and men. When some of Custer's men galloped up to engage the survivors in swordplay, other members of the legion, including Lt. Col. William G. Deloney, went down with saber slashes. Still other Confederates came to their aid, and the Yankees retreated under a covering fire, ending the frenetic contest.

By then, sixty-four Georgians had been killed or wounded, including five officers. The outcome should have been foreseeable and therefore avoidable. Charitable observers attributed Hampton's atypical behavior—his rashness, his faulty tactics—to the blow he had received on the head an hour or so earlier.[26]

>-+-◆>-+-O-+-◆>-+-◄

On the sultry morning of July 3, some six thousand horsemen under Stuart marched out the pike that led northeast from Gettysburg toward the reported position of the far right flank of the Army of the Potomac. While it continued to lack the men of Jones and Robertson, Stuart's organic command had been augmented by Jenkins's brigade, which had joined it upon Stuart's arrival the day before. The newcomers from western Virginia, who had supported Dick Ewell for the past three weeks, were now commanded by Col. Milton Ferguson of the 16th Virginia, Jenkins having been struck in the head by a sharpshooter's ball the previous day while returning from a conference at army headquarters.[27]

Jenkins was not Robert E. Lee's only visitor on July 2. Immediately upon reaching Gettysburg, Stuart had reported in person to his superior. He found Lee at the farmer's home his staff had appropriated for him on the Chambersburg Pike northwest of town. According to a later account, which is of dubious authenticity but has gained currency over the years, the meeting produced tension, embarrassment, harsh words, and wounded feelings. Lee excoriated Stuart for having rejoined the army so belatedly, in violation of his orders, and with the result that the army had lacked the eyes and ears that only cavalry could provide. Many of those who repeated the story maintained that Lee blamed Stuart's absence for the army's having stumbled upon the enemy at Gettysburg, and thus for precipitating a battle that required Lee, against his better judgment, to remain on the offensive throughout.[28]

While many of the details of the Lee-Stuart meeting will never be known, it can be said with some certainty that a bitter confrontation never took place. The issue of Stuart's tardiness, if it came up at all, would not have formed the basis of a complaint by Lee. The cavalryman could have been late only if his superior had fixed a date on which Stuart was to have made contact with Ewell in Pennsylvania—and no one outside of Stuart's most zealous detractors ever contended that such was the case. The charge that Stuart's absence caused Lee to grope blindly through Pennsylvania is equally specious. To suggest that Lee would have harbored this belief, much less have thrown it in Stuart's face, is to ignore the two thousand-some horsemen who accompanied Ewell into Pennsylvania and the five thousand others stationed in the army's rear when Stuart departed on his expedition. Those three and a half brigades would have given Lee more than enough cavalry to negotiate enemy territory safely. That he chose not to use Jenkins, White, or Brown to screen and scout for his main body, and that he ignored or forgot about the troopers in his rear, cannot be blamed on Stuart, the contentions of Longstreet and others to the contrary notwithstanding.

During the first two weeks of the campaign, Lee undoubtedly missed Stuart's veteran command. To a greater degree, he would have missed the talents and the "hard horse sense" of Stuart himself. When reunited with Stuart, he may well have expressed anxiety over not knowing the cavalry's whereabouts for several days. Even so, he would not have flayed Stuart for violating restrictions that had not been placed on him.

On the contrary, he would have been glad to see his subordinate. Most likely, he would have turned a sympathetic ear to the troubles the cavalryman had encountered on almost every leg of his journey. Under the circumstances, he would not have blamed Stuart even for failing to curtail the expedition in the face of Yankee interference. And he would gladly have accepted from him the 125 wagons taken at Rockville, the other war goods he had gathered en route to Gettysburg, and the many prisoners who had accompanied him—testimony to his success at Glascock's Gap, Fairfax Station, and Westminster.

At the end of their confab, Lee gave Stuart his orders for July 3. He was to circle north of Gettysburg toward the right rear of Meade's army, there to take the offensive. Lee had spent the previous day and a half battering both of Meade's flanks, achieving limited and temporary success. This day he intended to renew Ewell's aborted offensive against Culp's Hill, northeast of town, while sending Longstreet and Hill against the Union center on Cemetery Ridge. In conjunction with the latter offensive, Stuart should conform his movements to those of the infantry farther west. While Lee had not specifically directed him to attack in conjunction with Longstreet and Hill, he had suggested that if the frontal assault was successful, the cavalry might exploit and perhaps enlarge any breakthrough. Stuart might at least divert Union attention from the infantry's effort.[29]

As if anticipating the criticism his long absence would generate in some quarters, Stuart was determined to make an unambiguous display of his competence on this warm summer's afternoon. Everything he had done since sunup had been predicated on placing his men between the Hanover Road and the Baltimore Pike, behind Meade's center. He had the manpower for the job. Ferguson's brigade led his advance, followed at a distance by Chambliss and Hampton, with Fitz Lee bringing up the rear, escorting the division's ambulances. Captured men had been left with Lee's provost guards, and the wagons with his quartermasters. Between Chambliss's and Hampton's horsemen rumbled the batteries of Jackson and Griffin, the latter on loan from Jones's brigade.

Four other batteries assigned to the division were missing: the 1st and 2nd Stuart Horse Artillery had been left at army headquarters to refill their all-but-empty ammo chests, while Chew's and Moorman's guns were accompanying the brigades of Robertson and Jones. The absence of these experienced units was somewhat offset by the temporary addition to Hampton's brigade of Capt. C. A. Green's battery of mounted artillery. The Louisiana unit had been appropriated the previous afternoon to help the 1st Brigade compete with the cannons that had supported Custer at Hunterstown.[30]

At about 10:00 A.M., Stuart consulted his scouts and determined that he had come far enough up the pike—about three miles from Gettysburg. His troopers followed him onto a byroad that led southeastward across fields of clover and corn stubble. The scene was bucolic in the extreme. Although the sounds of combat had followed them from Gettysburg, by the time the vanguard reached open ground about a half mile from the pike, the troopers found themselves in a place where, it seemed, "no war existed."[31]

Stuart hoisted up his field glasses and surveyed the scene to the south and west, toward the intersection of the Hanover and Low Dutch (or Salem Church) Roads. The previous night, this sector had teemed with Union cavalrymen, who had engaged one of Ewell's brigades as it advanced to the initial attack on Culp's Hill. The ground in that direction was so cut up by ridges and farm fences and so dotted with trees that Stuart could not determine if Yankees lingered there. If there were any, almost any movement he made would flush them out.

Southwest of his position ran a long, fairly steep elevation known as Cress's Ridge. The trees atop it would conceal the road the cavalry had taken from the York Pike; thus Stuart moved Ferguson's men on top of it, there to wait for Hampton, Chambliss, and Lee to join them. While his aides rode back to speed up the other brigades, Stuart had three hundred-some members of Lt. Col. Vincent Witcher's 34th Virginia Battalion dismount and move south to occupy the strategically located farm of John Rummel. The western Virginians, who lacked the prejudices against fighting afoot that many of Stuart's men exhibited, responded with a rapid advance. The rest of their brigade closed up on their flanks, while Chambliss, upon arriving, formed on Witcher's left. Later, Hampton and Lee came up to extend the line along Cress's Ridge as far as the Daniel Stallsmith farm.[32]

As Witcher's skirmishers went forward to draw the fire of any Yankees in the area, Stuart called up a single Parrott rifle from Jackson's battery, placed it on top of the ridge, and had it fire four shots, one in each compass direction. Although he never explained his action, Major McClellan assumed it was a signal to Robert E. Lee that the cavalry had reached its assigned position. This explanation is consistent with the fact that less than an hour later, cannonading began on the main army's line. More than a hundred guns southwest of Gettysburg unleashed an unearthly roar as they began to soften up Meade's center preparatory to an attack by 12,500 infantry under Maj. Gen. George E. Pickett, Maj. Gen. Isaac Trimble, and Brig. Gen. J. Johnston Pettigrew. Years later, one of Stuart's staff officers recalled that "the very leaves on the trees seemed to tremble and vibrate from the tremendous thunder." Listening on another part of the field, a member of the Laurel Brigade called the cannonade "awful beyond anything I ever expect to see or hear until the judgment day."[33]

Stuart's attention was fixed on the cannonade only briefly; quickly it shifted to the grassy plain around the Hanover-Low Dutch Road junction, from which lines of dismounted Federals could now be seen advancing in response to Witcher's movement. As the Virginians engaged the newcomers at long range, Stuart had Jackson lob shells in their direction. In the enemy's midst, a battery—it proved to be the one that had opposed Hampton at Hunterstown—answered with a salvo. Jackson's shelling was accurate, but his opponent's was devastating. In time, the Union guns forced the Charlottesville Battery to duck into the trees atop the crest. Its withdrawal forced Stuart to bring up the cannons of Green.

Soon after Jackson's guns fell silent, so did the Union battery. Through his field glasses, Stuart could see additional groups of Yankees moving through the fields, exchanging positions with the sharpshooters farther forward. He would learn that the brigade of Col. John B. McIntosh of Gregg's division had been sent to relieve the pickets and skirmishers of Custer's brigade, Kilpatrick's division. Several companies of newcomers immediately pressed forward, occupying a line within carbine range of the Rummel farm. Stuart was pleased when Witcher's Virginians seized a parallel line of fencing and unleashed a volley that pinned the Yankees down.[34]

Their longer line enabled the Virginians to flank their opponents on the left, whereupon a rescue force came up, dismounted, in the Federals' rear. Witcher's men also took a toll of this force, which, by moving over open ground, made a compelling target. But when additional Yankees came up on foot, many of Witcher's men withdrew from their fences. Through some error probably attributable to Jenkins, his brigade had entered the fight so low on ammunition—about ten rounds of Enfield ammunition per man—that though they could take ground, they could not hold it for long.

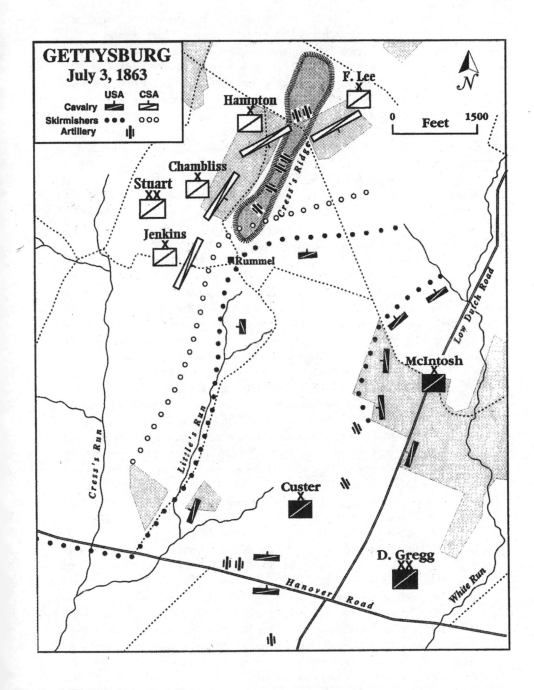

GETTYSBURG
July 3, 1863

Stuart spelled the withdrawing riflemen with members of Ferguson's remaining regiments, the 14th and 16th Virginia (the rest of the brigade, including Ferguson himself, was picketing and guarding prisoners in the rear), as well as with newly arrived units from Chambliss's and Hampton's brigades. The combined force threatened the stability of the ever-lengthening Union line, until General Gregg set up two of his own batteries and had them drop shells on the Rummel property and adjoining farmsteads. When the dismounted Yankees advanced under this barrage, Ferguson's men retreated, grudgingly and in good order, to the base of Cress's Ridge. Many of Chambliss's and Hampton's men pulled back as well.

Stuart had begun to consider himself in a tight corner when the resupplied batteries of Breathed and McGregor reached the field, although for a time they provided scant support to Green. Even so, their opponents' fire slackened noticeably. At the same time, the Federals opposite the Rummel farm fell back a short distance, and a lull settled over the field of battle.[35]

The fighting resumed, but only briefly, at about 2:00, by which time Fitz Lee's brigade had reached Cress's Ridge in force. With or without Stuart's blessing, Fitz suddenly advanced all four of his regiments down the ridge. They drew such a heavy and accurate shelling that he quickly recalled them to the shelter of the trees. About a half hour later, they went forward again along with some of Chambliss's units. The new advance responded to the withdrawal of many of the Federals opposite their line, whose ammunition had begun to run out.

The enemy—not only McIntosh's troopers, but also members of Custer's brigade, who had aborted their withdrawal to assist their embattled comrades—steeled themselves against Lee's advance. At least a couple dozen took position behind a post-and-rail fence that intersected the field from east to west. They became a target for Chambliss's advance regiment, the 9th Virginia, which went forward afoot, rifles ablaze. But then reinforcements rushed up to blast back Beale's men. The new additions also stymied Owen's 3rd Virginia, which had tried to advance on Beale's left. One of Stuart's aides described the action as utterly chaotic. It "looked like two high clouds, Gray and Blue, chasing each other to and fro across the big field."[36]

At this point, Fitz Lee launched the first mounted attack of the day. Col. James H. Drake's storied 1st Virginia came down from the ridge, aligned its ranks under a blistering skirmish fire, and as bugles blared, bounded forward. After riding down scores of Yankee skirmishers, the 1st directed its thrust toward the carbineers behind the post-and-rail fence.

Before the regiment could reach the barrier, the 7th Michigan came up at a full gallop, Custer at its head, to challenge it. Being green and awkward, many of the Yankees struck the wall head-on instead of skirting it, thereby transforming the outfit into a "mass of pulp." As soon as they recovered from the stunning blow, most of the Michiganders dismounted, pulled out their pistols, and fired into the head of Drake's regiment as it approached from the other side. Their opposition, and the wall itself, drained much of the momentum from the Confederate attack and sent the 1st Virginia galloping back to its ridge.

Some of the 1st's supports refused to accompany Drake's fugitives to the rear, but launched small-scale attacks of their own. Trooper Hudgins of the 3rd Virginia recalled:

> We advanced at the charge with drawn sabres as the enemy did the same toward us. We met near the center of that field where sabre met sabre and pistol shots followed in quick succession. Because we tried to ride the enemy down, the individual encounters were often decided by the weight and strength of animals. The battle grew hotter and hotter, horses and men were overthrown or shot and many were killed and wounded.[37]

Custer, with the portion of the 7th that had escaped the fence, tried to pursue the retreating Virginians, only to be taken in flank by two of Wade Hampton's outfits, both mounted—Baker's 1st North Carolina and Waring's Jeff Davis Legion. Desperate fighting swirled along the eastern edge of the Rummel farm as the 7th Michigan and dismounted supports on either side battled the men of the Deep South who had blindsided them. The outcome was not decided until newly mounted elements of the 9th Virginia, plus Phillips's 13th Virginia, charged up to force Custer and his rookies into retreat.[38]

Although wracked by pain from his Hunterstown wound, Wade Hampton, as senior victor on this part of the field, was in lofty spirits. But his euphoria died when he looked to his rear. To his surprise and dismay, the rest of his brigade had left its position on Cress's Ridge and was advancing toward him at a fast trot. Believing that his superior required additional reinforcement, and taking it upon himself to supply it, Hampton's adjutant, Capt. T. G. Barker, had ordered Lt. Col. John D. Twiggs's 1st South Carolina, Maj. Thomas J. Lipscomb's 2nd South Carolina, and the Phillips Legion under Lt. Col. Rich to the general's side.

This was the second time that day that a large portion of Hampton's brigade had moved forward, exposing itself to carbine and artillery fire, without its commander's permission. About an hour earlier, Hampton had been returning from an impromptu conference with Stuart when he discovered that someone—he suspected it was Fitz Lee—had ordered some of his regiments forward. Hampton, correctly judging the action premature, had recalled them before harm could befall them.[39]

This time, it was too late to recall anyone. Making the best of the situation, the brigadier placed himself at the head of the column and led it forward, intending to sweep away the last remnants of Yankee opposition, then gain Meade's rear on Cemetery Ridge. First at a trot, then at a gallop, and finally at an extended gallop, the horsemen thundered across the field on a diagonal heading, evading the obstacles that had broken the 7th Michigan. Those Federals in their path scrambled for cover, giving Hampton a wide berth.

The charging troops provoked expressions of admiration from the enemy. A typical reaction was voiced by one of Gregg's officers, Capt. William E.

Miller of the 3rd Pennsylvania: "They marched with well-aligned fronts and steady reins. Their polished saber-blades dazzled in the sun."[40]

The Confederates appeared to have acquired unstoppable momentum, although hazards were everywhere. One member of Baker's regiment wrote: "We charged them . . . across a field about a mile exposed to a most galling fire from their batteries. . . . The firing was so severe that but few expected to come out alive."

When nearly halfway to McIntosh's position at the road junction, Hampton's men were met in front by countercharging Yankees: Custer and his last uncommitted regiment, the veteran 1st Michigan. When the opposing ranks merged, Miller likened the impact to "the falling of timber . . . so sudden and violent . . . that many of the horses were turned end over end and crushed their riders beneath them." After recovering from the initial shock, individuals chose their antagonists, and hand-to-hand fighting gyrated across the plain.[41]

The larger size of Hampton's column gave it an advantage at the outset of the sword-and-pistol duel, but then other Federals joined the melee, charging in on the Confederates' flanks. One unit that did, Miller's squadron of Pennsylvanians, penetrated the Rebel left and sliced almost through the column, emerging near the Rummel farm. Another squadron, from Gregg's 1st New Jersey, also struck the left flank; its men made directly for the head of the line. One of its swordsmen singled out the massive Hampton and—probably because the general's attention was diverted elsewhere—inflicted another gash to his head. At about the same time, a pistol-wielding Yankee put a bullet in the general's thigh.[42]

The wounds eventually drove Hampton to the rear. When he left, much of his brigade—either through fear at being left leaderless or believing their commander was calling a retreat—went with him. Despite the Yankees who continued to thud into their flanks, the troopers retreated to Cress's Ridge at an unhurried pace and in good order. Within a half hour, the field between the lines was clear except for fallen men and scattered pockets of the able-bodied. The fallen were in greater supply. A Virginian recalled that "there were more men killed and wounded in this fight than I ever saw on any field where the fighting was done mounted."

By now it was 4:00 P.M., and R. E. Lee's attack on Cemetery Ridge had met a bloody repulse. Sensing that Hampton's withdrawal precluded a strike against the Union rear, Custer and McIntosh proclaimed victory and recalled their men. From Cress's Ridge, J. E. B. Stuart looked on with mixed emotions—chagrin at being prevented from accomplishing his assigned mission, and relief that an apparently hopeless effort had ended without taking an even greater toll of his command.[43]

Chapter Sixteen

"Carry Me Back to Old Va.'s Shore"

After dark on July 3, Stuart withdrew his weary squadrons to the York Pike, where they spent the night. Whether or not their day had ended in tactical or strategic success, officers and men had earned their rest. They had battled their enemy to a draw on one of the most hotly contested fields of the war, and at day's end they held that part of it they had occupied at the outset, including the Rummel farm. They had also inflicted more casualties on the enemy, in excess of 250, than they had absorbed—fewer than 200. The worst that could be said of Stuart's command was that it had achieved at least as much as the rest of the army.[1]

During the night, Robert E. Lee withdrew the equally battered, equally tired infantry to the high ground west of Gettysburg. Major McClellan contended that the fallback, of which Stuart was unaware until he visited army headquarters sometime after midnight, left this cavalry isolated and exposed. By the morning of July 4, the eighty-seventh anniversary of American independence, Stuart was in receipt of a communiqué explaining that the army would begin withdrawing from Gettysburg—indeed, from the North—at nightfall. Throughout that day, Lee hoped his opponent would repeat the mistake he had made in attacking head-on against well-defended positions. Meade may have been new to command, but he was no fool—he refused Lee's dare.[2]

With the campaign in Yankee territory now over, Stuart gave his full attention to getting his command back to Virginia in one piece. Lee had assigned him several missions on the road to the Potomac. He would, of course, guard the flanks and rear of the army as it disengaged. He would also devote a part of his force to escorting to Virginia the army's ambulances—whose hundreds of occupants included Wade Hampton, Will Deloney, several other cavalry officers, and dozens of troopers—as well as the supply wagons, whose contents constituted the army's most visible claim to a successful invasion.

Early on the fourth, Stuart learned that John Imboden, whose mixed bag of cavalry, mounted infantry, and partisans had recently closed up on Gettysburg, would provide immediate support to the larger of two wagon trains that would

make the return trip. To assist Imboden at long range, Stuart told off the men of
Hampton (now under Laurence Baker) and Fitz Lee. Upon leaving Gettysburg,
both brigades would move north and west to Cashtown, then south, guarding
not only the army's right flank, but also the wagons as they rolled down to the
river at Williamsport, Maryland. Shortly before Lee and Baker received their
instructions, orders went out to the detached brigades of Jones and Robertson to
occupy and hold the two passes that cut through the South Mountain spur
known as Jack Mountain.[3]

Jones and Robertson had been back with the army only since the previous
afternoon. Their failure to keep up with Robert E. Lee as he moved through
Maryland and into Pennsylvania was principally the fault of Robertson, the
senior officer, but his inept performance had been abetted by Jones. While carrying out one of the orders Stuart had given them—to block enemy access to
Ashby's and Snicker's Gaps in the Blue Ridge—the generals had failed to
maintain contact with each other. After Longstreet's rear guard crossed the
Potomac on June 26, they also failed to keep in touch with the main army. And
when Hooker left their front that same day, they failed to unite and attach themselves to Lee's right flank.

Nor had the pair accomplished any of the other missions assigned them.
They failed to observe and report Hooker's movements to and across the
Potomac; they did an indifferent job of refitting their commands and foraging in
the Shenandoah; and when, on the morning of July 1, they finally moved north,
they neither protected Lee's right (instead, they moved on his *left* flank) nor
made good time on the road to Gettysburg.

The upshot of these many errors of omission—in addition to Lee's ignorance of Hooker's movement into Maryland until he heard of it from one of
Longstreet's scouts—was that the two brigades, half the strength of the Cavalry
Division, A.N.V., did not report to Lee in Pennsylvania until 9:00 A.M. on July
3. By then the epic battle was nearly history, and Lee had no immediate need of
their services.[4]

But he did find a job for them. Just before 1:00 P.M., with the climactic
hour of the struggle drawing near, Lee took his attention from Pickett, Trimble,
and Pettigrew long enough to order Robertson and Jones to Fairfield, eight
miles to the southwest, to counter a body of Yankee cavalry that had been seen
heading toward a forage train in the army's rear. Lee wanted those wagons protected—he needed every ounce of rations, every pound of forage his men had
gathered from the breadbasket known as southern Pennsylvania.[5]

For unknown reasons, Robertson was absent from camp when Lee's order
arrived. Jones started off without him, and some time later Robertson followed
with his demibrigade. This day, the two brigades were close to equal strength;
Jones had on hand only the 6th, 7th, and 11th Virginia and Chew's battery.
White's Comanches remained on detached duty with Ewell, while Lt. Col.
Thomas B. Massie's 12th Virginia had been left in the Valley to keep watch

over the soon-to-be-abandoned garrison at Harpers Ferry—one of the few instructions from Stuart they had complied with fully.[6]

When within a few miles of his destination, Jones spied a small group of Yankee horsemen approaching from the southeast. Although it was difficult to determine numerical strength at such a distance, Jones could see he outnumbered the newcomers. They proved to be the four hundred members of the 6th U.S. Cavalry, Maj. Samuel H. Starr commanding. An hour before, the Regulars had been heading for Gettysburg along with the rest of the Reserve Cavalry Brigade of the Army of the Potomac. A few miles south of town, the brigade leader, Brig. Gen. Wesley Merritt, had detached them to capture the wagon train, whose location a civilian informant had reported that morning.

The fight that broke out in the shadow of South Mountain began when Jones charged the Regulars with his lead regiment, the 7th Virginia. Lieutenant Col. Marshall's troopers butted into Starr's advance squadron and began to force it back, but at a critical moment, another element of the 6th slammed into their flanks and thrust them back in turn. Simultaneously, Maj. Starr dismounted his main body behind roadside trees and fences inaccessible to mounted men. From those positions, his men raked both of Marshall's flanks with carbine fire. Reeling from the volley, the Virginians milled about in the road, horses edging toward panic. Several mounts bolted to the rear; others caught the frenzy, and soon the entire 7th Virginia was whirling to the rear, running a gauntlet of fire. One historian has speculated that by withdrawing, Marshall's men absorbed more casualties "than would have been lost had their onset been made with vigor and boldness."[7]

Mortified that one of his largest regiments should flee from so few opponents, Grumble Jones rode up to the next unit in line, Flournoy's 6th Virginia, and shouted in his shrill voice, "Shall one damned regiment of Yankees whip my whole brigade?" A chorus of voices replied in the negative, whereupon the general led the 6th up the road at a gallop.

By this time Major Starr had come to appreciate how badly he was outnumbered and outpositioned. He tried to remount his regiment and regain the road, either to flee or to launch a forlorn-hope counterattack. Before he could do either, Flournoy's Virginians swarmed over his position, and a slash-and-shoot contest erupted in the road and on both sides of it. Starr was wounded—he would lose an arm to amputation—and his little band was decimated. A few Regulars broke free of the writhing tangle and headed for the hills or for Fairfield in full retreat. Most, however, were shot down before they could reach safety. In the end, almost 250 Federals became casualties, most of them as POWs. The captives included Starr, two of his captains, four of his lieutenants, and two of his surgeons.

While the last fugitives were run to earth, Grumble Jones saw to it that the wounded portion of his fifty-five casualties received medical care, as did all injured prisoners. He also ensured that Starr and his luckless troopers were well guarded and questioned about their cavalry's strength and positions. Finally, he secured the wagon train he had been sent to protect and placed his brigade in bivouac not far from Jack Mountain, whose passes he and Robertson were soon tasked to guard.[8]

The passes—the shortest route from Gettysburg to Hagerstown and Williamsport, Maryland—had become extremely important to both armies by midday on July 4. The day before, when assigning John Imboden to escort his supply and ambulance train, Lee determined to march his main body, including all his infantry and a second, smaller supply train, through Jack Mountain. By heading in that direction after Imboden started out, Lee could reach the Potomac at Williamsport after the wagons and ambulances but before the enemy. A portion of the army could ford the river at Williamsport, while the rest, along with Imboden's column, could cross on a pontoon bridge that had been laid five miles downriver at Falling Waters. Lee was aware that a two-column retreat might prove a cumbersome operation. His ability to reach home without loss would depend largely on Jones's and Robertson's ability to secure the route through the mountains for as long as it was needed.[9]

Then nature and the enemy combined to complicate matters. Rain that began late in the afternoon of Independence Day and refused to stop caused the Potomac to overflow its banks, thereby preventing a fording operation at Williamsport. That same day a demolition party from Harpers Ferry raided the bridgehead at Falling Waters, chased off a guard detail from Massie's regiment, and rendered the pontoon span unusable.

Two days later, another mounted contingent from the Valley garrison wrecked other bridges on the river, preventing their use by the retreating Confederates. Meanwhile, troops of the Department of West Virginia had begun to advance on Williamsport and Falling Waters from Hancock, Maryland. Finally, other enemy forces, civilians as well as soldiers, made plans to waylay Imboden as soon as he left Gettysburg. If the Army of Northern Virginia returned home in one piece, it would not be due to a lack of effort on the enemy's part.[10]

>–⊹–O–⟨⊹–⟨

The first full-size element of Meade's army to set out in pursuit was Kilpatrick's division. Leaving Gettysburg early on the fourth, its three thousand men marched to Frederick, Maryland, where they learned that a wagon train was approaching Fairfield Gap. At their leader's order, they hastened west, reaching Jack Mountain sometime after dark. By then the small train, assigned to Dick Ewell, had passed through the gorge. Kilpatrick sent a single regiment on its trail, while he galloped southwestward with the main body in hopes of meeting the wagons on the other side of the mountain.

In the dark, both of his columns experienced rough going. The regiment sent after the train was roughly handled by Grumble Jones, most of whose men had been stationed inside Fairfield Gap. Meanwhile, near Monterey Pass on the other side of the mountain, Kilpatrick, at about 10:00 P.M., encountered a detachment of Brown's Maryland battalion, tried unsuccessfully to push it aside, then failed just as miserably to beat it down. For the next five hours, as Ewell's wagons rumbled through the gap, twenty Marylanders under Capt. G. M. Emack—later augmented by a dozen members of Robertson's 4th North Carolina—held back almost a hundred times as many Yankees, thanks to inspired tactics, a rainstorm that obscured the enemy's vision, and some of the roughest terrain Kilpatrick's men had ever trod—sheer cliffs, jagged rocks, and briar-infested underbrush.[11]

When the Yankees finally positioned themselves to threaten Emack's flanks and rear, his little band slipped away in the darkness. At last able to go forward, the attackers scrambled down the mountainside to a road that merged into the one Ewell's trains had taken from Fairfield Gap. Dozens of wagons were destroyed, while almost as many ambulances were rounded up and their occupants taken prisoner. Other vehicles had been ambushed by embattled farmers in advance of the defile and overturned, set afire, or chopped up with axes and hatchets. Still other wagons, however, had been saved by Emack's quick thinking, kept inside the pass until the main body of Jones's brigade came up to chase off the vandals and the saboteurs.[12]

While the fighting raged south of Gettysburg, Imboden's much longer train wended its way through the mountain passes west of town, then, at Cashtown, swerved southward. The entire trip was an ordeal that no member of the escort would ever forget. To begin with, the column was enormous, making it inherently difficult to protect. According to Pvt. Norval Baker of the 18th Virginia, it was "the longest wagon train I ever saw, some said it was 37 or 38 mile[s] long and hauled thousands of . . . wounded soldiers." Then there was the weather, so intense and so loud as to be frightening. Said Baker:

> It rained all night, one thunderstorm after another. The rain fell in sheets and vivid flashes of lightning and [it was] so dark we could not see our hands an inch from our eyes when there was no lightning. The roar of the water and heavy bursting thunder, the cries of the wounded and dying soldiers made it awful.[13]

Still another problem was that the train, like Ewell's supply column, became an inviting target for bands of marauders, including a roving body of Pennsylvania cavalry under a fire-eating aide from army headquarters, Capt. Ulric Dahlgren. This band attacked the wagons as they passed Waynesboro, twenty miles southwest of Gettysburg. By firing into the head of the column, they stopped it in its tracks. The men then bolted forward to damage wagon wheels and shoot or saber the teams, until chased away by soldiers under the brigade leader's brother, Col. George W. Imboden. An even larger force—two hundred members of the 1st New York Cavalry—attacked eight miles farther on, outside Greencastle. The toll they took included almost a hundred wagons overturned, burned, splintered, or otherwise rendered unserviceable. With the rest of the column, including the ambulances, Imboden plodded on to the Potomac, hoping that his ordeal was almost over. But he hoped in vain.[14]

>–+–‹›–O–‹›+–‹

Stuart had allowed his opponents to get the jump on him, but there was no help for it. The need to brief his officers on their many duties, the time it took to disengage from the field of July 3, and the problems posed by weather and unfamiliar territory prevented him from leaving Gettysburg until late in the afternoon of the fourth. As a result, the brigades he accompanied—Chambliss's and Ferguson's—did not reach Emmitsburg, Maryland, until early the next morning, by which time Kilpatrick had come and gone. From the start, it was rough going. On the first night out, reported one of Stuart's officers, "we marched behind the artillery—halting very often while the rains poured down and the roads were becoming very bad indeed." The rain continued into the morning, robbing rest stops of their value. "The only sleep I got that night," said the officer, "was one hour wrapped in a very wet blanket under a little apple tree so destitute of leaves that it didn't shelter me at all scarcely."[15]

Physical discomfort was bad enough, but some troopers also had to put up with insults and derision. On the way out of Gettysburg, a Virginia lieutenant passed a home whose inhabitants had grudgingly furnished him with breakfast the previous morning. Over flapjacks and coffee, the officer had bragged that if it chose to, his army could range at will across their state, from the Susquehanna to the Delaware. Now "the ladies were all out on the porch, when the old lady recognized me in the front of my command. She exclaimed, 'That is not the direction of Philadelphia,' but, pointing said, 'Philadelphia is in the opposite direction.' . . . After my boasting of the day before you may well imagine my feelings."[16]

After questioning the several dozen Federals he captured at Emmitsburg, Stuart declined to pursue Kilpatrick to Fairfield Gap and Monterey Pass. He reasoned that Jones was strong enough to protect Ewell's train. Besides, he had learned that Buford's division was hurrying toward the gaps west of Hagerstown; unless stopped, he would reach Williamsport and Imboden's train in advance of any other Confederates. Stuart did not trust Imboden's ragtag command to hold the enemy back; hence he had assigned Lee and Baker to cover its movements.

In midmorning, Stuart headed for the nearest stretch of the South Mountain range. Instead of coming to grips with Buford, however, just inside the mountains near Smithsburg he encountered Kilpatrick's division, fresh from its fight with Emack's band but apparently eager for more action. As if forewarned of the enemy's approach, Kilpatrick had assumed a defensive posture. His dismounted troopers and his horse artillery held commanding positions on some of the highest ground in the range.

Stuart had split his force to enter the defiles above and below Smithsburg, but Kilpatrick, who had been reinforced, had enough men to defend both. After both columns became engaged, Stuart tried to withdraw Ferguson's brigade in order to add its weight to Chambliss's effort, but the time it took negated the maneuver's effectiveness. To Stuart's immense relief, Kilpatrick suddenly abandoned his position, turned his back on his enemy, and galloped off. He might have gone west to Williamsport, where he could have attacked Imboden; instead, for no apparent reason, he marched south to Boonsboro, where he would be unable to contribute to Meade's pursuit.[17]

Thankful for large favors, Stuart pushed through the gaps Kilpatrick had vacated. On the far side of mountain, he met Captain Emack, who recounted his Thermopylae-like defense at Monterey and guided Chambliss and Ferguson to Leitersburg, where Jones and Robertson had congregated. At Leitersburg, bad news met Stuart. Jones reported that Imboden had reached Williamsport safely but had been trapped there by the rising of the Potomac. One observer later described the river as "madly rushing by, carrying logs and trees at a terrific rate, and of the color of yellow mud." What was worse, Buford was said to be closing in on Williamsport from the east; to oppose him, Imboden would have to rely on his small escort, several batteries that Lee had assigned him, ambulatory convalescents, and any teamsters willing to risk their necks for the Army of Northern Virginia. Neither Fitz Lee nor Baker was within supporting distance of the river.[18]

After mulling over Imboden's plight, Stuart added Robertson's two regiments to his column and started for Williamsport via Hagerstown. Jones's men he left near Funkstown to guard his flank and rear. Not long after, Stuart may have wished he had brought Jones along; scouts he had sent toward Boonsboro reported that Kilpatrick had also turned toward the river as if to team with Buford against the train.[19]

Before Stuart could assist him, Imboden found himself embattled. He had reached Williamsport in midafternoon on the fifth. With the river out of its banks and the bridge at Falling Waters reduced to kindling, the brigadier knew he was going nowhere for a while. Imboden was not a professional soldier—he had been a lawyer in Staunton and a member of the state legislature—but he was a man of imagination and energy, and he put both to good use on this occasion. Before anyone could threaten his position, he secured it with his artillery, including two horse batteries, Hart's and McClanahan's. He placed his guns in positions that commanded every road, with the largest number covering those from Hagerstown and Boonsboro. Then he dismounted most of his men, placed them behind whatever cover he could find, and handed a musket to every wounded man able and willing to fight.

To this force he added defenders who, left to their own inclination, would have remained with the wagons. Trooper Baker saw him "fetching out armed wagoners two and three hundred at a time and in every part of the field." Eventually Imboden's force approached three thousand, although nearly half were men whose physical and mental stamina could not be gauged. Before day's end, the general had also fashioned rafts by which he ferried the lighter wagons over to the Virginia side.[20]

By the time Buford approached Williamsport from Boonsboro early in the afternoon of the sixth, Imboden was as ready to meet him as he would ever be. Expecting that artillery alone would scatter the escort, Buford opened with the battery attached to his division. Private Baker noted that the Yankees "had the air full of flying shells in a very short time." To his surprise as well as Buford's, Imboden's guns replied with greater accuracy and intensity, blasting back almost every attempt to reach the wagons, which had been parked in rear of the strongest sector of his defense line. Buford was able to capture only seven wagons that by some mistake had been placed in a vulnerable position on the road to Downsville.[21]

One factor in Buford's repulse was the courage and determination of those wounded men who left the ambulances for the front. Lieutenant Colonel Deloney was one of these stalwarts; as he wrote his wife in Georgia:

> I was feeling very miserably, but the booming of their cannon aroused me and I gathered up the stragglers about the wagons & went to the field. . . . I managed very soon to inspire the men with confidence and led them in. They fought well, drove the enemy about 1/4 of a mile and about dark had completely flanked one of their batteries & if I had had a little more daylight I believe I should have taken it.

For the courage he showed on this field as well as on many others, Deloney became known as "a Georgia Henry of Navarre," a reference to the seventeenth-century warrior-king of France.[22]

Late in the day, a frustrated Buford sought help from Kilpatrick, then engaged to the north at Hagerstown. Kilpatrick responded as quickly as possible, but his lead brigade, Custer's, failed to reach Williamsport until close to dark. Giving up his attempt at a two-pronged attack, and upon learning that Fitz Lee was nearing Williamsport, Buford, as senior officer, had Kilpatrick's division and his own fall back and bivouac. The news of their withdrawal, as Imboden recalled, "was received with a wild and exultant yell." A similar response greeted Fitz's Lee's men when they arrived about an hour after dark.[23]

Kilpatrick's presence at Hagerstown had been the reason why Stuart, with Chambliss, Ferguson, and Robertson, had been unable to reinforce Imboden. Throughout the sixth, while the Federals made ineffective attempts to seize and destroy the Rebel train, Kilpatrick fought Stuart in the streets of Hagerstown, preventing him from moving south. For a time, Kilpatrick held the advantage, keeping Chambliss's brigade, at the head of Stuart's column, from gaining a foothold in the town. His sharpshooters took an especially heavy toll of the Confederate horse artillery. One gunner reported himself and his comrades "under a rapidly advancing line of sharpshooters' fire forty yards away. We

don't mind shell but these little bees zipping by make us nervous." Both sides
suffered heavily, the Confederates more so than Kilpatrick. Their losses
included Colonel Davis of the 10th Virginia, who was captured when his horse
was shot away beneath him. Not long afterward, however, the tactician was
paroled, exchanged, and returned to his regiment.[24]

Eventually, and to Stuart's dismay, Chambliss was forced to withdraw to
higher, more defensible ground about a mile west of Hagerstown, whereupon
Kilpatrick took full possession of the place. Yet his occupancy was short-lived.
Stuart, with the rest of his command—to which Jones's brigade had now been
added—gained enough momentum to thrust the Yankees through the streets in
the direction of Boonsboro. His new hold on Hagerstown was solidified late in
the day, when Lee's infantry advance, the Second Corps brigade of Alfred Iverson, Jr., reached the scene en route to the Potomac.

Iverson's arrival signified that R. E. Lee was intent on departing the North
with all possible speed. Next day, July 7, the rear of the army reached Hagerstown, only a few hours' march from Williamsport and Falling Waters. By contrast, Meade was moving so sluggishly that not for another three days would
every major element of his army be within striking distance of the Potomac. To
some observers, Meade gave the impression that he wished to escort Lee from
Maryland without further molestation.[25]

While Lee waited for the river to drop to fording depth, he ferried bridge
materials as well as pioneers and fatigue parties across the water to initiate construction of a new pontoon bridge. A rope ferry, making use of the rafts Imboden's men had built, was now in regular operation. On the eighth, it began to
carry across the artillery that had helped save the wagons and ambulances.

To protect the ferry and the bridge building, Lee had begun to construct a
line of works along a ten-mile stretch of river between Williamsport and
Downsville. The line, which he crowned with guns, both heavy and light,
enclosed several potential crossing sites, including Falling Waters. Until completed, it would be Stuart's job to keep away from those works the Union cavalry, the only element of Meade's army that showed any inclination to make
contact with the Confederates.[26]

Over the next week, the opposing horsemen fought a series of skirmishes,
some large enough to be considered battles. Usually the fighting ended inconclusively but on terms favorable to Stuart and his army. For the first four days of
that period, the fighting centered around Hagerstown, where the army's rear
guard continued to linger. On the first day, July 7, Buford advanced on the town
from the south. Near Funkstown, Merritt's brigade detached what remained of
the 6th United States, this day backed by the 1st U.S. Cavalry, and sent it to
monitor infantry movements farther north. As luck had it, Grumble Jones, also
engaged in a reconnaissance mission, was moving in the opposite direction on
the same road, the 7th Virginia in the van. The familiar antagonists met outside
Funkstown, and this time the 7th won the day, charging into and through the 6th,
then pouncing on its supports and pummeling both regiments without mercy.

Every Regular unit, at this stage of the war, was seriously understrength, the result of frequent detachments and lax recruiting. Not surprisingly, Jones's antagonists could not withstand the onslaught. They turned and raced back to their brigade, pursued for more than four miles by shouting, shooting Virginians.[27]

Stuart finally recalled Jones and his men to Hagerstown. The following morning, despite persistent rain, he led his reunited command—including the brigades of Lee and Baker—south to challenge Buford and Kilpatrick. Observing his approach, Stuart's opponents believed he intended to block the mountain passes from which Meade's infantry was about to emerge. But Stuart was merely feinting in that direction to keep his enemy at bay while Lee reeled in his rear guard, which remained in Hagerstown.

Drawing near Buford's position astride the Hagerstown Pike at about 5:00 A.M., the Confederates let loose with a barrage from McGregor's battery. Stuart had placed its guns on high ground, from which they enfiladed one of Buford's brigades and forced it, as well as a Yankee artillery unit, to withdraw. Then Chambliss's skirmishers advanced against other parts of Buford's line. The recent storms had left the ground too marshy to support a mounted advance, so the troopers moved up afoot. At the same time, Stuart sent dismounted members of Ferguson's brigade to menace the Union left via the Williamsport road.[28]

The one-two punch had the desired effect. Early in the afternoon, after repeated countermoves failed to dislodge the attackers, Buford's entire position began to waver. At a critical point, however, Kilpatrick arrived to strengthen both ends of his colleague's line, and Stuart's men were forced back in turn. Sometime after 5:00, with the available ammunition supply running low, Stuart pulled back toward Funkstown. By then his job was done: He had covered the move of Lee's infantry from Hagerstown to the river for several hours.

Heartened by their opponents' withdrawal, elements of Buford's and Kilpatrick's commands pursued across Beaver Creek—a tributary of another, better-known creek, the Antietam—until stopped on the outskirts of Funkstown by Jones's brigade and Chew's battery, whose accurate and incessant firing had much to do with the result. Suddenly glad to resume guarding the passes in their rear, the Yankees retired without complaint.[29]

Stuart believed his aggressive advance on the eighth "administered a *quietus* to the enemy on the 9th." Through most of the day, he was correct. Buford and Kilpatrick chose to spend the morning and the first half of the afternoon near Boonsboro, resting, refitting, and awaiting their friends in the infantry. Toward 5:00 P.M., however, one of Buford's brigades moved north to probe Stuart's dispositions behind Beaver Creek. One detachment, backed by two guns of a Regular battery, advanced across a bend in the stream and shoved in a portion of Stuart's line, but night fell before the stability of the position could be jeopardized.[30]

Late that day, Meade's advance emerged west of the mountains and moved within rifle distance of Lee's defenses, but did not challenge it. The Yankees

7-4 '63 GRANT!

attacked not with bullets, but with words, shouting across the lines the news that *29,000* on Independence Day, Ulysses Grant had forced the surrender of <u>Vicksburg.</u> *prisoners*

Early on the tenth, the Union cavalry resorted to more conventional weapons. Emboldened by the foot soldiers massing in their rear, Buford returned in force to Beaver Creek, threatening all parts of his enemy's line with a vigorous offensive. Soon the Confederate cavalry found hundreds of dismounted Yankees "crawling up on" them, and Stuart hauled them back to Funkstown.[31]

When Buford crossed Beaver Creek and came on with a full head of steam, Stuart's men were forced to ford the Antietam. In fact, they retreated until they were up against the infantry's entrenchments, which jutted east from Williamsport. Appreciating Stuart's predicament, the occupants came to his aid. Shortly after noon, the brigade of Brig. Gen. George T. Anderson of Longstreet's corps waded the creek and drove south. Near Funkstown, Fitzhugh Lee, at Stuart's behest, guided the foot soldiers against a critical sector of Buford's line. After several minutes of seesaw fighting, the Union troopers turned back to Beaver Creek.[32]

Even as they withdrew, Stuart had to admire the tenacity Buford's men had displayed, and not for the first time during this campaign. Cavalry was not supposed to hold the line, even briefly, against infantry—but Buford had done so not only this day, but also on July 1, when his dismounted troopers had held up A. P. Hill's advance on Gettysburg for more than two hours, until infantry arrived to relieve them. This ability was largely attributable to the abundance of breechloading carbines in Buford's command. Stuart must have wondered what his men might accomplish with such weaponry, in such quantity.

>─┼─◆〉─O─〈◆─┼─◄

On July 11, Meade began to close in on Lee's defenses. As the Army of the Potomac moved up, the cavalry led the way. Buford advanced northwestward toward Bakersville, seven miles below Williamsport. This was too close to his defenses for Robert E. Lee's comfort; at his order, infantry replaced Fitz Lee's brigade on the line between Bakersville and Stuart's new headquarters at Hagerstown. The foot soldiers slowed, then stopped the enemy advance.

Farther east, however, Kilpatrick's division pressed toward Funkstown, chasing out the last remnants of Stuart's division and propelling them toward Hagerstown. The next morning, he used the lodgment as a stepping-off point for an assault on Hagerstown itself. By now Stuart and his men had moved on to Williamsport—all but a few stragglers, which the Union troopers snatched up. Then Kilpatrick boldly turned west and started after Stuart. Backed by some infantry units, Stuart's re-formed ranks held off the advancing bluecoats with a heavy concentration of rifle and carbine fire.[33]

By the twelfth, Stuart was preparing another delaying action, this one to give the infantry the time it needed to cross the Potomac on its all-but-completed pontoons. The single bridge would not accommodate an entire army, but fording would soon be possible, for the river was receding steadily. Already, in fact, it had dropped low enough to permit some soldiers, including most of Imboden's brigade, to reach Virginia. A small portion of Stuart's command— notably Jones's 7th Virginia—had also crossed, via makeshift rafts and impro- vised ferryboats. Robert E. Lee figured he could afford to linger in Maryland for only one more day; still, his works were strong enough, and their defenders sufficiently numerous and vigilant, that he did not fear an attack by Meade. In truth, he would welcome it, for, given the open ground that surrounded his defenses, any assault would be a reprise of Pickett's Charge.[34]

Meade wished to oblige him. Throughout the twelfth he scrutinized Lee's defenses for weak points, maneuvered here and there, and telegraphed Wash- ington that he would strike all along the line the next morning. That night, how- ever, his subordinates persuaded him to make a more thorough reconnaissance the next day. The upshot was that little fighting was done on the thirteenth except by the cavalry. Buford probed the Confederate left flank, Kilpatrick the far right. Both gained some ground toward the river, but not enough to give Meade a clear path to his enemy's line. In moving up Buford suffered few casu- alties, but on the other end of the line, Stuart assisted his infantry brethren in repulsing Kilpatrick, with considerable loss.[35]

Lee, who had been expecting an attack for some days, prepared again on the thirteenth to receive it. By midafternoon, however, he doubted it would ever come. By now the river was low enough that Ewell's men might ford at Williamsport, while Longstreet, Hill, and the artillery trod the pontoons at Falling Waters. Lee decided to make for Virginia without further delay.

Stuart's role in the operation was critical to its success. At 4:15 P.M. Lee wrote him: "I wish you to place your cavalry in position before night so as to relieve the infantry along the whole extreme of their lines . . . and take the place of their sharpshooters when withdrawn." Stuart complied, but minus a part of his command. After dark, when the fording and crossing got under way, Jones's troopers, at Lee's order, accompanied Longstreet's column, walking their ani- mals across the narrow, swaying bridge.[36]

Stuart's men did an effective job of filling in for the infantry. Occupying the trenches that the foot soldiers had evacuated, they kept up such a steady rifle fire that for hours the nearest Yankees did not realize a troop transfer had occurred. Toward morning of July 14, Stuart finally got the word to pull out by crossing behind the infantry. While a few of his regiments used the pontoons at Falling Waters, most forded at Williamsport. Many of those who did not take the bridge wished they had, for although the river had fallen, in places it remained quite deep. The water, wrote Lieutenant Hubard of the 3rd Virginia, "took our horses within 12 inches of the top of the shoulders and wet our legs thoroughly eight inches above the knees at least."[37]

The Potomac continued to move along at a dangerous clip, and a couple of troopers were swept away by the current. A greater mistake was to send dozens of the wagons Stuart had captured at Rockville over at Williamsport. Many slid into deep water, carrying under their mule teams and, in a few instances, their drivers.[38]

The majority of Stuart's men had completed the fording by dawn on the fourteenth. The last to get over—a pair of squadrons of Fitz Lee's brigade, which crossed at Falling Waters—reached the Virginia side at around 8:00 A.M. Hours earlier, Custer's pickets near Hagerstown had detected their withdrawal, but the young general reached Williamsport too late to interrupt the fording. Stuart's men, the last to depart Maryland, "crossed just in time," a North Carolinian wrote, "for in a few hours after we got over the River was not fordable. The Yankees came up on the other side and seemed to be much provoked at our giving them the slip."[39]

Custer's men unleashed an impotent volley or two, then remounted and galloped south to Falling Waters. Reaching the bridgehead, they attacked Lee's rear guard, inflicting several casualties, including the mortal wounding of General Pettigrew. They also cut off dozens of straggling Confederates, but because Custer failed to coordinate operations with Buford, advancing from the east, a much larger haul eluded him. Before the Federals could unite to charge the bridge, Lee's engineers cut the pontoons loose from the Virginia shore, and they were carried away by the current.[40]

Many Confederates expressed relief at their safe return to the Old Dominion. Over the past week, the campaign in the North, which had begun as a bright, hopeful dream, had become a nightmarish combination of fatigue, suffering, and loss, and they wanted it to end, wanted to get back home where they could rest and recuperate. For the men of Stuart's cavalry, who had borne so much of the burden of invasion, the desire to put the Potomac behind them had burned with a desperate intensity. A typical trooper wrote home: "I am tired of Penn. and Md. and catch myself constantly humming—'Oh! carry me back, Oh! carry me back to old Va.'s shore'."[41]

Chapter Seventeen

Hairbreadth Escapes

The Yankees in the East get down to business

Stuart's soldiers returned from Maryland in wretched condition—"completely worn out and broken down," as one North Carolinian put it. The almost universal complaint was that they had gone too long without sleep and food, while ravaged by overexertion and constant travel. A member of the 4th Virginia complained, "[For] ten days and nights I did not unsaddle my horse." An enlisted man in the 9th Virginia fared worse: "I have been on my horse night and day for two weeks. I am completely worn up." A private in the 1st South Carolina had not had a change of clothing in three weeks.[1]

Many considered the lack of regular rations a greater privation than the long hours spent on horseback. "We not only had to fight the enemy every day," one trooper lamented, "but had also to contend with the pangs of hunger. We were kept so busy fighting that we hadn't time to go around and impress provisions as we intended to do." While they had captured numerous supply wagons on the road to Gettysburg, few had partaken of their contents. A 10th Virginia private complained that he had not eaten a meal of any kind until the third day of the march and had "not drawn a mouthfull from the government for a fortnight."[2]

The plethora of hardships would have been easier to bear had they helped produce a victory in the North, but few members of Stuart's command believed this was the case. The retreat from Gettysburg had been one indication of failure; another was the painful thinness of so many regiments. A private in the 5th Virginia informed a friend that at Aldie, all but five members of his company had been killed or taken prisoner, and of the five, two were wounded. "I tell you there was many a poor soldier killed in Maryland and Pennsylvania and there was no end to the wounded. I think we got the worst end of the bargain this time." The rank and file were not alone in expressing this opinion. In a letter written to his bride even before the campaign ended, Thomas Rosser wrote: "This trip to Penn. has done us no good—indeed I feel that it is quite a disaster."[3]

The situation moved some soldiers to despair. A lieutenant in Jackson's battery confided to his father:

237

The campaign we have just finished has not only been arduous & fruitless, but . . . terribly disastrous to our arms. . . . True, we have lived for nearly a month upon the enemies soil, we have killed as many, if not more of the foe, than we have lost, but we can look around & see no points of success, & this is a crisis when our cause cannot afford to lose without compensation.

Looking to the future made this man shudder:

The clouds around the Confederacy are darker & blacker than ever. This army is now regarded as the mainstay & prop of the countries cause, it is still dauntless in spirit, powerful & to be feared, but alas? how many thousands of its bravest will never more lift an arm or tramp the soil of their native land. They are now but a handful to cope with myriads. . . . One thing is proved beyond doubt that we are unable to carry on a war of invasion.[4]

But not everyone gave way to gloom or fear. Just as he seemed impervious to the discomforts of extended travel, J. E. B. Stuart appeared immune to the disheartening results of the recent campaign. On the afternoon of the fifteenth, he led his staff back to the Dandridge estate as if to recapture the gaiety of times past. At first the return seemed to rejuvenate everyone who accompanied him. "Our camp was pitched at the old place," William Blackford recalled, " . . . and our pleasant, gay life was resumed, with the lovely daughters and nieces of our host." But the engineer officer admitted that the mood was not as light as on their previous visit: "A shade of sadness hung over our meeting, however, when we thought how many who were with us during our former visit were dead or absent from wounds."[5]

More than the number of merrymakers present had changed. There would be no more parlor games, no more capering about the dance floor by von Borcke in drag, no more toe-tapping banjo solos, as Sam Sweeney had contracted smallpox (he would die of the disease during the coming winter). Symptomatic of the change of atmosphere was Blackford's collapse a few days after arriving at the Bower, from a malarialike condition triggered by fatigue and overexposure in the North. Within a week, he was carried from his sickroom in the Dandridge house to a hospital train that took him home to Abingdon. There, under his wife's care, he rapidly regained his health.[6]

Meanwhile, Blackford's comrades returned to the never-ending task of fighting Yankees. On the day Stuart reached the Bower, he learned that Union cavalry had crossed the Potomac near Harpers Ferry and had ranged toward Martinsburg, as if intending to move into Lee's rear. Annoyed to be torn from his hosts so soon after rejoining them, Stuart planned a coordinated counterattack involving Lee's, Chambliss's, Ferguson's, and Jones's brigades. It would be the first time he used these forces in combination.

Because he was called to a meeting at army headquarters that morning, Stuart could not oversee the execution of his strategy. For this reason, perhaps, the operation miscarried, with near-disastrous results.

Fitz Lee, who took over for his superior, attacked toward Leetown early on the sixteenth with his own brigade and Chambliss's. Meeting the Yankees—the brigade of J. Irvin Gregg—on the Martinsburg Road, he drove them rapidly toward the river. His thrust did not end till the enemy was within a mile of Shepherdstown. There Gregg's men, who outnumbered Lee's, rallied and shoved their assailants back in turn. At this point, Ferguson was supposed to have come in against the Yankees' left flank, with Jones in more remote support. But Alfred Jenkins's successor arrived late, throwing Fitz's plans out of kilter.[7]

By this time Stuart had reached the scene from army headquarters. At once he decided that "the ground was not practicable for cavalry"—not practicable, that is, for mounted operations. Almost any kind of terrain was conducive to fighting on foot, but Stuart continued to eschew this tactic whenever possible. He had already made up his mind to pull back when the Federals did so, taking shelter behind some stone fences. From that well-chosen position, the Yankees took a toll with their carbines. Among their targets was James Drake of the 1st Virginia, who received a wound from which he succumbed next day (the colonel died, said Fitz Lee, "as heroically as he had lived"). After that, Stuart was content to engage Gregg at long distance until darkness came on and the men in blue retired to the river. Stuart claimed that he was prepared to "renew the attack vigorously next morning but daybreak revealed that the enemy had retired towards Harper's Ferry."[8]

In later days, the rest of the Army of the Potomac followed its cavalry across the river. Unlike McClellan after Sharpsburg, Meade was determined to return quickly to Virginia and challenge Lee before he could withdraw to his old positions below the Rappahannock. By the nineteenth, Meade's rear echelon had gotten over and he was pushing the head of the army down the eastern rim of the Blue Ridge even as Lee hurried south on the other side. Meade hoped to force his way through the various gaps, cut off a part of his enemy's column, and finish the job of destruction that had begun at Gettysburg.[9]

Stuart, as always in his army's forefront, was determined to keep Meade well back from Lee's retreat route. When, on the nineteenth, Longstreet was hustled south in an effort to outrace the foe, Stuart split his command, sending a reinforced version of Robertson's brigade to escort the First Corps across the rain-swollen Shenandoah River near Front Royal, then through the Blue Ridge via Chester Gap. Meanwhile, Stuart assigned Baker's brigade the task of guarding Ewell's rear and ordered Jones's men to picket even farther north, safeguarding the Confederate left flank.

With the remainder of his division, Stuart hurried along the mountains to Manassas Gap, by which Meade hoped to gain entrance to the Valley. He found, however, that the Shenandoah River, having risen six feet under the recent rains, blocked his access to the defile. Left without any options, Stuart continued south to Front Royal, where he finally crossed the raging stream. On July 23, he moved east, on Longstreet's heels, through Chester Gap. That day his men helped evict a brigade of Yankee horsemen that had attempted to block the pass without infantry support.

Stuart's inability to reach Manassas Gap did not have dire repercussions. Although Union horsemen had seized the other side of the defile on the twenty-first, Meade's infantry moved too slowly to exploit their gains. The result—terribly disappointing to the Union commander—was that the rear of Lee's army had cleared that part of the Valley before the Federals finally poked through the gap on the twenty-third. The next day, Longstreet reoccupied the Culpeper Court House area, and the race to the Rappahannock was over.[10]

⋗⋅⊷⋅⊙⋅⊶⋅⋉

Only when settling into a fixed camp near Culpeper could Stuart attempt to fix the problems that had hampered his command during the campaigning in the North. Some of these were caused by the invasion itself; others predated it. Immediately after returning, he sent every man who could be spared from the picket and skirmish lines to forage for remounts and provisions throughout Culpeper County and beyond. He sternly advised regimental commanders to allow exhausted men and horses regular periods of rest in camp and bivouac. He dispatched representatives of various regiments to their home regions on the increasingly important job of recruiting. And he asked General Lee to use his influence with Jefferson Davis to increase the compensation awarded a trooper whose horse had been lost in combat. Stuart hoped a larger allowance would enable the members of Company Q to meet the inflationary prices that remounts commanded.[11]

When time permitted, he attended to personnel problems. He tried to find the best possible replacements for fallen officers, including some of his senior subordinates. Colonel Baker had done an effective job filling in for Wade Hampton—he would have to do so indefinitely. Hampton had been evacuated to the general hospital at Charlottesville, where his wounds were being treated. When well enough to travel, he would return to South Carolina to complete his recuperation. Stuart did not expect to see him in the field until the closing weeks of the year, at the earliest.[12]

Other replacements had likewise given satisfaction. Except for his tardiness at Shepherdstown, Ferguson had performed capably in command of Jenkins's brigade; this was fortunate, as its original commander would not return to the field until the fall. And by every indication, Chambliss had done splendidly while filling in for W. H. F. Lee. He, too, would continue in command for an indefinite period. In early July, during an abortive offensive against Richmond by Union forces on the south side of the James River, a party of horsemen had captured Rooney Lee while he convalesced from his Brandy Station wound, carrying him off, sickbed and all. He would spend the next eight months in a Union prison. For much of that period he would be held in solitary confinement as a hostage against the possibility that two Union captains, inmates of Libby Prison, would be executed in retaliation for the hanging of Confederate officers in Kentucky.[13]

At this time, Stuart worked hard to fulfill the wish of one subordinate and to foil the intent of a second. Two days after returning to Virginia, Beverly Robertson asked that he be assigned a larger command, one commensurate with his rank, or be permitted to rejoin the two regiments he had left in North Carolina. Stuart heartily endorsed the second course. On August 5, Robert E. Lee granted Robertson's request to leave the army but directed him to report to the Adjutant and Inspector General's Office for reassignment. Without casting aspersions on the man's abilities as a field leader, Lee recommended he be given command of a cavalry recruitment camp, which the army leader considered a "very important" priority. A few days later, when Robertson left the army for Richmond, Stuart, with heartfelt thanks, bade him farewell forever.[14]

The officer whose designs Stuart frustrated was Williams Wickham, who had recently been elected to the Confederate Congress from Virginia's Third Congressional District. For the second time in less than a year, Stuart petitioned the War Department to reject the colonel's resignation on the grounds that the service could not afford the loss of "as capable an officer" as he. Wickham, he maintained, "has displayed fine ability, zeal and bravery . . . and has been recommended for promotion." In the end, the government did not have to act; Wickham gave in to Stuart's pleas and his pledge that the officer would receive the first available promotion to brigadier general. Revoking his application, Wickham left his congressional seat vacant until the fall of 1864, when he finally quit the army to claim it.[15]

In addition to Wickham, Stuart had also recommended Rosser and Lomax for promotion, both of whom had shown aptitude for higher command throughout the recent campaign. A means of securing their elevation seemed at hand, for by the end of July, Robert E. Lee had come to consider the army's cavalry brigades, "even with the reduced numbers in the regiments," too large for their commanders to manage properly. On August 1, he recommended to Jefferson Davis that each brigade be reduced to no more than four regiments; the result would be a total of seven brigades, one more than previously. In Lee's mind, seven were enough to support a corps organization for the cavalry, a structure that had proved its value in the Army of the Potomac. He recommended that Wade Hampton and Fitzhugh Lee be made major generals, each to command a division under Stuart.[16]

Adding a brigade and promoting two generals, coupled with the loss of Robertson, would create vacancies for four brigadier generals. Lee recommended they be filled by promoting Colonels Butler, Wickham, Baker, and Lomax, saying, "I believe these four officers are the best qualified and . . . deserve promotion." Butler would take over Hampton's old brigade; Wickham would receive Fitz Lee's; Baker would command an expanded version of Robertson's brigade, in which all of the North Carolina regiments would be grouped; and Lomax would lead the new brigade. The existing brigades of Rooney Lee (commanded by Chambliss), Jones, and Jenkins (under Ferguson) would round out the corps.[17]

Many of Lee's proposals were based on the ideas of Stuart. The cavalry commander, therefore, was anxious that they be approved and acted on forthwith. His only regret was his inability to find a brigadier's slot for Tom Rosser, Pierce Young, and other subordinates just as deserving of promotion as the ones earmarked by Lee.

Stuart's preferences notwithstanding, implementation would have to wait for the resolution of a new round of fighting. On August 1, Buford's cavalry, for the second time in two months, crossed the Rappahannock at Beverly Ford, this time on a reconnaissance in force. It attacked the head of Baker's brigade, which had been patrolling the south bank toward Brandy Station, while a second column came in against the Confederate right flank. Badly outnumbered, Baker ordered a retreat, during which he took a severe wound. His successor, Pierce Young, fell wounded as well, as did the next officer to assume command, Col. John Logan Black of the 1st South Carolina.

Amid the carnage, the Federals pushed south, driving before them the troopers formerly led by Hampton. Their retreat finally ended about a mile and a half from Culpeper Court House. There, at about 3:00 P.M., Stuart counterattacked with Jones's horsemen, assisted by two brigades of foot soldiers from Richard H. Anderson's division, as well as by Hart's and Chew's batteries and a section of McGregor's. Against so heavy a force, the Yankees were compelled to retreat across the open plain on which Stuart had reviewed his legions almost two months before. The hot summer day ended with Buford's men holding the south bank of the river near the recently rebuilt railroad bridge at Rappahannock Station; they appeared in no hurry to retake the offensive. Reflecting on the history of the battlefield, a trooper of the 1st North Carolina noted, "The same field, that was sprinkled with the best blood of the land on the 9th of June . . . has again been made memorable."[18]

When Buford did not recross the river, Robert E. Lee wondered what his and Meade's intentions might be. On the evening of the fourth he sent Stuart to find out. Meeting the enemy troopers in advance of the bridge, Stuart drove them steadily back on their main force. An officer in the 6th Virginia described the action as "a very sharp hand to hand fight . . . conducted with a rush on the part of the Confederates." At a certain point cavalry skirmishing gave way to, as an officer in Moorman's battery described it, "the hottest Art[iller]y fight I have had for some time. The Yankees had a four gun Batty. playing on my one gun (Napoleon) and litterally ploughed up the ground all around the piece—every man at the Gun was struck & three of them badly wounded—still we held our ground." In the face of such determination, Buford fell back on the infantry supports in his rear, and the latest spate of fighting around Brandy Station came to a close.[19]

The next day, the Federals pushed another reconnaissance force—this from David Gregg's division—south of the river. The move toward Rixeyville ended short of its destination when a segment of Jones's brigade, principally Lomax and the 11th Virginia, prevented the Federals from crossing Muddy Run and forced them to retire.[20]

Following the fighting of August 1 through 5, a stalemate settled over the Rappahannock, as if the armies had agreed to a truce. For the next five weeks and more, the antagonists gave themselves over to minor skirmishing rather than close-quarters combat. On the twenty-second, Rosser's 5th Virginia escaped the monotony when sent on a secret mission to Middlesex County, on Virginia's Middle Peninsula. There the troopers joined a force of Confederate marines in capturing two gunboats and three transports in the Rappahannock and escorting their crews to Richmond.

To take part in the unusual operation, Rosser's men marched more than 150 miles, a heavy burden to place on overworked horses. Unfortunately, in some respects the success they had helped gain was short-lived. On September 2, a large portion of Kilpatrick's division, accompanied by two batteries, marched to the river opposite the captured gunboats. The guns opened on the vessels, riddled them with shells, and sent them to the bottom.[21]

Another diversion from field campaigning was the September 9 announcement of the organization of the Cavalry Corps, A.N.V. Because Ferguson's command had been returned to Samuel Jones's department on August 25, the new structure embraced six brigades, not the seven Robert E. Lee had envisioned. The table of organization looked like this:[22]

CAVALRY CORPS, ARMY OF NORTHERN VIRGINIA

(Maj. Gen. J. E. B. Stuart)

FIRST DIVISION (Maj. Gen. Wade Hampton)

Jones's Brigade (Brig. Gen. William E. Jones)
6th Virginia (Col. Julien Harrison)
7th Virginia (Col. Richard H. Dulany)
12th Virginia (Col. Asher W. Harman)
35th Virginia Battalion (Lt. Col. Elijah V. White)

Butler's Brigade (Brig. Gen. M. Calbraith Butler)
Cobb's Legion (Col. Pierce M. B. Young)
Jeff Davis Legion (Lt. Col. J. Frederick Waring)
Phillips Legion (Lt. Col. W. W. Rich)
2nd South Carolina (Col. Thomas J. Lipscomb)

Baker's Brigade (Brig. Gen. Laurence S. Baker)
1st North Carolina (Col. James B. Gordon)
2nd North Carolina (Lt. Col. W. G. Robinson)
4th North Carolina (Col. Dennis D. Ferebee)
5th North Carolina (Col. Stephen B. Evans)

SECOND DIVISION (Maj. Gen. Fitzhugh Lee)

Lee's Brigade (Brig. Gen W. H. F. Lee)
1st South Carolina (Col. John Logan Black)
9th Virginia (Col. Richard L. T. Beale)
10th Virginia (Col. J. Lucius Davis)
13th Virginia (Col. John R. Chambliss, Jr.)

Lomax's Brigade (Brig. Gen. Lunsford L. Lomax)
1st Maryland Battalion (Lt. Col. Ridgley Brown)
5th Virginia (Col. Thomas L. Rosser)
11th Virginia (Col. Oliver R. Funsten)
15th Virginia (Col. William B. Ball)

Wickham's Brigade (Brig. Gen. Williams C. Wickham)
1st Virginia (Col. Richard Welby Carter)
2nd Virginia (Col. Thomas T. Munford)
3rd Virginia (Col. Thomas H. Owen)
4th Virginia (Lt. Col. William H. F. Payne)

In outward appearance, the reorganization—which would not actually take effect for another two weeks—was a triumph of military administration, retaining as it did the existing unit composition of most of the brigades. Except for the presence of the 1st South Carolina in Lee's division, it also preserved the geographic distinctions that had marked the command since the time of Hampton's coming (by month's end, the South Carolinians would be transferred to Butler's brigade, which made more sense).

The new structure did not, however, please everyone. Among those who found elements of it wanting were three senior officers. One of these was Stuart himself, who in assuming command of the corps should have been promoted to lieutenant general. Robert E. Lee gave no reason for failing to recommend his cavalry chief for promotion, but one can assume that the smaller size of the cavalry in comparison with the army's infantry corps was a major factor. Because Stuart's responsibilities had not increased as a result of the reorganization, Lee saw no reason to elevate him.[23]

While he reacted to this situation with an outward show of indifference, the failure to win promotion seems to have bothered Stuart more deeply than he let

on. He was alert to rumors that he was about to be promoted, and on at least
one occasion, he believed he had been. He became upset when others viewed
his failure to move up in rank as a deliberate slight. One who did so was Peter
Hairston, Stuart's former volunteer aide, now a staff officer to Maj. Gen. Jubal
A. Early. Hairston, who bumped into Stuart about six weeks after the cavalry
corps came into being, found him "very much surprised to have not been made
Lt. Genl. I told him Genl Lee had complained of him about the Pennsylvania
campaign."[24] *Lee, himself, should have been relieved of high command*

A remark of this kind had the power to sting, for Stuart felt that for the past
three months a cloud had hovered over him despite his best efforts to remove it.
As he complained to an infantry colleague, in the aftermath of the invasion he
had "been much blamed by those who knew nothing about it." Other observers,
who appreciated the true state of affairs, sympathized with him. An officer in
the 4th Virginia warned his wife to avoid friends and relatives critical of the
way the Pennsylvania campaign had been conducted: "Gen. Stuart at this time
happens to be under the ban of the fickle populace without any just cause whatever. Those who draw sabre & ride with him in the charge, have lost none of
their confidence in him & he is today what he has ever been—one of our best &
most efficient officers." Stuart's fervent hope was that Robert E. Lee felt the
same way.[25]

If Stuart bore his apparent setback stoically, Munford and Rosser made no
attempt to hide their discontent. Munford may have had grounds for complaint;
he had long predicted that officers junior to him, such as Wickham and Rosser, *George Marshall was a V.M.I. grad!*
would be promoted over him because they were politicians or members of the
West Point clique, while he, as a graduate of V.M.I., was an outsider. Half of his
prediction came true when in September Wickham was announced as the successor to Fitz Lee. Three weeks later Stuart dropped the other shoe, informing
Munford—whom he realized had felt slighted by Wickham's promotion—that
the next vacancy would go to Rosser. Although Stuart gave no explanation for
his action, it appears that Munford's reputation continued to suffer—as did Stuart's—from the lingering effects of June 9.[26] *Brandy Station*

Soon after telling Munford not to expect the next promotion, Stuart
informed Rosser of his intention to recommend him in preference to Munford.
As he had on past occasions when recommending Rosser to Robert E. Lee's
good graces, Stuart continued to shower Rosser with praise:

> On the field of battle, in coolness and capacity to "control happen-
> ing events," and wield troops, you have no superior. . . . it would be
> impossible for me to even mention the various battles in which your
> right arm—upraised—has lent to the victory. . . . You deserve promo-
> tion more than any Col of a Va regt in my Command and if Brig Gen'l
> Jones should be sent elsewhere, you are my choice for the post.[27]

Perhaps more than any other subordinate, Rosser had benefited from Stuart's patronage. Stuart had made numerous efforts to increase his responsibilities and secure for him higher rank and stature. None of this, however, mattered to the commander of the 5th Virginia. He focused solely on Stuart's inability to make him a general officer, as if this could be done with the stroke of a pen or a word to army headquarters.

In letters to his wife of three months, Rosser unleashed his vituperation, calling Stuart a two-faced liar, an enemy, and worse. He denigrated the cavalry commander's contributions to the army, insisting that recent campaigning had applied "the finishing stroke to Stuart's declining reputation." He admitted that Stuart had talked several times of securing his promotion, but it was obvious that the man had not worked hard enough. So believing, Rosser was determined to leave his command: "<u>Nothing</u> will keep me."[28]

In fact, he went nowhere. He claimed that Dick Ewell, as well as the army's artillery commander, Brig. Gen. William N. Pendleton, had promised him higher rank if he transferred to their commands. He also predicted that by making a brief visit to the powers that be in Richmond, he would obtain for himself a promotion in the cavalry. When none of these prospects panned out, Rosser decided that there were worse fates than to command a regiment under Stuart.[29]

Sticking it out proved to be a wise move, for in the end he got what he wanted—with the help of the superior he had come to despise. Stuart's comment about promoting Rosser if Grumble Jones "should be sent elsewhere" referred to an incident in early August during which the long-simmering feud between the cavalry leader and his prickly subordinate boiled over. While the details of the confrontation are not known—neither of the antagonists publicized them—it appears that Stuart gave Jones an order and the subordinate responded with a barrage of expletives. Stuart had him arrested and preferred charges against him.

The following month, Jones was formally charged with disobedience of orders, conduct prejudicial to good order, and the use of disrespectful language to a superior. A court was quickly convened; it acquitted him of the first two charges but found him guilty of the third and allowed Robert E. Lee to fix the penalty. For months, Lee had hoped his cavalry generals would resolve their differences like gentlemen. Even now he respected Jones as a field leader and an administrator. But he could not condone the man's conduct, especially since Jones had loudly proclaimed that regardless of the court's verdict, he would never again serve under Stuart. Lee made the best of a bad situation when in mid-October he exiled Jones to the command of a cavalry brigade in the District of Southwestern Virginia and East Tennessee.[30]

Upon Jones's arrest, Lomax had been assigned temporary command of the Laurel Brigade. Once the court rendered its verdict, however, Stuart could assign a permanent leader. In mid-October, in fulfillment of his long-standing pledge, he tendered the command to Rosser, ensuring his promotion to brigadier general to rank from September 28.

Rosser the, ingrate

After what seemed a lifetime in quest of the wreathed stars of a general officer, Rosser had won the coveted prize. If he thanked Stuart for looking after him, it was never recorded.[31]

The all but forgotten non ANV fronts   *oh?*

On the day the cavalry reorganization was announced, events hundreds of miles to the south and west monopolized the attention of Lee's army. On September 9, Maj. Gen. William S. Rosecrans's Army of the Cumberland entered Chattanooga, Tennessee, having wrested that strategic citadel in the Cumberland Mountains from the Rebels of Braxton Bragg.

The authorities in Richmond were so alarmed by this turn of events, which threatened Confederate fortunes throughout the western theater, that they acted on a strategy formed during high-level conferences in Richmond. Lee would detach about one-third of his army and send it, under Longstreet, to Bragg's new headquarters in northern Georgia. The troop transfer would provide Bragg with the manpower he needed to turn back the pursuit that Rosecrans was certain to mount from Chattanooga. The trick was to accomplish the transfer in such secrecy as to prevent Lee's enemy from getting early wind of it and moving south to overpower him.

kinda of late, boys— Shiloh, Vicksburg hello!

Longstreet's troops began their march to the railroad on the ninth. Two days later, Meade's cavalry provided him with the first clue as to what was happening. The day after that, the Union commander crossed his horsemen over the Rappahannock, and on the thirteenth, he directed them to probe Lee's latest dispositions. If Lee's army was found to have been depleted, Meade would make him pay for his act of rashness.[32]

From scouts of his own, as well as from a civilian informant, Stuart learned of the Federals' crossing on the twelfth. That day he sent south all wagons, disabled horses, and other impediments to a rapid withdrawal, should one become necessary. It became necessary soon after 7:00 the next morning, when Pleasonton attacked his left and center with the troopers of Buford and Gregg, while sending Kilpatrick's division looping toward the Confederate right.

Stuart met the assault with Jones's brigade (still under Lomax) on the right; with Rooney Lee's brigade, this day under Colonel Beale, farther west; and with Chew's, Moorman's, and McGregor's batteries. Other elements of the division had been scattered along and below the Rappahannock. Some units were far afield, foraging, as they had been on other occasions when Stuart needed to concentrate his forces in a hurry. Once again, he had to scramble to find enough men to counter an enemy advance—and he had to do so on the run. The Federals were coming on so quickly and in such numbers that Stuart's force on hand was driven back to Culpeper Court House.

The game was in Pleasonton's hands even before he threw in his ace. By midafternoon, Stuart was hard-pressed near Culpeper, barely able to hold off Buford and Gregg. Then, without warning, Kilpatrick's division—troopers and horse artillerymen—came up on his right and assaulted the Laurel Brigade.

Lomax's men were unprepared for the onslaught; the flank swung precariously toward the rear and then gave way.[33]

At first the troops on the right withdrew in good order. They stood and fought from successive positions, but each effort ended more quickly than the previous one. Trooper Henry M. Trueheart of the 7th Virginia, fighting on foot as part of a skirmish detachment, reported:

> After the first stand, having held the position till the enemy got into our flank and rear on the right, we had to fall back down a steep hill for more than a mile under an awful fire of Artillery, and sharpshooter's rifles—the silent little sharpshooter's bullets cutting down a poor fellow here and there, and the shell, grape, canister and shrapnel crashing, and slashing above and around us, and in our midst most fearfully.[34]

After several minutes under this pounding, the men of the Laurel Brigade retreated at top speed, all semblance of formation gone. Their sprint to the rear caused Beale's brigade to fall back as well, especially after its leader was disabled by a leg wound. Carried off on a stretcher, Beale would be on convalescent leave for two months.

When Lomax's troopers fled, they uncovered Chew's battery. His attention fixed on events to the front, Chew discovered too late that his guns had been taken in flank. When Yankee horsemen swarmed over the position, it became every crew member for himself. Gunner George Neese "fired six rounds of canister, when we had to abandon our position and fall back double-quick to save ourselves from capture, for the enemy in our front was still pressing us, and their cavalry on our right flank were preparing to charge and cut us off." After the fight, Neese decided that even had they lacked the advantage of surprise, the Yankees would have been unstoppable. There were simply too many of them: "They far outnumbered us, and they well knew it, and that alone bears with it a kind of intoxicating inspiration which makes men bold, and boldness in danger is the foundation element of bravery."[35]

When the Yankees struck, many of Chew's men went down killed, wounded, or captured; the battery commander himself, along with his executive officer, Lt. James W. Thomson, barely escaped, Thomson by shooting down a charging Federal and taking his horse. Chew had to leave behind one of his guns; a second had been disabled. Moorman's and Griffin's batteries each lost a gun as well, along with several men.

Fighting as he fell back, Stuart moved what remained of his defense line below Culpeper Court House before pulling it back to Rapidan Station. He was preceded by Lee and the main army. When he learned that infantry was pressing south behind Meade's horsemen, Marse Robert realized that in his weakened condition, he could no longer hold the Rappahannock line. By late afternoon, he was retreating across the Rapidan, below which his soldiers frantically improved old works and built new ones.[36]   *Blame Stuart, Bobby?*

From his new position, which ran as far south as Liberty Mills on the North Fork of the Rapidan, Stuart spent the next several days overseeing an effort that kept the Union cavalry well back from the river. Until now, Pleasonton had credited reports that Lee's army was about to fall back on Richmond; Stuart's stubborn defense suggested otherwise and prompted him to withdraw. On the sixteenth, pressure on Stuart's line began to abate; by late in the day, the Union cavalry had drawn off to the north.

Stuart followed up the retreat, brushing aside screening patrols to discover that Meade's entire army was crossing to the south side of the Rappahannock, occupying the camps Lee's people had evacuated the week before. By September 20, the Army of the Potomac was sweeping toward the Rapidan, evidently to challenge Lee's new line. The advance heralded a critical confrontation in the countryside between the rivers.[37]

On the twenty-second, the struggle began. At about 8:00 A.M., scouts reported the approach of Buford's cavalry from the direction of Madison Court House. Hoping to prevent a penetration of Lee's lines, Stuart rode north at the head of almost two-thirds of Hampton's division—portions of Butler's brigade, this day led by James B. Gordon, and Baker's brigade, temporarily under Col. Dennis Ferebee. The provisional assignments indicated how badly the ranks of Stuart's subordinates had been depleted on the thirteenth.

Stuart encountered the head of Buford's column along a road that led north past a blacksmith's establishment, Jack's Shop. He began, as was his wont, by attacking mounted. According to his adjutant, Major McClellan, the tactic "failed to make any impression on his [Buford's] lines. A subsequent effort with dismounted men was equally unsuccessful." In the process, both of Stuart's brigades suffered considerably. Among the many men captured was Lt. Col. Deloney of Cobb's Legion, who had just rejoined Stuart after recovering from his Hunterstown wounds.[38]

Stuart's failure to drive the enemy was disheartening, but that was not the extent of his plight. While he and his men had been engaging Buford, Kilpatrick's division had outflanked them on the left by crossing the rapids upstream from Liberty Mills. Stuart must have considered himself at a doubly unfair disadvantage: It was not enough that the enemy outnumbered him so handily; now he also had to contend with guile and deception. That combination promised to be difficult to overcome.

Having made no headway in front, Stuart turned about to fight the fire in the rear. As he did, Buford's men became emboldened and pressed him even harder. McClellan remarked that it seemed "Stuart had at last been caught where he could not escape serious damage." Forced to fight in two directions at the same time, he lashed both forces with sharpshooter fire, as well as with case shot from Hart's battery, two guns of which faced to the front, two to the rear.

Then Gordon and Ferebee launched a series of mounted attacks that held Buford in check, at least momentarily.[39]

Grateful for the release of pressure in front, Stuart positioned the Laurel Brigade, this day led by Col. Oliver Funsten, for a do-or-die assault on Kilpatrick. To reach his main body, which had dismounted behind a network of fences, Funsten sent skirmishers forward afoot. According to Private Trueheart of the 7th Virginia:

> We were ordered to let down the lane fences on either side, and also a cross fence so as to enable our men to deploy on either side and give the enemy a check. In obeying the order I jumped from my horse leaving her tied in the lane and sprang over the lane fence. . . . the impulse of my motion in going over & the striking of the scabbard against the top rail—threw my sabre out, and I came with my whole force against its point . . . and only then discovered it had penetrated my leg.

With a mighty effort, Trueheart drew out the blade. At the sight of the blood pumping from the wound, he fainted and was carried to the rear for medical attention.[40]

His efforts and those of his comrades did not go for naught. As soon as the road was clear, the mounted portion of three regiments galloped through the fences and engaged the nearest Yankees. After a wild struggle, two of the outfits—Lt. Col. Mottrom D. Ball's 11th and Thomas Massie's 12th Virginia—pushed Kilpatrick's sharpshooters out of the way and hewed out an escape route.

Stuart seized the opening. Again turning his back to Buford, he sent his men plunging through the seam in Kilpatrick's line and across the stream in its rear. On the far side, the Confederates found infantry comrades rushing to their defense, members of Maj. Gen. Cadmus M. Wilcox's division of A. P. Hill's corps. With their assistance, the troopers dispersed the balance of Kilpatrick's command. Despite his colleague's retreat, Buford pursued his opponents across the river, halting only after he struck Wilcox's line. At that point, the Kentucky-born brigadier—waging one of his last fights before contracting a fatal dose of typhoid fever—turned about and withdrew.

Once again, Stuart had been battered and pushed around by the more numerous, and perhaps more aggressive, Union cavalry. Once again, he had escaped disaster by the thinnest of margins—and, truth to tell, only because of Wilcox's timely intervention. Had the infantry arrived a half hour later . . . Stuart shuddered at the thought.[41]

In fact, for a time Robert E. Lee feared his cavalry had been wiped out. According to H. B. McClellan, a report to that effect reached army headquarters at Orange Court House from a foreign officer who had taken part in the fight. When the Confederates found themselves surrounded, Lt. Col. George St. Ledger Grenfell, a British soldier of fortune attached to Stuart's staff, broke ranks and saved himself by taking to the bushes, then swimming the river. Shaking himself dry, he repaired to Lee's headquarters to report what he believed to be the truth: That Stuart and his troopers were doomed to extinction.

McClellan may have adorned or even fabricated this story, as he appears to have had a strong animus against Grenfell. But whether true or apocryphal, the _(CRAZY) ancedote underscores the resilience of Stuart's command, its leader's ability to think coolly and lead effectively in a crisis, and the interplay in his career of chance, timing, and good luck.[42] *(Post battle letter)*

Dear Pres J. Davis:

ENOUGH, ALREADY! You sorry wad!

John Doe, C.S.A

P.S. but the war is growing unpopular in the North, enlistments are faltering. maybe.

Chapter Eighteen

Up the Hill
and Then Down Again

In retrospect, the decision to send Longstreet's corps to Georgia was a master stroke." Thus reinforced, Bragg opposed an incautious, overconfident Rosecrans on even terms. The result was the bloody battle of Chickamauga, fought near Rossville on September 19 and 20. Thanks largely to Longstreet's participation—and to his timely exploitation of a weak point in the Federal line—the Army of the Cumberland was defeated, demoralized, and sent streaming back to Chattanooga. With stunning suddenness, the balance of power in the West had tilted in the Confederacy's favor.

President Lincoln and Secretary of War Stanton refused to permit the imbalance to endure. They dispatched Ulysses S. Grant, their most consistent field commander, with many of the troops that had captured Vicksburg, to relieve the siege Bragg had imposed on Rosecrans's stronghold. Fearing that this force might prove insufficient, the Union officials ordered Meade to detach the XI and XII Corps and send them west as well. The troop transfer began on September 25; it took a week to complete.[1]

Lincoln hoped to keep Robert E. Lee ignorant of the operation as long as possible. By the second week in October, however, the news had leaked out, thanks to newspaper editors more interested in readership than national security. By the ninth, Lee was alert to a series of movements on the enemy's side of the Rapidan. These suggested that Meade was shifting away from his headquarters at Culpeper Court House, but in what direction and in what strength Lee could not determine. To find out, he ordered an army-wide movement across the river toward Culpeper in hopes of bringing a weakened Meade to battle.[2]

As ever, the cavalry would lead the way. Stuart would march in advance of the army's right flank in company with Hampton's division and some guns of Beckham's battalion. Fitz Lee, backed by two brigades of infantry, would remain on the Rapidan until the movement was well under way. He would then press north to link with Stuart on the Rappahannock. If an opportunity to pincer the enemy arose, Stuart planned to take advantage of it.

253

What would become known as the Bristoe Campaign began on the chilly morning of the tenth, when Stuart's force crossed the river in the direction of Woodville, on the Sperryville Turnpike. Early on, Funsten's Laurel Brigade (minus White's battalion, which was on detached duty in the Loudoun Valley) was sent west toward Thornton's Gap in the Blue Ridge. His left flank thus covered, Stuart crossed Russell's Ford on Robertson's River, a Rapidan tributary, with the brigades of Gordon and Young. The former had been Laurence Baker's command; after Baker's disabling, his longtime subordinate had been quickly promoted to replace him. Young had been shifted to the command of Butler's brigade, but his appointment was temporary. Despite the severity of the wound he had taken the previous June, Butler was recuperating at his home in South Carolina and would rejoin the army in the spring.[3]

To this point, Stuart's march had been free of obstacles except for a small picket opposite Russell's Ford, which his advance had swatted aside. However, north of Robertson's River, near James City, his column approached a picket post manned by Kilpatrick's horsemen, with infantry within supporting distance. Using tried and true tactics, Stuart occupied the Yankees in front with Gordon's men, while sending Young's around their right. Once in Kilpatrick's rear, Young attacked with Twiggs's 1st South Carolina, which, as McClellan reported, "routed the whole line by one charge." Almost ninety troopers and foot soldiers fell into Young's hands. When they resumed the march, the Confederates encountered an even larger outpost near James City, situated on high ground and manned by troops of all arms, including six guns. This force Stuart engaged at long range, mostly with his own artillery. Late in the day, he repulsed a limited attack by cavalry; thereafter the Yankees seemed content to let him be.

Stuart bedded down for the night within sight of the outpost. Before morning, his scouts reported that the enemy had disappeared, apparently in retreat to the Rappahannock. His interest piqued, Stuart continued in that direction the next morning, but without Young's brigade, which he left behind to cover his rear. The loss was made good when, in midday, he struck the Sperryville Turnpike and made contact with three of Funsten's regiments. Adding two of them to his force (the third continued to guard the flank), he turned south toward his recent headquarters, Culpeper Court House. Three miles on, the head of his column sighted parties of pickets, but they were driven south with little difficulty. Then an infantry regiment appeared on a parallel road, hustling toward Culpeper to join its army. Geographical barriers prevented Stuart from bagging the entire outfit, but he put such a scare into the foot soldiers that they "broke and ran, dropping guns, knapsacks, and blankets, several of their number being captured."[4]

Approaching Culpeper, Stuart discovered that the Army of the Potomac was in full retreat. Most of it had crossed the Rappahannock, leaving Kilpatrick's troopers on the south bank, covered by some artillery on the hills beyond the river. Kilpatrick had drawn his men up in lines of battle, ready to engage the Confederates. Stuart wanted to oblige, but with only five regiments on hand, he thought it wise not to advance directly.

Showing commendable prudence, he had one of Gordon's regiments demonstrate strongly against the enemy's front. By means of a highly effective saber charge, Ferebee's 4th North Carolina chased a body of Kilpatrick's men across a Rappahannock tributary known as Mountain Run, Ferebee falling wounded in the process. Then, with Kilpatrick's attention riveted on Gordon, Stuart led Funsten's men southwestward toward Chestnut Fork Church to gain the enemy's left flank. His ultimate intent was to occupy Barbour House Hill, an expanse of high ground adjacent to Fleetwood Heights, where the climactic fighting on June 9 had taken place.

Stuart did not complete his movement, for the booming of cannons from the southeast told him that Fitz Lee was arriving from the direction of Stevensburg, driving another force of Yankee cavalry before him. At daylight, Fitz had encountered Buford's division as it reconnoitered below the Rapidan. Thanks to the aggressiveness of Lomax's, Chambliss's, and Wickham's brigades (the third commanded by Owen), as well as to the assistance of his infantry supports, Fitz had persuaded Buford to retire to the Rappahannock.[5]

It had not been easy going, for Buford had infused in his men a determination to hold their ground unless and until someone made them give it up. As William Corson of the 3rd Virginia described it:

> Col. Owen proceeded immediately to attack him [with] the 1st and 3rd in front. We charged the enemy under a galling fire from their sharpshooters and artillery but succeeded in driving him from his position with the loss of a few men and a number of horses. . . . Captain [William B.] Newton commanding the 4th was killed instantly. The Yankees now were rapidly retreating in the direction of Brandy Station, Col. Owen closely pursuing in the center, Wm. H. F. Lee's Brigade [under Chambliss] on the left, and Lomax on the right, our Sharpshooters supported by two small regiments of infantry.

Given the size of the opposition, the Federals had no alternative but to retreat. Even so, they halted several times, forcing their pursuers to pry them loose from woods, ridges, and streambeds. "The enemy made a stand at Stevensburg, and held a strong position," Corson wrote.

> Here we again charged them amidst a perfect shower of shot and shell and drove them across Mountain run. . . . Our regiment was exposed to a most terrific shelling at this place and we suffered heavily. . . . The Yankees made the next stand at Brandy Station on the Rail-Road where they were heavily reinforced with infantry and fought us stubbornly for several hours, but Southern Chivalry was more than a match for the Yankee hosts and we again had the enemy on the hip.[6]

Lee's approach gave Stuart the idea of combining forces and putting both Kilpatrick and Buford "on the hip." With judicious cooperation, they might crush the Yankees against the lower bank of the Rappahannock, their artillery cover notwithstanding. This would take some doing. Thanks to the distance between the Confederate columns, and the nondescript attire horsemen on both sides were wearing those days, Lee at first could not determine whether Stuart's men were Rebels or Yankees. In consequence, the shells his guns unleashed fell on Stuart and Funsten, as well as on the enemy. Stuart seemed not to mind; all that concerned him, as he disclosed in his after-action report, was that as Lee approached, "regiment after regiment of the enemy broke and dispersed." Much of the credit was due to the Laurel Brigade. Stuart claimed that a charge by the 12th Virginia alone cut off fifteen hundred Union horsemen. He was much less pleased, however, when the 4th and 5th North Carolina of Gordon's brigade, moving to the Virginians' support, were taken in flank and routed by a noticeably smaller force of Yankees.[7]

Stuart's inability to team effectively with Lee, and the dispersal of the two North Carolina regiments, bought Kilpatrick and Buford the time they needed to secure the high ground Stuart had been seeking to occupy. Still, when he finally made contact with the 2nd Division, the united forces delivered a series of blows that threatened the enemy's new position. Stuart applauded the men of Lomax and Chambliss, who charged the heights no fewer than five times, although each attack fell short of a permanent lodgment.

Under cover of these assaults, Fitz Lee moved to get between the heights and the river via another landmark of past combat, St. James Church. Detecting the effort, which, if successful, would cut them off from Meade, Buford and Kilpatrick relinquished their perch and bulled their way through to the river, where they began to cross. Stuart and Lee tried to threaten the operation, but gathering darkness limited their interference. By 8:00, the Federals were safely over, although they had left dozens of men and horses lying on the plains around Brandy Station.[8]

Stuart spent the night near the depot. Upon moving out in the morning, he left Rosser's 5th Virginia and a section of Chew's battery to guard Fleetwood Heights, and Pierce Young's brigade to cover Culpeper. After Stuart departed, Rosser placed his men on top of Barbour House Hill. There they made, as George Neese wrote, "a sort of feint to detain . . . deceive, and hold the Yankee cavalry in our front" and off Stuart's tail. The ruse "played very well until about three o'clock this afternoon, when the Yanks discovered the hollowness of our pretensions and advanced on us in force and cleared us off the hill in short order and in double-quick style."[9]

The Federals pursued Rosser and Chew toward Culpeper, where Young's brigade and five cannons were stationed. Apprised of their coming, Young established a battle line that stretched for a mile north and south of town. To draw the enemy to him, he sent Rosser, upon his arrival, to reengage them, then fall back slowly on Young's line. Rosser carried out his part of the deception with consummate skill: As soon as he retired, the Yankees eagerly pursued, ignorant of Young's presence. When they came within range, Young poured into them "a heavy volley . . . simultaneously from [his] artillery and dismounted troops."

The Federals scrambled backward, their ranks thinner than they had been moments before, to engage their opponents at longer range. Young held on at Culpeper through the night, to find the Yankees gone in the morning. He pursued them toward the Rappahannock, making prisoners of some thirty stragglers, before Rosser and he moved north to Rixeyville and then, at Robert E. Lee's direction, across the river to Bealton Station on the O & A. The combined force was recalled to Stuart's side on the evening of the fourteenth.[10]

After leaving Rosser at Brandy Station and Young at Culpeper, Stuart retraced his path up the Sperryville Pike toward its crossing of the Hazel River, another Rappahannock tributary. The infantry of the Army of Northern Virginia was moving to the same point. Making contact with the advance echelon, Stuart assigned Funsten's men to support the lead component, Ewell's corps, while attaching Gordon's brigade to the army's right flank. Then he accompanied Fitz Lee's horsemen across the Hazel and toward the Rappahannock.

On the road north, which led to Warrenton via Jeffersonton, Waterloo, and Hedgemann's River, the cavalry met resistance from the obligatory pickets and skirmishers, as well as from larger bodies of horsemen protecting Meade's rear. All were shoved out of position or flanked into retreat. They appeared willing, even eager, to go. Meade, bound by instructions from Washington to avoid a pitched battle in his reduced state, had decided to pull back to Bull Run, fully thirty miles from the Rappahannock. Above that famous stream, near Centreville, long, high ground approachable only across open terrain would afford him the position he needed to remain on the defensive in the face of Lee's aggression.[11]

Late in the day, the army forded the Rappahannock at several points, Stuart's column at Warrenton Springs. On the other side, Yankee infantry and artillery disputed his passage, but they gave way before a combination of dismounted sharpshooters from the Laurel Brigade and a barrage laid down by Ewell's artillery. Once over the river, Stuart's men helped repair the demolished bridge at the springs. They accomplished the job by nightfall, and in the dark, the infantry crossed it. Moving north to Warrenton—skirmishing all the way with detachments of mounted men—Stuart bivouacked near that town with the troopers of Gordon and Funsten.

By the morning of October 13, Lee's army had closed up on Warrenton, and Stuart's troopers were patrolling the roads that ran northeastward, the direction in which the enemy was moving. At 10:00 A.M. Lee ordered Stuart to reconnoiter toward one of the landmarks of his raiding career, Catlett's Station on the Orange & Alexandria. Lomax's brigade was dispatched to that vicinity, its rear covered by Funsten and Gordon.[12]

Discovering that Catlett's and other depots were in Union hands, Lomax halted short of the O & A at Auburn, where Stuart joined him and ordered him to remain. Proceeding toward the railroad with Funsten, Gordon, and seven of Beckham's cannons, Stuart moved close enough to study the long line of enemy troops moving alongside the tracks, some of them escorting an immense column of wagons that Stuart readily identified as the supply train of Meade's army. From the heading of the column, Stuart correctly discerned that the Army of the Potomac was heading for the Manassas Junction-Bull Run area. He so informed R. E. Lee, adding that if Lee dispatched an infantry force in timely fashion he could cut off Meade's train and perhaps capture it whole.

While waiting for the army to seize the opportunity he had offered it, Stuart kept his force well in hand within sight of Catlett's Station, but "carefully concealed" behind ridges and trees. He waited for several hours, to no purpose—the foot soldiers never appeared. Finally, late in the day, he turned back toward Warrenton to rejoin R. E. Lee.[13]

Approaching Auburn just after dark, Stuart suddenly understood why the infantry had not reached him. A steady stream of Yankees was passing through the village, heading north, cutting him off from the army and vice versa. In combination with the column passing up the railroad in his rear, the Yankees had hemmed him in quite neatly. To compound his predicament, an impassable woods lay off his right flank, while a several-mile-long millrace abutted his left. Stuart, his two brigades, and seven guns were caught in a four-sided trap, utterly at the mercy of their opponents.

They were, that is, if their opponents discovered their presence. Dispatches captured from passing couriers during the night convinced Stuart that, "notwithstanding the skirmishing that had taken place, the enemy was ignorant of my position." This set him to thinking—or, as one of his men said, putting "his Mentals to work." Characteristically, even with his back (and front and sides) to the wall, he thought of taking the offensive. He sent relays of couriers, garbed in Federal uniforms, through the enemy column to the west, whose men were "distinctly heard, passing within a few hundred yards of our position." Later Stuart learned that most of the messengers got through to Lee with their commander's proposal that the infantry attack the far side of the column while the cavalry struck from its perilous position. But the couriers had made such a wide circuit that for several hours—each of which passed with agonizing slowness—no rescue force reached Stuart.[14]

After the war, one of Gordon's men—who rode muleback, not horseback—called that nerve-racking night "one of the queerest" he had ever spent in the army, "with its tension, hunger, and its touch of the ridiculous. . . . We were in many tight places with Jeb Stuart, but that was the worst." He asked, rhetorically: "Did you ever try standing all night holding a mule by the halter, trying to keep him from braying and trying to keep your sabre and spurs from rattling; you were hungry, and so was the mule, and there were more Yankees around you than you believed were left in the world after Gettysburg?" He and his comrades endured more than fear and hunger. An officer in the 1st North Carolina recalled how they "suffered during the night. It was bitter cold, [and we] could have no fires."[15]

As on so many past occasions, good fortune befell Stuart and his cavaliers. After remaining undetected throughout the night, they were shrouded by a soupy fog in the morning. Still, the enemy was all around, and extremely close. Stuart's anxiety almost got the best of him when he found that a huge body of infantry—Maj. Gen. Gouverneur K. Warren's II Army Corps—had halted in a nearby field, where its men broke ranks and began to boil coffee. Just when he feared his luck had run out, volleys of musketry crashed forth from the direction of Warrenton.[16]

When he became convinced that the barrage signaled the approach of Lee's infantry, a relieved Stuart opened with his horse batteries—only to have the rifle fire die out and the nearest Yankees turn their guns on him. In minutes, Stuart's artillery had been silenced, and he had to drag it out of harm's way. Then the Federals began to threaten his left, which Gordon, at the cost of a wound, shored up with his 1st North Carolina, led by Lt. Col. Thomas Ruffin. The North Carolinians charged a regiment of Yankees and forced its surrender en masse. But before the prisoners could be corralled, a New Jersey outfit burst out of the woods and laced the attackers with a volley that mortally wounded Ruffin and scattered his men.[17]

With this exception, Stuart had surprisingly little trouble breaking free of encirclement. As the Yankees recoiled from Gordon's counterattack, he limbered up his artillery and led it south. While Funsten's men held the rear, Gordon's crossed the treacherous millrace, which, as Stuart wrote, "was soon bridged." By a roundabout route, the head of the column struck the road to Warrenton, which only a few hours before had teemed with Yankees. There Stuart capped his latest escape with a flourish, cutting off and capturing dozens of stragglers.[18]

With Warren's men now tangling with the cavalry's rescuers, Stuart was beyond the possibility of capture. With a confident air, he rode on to Auburn, where he fell in with Lee's infantry and sought out Lee himself. The army leader expressed relief and pleasure at his safety, even as he ordered Stuart to attach his men to the right flank of the main column as it continued after Meade. En route, the cavalry leader was reunited with Fitz Lee as well as with Lomax, who had joined Fitz after being cut off from Gordon and Chambliss. The following day, the fifteenth, Young and Rosser came up to join Stuart on the road to Centreville, completing the reunification of the corps.[19]

The northward march presented the cavalry with few opportunities to smite its foe, and none that would enable Stuart to exact revenge for his recent discomfiture and embarrassment. In truth, the race to overtake Meade had run its course. The Army of the Potomac was so far ahead of its opponents as to be home free at Centreville, while its elongated, unwieldy, and apparently vulnerable wagon train was too well guarded to permit its capture or destruction.

The previous afternoon, Lee's pursuit had been dealt a crippling blow when A. P. Hill's infantry, advancing toward the Union rear at Bristoe Station on the O & A, stumbled into battle against the well-entrenched, artillery-rich II Corps. Snugly ensconced behind the railroad embankment, the Federals poured a savage enfilade into Hill's men, nearly two thousand of whom were killed or wounded, as against a few hundred Union casualties.[20]

After the shocking defeat, which lowered the morale of the entire army and prompted calls for Hill's ouster, little good was expected of the pursuit. On the fifteenth, the army came up to Meade's new position atop the Centreville heights, and skirmishing broke out at familiar places, including Blackburn's and Mitchell's Fords on Bull Run. Lee probed determinedly for an opening, found none, and on the seventeenth began his return to the Rappahannock.[21]

That morning, Stuart joined in the withdrawal via the Little River Turnpike, Gum Springs, and Frying Pan. On this early leg of the return, he may have taken the time—as he had when returning from his raid to Dumfries—to visit Laura Ratcliffe and her mother, and perhaps to remove them from the path of enemy advance. One of his officers reported that two women, friends of the general, accompanied the retreat aboard an ambulance that Stuart used as his personal carriage. When the wagon crossed a stream, one of its wheels became wedged between rocks and could not be pulled clear by the mules. Along with Pierce Young and other subordinates, the gallant Stuart waded into the waist-deep water to help out. The high-ranking fatigue party succeeded in freeing the vehicle, but only after about a half hour of pushing. An officer who assisted in the effort called it "all very nice, until it came to riding in the wet clothes."[22]

During the withdrawal, Stuart finally got the chance to lash out at the foe, and he made the most of it. It came courtesy of the impetuosity of Judson Kilpatrick, whose division, supported by six guns and, at a distance, some foot soldiers, followed up Stuart's departure from Bull Run with ill-advised speed. Stuart took note of his approach along the Warrenton Turnpike and discovered that Kilpatrick had outdistanced his infantry friends. When, at dusk on the eighteenth, Kilpatrick attacked outriders along Stuart's right flank and drove them in on the column, his enemy plotted revenge.

As he neared Buckland Mills the next morning, Stuart sent word to Fitz Lee, whose division was moving on a parallel road to the south, to watch his flank and rear in case Kilpatrick repeated his uncivil behavior. In moving to comply, Fitz suggested that Stuart diverge from the main route and head toward Warrenton, in which case Kilpatrick would undoubtedly follow. Fitz would hang back near Auburn until Kilpatrick had passed him; then he would strike the Federal left and rear. His superior liked the idea at once and agreed to try it.[23]

As Stuart later noted, "The plan proved highly successful." Kilpatrick followed him to within three miles of Warrenton, casting not so much as a glance to left or rear. Late in the afternoon, as Stuart slowed to a stop near Chestnut

Hill and absorbed a new attack, Lee dashed up, gained the turnpike near Buckland, and crashed into Kilpatrick from the blind side. As the Yankees recoiled, Stuart wheeled Hampton's men about and charged down the pike. Gordon's brigade slammed into the head of Kilpatrick's column, while the troopers under Young and Rosser (the latter now in permanent command of the Laurel Brigade) laced Kilpatrick's flanks.

Under the many-sided pounding, the Yankee column accordioned in on itself, horses and riders squeezed into a compact mass, crushed under their own weight. Custer's brigade, much of which had passed the point of attack when *Fitz* Lee struck, suffered fairly heavily, losing several men, most of its baggage wagons and ambulances, and "many arms, horses, and equipments." Even so, the brigade of Brig. Gen. Henry E. Davies, in Custer's rear, had it much worse. Davies's men, who absorbed the brunt of the pressure, were simply overwhelmed. For a time they withstood the onslaught, but then, as Stuart succinctly observed, "they broke and the rout was soon complete."[24]

With a whoop and a holler, Stuart's men raced after the fugitives. They pursued at full speed for at least three miles, knocking every Yankee they overtook onto the hard earth with saber swipes and pistol shots. More than two hundred were rounded up as prisoners; others escaped only temporarily, wandering dazed and lost in roadside woods before stumbling inside Stuart's lines after dark.[25]

For every Confederate involved, the pursuit was an exhilarating experience, one that harked back to the good old days when the Yankees took to their heels whenever challenged. "It was very exciting," a North Carolinian exulted, "and afforded us as much amusement as a fox chase." A horse artilleryman regretted that his battery could not keep up with the other participants in "one of the most exciting races [he] ever saw." Kilpatrick, said another pursuer, "was completely outgeneraled and badly defeated." Stuart, his pride overflowing, claimed that "had his artillery been anywhere near the front, it would undoubtedly have fallen into our hands."[26]

Summing up the event that would forever be known, in both armies, as the "Buckland Races," the cavalry leader believed himself justified in calling the rout "the most signal and complete that any cavalry has suffered during the war." Few of those involved in it, regardless of the color of their uniforms, would have disputed him.[27]

⊱—⊶—◯—⊷—⊰

On the twentieth, Stuart followed his army over the Rappahannock and back to the camps it had abandoned almost six weeks before. The next several days were given over to picketing, skirmishing, scouting—the normal routine, rather than the often exciting, sometimes enervating experience of combat. Meade did not pursue across the river until early November, two days after Stuart reviewed his six thousand officers and men on the hallowed ground around Brandy Station.

The exhibition was less elaborately staged than the previous summer's trio of reviews, and it ended not with rapturous applause but in tragedy. According to one member of the 10th Virginia, the event "was a grand sight but I don't think it pays. One man was killed dead and three were badly hurt by their horses falling." The accident pointed up the sorry condition of the command's horseflesh, in contrast to the cavalry's well-mounted appearance the previous May and June.[28]

poor old horses!

When Meade advanced to the river on the seventh, he attacked the defenses Lee had established at Rappahannock Bridge. The assault was so quickly and skillfully executed that an entire brigade of Louisiana infantry was shot up and captured, while at Kelly's Ford, two regiments guarding the bridgehead from downstream were also gobbled up. The opposing cavalries were kept back from the river and saw only peripheral involvement in the proceedings. However, many of Stuart's units, including some under the command of Wade Hampton—just returned to the army after four months of post-Gettysburg recuperation—were poised to enter the fight if needed. Meanwhile, Breathed's, McGregor's, and Moorman's batteries took position atop and near Fleetwood Heights in support of Lee's front-line artillery.[29]

The added strength meant little, for once the Yankees muscled their way across the water, Robert E. Lee called a retreat to the Rapidan. Meade followed to ensure that his opponent remained south of that stream for an extended period. By the eleventh, the relative positions of the armies prior to the Bristoe Campaign had been reestablished. Lee had pitched his headquarters on well-worn ground outside Orange Court House, with Stuart's field quarters nearby. John Esten Cooke summarized the situation by telling his sister, "We have like the King of France 'marched up the hill and then down again.'" He was quick to add that this return to the status quo did not necessarily mean a long spell of inactivity: "We are waiting further developments which promise soon to occur."[30]

The "further developments" were two weeks in coming, and they were not precipitated by the Army of Northern Virginia, but by its suddenly aggressive enemy. On November 26—two days after Grant's forces in Tennessee, including those Meade had contributed, attacked and shattered Bragg's army outside Chattanooga—Meade, prodded by his civilian and military superiors, launched yet another offensive. Having studied Lee's recently strengthened defenses without finding an effective way of attacking them, the Union leader had decided to maneuver his opponent out of his position. He would do this by crossing the Rapidan at and near Germanna Ford, east of Lee's right flank, then sweeping west through the Wilderness toward the open ground beyond and into the enemy's rear. Meade's plan had its strong points, one being its reliance on maneuvering as much as on fighting. Simply to meet the threat, Lee would have to leave his near-impregnable defenses.[31]

Grant

The plan did depend, to a certain extent, on the element of surprise. Meade hoped to keep his opponent ignorant of the movement until the Army of the Potomac gained the high ground behind a north-south-running tributary of the

Rapidan known as Mine Run. Instead, Lee beat him into position, thwarting his strategy and bringing the offensive to a premature halt.

Many factors figured in Lee's quick and effective response, one being the vigilance of his cavalry. Even before the movement began, Stuart's scouts had picked up rumors that something big was afoot north of the Rapidan. Then, one day before Meade moved out, the newly minted General Rosser reported the significant news that he had clashed with David Gregg at Ely's Ford, downriver from Germanna Ford.

At 8:00 on the chilly morning of the twenty-sixth, Rosser informed Lee, through Stuart, that Gregg was crossing at Ely's and moving toward Chancellorsville, apparently leading the way for a large body of infantry. Later Rosser captured supply wagons marked with the insignia of Meade's I and V Corps, which Lee took as a sign that the Army of the Potomac was heading toward his right via the Orange Turnpike or the Orange Plank Road, quite possibly by both. That night he started his army east, intending to strike Meade while he was in motion. Instead, late the next morning, a meeting-engagement occurred just east of Mine Run, at a woodland crossroads called Locust Grove.[32]

Although the fighting at Locust Grove was mainly an infantry affair, another of Meade's columns, heading in the same direction as the first but three miles south of it, advanced in rear of Gregg's horsemen. The lower column moved more slowly than its comrades to the north; not till late afternoon did it reach New Hope Church, directly south of Locust Grove. At that point, Gregg encountered determined opposition from Stuart.[33]

The cavalry commander had left Fitz Lee's division on the Rapidan to guard the upper fords and deal with Kilpatrick, whose division was demonstrating against the Confederate left rear. With Hampton's cavalry—but at first without Hampton himself—Stuart set out to stop, or at least slow, Meade's progress toward Mine Run. He did so mainly with Gordon's brigade, augmented by the late-arriving brigade of Pierce Young under Hampton's supervision. The majority of the troopers advanced on foot over wooded, stream-crossed terrain that Robert E. Lee admitted was "very unfavorable for cavalry." In the end, neither Gordon nor Young could prevent the more numerous Federals, backed as they were by infantry, from pushing west. The arrival of foot soldiers in Stuart's rear finally arrested the movement and enabled both sides to solidify the positions they would occupy for the next several days.[34]

On the evening of the twenty-eighth, Lee acted to break the stalemate. He ordered Stuart to gain Meade's rear "and ascertain his purpose." Stuart dutifully left his field headquarters at Verdiersville—scene of his near capture sixteen months earlier—and circled south of the lower Union column. Reaching Hampton's command post on the Catharpin Road early the next morning, he found the division leader unaccountably absent. A perturbed Stuart appropriated Rosser's brigade and sent it north along a woods trace to Parker's Store on the Orange Plank Road. Upon his belated arrival, Hampton trailed Stuart with his remaining brigade.[35]

Arriving at Parker's, Rosser surprised and routed a rear-echelon camp inhabited by many of Gregg's troopers. While a portion of the Laurel Brigade pursued the escapees with wild abandon, other elements of Hampton's command ransacked the evacuated position. When Union reinforcements rushed down to the store, Stuart and Hampton mixed with them, giving at least as good as they got. Eventually, Stuart claimed, the Federals retreated, whereupon he began to pursue. He halted when scouts informed him that farther west, a large column of Meade's infantry was moving toward Mine Run on a line that overlapped the Confederate right. Fearing that a major assault was imminent, Stuart rushed word to Lee, then cleared the area via another looping detour.

The force whose presence Stuart brought to Lee's attention was Warren's corps. That morning, this command, eighteen thousand strong, had moved south from Locust Grove in hopes of getting around Lee's lower flank. Thanks to Stuart's warning, Lee was able to counter the maneuver before Warren attacked. The II Corps was to have gone forward at 9:00 the next morning, the thirtieth. But when the sun rose, Warren saw freshly built works crowning the high ground in his front. Reluctantly, he called off the assault, thereby killing his superior's last hope of salvaging his offensive. A sullen Meade remained in position for the rest of that day and throughout the next. On the morning of December 2, he commenced his withdrawal to the north side of the river. The final offensive of 1863 in the eastern theater was history.[36]

Despite having operated on ground inimical to the free movement of mounted forces, Stuart had done a commendable job in the brief but significant campaign just ended. He had kept Lee supplied with intelligence on Meade's and Warren's movements, and he had successfully resisted larger forces of both cavalry and infantry. His superior appreciated his contributions and indicated as much in a rare display of emotion. Learning that his cavalry chief had racked up so many accomplishments with only a couple hours of sleep over several days, Lee exclaimed within earshot of his staff, "What a hardy soldier!" Given that the army commander usually bestowed only quiet, understated praise on subordinates who had performed well, this was a truly memorable expression of gratitude and pride.[37]

Soon after returning from its latest confrontation with Meade, the Army of Northern Virginia went into winter quarters. Most of its infantry camped within easy reach of the Rapidan. The cavalry's encampments were more spread out, not only because it patrolled a wider stretch of river, but also because Stuart wished to maximize its access to those few areas where forage could be obtained. As on previous occasions, his forces became so widely dispersed that he could not have massed them in a hurry. He could get away with this because, with cold weather setting in, there seemed little chance that Meade would retake the offensive for weeks or months to come. With the A. N.V. firmly on the defensive, it was even less likely that Lee would initiate active operations.

Only a small portion of the cavalry would winter, like Stuart, near army headquarters at Orange Court House. On December 11, two-thirds of Fitz Lee's command—the brigades of Wickham and Chambliss—were placed in camp three miles outside Charlottesville. This was almost twenty miles distant from the nearest stretch of the Rapidan, which Lomax's brigade continued to picket. On the twenty-first, Beckham's horse artillery joined Fitz's troopers on the outskirts of the college town.[38]

Life in rear of the main army had its advantages. Grazing land was easier to find, and so were firewood and building materials. A member of the 1st Stuart Horse Artillery recalled that immediately upon arriving, his unit "became very busy building very comfortable homes (or shacks, in army parlance), topped off with tent flags and stick chimneys chinked with Albemarle [County] mud. This was the first time in the experience of the battalion that we had been . . . as comfortable as a 'bug in a rug.'"[39]

Few troopers enjoyed their snug cabins for long. Although Meade and Lee were content to remain stationary, other forces were not. Early in December, General Averell, who, after losing his command in the Army of the Potomac, had been active in West Virginia, commenced the third in a series of strategically successful raids. This time he led a large force of cavalry and infantry across the border to attack sections of the Virginia and Tennessee Railroad. As a diversion, an infantry force moved up the Shenandoah Valley from Winchester toward Staunton. The double threat overwhelmed General Imboden, now in charge of Confederate forces in the Valley; he asked Robert E. Lee to reinforce his small and scattered command.[40]

Lee responded by sending two brigades of Hill's corps, under Jubal Early, to Staunton by railroad. To counter the mounted portion of Averell's expedition, Fitz Lee, with the men of Wickham and Chambliss, was detached from Stuart on December 14 and sent to the Valley as well. Two days later, Rosser and the Laurel Brigade—probably because of the command's Valley background—were hauled out of their newly constructed cabins south of Fredericksburg and also sent to join Early and Imboden. The trip must have been an ordeal for Rosser, who was suffering the aftereffects of the previous night, when he had gotten drunk at a pre-Christmas party, embarrassing himself, his hostess, and the other guests—and prompting him to swear off liquor for life.[41]

Presumably he had recovered his faculties by the time he forded the Rappahannock and set off on his journey, for his chosen route brought him quickly into contact with the enemy. When crossing the Orange & Alexandria Railroad after dark on the seventeenth, the head of his column was challenged by guards inside a stockade near Sangster's Station. After Colonel Dulany's 7th Virginia, stymied by a deep stream, botched an attack on the Fairfax County outpost, Rosser sent in Mottrom Ball's 11th Virginia, which had recently returned to the brigade after brief service under Lomax. Ball's men cut through the frigid water, topped a hill fronting the stockade, surrounded it, and forced its garrison to surrender. After tending to his casualties and prisoners and burning the nearby railroad bridge, Rosser set out for Berry's Ferry on the Shenandoah River via the Loudoun Valley and Ashby's Gap.[42]

In the end, the reinforcements accomplished little of immediate significance. Both Yankee forces escaped, Averell after capturing 200 prisoners and 150 horses and laying waste to a vast amount of railroad property. After his return to West Virginia on December 22, Early, Lee, and Rosser did not immediately rejoin the Army of Northern Virginia. Taking a calculated risk, Lee temporarily discharged dozens of troopers "whose homes were accessible," enjoining them to reassemble when called back to duty at winter's end.[43]

The remainder of the cavalry was pressed into service farther west. A few days before the end of the year, at Early's order, Lee and Rosser crossed North Mountain, en route to Moorefield, West Virginia, to obtain rations and supplies, especially beef cattle, for the A.N.V. While on the march, they also attacked outposts, wagon trains, and railroad defenses. The brigades under Lee would not rejoin their army until mid-January; Rosser's men would remain active in West Virginia until both the war and the weather along the Rapidan warmed up.[44]

Upon his return to Charlottesville, Fitz Lee disbanded additional units of his division, including whole regiments, for the winter. As a result, Wickham's and Lomax's brigades virtually ceased to exist for two months or longer. Lee did this not only to force his men to subsist themselves, but also so they might recruit for their units. In many instances, the expedient, which was carefully monitored by Stuart's headquarters, proved highly effective. For example, when the 5th Virginia of Lomax's brigade was disbanded late in the winter, it consisted of 150 men and horses fit for service; when it reassembled early in May, it numbered almost 600.[45]

Of those regiments that did not disband, many were stationed far from the Rapidan. The 9th Virginia of now-Brigadier General Chambliss's brigade spent the winter on Virginia's Northern Neck and Middle Peninsula, spread over four counties. Other outfits were similarly dispersed. That left the burden of picketing the army's right flank to the two brigades that remained with Wade Hampton. The infantry covered the army's front and left, augmented by a handful of mounted units, such as the 15th Virginia, under Charles Collins, which guarded the line of Robertson's River.

Hampton's men found their workload onerous and never-ending. They also considered it unfair, since most of them were too far from home to avail themselves of the wholesale furloughs granted the Virginians. Hampton may have felt put upon before, but he was now consumed with anger and resentment over his situation. Following the detaching of the Laurel Brigade, he found himself, from his headquarters along the Richmond, Fredericksburg & Potomac Railroad, forced to cover both the Rapidan and the Lower Rappahannock with the men of Gordon and Butler (the latter still under Pierce Young). Casualties, sickness, and detachments had combined to reduce Hampton's total force to fewer than 750 officers and men "present for duty and with serviceable horses."[46]

Although said to be in good spirits, the men were in terrible condition. More than ever before, they lacked good weapons, sufficient ammunition, proper equipment, even basic items of attire. In a letter to his sister Hampton described them as "wanting clothing very much." Colonel Black of the 1st South Carolina recalled, "In the coldest part of the winter I had nearly 300 men without blankets," a problem he remedied by enlisting the help of a charitable organization in Columbia, which sent bedding and warm-weather wear to the regiment. Few officers, however, were as resourceful or as conscientious in providing for their troopers.[47]

More than the lack of clothing or blankets, the division's effectiveness was hampered by a general shortage of serviceable horses. Dozens of animals died during the winter from illness, exposure, and overwork, but mainly from a general lack of sustenance. Black noted that throughout the winter, Gordon's and Young's mounts "were poorly foraged. . . . Our corn issues for near two months did not exceed 3 lbs. to the horse as drawn from the Brigade Q. M. We procured thro our Regimental quartermasters . . . a little additional drawn from the lower banks of the Rappahannock. But with all this, it was little better than actual starvation to our poor horses." He would frequently tie his own horse to a white oak sapling, "that the poor creature might eat the bark from it."[48]

Hampton feared that his command's debility, especially its dearth of horses fit for service, would never improve in its present position. Early in December, he proposed to Stuart that both of his brigades be allowed to remount and refit in North Carolina, "where forage is abundant & where they will have an opportunity not only of procuring fresh horses but of doing good service." He must have realized the request was unrealistic and would not be granted, and it was not. But after Stuart rejected it for lack of suitable replacement troops, Hampton sent a similar petition to R. E. Lee, which the army commander regretfully disapproved. Later Lee relented to the extent of permitting two of Gordon's regiments, the 4th and 5th North Carolina, to return for a time to their home state to recruit, but because they were not replaced—just as Stuart had foreseen—Hampton's plight worsened. Thereafter, he had to handle his never-decreasing workload with one and a half brigades instead of two.[49]

If unable to succor his command, he tried to ease its burdens. In mid-January, he informed Stuart that Gordon's pickets on the Rapidan had to travel forty miles from their camps to their duty stations: "Forage has to be carried to these posts as none can be obtained near them & the mere travel is sufficient to prevent any improvement in the horses if not to break them down. I would respectfully recommend that my pickets may be relieved by Infantry as low down the River as Ely's Ford." That area could be covered by a relatively small force of foot soldiers. Their use would enable Hampton to conserve horseflesh, while leaving him a "much larger force to meet any incursion of the enemy."[50]

This request Stuart endorsed in a letter to Lee, noting that "infantry pickets could be more easily provided for than those on horseback." Again, however, the army commander disapproved, explaining that infantry picketing so far from their camps, and lacking the means for a quick getaway, were liable to be attacked, cut off, and captured. Again, Lee expressed his regret that guard duty "comes so heavy on the Cavalry & I wish I could relieve them," but there was no help for it. He also rejected a request Hampton submitted later in the winter, to move Young's horsemen from the lower Rappahannock to the Richmond area, where they would find it much easier to procure supplies, especially forage.[51]

Hampton, all of his efforts frustrated, began to verge on despair. More and more, he feared that his command would not be fit for duty in the spring. As he told his sister, "In this event, I shall ask to be transferred to some other army, or I will resign. I am thoroughly disgusted with the way things are managed here, and I have no doubt but that the Yankee cavalry will be better next spring, than ours."[52]

While Hampton's was not a wholly accurate assessment of the cavalry's situation, the problems he described were not exaggerations, and his complaint that they had not been adequately addressed was well taken. If nothing else, his gloomy view of affairs pointed up the magnitude of the difficulties facing the cavalry of the Army of Northern Virginia at the start of the last full year of the war.

Chapter Nineteen

The Ball Begins

As Wade Hampton had so forcefully observed, the cavalry's burdens in winter camp were many and onerous, and some may have been unnecessary. Even so, they kept coming. On the frigid morning of February 6, 1864, Brig. Gen. Isaac J. Wistar, the Union commander at Yorktown, started up the Peninsula at the head of four thousand troops of all arms. Wistar intended to exploit the relative isolation of Richmond, which lay forty miles in rear of Lee's army. His goals were to occupy the Confederate capital, free the inmates of Libby and Belle Isle Prisons, and destroy supply depots, ordnance caches, and foundries, including the venerable Tredegar Iron Works.

Thanks to the treachery of one of Wistar's own men, who had escaped from prison at Fort Monroe, the commander of the Department of Richmond, Maj. Gen. Arnold Elzey, had been forewarned of the raiders' coming. By unplanking Bottom's Bridge over the Chickahominy, about ten miles southeast of the city, and lining the far shore with hastily assembled defenders, Elzey foiled Wistar's plans and eventually forced his retreat.[1]

Although Elzey took effective precautions, at first he feared they would prove inadequate. With Jefferson Davis's permission, before the Federals could strike, he called on Robert E. Lee for support. Lee turned to Stuart, and Stuart ordered Hampton's command, its worn-down condition notwithstanding, to hasten to Elzey's side. Hampton responded with characteristic dispatch, but before he reached the capital, the crisis abated. Later he rued the effects of the "fruitless expedition," which resulted in "much harm" to his horses and their riders.

Being sent on one wild goose chase was bad enough, but four days after Wistar retreated, Elzey, reacting to rumors of another attempt on the capital by Peninsula-based Yankees, issued a second alarm. Again Lee was asked for assistance, and again Hampton was tasked to provide it. This time, however, the South Carolinian balked. He refused to send his men south until Elzey provided him with details of the new threat. As Hampton later explained to Robert E. Lee, "[I was] very unwilling to take my reduced and worn-out command on a march, unless there was an actual necessity for my doing so."[2]

269

    Lee upheld Hampton's decision to await further instructions, the wisdom
of which was proven when the new emergency quickly passed. Later Lee
chided Elzey for overreacting to baseless reports of enemy movements. He suggested that the departmental commander put his faith in "scouts who can be
relied upon," thus sparing the A.N.V. "the injury done to the troops morally and
physically by movements at this season."[3]

    Elzey may well have regretted crying wolf, for three weeks after Wistar's
failure, a much graver threat to the capital's security materialized. On February
28, Judson Kilpatrick, with the assistance of the fire-eating Ulric Dahlgren, led a
division-size force of troopers out of their winter camps near Stevensburg and
toward Richmond, which remained lightly defended. The raiders slipped over
the Rapidan at Ely's Ford after capturing picket posts manned by detachments of
Young's brigade—much to the Georgian's embarrassment. Below the river, Kilpatrick and his second-in-command parted ways. The brigadier led almost thirty-
six hundred troopers against the city from the north, while the colonel guided a
satellite force of five hundred across the James west of the capital. The columns
were supposed to link on March 1 for a two-pronged assault on the city. Like
Wistar, they intended to destroy government and private industry, while freeing
thousands of prisoners. Simultaneous movements well to the north and west by
hundreds of Meade's infantrymen and fifteen hundred troopers under George
Armstrong Custer were designed to divert Lee's attention from the raid.[4]

    The magnitude of the new threat was so great that the authorities were jus-
tified in sounding the tocsin. Despite having responded in vain to earlier alarms,
Stuart's cavalry leaped into action. Late on the twenty-eighth, Stuart, with the
few well-mounted companies he could gather on short notice, galloped toward
Albemarle County, Custer's reported destination. Advance bodies crossed the
Federals' path at Stanardsville, but Custer pushed them aside, crossed the
Rivanna River, and advanced on Charlottesville.

    There the Federal leader encountered the winter quarters of the Stuart
Horse Artillery. Only two weeks before, the battalion commander, Major Beckham, had left Virginia to take a higher position with the mounted artillery of the
Army of Tennessee; this day Marcellus Moorman was in charge of the batteries
hibernating outside the college town. Moorman, himself on the verge of transferring out of the horse artillery, apparently took little part in the fighting,
although Captains Chew and Breathed distinguished themselves throughout.

    Through quick maneuvering, effective firepower, and the support of Lee's
troopers, Moorman's subordinates hauled their cannons to the rear before they
could be overrun. A large detachment of Regulars attacked the camp, but
though they succeeded in burning and confiscating equipage, including caissons
and forges, the assailants failed to harm guns, teams, or crews. Reports of Stuart's approach and rumors that Rebel infantry was heading his way eventually
persuaded Custer to disengage, recross the Rivanna, and head homeward.[5]

    Custer's expedition and, to a lesser extent, Meade's infantry diversion did
assist Kilpatrick and Dahlgren, but in the end, not enough. Although the raiding

leaders encountered no concerted opposition between the Rapidan and Richmond, their well-planned expedition ended in disaster. Dahlgren's force was
blocked by an unfordable river and other obstacles, and failed to get to Richmond in time to cooperate with Kilpatrick, who reached the northern outskirts
of the city on the afternoon of March 1 and prepared to attack on his own. But
he lost some of his resolve when the local defense battalions—small as they
were—proved to be alert and combative. Bedeviled by artillery and rifle fire,
and buffeted by an icy rain, Kilpatrick ended his offensive after a weak attempt
on a section of works manned by a combination of regular troops, home guards,
and government clerks. Turning east, he crossed the Chickahominy to Mechanicsville and safety. There he bivouacked, waited in vain for Dahlgren's errant
column to join him, and tried to recapture the self-confidence his mostly unseen
opponents had stolen from him.[6]

During the first several hours Kilpatrick and Dahlgren were on the road,
Robert E. Lee's cavalry knew nothing of their movements. At midday on the
twenty-ninth, Hampton was finally alerted to Kilpatrick's presence by one of
his more enterprising scouts, Sgt. George Shadburne of the Jeff Davis Legion.
Hampton's initial response was to contact his superior, but because Stuart was
preoccupied with Custer, no reply was forthcoming. By late in the afternoon,
Hampton had come to see that only he was in a position to chase down the Yankees. With his available force—some three hundred members of the 1st and 2nd
North Carolina, plus a section of Hart's battery—he started south at a rapid clip.
En route, he picked up a few dozen reinforcements from the mounted portion of
the newly organized Maryland Line, under Col. Bradley T. Johnson, headquartered at Taylorsville on the Richmond, Fredericksburg & Potomac Railroad.

Hampton had no hope of overtaking Kilpatrick short of Richmond, but after
the raiding leader passed east of the city, his pursuer was able to strike a blow
both physical and psychological. After locating Kilpatrick's evening bivouac and
carefully positioning his few troops, Hampton sounded the attack. North Carolinians and Marylanders charged the Yankees from many directions, shooting
and screaming the Rebel yell. Sleep-fogged raiders panicked and ran for cover.
A few offered resistance, but most stampeded in the direction of Old Church.

Hampton, whose force had been so small that only under cover of darkness
could its attack have succeeded, had prevented Kilpatrick from launching a second, more carefully orchestrated offensive against Richmond. Utterly routed,
the Union leader lost the last vestiges of his nerve. The next morning, he led his
men on a retreat down the Peninsula to Yorktown. Hampton's troopers pursued
at a distance, unwilling to tempt fate with a daylight attack, but equally unwilling to give up the chase until certain Richmond was safe.[7]

The men under Stuart and Hampton were not the only members of the cavalry, A.N.V., to play a major role in pursuit of the Yankee raiders. After reaching Richmond too late to cooperate with Kilpatrick, a disheartened Dahlgren
also called a retreat. He led his little column eastward across the Chickahominy,
Pamunkey, and Mattapony Rivers, hoping by this roundabout route to join

Kilpatrick inside the Union defenses on the Peninsula. As he marched, however, he attracted dozens of pursuers: home guards, civilians toting shotguns and hunting rifles, and members of some of the companies that Fitz Lee had permitted to winter at home in the Virginia countryside.

One of these regular units, a twenty-five-man detachment of Company H, 9th Virginia, under Lt. James Pollard, helped corner what remained of Dahlgren's column (about half of its original force had become separated from Dahlgren and the rest) near the hamlet of Stevensville late on March 2. Finding himself virtually surrounded, the colonel opened fire on his pursuers and was shot dead, along with several of his men. Other raiders were rounded up and sent to Richmond to be incarcerated alongside the POWs they had hoped to liberate.

In the aftermath of the ambush, Lieutenant Pollard confiscated a memoranda book and a sheaf of papers that had been found on or near Dahlgren's body. The documents, which Pollard forwarded to Fitz Lee, revealed that Dahlgren's intent—and perhaps Kilpatrick's as well—had been not only to free prisoners in Richmond, but also to "destroy and burn the hateful city" and to seize and kill Jefferson Davis and other Confederate leaders.[8]

Lee forwarded the "Dahlgren Papers" to Richmond, where the raiders' intended victims perused their contents; later, excerpts were printed in the local newspapers. A firestorm of controversy erupted. Even as they condemned Yankee barbarity, Secretary of War Seddon and other high-ranking officials threatened to retaliate by hanging every captured raider. Kilpatrick, after returning to Meade's army, publicly disavowed the documents. Afterward, cooler heads such as Robert E. Lee—whose son continued to languish in a Union prison—counseled moderation.

Eventually, the crisis passed over. The captured Federals remained in prison, but none was executed. Only days after the raid ended, Rooney Lee was quietly released from captivity and permitted to rejoin his father's army. The only lasting legacy of the Kilpatrick-Dahlgren raid was the revelation that on the brink of the fourth spring of the war, the conflict had settled into a grim, win-at-any-cost struggle bereft of those trappings of civility and fair play it had appeared to wear in 1861–62.[9]

In the weeks following Kilpatrick's repulse and Dahlgren's demise, the troopers of Lee's army prepared—some willingly, some grudgingly—for the resumption of active campaigning. By early March, several units in the cavalry corps, including Lomax's brigade as a body, had reenlisted for the war. Since every Confederate was bound to service for the duration of the fight, the act was mainly a patriotic gesture, calculated to tell the enemy and the world that the Army of Northern Virginia was going to see the conflict through regardless of what hardships lay ahead.[10]

This same determination was evident in the personal expressions of many men. Lt. Col. Robert Randolph of the 4th Virginia declared in a letter home that

That old lie
. . . dulce et decorum est.
pro patria more . . .

he and his comrades were "anxious for the [spring] Campaign to commence. All hands seem to be getting tired of the monotony of Camp life." He added, "We are very confident that success will crown our efforts. . . & a decided majority consider that we are now in the last year of the war & that the time is not far distant when sitting around our fires at home we will spin long yarns of the deeds we have done."[11] *Good luck.*

Not only the officers expressed confidence and enthusiasm for the fight. A private in the 15th Virginia agreed that "we have no fears as to the coming conflict," for "something grand will turn up soon." One cause for optimism was the fact that "Genl. Lee's old army has recruited very largely during the past fall and winter, and it is now generally considered to be in better spirits & health, also better armed equipped &c, than at any previous time." This man may have hit the mark. As Wade Hampton observed when asking that his troopers be relieved on picket duty by better-conditioned comrades, many of the regiments Fitz Lee had disbanded at the start of the winter were returning to the army not only better equipped and better mounted than before, but also in greater numbers, the result of effective recruitment.[12]

But not every trooper awaited the return of campaigning with eager anticipation. Pvt. Ruben Hammon of the 7th Virginia spoke for many comrades when he wrote of being so tired of the war he hoped it would soon end, "one way or the other." Samuel Biddle of the 1st North Carolina doubted the recent influx of recruits would prove sufficient to the army's needs: "We want more Cavalry and I can't see how we can well get along without it." Biddle supposed that General Stuart "expects to accomplish something wonderful" in the weeks ahead, "but I am of the opinion that he will be . . . badly used up before the summer is over."[13] *oh, was he ever. Yellow Tavern.*

Trooper Biddle may have overestimated his commander's expectations for the spring campaign. In mid-April, Stuart wrote his wife (who was about to move into lodgings near Beaver Dam Station on the Virginia Central Railroad, not far from his headquarters) in an unusually subdued mood. At one point he reminded her that "tomorrow will bring its own cares without torturing the imagination today to divine what may happen." Perhaps he was only trying to lift Flora out of a melancholy mood. On the other hand, his words may have reflected a gloomy outlook, one he could share only with his spouse.[14]

Whatever its future, Stuart's corps would have a new look. When Rooney Lee rejoined the army on March 30, Stuart decided to reward him for his past services and compensate him for his long, stressful imprisonment by promoting him to major general and giving him a division. To stock the new command, on April 23 Stuart ordered the transfer of Rooney's old brigade, under Chambliss (now reduced to the 9th, 10th, and 13th Virginia) from Fitz Lee's division and Gordon's brigade (the 1st, 2nd, and 5th North Carolina) from Hampton's. Fitz complied readily, but Hampton did not; Gordon's brigade was not released until the first days of May. In the short term, Gordon's loss left Hampton with a single brigade, Pierce Young's, which now consisted of the Jeff Davis, Phillips, and Cobb Legions, as well as two newly acquired units, the 7th Georgia regiment and the 20th Georgia Battalion. Through his own and Hampton's efforts, Young had secured the transfer of both from Beauregard's Department of South Carolina, Georgia, and Florida—against the Creole's protests.[15]

Meanwhile, Rosser's brigade—now made up of the 7th, 11th, and 12th Virginia regiments and the 35th Virginia Battalion—continued to serve hundreds of miles from Hampton's side. Although briefly called east to help oppose Custer's foray through Albemarle County, the Laurel Brigade had been returned to the Shenandoah Valley; it would not be recalled to the Rapidan until the last days of April.[16]

Eventually, Hampton would be compensated for Rosser's continuing absence, as well as for the permanent loss of the 1st and 2nd South Carolina. Those regiments had recently been returned to their home state to recruit their strength, an action prompted by Hampton's repeated warnings that both had been dangerously reduced by hard campaigning. Toward the close of the winter, Hampton himself returned to South Carolina, hoping to rejoin the army in company with Calbraith Butler, who had nearly recovered from his Brandy Station wound. Hampton also hoped to bring north three large, well-equipped regiments that had been serving along the coast of his native state and with which he planned to build a new brigade for Butler: the 4th, 5th, and 6th South Carolina. In the first week of May, however, the approach of active operations caused Hampton to return to Virginia sooner than intended, and without his additions. Butler and his new outfits would not reach the fighting front in Virginia for another three weeks.[17]

Only Fitz Lee's division remained essentially unchanged from its configuration of the previous fall. Williams Wickham continued to command the oldest and most distinguished components of Stuart's corps, the 1st, 2nd, 3rd, and 4th Virginia. Lunsford Lomax's brigade had changed, but only slightly. Recently it had given up the 1st Maryland Battalion to Bradley Johnson's new command. Months earlier, on the eve of the Laurel Brigade's departure for the Valley, Lomax had traded the 11th Virginia to Rosser in exchange for the older but less battle-savvy 6th Virginia.[18]

Changes had also occurred in the ranks of the horse artillery, most of them the result of personnel transfers. Following Beckham's departure, Stuart had offered command of the battalion to Tom Rosser's groomsman, James Dearing. Months earlier, Dearing had transferred from the artillery to the cavalry; at the temporary grade of colonel, he had been assigned a mounted regiment in Maj. Gen. George E. Pickett's Department of North Carolina. In mid-March, Dearing agreed to Stuart's request to return to his original arm of the service, but he withdrew his consent when he learned he would have to accept a demotion to major.[19]

In place of Dearing, Stuart selected his senior battery commander, Chew, whom he promoted to major. To recognize the many contributions Jim Breathed had made to the battalion, he too was elevated to major, as Chew's second-in-command. James Thomson succeeded Chew in command of the Ashby Battery, while Breathed's 1st Stuart Horse Artillery went to Lt. Philip Preston Johnston; both were promoted to captain. So, too, was Lt. John J. Shoemaker, who succeeded Moorman in command of the Lynchburg Battery. James Hart continued to command the Washington (South Carolina) Battery, William McGregor the 2nd Stuart Horse Artillery.

Unit changes in the horse artillery during the winter were kept to a minimum. The Baltimore Light Artillery (Griffin's battery), which had been a part of the battalion since Gettysburg, was transferred to Johnson's Maryland Line. Its loss would be made good by the acquisition in the spring of Capt. Edward Graham's Petersburg Artillery, recently converted from mounted artillery service. While horses, forges, battery wagons, and other equipment remained, as always, in short supply, the Stuart Horse Artillery—bolstered by the memory of its stubborn defense of its winter camp—would serve honorably and effectively in the action-filled weeks to come.[20]

Over the winter, Stuart's opponents had also undergone changes—in fact, the Army of the Potomac appeared to have been transformed. It continued to be commanded by George Meade, but as of early March, Meade was accompanied by the new commanding general of United States Armies, Lt. Gen. Ulysses S. Grant. The most successful of Lincoln's field commanders, the hero of Vicksburg and Chattanooga, Grant would chart grand strategy not only for Meade's command, but also for another, smaller army operating in Virginia with the mission of capturing Richmond, the Army of the James, led by the politician-general Benjamin F. Butler. Grant's strategy would also shape the movements of every other Union army, including the three he had left behind in Tennessee under overall command of Maj. Gen. William T. Sherman.

Grant had brought with him from the West Maj. Gen. Philip H. Sheridan, a former infantry commander who had achieved distinction at Stones River, Perryville, Chattanooga, and in other battles. The fiery little Irishman also had cavalry experience; he was such a versatile performer that Grant had given him command of Meade's cavalry, the erratic Pleasonton being banished to the Trans-Mississippi. Also sent west during the winter—mainly the result of his debacle on the doorstep of Richmond—was Judson Kilpatrick. The 3rd Cavalry Division was now led by another Grant protégé, Brig. Gen. James Harrison Wilson, formerly a staff officer and desk general. Meanwhile, the 1st Cavalry Division, the late John Buford's, had been placed in the hands of an officer who, like Sheridan, had come over from the infantry, Brig. Gen. Alfred T. A. Torbert. The venerable David Gregg retained command of Sheridan's 2nd Division.[21]

➤━◆➤━○━◆━❮◆━❮

At dawn on May 4, the spring campaign got under way as Meade's army, under Grant's supervision, crossed the Rapidan about eight miles east of the Rebel lines along Mine Run. The V Army Corps, now under G. K. Warren, preceded by Wilson's cavalry, crossed at Germanna Ford; Maj. Gen. John Sedgwick's VI

Corps followed Warren; and the II Corps of Winfield Scott Hancock, screened by Gregg's horsemen, crossed at Ely's Ford, six miles below Germanna. Some hours later, the army's IX Corps, under the once disgraced but resurgent Ambrose Burnside, would leave its rear-guard position near Warrenton and ford the river at Germanna. Sheridan had placed Torbert's division behind the marching columns to guard their rear, as well as the army's immense and vital supply train.

In outward appearance, the movement was a reprise of Meade's failed offensive of the previous November. Grant, however, had no intention of attacking Lee's formidable position on Mine Run. He hoped that the army moved south quickly enough to skirt Lee's flank and get between him and Richmond. In so hoping, the commanding general was gambling that the troops could clear the movement-clogging, vision-obscuring Wilderness before Lee came up to challenge them.[22]

It was a gamble he would lose, thanks to the vigilance of Stuart and his troopers. Alert to stirrings in the camps above the Rapidan, the cavalry had been expecting a general movement for at least twenty-four hours. On the third, the master scout Stringfellow had returned from one of his excursions behind enemy lines to warn, as one of Stuart's staff officers reported, that "Grant's vast army is preparing to advance, that it numbers about one hundred and twenty thousand [nearly twice the size of the Army of Northern Virginia], and is magnificently equipped."

Stringfellow was right on all counts, and his timely warning permitted Stuart to break camp in record time. According to Alexander R. Boteler, Stuart's volunteer aide-de-camp, by the morning of the fourth, their "tents were struck, waggons [sic] loaded and long before noon everything was in its proper place and everybody about the camp ready for active operations." It did not take a seer to predict that "the ball [was] about to begin."

When, later in the morning, Stuart got definitive word that the enemy was crossing, he rode out along the turnpike from his headquarters near Orange Court House toward one of his old haunts, Verdiersville, below the Orange Plank Road and just west of Mine Run. To get there, he and his staff passed through some of the densest portions of the Wilderness, "a name that fitly applies," Boteler observed, " . . . for a gloomier, wilder and more forbidding region can hardly be found this side of the Alleghanies."[23]

Reaching the plank road early in the afternoon, Stuart found it filled with members of Hill's Third Corps, moving east to challenge Sedgwick's Federals near Brock Crossing. In that sector, he was in contact with some of Rooney Lee's troopers, who were covering the infantry's right flank. The rest of the cavalry corps appeared to be scattered to the corners of the earth. Hampton, with the few hundred troopers left to him, had been sent from his post on the Rapidan to Shady Grove Church, near Todd's Tavern. There Rosser's brigade, which had just reached Orange Court House from Charlottesville, was to join him. Meanwhile, Fitz Lee's recently reconstituted division was en route to Stuart from its position on the far right flank. Having broken camp at Hamilton's Crossing, below Fredericksburg, it was marching south and west along a round-about route that would also bring it to Todd's Tavern.[24]

Boteler recorded that when Stuart reached the plank road, he was recognized by Rooney Lee's men, "who greeted him with enthusiastic shouts . . . an impromptu ovation to the Chief of the Cavalry Corps." Hearing the cheers, Hill's foot soldiers, as they marched past, added their own "loud huzzas . . . in one grand chorus of twice ten thousand voices." The greeting was in marked contrast to the derisive cheers Stuart's infantry comrades had given him on the review field the previous June. It must have seemed a good note on which to begin a critical campaign.[25]

Stuart's initial mission was to gain intelligence on enemy movements and plans. Robert E. Lee had set in motion not only Hill's troops, but also those of Dick Ewell, who were moving along the Orange Turnpike, north of, and parallel to, Hill's route of advance. Longstreet's corps, the last to leave its winter camps, was moving to Hill's support via a less direct route, the Catharpin Road. Lee had made these dispositions, however, in almost total ignorance of his enemy's intentions. Meade's army might be planning to move downriver to Fredericksburg; it might also be preparing to turn west and confront him directly; or it might be up to something else entirely.

May 4 revealed that Stuart's scouting abilities were as sharp as ever. Shortly before midnight, he was able to confirm that the Federals had halted in the heart of the forest, Warren near Wilderness Tavern on the turnpike, Sedgwick on the plank road, and Hancock farther south between Chancellorsville and Todd's Tavern, near the lower edge of the forest. From what Stuart could gather, each column was heading south. When he passed the intelligence to Lee, the army leader realized that Grant wished to exit the Wilderness before offering battle. Meade's stationary position, however, offered Lee an opportunity to strike him in flank before he could clear the trees.[26]

Lee moved to seize that opportunity late on the morning of the fifth. Ewell advanced against Warren in line of battle, but before he could strike, shortly after noon, the V Corps attacked him. Farther south, Hill pressed forward on the plank road, but in that sector as well, the enemy seized the initiative. Shortly after 4:00 P.M., the Third Corps was assaulted by Sedgwick's corps and by thousands of troops under Hancock, who had countermarched to help defend the plank road. The result was bloody and sometimes desperate combat, which raged throughout the day, both sides gaining and losing ground. It ended inconclusively: When the fighting sputtered out after dark—with some exceptions—the antagonists held ground close to that which they had occupied when the struggle began.[27]

The cavalry action this day was sporadic and unplanned. Stuart, with half of Rooney Lee's division (Gordon's brigade had yet to join it), spent the day scouting rather than fighting. Hampton, Gordon, and Young had a few brushes with the Federals en route to Shady Grove Church, which they did not reach until the seventh. Meanwhile, the hard-marching troopers of Fitz Lee encountered Gregg's cavalry about two miles south of Todd's Tavern late in the afternoon. Fitz attacked with Lomax's brigade, which drove in some of Gregg's skirmishers but failed to dislodge his main body, at a cost of two Virginians killed and twenty wounded.[28]

In assailing Gregg, Lee was assisting Rosser's brigade, which had arrived from Orange Court House via the Catharpin Road early that morning to attack Wilson's division. Wilson, commanding the forwardmost element of Meade's army, had advanced to Craig's Meeting House, across the Po River from Todd's Tavern and dangerously far from his nearest supports. The encounter near Craig's was something that Rosser, a rival of Wilson's since their days together at West Point, had been looking forward to. It began with Rosser driving in Wilson's advance guard, only to be repulsed by his main body. Wilson claimed that he pursued his old antagonist for two miles before falling back to Craig's. While Rosser rallied his troops for a second attack, Wilson unwisely held his position, expecting to be relieved by the infantry. But the nearest troops, Hancock's, were too heavily engaged with Hill's Confederates to assist him.[29]

At about 2:00 P.M., Rosser again advanced, hurling the head of his column at Wilson "like the quivering arrow from the bowstring." A majority of the attackers—members of Thomas Marshall's 7th and Thomas B. Massie's 12th Virginia, supported by Lige White's Comanches—moved up afoot, lacking room to maneuver on horseback. The second assault was so well planned and launched with such force that it routed nearly half of Wilson's command, which fled to the rear in unseemly haste, some of its men not stopping till they reached Parker's Store, more than twenty miles to the north. Wilson was fortunate, however, to be supported by a pair of horse artillery batteries, whose crews doused the Laurel Brigade with enough short-range ammunition to stanch their assault. Even so, one of Massie's troopers noted, "we remained skirmishing with them for 1½ hours." The man added proudly that although Wilson's men had the advantage of numbers, "they never offered to advance."[30]

Again Rosser fell back, but only to plan a new offensive. This time, instead of attacking frontally, he sidled around to the north until, late in the afternoon, he interposed between Wilson's right flank and the rest of the Army of the Potomac. Concerned for his safety—especially after learning of Fitz Lee's approach to the south—Wilson disengaged and headed north and east toward Todd's Tavern. The Confederates pressed his rear as he withdrew; Wilson's rapid, almost panicky crossing of the Po River at Corbin's Bridge must have made even the taciturn Rosser smile.[31]

Hard-pressed as he was, and despite losing several men to capture, Wilson made good his escape. When he reached Todd's Tavern late in the day, he found to his relief that Meade, having learned of his plight, had rushed David Gregg's division to that point. A grateful Wilson led his embattled troopers behind the lines of breastworks that Gregg had constructed on all sides of the tavern.

By now Fitz Lee had arrived to augment Rosser. The newcomer saw at once that although Rosser had hunted Wilson down, he had been forced "to withdraw without his game." The combined forces rode north and struck at the tavern's defenses. Despite Lee's partial success on the right, however, Gregg's line held. Eventually Lee and Rosser fell back into the trees, whereupon Gregg counterattacked both on foot and in the saddle. The withdrawing Confederates remounted and, by divergent routes, dashed across the Po River until beyond pursuit. By hard marching and especially by hard riding, Wilson had avoided being cut off from his army and perhaps destroyed. As it was, he had suffered almost 100 men killed and more than four times as many wounded, against Rosser's casualty total of 114. This day had witnessed Wilson's maiden outing in field command—his classmate had made it an experience he would never forget.[32]

>-+-<>-O-<+-I-<

The fighting on the fifth had been fierce, but the battle of the Wilderness remained undecided. At daylight on May 6, Stuart, accompanied only by his staff, rode up to Rosser's field headquarters and ordered his men to saddle up. Rosser naturally expected to link with Fitz Lee, whose men had bivouacked well to the east. Instead, Stuart led the brigade westward, then up the Brock Road, a "narrow, blind road through the thick brush" that led to Todd's Tavern. As they rode, the men of the brigade heard clearly the racket of infantry combat. On the Orange Plank Road, Hill's men, now supported by Longstreet's, were again in action. Stuart hoped to assist them by threatening the south flank of their opponents, Hancock's corps. Rosser would not have to handle the job alone, however: En route he was joined by Thomson's (formerly Chew's) and Shoemaker's (recently Moorman's) batteries.[33]

The Laurel Brigade and its artillery supports never reached their target. South of Todd's Tavern, Stuart halted the column, sent forward scouts, made a personal reconnaissance, and discovered that a sizable body of Yankee horsemen had bivouacked inside a wide clearing astride the intersection of the Brock and Catharine Furnace Roads. These were the men of the Michigan Cavalry Brigade of George Custer, another West Point classmate of Rosser's, one he thought of as a friend. School ties put aside, Rosser prepared to carry out Stuart's order that he attack. For the assignment, he chose his smallest unit, Lige White's battalion, instructing its commander to "ride over everything in sight." Given the size of the opposition, White might have done a double-take. Instead, he saluted, formed an assault column four abreast—all the narrow road could accommodate—and spurred into a charge.

Shouting a facsimile of the war whoop their namesakes had made famous, the Comanches piled into Custer's picket line and the reserve force beyond, bowling over riders and horses and, as Rosser said, chasing "the remainder back into the thick underbrush whence they had come." But just as the Comanches hit their stride, White's horse took a bullet; in falling, it threw its rider. Thereafter, the assault lost momentum. Taking advantage, Custer's main body rushed up and, thanks largely to the firepower of their seven-shot Spencer carbines, sent their assailants reeling.[34]

White escaped without serious injury, but many of his men were killed, wounded, or captured. The remainder of Rosser's command, Funsten's 11th Virginia in front, immediately advanced on foot to cover the battalion's retreat. For a time, the 11th held off the rampaging Yankees, but after Custer was reinforced by Col. Thomas Devin's brigade of Torbert's division, Funsten's men allowed comrades in the 7th and 12th Virginia to relieve them. The newcomers eventually persuaded the Wolverines and their supports to fall back some distance. Thereafter Stuart allowed the guns of Thomson and Shoemaker to take over the fight. "The remainder of the day," Rosser observed, "was spent in wasting ammunition, firing into the woods at an unseen foe."[35]

At bottom, of course, this was Robert E. Lee's fault. By intercepting Grant's and Meade's southward passage, he had determined that the armies would grapple on terrain conducive to the operations of no arm of the service. On the other hand, only a battlefield of this nature could have enabled an army as small as his to take on a behemoth like Meade's.

>─┤─◆─○─◆─┤─◄

Day two in the Wilderness ended in much the same manner as day one, with the armies facing each other across rude entrenchments, although in much less strength than at battle's start. The savage nature of the fight, and the offensive posture the Federals had assumed throughout, were reflected in an uncommonly steep butcher's bill: Almost eighteen thousand Union casualties, fewer than half as many for Lee's army. Despite the cost, Grant seemed no closer to flanking Lee or interposing between him and his capital than he had been before crossing the Rapidan.

In similar situations, Grant's predecessors—including Meade after Mine Run—had retreated to recuperate and rethink, most often while putting a river between them and Lee. This Grant would not, or could not, do. His goal—to destroy the fighting effectiveness of the Army of Northern Virginia—could be attained only by drawing Lee out of his works and into the open for a stand-up fight. The most effective means of achieving this remained threatening his opponent's capital, which Lee would defend with his army's life. Therefore, rather than attacking for the third straight day, Grant on May 7 moved his army to the south and east, heading out of the forest on the road to Spotsylvania Court House. Thanks to Stuart, however, Lee divined his enemy's intent and exploited his interior lines of communication to get ahead of the Federals.[36]

The withdrawal of Meade's exhausted troops did not begin until mid-evening. Earlier in the day, the infantry of both armies engaged in sporadic, desultory combat. The cavalry saw more active service and suffered accordingly.

The previous afternoon, in response to erroneous reports that Confederate infantry had gotten between Sheridan's cavalry and Hancock's infantry, Meade had compelled the horsemen to withdraw from Todd's Tavern. The next morning, as a frustrated Sheridan had foreseen, Grant ordered him to reoccupy the position, which would serve as the jumping-off point for the advance to Spotsylvania. Heading south with two of his three divisions (Wilson's was recuperating from its battering on the fifth), "Little Phil" discovered that Rosser's men had evacuated the area, but that Fitz Lee's had occupied the works the Federals had abandoned above the tavern, adding log and fence-rail barricades of their own.[37]

Heedless of the obstacles, Sheridan attacked with the divisions of Torbert (temporarily under Wesley Merritt) and Gregg. Thanks to a well-crafted plan of cooperation, and to the power of their supporting artillery, the Federals, attacking dismounted, drove Lee's outgunned defenders from one line of works to another. Left with no alternative, the troopers of Lomax and Wickham abandoned their works and galloped back to the position, two miles south of the tavern, that they had taken up two days before. Left behind, strewn along dusty roads north and east of the tavern, were several dead, including the recently promoted Colonel Collins of the 15th Virginia, whose loss was openly mourned by Stuart and Fitz Lee. Another casualty was Colonel Owen of the 3rd Virginia, who took a severe wound.[38]

Below the tavern, fugitive Confederates took refuge in roadside trees, hoping the foliage would serve to lower the odds they were facing. It did not. Slowly but inexorably, Sheridan's troopers advanced south, their carbines ablaze. Through the balance of the day, they methodically evicted the occupants of the woods just as they had emptied the breastworks north of the tavern.

Given his less-than-cordial relations with Wade Hampton, Fitz Lee never admitted that all that saved his division from disaster was the arrival in late afternoon of Hampton's Virginians and Carolinians. Their commander, however, observed that "the reinforcement brought by me decided this affair to our advantage." Yet Hampton claimed too much for himself: By the time he came up, his opponents had accomplished their purpose, having secured the Todd's Tavern intersection for Meade's use come evening. Then, too, when Gordon's and Young's brigades reached the scene, Stuart, not Hampton, led them in an attack up the Catharpin Road. In response, Sheridan merely drew in his dismounted squadrons. With evening approaching, Little Phil was not about to risk squandering his daytime accomplishments with an after-dark attack against a reinforced enemy.[39]

Fitz Lee may have gotten the worst of it on May 7, but he would have his revenge the following day. Although forced to abandon Todd's Tavern, his men had reoccupied the breastworks south of the hostelry as soon as the Yankees withdrew. Their presence on the Brock Road ensured that when Sheridan's horsemen, followed by Warren's foot soldiers, pulled out of their positions after dark on the seventh, they found their march to Spotsylvania anything but the free-and-easy jaunt they had expected. For hours Lee's men stymied Merritt's division, which led the Yankee column. By 3:00 A.M. on the eighth, when the V Corps came up in the cavalry's rear, the horsemen had not progressed much beyond Todd's Tavern. Furious to find the Brock Road clogged with dismounted cavalry and horse artillery, Warren and his subordinates demanded that the way be cleared for them. After much wrangling and confusion, and only after Sheridan reached the scene from the rear, did the traffic snarl untangle.[40]

By then a golden opportunity for Grant and Meade had been lost. Shortly after Warren disengaged from the Wilderness, Lee had ordered Richard H. Anderson—commanding the First Corps in place of Longstreet, who had been wounded and disabled on the sixth—to Spotsylvania. Uncertain of Grant's immediate destination, Lee had instructed Anderson to begin his march in the morning. So late a start would have prevented the First Corps from beating its enemy to the strategic crossroads via the more direct road from Shady Grove Church. However, large portions of the tinder-dry Wilderness had been set afire by sparks from Rebel and Yankee firearms. The burning woods denied Anderson's men a secure bivouac; thus they marched on through the night. Toward morning, Stuart appeared on the road to hasten them into position outside Spotsylvania. The cavalry leader alone seemed to appreciate the necessity of speed. He was all too aware that the bulwark constructed by Fitz Lee could not long contain the blue tide building behind it.[41]

Under Stuart's prodding, at about 7:00 A.M. Anderson's men hustled into position northwest of the village and dug in across the Brock Road. As soon as he knew Anderson was up in force, Fitz Lee, sometime before 8:00, remounted his weary but triumphant troopers and led them south. Under the supervision of Lunsford Lomax, they took position behind the defenses above the courthouse. When Warren came up to challenge that line perhaps an hour later, Lee's men fought beside their infantry comrades to repulse him. Once again, the road to Richmond had been blocked to the invader. Round one of the new campaign had already gone to the Army of Northern Virginia; now round two had begun in promising fashion.[42]

The cavalry had accomplished great deeds this day, as it had during the previous two, and the high command was grateful. As his men filed into Anderson's works, Fitz Lee had ridden up to salute them. One trooper heard him say, "Boys, you have done fine! You have kept the Yankee infantry back for two days." Another man recalled Lee's praise as more effusive: "Boys, you have made the most glorious fight you ever made—the coolest I ever saw!"

However it was worded, the tribute was as much appreciated as it was deserved.[43]

Chapter Twenty

"Do Your Duty as I've Done Mine"

W arren's inability to make headway in the direction of Spotsylvania triggered an acrimonious exchange between Meade and Sheridan. The basis of their confrontation was the supposed ease with which Stuart's troopers had outmaneuvered and outfought their opponents over the past three days. The upshot was Sheridan's heated assertion that, if permitted to cut loose from the army, he would draw Stuart into an open fight and whip him soundly. When Grant learned of Sheridan's declaration, he gave the cavalry leader the authority he sought. Early on the ninth, Little Phil set out to make good on his boast.[1]

Sometime before 8:00 A.M., as the armies of Lee and Meade spread out to occupy every stretch of defensible ground outside Spotsylvania, scouts from Wickham's brigade along the extreme Confederate right flank south of Fredericksburg sent Stuart disturbing news. A heavy column of Yankee horsemen was moving through that sector, complete with batteries of horse artillery, ambulances, and pack mules. The troopers, who had come from the direction of Spotsylvania, were descending the Telegraph Road on a course that would carry them to Beaver Dam Station on the Virginia Central Railroad. Reaching that point, they would be only thirty miles from Richmond.

Stuart immediately relayed word of the movement to army headquarters, then pondered his course of action. Wickham's brigade would trail the Federals, but it had no hope of slowing, let alone halting, such an immense force. In trying to mount a larger pursuit, Stuart found his options limited. Hampton, with the brigades of Rosser and Young, was actively engaged with Union infantry along the Po River above Old Spotsylvania Court House; Fitz Lee, with Lomax's brigade, was similarly involved farther east. In midafternoon, however, Lomax became available for pursuit duty when relieved by Jubal Early's foot soldiers. By 3:00 P.M., Stuart had left his headquarters near the courthouse to lead the way south.[2]

By then Wickham, who had begun to pursue as soon as he reported the enemy's passage, had overtaken the rear of the twelve-mile-long column, which consisted of all three of Meade's mounted divisions, Sheridan in command. The Irishman's languid pace invited contact, for his express intent was to draw the Confederates after him. Early in the afternoon Wickham's force struck the Federal rear near Jerrell's Mill on the Ta River and kept up a running fight as far as Mitchell's Shop, five miles to the south. The pursuers enjoyed the chase, which gave them, as one Virginian said, "the satisfaction of harassing the enemy to our heart's content."[3]

Near Mitchell's Shop at about 5:00 P.M., satisfaction abruptly ceased as two Federal regiments, whose men had been hiding in trees on either side of a bend in the road, poured a murderous crossfire into the passing ranks of the 3rd Virginia. Wickham rallied the regiment and sent it into the trees, shouting, "Give them hell boys—damn 'em, give them hell!" But though his men chased down several of their ambushers, most escaped through the foliage to the safety of Sheridan's rear guard. Still shouting imprecations, Wickham recalled his troopers. He permitted Sheridan to proceed south while he waited for Stuart and Lee, with the rest of the pursuit force, to join him.[4]

It was close to nightfall when the cavalry leader, along with his favorite subordinate, reined in at Mitchell's Shop. Perhaps an hour later, they were joined by Lomax's brigade, with Johnston's battery and a two-gun section under James Hart. Well to the rear, Gordon's brigade was also en route, Stuart having ordered Rooney Lee to add the North Carolinians to the pursuit. To be sure, he could use the manpower: Even with Gordon on hand Sheridan would outnumber his pursuers by more than two to one. Given Stuart's preference for conducting an operation with the fewest possible troops, it seems unlikely he had even considered asking Robert E. Lee to allow him to add Rosser, Young, and Chambliss to the mission.[5]

Stuart's forces having assembled, "the next thing to [do]," as one of Fitz Lee's men observed, "was to get ahead of Sheridan." To accomplish this, Stuart decided to employ two pursuit columns. When Gordon's men reached his side late that evening, Stuart accompanied them westward toward Davenport's Bridge on the North Anna River. There they could detect any inclination by Sheridan to lay waste the Virginia Central. Meanwhile, Lee headed directly south with his own brigades, seeking to overtake the Federals, or at least keep a close watch on them.[6]

Stuart failed to cut off any Yankees short of the North Anna, although on the morning of the tenth, Lee's artillery shelled Sheridan's rear echelon, Gregg's division, as it crossed the river to join Merritt and Wilson on the south bank. After the Yankees had moved on, the pursuit columns crossed the stream and reunited at Beaver Dam Station. They found the depot a smoking ruin. Having captured the place at dusk the previous evening, Sheridan's men had torched most of it, but only after liberating almost four hundred captured Federals from trains that were conveying them to prison in Richmond.[7]

Although he had telegraphed the authorities in Richmond to prepare to repel another cavalry raid, Stuart was not convinced that Sheridan intended to attack the city. He might have learned from the mistakes of Kilpatrick, in which case he would probably strike, instead, the railroads above the capital. A well-delivered blow against those lines would do as much to disrupt the armies of the South as an attack on the nerve center of the Confederate government. To cover all possibilities, Stuart again split his command. Now Gordon would harass Sheridan's rear while Stuart, with Fitz Lee's men, raced southeastward to Hanover Junction, where the Virginia Central crossed the Richmond, Fredericksburg & Potomac.

Before Stuart's subordinates went their separate ways, he left them to run an impromptu errand. Accompanied by his aide Andrew Venable, the general headed for the plantation, one and a half miles from Beaver Dam, where Mrs. Stuart was staying as a guest of Col. Edmund Fontaine and his family. There, late in the morning, husband and wife had a brief reunion and Stuart kissed their four-year-old son, James, and the seventeen-month-old daughter they had christened Virginia Pelham in honor of the late, lamented artillerist.[8]

After bidding his family what Venable called "a most affectionate farewell," Stuart galloped back to Beaver Dam. Minutes after arriving, he was leading the way to Hanover Junction. The road was long and the going was frustrating, thanks to the slashings of trees with which the Federals had littered it—Sheridan may have wanted his pursuers to catch him, but he was not going to make it easy for them.

At 9:00 P.M., Stuart finally reached the depot village, where he learned that the Yankees had crossed the South Anna in the direction of Ashland Station on the R, F & P. After a four-hour layover to rest men and horses stressed by days of near-constant service, he pushed on. Hearing that Sheridan had damaged the railroad at Ashland, where his rear guard lingered, he sent thither Tom Munford and the 2nd Virginia. Upon arriving, the colonel chased off stragglers from the 1st Massachusetts Cavalry.[9]

After Munford galloped off, Stuart and Fitz Lee took a course slightly to the east, a more direct route to the capital than the one the Federals were following. A brisk march followed, enabling them to cross Sheridan's path at a point about six miles from Richmond. Stuart and Lee drew rein near Yellow Tavern, the abandoned hostelry at the junction of the Telegraph and Mountain Roads that they and many of their men had passed on the first leg of the Chickahominy Raid.

Immediately upon arriving, Stuart sized up the crossroads as a defensive site. At his command, Wickham and Lomax dismounted most of their men and had them take position on ridges, behind farm fences, and in woods astride the Telegraph Road, facing south and east. About 11:00 A.M., as they were hunkering down for a confrontation, Sheridan's advance came into view along the Mountain Road. Even as Gordon's North Carolinians thudded into its rear, the column advanced to the attack. One of Merritt's brigades went forward to seize the Brook Turnpike, the lower end of the Y formed by the junction of the roads occupied by the opposing forces.[10]

After that opening gambit, there was a lull in the fighting as Sheridan brought the rest of his force onto the field farther north. He did so against heavy opposition from Lomax, whose men scorched the ground on which the Yankees deployed with carbine fire. Meanwhile, Wickham's troopers, on Stuart's right, directed their attention, and their firepower, southward against the Yankees who had taken possession of the turnpike. When, early in the afternoon, newly arrived Federals advanced, dismounted, against Wickham's line, the 5th Virginia counterattacked, sending them scurrying for the cover of woodlots and ravines along the Mountain Road.

Wickham's counterthrust invited a response in turn, which Sheridan made in great strength. Some members of the 5th Virginia were staggered by the onslaught, whereupon Stuart rode up to try to steady their line. In so doing, he confronted their commander, perhaps his most bitter critic in the cavalry's officer corps. This day, however, he had nothing but praise for Henry Clay Pate, who, following the dismissal of the charges Stuart and Rosser had preferred against him, had become colonel of the 5th. Lauding Pate for so resolutely advancing his men, Stuart loudly asked him to maintain his position until Wickham sent up reinforcements. Pate replied, "[I will] hold it until I die, General," and then, unexpectedly, extended his hand to his superior. When Stuart grasped it, two years of antagonism and hard feelings fell away. Minutes after Stuart rode off, the Yankees renewed the attack in overwhelming numbers, swarming over Pate's regiment and killing him.[11]

In midafternoon, having made inroads against the enemy's position, Sheridan moved to exploit his advantage. Three-quarters of Custer's brigade advanced against Lomax on the left flank, hoping to stanch the accurate and nearly incessant fire of Griffin's battery which supported him. Two regiments of Wolverines advanced, dismounted, under cover of their own artillery, followed by a saber charge reminiscent of July 3 at Gettysburg, Custer at the head of the veteran 1st Michigan. Bounding across undulating ground riven with gullies and ridges, the attackers closed the distance to the battery with intimidating speed. In minutes, they were in among Griffin's guns, chasing off supporting troops, temporarily capturing two cannons, and spreading havoc along the Confederate left.[12]

Working closely with its dismounted comrades, the 1st Michigan caught hundreds of Rebels in the jaws of a vise. One Virginian recalled that "the federal lines moved down the road and another force from the opposite direction and a third force across the field, in our front, thus we were surrounded on three sides. The order was given to fall back up a ravine and all who could to save themselves."[13]

Concerned that his entire position would become untenable, Stuart again galloped forward to rally retreating men. But the point along the center of Wickham's line where he sat his gray charger was quickly overrun by the 5th Michigan, one of the regiments whose dismounted advance had paved Custer's way. Stuart had just ordered his old 1st Virginia to counterattack and was emptying

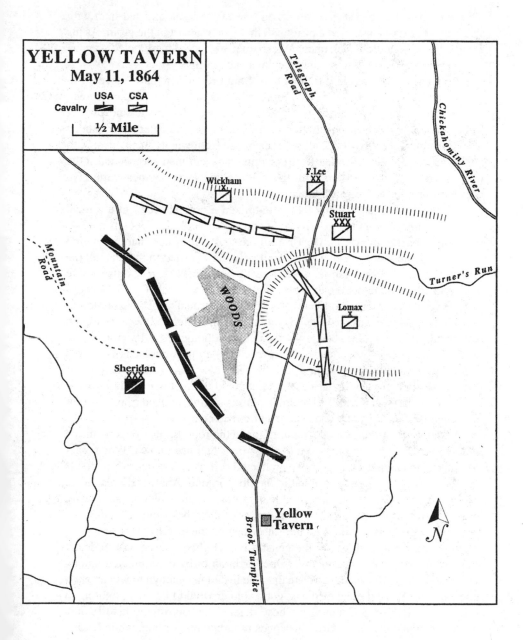

YELLOW TAVERN
May 11, 1864

Cavalry USA CSA

½ Mile

Telegraph Road

Chickahominy River

Wickham

F. Lee

Stuart

Mountain Road

WOODS

Turner's Run

Lomax

Sheridan

Yellow Tavern

Brook Turnpike

N

his revolver at the nearest Federals when one of them, an enlisted man with sharpshooter experience, fired a pistol ball that struck Stuart in the groin. As his assailant's regiment fell back under Wickham's advance, Stuart reeled precariously until one of his officers reached up to steady him.

When the officer asked if he was hurt, Stuart replied in a low voice, "I'm afraid they've killed me, Dorsey." Troopers who saw a crimson stain spread rapidly across the waist of his tunic silently agreed. As Custer and the 1st Michigan continued their penetration of the left flank, one enlarged by Sheridan's commitment of reserves, all sections of the Confederate line appeared to waver, exactly as Stuart had feared. Believing that every man was needed at the front, he resisted being taken from the field, telling everyone near him, "Go back to your men and drive the enemy!"

But it was too late; Custer had destabilized a critical sector at a critical time. In minutes, the gray line—its right and center, as well as its left flank—was falling back, uncovering the Brook Pike and giving Sheridan unfettered access to Richmond. By then Stuart had finally been carried to the rear, all the while exhorting officers and men: "Go back! Go back! Do your duty as I've done mine. I would rather die than be whipped!"[14]

He would experience both fates. As Sheridan gradually took possession of the field, the general was conveyed by ambulance to Richmond, where early on the twelfth he was put into bed at the Grace Street home of his brother-in-law, Dr. Charles Brewer. Brewer and, later, a couple of military surgeons examined the patient's wound and found it inoperable. The bullet had severed blood vessels and perforated Stuart's intestines. He lingered in great pain until 7:40 that night, when he succumbed to internal hemorrhaging and peritonitis—four hours before a hastily summoned Flora could reach his side.[15]

When word of the general's passing made the rounds, his troopers, mired in disastrous defeat, had little time to make their feelings known. When reactions began to circulate, however, they reflected sorrow and regret. "Our grief is real and deeply felt," wrote a diarist in the 9th Virginia. Another diarist, horse artilleryman George Neese, lamented that "a braver and nobler cavalier never drew a sword or wielded a saber." A member of the 5th Virginia called Stuart "the bravest of the brave and ever untiring when on the march."[16]

Many of those with whom the general had clashed praised him in death. Wade Hampton, who eulogized his superior in an order disseminated among the corps on May 16, noted in private that "he lived long enough to win an enviable name for himself & he died as a good soldier would like to do, fighting in a sacred cause & for a Country in whose defense he had offered his life on a hundred battlefields." Even Grumble Jones mourned his passing, while fearing its effects. As the crotchety brigadier, himself only weeks away from death in combat, told one of his officers, "You know I had no love for Stuart, and he just as little for me. But that is the greatest loss the army has ever sustained except the death of Jackson."[17]

Outside of Stuart's kin, the blow fell hardest on his staff officers. William Blackford spoke for the others when he noted that he felt as if he "had lost a brother. It was so hard to realize that he was gone." Many years later, he observed: "I can close my eyes and bring him before me as vividly as though he were there in life. General Stuart had his weaknesses—who has not?—but a braver, truer, or purer man than he has never lived."[18]

But if the general's image never faded from the hearts and minds of those who knew him well, later generations, along with more than a few historians, would recall him as the preening fop he sometimes appeared in life, or as the glory hunter whose grandstanding had cost his army a victory at Gettysburg. His most enduring image would be that of the raider, spreading terror behind enemy lines while laying waste to supply depots and wagon trains. This overemphasis on one facet of Stuart's career would obscure his primary contribution to Confederate fortunes—his unerring ability to provide his superiors with precise, accurate, timely intelligence from which they could deduce both their enemy's movements and intentions. Robert E. Lee defined the true value of his fallen lieutenant when, upon learning of Stuart's death, he exclaimed to his staff, *"He never brought me a piece of false information."*[19]

———◦———

At 3:00 on the stormy morning of May 12, as Stuart lay dying a few miles away, Sheridan's raiders departed the battlefield of Yellow Tavern, heading south. Even as he assimilated the duties and responsibilities that had been thrust upon him, Fitz Lee sought to regroup the brigades, regiments, and companies that Sheridan had uprooted and scattered. Fitz had to do what he could to protect a city that Secretary of War Seddon had recently described as in "hot danger." Richmond was threatened not only on the north by Sheridan, but also from the south by Ben Butler. The politician-general, who had sallied forth from Fort Monroe the day after Meade began crossing the Rapidan, had positioned his two army corps to attack the works at Drewry's Bluff, six miles below the city.[20]

It would have been natural if Fitz Lee had felt a bit overwhelmed by his new situation. Not surprisingly, he made no effort to pursue Sheridan until morning. By the time he had collected enough troops to do so, the raiders had reached some of the same defenses that had stymied Kilpatrick two months earlier. Sheridan elected not to attack them in force. Having bested Stuart, the raiding leader considered his job already done; he did not need to add a captured city to his list of accomplishments. When defenders on either side of the pike fired on the head of his column, Sheridan abruptly veered eastward until he gained the road to Mechanicsville, which led to Meadow Bridge on the Chickahominy. After crossing, he planned to head south to refit his command at Haxall's Landing, Butler's supply depot on the James; he would then return to Meade's army at the same casual pace he had taken to Yellow Tavern.

But when Sheridan reached Meadow Bridge in the murky hours of May 12, his advance found the span partially dismantled. Worse, Fitz Lee, with the few hundred troopers he had assembled thus far, held the far shore. Some of Lee's men occupied entrenchments, while others were dug in along a series of ridges in their rear. To complete the raiders' predicament, James Gordon, whose North Carolinians had been sniping at their heels for the past two days, again came up to flay Sheridan's rear guard.[21]

Demonstrating the strength and confidence they had gained in Sheridan, the Federals shrugged off the gloom and set to work stripping roadside houses for timber with which to shore up the bridge. As the repair crews worked, enough dismounted men crept across the intact portion of the trestle to hold Fitz Lee's followers at bay. At the same time, Gregg turned his division about and lashed out at his tormentors. Several North Carolinians fell, including Gordon himself, who stopped a ball with his left arm. The wound appeared minor, but Gordon died six days later of a hospital-borne infection.[22]

The time having come to fold his hand, Fitz Lee withdrew, allowing his enemy to cross the Chickahominy. As the mighty Union column started on its journey to the James, Confederate scouts followed at a respectful distance. With the remainder of his force, Fitz took position at Mechanicsville, where he was joined by Gordon's men, under Col. Clinton M. Andrews. For the next several days, Robert E. Lee's nephew continued to collect the remnants of the once-mighty Cavalry Corps, A.N.V. He also strove to overcome the effects of nine consecutive days of marching and fighting without adequate rations or ammunition.[23]

For a portion of that period, he stood ready to defend the capital against the Army of the James. After the sixteenth, however, the threat to the south dissipated. On that fog-shrouded morning, troops that had been rushed up from Petersburg and the Carolinas under P. G. T. Beauregard attacked Butler at Drewry's Bluff, dislodged his right flank, and rolled up his battle line like a blue carpet. By late afternoon, the politician-general was heading back to Bermuda Hundred, a fortified peninsula formed by the James and Appomattox Rivers. Beauregard followed and effectively trapped his opponent there.[24]

After Butler's overthrow, there seemed to be nothing to keep Fitz Lee from returning to his relative's army. By the third week in May, the armies above Richmond were nearing the end of one of the war's bloodiest fortnights. Since the eighth, they had been slugging it out on all sides of Spotsylvania, running up long casualty lists without producing the breakthrough Grant desired or the overwhelming counterpunch Lee needed. In a few days, both armies would emulate Sheridan and Stuart by breaking contact and heading for the North Anna, Lee once again hoping to bar his enemy's path to Richmond. Another round of movements, countermovements, and bloodletting would follow.

Throughout this period, Fitz Lee remained miles apart from his army. With Sheridan on the James, and therefore within striking distance of the capital, the officials in Richmond wanted him watched closely. Meanwhile, the A.N.V.

appeared to get along very nicely without a large part of its cavalry arm, supported as it was by the two brigades under Hampton and the single brigade with Rooney Lee. Fitz may have preferred it that way, given that as soon as he rejoined the army, he would come under the authority of Wade Hampton, who, as Stuart's senior subordinate, stood to replace the fallen leader.

In fact, Robert E. Lee held off assigning Hampton to the position until he was certain the planter-turned-soldier was the right man for it. Pending the army leader's ability to render a well-informed evaluation, Fitz would report to Hampton only when their divisions served together. Whenever they operated apart, each man would report directly to army headquarters. While this arrangement appears to have been somewhat awkward and unwieldy, Hampton apparently accepted it with good grace. Fitz embraced it as redounding to his benefit.[25]

The two officers could not indefinitely serve apart. On the seventeenth, Sheridan began his return to Meade's side. When Fitz Lee's scouts informed him that the movement had begun, he placed his reassembled force parallel to the raiders' line of march, keeping between them and Richmond. Sheridan made no attempt to strike the capital; he crossed the Chickahominy at Jones's Bridge and then moved on to the Pamunkey at White House. While sending patrols to harass his enemy, Fitz moved his main body back to Mechanicsville, then to Atlee's Station on the Virginia Central. By the twenty-fourth, Sheridan had rejoined Meade near Chesterfield Station on the R, F & P as the Army of the Potomac poised to leave the North Anna for points unknown to its enemy.[26]

After Sheridan passed him by, Fitz Lee took on a mission at the request of Jefferson Davis's military advisor, Braxton Bragg. On the twenty-third, a large detachment from Lee's division followed the north bank of the James all the way to Charles City County. There it prepared to attack Wilson's Wharf, a fortified outpost recently established by Ben Butler. The position, which one Confederate described as a "formidable octagonal earthwork mounting six guns surrounded by a moat 9 to 12 feet wide," was held by several hundred U.S. Colored Troops, who, simply by being in the neighborhood, had made themselves obnoxious to local secessionists.

Assaulting fixed fieldworks was not a proper mission of cavalry—Bragg should have known it; assuredly Fitz Lee did. But Fitz had agreed to the assignment, like the good soldier he was. Late on the morning of the twenty-fourth, following an all-night, twenty-five-mile trek from Atlee's Station, he confronted the fort and found it inherently stronger and held in greater force that he had been led to believe by citizens "upon whose accounts the expedition had been sent. [I] nevertheless resolved to make an attempt for the capture of the place now that the march had been made."[27]

He lived to regret his decision, but not all of his men did. After a surrender demand was rejected by the fort's commander, Brig. Gen. Edward A. Wild, Fitz made a brief demonstration against its west face, then struck from the east with several hundred men, most of them from Wickham's brigade. Before well across the moat-bordered plain that fronted the works, dozens of troopers fell to rifle fire and the salvos of gunboats anchored in the James. When survivors turned around, they found it more deadly to retreat than to advance. The first wave of attack cost Lee ten men killed and almost fifty wounded. There was no second wave—he called off the effort following a personal reconnaissance that he should have made much sooner. Not long afterward, a somber group of cavalrymen trotted back to Richmond to the accompaniment of the triumphal cheers of black soldiers. The participants would not soon forget their experience this day. Forty years later, one recalled it as "the most useless sacrifice of time and men and horses made during the war."[28]

>─┤◆>─○─<◆┤─<

As it turned out, Fitz Lee did not have to leave the Richmond area to rejoin the army; the army rejoined him. On the evening of the twenty-seventh, Robert E. Lee, while pursuing Grant and Meade toward the Pamunkey, halted adjacent to his nephew's headquarters at Atlee's Station. When Hampton and Rooney Lee arrived soon afterward, the cavalry corps was united for the first time since the Yankees crossed the Rapidan. For the first time, too, Fitz found himself, at least temporarily, under Wade Hampton's authority. He also found his division reduced to its original size, with Gordon's brigade being returned to his cousin Rooney.[29]

Comparing notes with the new arrivals, Fitz learned that for the past eighteen days, they had been guarding the army's flanks and rear while seeking to attack those same sectors of Meade's army. A good deal of their time had been taken up observing enemy movements and reporting them to Robert E. Lee. The thoroughness with which the cavalry had performed the intelligence-gathering mission was a tribute to J. E. B. Stuart's memory and a mark of his legacy to the army.

At Spotsylvania, Lee had relied on his horsemen to follow the many shifts of position Meade's army underwent in response to Grant's strategy. On the fifteenth, Rosser's brigade had made a dangerous reconnaissance along the plank road toward Fredericksburg to bring Lee critical information on the position and movements of the Union right flank. Intelligence gathering had become especially important after Grant and Meade left Spotsylvania. On the twenty-first, as they began to swing toward the North Anna, Hampton and Rooney Lee not only had monitored the Union movement toward Hanover Junction, but also had slowed and diverted it whenever opportunity arose.[30]

When the three mounted divisions of the A.N.V. came together at Atlee's, the Army of the Potomac was again on the march, having quietly vacated the North Anna on the evening of the twenty-sixth. Grant's opponent had been left in the dark as to his intentions; again he had asked the cavalry to determine where the Army of the Potomac was going, and by which route. Now Fitz Lee could join the hunt.

For several hours after the army reached Atlee's Station, Fitz's inclusion did not appear to help. By the morning of the twenty-eighth, the rationale behind the Federals' maneuvering continued to escape Robert E. Lee. Lee knew that the previous morning Torbert's and Gregg's divisions of cavalry had crossed the Pamunkey at Hanovertown Ferry, about seven miles east of Atlee's Station. A division of infantry had accompanied the troopers but had remained on the riverbank while the horsemen ranged inland. The rest of Meade's army had not shown up. Perhaps it never would—perhaps the cavalry movement was a blind to mask the real crossing somewhere else. If so, where? To plot countermoves, Lee needed to know, and quickly.[31]

This, then, was the basis of Wade Hampton's first assignment in command of more than a single division of horsemen. Early on the twenty-eighth, he started for the Pamunkey with Rosser's brigade, Wickham's brigade of Lee's division, and half of Rooney Lee's command (the other half, formerly Gordon's brigade, was already in contact with Torbert and Gregg). Another participant in the mission was the main body of the brigade Hampton had carved out for his old subordinate, Butler. Although Butler himself, who was again fit for field duty, was still on the road to Virginia, two of the regiments earmarked for him—the 4th and 5th South Carolina Cavalry—had reached Richmond by train on the twenty-third and twenty-fourth. The entire 5th was available for active service, along with about half the 4th. The remainder of the 4th and the entire 6th South Carolina were en route from their home state along with Butler. In his absence, the new arrivals were led by Col. B. Huger Rutledge of the 4th.[32]

The 5th South Carolina, under Col. John Dunovant, had already seen action in Virginia, having accompanied Fitz Lee on the expedition to Wilson's Wharf. While the disastrous assault of the twenty-fourth was a poor way to begin its association with the Army of Northern Virginia, Dunovant's outfit had not made the day's casualty list. Having survived its initial outing, its men hoped they would enjoy a more promising opportunity to contribute to the fortunes of Robert E. Lee.

Some of their new comrades did not like the South Carolinians' prospects. They were, to use a common term of derision, "bandbox" regiments, not only because they stocked a full complement of officers and men, in contrast to the thinned ranks of Hampton's veteran outfits, but also because they were garbed in neat, even snazzy uniforms, their officers wearing white cotton gloves. In addition to a shiny new Enfield, each newcomer toted enough equipment to outfit a squadron. Yet the rookies would soon prove they were not afraid to get *Grant's* their hands, uniforms, or weapons dirty.[33] *pontoon bridge*

About 10:00 on that pleasant morning in late May, Hampton's mixed force neared Hanovertown, where a freshly laid pontoon bridge suggested—but did not prove—that Grant was about to cross the Pamunkey in force. A few miles from the ferry, the Confederates met the head of Sheridan's column, which appeared to be engaged in a reconnaissance of its own. In fact, Grant was as ignorant of his enemy's position and heading as Lee was of his; he had dis-patched the cavalry toward Mechanicsville to determine which, if any, Confed-erates were in his front. The opposing horsemen collided near a crossroads landmark familiar from the Peninsula Campaign, Haw's Shop.

Sheridan's men had gotten there first. David Gregg, leading Sheridan's advance, had sized up the place, where several roads connected the Pamunkey River country with the Richmond vicinity, as a possible staging area for Grant's continuing journey toward the James. But before Gregg could secure the cross-roads, Hampton's men arrived and drove in the Yankee pickets stationed on the road to Mechanicsville. The vedettes retreated to a point west of Haw's Shop, where high ground made for a good defensive position. As Gregg dug in to await reinforcement by Torbert—who, with Sheridan, was well to the rear— Hampton staked out a position atop a parallel ridge a few hundred yards farther west. Beside a whitewashed chapel known as Enon Church, his men con-structed fallen-log and fence-rail breastworks. As soon as the barricades had taken shape, Hampton stocked them with dismounted men—hundreds of them. In fact, he unhorsed almost every trooper within his range of vision and had them pop away at the enemy with their rifles and carbines.[34]

His men appreciated the novelty of the deployment. In every fight they had waged since 1861, a certain percentage of them had always served on foot. Usually, however, it had been only a couple of companies per regiment, a few squadrons per brigade. Over the years, Stuart had slowly increased the number he committed to battle dismounted, but nothing like this. Within minutes of the opening shots at Haw's Shop, more than half of Hampton's three thousand troopers were rooted to the ground, opposed by approximately equal numbers of dismounted Yankees. Fitz Lee's division held the right of the line, with Rosser's brigade on its left and W. H. F. Lee to the left and rear of Rosser. Later in the fight, however, Rooney Lee led most of his men on a circuitous attempt to turn Gregg's right, effectively removing his command from the fight.

Many Confederates would mark this day as the start of a new regime—the first of many engagements in which their enemy wondered whether they were facing foot soldiers. In fact, Hampton's men would learn to think of themselves as "Riding Infantry." Once a pejorative term in the Cavalry, A.N.V., it would take on a new connotation under Stuart's successor. The men would come to glory in their ability not merely to seize a position for other troops to occupy, but also to "hold a line of battle as well as our veteran infantry."[35]

Some troopers identified another feature of Hampton's generalship. They were impressed that when starting for Haw's Shop, he had taken not just a por-tion of the force available to him, but everyone Robert E. Lee did not hold back to support the main army. As Capt. Frank Myers of the 35th Virginia put it, on the twenty-eighth of May, he and his comrades discovered "a vast difference between the old and the new, for while General Stuart would attempt his work with whatever force he had at hand, and often seemed to try to accomplish a given result with the smallest possible number of men, Gen. Hampton always endeavored to carry every available man to his point of operation, and the larger the force the better he liked it." The better the men liked it, too: In strength there was security. In the past, they sometimes had the uncomfortable feeling that Stuart deliberately minimized his field force to show contempt for the enemy or to demonstrate that the Confederate trooper sneered at long odds.[36]

On the present occasion, the power generated by Hampton's sizable force won the day, although the outcome may not have been evident to everyone. For the better part of six hours, the opposing cavalries slugged it out from behind their barriers. Each alternately seized, then lost, the initiative. At first Gregg's men were roughly handled and portions of their line were driven in, especially when, in the middle of the afternoon, Rosser's brigade made a strong advance against the Union center under a barrage from several batteries of what was still known as the Stuart Horse Artillery. Twice, however, the hard-pressed Federals were reinforced, first by another element of Gregg's division, and late in the afternoon by Custer's brigade of Torbert's newly arrived command.

The battle appeared to turn when, sometime after 4:00 P.M., Custer's Wolverines charged forward afoot on both sides of the road, overrunning a position whose occupants had run low on ammunition. But by now Hampton had acquired a large number of prisoners, some of whom turned out to be infantrymen. Their presence in Gregg's sector told the cavalry commander what his superior had sent him to discover: that Meade's army was crossing the river at Hanovertown. "The object of the reconnaissance having been accomplished," Hampton observed, "I ordered my command to withdraw."[37]

Wickham's and Rosser's men, being veterans, promptly disengaged. The process was speeded up when Custer attacked. Struck while in motion, an unusually large number of Confederates fell into Union hands. Hampton's pullback and the losses it incurred made many Federals believe they had won the day, whereas Hampton's men had demonstrated a remarkable tenacity throughout the fight. Some were still showing it: Even when Hampton called retreat, Rutledge's South Carolinians refused to abandon their position on the right. With their long-range Enfields, they continued to take a toll of Custer's men long after their comrades had uncovered both of their flanks. Among those who fell to their fire was Pvt. John Huff of the 5th Michigan, who had been credited with mortally wounding Stuart.[38]

The South Carolinians exasperated Hampton, who personally went forward to haul them to the rear minutes before they could be surrounded and cut off. Their stubbornness cost them a long casualty list, but it also impressed many veterans. They had made an impression on their enemy as well. Once Hampton quit the field, burial details worked past midnight to inter the 127 dead who had been left behind. The gravediggers commented on the fact that so many of those they shoveled under wore white gloves.

[handwritten margin notes: COLD HARBOR / Grant's biggest mistake]

After Haw's Shop, Grant had Sheridan fall back to the Pamunkey, where the cavalry reestablished contact with the rest of Meade's army. Then, on the twenty-ninth, Sheridan was sent southeastward toward Cold Harbor. That nondescript cluster of dwellings, only lightly held by the enemy, would provide a stepping-stone for what Grant hoped would be the last leg of his journey to Richmond, only ten miles to the southwest. Troops holding the roads that ran through the Cold Harbor vicinity would command access to White House on the lower Pamunkey; Grant planned to make that venerable site, for the second time in this war, a supply base for the Army of the Potomac.

Sheridan's enemy anticipated his movement. On the thirty-first, Fitz Lee, whose division had returned to Atlee's Station after the fight at Haw's Shop, took up picket duties at Cold Harbor, relieving a detachment of those green but gritty South Carolinians. The newcomers were now under their designated leader, Brigadier General Butler, who had reached Richmond on the evening of the recent battle, two weeks short of a year after losing his foot at Brandy Station. His new cork limb tucked inside high-topped boots, Butler climbed into the saddle minutes after alighting from the train at Atlee's. To those who came out to welcome him back, he joked, "I am not much of a pedestrian, but in the saddle, I am as good as ever."[39] *Manly bravado*

While Butler and his new command went to the rear to get acquainted, Fitz Lee's men dug in north of Cold Harbor, sensing that the enemy was about to challenge them. At 3:30 that afternoon, Sheridan's advance, Torbert's division, came calling, only to withdraw under a torrent of carbine and rifle fire. Soon after the Yankees drew off, Lee was joined by the advance of Maj. Gen. Robert F. Hoke's infantry division. But before the infantry could fashion a new set of fieldworks, Torbert renewed his attack. This time he was supported by Gregg's division and, at greater distance, by the V Corps. After an "obstinate fight," lasting upward of three hours, Lee and his infantry friends were driven from their works, shortly before the balance of Hoke's command could come up to secure it. Sheridan claimed his opponents retreated a mile or more; Fitz Lee insisted he fell back a quarter of a mile.[40]

Fitz's division held its new position into the early afternoon of June 1, when Sheridan's men abruptly vacated their ground. Aware that Union infantry was pouring into the area, Fitz did not reoccupy his old works, but Sheridan did, later in the day, after Meade ordered him back to the village. Afterward Fitz, along with Butler's brigade, fell back to Bottom's Bridge to block any attempt by Meade to cross the Chickahominy. He remained in that area for the next two days, picketing up and down the river, while the main bodies of both armies staged a violent confrontation outside Cold Harbor. On the first, the Army of the Potomac attacked Lee's well-entrenched position, gaining some ground but not enough to claim victory. Two days later Grant had Meade attack in greater force—with catastrophic results. Secure behind their artillery-studded works, Lee's troops blew apart a series of uncoordinated attacks, killing or wounding almost seven thousand Yankees while absorbing fewer than fifteen hundred casualties.[41]

[handwritten margin notes: 7000 U.S. cas. no lie]

While Fitz Lee guarded the far right of the army, Hampton's old division had been holding the center near Atlee's, and W. H. F. Lee's the left, or upper, flank, in the vicinity of Hanover Court House. On the thirty-first, Rooney's men were attacked near the courthouse by Wilson's division. Aware that infantry lurked in Wilson's rear, the army leader's son withdrew across the tracks of the Virginia Central toward Ashland Station on the R, F & P, site of the camp of instruction where thousands of Southern boys had learned the basics of cavalry life in 1861–62. Hampton promptly reinforced Rooney with three of Rosser's regiments, which struck the rear of Wilson's column while it was in motion.

For the second time in less than a month, the Laurel Brigade threw Wilson's command into disorder and panic. Hampton, who had assumed command of a portion of Rooney Lee's division, noted, "[The] combined assaults were completely successful, the enemy giving way at all points . . . [and we] pursued until night forced us to halt." One of Rosser's troopers summed up the fight in his own way: "We went around and got into the rear and charged them and what we did not capture or kill, we ran . . . for several miles." The only shadow on the day's success was the severe wounding of Pierce Young, whom Hampton had placed in command of Lee's North Carolina brigade until a permanent successor to Gordon could be appointed. Young's loss forced state and Confederate officials to agree on a replacement, one from North Carolina. On June 6, Rufus Barringer was appointed brigadier general to lead the brigade.[42]

Following the fight at Ashland, Hampton's troopers resumed their position in the center of the army and Rooney Lee's on the left. On the third, while the fighting raged at Cold Harbor, Rooney's troops reconnoitered toward Haw's Shop, under Hampton's supervision. Upon arriving, they confirmed the accuracy of a report that Wilson's horsemen had reoccupied the breastworks the antagonists had thrown up on the twenty-eighth. At Hampton's order, Lee dismounted his North Carolinians and sent them, under Col. John A. Baker, to drive the Yankees out. Through inspired use of the dismounted tactics that Hampton favored, Baker's men maneuvered the Yankees out of three lines of works and into full retreat.

It was only the latest in a series of successes that had begun with Hampton's rise to cavalry seniority—successes that appeared to have defied all the odds. As one of Fitz Lee's officers put it, Sheridan had crossed the Pamunkey expecting to pave Grant's way to Richmond, only to run aground against "Hampton's half fed, half armed, half mounted, ill-disciplined yet ubiquitous and resolute cavalry."[43]

>—+—◆>—O—<◆—+—◄

Sobered by the carnage on the first and third, the armies did not clash again at full strength at Cold Harbor, but neither did they break contact. For several days, they glowered at each other across the sun-baked meadows that held the bodies of hundreds of Union soldiers. Not until the seventh did the antagonists agree to a truce during which to inter the rotting corpses. Throughout this period, their mounted forces were largely quiescent, catching their breath after weeks of incessant activity.

After June 4, Hampton began to suspect that the Yankees in his front had fallen back; fewer and fewer of them were in evidence. But it was the eighth before he had an inkling of what was going on. That day his scouts reported that Sheridan had crossed most or all of his command to the north side of the Pamunkey, preparatory to moving—somewhere. Later reports had the Yankees moving up the south side of the Mattapony River in the direction of Gordonsville. At once Hampton suspected what was afoot. By signal and by written dispatch, he communicated the information to army headquarters along with his opinion that Sheridan intended to raid the Virginia Central near Gordonsville or Charlottesville, perhaps in cooperation with Union forces operating near Lynchburg.

Years later, the South Carolinian succinctly explained what followed: "I urged the Genl. Comdg. to allow me to concentrate the cavalry & pursue him. After a full consultation, he directed me to carry out the plan I had proposed."[44]

Chapter Twenty-one

Under New Management

Those same interior lines that had saved Lee's army so often over the past three weeks served Hampton well as he pursued Sheridan's latest raid. The Yankees had to move well to the north before turning west and marching fifty miles to reach that stretch of the Virginia Central that Grant wished destroyed. For Hampton, it was a quicker and simpler matter to follow the railroad, not merely shadowing Little Phil but keeping ahead of him. When Sheridan slowed his march to strike targets of opportunity such as the R, F & P, which he crossed at Polecat Station on June 8, Hampton was able to get even farther ahead of him. The result was that on the tenth, when the raiders finally turned south toward the Virginia Central, their pursuers were squarely across their path.

Because Hampton and Fitz Lee had begun the pursuit miles apart, they were miles apart still. Hampton, with the brigades of Rosser, Butler, and Young (the last-named led by Colonel Wright of Cobb's Legion), took position just below Sheridan's presumed target, Trevilian Station, twenty-five miles northeast of Charlottesville. Lee, with the brigades of Wickham and Lomax, was stationed a little more than four miles to the southeast, outside Louisa Court House. Rooney Lee's division remained with the main army, a concession Hampton had made to Rooney's father because it had become known that Sheridan had left Wilson's division behind to screen Meade's march toward Richmond.[1]

On the morning of the eleventh, as the Yankees approached the railroad, Hampton prepared to link with the just-arrived Lee to defend as wide a stretch as possible of this railroad, the Army of Northern Virginia's principal link with the Shenandoah Valley, the "Breadbasket of the Confederacy." When he and Fitz joined hands, Hampton would be able to pit close to sixty-five hundred troopers against the more than nine thousand following Sheridan. The disparity appeared to place the Confederates at a severe disadvantage, but it was a condition that Hampton, like every Confederate cavalry leader, had learned to live with long ago.

Outnumbered or not, Hampton resolved to land the first blow. According to his plan, which he had carefully communicated to his subordinates, including

Fitz, the brigades of Butler and Wright would engage the head of Sheridan's column, occupying it until, at an opportune moment, Lee came in on the Union left flank. It was a tried-and-true strategy that had proven effective on several occasions, notably at Buckland Mills. Since it had succeeded for Lee and Stuart, Hampton saw no reason why it would not work for Lee and him. And to prevent Sheridan from employing the same tactic, Hampton had stationed Rosser's brigade west of Trevilian to guard his left rear.[2]

So promising a plan should not have broken down early in the execution, but it did. When Merritt's brigade of Torbert's division approached the depot just after 5:00 A.M., Hampton's men galloped up the Clayton's Store Road to meet it. Two miles above Trevilian, they halted the long blue column by cutting loose with carbines, rifles, and pistols; a few traditionalists flailed about with sabers. Almost immediately, men on both sides jumped from their saddles to fight on foot behind cover. And cover here was plentiful, for the road was lined on both sides with what one Union officer called "one of the thickest tangles of brush that I have ever seen." For a time, it was the madness of the Wilderness all over again, with troopers enclosed on all sides by rank vegetation, unable to distinguish friend from foe even at arm's length.[3]

The confused fighting went on for several hours under a blistering sun, neither side able to gain the upper hand, principally because neither commander was willing to commit his entire force. Late in the morning, Sheridan added Devin's brigade to the fray, but he kept Gregg's division well in the rear, guarding his column's ambulance train. For his part, Hampton was reluctant to call in Rosser unless the fight clearly appeared to go against him. The one component he did intend to add to the fight—Fitz Lee's division—failed to come up as planned. Hampton's staff officers, if not Hampton himself, regarded Lee's non-appearance as proof of his unwillingness to support any superior other than J. E. B. Stuart.[4] (west point men)

The situation worsened when, in midmorning, Hampton discovered that Custer's brigade had interposed between the rail depot and Louisa Court House via a diagonal track through the forest that placed it in rear of Butler and Wright. South of the railroad, Custer's advance was struck a glancing blow by Lee's division, which made a belated appearance from the vicinity of the courthouse. Leaving one of his four regiments to deal with Lee, Custer continued south until he was in position to strike Hampton from behind while the rest of Torbert's men continued to press him in front. Then a more tempting objective came into view: the hundreds of mounts being held in rear of Hampton's firing line, whose vulnerability constituted one of the few drawbacks of dismounted fighting. Quickly changing direction, Custer made for the horse herds; within minutes, fifteen hundred or more animals were being led away from their owners.[5]

But they were not moved far enough, or fast enough, from the front. Before the herd could be placed in a position where its recovery seemed unlikely, a wave of dismounted Rebels swept down from the north and east. Having been dislodged from their brush-covered position when Sheridan finally reinforced

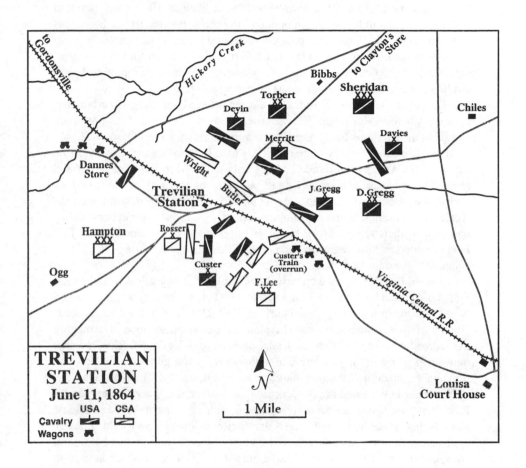

to Gordonsville

to Clayton's Store

Hickory Creek

Bibbs

Sheridan
XXX

Chiles

Torbert
XX

Devin
X

Merritt
X

Davies
X

Wright

Dannes
Store

Trevilian
Station

Butler

J.Gregg
X

D.Gregg
XX

Hampton
XXX

Rosser
X

Custer's
Train
(overrun)

Ogg

Custer
X

F.Lee
XX

Virginia Central R.R

Louisa
Court House

**TREVILIAN
STATION**
June 11, 1864

        USA   CSA
Cavalry
Wagons

N

1 Mile

Merritt and Devin with a brigade from Gregg's division, the Confederates were making a mad dash to the rear, and their mounts. On the way, they sliced through Custer's ranks, isolating regiments and companies from each other. To make matters worse for the Wolverines, the troopers of Custer's old friend Rosser galloped up from the northwest, having been sent for after Hampton spied dust clouds in his rear. Hampton and Rosser, supported by the horse batteries of Hart and Thomson, pressed their opponents simultaneously from north, west, and southwest, while Fitz Lee's men flooded in from Louisa to prevent Custer from fleeing eastward. The cooperative venture Hampton had plotted had come into being, albeit not as he had envisioned.[6]

Caught in the jaws of a gray vise, Custer suffered upward of four hundred casualties before Merritt and Devin broke through to him in late afternoon, releasing the pressure being applied from the north. By then Custer's supply train had been captured. His horse artillery avoided the same fate by a narrow margin. The Wolverine Brigade had not only survived to fight again, but had also done considerable damage with its seven-shooters; Confederate casualties included Rosser, who received a leg wound from which he spent the next ten weeks convalescing. Some of Hampton's men sensed that a great opportunity had slipped their grasp. "If we had been supported," complained one of Fitz Lee's troopers, whose regiment had come within an ace of carting off a Union cannon, "we would have destroyed Custer's brigade."[7]

The Wolverines' escape effectively ended the fighting this day; thereafter, both sides pulled back to the positions they had held at the outset and remained there, sparring at long range, until darkness fell. Despite the day's listless conclusion, Hampton suspected that Sheridan had not given up hope of damaging the railroad; thus the Confederate leader planned to defend the tracks for a second day. During the night, Fitz Lee, supported by the guns of Johnston and Shoemaker, made a circuitous march to join him west of Trevilian. One can only wonder how heated the conversation grew when the generals met face-to-face. Hampton could not have been pleased with Lee's performance this day, and whether or not he believed Lee's dereliction deliberate, he would certainly have demanded the reasons for it. In his report of the action, which he did not compile until after the war, Fitz stated only that the point at which he was to join Hampton was "too distant" from Louisa Court House. He would have had to do better than that when Hampton confronted him.[8]

In marching to Trevilian, Sheridan had intended not only to damage the railroad, but also to link near Charlottesville with the small army of Maj. Gen. David Hunter, who was to have accompanied him to Meade's army. Now, however, Sheridan learned from his prisoners that the undependable Hunter was nowhere near Charlottesville, thus defeating Grant's strategy. Therefore, come daylight, Little Phil intended to damage the railroad on either side of the depot—his men had already done so to a limited extent—and then return to Meade's side.[9]

On the morning of June 12, Hampton patiently waited for his opponents to finish their rail wrecking. But the work was still under way when, about 3:00 P.M., Sheridan detached Torbert's division and sent it out the Gordonsville road toward a perpendicular byway that led north to Mallory's Ford. At that commodious crossing point, Little Phil wished to cross the North Anna to start his homeward jaunt. Instead, two and a half miles west of Trevilian, Torbert encountered the Confederates, most of whom had dug in along the railroad embankment and behind adjacent earthworks that looked as if they had been built with care.

At Sheridan's order, but against the better judgment of some of his officers, Torbert attacked all along the Rebel line. He gained a modicum of ground to the south against Fitz Lee's works, but the success there was short-lived. When he attempted to skirt the upper flank of Hampton's division along the right-of-way, he found the going just as tough. Hampton would claim to have repulsed no fewer than five assaults, without incurring heavy loss.

One reason for Hampton's success was that with all his forces on hand, he could compel Lee's cooperation. When, late in the day, Torbert bolstered Merritt's efforts against the Rebel left with portions of Devin's brigade, Custer's men, weakened from their recent pummeling, failed to contain Lee's division. While Lomax's men remained in position to occupy the Wolverines, Wickham's rushed north to reinforce Rosser, Butler, and Wright. The result was that Merritt was repulsed even more decisively than before. Many of Hampton's men applauded the realization that they were fighting "infantry style." That mode of warfare appealed especially to the veterans in Butler's brigade, who favored marksmanship over horsemanship: "We understood the art of shooting, and we shot to kill and did kill lots of them. Next morning, the 13th, we found the field in our front covered with their dead and wounded."[10]

Although unable to make headway toward Mallory's Ford, Sheridan and Torbert maintained contact with their enemy until after dark. Dawn, however, found them gone, having retreated by the same road they had taken to Trevilian. They had carried off four hundred wounded, while leaving another fifty or so on the field, along with almost a thousand dead and four hundred-some prisoners. By all indications, Sheridan's raid had been a failure. He had broken the Virginia Central, but the damage was readily repairable. Moreover, Hampton and Lee had whipped him as soundly as he had whipped Stuart at Yellow Tavern, and with two-thirds the resources Sheridan had enjoyed on May 11.[11]

>─┼─◇─○─◇─┼─◄

After the raiders departed, burial details gathered up the dozens of corpses that strewed the dusty ground leading to Hampton's breastworks. Before morning was over, the Confederates had started on their homeward pursuit. They moved in two parallel columns, Hampton by the way he had come, Fitz Lee following the track Sheridan had taken to Trevilian via Chilesburg and New Market.

Fitz's route may have been Hampton's idea, as it was found to be "perfumed with dead horses abandoned and shot by the enemy."[12]

Sheridan was also traveling on a parallel road, although he had placed an additional barrier between him and his opponents by crossing the Mattapony River, as well as the North Anna. Still, he was near enough to tangle with the Confederates had he wished to. Several times on the return, Hampton gave him the opportunity to do so, but each time Little Phil declined. Hampton then decided to attack a position Sheridan would have to defend. Late on the nineteenth, he forged ahead of the Yankees en route to White House. That landing on the Pamunkey had completed its second stint as a supply depot for Union forces operating against Richmond. All but abandoned, it still held the nine hundred-wagon train of Sheridan's corps, which he had been ordered to escort to the rear of the army, now well to the south of White House.

Hampton reached the landing half a day ahead of Sheridan but did not move against it till the next morning. At 7:00 A.M. on the twentieth, having positioned the guns of Hart, Shoemaker, Johnston, and Thomson on an elevation west of White House, he opened fire on all parts of the base, as well as on the caretaker force under Brig. Gen. John J. Abercrombie. While Hampton's troopers awaited the word to attack, for two hours the horse batteries rained shells on warehouses, wharves, and railroad facilities while also exchanging fire with land-based artillery and with a couple of gunboats that had ventured up from the York River.

The naval vessels provided the most formidable opposition. One of Thomson's men, who had a flair for imagery, observed, "The gun boats have opened on us with 150 pound shells, crashing [into] the trees over us. . . . It looks like an angry devil as she vomits forth her fiery hell."[13]

By late morning, Hampton believed the garrison had been sufficiently softened to take by storm. He was about to give the order to go forward when Fitz Lee, for whom the undertaking was all too reminiscent of Wilson's Wharf, objected. Lieutenant Hubard of the 3rd Virginia could understand why: "We had no scaling ladders, our guns [were] a good way off . . . [and] our two divisions had been smartly cut up & so many horses broken down that taking 1/4 to hold horses we hadn't more than 1500 in line." Hubard, for one, was glad when "the remonstrances of Genl. Lee prevailed, [and] the assault was given up." The men went into camp a short distance south of the base, near St. Peter's Church. A few hours later, Sheridan's advance crossed the Pamunkey to secure the landing, chasing away Hampton's rear guard.[14]

By now Hampton had relinquished his hopes of corralling the immense supply train that Sheridan was about to escort south. He was not willing, however, to give the Federals a clear path to the Chickahominy and the James. Hampton realized that his adversary intended to cross both rivers because they barred him from Grant's and Meade's latest position. During the twelve days Hampton and Sheridan had traveled to and from Trevilian Station, the war had moved well south of where they had left it. After the repulse at Cold Harbor, Grant realized that Lee had shoved him too far northeast of Richmond to continue his drive on the Rebel capital—he lacked the room for another attempt to outflank his opponent. After much deliberation, on the twelfth he began pulling out of Cold Harbor with as much stealth as a one hundred thousand-man army could muster. Various stratagems permitted Grant to steal a long march on Lee. By the thirteenth, he put some of Meade's troops across the James on pontoons and transports. Two days later, a mighty attack column was hammering at the door to Petersburg, twenty-two miles south of Richmond, the supply center that linked the capital to the Confederate interior. Petersburg's geography was such that its fall would probably cause Richmond to be evacuated—it should at least force Lee's army to wander across the countryside in search of substitute supply lines, leaving itself vulnerable to the forces of Meade and Butler.

[handwritten margin note: Defended by P.G.T's 8,000 Men. My God.]

All of this Wade Hampton knew, or had discerned, by the third week of June. He was also aware that the surprise assault on Petersburg had failed through a chain of circumstances that might be described as divine intervention in the Confederacy's behalf. For three days after his enemy left his front, R. E. Lee, his reconnaissance capabilities depleted by Hampton's detaching, had remained ignorant of Grant's destination. Eventually, the pleas of Petersburg's commander galvanized him into action. By the fifteenth, he had begun to move south, and by the eighteenth—granted the necessary time by Meade's poorly coordinated, error-plagued offensive—his army had secured the "Cockade City."[15]

[handwritten margin note: P.G.T]

On the twenty-first, Sheridan began moving south, his march slowed almost to a crawl by the wagons. Most of his adversaries followed, sniping at the train. Fitz Lee's men, meanwhile, had been returned to the banks of the Chickahominy, where they might block Sheridan's access to the stream. On the river, Fitz connected with the troopers of his cousin. For the past two weeks, Rooney Lee had been dogging Meade's advance to the Chickahominy and the James, seeking to penetrate the counterreconnaissance screen that Wilson's horsemen had erected. Although unable to stop the Army of the Potomac short of its destination, his men had earned their pay in sweat and blood, especially when opposed by the foot soldiers in Wilson's rear, as occurred frequently.[16]

Now the job of stopping a Yankee drive to the James had been entrusted to Wade Hampton. He looked forward to the opportunity, although after the twenty-second, he feared he would be able to devote only a portion of his attention and resources to it. That morning, as Sheridan left White House for Jones's Bridge on the Chickahominy, Wilson, now ensconced southeast of Petersburg with the bulk of Meade's army, started on a raid of his own, against the railroads that served the Cockade City. Those communications were so vital to the continued existence of the Army of Northern Virginia that Rooney Lee, with a portion of his command, was quickly put on Wilson's trail.

Before his own division could be ordered to assist in the effort, Hampton moved to strike Sheridan. He would do so with Butler's and Rosser's brigades (the latter led by Col. Richard H. Dulany following Rosser's wounding), plus Wickham's brigade of Fitz Lee's division and Chambliss's brigade, which

Rooney Lee had left behind when starting after Wilson. To this force, Hampton added a cavalry brigade formed eleven days earlier, consisting of the "mounted infantry" of the Hampton Legion and two cavalry regiments recently arrived in Richmond, the 7th South Carolina and the 24th Virginia. This slightly ragtag force, which would continue to serve north of the James after the rest of Robert E. Lee's cavalry moved to Petersburg, had been entrusted to a fellow South Carolinian—in fact, a protégé of Hampton's—Brig. Gen. Martin W. Gary.[17]

Hampton found no opportunity to pitch into Sheridan short of Jones's Bridge, so he crossed the Chickahominy farther upstream, then hastened south. On the afternoon of the twenty-fourth, he landed hard on Gregg's division, which had dug in near Nance's Shop and Samaria (the Yankees called it "St. Mary's") Church, on the road to Charles City. Gregg, who had been assigned to guard the rear while Sheridan ferried Torbert's division and the supply train across the James at Douthat's Landing, was so far from the nearest support he was virtually isolated—in other words, a ready-made target.

With horse batteries and dismounted carbineers up front, mounted men held ready in the rear, Hampton attacked Gregg's works at Samaria Church from several directions, while moving to interpose between the enemy and the river. From the start, the several-hour fight had a desperate quality to it, Gregg fighting for the life of his command, Hampton for the security of Petersburg and Richmond. The Confederates' desperation proved mightier; as one of them explained, "The enemy position was a strong one . . . [and] they fought vigorously for a while but as our boys closed in on them they fled and when they broke the mounted cavalry was order[ed] to charge which they did driving pell mell for 3 miles capturing quite a number of prisoners, they leaving their dead and wounded in our care." Other than those he left behind, Gregg escaped with his division intact. Hampton's attempt to cut the road to Charles City had come up short by a few hundred yards.[18]

As he had after the fight at Trevilian Station, Hampton bivouacked on the field of victory. While some of his men buried the dead and tended to the wounded on both sides—fewer than 300 Confederates had become casualties, more than 350 for Gregg—patrols followed the retreating Yankees to the James. For most of Hampton's troopers, however, their service north of the James was almost over. The next morning, as their leader had anticipated, R. E. Lee urged—but did not order—him to join the effort to run down Wilson's raiders. Following Chambliss's detaching, Rooney Lee had taken on that chore with Barringer's brigade, augmented by a Petersburg-based brigade of North Carolina and Georgia troopers of which James Dearing had taken command.[19]

That afternoon, leaving a part of Gary's brigade on the Northside, Hampton led everyone else southwestward toward Richmond. He lingered on the north bank for another day while Sheridan's men boarded transports for a crossing farther downriver. On the twenty-seventh, at Robert E. Lee's imperative order to report at Petersburg, Hampton sent the men and horses of Butler, Dulany, and Chambliss across the pontoon bridge that had been laid near Ben

Butler's old objective, Chaffin's Bluff. Lee's division covered the crossing before following the others over on the twenty-eighth.[20]

While Sheridan put his men in camp near Windmill Point, Hampton's equally weary troopers kept moving. Guides from the main army conducted them to Petersburg across the rear of the forces confronting Butler's enclave at Bermuda Hundred. The horsemen enjoyed no rest stops; their journey did not end until they reached Sappony Church, a crossroads chapel west of Stony Creek Station on the Petersburg & Weldon Railroad. The Weldon line was one of two railroads that Wilson had recently struck in cooperation with Ben Butler's division of cavalry, under Brig. Gen. August V. Kautz.

Hampton, who would be joined near Sappony by two infantry brigades under Maj. Gen. William Mahone, arrived shortly before Wilson and Kautz, returning from damaging the Petersburg & Lynchburg (or Southside) Railroad, came into view from the west, trailed by Rooney Lee, Barringer, and Dearing. A member of Chambliss's brigade observed that "it was an hour or so from the time of our first observation of the enemy before he undertook to force the position—but when he began it seemed as if he would never stop." The strength of the raiding force—thirty-three hundred horsemen and twelve cannons—made it a match for any defender, even infantry. Not surprisingly, the fight lasted, as Wilson himself commented, "with alternating charge and countercharge till nearly midnight without either side gaining any substantial advantage."[21]

Hampton and his comrades intended to continue the fight at daylight, but during the night they learned that Wilson had sent Kautz north to Reams's Station. Kautz's long detour enabled Hampton's main body, along with the more fleet-footed members of Mahone's command, to reach Reams's in time to cut off Kautz's retreat. When the Yankees approached his position in the wee hours of the twenty-ninth, Hampton tore into them, while the troopers he had left at Sappony Church harassed Wilson's withdrawal. When the hard pressed Wilson came up in Kautz's rear, Hampton, with support from Mahone, pummeled him as well.

After a valiant attempt to hold their position, both Union divisions were forced to scatter, every man for himself. To speed their flight, they abandoned every artillery piece, thirty supply wagons (which held a fantastic cache of booty), hundreds of their own men, and an equal number of recently liberated slaves. Because Hampton's troopers were too tired to pursue, and Mahone's too slow, most of the fugitives eventually found their way inside Meade's lines below Petersburg. But theirs had been a narrow escape indeed—another tribute to the power and endurance of soldiers who, while cherishing the memory of J. E. B. Stuart, now thought of themselves as Wade Hampton's cavalry.[22]

>─┤◆>─O─<◆┤─<

The troopers of the A.N.V. had been on the go almost constantly for more than two months; even the hard-driving Hampton recognized their need for a break. So did his superior: When the Federal cavalry began a long, quiet period in rear of their army, Robert E. Lee decreed a time of rest and refurbishment for his horsemen. For the next six weeks, with a single exception, they performed only the routine duties of picketing and reconnoitering. The remainder of each day they spent in their camps south of Petersburg, reacquainting themselves with sleep and food. During this period, Hampton's division held the extreme right of the cavalry's lines in the vicinity of its triumph at Sappony Church; Fitz Lee's horsemen guarded the center, opposite Reams's Station; and Rooney Lee, to whose division Dearing's brigade had been more or less permanently attached, protected the left flank, connecting with the infantry's line below Petersburg.[23]

The only interruption occurred during the last days of July, when Grant sent a mixed force from Meade's and Butler's commands, including two of Sheridan's divisions, to Bermuda Hundred and then over the James opposite a swampy creek mouth known as Deep Bottom. Lee had no way of knowing that the movement was not a raid on Richmond, but a diversion for the detonation of a powder-filled tunnel that coal miners in Burnside's corps had dug under a Confederate salient east of Petersburg. On the twenty-eighth, the Confederate commander responded by hustling over the pontoons near Drewry's Bluff two infantry divisions supported by heavy detachments from Fitz and Rooney Lee's commands, plus McGregor's battery. On the Northside, the troopers joined with the cavalry of Gary to impede the enemy's progress northward and westward. There followed three days of intermittent combat, punctuated by what a member of the 9th Virginia called "spirited action" near Malvern Hill. In that fight, the 9th wrested two battle flags from the hands of enemy infantry. The captured banners were later presented to Wade Hampton as a token of the regiment's esteem.[24]

When the enemy suddenly recrossed to Bermuda Hundred on the thirtieth, the Southerners followed suit. En route to their old camps, they heard—and felt—the explosion of Burnside's mine. The blast, which failed to produce the military breakthrough that Grant had hoped for, was nevertheless impressive in its effects. A member of the 35th Virginia Battalion, who had remained at Petersburg throughout the fighting at Deep Bottom, reported that shock waves "shook the ground for miles," leaving him and his comrades wondering "whether it was the day of judgment or an earthquake." It was neither—merely a sign that the war would be won through continued bloodletting, not technological intervention.[25]

>-+‹›-O-‹›+‹

As August came in, the siege that had settled over the Petersburg front seemed destined to continue indefinitely. But not every member of Lee's army had to endure the drudgery, boredom, and danger of trench warfare. Many were able to escape the investment lines for the picturesque vistas of the Shenandoah Valley. Even in those lovely surroundings, however, they found death and destruction all around them.

...er to the Valley.
...choice to lead the army's
...ritten Jefferson Davis:

...en Hampton, and my
...is late expedition [to
...nd good conduct, and
...ve that activity and
...and so entirely pos-
...ace him in the com-

...icantly, perhaps, a few
...ampton's chief rival for

...cavalry, Lee ordered
...e hands of M. C. But-
...ingered there, within
...elieve that additional
...ion to add Wilson's
...uded a contingency
...g his capital uncov-
...much as Early had
...Hampton returned
...fifteenth.[31]

...n saw less action
...uctance to offer
...f determined to
...d fairly begun.
...alley, his retro-
...ly assigned to

...er, he would
...him; the next
...s reinforced,
...n terms—to
...Little Phil,
...d faced his
...pers Ferry.
...nderson's
...erved that
...gs, Lee's

...ent
...inclu...
...orth Car...
...e city from

...hereafter, he
...r, and invaded
...C., prompting
...sist. Since then,
...roam freely. By
...ly depots, he con-
...r were applying to
...able than Richmond.
...e ordered Sheridan to
...newcomers would join
...the cavalry of William
...sion was to lay waste to
...cy, thereby depriving Lee
...rovided him.[27]

...—Sheridan would start out
...ded a countermove. On the
...lready-reinforced army with
...on, thus increasing Confeder-
...e thousand. The reinforcements
...s infantry division and Fitzhugh
...by overland march, the foot sol-
...under way on the fifth and sixth.
...venteenth at Winchester, where he
...northeast.[28]

...he horsemen in Early's department.
...en serving Old Jube for the past six
...ohn Imboden, Bradley Johnson, John
...ll") Jackson. None of these units was of
...te the best efforts of Ransom, they were
...rmed, and poorly equipped troopers who
...field.

...on no doubt aggravated by the problems the
...nsom had recently retired from active service.
... 10 Lunsford Lomax was appointed a major
..., at least, Fitz would have a trusted subordinate
...ming campaign. Another dependable lieutenant,
...to command Fitz's division.[29]

...her promotion may have resulted from Fi...

...early July, Robert E. Lee had made known...

...men on a regular basis. At that time, he had w...

> You know the high opinion I entertain of (...
> appreciation of his character and services. In...
> Trevilian Station] he has displayed both energy a...
> although I have feared that he might not ha...
> endurance so necessary in a cavalry commander...
> sessed by Gen Stuart . . . I request authority to p...
> mand.

Approval finally came through on August 11—signi...
days after the officer who might have been considered H...
the position was detached from the army.[30]

On the day Hampton was appointed commander o...
him, with his old division (which would soon pass into th...
ler), toward Culpeper Court House. Anderson's infantry...
marching distance of Winchester. Lee wished Sheridan to...
cavalry was on its way to Early, countering Grant's deci...
division to the Valley forces. Lee's orders to Hampton inc...
mission: "Should the enemy move up the Potomac, leavin...
ered," he was authorized to threaten Abraham Lincoln's city...
the month before. No such opportunity arose, however, and...
men and horses to Petersburg, by train via Richmond, on the...

>-+>-O-<+-<

During their first six weeks in the Shenandoah, Fitz Lee's me...
than they had expected. The reason was Sheridan's initial rel...
battle. He advanced south from Harpers Ferry on the tenth as...
take Winchester, smash Early, and end the campaign before it h...
In the face of Sheridan's movement, Early withdrew down the V...
grade covered, albeit clumsily, by two of the brigades recent...
Lomax.

Although Early's retreat meant the evacuation of Winches...
soon reoccupy the place. By the seventeenth, Fitz Lee had joined...
day, Early made contact with Anderson near Front Royal. Thu...
Early turned north to confront Sheridan on something closer to eve...
find that his opponent had gone on the defensive. On the sixteenth...
who had occupied a line along Cedar Creek south of Winchester, ha...
army about: Now he was heading north to Halltown, just below Ha...

Fitz Lee's troopers made their Valley debut by supporting A...
attack on Merritt's cavalry, covering Sheridan's retreat. Merritt obs...
despite lacking the time to orient themselves to their new surroundin...

men struck Devin's brigade "with great violence." Only by prompt maneuvering were the Federals able to ward off the blow. Then they, too, hastened north, giving their enemy the impression they were running scared. The gray horsemen followed closely; the next day, with their support, Anderson assaulted Merritt's division "with such overwhelming numbers," Merritt reported, "as completely to overthrow it, and with considerable loss, and drive it from Winchester."[32]

It was on the seventeenth that Early started down the Valley with his main army. Sheridan's behavior suggested timidity and indecision, leading Old Jube to underestimate the man. In fact, Sheridan was heeding the instructions and advice of his superiors, who feared that Early's additions had given him a numerical advantage. Then, too, there was a political dimension to Sheridan's movements. Before leaving for the Valley, he had been warned by Grant, as well as by General-in-Chief Halleck, to avoid miscues that might add to the pessimism the North was feeling in the wake of the missed opportunities and stalemate at Petersburg. A presidential race was on; another blunder might doom Lincoln's chances for reelection.[33]

As Sheridan continued north, Early jabbed spitefully at his flanks and rear. When the Union commander dug in around Halltown, near the point at which the campaign had begun, his opponent spent three days trying but failing to draw him into a fight. Aware that unless he committed all his forces to battle, Lee would recall Anderson and perhaps Fitz Lee as well, on the twenty-fifth Early veered eastward with a part of his army as if to invade Maryland for the second time in two months. He moved to Leetown, and from there ranged north to Kearneysville on the B & O Railroad, as well as to Shepherdstown on the upper Potomac. Meanwhile, Fitz Lee, with all of Early's cavalry save elements of two brigades, rode north to a point opposite Williamsport, where the A.N.V. had escaped to Virginia following Gettysburg. There, as he reported, he spent the twenty-sixth "making demonstrations as if to cross the river" and sparring with Averell's cavalry, part of which he drove for a considerable distance.[34]

As these feints suggested, Early had no intention of leaving the Valley; the move east was a ploy to draw Sheridan into the open. When only Torbert's cavalry came up to challenge him at Kearneysville and Shepherdstown, the Confederate commander retraced his steps in frustration until going into position west of the Opequon and east of Winchester. En route to join him, Torbert's men attacked Lomax's portion of Lee's column near Smithfield, but, as Fitz noted with gratification, "his attack was successfully resisted." Their well-fed horses and repeating arms notwithstanding, thus far Sheridan's troopers had shown Lee's men nothing to indicate that they were a skillful, let alone formidable, foe.

The pattern of operations in the Valley did not change until after August 28, when Grant informed Sheridan by wire that Anderson would soon return to Petersburg in response to a coordinated offensive by Meade and Butler. Thereafter, Sheridan began a cautious advance from Halltown to Charles Town, less than twenty miles from Early's position. That day Merritt pushed Lomax's less-than-steadfast cavalry out of Leetown and across the Opequon to Bunker Hill.

The Yankee troopers appeared to have regained their aggressiveness. Still, Early knew that cavalry alone could not drive him from the Valley, and he doubted that Sheridan had the ability, or the gumption, to do so with his main army.[35]

Early's opinion of his adversary was so low he believed he could get along without the extra infantry Robert E. Lee had sent him. On September 3, his own foot soldiers, assisted by Lomax's horsemen, made a demonstration near Bunker Hill to cover Anderson's withdrawal from the Valley. On the fourteenth, Kershaw's division started back to Petersburg; almost as soon as he had left, Sheridan firmed up plans for attacking Early's poorly defended position outside Winchester. Five days later, he put his army, and his strategy, in motion.

At daylight on the nineteenth, Lomax's pickets at the Berryville Road's crossing of the Opequon were driven in by Sheridan's advance. Soon afterward, skirmishing broke out along Early's right flank. The Confederate leader took steps to shore up the position, but by 9:00 A.M., Wilson's troopers, leading the Union advance in that sector, had secured a lodgment close to Winchester, permitting Sheridan's VI and XIX Corps to move forward in their right rear. After some confusion caused by the errant passage of supply wagons across their route of advance, Sheridan's foot soldiers poured through a ravine toward the enemy line, overwhelming Lomax's men and threatening to do the same to the infantry in their rear, the division of Maj. Gen. Stephen D. Ramseur, supported to the north by Maj. Gen. Robert E. Rodes's division. Then the Federals ranged northward to link with the upper column of Sheridan's attack force.[36]

It took several hours for the right half of the Union assault force—which had made a long, forced march—to get in position to advance toward Winchester. About noon, the push finally began opposite Early's left, defended by the infantry of Maj. Gen. John Brown Gordon and, later, Maj. Gen. John C. Breckinridge. That sector had been picketed by Wickham's division, consisting of his old brigade, and the brigade formerly led by Lomax and now by William Payne. The troopers fought long and hard to hold back the blue tide, assisted greatly by five of the six guns under Major Breathed, commanding Fitz Lee's horse artillery. In time, however, converging attacks by separate columns of cavalry and infantry along the Charles Town road, and by Averell's horseman on the Martinsburg Pike, proved too much for the understrength squadrons, which fell back with alacrity. As Fitz Lee put it succinctly, "The odds were too great."[37]

Typical was the experience of Colonel Owen and his 3rd Virginia—117 officers and men—who, when Merritt's troopers surged over the Opequon, were thrown into the breach. Now-Capt. Robert Hubard, who rode in the first rank of the forlorn-hope effort, wrote: "[We] charged through a storm of shell and small [arms' fire] upon & repulsed the skirmish line. . . . Three regiments now came forward with drawn sabres to the charge. There we were 1/2 mile from supports charged by a force of at least five to one. Of course we beat a hasty retreat."[38]

The situation on Early's left deteriorated rapidly after Fitz Lee took a bullet in the leg and was carried from the field. His successor, Wickham, proved

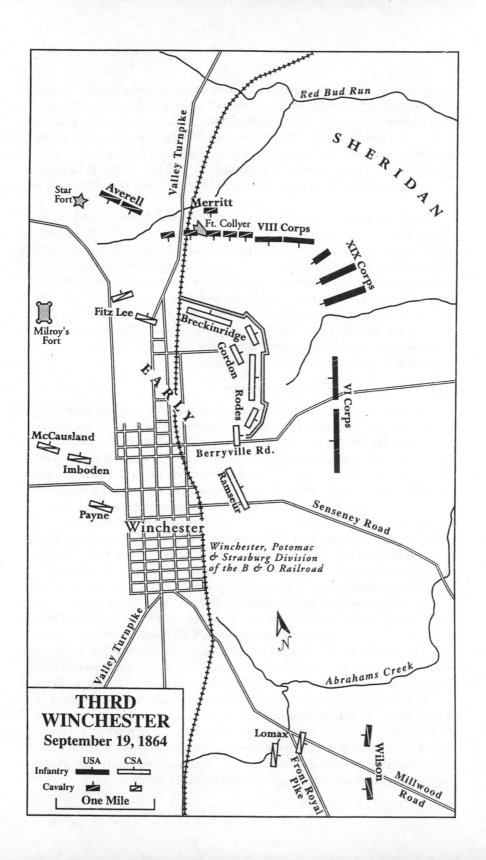

Red Bud Run

S H E R I D A N

Valley Turnpike

Star
Fort

Averell

Merritt

Ft. Collyer   VIII Corps

XIX Corps

Milroy's
Fort

Fitz Lee

Breckinridge

Gordon

Rodes

VI Corps

E A R L Y

McCausland

Imboden

Berryville Rd.

Ramseur

Payne

Winchester

Senseney Road

Winchester, Potomac
& Strasburg Division
of the B & O Railroad

N

Valley Turnpike

Abrahams Creek

THIRD
WINCHESTER
September 19, 1864

Infantry   USA   CSA

Cavalry

One Mile

Lomax

Front Royal Pike

Wilson

Millwood Road

unequal to the enlarged responsibility (Hubard blamed him for the "stupid bungling way in which this fight was directed" after Lee's departure). Yet, even if Wickham had shouldered the burden squarely, it seems unlikely that the offensive—especially after Sheridan threw in heavy reinforcements—could have been contained. When a series of counterattacks fell short of decisive success, Early must have known the day was lost. By 5:00 P.M., his troops had been squeezed into a compact pocket abutting Winchester. Only then did he call a retreat.

Darkness was coming as the weary, bloodied Confederates poured out the Valley Pike toward Strasburg, their flanks and rear covered by the equally exhausted troopers of Wickham and Lomax. Early's plucky army had fought gamely; it had inflicted more than five thousand casualties on Sheridan while it had lost fewer than four thousand, but Sheridan's costly attack had also been overwhelming. Little Phil had won by deceiving his opponent, making Early believe he lacked the stomach for a confrontation. In the end, more than any other factor, including the "stupid bungling" of his subordinates, Old Jube's overconfidence and his underestimation of Sheridan had cost him the battle, as it would the entire campaign in the Shenandoah.[39]

>─┼─◀▶─O─◀▶─┼─◀

The demoralized Rebels did not halt until Early placed as many of them as he could collect atop Fisher's Hill, nearly twenty miles south of the battlefield. Sheridan followed and attacked the ragged, four-mile-long line late on the twenty-second. Again he engulfed his opposition via a sweeping envelopment of Early's left. This time the blow landed hardest on Lomax's cavalry, which Early had placed, dismounted, in a vulnerable position. Lomax's overthrow confirmed the worst suspicions of his superior, who doubted the effectiveness of all horse soldiers. After the battle, Early sent a message to Robert E. Lee in which he unfairly branded the Valley cavalry "the cause of all my disasters."[40]

Lomax's command was the only element of Early's mounted arm to suffer through the defeat at Fisher's Hill, which cost the Valley army at least twelve hundred casualties and the loss of twelve cannons, while sending the survivors fleeing toward Mount Jackson. To complete his victory, in advance of his attack Sheridan had sent Torbert, with the majority of Merritt's division and all of Wilson's, across the Shenandoah River and up the Luray Valley (formed by Massanutten Mountain on the west and the Blue Ridge to the east). The maneuver was designed to permit Torbert to curl around Early's left flank as he retreated, trapping the Rebels between two heavy forces and thereby destroying them.

It did not work out that way. Torbert failed due to the determination of Early's cavalry to clear its reputation of any stain it had picked up at Winchester. Twice in as many days, two brigades, under overall command of Wickham, halted and held back their more numerous, better-armed and -mounted opponents. Torbert was prevented from reaching the Rebel rear until it had passed below the point at which his troopers exited the Luray Valley.

Wickham had administered the check late on the morning of the twenty-second, when, having anticipated Torbert's movement, his troopers dug in along the south bank of Overall's Run. They made excellent use of terrain to solidify their position, their left flank secured by the Shenandoah River, their right by a spur of the Massanutten. Further, the men had erected "loop-hole" breastworks across their front. Torbert was so impressed by the strength of the position that he withdrew after a brief reconnaissance. While en route to Sheridan, however, he learned that the attack on Fisher's Hill had been successful and that Early's infantry was in rapid retreat. A communiqué from Sheridan demanded that Torbert retrace his steps and make another attempt to cut through the mountains into the enemy's rear.

The long-suffering subordinate moved to comply on the twenty-fourth. This time he got as far as the village of Luray, about ten miles below the line Wickham had abandoned on Overall's Run. Again, however, he found the enemy massed in his front, blocking the local pass. This time Wickham's position was not impregnable; eventually, Custer's brigade charged his men into retreat, taking several prisoners. But again the Confederates had mounted an effective delaying action. By the time Torbert pushed through the gap, Early's fugitives had passed the point at which they could be intercepted. The cavalry's failure was a great disappointment to Sheridan, who never forgave Torbert's slowness or his initial reluctance to engage Wickham. The episode contributed to Torbert's loss of his command on the eve of the war's final campaign.[41]

>─┼─◆>──◇──◆>─┼─◄

Even before the magnitude of the defeats at Winchester and Fisher's Hill had become clear, reinforcements were again on their way to Early. On September 24, Kershaw's infantry returned, this time without Anderson. Two days later, the Laurel Brigade was also summoned west. Its commander had just returned to field service after recuperating from his Trevilian Station wound. When he started for the Valley, Tom Rosser was in an ebullient mood, not only because his health had been restored, and not merely because an enlarged command and a promotion awaited him at the end of his five-day journey. The brigadier was fresh from a leading role in one of the most dramatic successes of his military career, a raid behind the Union lines at Petersburg aimed not at the enemy's communications or troop concentrations, but at its stomach.[42]

The unique expedition had originated with Hampton's most enterprising scout, George Shadburne. On September 5, the sergeant had returned from a mission behind Meade's lines to report the vulnerability of the immense herd of cattle that had been corralled near Coggins's Point on the James—"3,000 beeves, attended by 120 men and 30 citizens, without arms." Cavalry from both Meade's and Butler's armies picketed the river, but no closer than two miles from the herd. Hampton, whose men, habitually low on rations, were facing a winter of near starvation, perceived an opportunity to capture at least some of the cattle before they could be slaughtered for benefit of the enemy.[43]

On the morning of the fourteenth, following a week of careful planning, the cavalry commander led four thousand officers and men from their camps along the Weldon railroad toward Meade's left flank. Splitting off from the column, Rooney Lee, with the main body of his division, demonstrated west of their objective while Dearing's brigade created a commotion in the opposite direction. Marching between these forces, Shadburne guided Hampton, with Rosser's brigade, toward Coggins's Point before dawn on the sixteenth. Near Sycamore Church, the raiders swept down on an unsuspecting regiment of Yankee cavalry, capturing it en masse. Then they hastened to the cattle ranch on the river.

On arriving, they found that the herd's civilian drovers, having learned of their approach, had stampeded the cattle by knocking down corral walls and firing pistols into the air. Rosser's troopers galloped after the rampaging beasts for a mile or more before being able to get in front of them, slow them down, and round them up. While Lige White's Comanches conducted a delaying action at Belchers Mill, beating back a pursuit by the cavalry of Gregg and Kautz, the cavalrymen-turned-drovers hastened the herd south, across a bridge over the Blackwater River and inside Lee's lines below Petersburg. On the homeward journey, Rosser had a count taken and found that Hampton and he had snatched almost 2,500 head of cattle. As he proudly reported, they "delivered to General Lee's commissary every one of the 2,486 beeves." While their haul kept the army fed for only a few weeks, the daring feat long remained a source of pride and satisfaction to Rosser and to everyone else involved in the war's only recorded episode of cattle rustling.[44]

Unfortunately, hard on the heels of this dramatic success, Rosser's command experienced the most lopsided defeat ever suffered by cavalry in Virginia.

Their leader did not see it coming. In fact, his service in the Valley started off in fine fashion: Upon reporting to Early's current headquarters at New Market on October 2, Rosser found himself appointed a major general and installed as successor to Wickham, commanding every horseman Fitz Lee had brought from Petersburg the previous month. Wickham—perhaps as a result of his jarring experience at Winchester—had quit the field to take that congressional seat he had left vacant for the past year.

Rosser's initial field service in the Valley entailed jabbing at Torbert's horsemen, who would strike, then fall back as if trying to lure the Confederates into a fight—just as Early had tried to force Sheridan's hand before Winchester. After October 6, however, the tables turned once again. Frustrated by Early's unwillingness to venture from his stronghold in the foothills of the Massanutten, Sheridan turned his back on him and headed down the Valley, eventually establishing a position along Cedar Creek, near Middletown.

Early ordered both Rosser and Lomax, who still commanded the Valley cavalry, to "pursue the enemy, to harass him and ascertain his purposes," while the rest of the army remained at New Market. Rosser required little urging; his desire to damage, demoralize, and defeat his enemy burned as strongly as ever. His urge to lash out grew when Sheridan's army, as it withdrew to Cedar Creek, applied the torch to the farms of the upper Valley, while confiscating livestock and crops. Rosser and Lomax retaliated by taking small pieces out of Sheridan's hide. For three days, they sniped mercilessly at the flanks and rear of his moving column, cutting off and killing or wounding as many of his men as possible. At length, Sheridan had had enough. On the evening of the eighth, he gave Torbert explicit instructions to confront his tormentors, to either whip them or take a whipping at their hands.[45]

The next day, Torbert found Rosser's men bivouacked on the Back Road just south of Tom's Brook and Lomax's about three miles farther east, on the Valley Pike near Woodstock. Both officers expected to continue their hit-and-run tactics this day; thus they were unprepared for the hordes of Yankee cavalry who charged them just after daylight, screaming like banshees—Merritt's division on the turnpike, Custer's along the Back Road. Outnumbered perhaps three to one, the Confederates had no recourse but to flee. But they put spurs to their horses too late; before their men could get away, the attackers were all over them, cutting them out of the saddle with sabers and pistols, silencing their horse artillery, capturing their caissons, ambulances, and baggage wagons.

When they finally started running, Rosser and Lomax found it hard to stop, swept up as they were in a tidal wave of horses, riders, and vehicles. At a few points, both divisions attempted to make a stand, but their defenses quickly collapsed and the retreat resumed. By day's end, Rosser and Lomax had been shoved at least twenty-five miles from the point of contact, suffering perhaps one hundred men killed or wounded while eleven cannons, seventy horses, forty baggage wagons, four caissons, and three ambulances had been captured.[46]

The rout was so complete that Early feared his cavalry had been irreparably demoralized. After Torbert's pursuit reached a merciful conclusion, Old Jube's concern turned to bitterness. In a telegram to Robert E. Lee the army leader condemned his horsemen as utterly worthless, adding, "It would be better if they could all but put into the infantry; but if that were tried I am afraid they would all run off."[47]

Chapter Twenty-two

No Surrender

Early and Sheridan would face each other for four months after Tom's Brook (or, as Rosser's and Lomax's defeat became known among the rank and file of both armies, "the Woodstock Races"). By mid-October, however, the drama that was the Shenandoah Valley campaign was approaching its finale.

The climactic scene began with a three-day absence from the front by Sheridan, who on the fifteenth left Cedar Creek for conferences in Washington with Halleck and Secretary of War Stanton. Shortly after he departed, Early, who had cautiously returned to Fisher's Hill, determined on a risky offensive. His enemy's efforts to "peel" the Valley had been so successful that Early could not remain long in his present position for lack of rations and forage. Forced to gamble, he would advance against the army that was led in Sheridan's absence by Maj. Gen. Horatio G. Wright, commander of the VI Corps. Early's horsemen would have roles to play in his plan, but—reflective of his low opinion of them—not critical ones. Rosser was assigned to hold the attention of Torbert's cavalry, which had massed along the Union right above Cedar Creek—and Early intended to turn the *left* flank. Meanwhile, Lomax's division, which, unlike Rosser's, appeared not to have recovered from the disaster of the ninth, was assigned a detached mission that would virtually remove it from the field of battle.[1]

After dark on the eighteenth, less than twenty-four hours before Sheridan was expected to rejoin his troops, Early moved his men in two columns past Strasburg and into position south of Cedar Creek. In accordance with his plan, promptly at 5:00 A.M., two columns of infantry waded the creek. One hit the Union left head-on; the other, larger, column, which had made a concealed march around the base of Massanutten Mountain, struck the same sector but at an oblique angle toward the rear.

Literally caught napping, bleary-eyed defenders were routed, and the left flank caved in. The VIII Corps went under completely, along with a portion of the XIX Corps on its right. At first the scene was the same on Rosser's part of the field, where a member of Shoemaker's battery saw Yankees "killed & wounded [while] running from their tents 'en dishabille.'" Within minutes, "the victory was complete. The captures were as follows: 16 pieces of artillery, 19 wagons, 12 ambulances, 1600 prisoners."[2]

In fact, it was far from complete. By late morning, the Union left was in shambles. The only mounted force to attack that sector, Payne's brigade, "drove the enemy," as one participant wrote, "in a beautiful charge through & a half mile beyond Newtown," some miles to the north. Even so, the VI Corps continued to hold the center of Wright's line, steadying that part of the XIX Corps that had not fled on first contact.[3]

Meanwhile, at Cupp's Ford, on the Union right, Rosser failed to make headway against the troopers of Custer, whom he must have felt he had been battling forever. Nor could he hold the Federals in place; late in the morning, Custer slipped away from him to shore up another part of Wright's line. Later Rosser blamed his failure on Early, as he had after Tom's Brook. On the earlier occasion, he had faulted his superior for sending him too far in advance of the main army (thereby implying that only when braced with infantry could his troopers compete successfully with their counterparts in blue). This day, he criticized Early for compelling him to confront Custer instead of the troops fleeing from the Union left (another admission that his command was no match for their ordained opponents in the Federal cavalry).

Rosser's complaints aside, and the efforts of the VI Corps to stand firm notwithstanding, Early's turning movement had been a smashing success, literally and figuratively. Given impetus by his surprise assault, he should have hurled the remaining Yankees from the field. Instead, he and his subordinates forfeited victory by permitting their men to halt and loot the enemy's camps instead of pursuing their occupants. As an officer in the 4th Virginia put it, victory was lost because "the rich Yankee camps offer too great a temptation for our men to withstand."[4]

While Early's troops plundered, the routed foe rallied, re-formed, and prepared to counterattack. At a critical moment, Phil Sheridan returned to the army after a twenty-mile gallop from Winchester, accompanied only by his escort. Before Early's horrified eyes, Little Phil engineered an attack of his own that rolled forward at about 4:00 P.M. with unstoppable power. On the right, Custer's men smashed into the Rebel north flank as if Rosser's men posed no barrier at all. On the left, mixed forces of foot and horse units surged forward, uprooted their flabbergasted opponents, and flung them back across the creek. By sundown, Early's troops—those not killed, disabled, or captured—were heading back to Strasburg with singleminded determination.

The cavalry did their utmost to stem the rout, but from the start, it was a losing proposition. When darkness came on, the future of the Valley army had turned as black as the night. Early had lost almost two thousand men, another two dozen guns, and every ambulance and ammunition wagon not captured at

Winchester, Fisher's Hill, or Tom's Brook. Old Jube's last offensive had collapsed, and with it the Confederacy's hope of hanging on to the fertile crescent known as the Shenandoah.[5]

If Sheridan's dramatic victory at Winchester, or the earlier capture of Atlanta by William T. Sherman, had not already done so, Cedar Creek made the reelection of Abraham Lincoln a *fait accompli*. In turn, Lincoln's victory doomed the Confederacy to extinction. By the time the president retook his oath of office in March, the life of the Southern nation could be measured in weeks.

Abe's opponent, Retid Gen. George Mc clellan (D)

>—•◊—O—◊•—<

Service in the Valley after Cedar Creek was decidedly anticlimactic. Even so, most of the cavalry sent to Early from Lee's army remained with him at and near his headquarters at New Market (which he later transferred to Waynesboro). Many endured the frigid, starving winter of 1864–65, while Sheridan's soldiers lay warm and well-fed in their winterized cabins outside Winchester. But when active operations shut down for the season, some troopers sought other, more active, if not necessarily warmer, venues. Late in November, Rosser set out for West Virginia with a portion of his command, including the Laurel Brigade. There he raided New Creek and other Union outposts, collecting not only critically needed forage, but also hundreds of prisoners. He returned east in time to counter successfully the single large-scale operation Sheridan launched that winter, a late-December raid by Torbert's men against the Virginia Central and other communication lines in the Gordonsville-Charlottesville area.[6]

The majority of the Confederate troopers who had come to the Valley in August and September did not return to the Petersburg front until Sheridan did. In late February 1865, even before the snow had melted at Winchester, the Union commander began moving up the Valley at the head of a column ten thousand strong to rejoin Grant and Meade in time to take part in the final campaign of the war in the East. His route led through Waynesboro, where, on March 2, he had a final confrontation with Early. Its rout at Cedar Creek had reduced the Valley army to a shadow of its former self; after the brief, one-sided encounter at Waynesboro, even the shadow was gone.[7]

Wiping the blood from his hands, Sheridan continued on to Petersburg via Charlottesville, Columbia, and the banks of the James River, leaving behind scorched earth and the charred ruins of Confederate property. Elements of Rosser's command—which had been present at Waynesboro but whose mobility had saved it from annihilation—shadowed Little Phil to Petersburg, making fitful and ineffective efforts to bring him to bay or at least limit the damage he inflicted on railroads, bridges, and canals. It was desperate, futile work, and most of Sheridan's pursuers were glad when it ended in the last days of March with the Yankees slipping inside their army's lines east of Petersburg.[8]

A la Sherman

Once Rosser saw he had no legitimate chance at overhauling Sheridan's main force, he began to tail the detachment that had started back to Winchester as an escort for the prisoners taken at Waynesboro. Even these Federals were more than a match for the general, whose every attempt to free the captives was repulsed.[9]

iT ain't over til its over. It is so over, Jeff.

After this latest failure, a thoroughly disgusted Rosser proceeded to Petersburg, reaching Robert E. Lee's lines on the fifteenth. Upon arriving, he found himself reduced to brigade command, being forced to relinquish to Fitz Lee most of the units he had brought with him, including McCausland's brigade. Fitz, who had fully recovered from the wound he had taken at Winchester but had not returned to the Valley, was serving north of the James, his command primarily consisting of Gary's brigade. Now he would add to it Payne's and Wickham's horsemen. The latter brigade he assigned to Tom Munford.

By rights, Munford, who had served in Early's army throughout the Valley operations, should have occupied the position much sooner: Upon Wickham's resignation in October, he had been the senior colonel in his brigade. The post had been denied him by Rosser, with whom Munford had quarreled since the days when Rosser, then a junior officer, had served under him. In the Valley, the spiteful Rosser had also court-martialed Munford for some trivial offense, although the charges were so flimsy a tribunal had immediately dismissed them. Now, finally, Munford's fortunes appeared to have reversed. Not only had he been given a more prestigious command, one separated from his adversary, but in the campaign that lay ahead, Fitz Lee would secure a brigadier's rank for him—a prize made all the more desirable by the fact that Munford had been passed over for promotion so many times. In one more cruel twist of fate, however, the war would end before the Confederate Congress could confirm his appointment.[10]

A new division was immediately assigned to Rosser, consisting of the Laurel Brigade and McCausland's erstwhile Valley cavalry. Rounding out the corps, Rooney Lee, who was stationed along the railroad south of Petersburg, commanded the brigades of Barringer, Dearing, and Beale (formerly Chambliss's, its leader having been killed, as a brigadier general, during a mid-August skirmish outside Richmond). The entire mounted arm, as of late February, numbered perhaps four thousand officers and troopers.[11]

Once back with the A.N.V., Rosser and the other returnees from the Valley noticed some conspicuous absentees. Wade Hampton had gone to South Carolina, as had Calbraith Butler, who had taken over Hampton's former division when the latter moved up to corps command. Gone, too, was Pierce Young, who had not returned from a November remount operation in Georgia.

In late January, Hampton and Butler, along with subordinates, enlisted personnel, mounts, equipments, and appurtenances, had entrained for their home state. South Carolina was the next target of Sherman, whose armies had recently completed their rampage across Georgia, spreading destruction and terror wherever they went. Robert E. Lee, who recently had been named com-

Ha!

mander of all the Confederate armies, had decided to make Butler's division, including Young's brigade, available to the military commander at Columbia, Lt. Gen. William J. Hardee, and Hardee's cavalry chief, Maj. Gen. Joseph Wheeler. As Lee informed President Davis, the transfer would be a package deal: "I should have to send Gen. Hampton, or [the division] might be merged in Wheeler's cavalry and thus lost." Lee acted on the condition that Hampton and Butler would return to the Army of Northern Virginia in time to take part in the spring campaign. Neither officer, however, did so.[12]

Lee's rationale was a bit obscure, yet Davis not only approved the transfer, but also saw to it that on the eve of his departure Hampton received a promotion to lieutenant general. After the command had gone, however, Lee would second-guess his generosity. That summer, after the war was over, he admitted in reply to a letter from Hampton: "You cannot regret as much as I did that you were not with us at our final struggle. The absence of the troops which I had sent to North & South Carolina, was I believe the cause of our immediate disaster."[13] *Lee had lost His mind, when? what?*

During the five months preceding Hampton's departure for the Carolinas, his old division had teamed with that of Rooney Lee, as well as with Gary's brigade, to support the Army of Northern Virginia on both sides of the James. An especially heavy period of activity had begun within days of Fitz Lee's transfer to the Valley. From August 14 to 18, the cavalry had returned to the area above the James to help block a second Union incursion through the Northside, this aimed at testing the defenses of Richmond. The unsuccessful offensive, which had involved Butler's army as well as Meade's, had contributed to Hampton's recall from Culpeper. Without this distraction, Hampton might have been dispatched to the Valley, where he would have led Early's cavalry, a situation he would not have relished, if only because it would mean reestablishing close contact with Fitz Lee.[14]

From the Northside, Hampton and his two divisions had hastened back to the Weldon Railroad to help defend that vital communication line. On the twenty-fifth, the cavalry lent its power and mobility to an attack by A. P. Hill on Yankees trying to gain possession of the rail line in the vicinity of Reams's Station. They wrested a well-fortified position from the astonished II Corps, Army of the Potomac, and sent its troops hurtling north. Through the rest of the year, Hampton's troopers warded off other attempts by Meade to seize strategic sections of the line, especially along the twenty-mile stretch between Stony Creek Station and Belfield.[15]

Two weeks after their spectacular raid on Grant's cattle herd, Hampton's men were less successful in opposing Meade's half of a major offensive aimed at taking and holding ground on both sides of the James. Hampton, Butler, and Rooney Lee, backed by two batteries under Major Chew, fought long and hard on September 30 to hold positions on the Boydton Plank Road southwest of Petersburg and late the following day along the hotly contested Vaughan Road, directly south of the city. The fighting on October 1 was especially sanguinary; among the killed was John Dunovant, who had received command of Butler's brigade when Butler moved up to lead Hampton's division. While not uniformly successful in stopping Meade's thrust toward Lee's rear, the troopers did their part in slowing and, at some points, containing it.[16]

Hampton fended off yet another thrust toward the Boydton Road three weeks later. His support eventually forced the Yankees to relinquish a foothold dangerously close to the Southside Railroad, the Army of Northern Virginia's last functional supply line. Hampton's role in that autumn confrontation came at great personal cost: the death of his twenty-two-year-old son, Preston, and the severe wounding of twenty-four-year-old Wade Hampton, Jr., both of whom served on their father's staff.[17]

Mercifully, Hampton, as also Butler and Young, was gone from Petersburg when the Federals on February 5, 1865, finally secured a lodgment on the Boydton Road. With the Southside line all but lost, the end was not far off for the army the generals had bade farewell to. They could not escape the inevitable: In South Carolina, Hampton and his subordinates would also be caught up in a losing struggle. But at least they would go down fighting close to home and kin, instead of on the killing ground of Virginia, where each had suffered grievous wounds and Hampton had buried a son and a brother.

➤━◆━●━◆━◄

The "immediate disaster" to which Robert E. Lee made reference in his postwar letter to Hampton engulfed Richmond and Petersburg soon after spring arrived. On March 25, Lee launched his final offensive, a surprise assault that captured Fort Stedman and other, smaller, works along the right flank of the siege lines at Petersburg. When a series of counterattacks erased all his gains, however, Lee withdrew his shattered ranks and began to plan the evacuation of the city.[18]

Upon Sheridan's return from the Valley, Grant moved in for the kill. On the morning of March 29, he dispatched Little Phil with three divisions of Meade's cavalry, a total of nine thousand effectives, across the Weldon Railroad to Dinwiddie Court House on the plank road, a dozen miles southwest of Petersburg. In that area, opposite the extreme right flank of the Army of Northern Virginia, Little Phil was to cooperate with Meade's infantry to seize and hold the railroad in Robert E. Lee's rear. If Sheridan succeeded, Petersburg and, by extension, Richmond were doomed.[19]

Lee, always alert to his enemy's strategy, anticipated Sheridan's movement. On the twenty-eighth, he ordered every mounted member of his nephew's division who still had a horse to move to Petersburg. Fitz marched promptly down the Nine Mile Road with the brigades of Munford, Payne, and Gary. The next morning, he reached his assigned destination, Sutherland Station on the Southside Railroad, nineteen miles southwest of the besieged city.

Upon arriving, Fitz Lee gained a long-coveted promotion. Following Hampton's departure for the Carolinas, Robert E. Lee had once again permitted months to pass without naming an officer to command his horsemen. This day,

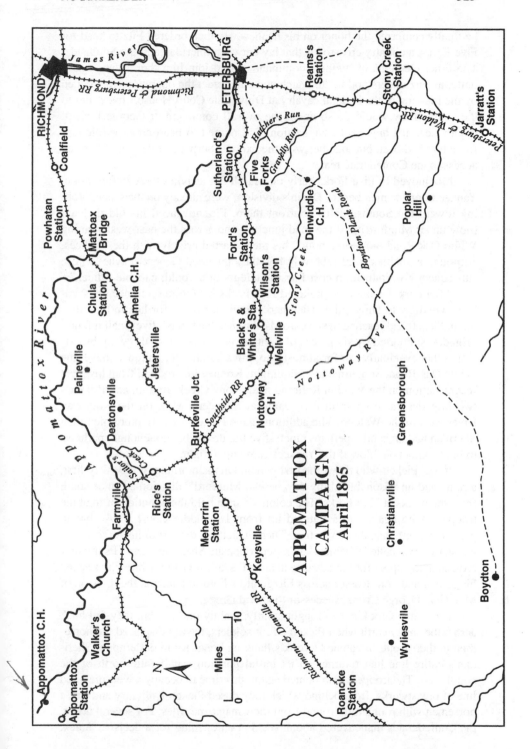

APPOMATTOX
CAMPAIGN
April 1865

he finally conferred the honor on his nephew. He then ordered Fitz to head for Five Forks, a country crossroads that lay between Sheridan and the Southside. The other elements of his new command would join him there; they would unite, as Fitz understood it, "to watch and counteract the operations threatened by the massing of the Federal cavalry at Dinwiddie Court House," five miles to the south. They would do so under the overall command of George Pickett, whom Lee, at Longstreet's suggestion, had named to head an expeditionary force that had been put together with the express purpose of denying Sheridan access to the Confederate rear.

Fitz moved to Five Forks early on March 30, arriving there before noon. Yankee troopers, members of Devin's division, were already on the scene, probing toward the Southside. To confront them, Fitz advanced his old division (now under Munford) past the road junction and across the east-west-running White Oak Road. For some hours, his men sparred briskly with the Yankees. Although casualties were relatively few they included General Payne, whose subsequent hospitalization cost Fitz the talents of a "bold, capable officer."[20]

After dark, having reconnoitered Five Forks for future reference, the Yankees withdrew to Dinwiddie. They had gotten an eyeful, for late in the afternoon, Pickett had reached the crossroads. At once his force—five small infantry brigades, supported by six pieces of light artillery—began to throw up breastworks that eventually ran for almost two miles parallel to, and just above, the White Oak Road. Sometime after midnight, Rooney Lee rode in from his most recent station on the Weldon Railroad near Stony Creek Station, and Rosser's two brigades came up from their camp at Spencer's Mill, on the Nottoway River west of the Weldon. The additions gave Pickett slightly more men than Sheridan had on hand—perhaps ninety-five hundred—but not enough, perhaps, to land a knockout blow if the Yankees came up to fight.[21]

It was Pickett who threw the first punch. On the morning of the thirty-first, a rainy and unseasonably chilly day, he had Munford's division advance south from the works at Five Forks. The colonel's men held the attention of the blue troopers, who again had sauntered up from Dinwiddie Court House but in greater strength than the day before. Then Pickett led the rest of his force across a marshy creek called Chamberlain's Bed, opposite Sheridan's left. His infantry crossed at the upper ford to advance against Devin's division, while Fitz Lee led his cousin and Tom Rosser across Fitzgerald's Ford to confront the division of Maj. Gen. George Crook, successor to David Gregg.

For a time Crook's men fought stoutly, mainly on foot, but they fell back across the soggy earth when Pickett's foot soldiers, having displaced the horsemen in their front, threatened Crook's flank and rear. By midafternoon, Sheridan's entire line had returned to its initial position a half mile north of the courthouse. The troopers dismounted again, this time to occupy a well-prepared line of breastworks, from behind which they dosed Pickett's infantry and Lee's horsemen with round after round from their magazine rifles. For several hours, the Confederates maneuvered about, seeking an opening for a decisive attack, but found none. Yet Pickett held his position north of the courthouse through most of the night. At dawn he realized that by advancing so far from his works, he had left his command vulnerable to assault by the Union infantry operating not far to the east of him. Belatedly, he retreated to the crossroads, his flanks and rear covered by Lee's horsemen.[22]

That evening, Sheridan, who refused to admit that he had been outmaneuvered and outfought this day, called on Grant for infantry support. He hoped to be assigned Wright's VI Corps, which had fought gamely at Cedar Creek and had done so again this day, farther north. Instead Grant sent him Warren's V Corps, the advance element of which did not reach him until 7:00 A.M., seven hours later than Sheridan had anticipated. Throughout the early part of April 1, Little Phil made plans to strike along the length of the Five Forks line. He moved his horsemen toward the position at about 1:00, although his slow-footed infantry friends were not in opposition to attack for another three hours.[23]

By then Pickett's infantry and artillery and Fitz Lee's troopers had had time to make their position quite strong. Yet it appears that Pickett did not greatly improve the slim line of pine logs, with a shallow ditch in front, that had been erected soon after he had arrived the previous afternoon. This was bad enough, but the Gettysburg hero—who ought to have anticipated a general attack at some point—was lax in his dispositions, especially in his placement of the cavalry. The position he had chosen for his command was so heavily wooded and so inundated by streams that Rooney Lee, whose division he had assigned to guard his far right, and Munford, whom Pickett placed on the 90-degree-angled left flank, could reach the front solely by way of a road so narrow only a few men could ride abreast.

Furthermore, at its commander's request, Pickett had permitted Rosser's command—the brigades of McCausland and Dearing, the latter recently assigned to lead the Laurel Brigade—to deploy in rear of the rest of the expeditionary force, along Hatcher's Run. In his new position, Rosser's primary mission was to guard Pickett's rear wagon train, but he ought to have been closer to the front. An additional mounted force available to Pickett—one regiment and one battalion, both from North Carolina, under Brig. Gen. William P. Roberts—connected Pickett's works, via a paper-thin skirmish line, with the right flank of Robert E. Lee's defenses at Petersburg, five miles away.[24]

Pickett's questionable decision-making did not end at this point, although in making his next blunder, he was aided by the cavalry. While in bivouac at Spencer's Mill, Rosser had employed a borrowed seine to catch a mess of Nottoway River shad. He had transported the tasty morsels, packed in ice, to Five Forks in his personal baggage wagon. Early on the afternoon of the first, when all concerned ought to have been on the alert for Sheridan's advance, Rosser invited Pickett and Fitz Lee to a shad bake in a secluded spot north of Hatcher's Run. Both commanders accepted the hospitality; they compounded their poor judgment by failing to tell the next in rank, Rooney Lee, where they were going and how they could be reached.[25] "who cares?"

In their luncheon nook, the expeditionary commander and the two cavalry generals whiled away the late morning and much of the afternoon of April 1, devouring shad and sipping spirits. This was perhaps to be expected. Pickett and Lee had never made any pretense of being teetotalers, while the promises Rosser had made to his wife that he would ride the water wagon for the duration of his military career seem to have been in the realm of wishful thinking. Sated, perhaps a bit sleepy, perhaps also a bit befogged, the ranking triumvirate remained happily in the rear until sometime after 4:00 P.M., when a courier galloped across the run to inform them that the Yankees had attacked all sections of the works at Five Forks. They had also shoved aside Roberts's pickets, thereby isolating Pickett from Petersburg.

The reactions of Lee and Rosser to the news, and their subsequent movements, remain shrouded in mystery. Pickett, his face showing panic, mounted and rode wildly to the front, running a gauntlet of rifle fire, only to find his line unhinged and most of its defenders falling back. Then he turned and rode for his life. Lieutenant Robertson, formerly of Stuart's staff, now of Rooney Lee's, saw Pickett ride past and was about to call to him when the general snapped: "Don't talk to me. My lines are broken!" Then he rode off, whipping his black horse into a lather, his command and his reputation gone up in cannon smoke.[26]

Pickett's line had gone under both because the Federals were in overwhelming force and also because of Pickett's faulty troop placement. On the left, Tom Munford had been unable to bring up enough troopers to help the infantry hold the flank. Consequently, V Corps troops had flooded over the angle, smashing it to pieces, before turning west and rolling up the Rebel center. Only on the right, where Rooney Lee and a portion of Pickett's own division held on stubbornly, did any semblance of defense remain. Even that sector was lost once Sheridan reinforced the mounted and dismounted horsemen assaulting it.

Before dusk, Pickett's position had been obliterated. Hundreds had been killed or wounded, and two thousand-some captured. Most of the rest of the defenders were racing across Hatcher's Run in full flight. Unwilling to join them, but bereft of other options, Rooney Lee and Tom Munford gathered what troops remained to them and reluctantly joined the exodus, at the same time trying to guard the escapees' rear. They discovered, however, that locating, let alone protecting, any portion of such a formless mass of terrified humanity as Pickett's command had become required more skill than either officer possessed.[27]

>─┼─◆>─O─<◆─┼─<

The loss of Pickett's position necessitated Petersburg's evacuation, which began after dark on the second, following a series of devastating attacks on the city's outer and intermediate works by Meade's army and elements of the Army of the James, now under Edward O. C. Ord, a solid professional rather than a political general. Lee realized that his opponents would carry the remaining works by morning; he must retreat, and soon. His troops began to evacuate at about 8:00 P.M.; soon after, the defenders of Richmond also abandoned their lines. By morning, retreat columns were flooding out of both cities, converging toward the line of the Appomattox River.[28]

After hastily departing the shad feast, Fitz Lee, like every other Confederate able to flee the scene of disaster, had crossed Hatcher's Run, putting that barrier between himself and his enemy. He continued north to the Southside line, striking the tracks at the Church Road Crossing, about two and a half miles north of Five Forks. He was able to remain in that vicinity without molestation until early on the second. During the night and on the following morning, he was joined there by Rooney Lee, Rosser, Munford, and those of their officers and men who had managed to evade capture at Five Forks—many by a razor-thin margin. Also on hand by morning was McGregor's old battery. The previous day this unit, with a section of Graham's Petersburg Artillery, which had been captured in the battle, had tried valiantly but futilely to sore up Pickett's line. Pickett, with the pitiful remnants of his expeditionary force, rounded out the motley group that congregated at Church Road Crossing.[29]

The conglomeration of fugitives from the different service arms was not strong enough to hold its position should Sheridan move against it in force. Late in the morning of April 2, however, it was augmented by Maj. Gen. Bushrod R. Johnson and two brigades of infantry, part of a force that Lee's colleague from the Shenandoah Valley, Richard Anderson, had led too late to Pickett's relief the day before. Lee and Pickett compared notes with the new arrival. They decided to leave the railroad, head north, cross the Appomattox River, and make for Amelia Court House on the Richmond & Danville Railroad, the location toward which all other retreat columns appeared to be heading.

Throughout the day, Johnson, Pickett, the cavalry, and Chew's horse artillery plodded north on Brown's Road, then west along the road to Namozine Church. Per standard procedure, the infantry moved in front while Lee's troopers and artillerists covered the rear, sparring with increasing numbers of Yankee cavalry. By midafternoon, Fitz discovered that a sizable force of blue riders was fast approaching his position. He relayed the news to Johnson, who had his foot soldiers erect breastworks across the road. By the time Tom Devin's division came up just before dark, Johnson's men were well enough situated that they repulsed a series of dismounted attacks. But the Yankees kept coming, and the fighting did not cease till well after dark.[30]

On the third, the weary march across Namozine Creek toward Amelia Court House resumed. This day, it was opposed not only by Devin's division, but by those under Crook and Custer as well. At this point, Roberts's cavalry brigade what remained of it—fell in with the column, and Fitz Lee placed it in the extreme rear. Roberts's men tried gamely to prevent Custer, who had taken over Sheridan's advance, from crossing Namozine Creek, but after one clash with their enemy, the Tarheels were forced into quick retreat.

Once on the far shore, Custer rushed toward the main body of Johnson's column near Namozine Church, his path now barred by Barringer's brigade of Rooney Lee's division. Two, and later three, of Custer's regiments rushed Barringer's little command, breaking the formation of the once-formidable 1st North Carolina and blunting a counterattack by the 2nd North Carolina. Suddenly and unexpectedly, the brigade fell apart before Barringer's eyes, 350 of its men either surrendering or being captured. Most of the remaining troopers fled down the road to Fitz Lee's main body, leaving their commander behind. On his way back to his own lines, Barringer was taken prisoner by a band of Sheridan's scouts wearing gray uniforms. Fitz Lee wrote that his capture, which proved a humiliating experience to the brigadier, "was keenly felt by the command."[31]

Minus Barringer and the better part of his command, the infantry-cavalry column continued on, for a time on two parallel roads, before turning north late in the afternoon and crossing the bridge over Deep Creek, an Appomattox tributary. The next day, the fugitives reached the Amelia Court House vicinity, where they joined the other columns out of Petersburg and Richmond, all of which were now heading toward a common destination, Lynchburg. The famished troops of Pickett, Johnson, and Lee, as well as many of their embattled comrades, had been led to believe that when they reached Amelia, rations and forage would be waiting for them. Instead, they found only a little cornmeal for the men, no grain or hay for the horses.[32]

Despite the meager diet, Lee's troopers were expected to stay alert and stand ready to fight. Fighting was required of them on each of the next two days. By the fifth, Sheridan's cavalry, with Ord's infantry in its rear, had gotten ahead of its quarry, striking the R & D at Jetersville, eight miles southwest of Amelia Court House. That day, too, one of Sheridan's brigades, under Henry E. Davies, pressed up the railroad toward Painesville, where it discovered and attacked a Confederate supply train, trundling westward. Davies's men set fire to dozens of wagons, but before they could do a truly thorough job of destruction, Fitz Lee galloped up with the men of Rosser and Munford. Confronting the wagon burners near Painesville, Rosser hit them with an old-fashioned saber charge. Proving that although reduced in numbers and stamina, they still were capable of great power, the attackers killed thirty Yankees, wounded or captured nearly 150 others, and sent the rest flying back on their supports at Jetersville. When Sheridan's main body hustled up to halt Davies's retreat, Fitz marched his men north, bivouacking for the night at Amelia Springs, seven miles west of the courthouse of the same name.[33]

On the sixth, Fitz Lee's men were called on to attack another band of Yankee vandals, this dispatched by General Ord to get ahead of the retreating Confederates at Farmville. That village on the meandering Appomattox lay roughly ✓ equidistant between Amelia Court House and the last major settlement on the road to Lynchburg, Appomattox Court House. At Farmville, a combination railroad-wagon bridge, 2,400 feet long and 125 feet high, crossed the river. Hoping to deny this span to the Confederates and thereby halt their march, Ord, at dawn on April 6, dispatched two infantry outfits, supported by three companies of a Massachusetts cavalry regiment, to seize and burn High Bridge. Soon after the demolition party set out, however, Robert E. Lee got wind of it and ordered his cavalry to stop it short of its destination.

As soon as he received his orders, Fitz Lee galloped west, again at the head of Rosser's and Munford's men. Reaching Farmville after Ord's troops, but before the span could be torched, the troopers piled into the infantry portion of the Union column, Munford attacking its front and Rosser lashing its right flank. The foot soldiers promptly scattered, whereupon their plucky but indiscreet cavalry comrades charged Lee's line. The Confederates met them head-on, shooting and sabering right and left. At first the Massachusetts troopers resisted fiercely and took a toll of their attackers. At the height of the melee, James Dearing was mortally wounded (he would succumb on April 23, thus ← becoming the last Confederate general officer to die from combat wounds). Col. Rueben Boston of the 5th Virginia, commanding Payne's brigade, and Major Thomson of the horse artillery were killed outright, and Rosser took a slight wound. Then the Confederates rallied, and in a matter of minutes, the Massa- ← chusetts unit ceased to exist. All of its men were killed, wounded, or captured, while Ord's chief of staff, Maj. Theodore Read, took a mortal wound as well.[34]

When the fight ended, Munford and Rosser corralled eight hundred prisoners, whom they held until other gray columns reached Farmville. When they came up, the retreat resumed, now in the direction of Rice's Station on the Southside Railroad. Later on the sixth, however, the Army of Northern Virginia's chances of long-term survival winked out when Sheridan's troopers and Meade's infantry destroyed one of Robert E. Lee's columns on Little Sailor's 8,000 Creek, making casualties of almost eight thousand Confederates, including six general officers. Then, on the seventh, the command that had crossed the Appomattox at High Bridge did an imperfect job of torching the span, enabling their pursuers to put out the fire, save the structure, and cross it, foiling a last-ditch attempt to put space between fugitives and pursuers.[35]

By late on the seventh, the hounds were at the Confederates' heels, and Grant was sending messages through the lines calling on Lee to surrender. Final defeat lay just ahead, but most Confederates kept moving west, hoping against hope that a safe haven could be found in, or short of, Lynchburg. Some even seemed optimistic despite the lengthening odds, buoyed up by small triumphs. On the afternoon of the seventh, for instance, the cavalry brigade of John Irvin Gregg pressed the rear of Fitz Lee's command too closely near Farmville, and its leader paid the price. Advancing well in front of his main body, Gregg was cut off from his men when Rosser charged his advance. Rosser later released his prisoner, but only after humiliating the colonel by stealing his boots.[36]

This was, in a sense, the last triumph of the cavalry of the Army of Northern Virginia. While its troopers plodded onward as before, the effects of physical and nervous exhaustion were beginning to tell, and the march proceeded more slowly than before. In contrast, Sheridan's troopers, and Ord's infantrymen to their rear, were marching faster than ever, galvanized by the image of a final victory just up the road. Late in the day, Sheridan's men managed to pass around the Confederates' left flank and, by heading north from Appomattox Station, got in front of them. On the evening of the eighth, as Fitz Lee's men approached Appomattox Court House, their scouts reported that a force of Yankee cavalry, size unknown, had taken position across their path on the Richmond-Lynchburg Stage Road.[37]

This was a matter of mild concern to Robert E. Lee, who saw the end approaching but doubted that it was at hand already. That night, the army leader held a council of war at his field headquarters a mile east of the village. Attendees included the few high-ranking infantry officers remaining with him, including Longstreet and John Brown Gordon, as well as Fitz Lee. All decided that on the morrow, both infantry and horsemen would press the Yankee force; if it turned out to be cavalry alone, as the army leader believed, they would attempt a breakthrough toward Lynchburg. If Meade's or Ord's infantry had come up in the horsemen's rear, however, Lee might have to entertain the surrender proposals that Grant had been sending him for the past three days.[38]

On that bright, cool Palm Sunday morning, April 9, Gordon formed his foot soldiers west of Appomattox Court House, ready to spearhead the movement that Robert E. Lee had decreed. Fitz Lee, as per the agreed-on plan, placed his troopers on Gordon's right flank, about a half mile northeast of the village. Munford's division held the far right, Rosser's the center, and Rooney Lee's the left, connecting with the foot soldiers. At daybreak, bugles squalled and the lines moved forward to attack what Robert E. Lee supposed was a thin, unsupported line of Union cavalry—a force capable of being brushed aside or run over. He had no inkling that behind the roadblock set up by the brigade of Col. Charles H. Smith of Sheridan's cavalry corps, Ord's foot soldiers, who had maintained a killing pace through the night to reach the scene before Sheridan could be overthrown, were less than a mile from the Lynchburg road.[39]

When the bugles blew, Gordon's line advanced slowly, his cavalry supports more rapidly. Gradually the combined force pressed Smith's troopers westward along the road. On the cavalry's part of the line, Rooney Lee's men moved straight ahead in close cooperation with Gordon's infantry, but Fitz Lee, with Rosser and Munford, swung farther north and west. Coming up to another line of cavalry—the main body of George Crook's division, of which Smith's brigade was a part—the Confederates spurred forward in the last saber charge most of them would ever conduct. Keening the Rebel yell, they crashed into the Union line, pushing it back through a combination of momentum and determination.

Suddenly, unexpectedly, the Yankees were gone from their front, and the road to Lynchburg lay open. Swinging back south, the gray troopers found themselves well in rear of the force that Gordon's men continued to oppose farther east. Then a crash of gunfire caused everyone to turn in that direction. Glancing over their shoulders, Fitz Lee's men saw ranks of Union infantry racing across the fields from the south and into position behind Smith's troopers. Ord's advance had reached Appomattox just in time to deny the road to Robert E. Lee's infantry. Fitz, his subordinates, and most of their officers and men saw at once that the war was over. Even before white flags went up across the lines, they realized that surrender was inevitable. His progress to the west cut off, with slower-footed Yankees coming up in his rear, Robert E. Lee had been caught in an inescapable trap.[40]

But Rosser, Munford, and their men had an option that their commander did not. As far afield as they were from the Union line, they were home free on the road to Lynchburg—if they chose to be. Most chose to be; they expressed a desire to return to their homes without experiencing the ignominy of surrender.

If the Yankee cavalry had their way, however, the escape route would not remain open for long. For several minutes the troopers under Rosser and Munford remained alongside the Richmond-Lynchburg Stage Road, many of them standing beside their horses, while their commanders debated their next move. Presently, a line of enemy horsemen appeared in rear of Munford's division, about two miles west of Appomattox Court House, and prepared to attack. The last regiment in Munford's column, the 2nd Virginia, coolly turned about, charged the Federals before they could form, and scattered them across the fields.

A few minutes later, another body of Yankee cavalry made an effort to strike the head of Munford's command, only to be repulsed by the charging 1st Maryland Battalion. In this action, Private C. W. Price of the 1st was killed— apparently the last battle fatality in the Army of Northern Virginia. At about the same time, however, the 14th Virginia of Rooney Lee's division charged a Union battery near the courthouse; in the ensuing fight, the color-bearer of the 14th, Private Samuel Walker, fell mortally wounded.

Soon after the 1st Maryland and 14th Virginia made their assaults, truce flags entered the Confederate lines, along with word that Lee was going to meet with Grant in the courthouse village. Rosser, for one, feared that Lee was going to capitulate: "The possibility of such a thing seemed to be doubly denied by the calm, manly and heroic bearing of every man in our little army, and I felt that the only answer which such a proposition should receive would be that of the Old Guard: We can die, but we cannot surrender!"

During the lull that ensued, officers on both sides crossed the lines to mingle and discuss the situation with their enemy, some of whom had been their comrades in the Old Army. Tom Munford fraternized with two of Sheridan's ranking lieutenants, Brig. Gens. Henry E. Davies and Ranald S. Mackenzie. The trio even shared a canteen filled with peach brandy, a gift of the chief quartermaster of the 2nd Virginia.

Though convivial, the confab was short. Before word of Lee's action could reach him, Munford returned to his division for a hurried consultation with his senior subordinates. They agreed that, whatever course the army commander adopted, they would not surrender—not today, not on this field. Instead, along with the majority of Rosser's command, they started off for the town that so many of them hailed from, where numerous companies and whole regiments had been organized.[41]

Their gesture of defiance may have seemed short-lived. As soon as they reached Lynchburg, most of the fugitive units disbanded, although many of their officers held out to the last. Some sought to slip into North Carolina to fight on with what remained of Joe Johnston's Army of Tennessee, but that idea died with Johnston's surrender at Durham Station on April 26. Munford and a few other commanders tried to reconstitute their units and fight on indefinitely, only to find most of their men too weary of the war to continue it. Still others hid out, eluding enemy soldiers and marshals until, tired and heartsick, they came out of the woods or mountains to sign their parole papers.[42]

4-26-'65

The true diehards, like Rosser, resorted to each of these tactics, but in the end, even he made his peace with the representatives of his enemy's government. On May 10, a full month after Robert E. Lee laid down his arms, and his army, at Appomattox, Rosser, one of the last holdouts among high-ranking Confederate leaders in Virginia, formally surrendered what remained of his command at Staunton and took the oath of allegiance to the U.S. government. For Lee's cavalrymen, the war was finally over.[43]

ROSSER

After Lee's surrender In N.C, Jefferson Davis met in a railroad car with Johnston and Beauregard insisting they fight on. He had planned on merging the C.S.A. with and extending colored slavery into Mexico! They told him "the Cause" was lost. He never liked either. P.G.T was a Catholic, populer, and heavily reported even in Northern papers. But he, unlike R.E. Lee, did not kiss Davis' butt. After every P.G.T. triumph Davis would "shit-can him" to a lesser command. P.G.T had been appointed supt. of West Point, but elected to go with the C.S.A. He is the most underrated and R.E. Lee the most over-rated of C.S.A. generals. Davis & Lee lost the war. D.C. was ripe for the taking after MANASSA I & II Early on Davis called for a defensive war as though the North would accept secession some day.

AFTERWORD

The cavalry of the Army of Northern Virginia entered the war at a distinct ?
disadvantage to its opponent, except in two areas: Familiarity with horses
and firearms, and confidence in its ability to prevail in the field. Yet it ended the
conflict in even direr straits than four years earlier, having been outmanned,
outmaneuvered, and in the final analysis, outperformed by a gaggle of erstwhile
mechanics and store clerks whose incompetence had long made them the
objects of ridicule and scorn.

In the minds of many Southerners—as well as many latter-day historians—
this outcome was the inevitable result of resource limitations and materiel deficiencies too great to be overcome. The relatively narrow population base from
which Robert E. Lee's army drew its manpower, the South's tiny industrial
capacity, its limited supplies of horseflesh and forage all contributed to a defeat
the arm shared with the other combat branches of the A.N.V. At the outset,
these unhappy facts had been regarded merely as raising the stakes so as to render Confederate triumph, when it came, all the more impressive. But as the war
dragged on, as the cavalry of the Army of the Potomac grew more numerous
and powerful, and as the troopers of Robert E. Lee grew fewer, rode poorer
horses, and made do with antiquated or obsolete weapons, the gray cavaliers _(DAVIS)_
realized how wrong they had been to assume that honor and courage alone
would carry the day.

While it has some merits, this view of things does not withstand scrutiny.
For the first two years of the war, the cavalry of Maj. Gen. J. E. B. Stuart was
consistently successful, despite its paucity of resources. Then, during a period
of relative prosperity, its fortunes suddenly plummeted. Throughout the Gettysburg campaign, when the Southern cavalry's manpower actually exceeded that
of its enemy, it was beaten, or at least held to a draw, by its upstart opponents.
The decline accelerated in 1864–65, but not because the gap between haves and
have-nots had widened dramatically. Inherent flaws in Confederate cavalry
management and operations were largely to blame for the downward spiral.

To begin with, Stuart's men never developed a consistently effective body of tactics. Their opponents learned to adopt, with some modifications, the U.S. Army's venerable dragoon tradition, which stressed tactical versatility and mission flexibility. By contrast, the Confederates fought according to a prewar militia tradition peculiar to their region, one that stressed horsemanship above all else and favored mounted fighting in almost every battlefield situation. Stuart and his followers refused to acknowledge the limitations of a mounted charge—the foremost being the inevitability of its repulse, often with heavy loss, by a skillfully mounted countercharge. Moreover, the average Confederate eschewed the use of the saber, which he regarded as a terror weapon from antiquity, putting his faith, instead, in firearms that could not be used on horseback with effectiveness except in extremely close-quarters combat.

A few commanders realized too late the fallacy of relying on the offensive and inappropriate weaponry. Following his cavalry's embarrassing defeat at Tom's Brook, October 9, 1864, Lt. Gen. Jubal A. Early rendered a judgment that Stuart would never have arrived at:

> The enemy's cavalry is so much superior to ours, both in numbers and equipment, and the country [in the upper Shenandoah Valley] is so favorable to the operations of cavalry, that it is impossible for ours to compete with his . . . [Our] cavalry are armed entirely with rifles and have no sabers, and the consequence is that they cannot fight on horseback, and in this open country they cannot successfully fight on foot against large bodies of cavalry.

Stuart and his disciples were, to a certain extent, prisoners of their early success, which extended to their horse batteries, commanded as they were by some of the South's finest artillerists, including Pelham, Chew, and Breathed. In 1861–62, their adversaries fled in panic and disarray from the saber charge (often minus the saber). In later months, however, the erstwhile victors found themselves at the mercy of experienced Yankees who disrupted their attacks with dismounted tactics or, when mounted, had the manpower to repulse every offensive and maintain a reserve. This situation first developed in early and mid-1863 at Kelly's Ford and Brandy Station; it assumed a pattern in the latter stages of the Gettysburg campaign; and it became the permanent order of things by late 1863 and early 1864.

Stuart's mortal wounding at Yellow Tavern spawned a trend toward tactical versatility. His successor, Wade Hampton, was more pragmatic, less bound to tradition. Thus, at Haw's Shop, Trevilian Station, and in later battles, the troopers of the Army of Northern Virginia made greater use of dragoon tactics, sometimes with dramatic results. But by 1864, the overreliance on the mounted offensive had taken a grievous toll. Regiments had shrunk to the size of battalions, companies had been skeletonized, and "Company Q"—the dismounted ranks maintained by every brigade—had grown to alarming proportions.

By late in the year, if not sooner, the contest was over. The war of maneuver of 1861–63 had become a war of attrition that gnawed at the vitals of the Confederate cavalry as it did at its army and its nation as a whole. Yet defeat was as much the result of internal failings as of external pressures. From start to finish, Lee's cavalrymen faced daunting odds, but the way in which they chose to fight not only added to their problems, but made them insurmountable.

Lots of research cited but — (90% wrong)
conclusions

The CSA was outmanned, outgunned, out provisioned, out-rested and saddled with an inept, fool President. The yankees improved in leadership, numbers, supplies as the CSA ran down. There were 19 million whites in the North, 8,000 in the South. 200,000 blacks, North, 4 million in the South. Few factories in the South. England & France did not aid the South as expected and the cotton export market dried up. Davis-Lee et al should have known better. Sherman did. He had been the Supt of the LA Mil. ACAD. (now LSU) but knew the CSA was doomed to a bitter, ruinous defeat, resigned and went north-after personally escorting Beauregard's two student sons home "Bory, its a noble cause but theres no way the CSA can win the war"

Face it, J.E.B Stuart and N.B Forrest had no yankee equals.

NOTES

CHAPTER 1

1. Joseph E. Johnston, *Narrative of Military Operations during the Civil War* (New York, 1874), 32–34; Henry B. McClellan, *The Life and Campaigns of Maj. Gen. J. E. B. Stuart . . .* (Boston, 1885), 34.

2. Frank Moore, ed., *The Rebellion Record: A Diary of American Events* (New York, 1861–68), 2: 303–4; Craig L. Symonds, *Joseph E. Johnston: A Civil War Biography* (New York, 1994), 111.

3. *OR,* I, 2: 473; Johnston, *Narrative of Military Operations,* 33–34.

4. *OR,* I, 2: 473; William C. Davis, *Battle at Bull Run: A History of the First Major Campaign of the Civil War* (Garden City, N.Y., 1977), 132–43.

5. Marcus Cunliffe, *Soldiers & Civilians: The Martial Spirit in America, 1775–1865* (Boston, 1968), 340–41, 368–69, 416–19.

6. Janet Hewett et al., eds., *Supplement to the Official Records of the Union and Confederate Armies* (Wilmington, N.C., 1994–), II, 69: 647–68.

7. *OR,* I, 2: 822, 853, 858–59; Rufus H. Peck, *Reminiscences of a Confederate Soldier of Co. C, 2nd Va. Cavalry* (Fincastle, Va., 1913), 2–3; Robert J. Driver, Jr., and H. E. Howard, *2nd Virginia Cavalry* (Lynchburg, Va., 1995), 1–10; Fletcher B. Moore to "Dear Ann," June 7, 1861, Moore MSS, USAMHI; Jeffry Wert, "His Unhonored Service," *CWTI* 24 (June 1985): 29–30.

8. John Esten Cooke, *Wearing of the Gray: Being Personal Portraits, Scenes and Adventures of the War* (Baton Rouge, La., 1997), 60–71; Charles L. Dufour, *Nine Men in Gray* (Garden City, N.Y., 1963), 43–48; Robert G. Tanner, *Stonewall in the Valley: Thomas J. "Stonewall" Jackson's Shenandoah Valley Campaign, Spring 1862* (Garden City, N.Y., 1976), 56–58; John Richard Kerwood, "His Daring Was Proverbial," *CWTI* 7 (Aug. 1968): 19–23.

9. Dufour, *Nine Men in Gray,* 48–49; James B. Avirett et al., *The Memoirs of General Turner Ashby and His Compeers* (Baltimore, 1867), 395–99; Clarence Thomas, *General Turner Ashby, the Centaur of the South* (Winchester, Va., 1907), 24–28.

10. John D. Imboden, "Jackson at Harper's Ferry in 1861," *B&L* 2: 123–34.

11. Davis, *Battle at Bull Run,* 34.

12. Ibid., 33–34; *OR,* I, 2: 62, 64.

13. Daniel A. Grimsley to "D[ea]r Cousin Bettie," June 3, 1861, LV.

14. Francis W. Chamberlayne memoirs, 3, VHS.

15. *OR,* I, 2: 63–64; John W. Thomason, Jr., *Jeb Stuart* (New York, 1930), 96.

16. *OR,* I, 2: 128–30.

17. Ibid., 124–30; Davis, *Battle at Bull Run,* 70–72; Thomason, *Jeb Stuart,* 96–97.

18. Edward G. Longacre, *Lincoln's Cavalrymen: A History of the Mounted Forces of the Army of the Potomac, 1861–1865* (Mechanicsburg, Pa., 2000), 1–3.

19. Hewett et al., *Supplement to the Official Records,* II, 69: 730–31; *OR,* I, 2: 440–41, 486–87, 532–35, 842.

20. John Scott, "The Black Horse Cavalry," in *The Annals of the War, Written by Leading Participants, North and South* (Philadelphia, 1879), 590–93; William H. F. Payne to "My Dear Miss Janet," Sept. 28, 1897, Payne MSS, MC; "The Black Horse Troop: The Members of the [Virginia] House of Delegates Who Served in the Famous Body . . .," *SHSP* 24 (1896): 218–19.

21. *OR,* I, 2: 36–37, 865.

22. Hewett et al., *Supplement to the Official Records,* II, 69: 700–05.

23. *OR,* I, 2: 75–77.

24. Ibid., 77–78, 82–83, 91, 93–94, 917–18.

25. Ibid., 94–96; Robert S. Hudgins II, *Recollections of an Old Dominion Dragoon: The Civil War Experiences of Sgt. Robert S. Hudgins II, Company B, 3rd Virginia Cavalry,* ed. Garland C. Hudgins and Richard B. Kleese (Orange, Va., 1993), 23–27.

CHAPTER 2

1. *OR,* I, 2: 880–81.

2. Hewett et al., *Supplement to the Official Records,* I, 1: 182–83.

3. John H. Ervine to his wife, June 18, 1861, Ervine MSS, Preston Lib., V.M.I., Lexington.

4. Davis, *Battle at Bull Run,* 45–48; Thomason, *Jeb Stuart,* 88; *OR,* I, 51, pt. 2: 143.

5. *OR,* I, 2: 185–86; McClellan, *Life and Campaigns of Stuart,* 32–33.

6. McClellan, *Life and Campaigns of Stuart,* 33–34; Johnston, *Narrative of Military Operations,* 30–31; Hewett et al., *Supplement to the Official Records,* I, 1: 182–83; Robert J. Trout, ed., *With Pen and Saber: The Letters and Diaries of J. E. B. Stuart's Staff Officers* (Mechanicsburg, Pa., 1995), 14; Robert J. Driver, Jr., *1st Virginia Cavalry* (Lynchburg, Va., 1991), 6–7.

7. J. E. B. Stuart to Flora Cooke Stuart, July 4, 1861, Stuart MSS, Robert W. Woodruff Lib., Emory Univ., Atlanta.

8. Johnston, *Narrative of Military Operations,* 32; McClellan, *Life and Campaigns of Stuart,* 34; John Singleton Mosby, *The Letters of John S. Mosby,* ed. Adele H. Mitchell (n. p., 1986), 6–7; Moore, *Rebellion Record,* 2: 303–4; Davis, *Battle at Bull Run,* 85–89, 133.

9. Davis, *Battle at Bull Run,* 91–95; *OR,* I, 2: 449–50, 457–58.

10. *OR,* I, 2: 440–47, 458; Alfred Roman, *The Military Operations of General Beauregard in the War Between the States, 1861–1865* (New York, 1884), 1: 92–93; Francis W. Chamberlayne memoirs, 5–8; James K. Munnerlyn to his sister, Aug. 7, 1861, Munnerlyn MSS, UNC; William S. Ball memoirs, 20, VHS; Driver and Howard, *2nd Virginia Cavalry,* 12–14; Woodford B. Hackley, *The Little Fork Rangers: A Sketch of Company "D," Fourth Virginia Cavalry* (Richmond, Va., 1927), 36; Kenneth L. Stiles, *4th Virginia Cavalry* (Lynchburg, Va., 1985), 5.

11. *OR,* I, 2: 473–74, 485–87; Davis, *Battle at Bull Run,* 134–47, 154–58.

12. *OR,* I, 2: 486–87; Hewett et al., *Supplement to the Official Records,* I, 69: 732, 771; Robert K. Krick, *Lee's Colonels: A Biographical Register of the Field Officers of the Army of Northern Virginia* (Dayton, 1979), 167–68.

13. *OR,* I, 2: 483, 487, 532, 534; Roman, *Military Operations of Beauregard,* 1: 97; Davis, *Battle at Bull Run,* 162–98.

14. William W. Blackford, *War Years with Jeb Stuart* (New York, 1945), 24–26; Davis, *Battle at Bull Run,* 184, 205–6.

15. Blackford, *War Years with Jeb Stuart,* 27; Mosby, *Letters of John S. Mosby,* 11; Cooke, *Wearing of the Gray,* 47–48; Manly Wade Wellman, *Giant in Gray: A Biography of Wade Hampton of South Carolina* (New York, 1949), 61–65.

16. Blackford, *War Years with Jeb Stuart,* 27.

17. Ibid., 27–29; *OR,* I, 2: 483; William W. Blackford to "Dear Uncle John," Aug. 6, 1861, USAMHI; Driver, *1st Virginia Cavalry,* 13–14.

18. Bushrod W. Lynn, "In the [First] Battle of Manassas," *CV* 26 (1918): 192.

19. Blackford, *War Years with Jeb Stuart,* 30–31.

20. *OR,* I, 2: 483.

21. Davis, *Battle at Bull Run,* 208–36; James B. Fry, "McDowell's Advance to Bull Run," *B&L* 1: 192–93.

22. *OR,* I, 2: 483, 497; Blackford, *War Years with Jeb Stuart,* 32–33; *Daily Constitutionalist* (Augusta, Ga.), Aug. 20, 1861.

23. John Singleton Mosby, *The Memoirs of Colonel John S. Mosby,* ed. by Charles Wells Russell (Boston, 1917), 48–49; Krick, *Lee's Colonels,* 338.

24. *OR,* I, 2: 532; Charles M. Blackford and Susan Leigh Blackford, *Letters from Lee's Army . . .,* ed. Charles Minor Blackford III (New York, 1947), 31–32; Peck, *Co. C, 2nd Va. Cavalry,* 5.

25. *OR,* I, 2: 532–34; Blackford, *War Years with Jeb Stuart,* 41; Driver and Howard, *2nd Virginia Cavalry,* 16–23; Blackford and Blackford, *Letters from Lee's Army,* 31–32; Davis, *Battle at Bull Run,* 236–37.

26. *OR,* I, 2: 534.

27. Blackford, *War Years with Jeb Stuart,* 31; William H. F. Payne to "My Dear Miss Janet," Sept. 28, 1897, Payne MSS, MC; William H. F. Payne to Joseph R. Anderson, Dec. 13, 1903, Payne MSS, MC; John J. Hennessy, *The First Battle of Manassas: An End to Innocence, July 18–21, 1861* (Lynchburg, Va., 1989), 119; Stiles, *4th Virginia Cavalry,* 6.

28. *OR,* I, 2: 533.

29. Blackford and Blackford, *Letters from Lee's Army,* 32; Maurice Evans to his mother, July 26, 1861, Evans MSS, VHS.

CHAPTER 3

1. Allen C. Redwood, "Following Stuart's Feather," *JMSIUS* 49 (1911): 113–14.

2. Blackford, *War Years with Jeb Stuart,* 15.

3. George Cary Eggleston, *A Rebel's Recollections* (New York, 1878), 19–20.

4. Samuel A. Riddick to his father, Nov. 23, 1861, MC; J. W. Biddle to his father, Feb. 3, 1862, Biddle MSS, DU.

5. Robert L. Dabney, *A Memorial of Lieut. Colonel John C. Thornton, of the Third Virginia Cavalry, C.S.A.* (Richmond, Va., 1864), 20; Richard H. Dulany to his sister, Sept. 21, 1861, Dulany MSS, VHS; Fletcher B. Moore to "Dear Ann," June 7, 1861, Moore MSS.

6. Dennis E. Frye, *12th Virginia Cavalry* (Lynchburg, Va., 1988), 3.

7. Micajah Woods to his mother, Aug. 14, 1862, Woods MSS, UV; Samuel S. Biddle to "My Dear Rosa," Jan. 27, 1862, Biddle MSS, DU; William H. Darden to "My Dear Beck," July 2, 1861, Darden MSS, VHS; Bell Irvin Wiley, *The Life of Johnny Reb: The Common Soldier of the Confederacy* (Indianapolis, 1943), 341.

8. Robert T. Hubard memoirs, 70, DU.

9. James K. Munnerlyn to his sister, Sept. 8, 1862, Munnerlyn MSS.

10. William Clark Corson, *My Dear Jennie: A Collection of Love Letters from a Confederate Soldier to His Fiancée during the Period 1861–1865,* ed. Blake W. Corson, Jr. (Richmond, 1982), 7.

11. Leiper M. Robinson memoirs, 8, VHS; Anon. to "Dear Cousin Laura," May 26, 1861, VHS; Henry F. Jones to his sister, Oct. 27, 1861, Jones MSS, USAMHI.

12. St. George T. Brooke autobiography, 34, VHS; James K. Munnerlyn to his sister, Aug. 18, 1861, Munnerlyn MSS.

13. John H. Ervine to his wife, June 18, 1861, Ervine MSS; Charles K. Pendleton to his father, Mar. 27, 1862, VHS.

14. Edward L. Wells, *Hampton and His Cavalry* (Richmond, Va., 1899), 83.

15. Ibid., 84–85.

16. Eggleston, *A Rebel's Recollections,* 46; Thomas L. Rosser, *Addresses of Gen'l T. L. Rosser, at the Seventh Annual Reunion of the Association of the Maryland Line . . .* (New York, 1889), 25.

17. Fairfax Downey, *Clash of Cavalry: The Battle of Brandy Station, June 9, 1863* (New York, 1959), 17–18.

18. Hudgins, *Old Dominion Dragoon,* 19; R. L. T. Beale, *History of the Ninth Virginia Cavalry, in the War Between the States* (Richmond, Va., 1899), 10–11.

19. *OR,* I, 11, pt. 2: 522–23; David Knapp, Jr., *The Confederate Horsemen* (New York, 1966), 50–53; Fitzgerald Ross, *Cities and Camps of the Confederate States,* ed. Richard B. Harwell (Urbana, Ill., 1958), 173. Although filled with invented conversation, the most satisfying biography of Stringfellow is R. Shepard Brown, *Stringfellow of the Fourth* (New York, 1960). See also James D. Peavey, *Confederate Scout: Virginia's Frank Stringfellow* (Onancock, Va., 1956) and Stringfellow's own *War Reminiscences: The Life of a Confederate Scout inside the Enemy's Line* (n. p., 1882). To follow the exploits of the largely unsung Rob Towles, see his

diary in the Earl Gregg Swem Library, College of William and Mary, Williamsburg, Va.

20. Cooke, *Wearing of the Gray*, 130–40. The best biography of Farley is J. Tracy Power, "The Confederate as Gallant Knight: The Life and Death of William Downs Farley," *Civil War History* 37 (1991): 247–55.

21. William L. Royall, *Some Reminiscences* (New York, 1909), 11.

22. McClellan, *Life and Campaigns of Stuart*, 258.

23. Although marred by halting attempts at psychoanalysis, the best biography of Stuart is the most recent: Emory M. Thomas, *Bold Dragoon: The Life of J. E. B. Stuart* (New York, 1986). Earlier, adequate life studies include McClellan, *Life and Campaigns of Stuart;* Thomason, *Jeb Stuart;* and Burke Davis, *Jeb Stuart, the Last Cavalier* (New York, 1957).

24. Cooke, *Wearing of the Gray*, 7; John Esten Cooke, "General Stuart in Camp and Field," 665.

25. Cooke, *Wearing of the Gray*, 9, 14–17; Thomas L. Rosser to Elizabeth Winston Rosser, Sept. 15, 1863, Rosser MSS, UV.

26. Franklin M. Myers, *The Comanches: A History of White's Battalion, Virginia Cavalry, Laurel Brig., Hampton['s] Div., A.N.V., C.S.A.* (Baltimore, 1871), 291. The author acknowledges the assistance of Dr. Gary Leak, Deptartment of Psychology, Creighton University, in developing a psychological profile of Stuart using modern techniques of personality psychology.

27. The only published study of Fitzhugh Lee, although heavily concerned with the general's postwar career, is James L. Nichols, *General Fitzhugh Lee: A Biography* (Lynchburg, Va., 1989). See also Henry W. Readnor, "General Fitzhugh Lee, 1835–1915" (Ph.D. diss., University of Virginia, 1958) and Ardyce Kinsley, comp., *The Fitzhugh Lee Sampler* (Lively, Va., 1992).

28. For brief biographies of each of these officers, see Ezra J. Warner, *Generals in Gray: Lives of the Confederate Commanders* (Baton Rouge, La., 1959). Munford is the only one of the group to have received a full–length study: Robert N. Thomas, "Brigadier General Thomas T. Munford and the Confederacy" (Master's thesis, Duke University, 1958). For biographical information on Baker and Gordon, see Chris J. Hartley, *Stuart's Tarheels: James B. Gordon and His North Carolina Cavalry* (Baltimore, 1996). On Martin and his original unit, see Donald A. Hopkins, *The Little Jeff: The Jeff Davis Legion, Cavalry, Army of Northern Virginia* (Shippensburg, Pa., 1999).

29. Jones's career is traced, albeit sketchily, in Dobbie Edward Lambert, *Grumble: The W. E. Jones Brigade of 1863–1864* (Wahiawa, Hawaii, 1992). Although he died midway through the war, Pelham is represented by more life studies than most Confederate generals. The best is Charles G. Milham, *Gallant Pelham, American Extraordinary* (Washington, D. C., 1959). Other biographies include William W. Hassler, *Colonel John Pelham, Lee's Boy Artillerist* (Chapel Hill, N.C., 1965); Philip Mercer, *The Life of the Gallant Pelham* (Macon, Ga., 1929); and Walter B. Jones, *The Great Cannoneer:*

An Address on the Life and Military Genius of Major John Pelham, C.S.A. ... (Montgomery, Ala., ca. 1929).

30. Each of these officers is represented by at least one substantial biography. For Butler, see Samuel J. Martin, *Southern Hero: Matthew Calbraith Butler, Confederate General, Hampton Red Shirt, and U.S. Senator* (Mechanicsburg, Pa., 2001). Young's biography is Lynwood M. Holland, *Pierce M. B. Young, the Warwick of the South* (Athens, Ga., 1964). The best biography of Hampton, although now out–of–date, is Wellman, *Giant in Gray.* For Rosser see Millard K. and Dean M. Bushong, *Fightin' Tom Rosser, C.S.A.* (Shippensburg, Pa., 1983), and Thomas O. Beane, "Thomas Lafayette Rosser: Soldier, Railroad Builder, Politician, Businessman (1836–1910)" (Master's thesis, University of Virginia, 1957).

31. J. E. B. Stuart to Flora Cooke Stuart, Aug. 28, 1863, Stuart MSS, VHS. The most comprehensive source on Stuart's military family is Robert J. Trout, *They Followed the Plume: The Story of J. E. B. Stuart and His Staff* (Mechanicsburg, Pa., 1993). See also Trout, *With Pen and Saber.*

CHAPTER 4

1. E. B. Long and Barbara Long, *The Civil War Day by Day: An Almanac, 1861–1865* (Garden City, N.Y., 1971), 700–02.

2. For a tactical and organizational history of Stuart's opponents, see Charles D. Rhodes, *History of the Cavalry of the Army of the Potomac* (Kansas City, Mo., 1900); and Longacre, *Lincoln's Cavalrymen,* especially chapters 5 through 10.

3. John T. Chappell, Memoir of Yorktown–Williamsburg Operations, [9], VHS; Hudgins, *Old Dominion Dragoon,* 20; G. B. Philpot, "A Maryland Boy in the Confederate Army," *CV* 24 (1916): 312; James L. Powell, Jr., memoirs, 7, VHS; Robert K. Krick, *9th Virginia Cavalry* (Lynchburg, Va., 1982), 3.

4. Hackley, *Little Fork Rangers,* 28, 35.

5. Joseph G. Bilby, *Civil War Firearms: Their Historical Background, Tactical Use and Modern Collecting and Shooting* (Conshohocken, Pa., 1996), 129–55.

6. McClellan, *Life and Campaigns of Stuart,* 260; Francis A. Lord, "Confederate Cavalrymen Found Revolvers Better than Sabers or Rifles," *CWTI* 1 (Jan. 1963): 46.

7. Richard D. Steuart, "Armories of the Confederacy," *CV* 35 (1927): 9–10; *OR,* I, 27, pt. 3: 873; 29, pt. 2: 648–49; Joseph G. Bilby to the author, Dec. 22, 2000.

8. John Lamb, "The Confederate Cavalry: Its Wants, Trials, and Heroism: An Address by Hon. John Lamb, Late Captain of Cavalry, C.S. Army," *SHSP* 26 (1898): 361; Wells, *Hampton and His Cavalry,* 92.

9. Wells, *Hampton and His Cavalry,* 93–94; Bilby, *Civil War Firearms,* 205.

10. Lamb, "Confederate Cavalry," 361; Wells, *Hampton and His Cavalry*, 92, 94.

11. *OR,* 11, pt. 3: 390; Rosser, *Addresses of Gen'l T. L. Rosser,* 30.

12. Robert J. Driver, Jr., *10th Virginia Cavalry* (Lynchburg, Va., 1992), 35.

13. Wiley, *Life of Johnny Reb,* 296–97; Richard D. Steuart, "A Pair of Navy Sixes," *CV* 33 (1925): 92; Carlton McCarthy, *Detailed Minutiae of Soldier Life in the Army of Northern Virginia, 1861–1865* (Richmond, Va., 1882), 27; Rufus Barringer, *The First North Carolina–A Famous Cavalry Regiment* (n.p., ca. 1866), 8.

14. Royall, *Some Reminiscences,* 11–12.

15. Mosby, *Memoirs of John S. Mosby,* 30; *Pennsylvania at Gettysburg* (Harrisburg, Pa., 1893), 2: 779.

16. McClellan, *Life and Campaigns of Stuart,* 261.

17. Lord, "Confederate Cavalrymen Found Revolvers Better," 46; Randy Steffen, *The Horse Soldier, 1776–1943: The United States Cavalryman—His Uniforms, Arms, Accoutrements, and Equipments* (Norman, Okla., 1977–80), 1: 73–76; St. George T. Brooke autobiography, 27, 29.

18. Wells, *Hampton and His Cavalry,* 99.

19. McClellan, *Life and Campaigns of Stuart,* 257–60; John N. Opie, *A Rebel Cavalryman with Lee, Stuart, and Jackson* (Chicago, 1899), 158–59; Lamb, "Confederate Cavalry," 359–60; Wiley, *Life of Johnny Reb,* 139.

20. Wells, *Hampton and His Cavalry,* 97; Redwood, "Following Stuart's Feather," 115.

21. Redwood, "Following Stuart's Feather," 115, 117; Wells, *Hampton and His Cavalry,* 97–98; Patrick Brennan, "The Best Cavalry in the World," *North & South* 2 (Jan. 1999): 13.

22. Wells, *Hampton and His Cavalry,* 99–101.

23. Richard D. Goff, *Confederate Supply* (Durham, N.C., 1969), 72–75; Redwood, "Following Stuart's Feather," 117–18; *OR,* I, 51, pt. 2: 859–60.

24. For an overview of cavalry training in the Army of the Potomac, see Longacre, *Lincoln's Cavalrymen,* chapters 3 and 4, especially pp. 35, 49–52.

25. Eggleston, *A Rebel's Recollections,* 20–21.

26. Author's interview of Perry D. Jamieson, Jan. 3, 2000.

27. Ibid.; Grady McWhiney and Perry D. Jamieson, *Attack and Die: Civil War Military Tactics and the Southern Heritage* (University, Ala., 1982), 126–32.

28. W. H. Ware, *The Battle of Kelly's Ford, Fought March 17, 1863* (Newport News, Va., 1922), 9.

29. McWhiney and Jamieson, *Attack and Die,* 132, 139.

30. Ibid., 136–38; Thomason, *Jeb Stuart,* 80; Redwood, "Following Stuart's Feather," 116–17.

31. James Parker, "Mounted and Dismounted Action of Cavalry," *JMSIUS* 39 (1906): 381–82; William Y. Chalfant, *Cheyennes and Horse Soldiers: The 1857 Expedition and Battle of Solomon's Fork* (Norman, Okla., 1989), 192.

32. Hewett et al., *Supplement to the Official Records,* II, 69: 647–52, 803–8; 70: 49–55, 181–94, 223–27.
33. Redwood, "Following Stuart's Feather," 116.
34. Hudgins, *Old Dominion Dragoon,* 20.

CHAPTER 5

1. Blackford, *War Years with Jeb Stuart,* 38–39; Davis, *Battle at Bull Run,* 243–44.
2. Davis, *Battle at Bull Run,* 256–57; William W. Blackford to "Dear Uncle John," Aug. 6, 1861, USAMHI; William B. Gallaher to his father, July 22, 1861, Gallaher MSS, LV; Eggleston, *A Rebel's Recollections,* 44; Thomas, *Bold Dragoon,* 82–83; "Letters to Laura," *CWTI* 32 (July–Aug. 1992): 12, 58.
3. Mosby, *Memoirs of John S. Mosby,* 84–85; Dufour, *Nine Men in Gray,* 52.
4. Cooke, *Wearing of the Gray,* 63–71; Kerwood, "His Daring Was Proverbial," 20–23, 28–30.
5. *OR,* I, 5: 77.
6. Personnel returns, 1861, CSR of J. E. B. Stuart, M–331, R–238, NA; McClellan, *Life and Campaigns of Stuart,* 32, 42; Avirett et al., *Memoirs of Ashby,* 383; *OR,* I, 51, pt. 2: 320.
7. Driver, *1st Virginia Cavalry,* 20; Driver and Howard, *2nd Virginia Cavalry,* 25; Wert, "His Unhonored Service," 30.
8. *OR,* I, 5: 889–90, 913–14, 922, 930, 934–35; Robert G. Hartje, *Van Dorn: The Life and Times of a Confederate General* (Nashville, Tenn., 1967), 91–105.
9. Stiles, *4th Virginia Cavalry,* 1–7; Warner, *Generals in Gray,* 259–60; Beverly H. Robertson to his brother, May 14, 1861, Letters Recd. by the Adj. Gen.'s Office, RG–393, NA; Patrick A. Bowmaster, "Brig. Gen. B. H. Robertson, C.S.A." (typescript in possession of the author), 15–16; Williams C. Wickham to his father, Sept. 8, 1861, Wickham MSS, LV; J. E. B. Stuart to Flora Cooke Stuart, Oct. 21, 1861, Stuart MSS, Robert W. Woodruff Lib., Emory Univ.
10. *OR,* I, 5: 932; Thomas P. Nanzig, *3rd Virginia Cavalry* (Lynchburg, Va., 1989), 10; Driver and Howard, *2nd Virginia Cavalry,* 29; Krick, *9th Virginia Cavalry,* 1–3; Driver, *10th Virginia Cavalry,* 1–7.
11. Walter Clark, ed., *Histories of the Several Regiments and Battalions from North Carolina in the Great War, 1861–'65 . . .* (Goldsboro and Raleigh, N.C., 1901), 1: 417–18; Hopkins, *The Little Jeff,* 12–26, 38; Robert H. Moore, II, *The 1st and 2nd Stuart Horse Artillery* (Lynchburg, Va., 1985), 1.
12. Moore, *Stuart Horse Artillery,* 1–2; Personnel returns, 1861, CSR of John Pelham, M–331, R–195, NA; John Pelham to Jefferson Davis, Feb. 27, 1861, ibid.; Robert J. Trout, "Galloping Thunder: The Stuart Horse Artillery Battalion . . .," *North & South* 3 (Sept. 2000): 78.

13. Trout, "Galloping Thunder," 77–78; Jennings Cropper Wise, *The Long Arm of Lee; or, The History of the Artillery of the Army of Northern Virginia* . . . (Lynchburg, Va., 1915), 1: 162–63; Avirett et al., *Memoirs of Ashby,* 267–68; Tanner, *Stonewall in the Valley,* 56.

14. Longacre, *Lincoln's Cavalrymen,* 53–58; *OR,* I, 5: 182; 51, pt. 1: 38.

15. Alexander H. Boykin to his wife, Aug. 17, 1861, Boykin MSS, UNC.

16. *OR,* I, 5: 183–84, 848; 51, pt. 2: 291; McClellan, *Life and Campaigns of Stuart,* 41–42; Driver, *1st Virginia Cavalry,* 19; Beane, "Thomas Lafayette Rosser," 15–16; Mosby, *Letters of John S. Mosby,* 15–16.

17. J. E. B. Stuart to Thomas L. Rosser, Jan. 22, 1862, Rosser MSS, UV.

18. *OR,* I, 5: 305–6, 348–53, 368–72.

19. J. E. B. Stuart to Flora Cooke Stuart, Oct. 18, 1861, Stuart MSS, Robert W. Woodruff Lib., Emory Univ.; *OR,* I, 5: 929–30; Thornton R. Baxter to his mother, Oct. 25, 1861, Baxter MSS, James Graham Leyburn Library, Washington and Lee Univ., Lexington, Va.

20. J. E. B. Stuart to Flora Cooke Stuart, Nov. 20, 1861, Stuart MSS, Robert W. Woodruff Lib., Emory Univ.; *OR,* I, 5: 439–41; Hopkins, *The Little Jeff,* 29–30; Hewett et al., *Supplement to the Official Records,* I, 1: 408.

21. Davis, *Battle at Bull Run,* 207–9.

22. J. E. B. Stuart to Flora Cooke Stuart, Nov. 20, 1861, Stuart MSS, Robert W. Woodruff Lib., Emory Univ.; *OR,* I, 5: 441–43; Hewett et al., *Supplement to the Official Records,* I, 1: 407–8; Frank A. Bond, "Fitz Lee in [the] Army of Northern Virginia," *CV* 6 (1898): 420–21; Mosby, *Letters of John S. Mosby,* 18; Driver, *1st Virginia Cavalry,* 25–26.

23. *OR,* I, 5: 443–47; Hewett et al., *Supplement to the Official Records,* I, 1: 408; Jacob A. Fisher to his parents, Dec. 8, 1861, USAMHI; Barringer, *First North Carolina,* 2; Clark, *Regiments and Battalions from North Carolina,* 1: 419.

24. Hewett et al., *Supplement to the Official Records,* I, 1: 408; Daniel A. Grimsley to "D[ea]r Cousin," Dec. 6, 1861, Grimsley MSS, LV; Robert W. Pritchett to his wife, Dec. 5, 1861, Pritchett MSS, MC.

25. Hewett et al., *Supplement to the Official Records,* I, 1: 409; *OR,* I, 5: 448–51.

26. *OR,* I, 5: 490–91; McClellan, *Life and Campaigns of Stuart,* 43–44; Johnston, *Narrative of Military Operations,* 83–84; Driver and Howard, *2nd Virginia Cavalry,* 31–32.

27. *OR,* I, 5: 491–92; McClellan, *Life and Campaigns of Stuart,* 44–45; Clark, *Regiments and Battalions from North Carolina,* 1: 419–20.

28. *OR,* I, 5: 492–94; McClellan, *Life and Campaigns of Stuart,* 45.

29. Fletcher B. Moore to "Dear Par," Dec. 30, 1861, Moore MSS; J. B. Jones, *A Rebel War Clerk's Diary at the Confederate States Capital,* ed. Howard Swiggett (New York, 1935), 1: 97–98.

30. George H. Caperton diary, Dec. 25, 1861, VHS; Driver and Howard, *2nd Virginia Cavalry,* 32; Fletcher B. Moore to "Dear Par," Dec. 30, 1861, Moore MSS.

CHAPTER 6

1. "Letters to Laura," 12, 58, 60–61.
2. Driver, *1st Virginia Cavalry,* 29.
3. Holmes Conrad to his mother, Dec. 29, 1861, Conrad MSS, VHS; *OR,* I, 5: 1030; J. E. B. Stuart to Flora Cooke Stuart, Dec. 11, 1861, Stuart MSS, Robert W. Woodruff Lib., Emory Univ.; J. E. B. Stuart to John R. Cooke, Jan. 18, 1862, Cooke MSS, VHS; Moore, *Stuart Horse Artillery,* 3–5.
4. H. H. Matthews, "A Maryland Confederate . . . Recollections of Major James Breathed," *SHSP* 30 (1902): 346–48; "A Model U.C.V. Camp," *CV* 7 (1899): 167–68; Wise, *Long Arm of Lee,* 1: 352–53; Moore, *Stuart Horse Artillery,* 1–4; Milham, *Gallant Pellham,* 59; Hassler, *Colonel John Pelham,* 26.
5. *OR,* I, 5: 1025; 9: 111–12; Samuel S. Biddle to his father, Feb. 3, 1862, Biddle MSS; Benjamin C. Yancey to his wife, Feb. 11, 1862, Yancey MSS, UNC; John B. Fontaine to his sister, Feb. 16, 1862, Fontaine MSS, USAMHI; James K. Munnerlyn to his sister, Feb. 27, 1862, Munnerlyn MSS.
6. Clark, *Regiments and Battalions from North Carolina,* 1: 420; Warner, *Generals in Gray,* 87, 253–54.
7. James K. Munnerlyn to his sister, Jan. 18, 1862, Munnerlyn MSS; Holmes Conrad to his father, Jan. 20, 1862, Conrad MSS; Driver, *1st Virginia Cavalry,* 28–29.
8. Mosby, *Memoirs of John S. Mosby,* 99–102.
9. Johnston, *Narrative of Military Operations,* 102–3; Blackford, *War Years with Jeb Stuart,* 59–60.
10. *OR,* I, 5: 1091, 1093–94; Symonds, *Joseph E. Johnston,* 145.
11. Johnston, *Narrative of Military Operations,* 103–4; Driver, *1st Virginia Cavalry,* 30; Driver and Howard, *2nd Virginia Cavalry,* 38–39; Peck, *Co. C, 2nd Va. Cavalry,* 12.
12. John Singleton Mosby, *Mosby's War Reminiscences and Stuart's Cavalry Campaigns* (Boston, 1887), 212.
13. *OR,* I, 5: 550–51, 1101–2.
14. Ibid., 11, pt. 3: 415.
15. Stephen W. Sears, *To the Gates of Richmond: The Peninsula Campaign* (New York, 1992), 28–32; *OR,* I, 11, pt. 3: 402.
16. Driver, *1st Virginia Cavalry,* 31; *OR,* I, 11, pt. 3: 406–7, 415–17.
17. *OR,* I, 11, pt. 3: 390, 395.
18. Ibid., 396; Krick, *9th Virginia Cavalry,* 4; Driver, *10th Virginia Cavalry,* 17.
19. *OR,* I, 11, pt. 3: 415–16; Sears, *To the Gates of Richmond,* 34–36.
20. Sears, *To the Gates of Richmond,* 28–32.
21. *OR,* I, 11, pt. 1: 8–9, 284–85, 358.
22. Ibid., 409; Sears, *To the Gates of Richmond,* 37–38.
23. Sears, *To the Gates of Richmond,* 43–45.

24. Moore, *Stuart Horse Artillery,* 9–10; J. E. B. Stuart to Jefferson Davis, Apr. 4, 1862, CSR of Stuart, M–331, R–216, NA; *OR,* I, 11, pt. 3: 423.

25. Trout, *With Pen and Saber,* 58–59.

26. Thomas, *Bold Dragoon,* 103–4.

27. Driver and Howard, *2nd Virginia Cavalry;* 40–41; Krick, *9th Virginia Cavalry,* 4; Edwin C. Claybrook diary, Apr. 17–18, 1862, MC; Lomax Tayloe to his father, Apr. 24, 1862, Tayloe MSS, Hist. Soc. of Southwestern Virginia, Roanoke; *OR,* I, 12, pt. 1: 427–40.

28. Tanner, *Stonewall in the Valley,* 155–60.

29. Hudgins, *Old Dominion Dragoon,* 52; Lamb, "Confederate Cavalry," 360; Hackley, *Little Fork Rangers,* 41; John T. Thornton to his wife, Apr. 27, 1862, Thornton MSS, UV.

30. Driver, *1st Virginia Cavalry,* 32; Nanzig, *3rd Virginia Cavalry,* 13; Stiles, *4th Virginia Cavalry,* 10; Bowmaster, "Brig. Gen. B. H. Robertson," 15.

31. Sears, *To the Gates of Richmond,* 61–62, 65–68.

32. *OR,* I, 11, p. 1: 444; Cooke, *Wearing of the Gray,* 423.

33. *OR,* I, 11, pt. 1: 444–45, 574.

34. Ibid., 444, 564; McClellan, *Life and Campaigns of Stuart,* 48–49; Hackley, *Little Fork Rangers,* 42; Driver, *10th Virginia Cavalry,* 18; John Z. H. Scott memoirs, 8, VHS; John T. Chappell, Memoir of Yorktown–Williamsburg Operations, [8]–[9].

35. *OR,* I, 11, pt. 1: 444, 574; McClellan, *Life and Campaigns of Stuart,* 49; Hudgins, *Old Dominion Dragoon,* 52–53; John T. Thornton to his wife, May 10, 1862, Thornton MSS; Robert T. Hubard memoirs, 43.

36. *OR,* I, 11, pt. 1: 444–45; McClellan, *Life and Campaigns of Stuart,* 49–50; Cooke, *Wearing of the Gray,* 425–26; Nanzig, *3rd Virginia Cavalry,* 16; Stiles, *4th Virginia Cavalry,* 10.

CHAPTER 7

1. *OR,* I, 11, pt. 1: 570.

2. Ibid., 564–68, 570–71; McClellan, *Life and Campaigns of Stuart,* 50; Sears, *To the Gates of Richmond,* 68–78.

3. Sears, *To the Gates of Richmond,* 78–79; *OR,* I, 11, pt. 1: 571.

4. *OR,* I, 11, pt. 1: 571–72, 574–75; Moore, *Stuart Horse Artillery,* 12–13.

5. *OR,* I, 11, pt. 1: 450, 569.

6. Ibid., 572; William H. F. Payne to Joseph R. Anderson, Dec. 13, 1903, Payne MSS, MC; Stiles, *4th Virginia Cavalry,* 11; Scott, "Black Horse Cavalry," 595; Henry W. Coons to "Dear Sister Mollie," May 18, 1862, Coons MSS, VHS.

7. J. E. B. Stuart to Flora Cooke Stuart, May 9, 1862, Stuart MSS, VHS.

8. Driver, *1st Virginia Cavalry,* 34; Trout, *With Pen and Saber,* 66.

9. *OR,* I, 11, pt. 1: 628; Johnston, *Narrative of Military Operations,* 126; McClellan, *Life and Campaigns of Stuart,* 50–51.

10. Moore, *Stuart Horse Artillery,* 14; Hackley, *Little Fork Rangers,* 43; Driver, *1st Virginia Cavalry,* 34; Corson, *My Dear Jennie,* 77–78; John T. Thornton to his wife, May 10, 1862, Thornton MSS; Henry W. Coons to "Dear Sister Mollie," May 18, 1862, Coons MSS.
11. *OR,* I, 11, pt. 3: 515.
12. Long and Long, *Civil War Day by Day,* 211–13; *OR,* I, 11, pt. 1: 27.
13. Hudgins, *Old Dominion Dragoon,* 53.
14. Johnston, *Narrative of Military Operations,* 129–31; *OR,* I, 11, pt. 1: 27–33.
15. Tanner, *Stonewall in the Valley,* 209–15.
16. Driver and Howard, *2nd Virginia Cavalry,* 41–45; *OR,* I, 12, pt. 1: 729–34; Hewett et al., *Supplement to the Official Records,* I, 2: 573–74.
17. Tanner, *Stonewall in the Valley,* 225–33.
18. *OR,* I, 11, pt. 1: 31–32; Johnston, *Narrative of Military Operations,* 131–32; Joseph E. Johnston, "Manassas to Seven Pines," *B&L* 2: 211.
19. Sears, *To the Gates of Richmond,* 117–45.
20. McClellan, *Life and Campaigns of Stuart,* 51; *OR,* I, 11, pt. 1: 941, 993–94; Gustavus W. Smith, *The Battle of Seven Pines* (New York, 1891), 127.
21. Corson, *My Dear Jennie,* 80.
22. *OR,* I, 11, pt. 3: 570; J. E. B. Stuart to Robert E. Lee, June 4, 1862, Douglas Southall Freeman MSS, LC.
23. J. E. B. Stuart to Robert E. Lee, June 4, 1862, Douglas Southall Freeman MSS, LC.
24. Douglas Southall Freeman, *Lee's Lieutenants: A Study in Command* (New York, 1942–44), 1: 275–77.
25. Ibid., 277–78; *OR,* I, 11, pt. 3: 590–91.
26. *OR,* I, 11, pt. 1: 1036, 1042–44; McClellan, *Life and Campaigns of Stuart,* 53–54; Hackley, *Little Fork Rangers,* 43; Stiles, *4th Virginia Cavalry,* 12; Moore, *Stuart Horse Artillery,* 15.
27. W. T. Robins, "Stuart's Ride around McClellan," *B&L* 2: 271; *OR,* I, 11, pt. 1: 1036; George W. Beale, *A Lieutenant of Cavalry in Lee's Army* (Boston, 1918), 24–25.
28. *OR,* I, 11, pt. 1: 1036; McClellan, *Life and Campaigns of Stuart,* 54–55; Freeman, *Lee's Lieutenants,* 1: 282–84; Cooke, *Wearing of the Gray,* 167.
29. *OR,* I, 11, pt. 1: 1020–22, 1037, 1043; McClellan, *Life and Campaigns of Stuart,* 55; Robins, "Stuart's Ride," 271; Cooke, *Wearing of the Gray,* 168; Beale, *Ninth Virginia Cavalry,* 17; Charles R. Chewning diary, June 13, 1862, Handley Regional Lib., Winchester, Va.
30. *OR,* I, 11, pt. 1: 1020–21, 1023–24, 1037, 1043; McClellan, *Life and Campaigns of Stuart,* 56; Robins, "Stuart's Ride," 272; Beale, *Ninth Virginia Cavalry,* 18; W. W. Scott, ed., "Two Confederate Items," *Bulletin of the Virginia State Library* 16 (July 1927): 68; Charles R. Chewning diary, June 13, 1862; Robert P. Baylor to his father, June 15, 1862, VHS; Chiswell Dabney to his mother, June 18, 1862, Dabney MSS, VHS; John W. Murray

to his wife, June 17, 1862, Murray MSS, LV; William Campbell, "Stuart's Ride and Death of Latane . . .," *SHSP* 39 (1914): 86–90.

31. McClellan, *Life and Campaigns of Stuart,* 57–58.

32. *OR,* I, 11, pt. 1: 1038; McClellan, *Life and Campaigns of Stuart,* 58; Freeman, *Lee's Lieutenants,* 1: 288.

33. *OR,* I, 11, pt. 1: 1006–8, 1010–11, 1015–17, 1019, 1021, 1023–27, 1029–30, 1037; Longacre, *Lincoln's Cavalrymen,* 87–89; McClellan, *Life and Campaigns of Stuart,* 58–60; Robins, "Stuart's Ride," 272; Cooke, *Wearing of the Gray,* 169–70; Beale, *Lieutenant of Cavalry,* 27; John H. Cameron memoirs, 9, Preston Lib., V.M.I.

34. *OR,* I, 11, pt. 1: 1027–28, 1032–34, 1038, 1044; McClellan, *Life and Campaigns of Stuart,* 60; Robins, "Stuart's Ride," 273; Beale, *Ninth Virginia Cavalry,* 19.

35. *OR,* I, 11, pt. 1: 1031–32, 1039–45; McClellan, *Life and Campaigns of Stuart,* 60–61; Robins, "Stuart's Ride," 272–73; Cooke, *Wearing of the Gray,* 172–74; Freeman, *Lee's Lieutenants,* 1: 292–93; Beale, *Ninth Virginia Cavalry,* 19–20; Beale, *Lieutenant of Cavalry,* 28–29; George E. Turner, *Victory Rode the Rails: The Strategic Place of the Railroads in the Civil War* (Indianapolis, 1953), 163–64.

36. *OR,* I, 11, pt. 1: 1038–39; McClellan, *Life and Campaigns of Stuart,* 62–63; Freeman, *Lee's Lieutenants,* 1: 293; Cooke, *Wearing of the Gray,* 174.

37. *OR,* I, 11, pt. 1: 1039; McClellan, *Life and Campaigns of Stuart,* 63–64; Robins, "Stuart's Ride," 273; Cooke, *Wearing of the Gray,* 174–78; Beale, *Ninth Virginia Cavalry,* 20; Beale, *Lieutenant of Cavalry,* 29; Freeman, *Lee's Lieutenants,* 1: 295–97.

38. *OR,* I, 11, pt. 1: 1039; McClellan, *Life and Campaigns of Stuart,* 64–65; Robins, "Stuart's Ride," 274–75; Cooke, *Wearing of the Gray,* 178–79; Beale, *Ninth Virginia Cavalry,* 21; Beale, *Lieutenant of Cavalry,* 30; Freeman, *Lee's Lieutenants,* 1: 297–99.

39. *OR,* I, 11, pt. 1: 1039; McClellan, *Life and Campaigns of Stuart,* 65–67; Robins, "Stuart's Ride," 275; Cooke, *Wearing of the Gray,* 180.

40. *OR,* I, 11, pt. 1: 1039; Driver, *1st Virginia Cavalry,* 39; Hudgins, *Old Dominion Dragoon,* 55; Charles R. Chewning diary, June 16, 1862.

41. John Letcher to Jefferson Davis, June 15, 1862, CSR of J. E. B. Stuart, M–331, R–238, NA; Moore, *Rebellion Record,* 5: 195–202.

CHAPTER 8

1. Charles R. Chewning diary, June 16, 1862; *OR,* I, 11, pt. 1: 1041.

2. Hudgins, *Old Dominion Dragoon,* 59.

3. Ibid.; *OR,* I, 11, pt. 2: 552; Driver and Howard, *2nd Virginia Cavalry,* 51; Freeman, *Lee's Lieutenants,* 1: 493–98.

4. Freeman, *Lee's Lieutenants,* 1: 496–98; Sears, *To the Gates of Richmond,* 175–77.

5. Clark, *Regiments and Battalions from North Carolina*, 1: 420; Hewett et al., *Supplement to the Official Records*, II, 48: 29; Warner, *Generals in Gray*, 56, 348.

6. Robert J. Driver, Jr., *5th Virginia Cavalry* (Lynchburg, Va., 1997), 22–23, 28, 31; J. E. B. Stuart to Thomas L. Rosser, June 23, 1862, Rosser MSS, UV; Milham, *Gallant Pellham*, 90; Personnel return, June 1862, CSR of Thomas L. Rosser, M–331, R–216, NA; Bushong and Bushong, *Fightin' Tom Rosser*, 20.

7. Driver, *5th Virginia Cavalry*, 22–23, 32–34, 46; Thaddeus Fitzhugh memoirs, 18, MC. The case against Pate is summarized in *Proceedings of the General Court Martial, in the Case of Lieut. Col. H. Clay Pate, 5th Va. Cavalry* (Richmond, 1863).

8. Sears, *To the Gates of Richmond*, 183–89.

9. *OR*, I, 11, pt. 2: 513, 525, 532; McClellan, *Life and Campaigns of Stuart*, 72–73; Charles R. Chewning diary, June 25–26, 1862; Beale, *Lieutenant of Cavalry*, 33–34; Hudgins, *Old Dominion Dragoon*, 60.

10. *OR*, I, 11, pt. 2: 490, 513–14.

11. Ibid., 514–15; Blackford, *War Years with Jeb Stuart*, 72; Beale, *Lieutenant of Cavalry*, 34.

12. *OR*, I, 11, pt. 2: 515, 528; McClellan, *Life and Campaigns of Stuart*, 76; Moore, *Stuart Horse Artillery*, 17; Jones, *Great Cannoneer*, 9; Wiley C. Howard, *Sketch of Cobb Legion Cavalry and Some Incidents and Scenes Remembered . . .* (Atlanta, 1901), 1–2; John Esten Cooke diary, June 28, 1862, UV.

13. *OR*, I, 11, pt. 2: 515.

14. Ibid., 515–16, 524, 528; Moore, *Stuart Horse Artillery*, 18.

15. *OR*, I, 11, pt. 2: 529.

16. Ibid., 516–17; McClellan, *Life and Campaigns of Stuart*, 78; Moore, *Stuart Horse Artillery*, 18–19.

17. *OR*, I, 11, pt. 2: 516; Blackford, *War Years with Jeb Stuart*, 75–76; Charles R. Chewning diary, June 29, 1862.

18. *OR*, I, 11, pt. 2: 517–18, 529–30, 627, 685; McClellan, *Life and Campaigns of Stuart*, 79; Charles R. Chewning diary, June 30, 1862; Beale, *Lieutenant of Cavalry*, 37; John Esten Cooke diary, July 7, 1862; Driver, *1st Virginia Cavalry*, 41.

19. *OR*, I, 11, pt. 2: 518; McClellan, *Life and Campaigns of Stuart*, 79–80; Driver, *1st Virginia Cavalry*, 41. For a contemporary criticism of Stuart's expedition to White House, see Charles Marshall, *An Aide–de–Camp of Lee: Being the Papers of Colonel Charles Marshall . . .*, ed. Sir Frederick Maurice (Boston, 1927), 99n.

20. *OR*, I, 11, pt. 2: 519, 530; J. E. B. Stuart to Robert E. Lee, July 2, 1862, Stuart MSS, Gilder Lehrman Coll., New York; McClellan, *Life and Campaigns of Stuart*, 82; Blackford, *War Years with Jeb Stuart*, 78–79; James

Hardeman Stuart diary, July 2, 1862, Mississippi Dept. of Arch. and Hist., Jackson.

21. *OR,* I, 11, pt. 2: 519–20, 530–31; Wise, *Long Arm of Lee,* 1: 233; Robert Stiles, *Four Years under Marse Robert* (New York, 1903), 106–07; Moore, *Stuart Horse Artillery,* 20.

22. Walter H. Taylor, *Four Years with General Lee . . .* (New York, 1877), 41; McClellan, *Life and Campaigns of Stuart,* 83–85; Fitzhugh Lee, *General Lee* (New York, 1894), 165–66; Edward Porter Alexander, *Fighting for the Confederacy: The Personal Recollections of General Edward Porter Alexander,* ed. Gary A. Gallagher (Chapel Hill, N.C., 1989), 114–15; Freeman, *Lee's Lieutenants,* 1: 641–43.

23. John J. Hennessy, *Return to Bull Run: The Campaign and Battle of Second Manassas* (New York, 1993), 5–26.

24. Ibid., 23–26; Blackford, *War Years with Jeb Stuart,* 87.

25. *OR,* I, 11, pt. 2: 525, 532; Corson, *My Dear Jennie,* 87; Nanzig, *3rd Virginia Cavalry,* 17.

26. *OR,* I, 11, pt. 1: 525; McClellan, *Life and Campaigns of Stuart,* 79; Chris J. Hartley, "Artillery Ambush at Willis Church," *America's Civil War* 14 (May 2001): 51–55.

27. *OR,* I, 11, pt. 1: 525; Clark, *Regiments and Battalions from North Carolina,* 1: 420; Albert F. Williams, "A. F. Williams Diary, 1862," *Lower Cape Fear Historical Society Bulletin* 17 (1974): 1–2; Hartley, "Willis Church," 55–56. While some accounts date the fight as occurring on June 30, other, more reliable sources, describe it as taking place the previous day.

28. Blackford, *War Years with Jeb Stuart,* 88; Register of appointment, CSR of J. E. B. Stuart, M–331, R–238, NA; *OR,* I, 11, pt. 3: 655.

29. *OR,* I, 11, pt. 3:, 645.

30. Ibid., 652, 657; McClellan, *Life and Campaigns of Stuart,* 86.

31. *OR,* I, 11, pt. 1: 1041; pt. 3: 655.

32. Ibid., pt. 3: 655; Wellman, *Giant in Gray,* 81–85.

33. Wellman, *Giant in Gray,* , 83–84; Warner, *Generals in Gray,* 122; Cooke, *Wearing of the Gray,* 51–55.

34. Cooke, *Wearing of the Gray,* 48–49, 52.

35. Wellman, *Giant in Gray,* 84; *OR,* I, 11, pt. 3: 657; 12, pt. 3: 920.

36. *OR,* I, 12, pt. 2: 550n, 725; Robert E. Lee, *The Wartime Papers of Robert E. Lee,* ed. Clifford Dowdey and Louis H. Manarin (Boston, 1961), 255.

37. *OR,* I, 12, pt. 2: 177.

38. Cooke, *Wearing of the Gray,* 335–36; Hugh C. Keen and Horace Mewborn, *43rd Battalion, Virginia Cavalry, Mosby's Command* (Lynchburg, Va., 1993), 4–5; James A. Ramage, *Gray Ghost: The Life of Col. John Singleton Mosby* (Lexington, Ky., 1999), 50–51; *OR,* I, 51, pt. 2: 594.

39. *OR,* I, 51, pt. 2: 51–54; Mosby, *Memoirs of John S. Mosby,* 134; "An Appraisal of John S. Mosby," *CWTI* 4 (Nov. 1965): 6.

40. *OR,* I, 12, pt. 2: 119–20; McClellan, *Life and Campaigns of Stuart,* 87–88.

41. *OR,* I, 12, pt. 2: 118, 120; McClellan, *Life and Campaigns of Stuart,* 88; Blackford, *War Years with Jeb Stuart,* 95; James Hardeman Stuart diary, Aug. 6, 1862; Henry W. Coons to "Dear Sister Mollie," Aug. 9, 1862, Coons MSS; Edwin C. Claybrook diary, Aug. 6, 1862.
42. *OR,* I, 12, pt. 2: 121; McClellan, *Life and Campaigns of Stuart,* 88–89.

CHAPTER 9
1. Blackford, *War Years with Jeb Stuart,* 97.
2. *OR,* I, 12, pt. 2: 184; Hennessy, *Return to Bull Run,* 28–29.
3. *OR,* I, 12, pt. 2: 184; Chiswell Dabney to his mother, Aug. 13, 1862, Dabney MSS.
4. Blackford, *War Years with Jeb Stuart,* 97; J. E. B. Stuart to Robert E. Lee, Aug. 13, 1862, Stuart MSS, VHS; Bowmaster, "Brig. Gen. B. H. Robertson," 17–18.
5. Bowmaster, "Brig. Gen. B. H. Robertson," 15; Blackford, *War Years with Jeb Stuart,* 229.
6. Blackford, *War Years with Jeb Stuart,* 97; *OR,* I, 12, pt. 2: 725; McClellan, *Life and Campaigns of Stuart,* 89; Thomas, *Bold Dragoon,* 142.
7. *OR,* I, 11, pt. 3: 676; 12, pt. 2: 725; pt. 3: 929–30.
8. Ibid., pt. 2: 725–26; Cooke, *Wearing of the Gray,* 195–96.
9. Cooke, *Wearing of the Gray,* 196–99; McClellan, *Life and Campaigns of Stuart,* 89–90; Lee, *General Lee,* 183; Mosby, *Memoirs of John S. Mosby,* 136–37; James Hardeman Stuart diary, Aug. 18, 1862; James Longstreet, *From Manassas to Appomattox: Memoirs of the Civil War in America* (Philadelphia, 1896), 161, 166; William Y. Thompson, "Robert Toombs, Confederate General," *Civil War History* 7 (1961): 415–16.
10. McClellan, *Life and Campaigns of Stuart,* 90; Blackford, *War Years with Jeb Stuart,* 97; B. J. Haden, *Reminiscences of J. E. B. Stuart's Cavalry . . .* (Charlottesville, Va., ca. 1890), 14–15.
11. McClellan, *Life and Campaigns of Stuart,* 90–91; Walter H. Taylor, *General Lee: His Campaigns in Virginia, 1861–1865 . . .* (Norfolk, Va., 1906), 92.
12. *OR,* I, 12, pt. 2: 728; pt. 3: 934.
13. McClellan, *Life and Campaigns of Stuart,* 91; Marshall, *Aide-de-Camp of Lee,* 126–27; Freeman, *Lee's Lieutenants,* 2: 61.
14. *OR,* I, 12, pt. 2: 728–29.
15. Ibid., 726–27; McClellan, *Life and Campaigns of Stuart,* 92; Daniel A. Grimsley, *Battles in Culpeper County, Virginia, 1861–1865* (Culpeper, Va., 1900), 3; George M. Neese, *Three Years in the Confederate Horse Artillery* (New York, 1911), 96; John T. Thornton to his wife, Aug. 25, 1862, Thornton MSS.
16. *OR,* I, 12, pt. 2: 727; Heros von Borcke, *Memoirs of the Confederate War for Independence* (New York, 1938), 1: 111–13; Hewett et al., *Supplement to the Official Records,* I, 2: 783.

17. *OR,* I, 12, pt. 2: 727–28; McClellan, *Life and Campaigns of Stuart,* 93; Hewett et al., *Supplement to the Official Records,* I, 2: 594, 784; von Borcke, *Memoirs,* 1: 113–15; Richard L. Armstrong, *7th Virginia Cavalry* (Lynchburg, Va., 1992), 40–41; Richard L. Armstrong, *11th Virginia Cavalry* (Lynchburg, Va., 1989), 12; Frye, *12th Virginia Cavalry,* 8–9; Moore, *Stuart Horse Artillery,* 25–26.

18. *OR,* I, 12, pt. 2: 727.

19. James L. Powell, Jr., memoirs, 9.

20. *OR,* I, 12, pt. 2: 730; McClellan, *Life and Campaigns of Stuart,* 93; Hennessy, *Return to Bull Run,* 62–63.

21. Hennessy, *Return to Bull Run,* 63–67; *OR,* I, 12, pt. 2: 730; Blackford and Blackford, *Letters from Lee's Army,* 119.

22. *OR,* I, 12, pt. 2: 730.

23. Ibid., 730–31; McClellan, *Life and Campaigns of Stuart,* 94; Blackford, *War Years with Jeb Stuart,* 99–100; James D. Peavey, *Confederate Scout: Virginia's Frank Stringfellow* (Onancoc, Va., 1956), 44–45.

24. Blackford, *War Years with Jeb Stuart,* 100.

25. *OR,* I, 12, pt. 2: 731; McClellan, *Life and Campaigns of Stuart,* 94; Blackford, *War Years with Jeb Stuart,* 100–101; Neese, *Confederate Horse Artillery,* 101; Robert H. Moore, II, *Chew's Ashby, Shoemaker's Lynchburg, and the Newtown Artillery* (Lynchburg, Va., 1995), 15–16.

26. Blackford, *War Years with Jeb Stuart,* 102; Haden, *Reminiscences,* 15; Hennessy, *Return to Bull Run,* 77–78.

27. Blackford, *War Years with Jeb Stuart,* 103.

28. *OR,* I, 12, pt. 2: 732; pt. 3: 942; Freeman, *Lee's Lieutenants,* 2: 71; Douglas Southall Freeman, *R. E. Lee: A Biography* (New York, 1934–35), 2: 297n.; Hennessy, *Return to Bull Run,* 80–81; L. Van Loan Naisawald, "Stuart as a Cavalryman's Cavalryman," *CWTI* 1 (Feb. 1963): 44–45.

29. Rosser, *Addresses of Gen'l T. L. Rosser,* 30; Beane, "Thomas Lafayette Rosser," 21–22; Bushong and Bushong, *Fightin' Tom Rosser,* 24–25; William N. McDonald, *A History of the Laurel Brigade, Originally the Ashby Cavalry of the Army of Northern Virginia, and Chew's Battery,* ed. Bushrod C. Washington (Baltimore, 1907), 84; Driver, *5th Virginia Cavalry,* 36–37.

30. *OR,* I, 12, pt. 2: 731; McClellan, *Life and Campaigns of Stuart,* 94–95; Blackford, *War Years with Jeb Stuart,* 105–8; Lee, *Wartime Papers,* 262; Hackley, *Little Fork Rangers,* 44.

31. Hennessy, *Return to Bull Run,* 92–94; Marshall, *Aide-de-Camp of Lee,* 129.

32. *OR,* I, 12, pt. 2: 732–33; James Hardeman Stuart diary, Aug. 24, 1862.

33. *OR,* I, 12, pt. 2: 733–34, 747–48; McClellan, *Life and Campaigns of Stuart,* 95–96; Blackford, *War Years with Jeb Stuart,* 108–15; Hackley, *Little Fork Rangers,* 44–45; W. B. Taliaferro, "Jackson's Raid Around Pope," *B&L* 2: 502; McDonald, *Laurel Brigade,* 85; Angus James Johnston, II, *Virginia Railroads in the Civil War* (Chapel Hill, N.C., 1961), 85–86.

34. *OR,* I, 12, pt. 2: 720, 734; McClellan, *Life and Campaigns of Stuart,* 96.
35. *OR,* I, 12, pt. 2: 734, 739; McClellan, *Life and Campaigns of Stuart,* 96–99; Taliaferro, "Jackson's Raid," 503; Hennessy, *Return to Bull Run,* 113–15; Stiles, *4th Virginia Cavalry,* 18.
36. *OR,* I, 12, pt. 2: 720–25, 741–43; McClellan, *Life and Campaigns of Stuart,* 99–102.
37. *OR,* I, 12, pt. 2: 643–44.
38. Ibid., 554–55; Hennessy, *Return to Bull Run,* 117–20.
39. *OR,* I, 12, pt. 2: 554–55, 734–35, 748–50; McClellan, *Life and Campaigns of Stuart,* 103; Moore, *Stuart Horse Artillery,* 26–27; Hewett et al., *Supplement to the Official Records,* I, 2: 597; Stiles, *4th Virginia Cavalry,* 18–19; Taliaferro, "Jackson's Raid," 504.
40. *OR,* I, 12, pt. 2: 733, 735, 738–39, 750, 753–55; McClellan, *Life and Campaigns of Stuart,* 104, 107–8; Blackford, *War Years with Jeb Stuart,* 116; Hewett et al., *Supplement to the Official Records,* I, 2: 598; Moore, *Stuart Horse Artillery,* 27–28.
41. *OR,* I, 12, pt. 2: 735–36; McClellan, *Life and Campaigns of Stuart,* 105; Hewett et al., *Supplement to the Official Records,* I, 2: 599; Jasper Hawse diary, Aug. 31, 1862, UV; Andrew C. L. Gatewood to his sister, Sept. 3, 1862, Gatewood MSS, Preston Lib., V.M.I.; McDonald, *Laurel Brigade,* 87 and n.
42. *OR,* I, 12, pt. 2: 736; McClellan, *Life and Campaigns of Stuart,* 105; Blackford, *War Years with Jeb Stuart,* 124–28; Longstreet, *From Manassas to Appomattox,* 183.
43. *OR,* I, 12, pt. 2: 736; McClellan, *Life and Campaigns of Stuart,* 105; Blackford, *War Years with Jeb Stuart,* 130–33.
44. *OR,* I, 12, pt. 2: 736–37, 746–52, 754–55; McClellan, *Life and Campaigns of Stuart,* 106–7; Blackford, *War Years with Jeb Stuart,* 133–34; Lee, *Wartime Papers,* 285; McDonald, *Laurel Brigade,* 89; J. B. Fry, "Cavalry Fight at Second Manassas," *CV* 23 (1915): 263–64; Hewett et al., *Supplement to the Official Records,* I, 2: 600; Driver and Howard, *2nd Virginia Cavalry,* 56–57; Frye, *12th Virginia Cavalry,* 10–12; Thornton R. Baxter to "My Dear Aunt," Sept. 6, 1862, Baxter MSS; Andrew C. L. Gatewood to his sister, Sept. 3, 1862, Gatewood MSS.

CHAPTER 10
1. *OR,* I, 12, pt. 2: 737–38.
2. Ibid., 738, 743, 751; Bushong and Bushong, *Fightin' Tom Rosser,* 26.
3. *OR,* I, 12, pt. 2: 743–44; Blackford, *War Years with Jeb Stuart,* 134; George B. McClellan, *The Civil War Papers of George B. McClellan: Selected Correspondence, 1860–1865,* ed. Stephen W. Sears (New York, 1999), 425–26.
4. McClellan, *Civil War Papers,* 425–26; Stephen W. Sears, *Landscape Turned Red: The Battle of Antietam* (New Haven, Conn., 1983), 15–17.

5. *OR,* I, 12, pt. 2: 744; Hennessy, *Return to Bull Run,* 448–51.

6. *OR,* I, 12, pt. 2: 744; Samuel E. Mays, *Genealogical Notes on the Family of Mays and Reminiscences of the War Between the States from Notes Written around the Campfires* (Plant City, Fla., 1927), 89.

7. Trout, "Galloping Thunder," 78.

8. *OR,* I, 12, pt. 2: 744; Moore, *Stuart Horse Artillery,* 31.

9. *OR,* I, 19, pt. 1: 144.

10. Ibid., 814; R. Channing Price to his mother, Sept. 5, 1862, Price MSS, UNC; McClellan, *Life and Campaigns of Stuart,* 110; Driver, *1st Virginia Cavalry,* 46; James K. Munnerlyn to his sister, Sept. 8, 1862, Munnerlyn MSS.

11. R. Channing Price to his mother, Sept. 10, 1862, Price MSS, UNC.

12. *OR,* I, 18: 900; 19, pt. 1: 814; pt. 2: 595; James Ewell Brown Stuart, *The Letters of Major General James E. B. Stuart,* ed. Adele H. Mitchell (n.p., 1990), 266; McClellan, *Life and Campaigns of Stuart,* 109; Bowmaster, "Brig. Gen. B. H. Robertson," 19–20.

13. *OR,* I, 19, pt. 1: 814.

14. Ibid., 815; William R. Carter diary, Sept. 8, 1862, LV.

15. *OR,* I, 19, pt. 1: 814–15.

16. Blackford, *War Years with Jeb Stuart,* 140.

17. Ibid., 140–41; Thomas, *Bold Dragoon,* 164–65.

18. Blackford, *War Years with Jeb Stuart,* 141–42.

19. *OR,* I, 19, pt. 1: 145, 815, 822–23.

20. Ibid., 815–16, 823, 825; McClellan, *Life and Campaigns of Stuart,* 110–14; Hopkins, *The Little Jeff,* 91–92; Driver and Howard, *2nd Virginia Cavalry,* 59; Armstrong, *7th Virginia Cavalry,* 42; Frye, *12th Virginia Cavalry,* 14; George B. Davis, "The Antietam Campaign," *Papers of the Military Historical Society of Massachusetts* 3 (1903): 36; James K. Munnerlyn to his sister, Oct. 9, 1862, Munnerlyn MSS; D. B. Rea, "Cavalry Incidents of the Maryland Campaign," *Maine Bugle* 2 (1895): 117–20.

21. *OR,* I, 19, pt. 1: 816–17; Sears, *Landscape Turned Red,* 90–91, 112–13.

22. *OR,* I, 19, pt. 1: 817, 823–24; McClellan, *Life and Campaigns of Stuart,* 114–15; Hopkins, *The Little Jeff,* 93–94.

23. *OR,* I, 19, pt. 1: 608, 1052; McClellan, *Life and Campaigns of Stuart,* 119; Daniel H. Hill, "The Battle of South Mountain, or Boonsboro'," *B&L* 2: 561–81; Driver, *5th Virginia Cavalry,* 39–40; Moore, *Stuart Horse Artillery,* 33; Bushong and Bushong, *Fightin' Tom Rosser,* 28–29.

24. *OR,* I, 19, pt. 1: 817; McClellan, *Life and Campaigns of Stuart,* 117; Hill, "Battle of South Mountain," 561.

25. *OR,* I, 19, pt. 1: 817–18, 824, 826; McClellan, *Life and Campaigns of Stuart,* 117–18; Rea, "Cavalry Incidents," 121–23.

26. *OR,* I, 19, pt. 1: 818, 854; R. Channing Price to his mother, Sept. 18, 1862, Price MSS, UNC.

27. *OR,* I, 19, pt. 1: 818–19, 826–27, 854; McClellan, *Life and Campaigns of Stuart,* 115, 120–23; McDonald, *Laurel Brigade,* 93–94; Driver and Howard, *2nd Virginia Cavalry,* 60–61; Frye, *12th Virginia Cavalry,* 16; Moore, *Chew's, Shoemaker's, Newtown Artillery,* 18.

28. *OR,* I, 19, pt. 1: 819, 855; McClellan, *Life and Campaigns of Stuart,* 123; Blackford, *War Years with Jeb Stuart,* 148; R. Channing Price to his mother, Sept. 18, 1862, Price MSS, UNC.

29. *OR,* I, 19, pt. 1: 819; Sears, *Landscape Turned Red,* 174–82.

30. *OR,* I, 19, pt. 1: 819; McClellan, *Life and Campaigns of Stuart,* 124–25; Lee, *General Lee,* 205; Davis, "Antietam Campaign," 37.

31. McClellan, *Life and Campaigns of Stuart,* 125–26; "Maryland Campaign: The Cavalry Fight at Boonsboro' Graphically Described . . .," *SHSP* 25 (1897): 276–78; William R. Carter diary, Sept. 15, 1862; Robert T. Hubard memoirs, 56–57; Beale, *Lieutenant of Cavalry,* 44–46; Nanzig, *3rd Virginia Cavalry,* 20–21; Krick, *9th Virginia Cavalry,* 10.

32. *OR,* I, 19, pt. 1: 819–20; McClellan, *Life and Campaigns of Stuart,* 127–29; James V. Murfin, *The Gleam of Bayonets: The Battle of Antietam and the Maryland Campaign of 1862* (New York, 1965), 213–14; Milham, *Gallant Pellham,* 160–62. The definitive source on Stuart at Antietam is Robert E. L. Krick, "Defending Lee's Flank: J. E. B. Stuart, John Pelham, and Confederate Artillery on Nicodemus Heights," in Gary A. Gallagher, ed., *The Antietam Campaign* (Chapel Hill, N.C., 1999), 192–222.

33. *OR,* I, 19, pt. 1: 819–20; William R. Carter diary, Sept. 17, 1862; Robert T. Hubard memoirs, 57; Beale, *Lieutenant of Cavalry,* 48; "Maryland Campaign," 280; Sears, *Landscape Turned Red,* 190–91.

34. *OR,* I, 19, pt. 1: 820, 971; McClellan, *Life and Campaigns of Stuart,* 129–30; Murfin, *Gleam of Bayonets,* 231, 240; Milham, *Gallant Pellham,* 162–67; Moore, *Stuart Horse Artillery,* 34–35.

35. *OR,* I, 19, pt. 1: 874, 1010; R. Channing Price to his mother, Sept. 18, 1862, Price MSS, UNC; John G. Walker, "Sharpsburg," *B&L* 2: 679–80; Beale, *Lieutenant of Cavalry,* 48–50; Sears, *Landscape Turned Red,* 274–76, 291.

36. Sears, *Landscape Turned Red,* 258–68, 276–92.

37. *OR,* I, 19, pt. 1: 151, 820; McClellan, *Life and Campaigns of Stuart,* 132; Blackford, *War Years with Jeb Stuart,* 151; Robert T. Hubard memoirs, 58; Sears, *Landscape Turned Red,* 303–4.

38. *OR,* I, 19, pt. 1: 142, 151; Sears, *Landscape Turned Red,* 306–8.

39. Thomas M. Garber to his sister, Sept. 17, 1862, Garber MSS, LV.

40. *OR,* I, 19, pt. 1: 820, 824; McClellan, *Life and Campaigns of Stuart,* 133; Blackford, *War Years with Jeb Stuart,* 152.

41. *OR,* I, 19, pt. 1: 68, 820–21, 824, 828; McClellan, *Life and Campaigns of Stuart,* 133–35; Blackford, *War Years with Jeb Stuart,* 153–54; William R. Carter diary, Sept. 19, 1862; James K. Munnerlyn to his sister, Oct. 9, 1862, Munnerlyn MSS; Driver and Howard, *2nd Virginia Cavalry,* 61.

CHAPTER 11

1. *OR,* I, 19, pt. 1: 68–87, 151–53; von Borcke, *Memoirs,* 1: 289–92; Blackford, *War Years with Jeb Stuart,* 154–55.
2. A. L. Long, *Memoirs of Robert E. Lee: His Military and Personal History* . . . (New York, 1886), 229.
3. Henry Kyd Douglas, *I Rode with Stonewall: Being Chiefly the War Experiences of the Youngest Member of Jackson's Staff* . . . (Chapel Hill, N.C., 1940), 196.
4. Blackford, *War Years with Jeb Stuart,* 156–58.
5. Ibid., 158–59; von Borcke, *Memoirs,* 1: 293–94.
6. Blackford, *War Years with Jeb Stuart,* 162; John Bolling to "Dear Sir," Sept. 24, 1862, Bolling MSS, VHS; William R. Carter diary, Sept. 25, Oct. 1, 1862; Nanzig, *3rd Virginia Cavalry,* 22; Krick, *9th Virginia Cavalry,* 11.
7. *OR,* I, 19, pt. 2: 13–14; von Borcke, *Memoirs,* 1: 273–76; Lafayette J. Carneal to his father, Oct. 3, 1862, Carneal MSS, VHS; Driver, *1st Virginia Cavalry,* 47–48.
8. *OR,* I, 19: pt. 2: 55.
9. Driver and Howard, *2nd Virginia Cavalry,* 62–63; McDonald, *Laurel Brigade*, 105; Wert, "His Unhonored Service," 32.
10. *OR,* I, 19, pt. 2: 55.
11. Ibid., 52, 55; McClellan, *Life and Campaigns of Stuart,* 136; R. Channing Price to his mother, Oct. 15, 1862, Price MSS, UNC.
12. *OR,* I, 19, pt. 2: 52, 55–56; Freeman, *Lee's Lieutenants,* 2: 286; Julian T. Edwards to his parents, Oct. 15, 1862, VHS.
13. *OR,* I, 19, pt. 2: 52, 57; McClellan, *Life and Campaigns of Stuart,* 138; Blackford, *War Years with Jeb Stuart,* 165.
14. *OR,* I, 19, pt. 2: 52; McClellan, *Life and Campaigns of Stuart,* 138–39; Blackford, *War Years with Jeb Stuart,* 165.
15. *OR,* I, 19, pt. 2: 56; Davis, *Last Cavalier,* 218.
16. *OR,* I, 19, pt. 2: 52, 57; McClellan, *Life and Campaigns of Stuart,* 140; Blackford, *War Years with Jeb Stuart,* 165–68; Corson, *My Dear Jennie,* 96; Chiswell Dabney to his mother, Oct. 21, 1862, Dabney MSS.
17. Corson, *My Dear Jennie,* 96–97; Julian T. Edwards to his parents, Oct. 15, 1862.
18. *OR,* I, 19, pt. 2: 57; McClellan, *Life and Campaigns of Stuart,* 141; Blackford, *War Years with Jeb Stuart,* 168.
19. *OR,* I, 19, pt. 2: 52; McClellan, *Life and Campaigns of Stuart,* 141.
20. *OR,* I, 19, pt. 2: 52; Davis, *Last Cavalier,* 221.
21. *OR,* I, 19, pt. 2: 52–53, 58; Julian T. Edwards to his parents, Oct. 15, 1862.
22. Driver, *10th Virginia Cavalry,* 25; Davis, *Last Cavalier,* 221.
23. *OR,* I, 19, pt. 2: 53; McClellan, *Life and Campaigns of Stuart,* 148; Blackford, *War Years with Jeb Stuart,* 169–70.
24. Blackford, *War Years with Jeb Stuart,* 149; R. Channing Price to his mother, Oct. 15, 1862, Price MSS, UNC.

25. *OR,* I, 19, pt. 2: 53; McClellan, *Life and Campaigns of Stuart,* 149; Blackford, *War Years with Jeb Stuart,* 172–73.

26. Blackford, *War Years with Jeb Stuart,* 174, 179–80; Clark, *Regiments and Battalions from North Carolina,* 1: 422.

27. *OR,* I, 19, pt. 2: 53; McClellan, *Life and Campaigns of Stuart,* 150–53, 156; Blackford, *War Years with Jeb Stuart,* 175; Longacre, *Lincoln's Cavalrymen,* 109–10.

28. Longacre, *Lincoln's Cavalrymen,* 110–11; *OR,* I, 19, pt. 2: 53; McClellan, *Life and Campaigns of Stuart,* 155.

29. Blackford, *War Years with Jeb Stuart,* 171–72.

30. McClellan, *Life and Campaigns of Stuart,* 155; Wilbur S. Nye, "How Stuart Recrossed the Potomac," *CWTI* 4 (Jan. 1966): 45–46.

31. *OR,* I, 19, pt. 2: 53–54, 58; McClellan, *Life and Campaigns of Stuart,* 155–58; Blackford, *War Years with Jeb Stuart,* 175; Driver, *1st Virginia Cavalry,* 49; Moore, *Stuart Horse Artillery,* 40–42; R. Channing Price to his mother, Oct. 15, 1862, Price MSS, UNC; Julian T. Edwards to his parents, Oct. 15, 1862; Nye, "How Stuart Recrossed," 46–47.

32. *OR,* I, 19, pt. 2: 53, 58; McClellan, *Life and Campaigns of Stuart,* 158–60; Blackford, *War Years with Jeb Stuart,* 176–78.

CHAPTER 12

1. Edward D. Cottrell to his wife, Oct. 16, 1862, VHS; R. Channing Price to his mother, Oct. 15, 1862, Price MSS, UNC.

2. R. Channing Price to his mother, Oct. 15, 1862, Price MSS, UNC; *OR,* I, 19, pt. 2: 52–56.

3. Moore, *Rebellion Record,* 6: 1–5, 17–18.

4. Robert T. Hubard memoirs, 59; W. Bailey Clement to "Dear Mattie," Oct. 20, 1862, Clement MSS, NCSDA&H.

5. Blackford, *War Years with Jeb Stuart,* 181–83; Thomas, *Bold Dragoon,* 171, 192.

6. *OR,* I, 19, pt. 1: 152; Blackford, *War Years with Jeb Stuart,* 183.

7. *OR,* I, 19, pt. 1: 87, 152.

8. Ibid., pt. 2: 140–41.

9. Wise, *Long Arm of Lee,* 1: 346; Trout, "Galloping Thunder," 78–79.

10. John Esten Cooke to S. D. Duval, Dec. 3, 1862, Cooke MS, UV.

11. Beale, *Lieutenant of Cavalry,* 53.

12. *OR,* I, 19, pt. 2: 141; 51, pt. 1: 171–72; Cooke, *Wearing of the Gray,* 279–80; McClellan, *Life and Campaigns of Stuart,* 169–71; Beale, *Ninth Virginia Cavalry,* 46–47; Robert T. Hubard memoirs, 59–60.

13. *OR,* I, 19, pt. 2: 141–42, 692–93; McClellan, *Life and Campaigns of Stuart,* 172–76; Wise, *Long Arm of Lee,* 1: 349–50; Moore, *Stuart Horse Artillery,* 43–44; Beale, *Ninth Virginia Cavalry,* 47–48; Robert T. Hubard memoirs, 60.

14. *OR,* I, 19, pt. 2, 143; McClellan, *Life and Campaigns of Stuart,* 176–80; Stiles, *4th Virginia Cavalry,* 21; Beale, *Ninth Virginia Cavalry,* 49–50; Wise, *Long Arm of Lee,* 1: 352–53; Robert T. Hubard memoirs, 60; John H. Cameron memoirs, 14–15; William R. Carter diary, Nov. 3, 1862.

15. *OR,* I, 19, pt. 2: 143–46; McClellan, *Life and Campaigns of Stuart,* 180–84; Hartley, *Stuart's Tarheels,* 164–68; Stiles, *4th Virginia Cavalry,* 21–22; Driver, *5th Virginia Cavalry,* 41; Beale, *Ninth Virginia Cavalry,* 49–53; Moore, *Stuart Horse Artillery,* 44; Moore, *Rebellion Record,* 6: 177–79; William R. Carter diary, Nov. 4–5, 1862.

16. *OR,* I, 19, pt. 2: 144; Robert T. Hubard memoirs, 60.

17. *OR,* I, 19, pt. 1: 88; pt. 2: 144–45, 551.

18. Ibid., 701; Longacre, *Lincoln's Cavalrymen,* 125.

19. Cooke, *Wearing of the Gray,* 16; von Borcke, *Memoirs,* 2: 48–49, 62; J. E. B. Stuart to Flora Cooke Stuart, Nov. 6, 1862, Stuart MSS, VHS.

20. *OR,* I, 19, pt. 2: 712; 21: 544; McClellan, *Life and Campaigns of Stuart,* 186n–87n; Daniel T. Balfour, *13th Virginia Cavalry* (Lynchburg, Va., 1986), 1–11; John Fortier, *15th Virginia Cavalry* (Lynchburg, Va., 1993), 1–20.

21. Hopkins, *The Little Jeff,* 112; Charles E. Cauthen, ed., *Family Letters of the Three Wade Hamptons, 1782–1901* (Columbia, S.C., 1953), 87–88.

22. *OR,* I, 21: 545; McDonald, *Laurel Brigade,* 105.

23. *OR,* I, 19, pt. 2: 145; 21: 1019.

24. Ibid., I, 19, pt. 2: 145; 21: 1014–15, 1019–21; Driver, *1st Virginia Cavalry,* 51; Moore, *Stuart Horse Artillery,* 45.

25. *OR,* I, 21: 1020–22; 51, pt. 2: 647; Beale, *Ninth Virginia Cavalry,* 54; Fortier, *15th Virginia Cavalry,* 22; Charles R. Chewning diary, Nov. 19, 1862.

26. *OR,* I, 21: 84–87, 550–51.

27. Ibid., 13–16; 51, pt. 2: 653; McClellan, *Life and Campaigns of Stuart,* 187–88; R. Channing Price to his mother, Nov. 30, 1862, Price MSS, UNC.

28. *OR,* I, 21: 27–28; Lee, *Wartime Papers,* 354; Beale, *Lieutenant of Cavalry,* 59–62; Beale, *Ninth Virginia Cavalry,* 54–56; Krick, *9th Virginia Cavalry,* 13–14.

29. *OR,* I, 21: 36–37.

30. Ibid., 37–38; J. E. B. Stuart to John R. Cooke, Feb. 28, 1863, Cooke MSS; Lee, *Wartime Papers,* 354; Moore, *Stuart Horse Artillery,* 46; Moore, *Chew's, Shoemaker's, Newtown Artillery,* 72; John J. Shoemaker, *Shoemaker's Battery, Stuart's Horse Artillery, Pelham's Battalion . . .* (Memphis, 1908), 25.

31. *OR,* I, 21: 88–92, 558; R. Channing Price to his mother, Dec. 17, 1862, Price MSS, UNC; Blackford, *War Years with Jeb Stuart,* 192–93; William H. Mills to "Dear Brother," Dec. 25, 1862, Mills MSS, J. Y. Joyner Lib., East Carolina Univ., Greenville; Beale, *Ninth Virginia Cavalry,* 56–57;

Irvin C. Wills to "Dear Brother," Jan. 1, 1863, Wills MSS, VHS; Driver, *1st Virginia Cavalry,* 51–52; Driver and Howard, *2nd Virginia Cavalry,* 65–66; Balfour, *13th Virginia Cavalry,* 11.

32. Wise, *Long Arm of Lee,* 1: 382–85; Milham, *Gallant Pelham,* 210; Moore, *Stuart Horse Artillery,* 46.

33. R. Channing Price to his mother, Dec. 17, 1862, Price MSS, UNC; McClellan, *Life and Campaigns of Stuart,* 195; Wise, *Long Arm of Lee,* 1: 404; Milham, *Gallant Pelham,* 211–17; Hassler, *Colonel John Pelham,* 145–49; Moore, *Stuart Horse Artillery,* 47–48; Beale, *Lieutenant of Cavalry,* 65; Robert T. Hubard memoirs, 63; A. Wilson Greene, "Opportunity to the South: Meade versus Jackson at Fredericksburg," *Civil War History* 33 (1987): 303.

34. *OR,* I, 21: 547, 553; Moore, *Stuart Horse Artillery,* 48.

35. J. E. B. Stuart to G. W. Custis Lee, Dec. 18, 1862, Stuart MSS, DU; *OR,* I, 21: 555.

36. *OR,* I, 21: 689–97; McClellan, *Life and Campaigns of Stuart,* 188–90; R. Channing Price to his mother, Dec. 23, 1862, Price MSS, UNC; Cauthen, *Letters of Three Wade Hamptons,* 89–90; D. B. Rea, *Sketches from Hampton's Cavalry, Embracing the Principal Exploits of the Cavalry in the Campaigns of 1862 and 1863* (Columbia, S.C., 1864), 62; U. R. Brooks, *Butler and His Cavalry in the War of Secession, 1861–1865* (Columbia, S.C., 1909), 85–87; E. Prioleau Henderson, *Autobiography of Arab* (Columbia, S.C., 1901), 100–05; Alfred Adams to his parents, Dec. 22, 1862, Adams MSS, DU.

37. Edwin R. Sloan to his wife, Dec. 21, 1862, Sloan MSS, DU.

38. *OR,* I, 21: 731, 735, 737, 741, 1075–76; McClellan, *Life and Campaigns of Stuart,* 197; Freeman, *Lee's Lieutenants,* 2: 399 and n–400 and n; Moore, *Stuart Horse Artillery,* 50; Edward G. Longacre, "Stuart's Dumfries Raid," *CWTI* 15 (July 1976): 18–22.

39. *OR,* I, 21: 731–32; McClellan, *Life and Campaigns of Stuart,* 198; Fortier, *15th Virginia Cavalry,* 24; Robert T. Hubard memoirs, 63–64.

40. *OR,* I, 21: 732, 738, 740–42; McClellan, *Life and Campaigns of Stuart,* 198; Driver, *1st Virginia Cavalry,* 52.

41. *OR,* I, 21: 732–33, 736–37; McClellan, *Life and Campaigns of Stuart,* 199; Rea, *Sketches from Hampton's Cavalry,* 64; Brooks, *Butler and His Cavalry,* 87; Longacre, "Stuart's Dumfries Raid," 22.

42. Freeman, *Lee's Lieutenants,* 2: 402–3.

43. *OR,* I, 21: 733, 736–37, 739–41; McClellan, *Life and Campaigns of Stuart,* 199–201; Driver, *5th Virginia Cavalry,* 43–44; Brooks, *Butler and His Cavalry,* 88; R. Channing Price to his sister, Jan. 20, 1863, Price MSS, UNC; Robert B. Jones to his wife, Jan. 3, 1863, Jones MSS, VHS; Robert T. Hubard memoirs, 64.

44. *OR,* I, 21: 733–34, 738–39; McClellan, *Life and Campaigns of Stuart,* 201–2; R. Channing Price to his sister, Jan. 20, 1863, Price MSS, UNC.

45. *OR,* I, 21: 734–35, 739; McClellan, *Life and Campaigns of Stuart,* 202; R. Channing Price to his sister, Jan. 20, 1863, Price MSS, UNC; John Z. H. Scott memoirs, 12.

CHAPTER 13

1. Driver, *1st Virginia Cavalry,* 54; Nanzig, *3rd Virginia Cavalry,* 27; Driver, *10th Virginia Cavalry,* 31–32; Balfour, *13th Virginia Cavalry,* 12; Shoemaker, *Shoemaker's Battery,* 26; Robert T. Hubard memoirs, 65; Robert B. Jones to his wife, Jan. 3, 1863, Jones MSS; John Bolling to "My dear Sir," Jan. 21, 1863, Bolling MSS.

2. *OR,* I, 25, pt. 1: 795, 1045; Robert E. Lee, *Lee's Dispatches: Unpublished Letters of General Robert E. Lee, C.S A., to Jefferson Davis and the War Department of the Confederate States of America,* ed. Douglas Southall Freeman and Grady McWhiney (New York, 1957), 71 and n–73 and n; McClellan, *Life and Campaigns of Stuart,* 204; Driver, *1st Virginia Cavalry,* 54; Driver and Howard, *2nd Virginia Cavalry,* 69; Stiles, *4th Virginia Cavalry,* 23; R. Channing Price to his sister, Feb. 17, 1863, Price MSS, VHS; Thaddeus Fitzhugh memoirs, 19.

3. Cauthen, *Letters of Three Wade Hamptons,* 91–92.

4. Wade Hampton to P. G. T. Beauregard, Apr. 6, 1863, CSR of Hampton, M–331, R–115, NA.

5. Lee, *Lee's Dispatches,* 72.

6. *OR,* I, 21: 752–55, 1101; Halsey Wigfall to his mother, Jan. 22, 1863, Wigfall MSS, LC.

7. Williams Wickham to Jefferson Davis, Jan. 15, 1863 (and endorsements), CSR of Wickham, M–331, R–267, NA.

8. J. E. B. Stuart to Samuel Cooper, Jan. 13, 1863, Thomas L. Rosser MSS, UV; Thomas L. Rosser to Alexander R. Boteler, Mar. 12, 1863, CSR of Rosser, M–331, R–216, NA; Halsey Wigfall to his father, Feb. 7, 1863, Wigfall MSS; J. E. B. Stuart to Samuel Cooper, Feb. 10, 1863 (and endorsements), CSR of John Pelham, M–331, R–195, NA.

9. *OR,* I, 21: 1079–81; 25, pt. 2: 621–22; McDonald, *Laurel Brigade,* 109; Robert E. Lee to J. E. B. Stuart, Feb. 13, 15, 1863, CSR of Henry B. McClellan, M–331, R–169, NA; Lee, *Wartime Papers,* 402–3; Halsey Wigfall to his mother, Jan. 29, 1863, Wigfall MSS.

10. *OR,* I, 25, pt. 1: 25; McClellan, *Life and Campaigns of Stuart,* 204; Driver, *1st Virginia Cavalry,* 55; Lee, *Wartime Papers,* 409.

11. *OR,* I, 25, pt. 1: 25–26; J. E. B. Stuart to John R. Cooke, Feb. 28, 1863, Cooke MSS; Robert T. Hubard memoirs, 65–66; R. Channing Price to his mother, Mar. 2, 1863, Price MSS, UNC; Driver and Howard, *2nd Virginia Cavalry,* 70–71; William R. Carter diary, Feb. 25, 1863.

12. *OR,* I, 25, pt. 1: 47–48; McClellan, *Life and Campaigns of Stuart,* 217; Freeman, *Lee's Lieutenants,* 2: 455–57 and n; Driver, *5th Virginia Cavalry,* 46; R. Channing Price to his sister, Mar. 15, 1863, Price MSS, VHS.

13. *OR,* I, 25, pt. 1: 48, 61; McClellan, *Life and Campaigns of Stuart,* 205–8.

14. *OR,* I, 25, pt. 1: 48–49; Thaddeus Fitzhugh memoirs, 19.

15. *OR,* I, 25, pt. 1: 49, 58, 61; McClellan, *Life and Campaigns of Stuart,* 209; Ware, *Battle of Kelly's Ford,* 6; Driver and Howard, *2nd Virginia Cavalry,* 75.

16. *OR,* I, 25, pt. 1: 59; McClellan, *Life and Campaigns of Stuart,* 210–11; Nanzig, *3rd Virginia Cavalry,* 30; Hudgins, *Old Dominion Dragoon,* 65; Driver, *5th Virginia Cavalry,* 48–49; Thaddeus Fitzhugh memoirs, 19–20; William R. Carter diary, Mar. 17, 1863.

17. *OR,* I, 25, pt. 1: 50, 56–57; Blackford, *War Years with Jeb Stuart,* 201–2; Ware, *Battle of Kelly's Ford,* 7; Cooke, *Wearing of the Gray,* 116–19; R. Channing Price to his mother, Mar. 21, 1863, Price MSS, UNC; Thaddeus Fitzhugh memoirs, 20; Freeman, *Lee's Lieutenants,* 2: 463–66; Mercer, *Life of the Gallant Pelham,* 160–64; Jones, *Great Cannoneer,* 10–11; Lee, *Wartime Papers,* 414.

18. *OR,* I, 25, pt. 1: 50, 54–55; McClellan, *Life and Campaigns of Stuart,* 212–13.

19. McClellan, *Life and Campaigns of Stuart,* 213–14; Driver and Howard, *2nd Virginia Cavalry,* 76; Nanzig, *3rd Virginia Cavalry,* 31; Robert T. Hubard memoirs, 66–67.

20. McClellan, *Life and Campaigns of Stuart,* 214–15; Stiles, *4th Virginia Cavalry,* 25; Balfour, *13th Virginia Cavalry,* 13; William H. F. Payne to J. D. Ferguson, Mar. 20, 1863, Payne MSS, MC; William H. F. Payne to Joseph R. Anderson, Dec. 13, 1903, ibid.

21. *OR,* I, 25, pt. 1: 50; McClellan, *Life and Campaigns of Stuart,* 215–16; Wiley Sword, "Cavalry on Trial at Kelly's Ford," *CWTI* 13 (Apr. 1974): 39–40.

22. Longacre, *Lee's Cavalrymen,* 137–38.

23. *OR,* I, 25, pt. 1: 59, 64; 51, pt. 2: 686.

24. William R. Carter diary, Apr. 7, 1863.

25. Appointment Certificate of R. Channing Price, Mar. 21, 1863, Price MSS, UNC; R. Channing Price to his mother, Mar. 25, 1863, ibid.; Blackford, *War Years with Jeb Stuart,* 204–5.

26. *OR,* I, 25, pt. 2: 858; J. E. B. Stuart to Samuel Cooper, Mar. 26, 1863 (and endorsements), CSR of Robert F. Beckham, M–331, R–20, NA; Wise, *Long Arm of Lee,* 1: 460–61; 2: 578; Trout, "Galloping Thunder," 79–80; R. Channing Price to his sister, Apr. 8, 1863, Price MSS, VHS.

27. Trout, "Galloping Thunder," 80; Wise, *Long Arm of Lee,* 2: 576–78.

28. *OR,* I, 25, pt. 2: 724; Stiles, *4th Virginia Cavalry,* 26; Krick, *9th Virginia Cavalry,* 16; Balfour, *13th Virginia Cavalry,* 13.

29. *OR,* I, 25, pt. 1: 1066; Stephen W. Sears, *Chancellorsville* (Boston, 1996), 120–21.

30. *OR,* I, 25, pt. 1: 85, 87–89, pt. 2: 725, 730; Lee, *Wartime Papers,* 434–36; McClellan, *Life and Campaigns of Stuart,* 219–20; R. Channing Price to his

mother, Apr. 16, 1863, Price MSS, UNC; Longacre, *Lincoln's Cavalrymen,* 140; Beale, *Lieutenant of Cavalry,* 78; Charles R. Phelps to "Dear Aunt," Apr. 16, 1863, Phelps MSS, UV; Irvin C. Wills to "Dear Brother," Apr. 17, 1863, Wills MSS.

31. *OR,* I, 25, pt. 1: 1045, 1057–58, 1065; Sears, *Chancellorsville,* 131–32, 166; Lee, *Wartime Papers,* 444–45.

32. McClellan, *Life and Campaigns of Stuart,* 226; Sears, *Chancellorville,* 154–76.

33. *OR,* I, 25, pt. 1: 796.

34. Ibid., 1045–46, 1048, 1098; McClellan, *Life and Campaigns of Stuart,* 224–25; George W. Jones memoirs, 10, MC; Shoemaker, *Shoemaker's Battery,* 29.

35. *OR,* I, 25, pt. 1: 804, 1046–47; McClellan, *Life and Campaigns of Stuart,* 227.

36. *OR,* I, 25, pt. 1: 1072–73, 1075, 1078–79, 1098; Krick, *9th Virginia Cavalry,* 17; Beale, *Lieutenant of Cavalry,* 70–72.

37. *OR,* I, 25, pt. 1: 1085, 1098; Beale, *Lieutenant of Cavalry,* 73.

38. *OR,* I, 25, pt. 1: 1061–62, 1089, 1093, 1097–99; Beale, *Lieutenant of Cavalry,* 73–74.

39. *OR,* I, 25, pt. 1: 1046; Robert J. Trout, *In the Saddle with Stuart* (Gettysburg, Pa., 1998), 26–31, 36; Fortier, *15th Virginia Cavalry,* 29; Trout, *With Pen and Saber,* 199–200.

40. *OR,* I, 25, pt. 1: 1046–47; McClellan, *Life and Campaigns of Stuart,* 227–30; Sears, *Chancellorsville,* 175–76; Driver, *5th Virginia Cavalry,* 50–51; Haden, *Reminiscences,* 18–19; Alfred Pleasonton, "The Successes and Failures of Chancellorsville," *B&L* 3: 175; Hewett et al., *Supplement to the Official Records,* I, 4: 678–79.

41. Robert T. Hubard memoirs, 69.

42. *OR,* I, 25, pt. 1: 1047; McClellan, *Life and Campaigns of Stuart,* 230–31.

43. *OR,* I, 25, pt. 1: 1047–49; McClellan, *Life and Campaigns of Stuart,* 231–32; Sears, *Chancellorsville,* 222–23; Moore, *Stuart Horse Artillery,* 59–60.

44. McClellan, *Life and Campaigns of Stuart,* 232; J. E. B. Stuart to Mrs. Thomas Randolph Price, Sr., May 11, 1863, Price MSS, UNC; J. E. B. Stuart to Henry B. McClellan, Apr. 13, 1863, Douglas Southall Freeman MSS; J. E. B. Stuart to Samuel Cooper, Apr. 29, 1863, CSR of Henry B. McClellan, M–331, R–169, NA.

45. McClellan, *Life and Campaigns of Stuart,* 233; Sears, *Chancellorsville,* 224–35.

46. McClellan, *Life and Campaigns of Stuart,* 232–33; Alexander, *Fighting for the Confederacy,* 201–2.

47. *OR,* I, 25, pt. 1: 886–87, 1049–50; McClellan, *Life and Campaigns of Stuart,* 234–35, 247; Wise, *Long Arm of Lee,* 1: 471, 478, 480; Moore, *Stuart Horse Artillery,* 60–61; Shoemaker, *Shoemaker's Battery,* 34; J. E. B. Stu-

art to Samuel Cooper, May 21, 1863 (and endorsements), CSR of Robert F. Beckham, M–331, R–20, NA; Halsey Wigfall to his parents, May 2, 1863, Wigfall MSS.

48. *OR,* I, 25, pt. 1; 887–89; McClellan, *Life and Campaigns of Stuart,* 235–56; Thomas, *Bold Dragoon,* 210–12; Davis, *Last Cavalier,* 294–97; Sears, *Chancellorsville,* 324–47; Ernest B. Furgurson, *Chancellorsville: The Souls of the Brave* (New York, 1992), 207–47.

CHAPTER 14

1. *OR,* I, 25, pt. 2: 782, 824, 827.
2. John T. Gaston, *Confederate War Diary of John Thomas Gaston,* comp. Alifaire Gaston Walden (Columbia, S.C., 1960), xiii; Haden, *Reminiscences,* 21; Jacob K. Langhorne to his parents, May 4, 8, 1863, Preston Library, V.M.I.
3. *OR,* I, 25, pt. 2: 788–89, 792; Edward G. Longacre, *The Cavalry at Gettysburg: A Tactical Study of Mounted Operations during the Civil War's Pivotal Campaign, 9 June–14 July 1863* (Rutherford, N.J., 1986), 61.
4. Longacre, *Cavalry at Gettysburg,* 37, 39; John Singleton Mosby, *Stuart's Cavalry in the Gettysburg Campaign* (New York, 1908), 5.
5. Edwin B. Coddington, *The Gettysburg Campaign: A Study in Command* (New York, 1968), 5–7.
6. *OR,* I, 25, pt. 2: 789–90, 804–5, 819–21, 825–26, 836, 848.
7. Redwood, "Following Stuart's Feather," 117.
8. *OR,* I, 25, pt. 2: 831, 837, 852, 854; Longacre, *Cavalry at Gettysburg,* 30.
9. *OR,* I, 25, pt. 2: 846.
10. Wilbur S. Nye, *Here Come the Rebels!* (Baton Rouge, La., 1965), 30–32; Longacre, *Cavalry at Gettysburg,* 61–62.
11. McClellan, *Life and Campaigns of Stuart,* 261; Trout, *In the Saddle with Stuart,* 50–51; Irvin C. Wills to "Dear brother," May 22, 1863, Wills MS.
12. Thaddeus Fitzhugh memoirs, 21; Thomas L. Rosser, Jr., to Douglas Southall Freeman, May 17, 1938, Freeman MSS; Bushong and Bushong, *Fightin' Tom Rosser,* 42–43; James H. Allen, "The James City Cavalry: Its Organization and Its First Service . . .," *SHSP* 24 (1896): 354; Halsey Wigfall to anon., June 4, 1863, Wigfall MSS.
13. Media Evans memoirs, 7, UNC; Charles McVicar memoirs, 8, LC; Neese, *Confederate Horse Artillery,* 165–66; Halsey Wigfall to anon., June 4, 1863, Wigfall MSS.
14. Freeman, *Lee's Lieutenants,* 3: 2; Blackford, *War Years with Jeb Stuart,* 211–12; Heath J. Christian to his mother, May [June] 6, 1863, Christian MSS, VHS; Lewis T. Nunnelee memoirs, 73, MC; Richard P. Allen to "Dear Captain," June 6, 1863, Allen MSS, MC; Charles McVicar memoirs, 9; Ephram Bowman to his father, June 6, 1863, Bowman MSS, UV; Hudgins, *Old Dominion Dragoon,* 75–76; Neese, *Confederate Horse Artillery,*

166–69; John E. Divine, *35th Battalion Virginia Cavalry* (Lynchburg, Va., 1985), 27.

15. *OR,* I, 27, pt. 3: 5–8, 12–14; Nye, *Here Come the Rebels,* 33–36.

16. Coddington, *Gettysburg Campaign,* 51–52.

17. James D. Ferguson to James H. Drake, June 8 [1863], Drake MSS, LC; McClellan, *Life and Campaigns of Stuart,* 261–62; Daniel B. Coltrane, *The Memoirs of Daniel Branson Coltrane, Co. I, 63rd Reg., N.C. Cavalry, C.S.A.* (Raleigh, N.C., 1956), 11–12; William L. Wilson, *A Borderland Confederate,* ed. Festus P. Summers (Pittsburgh, Pa., 1962), 71; G. Moxley Sorrel, *Recollections of a Confederate Staff Officer* (New York, 1905), 161; Opie, *Rebel Cavalryman,* 145–46; Neese, *Confederate Horse Artillery,* 169–70.

18. McClellan, *Life and Campaigns of Stuart,* 262; William V. Kennedy, "The Cavalry Battle at Brandy Station," *Armor* 65 (1956): 28–29; Downey, *Clash of Cavalry,* 84–86; *OR,* I, 27, pt. 2: 680, 727.

19. *OR,* I, 27, pt. 1: 170; pt. 3: 15–17, 27–30, 34–35, 45; 51, pt. 1: 1047; Nye, *Here Come the Rebels,* 45–48; Coddington, *Gettysburg Campaign,* 54–57, 615n, 618n; Mosby, *Stuart's Cavalry in the Gettysburg Campaign,* 9–16, 27–28, 28n., 139.

20. *OR,* I, 27, pt. 1: 1047; pt. 2: 748–49, 754–55, 757; Opie, *Rebel Cavalryman,* 147; Ephraim Bowman to his father, June 11, 1863, Bowman MSS; Ephraim Bowman diary, June 9, 1863, ibid.; Luther W. Hopkins, *From Bull Run to Appomattox: A Boy's View* (Baltimore, 1908), 90–91; Beale, *Lieutenant of Cavalry,* 84; Neese, *Confederate Horse Artillery,* 170–73; George M. Neese diary, June 9, 1863, LV; Charles McVicar memoirs, 11–12; Wise, *Long Arm of Lee,* 2: 585–86.

21. *OR,* I, 27, pt. 1: 1047–48; pt. 2: 749, 762–63, 765, 768; Heros von Borcke and Justus Scheibert, *Die Grosse Reiterschlacht bei Brandy Station, 9. Juni 1863* (Berlin, 1893), 86–87; Hopkins, *Bull Run to Appomattox,* 91; Neese, *Confederate Horse Artillery,* 172; Opie, *Rebel Calvaryman,* 152; McDonald, *Laurel Brigade,* 135; George Baylor, *Bull Run to Bull Run; or, Four Years in the Army of Northern Virginia . . .* (Richmond, Va., 1900), 142.

22. *OR,* I, 27, pt. 2: 737, 743–44; McClellan, *Life and Campaigns of Stuart,* 283; Hackley, *Little Fork Rangers,* 47; William R. Carter diary, June 9, 1863; Driver and Howard, *2nd Virginia Cavalry,* 82; Nanzig, *3rd Virginia Cavalry,* 36; William H. Peek to "Dear Sis," June 11, 1863, Peek MSS, VHS; Robert B. Jones to his wife, June 11, 1863, Jones MSS; Halsey Wigfall to "Dear Lou," June 13–14, 1863, Wigfall MSS; Wert, "His Unhonored Service," 32.

23. *OR,* I, 27, pt. 2: 680, 721, 727, 729, 733; McClellan, *Life and Campaigns of Stuart,* 268–69; Beale, *Lieutenant of Cavalry,* 86; Opie, *Rebel Calvaryman,* 152; Cadwallader J. Iredell to anon., June 13, 1863, Iredell MSS, UNC.

24. *OR,* I, 27, pt. 1: 1043–45, McClellan, *Life and Campaigns of Stuart,* 266–67; Beale, *Lieutenant of Cavalry,* 86; Neese, *Confederate Horse Artillery,* 172–74; Baylor, *Bull Run to Bull Run,* 143; Beale, *Ninth Virginia Cavalry,* 69.

25. *OR,* I, 27, pt. 1: 950, 961, 1054; pt. 2: 734–36; pt. 3: 42; Blackford, *War Years with Jeb Stuart,* 214–15; David M. Gregg to Henry B. McClellan, Jan. 21, 1878, McClellan MSS, VHS; Downey, *Clash of Cavalry,* 106–7.

26. *OR,* I, 27, pt. 1: 965, 1024, 1053; 51, pt. 2: 722; McClellan, *Life and Campaigns of Stuart,* 269–70.

27. *OR,* I, 27, pt. 1: 961, 975; pt. 2: 683, 729–31, 744; McClellan, *Life and Campaigns of Stuart,* 289–92; Beale, *Lieutenant of Cavalry,* 89; Brooks, *Butler and His Cavalry,* 53, 152–53, 165–69; Lawson Morrissett diary, June 9, 1863, MC; Chiswell Dabney to his father, June 14, 1863, Dabney MSS; Wellman, *Giant in Gray,* 108–9.

28. *OR,* I, 27, pt. 1: 950–51, 965–66, 1053; pt. 2: 681, 684, 755, 769; Blackford, *War Years with Jeb Stuart,* 216; Opie, *Rebel Calvaryman,* 153–54; von Borcke, *Memoirs,* 2: 273–74; Grimsley, *Battles in Culpeper County,* 11; Edward A. Green memoirs, 38, MC.

29. *OR,* I, 27, pt. 1: 985–86, 996–97, 1024–25, 1027; pt. 2: 722, 732, 755, 763, 769; Myers, *The Comanches,* 184–85; von Borcke, *Memoirs,* 2: 276; Beale, *Lieutenant of Cavalry,* 94; Holland, *Pierce M. B. Young,* 72.

30. *OR,* I, 27, pt. 1: 170, 1044; pt. 2: 682–83, 771, 794, 796; James M. Scott memoirs, 10, VHS; Grimsley, *Battles in Culpeper County,* 12; Beale, *Lieutenant of Cavalry,* 95–96; Benjamin F. Parker to "Dear Sister," June 10, 1863, Fredericksburg–Spotsylvania National Military Park Lib., Fredericksburg, Va.

31. *OR,* I, 27, pt. 1: 168–70, 904; pt. 2: 718–20; pt. 3: 39–40, 609, 903–4, 951, 962, 1045; pt. 2: 564; pt. 3: 49, 876; McClellan, *Life and Campaigns of Stuart,* 266, 294–95; Blackford, *War Years with Jeb Stuart,* 216; Mosby, *Stuart's Cavalry in the Gettysburg Campaign,* 35, 38–39, 46–48; Coddington, *Gettysburg Campaign,* 54, 58, 61–63, 66, 615n–16n; *Daily Richmond Examiner,* June 12, 1863.

32. *OR,* I, 27, pt. 2: 313, 340; Freeman, *Lee's Lieutenants,* 3: 20; Mosby, *Stuart's Cavalry in the Gettysburg Campaign,* 59; Nye, *Here Come the Rebels,* 165; Thomason, *Jeb Stuart,* 412; Myers, *The Comanches,* 103–4, 188.

33. *OR,* I, 27, pt. 2: 719–20; Grimsley, *Battles in Culpeper County,* 13.

34. Jones, *Rebel War Clerk's Diary,* 1: 345; Freeman, *Lee's Lieutenants,* 3: 19, 51–52; Nye, *Here Come the Rebels,* 311–12.

35. William H. Peek to "Dear Sis," June 11, 1863, Peek MSS; McClellan, *Life and Campaigns of Stuart,* 294.

36. *OR,* I, 27, pt. 2: 306, 315, 357, 366, 613, 652, 673–77, 687–88, 873, pt. 3: 71–72, 80–84, 87–89, 106, 116–17, 887–88; 51, pt. 1: 1054–55; pt. 2: 723;

John Swann to "Dear Bettie," June 20, 1863, Swann MSS, Georgia Dept. of Arch. and Hist., Atlanta.

37. *OR,* I, 27, pt. 3: 186, 201, Hermann Schuricht, "Jenkins' Brigade in the Gettysburg Campaign," *SHSP* 24 (1896): 340; Moore, *Rebellion Record,* 7: 196–98; Nye, *Here Come the Rebels,* 136–48.

38. *OR,* I, 27, pt. 2: 688; 52, pt. 1: 723; McClellan, *Life and Campaigns of Stuart,* 314; von Borcke, *Memoirs,* 2: 285; Thaddeus Fitzhugh memoirs, 22.

39. *OR,* I, 27, pt. 2: 739, 747.

40. Ibid., pt. 1: 906, 953, 1052; pt. 2: 739, 745, 747; Nye, *Here Come the Rebels,* 171–77; Robert B. Jones to his wife, July 15, 1863, Jones MSS.

41. *OR,* I, 27, pt. 1: 972–73; pt. 2: 740, 742; Nye, *Here Come the Rebels,* 177–78; Haden, *Reminiscences,* 23; St. George T. Brooke autobiography, 27–29.

42. *OR,* I, 27, pt. 1; 171, 1052; Robert T. Hubard memoirs, 74.

43. *OR,* I, 27, pt. 1: 979–80, 1052; pt. 2: 741–43, 746; McClellan, *Life and Campaigns of Stuart,* 300–301; *New York Times,* June 22, 1863.

44. *OR,* I, 27, pt. 1: 907, 953, 1052; pt. 2: 357, 366, 741; pt. 3: 173; Trout, *With Pen and Saber,* 214–15; Thomas L. Rosser to Elizabeth Winston Rosser, June 18, 1863, Rosser MSS, UV.

45. *OR,* I, 27, pt. 1: 961–63, 1055; McClellan, *Life and Campaigns of Stuart,* 303–4; Davis, *Last Cavalier,* 316; von Borcke, *Memoirs,* 2: 285–86.

46. *OR,* I, 27, pt. 1: 963–65, 1056; pt 2: 688; Mosby, *Stuart's Cavalry in the Gettysburg Campaign,* 71; von Borcke, *Memoirs,* 2: 287–88; Beale, *Ninth Virginia Cavalry,* 71; Coddington, *Gettysburg Campaign,* 77–78; *New York Times,* June 22, 1863; Archibald Atkinson, Jr., memoirs, 14, Carol M. Newman Lib., Virginia Polytechnic Institute and State Univ., Blacksburg.

47. von Borcke, *Memoirs,* 2: 288–90; Thomason, *Jeb Stuart,* 416.

48. Mosby, *Stuart's Cavalry in the Gettysburg Campaign,* 65–66; McClellan, *Life and Campaigns of Stuart,* 306; *OR,* I, 27, pt. 1: 142, 910; pt. 2: 689; pt. 3: 192.

49. *OR,* I, 27, pt. 1: 909, 953, 975; pt. 2: 690; Nye, *Here Come the Rebels,* 190–91; Lewis T. Nunnelee memoirs, 77–78.

50. *OR,* I, 27, pt. 1: 953, 972, 975–76, 1034; Nye, *Here Come the Rebels,* 190–92; Media Evans memoirs, 8.

51. *OR,* I, 27, pt. 1: 976; pt. 2: 689; McClellan, *Life and Campaigns of Stuart,* 306–7; Blackford, *War Years with Jeb Stuart,* 218–20; Beale, *Ninth Virginia Cavalry,* 72–73; von Borcke, *Memoirs,* 2: 291–93.

52. *OR,* I, 27, pt. 1: 911–13; pt. 3: 213, 227–30; Neese, *Confederate Horse Artillery,* 181–82; Nye, *Here Come the Rebels,* 197, 201.

53. *OR,* I, 27, pt. 1: 614, 1035; pt. 2: 690; Brooks, *Butler and His Cavalry,* 177.

54. *OR,* I, 27, pt. 1: 614, 616, 954, 972–73, 1055; pt. 2: 688, 690–91; McClellan, *Life and Campaigns of Stuart,* 303–4, 311–12; von Borcke, *Memoirs,*

2: 285–86; Nye, *Here Come the Rebels,* 183, 198–200, 205; Baylor, *Bull Run to Bull Run,* 149; Brooks, *Butler and His Cavalry,* 180–82; Wade Hampton to Henry B. McClellan, Jan. 14, 1878, McClellan MSS; Beale, *Ninth Virginia Cavalry,* 71; Charles R. Phelps to "Dear Aunt," June 25, 1863, Phelps MSS; Edwin R. Sloan to his wife, June 24, 1863, Sloan MSS; Media Evans memoirs, 8–9.

55. *OR,* I, 27, pt. 1: 920–21, 932–33, 1029; pt. 2: 750–51, 756, 759, 766; Ephraim Bowman to his father, June 21, 1863, Bowman MSS; Ephraim Bowman diary, June 21, 1863, ibid.; Charles McVicar memoirs, 14.

56. Marshall E. Decker to his wife, June 22, 1863, Decker MSS, LV; Media Evans memoirs, 9; Lewis T. Nunnelee memoirs, 79–80.

57. *OR,* I, 27, pt. 1: 171–72, 193, 913; pt. 2: 713, 719, 741; Coddington, *Gettysburg Campaign,* 121–22; Longacre, *Cavalry at Gettysburg,* 132.

CHAPTER 15

1. *OR,* I, 27, pt. 1: 171–72, 193; pt. 2: 692; pt. 3: 913, 915, 923; Marshall, *Aide-de-Camp of Lee,* 201–2, 205–6, 208; Freeman, *Lee's Lieutenants,* 3: 41 and n, 47–48, 550; Coddington, *Gettysburg Campaign,* 107–8; Longstreet, *From Manassas to Appomattox,* 336, 342–43; Randolph H. McKim, "The Confederate Cavalry in the Gettysburg Campaign," *JMSIUS* 46 (1910): 418.

2. *OR,* I, 27, pt. 2: 692, 696, 708–9; McClellan, *Life and Campaigns of Stuart,* 315–17; John S. Mosby to Lunsford L. Lomax, Feb. 19, 1896, Mosby MSS, USAMHI; John S. Mosby to the editor of the *Philadelphia Weekly Times,* Mar. 8, 1896, Mosby MSS, Missouri Hist. Soc., St. Louis.

3. *OR,* I, 27, pt. 2: 915; J. E. B. Stuart to Beverly H. Robertson ("Confidential"), June 24, 1863, Stuart MSS, Gilder Lehrman Coll.; Mosby, "Confederate Cavalry in the Gettysburg Campaign," 251–52; Mosby, *War Reminiscences and Stuart's Campaigns,* 178–82; Longstreet, *From Manassas to Appomattox,* 343; Bowmaster, "Brig. Gen. B. H. Robertson," 36–41; Patrick A. Bowmaster, ed., "Confederate Brig. Gen. B. H. 'Bev' Robertson Interviewed on the Gettysburg Campaign," *Gettysburg Magazine* 20 (1998): 19–26; Wise, *Long Arm of Lee,* 1: 691.

4. *OR,* I, 27, pt. 2: 692, 915; Miles A. Cavin to his sister, June 27, 1863, Cavin MSS, NCSDA&H; William R. Carter diary, June 25, 1863; McClellan, *Life and Campaigns of Stuart,* 318–21, 336; Blackford, *War Years with Jeb Stuart,* 223; Cooke, *Wearing of the Gray,* 226–31; Freeman, *Lee's Lieutenants,* 3: 61; Longstreet, *From Manassas to Appomattox,* 343.

5. *OR,* I, 27, pt. 3: 923; McKim, "Confederate Cavalry in the Gettysburg Campaign," 420; Freeman, *Lee's Lieutenants,* 3: 48, 550–51; Coddington, *Gettysburg Campaign,* 112–13.

6. *OR,* I, 27, pt. 2: 692–93; pt. 3: 309–10, 318; McClellan, *Life and Campaigns of Stuart,* 321; Cooke, *Wearing of the Gray,* 230–33; Coddington, *Gettysburg Campaign,* 113; Lawson Morrissett diary, June 25, 1863.

7. *OR,* I, 27, pt. 2: 693; pt. 3: 376–77; Blackford, *War Years with Jeb Stuart,* 223; Cooke, *Wearing of the Gray,* 235; Thaddeus Fitzhugh memoirs, 22; Beale, *Ninth Virginia Cavalry,* 78; Kenneth W. Holt to the author, May 17, 1994.

8. *OR,* I, 27, pt. 2: 694; Haden, *Reminiscences,* 23; Thaddeus Fitzhugh memoirs, 22; Lawson Morrissett diary, June 26, 1863; William R. Carter diary, June 26, 1863.

9. Beale, *Ninth Virginia Cavalry,* 78; Blackford, *War Years with Jeb Stuart,* 225; Cooke, *Wearing of the Gray,* 236.

10. Beale, *Ninth Virginia Cavalry,* 79–80; McClellan, *Life and Campaigns of Stuart,* 324; Blackford, *War Years with Jeb Stuart,* 224; Cooke, *Wearing of the Gray,* 238; Beale, *Lieutenant of Cavalry,* 112–13; William R. Carter diary, June 28, 1863.

11. *OR,* I, 27, pt. 2: 694; pt. 3: 396, 403–4; Freeman, *Lee's Lieutenants,* 3: 67.

12. *OR,* I, 27, pt. 2: 202, 695; Cooke, *Wearing of the Gray,* 239; Nye, *Here Come the Rebels,* 319–20; Everett I. Pearson, "Stuart in Westminster," *Transactions of the Southern Historical Society* 2 (1875): 20–22; St. George T. Brooke autobiography, 30; William R. Carter diary, June 29, 1863. For a more detailed account of this affair, see James Harrison Wilson, *Captain Charles Corbit's Charge at Westminster . . . An Episode of the Gettysburg Campaign* (Wilmington, Del., 1913).

13. *Encounter at Hanover: Prelude to Gettysburg* (Hanover, Pa., 1963), 22; William H. Shriver, "My Father Led J. E. B. Stuart to Gettysburg," 3–4, Gettysburg National Military Park Lib., Gettysburg, Pa.

14. McClellan, *Life and Campaigns of Stuart,* 327; *Encounter at Hanover,* 22, 24; Shriver, "My Father Led Stuart," 3.

15. *OR,* I, 27, pt. 2: 695–96; McClellan, *Life and Campaigns of Stuart,* 328; Blackford, *War Years with Jeb Stuart,* 225–26; Beale, *Ninth Virginia Cavalry,* 82; *Encounter at Hanover,* 61, 66, 93.

16. *OR,* I, 27, p. 2: 696; McClellan, *Life and Campaigns of Stuart,* 328–29; Blackford, *War Years with Jeb Stuart,* 226–27; Cooke, *Wearing of the Gray,* 241–42; William R. Carter diary, June 30, 1863.

17. *OR,* I, 27, pt. 2: 696; George W. Beale, "A Soldier's Account of the Gettysburg Campaign: Letter from George W. Beale," *SHSP* 11 (1883): 322–23.

18. *OR,* I, 27, pt. 2: 467–68, 696; McClellan, *Life and Campaigns of Stuart,* 330; Freeman, *Lee's Lieutenants,* 3: 71, 136; Mosby, *Stuart's Cavalry in the Gettysburg Campaign,* 183 and n, 184n.

19. *OR,* I, 27, pt. 2: 307, 316–17, 696; Mosby, *Stuart's Cavalry in the Gettysburg Campaign,* 182–83.

20. *OR,* I, 27, pt. 2: 220, 696; Nye, *Here Come the Rebels,* 347–49; Codding-ton, *Gettysburg Campaign,* 206, 660n–61n; Beale, *Lieutenant of Cavalry,* 114; William R. Carter diary, July 1, 1863.

21. *OR,* I, 27, pt. 2: 224, 696–97; *New York Times,* July 3, 1863; Nye, *Here Come the Rebels,* 325; Davis, *Last Cavalier,* 331.

22. *OR,* I, 27, pt. 2: 221, 697; Cooke, *Wearing of the Gray,* 245; Peck, *Co. C, 2nd Va. Cavalry,* 32; Thaddeus Fitzhugh memoirs, 23.

23. *OR,* I, 27, pt. 2: 221, 224, 697; McClellan, *Life and Campaigns of Stuart,* 330–31; *Encounter at Hanover,* 240; Wilbur S. Nye, "The Affair at Hunters-town," *CWTI* 9 (Feb. 1971): 29; William R. Carter diary, July 2, 1863.

24. T. J. Mackey, "Duel of General Wade Hampton on the Battle–Field at Get-tysburg with a Federal Soldier," *SHSP* 22 (1894): 125–26; Wellman, *Giant in Gray,* 115–16.

25. *OR,* I, 27, pt. 1: 992, 999; McClellan, *Life and Campaigns of Stuart,* 331; Nye, "Affair at Hunterstown," 30–33; W. C. Storrick, "The Hunterstown Fight," 3–4, Gettysburg National Military Park Lib.; *New York Times,* July 21, 1863.

26. *OR,* I, 27, p. 2: 497, 724; William G. Deloney to his wife, July 4, 7, 1863, Deloney MSS, Hargrett Lib., Univ. of Georgia, Athens; Nye, "Affair at Hunterstown," 23; Holland, *Pierce M. B. Young,* 73; Howard, *Cobb Legion Cavalry,* 9.

27. Edwin E. Bouldin to John Bachelder, July 19, 1886, Bachelder MSS, New Hampshire Hist. Soc., Concord; Jack L. Dickinson, *16th Virginia Cavalry* (Lynchburg, Va., 1989), 27.

28. *OR,* I, 27, pt. 2: 307, 321; Coddington, *Gettysburg Campaign,* 207; Sorrel, *Confederate Staff Officer,* 154; Edward Porter Alexander, *Military Mem-oirs of a Confederate: A Critical Narrative* (New York, 1907), 377.

29. *OR,* I, 27, pt. 2: 697, 699; Royall, *Some Reminiscences,* 25; Coddington, *Gettysburg Campaign,* 520; J. G. Harbord, "The History of the Cavalry of the Army of Northern Virginia," *JUSCA* 14 (1904): 456–57.

30. McClellan, *Life and Campaigns of Stuart,* 337; Wise, *Long Arm of Lee,* 2: 691; Fairfax Downey, *The Guns at Gettysburg* (New York, 1958), 161–62.

31. *OR,* I, 27, pt. 2: 697; McClellan, *Life and Campaigns of Stuart,* 338.

32. McClellan, *Life and Campaigns of Stuart,* 339; Edwin E. Bouldin to John Bachelder, July 29, 1886; Bachelder MSS; Vincent A. Witcher to William C. Endicott, Mar. 27, 1887, ibid.; Vincent A. Witcher to Lunsford L. Lomax, Aug. 20, 1908, William Brooke Rawle MSS, Hist. Soc. of Penn-sylvania, Philadelphia; Scott C. Cole, *34th Virginia Cavalry* (Lynchburg, Va., 1993), 48–49.

33. McClellan, *Life and Campaigns of Stuart,* 338–39; Trout, *In the Saddle with Stuart,* 83; Jasper Hawse diary, July 3, 1863.

34. *OR,* I, 27, pt. 1: 956, 1050; pt. 2: 697–98; McClellan, *Life and Campaigns of Stuart,* 339–40; William E. Miller, "The Cavalry Battle near Gettysburg,"

B&L 3: 400–403; Cole, *34th Virginia Cavalry,* 51–52; Henry B. McClellan to John Bachelder, Apr. 12, 1886, Bachelder MSS.

35. *OR,* I, 27, pt. 1: 956; pt. 2: 697–98; McClellan, *Life and Campaigns of Stuart,* 339–40; Miller, "Cavalry Battle near Gettysburg," 400–402; Moore, *Stuart Horse Artillery,* 70–71; Micajah Woods to his father, July 10, 16, 1863, Woods MSS; Charles R. Phelps to "Dear Aunt," July 9, 1863, Phelps MSS; Edwin E. Bouldin to John Bachelder, July 29, 1886, Bachelder MSS; Vincent A. Witcher to William C. Endicott, Mar. 27, 1887, ibid.; Henry B. McClellan to John Bachelder, Apr. 12, 1886, ibid.

36. Henry B. McClellan to John Bachelder, Apr. 12, 1886, Bachelder MSS; Krick, *9th Virginia Cavalry,* 24; Trout, *In the Saddle with Stuart,* 82.

37. *OR,* I, 27, pt. 1: 957; Miller, "Cavalry Battle near Gettysburg," 403; Hudgins, *Old Dominion Dragoon,* 82, 84.

38. *OR,* I, 27, pt. 2: 698; Miller, "Cavalry Battle near Gettysburg," 403–4; Hopkins, *The Little Jeff,* 154–55; J. W. Biddle to his father, July 16, 1863, Biddle MSS.

39. *OR,* I, 27, pt. 2: 724–25; Wellman, *Giant in Gray,* 118–19.

40. Miller, "Cavalry Battle near Gettysburg," 404.

41. Ibid.; Wellman, *Giant in Gray,* 118–19; J. W. Biddle to his father, July 16, 1863, Biddle MSS.

42. *OR,* I, 27, pt. 1: 1051; Cooke, *Wearing of the Gray,* 247; William E. Miller to William Brooke Rawle, June 5, 1878, William Brooke Rawle MSS; William E. Miller to John B. McIntosh, June 8, 1878, ibid.; Miller, "Cavalry Battle near Gettysburg," 404–5; Wellman, *Giant in Gray,* 120; Cauthen, *Letters of Three Wade Hamptons,* 94; Barringer, *First North Carolina,* 5; William G. Deloney to his wife, July 4, 1863, Deloney MSS; Mackey, "Duel of General Wade Hampton," 125.

43. *OR,* I, 27, pt. 1: 186, 193, 957–58; pt. 2: 699, 714–15; McClellan, *Life and Campaigns of Stuart,* 341–49; Miller, "Cavalry Battle near Gettysburg," 405 and n–406; Driver, *1st Virginia Cavalry,* 67.

CHAPTER 16

1. *OR,* I, 27, pt. 1: 186, 193, 957–58; pt. 2: 699, 714–15.

2. Ibid., 699; McClellan, *Life and Campaigns of Stuart,* 349; Coddington, *Gettysburg Campaign,* 535–39.

3. Coddington, *Gettysburg Campaign,* 538; John D. Imboden, "The Confederate Retreat from Gettysburg," *B&L* 3: 420–22; *OR,* I, 27, pt. 2: 699.

4. *OR,* I, 27, pt. 3: 923, 927–28; McClellan, *Life and Campaigns of Stuart,* 336, 347; Coddington, *Gettysburg Campaign,* 184–86; Mosby, *Stuart's Cavalry in the Gettysburg Campaign,* 195, 198–201, 215–18; Mosby, "Confederate Cavalry in the Gettysburg Campaign," 251–52; Beverly H. Robertson, "The Confederate Cavalry in the Gettysburg Campaign," *B&L* 3: 253; Jasper Hawse diary, July 3, 1863; Bowmaster, "B. H. Robertson Interviewed," 22; John S. Mosby to the "Editor of the [*Philadelphia*

Weekly] Times," Mar. 2, 1896, Mosby MSS, Missouri Hist. Soc.; John S. Mosby to Lunsford L. Lomax, Feb. 19, 1896, Mosby MSS, USAMHI; Neese, *Confederate Horse Artillery,* 184–86; McDonald, *Laurel Brigade,* 153; Hopkins, *Bull Run to Appomattox,* 109.

5. *OR,* I, 27, pt. 2: 752, 756, 760; pt. 3: 947–48.

6. Frye, *12th Virginia Cavalry,* 43; Baylor, *Bull Run to Bull Run,* 150; McDonald, *Laurel Brigade,* 153; Myers, *The Comanches,* 201–3.

7. *OR,* I, 27, pt. 1: 943, 948; McClellan, *Life and Campaigns of Stuart,* 347–48; Armstrong, *7th Virginia Cavalry,* 55; *New York Times,* July 8, 1863; John Purifoy, "Cavalry Action near Fairfield, Pa., July 3, 1863," *CV* 32 (1924): 345.

8. *OR,* I, 27, pt. 1: 948; 2: 756; Opie, *Rebel Calvaryman,* 172–73; McDonald, *Laurel Brigade,* 155–56; Hopkins, From *Bull Run to Appomattox,* 113; Neese, *Confederate Horse Artillery,* 188; Michael P. Musick, *6th Virginia Cavalry* (Lynchburg, Va., 1990), 45.

9. *OR,* I, 27, pt. 2: 299, 309, 311, 322, 699; pt. 3: 531; Coddington, *Gettysburg Campaign,* 535–41; Longacre, *Cavalry at Gettysburg,* 247.

10. Imboden, "Confederate Retreat from Gettysburg," 423–24; *OR,* I, 27, pt. 1: 81, 85, 489; pt. 2: 221–22, 238, 246; pt. 3: 506–8, 549–50; *New York Times,* July 21, 1863; Coddington, *Gettysburg Campaign,* 452–43; Longacre, *Cavalry at Gettysburg,* 247–48.

11. *OR,* I, 27, pt. 1: 970, 993–94, 998; pt. 2: 326, 752–53; McClellan, *Life and Campaigns of Stuart,* 352–55; George Wilson Booth, *Personal Reminiscences of a Maryland Soldier in the War Between the States, 1861–65* (Baltimore, 1898), 93; Musick, *6th Virginia Cavalry,* 45–46; Robert J. Driver, Jr., *First & Second Maryland Cavalry, C.S.A.* (Charlottesville, Va., 1999), 56–59.

12. *OR,* I, 27, pt. 1: 970, 994; pt. 2: 700–701, 753; Hopkins, *Bull Run to Appomattox,* 105; Opie, *Rebel Calvaryman,* 173; Neese, *Confederate Horse Artillery,* 190–91.

13. Isaac N. Baker Memoir of the Retreat from Gettysburg, 1, Preston Lib., V.M.I.

14. *OR,* I, 27, pt. 2: 214, 280, 347, 703; pt. 3: 547–49; Coddington, *Gettysburg Campaign,* 542–43, 552; Imboden, "Confederate Retreat from Gettysburg," 425; Milton B. Steele diary, July 5, 1863, MC; *New York Times,* July 21, 1863.

15. *OR,* I, 27, pt. 2: 311, 700; Robert T. Hubard memoirs, 77.

16. Thaddeus Fitzhugh memoirs, 24.

17. *OR,* I, 27, pt. 1: 971, 994–95, 1006, 1014; pt. 2: 700; *New York Times,* July 21, 1863.

18. *OR,* I, 27, pt. 2: 700–01, 753–54; pt. 3: 548; *New York Times,* July 6, 1863; Longacre, *Cavalry at Gettysburg,* 253–54.

19. *OR,* I, 27, pt. 2: 701.

20. Ibid, 436–38, 488–89, 653, 655; Imboden, "Confederate Retreat from Gettysburg," 425–27; Coddington, *Gettysburg Campaign,* 554; Isaac N. Baker memoir, 1.

21. Isaac N. Baker memoir, 1; *OR,* I, 27, pt. 1: 916, 928, 935, 939–40, 943, 995; p. 2: 436–38; pt. 3: 586; Imboden, "Confederate Retreat from Gettysburg," 427–28; Jasper Hawse diary, July 6, 1863; W. Bailey Clement to his wife, July 9, 1863, Clement MSS; Halsey Wigfall to his father, July 7, 1863, Wigfall MSS; John H. Cameron memoirs, 19–20; George B. Davis, "From Gettysburg to Williamsport," *Papers of the Military Historical Society of Massachusetts* 3 (1903): 457; John Purifoy, "A Unique Battle," *CV* 33 (1925): 132–35.

22. William G. Deloney to his wife, July 7, 1863, Deloney MSS; Frances Letcher Mitchell, "A Georgia Henry of Navarre," *CV* 23 (1915): 363.

23. *OR,* I, 27, pt. 1: 928, 995, 999–1000; pt. 2: 702; Imboden, "Confederate Retreat from Gettysburg," 427–28.

24. *OR,* I, 27, pt. 1: 928, 995; pt. 2: 322, 361, 370, 701–3, 764–65; McClellan, *Life and Campaigns of Stuart,* 359; Neese, *Confederate Horse Artillery,* 193–94; Coddington, *Gettysburg Campaign,* 553; W. W. Goldsborough, *The Maryland Line in the Confederate States Army* (Baltimore, 1869), 218–19; Charles McVicar memoirs, 19; W. Bailey Clement to his wife, July 9, 1863, Clement MSS; James A. Jeter to "Bettie," Aug. 8, 1863, Jeter MSS, VHS.

25. *OR,* I, 27, pt. 1: 1006, 1010–11, 1014–15; pt. 2: 365, 370, 702, 754–65; Longacre, *Cavalry at Gettysburg,* 257–58.

26. *OR,* I, 27, pt. 2: 299–301, 322–23, 438, 493; Coddington, *Gettysburg Campaign,* 565–66, 818n.

27. *OR,* I, 27, pt. 1: 928, 944, 948–49, 966; pt. 2: 703, 754, 760–61; *New York Times,* July 12, 21, 1863; Hewett et al., *Supplement to the Official Records,* I, 5: 473–74; Armstrong, *7th Virginia Cavalry,* 57.

28. *OR,* I, 27, pt. 1: 929, 935, 940–41; pt. 2: 703; Moore, *Stuart Horse Artillery,* 71.

29. *OR,* I, 27, pt. 2: 703–4; Thaddeus Fitzhugh memoirs, 25; Charles McVicar memoirs, 19–20; Charles R. Phelps to "Dear Aunt," July 9, 1863, Phelps MSS.

30. *OR,* I, 27, pt. 1: 929, 941, 958, 1007; pt. 2: 704; Neese, *Confederate Horse Artillery,* 197; Charles McVicar memoirs, 20; Shoemaker, *Shoemaker's Battery,* 47; J. W. Biddle to his father, July 16, 1863, Biddle MSS; Micajah Woods to his father, July 10, 1863, Woods MSS; Joseph P. Webb diary, July 9, 1863, UV; Lewis T. Nunnelee memoirs, 88.

31. *OR,* I, 27, pt. 1: 146, 925–26, 929, 936, 941–42, 1033; pt. 3: 621.

32. Ibid., pt. 1: 663–64, 929, 936, 942; pt. 2: 398–99, 704; Neese, *Confederate Horse Artillery,* 197–98; Joseph P. Webb diary, July 10, 1863; Charles McVicar memoirs, 20; Lawson Morrissett diary, July 10, 1863.

33. *OR,* I, 27, pt. 1: 664, 988–89, 929, 971, 999–1000; pt. 2: 704–5; pt. 3: 649, 651, 657–58, 660, 664, 994–95, 998; Robert E. Lee to J. E. B. Stuart, July 11, 1863 (two letters), July 13, 1863 (four letters), Stuart MSS, Henry E. Huntington Lib., San Marino, Calif. (copies in CSR of Henry B. McClellan, M–331, R–169, NA); Joseph P. Webb diary, July 11–12, 1863; T. W. Grussell diary, July 11–12, 1863, DU; Robert T. Hubard memoirs, 78; Louis T. Nunnelee memoirs, 89.

34. *OR,* I, 27, pt. 2: 753, 762; pt. 3: 657–58, 664–65, 669, 987–88; Coddington, *Gettysburg Campaign,* 566.

35. *OR,* I, 27, pt. 1: 118, 929, 996, 1016–17; pt. 2: 226, 246, 1008; pt. 3: 675; Robert E. Lee to John D. Imboden, July 13, 1863, Lee MSS, Gilder Lehrman Coll.; Coddington, *Gettysburg Campaign,* 567.

36. *OR,* I, 27, pt. 2: 705; pt. 3: 1001; Robert E. Lee to J. E. B. Stuart, July 13, 1863, Stuart MSS, Henry E. Huntington Lib.

37. Robert T. Hubard memoirs, 79.

38. *OR,* I, 27, pt. 2: 327; Neese, *Confederate Horse Artillery,* 199; Blackford, *War Years with Jeb Stuart,* 234–35.

39. J. W. Biddle to his father, July 16, 1863, Biddle MSS.

40. *OR,* I, 27, pt. 1: 929, 936–37, 942, 990, 998–1000; pt. 2: 640–42, 705; pt. 3: 685; *New York Times,* July 21, 1863.

41. Heath J. Christian to his father, July 13, 1863, Christian MSS.

CHAPTER 17

1. J. W. Biddle to his father, July 16, 1863, Biddle MSS; Stiles, *4th Virginia Cavalry,* 34; Krick, *9th Virginia Cavalry,* 27; Turner W. Holley to anon., July 10, 1863, Holley MSS, DU.

2. J. W. Biddle to his father, July 16, 1863, Biddle MSS; Driver, *10th Virginia Cavalry,* 45.

3. Jacob B. Click to "Dear Old Friend Lucius," July 17, 1863, USAMHI; Thomas L. Rosser to Elizabeth Winston Rosser, July 7, 1863, Rosser MSS, UV.

4. Micajah Woods to his father, July 16, 1863, Woods MSS.

5. Blackford, *War Years with Jeb Stuart,* 235.

6. Ibid., 235–36; J. E. B. Stuart to "Mrs. Grinnan," Apr. 30, 1864, Stuart MSS, UV.

7. *OR,* I, 27, pt. 2: 706; Driver and Howard, *2nd Virginia Cavalry,* 94–95; Andrew A. Humphreys, *Gettysburg to the Rapidan: The Army of the Potomac, July, 1863, to April, 1864* (New York, 1883), 8; Robert T. Hubard memoirs, 79; Joseph P. Webb diary, July 15, 1863.

8. *OR,* I, 27, pt. 2: 706; Driver, *1st Virginia Cavalry,* 69–70; T. W. Grussell diary, July 14, 1863.

9. *OR,* I, 27, pt. 1: 147–50; Humphreys, *Gettysburg to the Rapidan,* 8–9.

10. *OR,* I, 27, pt. 2: 706–7; pt. 3: 734–35, 741–42, 752.

11. J. E. B. Stuart to Walter H. Taylor, July 27, 1863 (and endorsements), CSR of Fitzhugh Lee, ibid.

12. Surgeon's Certificates, July 20, Aug. 7, 1863, CSR of Wade Hampton, M–331, R–115, NA; J. E. B. Stuart to Robert E. Lee, Aug. 14, 1863 (and endorsements), ibid.

13. *OR,* I, 27, pt. 2: 794, 796, 821; II, 6: 69, 118, 219, 358, 362, 364, 484–85, 488, 500, 706, 927.

14. *OR,* I, 27, pt. 3: 1006–7.

15. Williams C. Wickham to James A. Seddon, July 14, 1863 (and endorsements), CSR of Wickham, M–331, R–267, NA; Stiles, *4th Virginia Cavalry,* 36.

16. *OR,* I, 27, pt. 3: 1068–69.

17. Ibid.; Thomas, *Bold Dragoon,* 258–59.

18. Moore, *Stuart Horse Artillery,* 73–74; Moore, *Chew's, Shoemaker's, New-town Artillery,* 31; Charles McVicar memoirs, 21–22; Halsey Wigfall to his mother, Aug. 13, 1863, Wigfall MSS; Mays, *Genealogical Notes,* 109–13; Cadwallader J. Iredell to "My dear Mattie," Aug. 2, 1863, Iredell MSS.

19. Halsey Wigfall to his mother, Aug. 13, 1863, Wigfall MSS; Charles R. Phelps to "Dear Aunt," Aug. 10, 1863, Phelps MSS; Grimsley, *Battles in Culpeper County,* 14.

20. Grimsley, *Battles in Culpeper County,* 14–15.

21. Driver, *5th Virginia Cavalry,* 60–61; Robert B. Jones to his wife, Aug. 24, 1863, Jones MSS; Robert T. Hubard memoirs, 81; Longacre, *Lincoln's Cavalrymen,* 222–23.

22. *OR,* I, 29, pt. 2: 707–8; Robert J. Driver, Jr., *14th Virginia Cavalry* (Lynchburg, Va., 1988), 26.

23. Freeman, *Lee's Lieutenants,* 3: 211–12; Thomas, *Bold Dragoon,* 258–59.

24. J. E. B. Stuart to Flora Cooke Stuart, Sept. 11, 28, Aug. 4, 1863, Stuart MSS, VHS; Peter W. Hairston to his wife, Oct. 30, 1863, Hairston MSS, UNC.

25. Hewett et al., *Supplement to the Official Records,* I, 5: 563; Rawleigh W. Downman to his wife, Aug. 7, 1863, Downman MSS, VHS.

26. Driver and Howard, *2nd Virginia Cavalry,* 95; J. E. B. Stuart to Thomas L. Rosser, Sept. 30, 1863, Rosser MSS, UV.

27. J. E. B. Stuart to Thomas L. Rosser, Sept. 30, 1863, Rosser MSS, UV.

28. Thomas L. Rosser to Elizabeth Winston Rosser, Sept. 15, 16, 24, 1863, Rosser MSS, UV.

29. Ibid., Sept. 24, 1863.

30. Musick, *6th Virginia Cavalry,* 48; Armstrong, *7th Virginia Cavalry,* 58; McDonald, *Laurel Brigade,* 168–69; Lambert, *Grumble,* 9; "'Grumble' Jones: A Personality Profile," *CWTI* 7 (June 1968): 40.

31. Baylor, *Bull Run to Bull Run,* 154–55; *OR,* I, 29, pt. 2: 771–72; Register of Appointment, Oct. 10, 1863, CSR of Thomas L. Rosser, M–331, R–216,

NA; Thomas L. Rosser, *Riding with Rosser*, ed. S. Roger Keller (Shippensburg, Pa., 1997), 2; Driver, *5th Virginia Cavalry*, 62.

32. *OR*, I, 29, pt. 2: 167, 169, 172, 706, 720–21.

33. McClellan, *Life and Campaigns of Stuart*, 372–74; Musick, *6th Virginia Cavalry*, 48–49; Armstrong, *11th Virginia Cavalry*, 51; Opie, *Rebel Calvaryman*, 195; Grimsley, *Battles in Culpeper County*, 15–17.

34. Charles W. and Henry M. Trueheart, *Rebel Brothers: The Civil War Letters of the Truehearts*, ed. Edward B. Williams (College Station, Tex., 1995), 172–73.

35. Krick, *9th Virginia Cavalry*, 28; Fortier, *15th Virginia Cavalry*, 40–41; Neese, *Confederate Horse Artillery*, 208–10.

36. Neese, *Confederate Horse Artillery*, 210–11; Moore, *Stuart Horse Artillery*, 75; Moore, *Chew's, Shoemaker's, Newtown Artillery*, 31–32.

37. *OR*, I, 29, pt. 1: 195–96, 200–202, 207–8, 215, 730–31, 742–43.

38. McClellan, *Life and Campaigns of Stuart*, 374; Armstrong, *7th Virginia Cavalry*, 58–59; Armstrong, *11th Virginia Cavalry*, 53; Hewett et al., *Supplement to the Official Records*, I, 5: 585–89; Mays, *Genealogical Notes*, 115–17; Coltrane, *Memoirs*, 20–21.

39. McClellan, *Life and Campaigns of Stuart*, 375.

40. Trueheart and Trueheart, *Rebel Brothers*, 177.

41. Baylor, *Bull Run to Bull Run*, 156–57; Armstrong, *11th Virginia Cavalry*, 54; Frye, *12th Virginia Cavalry*, 48.

42. *OR*, I, 29, pt. 2: 743; McClellan, *Life and Campaigns of Stuart*, 375n–76n; Mays, *Genealogical Notes*, 118–19.

CHAPTER 18

1. *OR*, I, 29, pt. 1: 146–95; pt. 2: 220, 227.

2. Ibid., pt. 1: 439; 51, pt. 2: 772–73.

3. Ibid., 775; 29, pt. 1: 410, 439, 455.

4. *OR*, I, 29, pt. 1: 410, 440–41, 455, 458, 460; McClellan, *Life and Campaigns of Stuart*, 377–78.

5. *OR*, I, 29, pt. 1: 441, 460, 463; McClellan, *Life and Campaigns of Stuart*, 378.

6. *OR*, I, 29, pt. 1: 410, 442, 463, 465; Hackley, *Little Fork Rangers*, 48–49; Driver, *1st Virginia Cavalry*, 72; Driver and Howard, *2nd Virginia Cavalry*, 97–100; Nanzig, *3rd Virginia Cavalry*, 41–43; Stiles, *4th Virginia Cavalry*, 36–37; Robert T. Hubard memoirs, 82; Milton B. Steele diary, Oct. 11, 1863; Beale, *Lieutenant of Cavalry*, 129; Corson, *My Dear Jennie*, 111–12.

7. *OR*, I, 29, pt. 1: 442–43; McClellan, *Life and Campaigns of Stuart*, 378–79; Neese, *Confederate Horse Artillery*, 217–18; Musick, *6th Virginia Cavalry*, 50–51; Halsey Wigfall to his mother, Oct. 13, 1863, Wigfall MSS; Beale, *Lieutenant of Cavalry*, 130.

8. *OR,* I, 29, pt. 1: 443–44, 465, 474; McClellan, *Life and Campaigns of Stuart,* 382–83; Fortier, *15th Virginia Cavalry,* 45–48; James M. Scott memoirs, 12.

9. *OR,* I, 29, pt. 1: 458; McClellan, *Life and Campaigns of Stuart,* 381–82; Neese, *Confederate Horse Artillery,* 221.

10. *OR,* I, 29, pt. 1: 446, 458; McClellan, *Life and Campaigns of Stuart,* 383–84; Neese, *Confederate Horse Artillery,* 222–23.

11. *OR,* I, 29, pt. 1: 444; Martin T. McMahon, "From Gettysburg to the Coming of Grant," *B&L* 4: 83–84.

12. *OR,* I, 29, pt. 1: 447, 456; 51, pt. 2: 776–77; McClellan, *Life and Campaigns of Stuart,* 385–87.

13. *OR,* I, 29, pt. 1: 447; McClellan, *Life and Campaigns of Stuart,* 388.

14. *OR,* I, 29, pt. 1: 447–48, 461; W. Gordon McCabe, *A Brief Sketch of Andrew Reid Venable, Jr., Formerly A.A. and Inspector General, Cavalry Corps, A.N.V.* (Richmond, 1909), 8–9; Robert T. Hubard memoirs, 82; Cadwallader J. Iredell to "My dear Mattie," Oct. 23, 1863, Iredell MSS.

15. Cadwallader J. Iredell to "My dear Mattie," Oct. 23, 1863, Iredell MSS; Coltrane, *Memoirs,* 22–23.

16. *OR,* I, 29, pt. 1: 448.

17. Ibid., 448, 461; McClellan, *Life and Campaigns of Stuart,* 392; Clark, *Regiments and Battalions from North Carolina,* 1: 426–27.

18. *OR,* I, 29, pt. 1: 448–49.

19. Ibid., 449, 459, 466.

20. Ibid., 426–27, 430–32.

21. Ibid., 449–50, 466; Rosser, *Riding with Rosser,* 3–4; Halsey Wigfall to his father, Oct. 23, 1863, Wigfall MSS; Driver, *5th Virginia Cavalry,* 64–67; Fortier, *15th Virginia Cavalry,* 48–49; Robert T. Hubard memoirs, 83; Milton B. Steele diary, Oct. 15–17, 1863.

22. Cadwallader J. Iredell to "My dear Mattie," Oct. 23, 1863, Iredell MSS.

23. *OR,* I, 29, pt. 1: 451, 464; McClellan, *Life and Campaigns of Stuart,* 393–94.

24. *OR,* I, 29, pt. 1: 411, 451–52, 461; McClellan, *Life and Campaigns of Stuart,* 394–95; Clark, *Regiments and Battalions from North Carolina,* 1: 427; Cooke, *Wearing of the Gray,* 265–66; Driver, *1st Virginia Cavalry,* 73–74; Nanzig, *3rd Virginia Cavalry,* 44; Rosser, *Riding with Rosser,* 4–5; Halsey Wigfall to his father, Oct. 19, 23, 1863, Wigfall MSS; Robert T. Hubard memoirs, 82–84.

25. *OR,* I, 29, pt. 1: 452

26. Ibid., 51, pt. 2: 778; Cadwallader J. Iredell to "My dear Mattie," Oct. 23, 1863, Iredell MSS; Lewis T. Nunnelee memoirs, 112–13; William R. Carter diary, Oct. 19, 1863.

27. *OR,* I, 29, pt. 1: 452.

28. Hewett et al., *Supplement to the Official Records,* I, 5: 566–67; Driver, *1st Virginia Cavalry,* 74; Driver, *10th Virginia Cavalry,* 50.

29. Moore, *Stuart Horse Artillery,* 83; Shoemaker, *Shoemaker's Battery,* 59–60; J. Frederick Waring to "Dear Wilby," Nov. 12, 1863, Waring MSS, UNC; Grimsley, *Battles in Culpeper County,* 23.
30. John Esten Cooke to "My dearest Sal," Nov. 14, 1863, Cooke MSS, UV.
31. *OR,* I, 29, pt. 1: 11–13.
32. Ibid., 898, 903–4.
33. Ibid., 806–7.
34. Ibid., 825–30, 898–99, 902–3, 906–7; 51, pt. 2: 788–89; Driver, *1st Virginia Cavalry,* 75; Stiles, *4th Virginia Cavalry,* 39; Thornton R. Baxter to his mother, Nov. 29, 1863, Baxter MSS.
35. *OR,* I, 29, pt. 1: 899, 901–2, 905–6.
36. Ibid., 899–900, 903, 905–7; 51, pt. 2: 790–92; Lee, *Wartime Papers,* 630; Cauthen, *Letters of Three Wade Hamptons,* 97; McDonald, *Laurel Brigade,* 206–7; Baylor, *Bull Run to Bull Run,* 181; Myers, *The Comanches,* 237; Armstrong, *7th Virginia Cavalry,* 62; Armstrong, *11th Virginia Cavalry,* 60–61; Divine, *35th Battalion Virginia Cavalry,* 42.
37. Long, *Memoirs of Lee,* 314.
38. *OR,* I, 29, pt. 1: 971; 33: 1119; Rawleigh W. Downman to his wife, Dec. 8, 1863, Downman MSS; Musick, *6th Virginia Cavalry,* 52; Halsey Wigfall to his father, Dec. 20, 1863, Wigfall MSS; Neese, *Confederate Horse Artillery,* 244; Shoemaker, *Shoemaker's Battery,* 65; Moore, *Stuart Horse Artillery,* 84.
39. Moore, *Stuart Horse Artillery,* 85.
40. Jubal A. Early, *War Memoirs: Autobiographical Sketch and Narrative of the War Between the States,* ed. Frank E. Vandiver (Bloomington, Ind., 1960), 326–27.
41. Ibid., 328; *OR,* I, 29, pt. 1: 971; T. W. Grussell diary, Dec. 11, 1863; Milton B. Steele diary, Dec. 14, 1863; Rawleigh W. Downman to his wife, Dec. 16, 1863, Downman MSS; Lafayette J. Carneal to his father, Jan. 9, 1864, Carneal MSS; Halsey Wigfall to his mother, Dec. 15, 1863, Wigfall MSS.; Thomas L. Rosser to Elizabeth Winston Rosser, Dec. 27, 1863, Rosser MSS, UV.
42. Hewett et al., *Supplement to the Official Records,* I, 5: 640–43; Thomas L. Rosser to Elizabeth Winston Rosser, Dec. 24, 1863, Rosser MSS, UV; Rosser, *Riding with Rosser,* 14; Edward H. McDonald, "The Laurel Brigade Raid across Northern Virginia," *CWTI* 5 (Nov. 1966): 44.
43. *OR,* I, 29, pt. 1: 924–25; St. George T. Brooke autobiography, 35; Cary Breckinridge, "The Second Virginia Cavalry Regt. from Five Forks to Appomattox," 2, VHS; Rawleigh W. Downman to his wife, Jan. 16, 1864, Downman MSS; Thornton R. Baxter to "My Dear Aunt Lou," Jan. 4, 1864, Baxter MSS; Haden, *Reminiscences,* 29.
44. Thomas L. Rosser to Elizabeth Winston Rosser, Dec. 24, 27, 1864, Jan. 8, 1865, Rosser MSS, UV; Rosser, *Riding with Rosser,* 15–18; Heath J. Christian to his mother, Dec. 29, 1864, Christian MSS; McDonald, *Laurel*

Brigade, 215–21; McDonald, "Laurel Brigade Raid," 44–45; T. W. Grussell diaries, Dec. 14, 1863–Jan. 5, 1864; John Wise to his sister, Jan. 12, 1865, Wise MSS, UV; Richard H. Dulany et al., *The Dulanys of Welbourne: A Family in Mosby's Confederacy,* ed. Margaret Ann Vogtsberger (Berryville, Va., 1995), 127.

45. J. E. B. Stuart to Flora Cooke Stuart, Jan. 27, 1864, Stuart MSS, VHS; Driver, *5th Virginia Cavalry,* 71.
46. Krick, *9th Virginia Cavalry,* 32; Fortier, *15th Virginia Cavalry,* 56, 59.
47. Cauthen, *Letters of Three Wade Hamptons,* 102; John L. Black, *Crumbling Defenses; or, Memoirs and Reminiscences of John Logan Black, Colonel, C.S.A.,* ed. Eleanor D. McSwain (Macon, Ga., 1960), 70.
48. Black, *Crumbling Defenses,* 70.
49. *OR,* I, 33: 1153–55, 1162–64; Wade Hampton memoirs, 9–12, USC; Cauthen, *Letters of Three Wade Hamptons,* 99–100.
50. Wade Hampton memoirs, 13–15.
51. Ibid., 38–42.
52. Cauthen, *Letters of Three Wade Hamptons,* 100.

CHAPTER 19
1. *OR,* I, 33: 143–50; J. E. B. Stuart to Flora Cooke Stuart, Feb. 8, 1864, Stuart MSS, VHS.
2. Wade Hampton memoirs, 21–25.
3. Lee, *Wartime Papers,* 673–74.
4. Edward G. Longacre, *Mounted Raids of the Civil War* (South Brunswick, N.J., 1975), 225–37. The fullest account of Kilpatrick's and Dahlgren's expedition remains Virgil Carrington Jones, *Eight Hours before Richmond* (New York, 1957).
5. *OR,* I, 33: 167–68; 51, pt. 2: 823; Moore, *Stuart Horse Artillery,* 88–91; Shoemaker, *Shoemaker's Battery,* 65–68; Hewett et al., *Supplement to the Official Records,* I, 6: 284–85; Beverly K. Whittle to "Dear all," Mar. 3, 1864, Whittle MSS, UV.
6. Longacre, *Mounted Raids,* 237–44.
7. *OR,* I, 33: 199–204; Wade Hampton memoirs, 31–32; McClellan, *Life and Campaigns of Stuart,* 403–4; Samuel S. Biddle to his father, Mar. 4, 1864, Biddle MSS; Noah P. Ford, "Wade Hampton's Strategy: An Attack on Richmond Foiled . . . .," *SHSP* 24 (1896): 278–84.
8. *OR,* I, 33: 205–10, 219–24; Lee, *Wartime Papers,* 678; J. William Jones, "Kilpatrick–Dahlgren Raid Against Richmond," *SHSP* 13 (1885): 515–60; Krick, *9th Virginia Cavalry,* 33; Wade Hampton memoirs, 36–37.
9. *OR,* I, 33: 218, 222. For the most recent scholarship on the Dahlgren Papers, including some dubious speculation on their origin, see Duane Schultz, *The Dahlgren Affair: Terror and Conspiracy in the Civil War* (New York, 1998).
10. *OR,* I, 33: 1152–53, 1170, 1180.

11. Robert Randolph to "Dear Sister Donie," Mar. 30, 1864, Randolph MSS, VHS.
12. Robert P. Tutwiler to "Dearest Aunt," Apr. 24, 1864, UNC; Wade Hampton memoirs, 40.
13. Ruben E. Hammon to anon., Apr. 13, 1864, Hammon MSS, DU; Samuel S. Biddle to his father, Apr. 11, 1864, Biddle MSS.
14. J. E. B. Stuart to Flora Cooke Stuart, Apr. 16, 1864, Stuart MSS, Gilder Lehrman Coll.
15. Register of appointment, CSR of W. H. F. Lee, M–331, R–155, NA; J. E. B. Stuart to "Mrs. Grinnan," Apr. 30, 1864, Stuart MSS, UV; Wade Hampton memoirs, 6, 11, 44–45.
16. Armstrong, 7th Virginia Cavalry, 66; Thomas L. Rosser to Elizabeth Winston Rosser, Mar. 1, 1864, Rosser MSS, UV; Holmes Conrad to his father, Mar. 26, 1864, Conrad MSS; OR, I, 51, pt. 2: 773–75.
17. Black, Crumbling Defenses, 71; Wade Hampton memoirs, 19–20, 42; OR, I, 33: 1258–59.
18. OR, I, 36, pt. 1: 1027.
19. Ibid., 33: 1236, 1264; Wise, Long Arm of Lee, 2: 725; Moore, Stuart Horse Artillery, 93; Trout, "Galloping Thunder," 81; J. E. B. Stuart to Robert E. Lee, April 21, 1864, CSR of James Dearing, M–331, R–74, NA.
20. Trout, "Galloping Thunder," 81–82; Wise, Long Arm of Lee, 2: 725n, 740.
21. Gordon C. Rhea, The Battle of the Wilderness, May 5–6, 1864 (Baton Rouge, La., 1994), 40–49.
22. Ibid., 49–64.
23. OR, I, 51, pt. 2: 887–88; Alexander R. Boteler diary, May 3–4, 1864, LC.
24. OR, I, 51, pt. 2: 888; Wade Hampton memoirs, 43–44; Fitzhugh Lee, Report of Lee's Division, Cavalry Corps, Army of Northern Virginia, May 1864–April 1865, [1]–[4], MC.
25. Alexander Boteler diary, May 4, 1864.
26. Rhea, Battle of the Wilderness, 79–90.
27. Ibid., 91–282.
28. Wade Hampton memoirs, 46; Fitzhugh Lee, Report of Lee's Division, [3]–[4].
29. Thomas L. Rosser to J. E. B. Stuart, May 5, 1864, CSR of Henry B. McClellan, M–331, R–169, NA; Jasper Hawse diary, May 5, 1864; Baylor, Bull Run to Bull Run, 202–3; Beane, "Thomas Lafayette Rosser," 37; James Harrison Wilson, Under the Old Flag: Recollections of Military Operations in the War for the Union, the Spanish War, the Boxer Rebellion, etc. (New York, 1912), 1: 380–81; Armstrong, 11th Virginia Cavalry, 67; Frye, 12th Virginia Cavalry, 64; Rosser, Riding with Rosser, 19.
30. Divine, 35th Battalion Virginia Cavalry, 47; Edward A. Green memoirs, 79.
31. Rosser, Riding with Rosser, 20; Wilson, Under the Old Flag, 1: 382–83; Armstrong, 11th Virginia Cavalry, 69; Frye, 12th Virginia Cavalry, 64.

32. *Richmond Daily Dispatch,* May 7, 1864; *Richmond Sentinel,* May 7, 1864; Robert T. Hubard memoirs, 88.

33. Rosser, *Riding with Rosser,* 21; Armstrong, *11th Virginia Cavalry,* 69; Moore, *Chew's, Shoemaker's, Newtown Artillery,* 42–43.

34. Rosser, *Riding with Rosser,* 22; Divine, *35th Battalion Virginia Cavalry,* 48–49.

35. Rosser, *Riding with Rosser,* 22; Jasper Hawse diary, May 6, 1864; Edward H. McDonald, "We Drove Them from the Field," *CWTI* 6 (Nov. 1967): 30–31; Armstrong, *11th Virginia Cavalry,* 70.

36. Rhea, *Battle of the Wilderness,* 430–39.

37. *OR,* I, 36, pt. 1: 774–76, 778–89; Fitzhugh Lee, Report of Lee's Division, [4]–[5].

38. Fitzhugh Lee, Report of Lee's Division, [5]–[6]; McClellan, *Life and Campaigns of Stuart,* 408; Driver and Howard, *2nd Virginia Cavalry,* 112–13; Driver, *5th Virginia Cavalry,* 73; Fortier, *15th Virginia Cavalry,* 66; Alexander, *Fighting for the Confederacy,* 366.

39. Wade Hampton memoirs, 46; *OR,* I, 51, pt. 1: 248–49; pt. 2: 897–98.

40. *OR,* I, 36, pt. 1: 540–41; Stiles, *4th Virginia Cavalry,* 45–46; Driver, *5th Virginia Cavalry,* 73–74; Lewis T. Nunnelee memoirs, 128; Wise, *Long Arm of Lee,* 2: 794–96.

41. McClellan, *Life and Campaigns of Stuart,* 408–9; John Cheves Haskell, *The Haskell Memoirs,* ed. Gilbert E. Govan and James W. Livingood (New York, 1960), 67.

42. Fitzhugh Lee, Report of Lee's Division, [6]–[10].

43. Samuel B. Rucker, Jr., memoirs, 2, Jones Memorial Lib., Lynchburg, Va.; Robert T. Hubard memoirs, 89.

CHAPTER 20

1. Philip H. Sheridan, *Personal Memoirs of P. H. Sheridan* (New York, 1888), 1: 366–67; *OR,* I, 36, pt. 1: 788–89; pt. 2: 553.

2. Gordon C. Rhea, *The Battles for Spotsylvania Court House and the Road to Yellow Tavern, May 7–12, 1864* (Baton Rouge, La., 1997), 114; McDonald, "We Drove Them from the Field," 28.

3. Rhea, *Battles for Spotsylvania,* 114–15.

4. *OR,* I, 36, pt. 1: 853, 857, 861; Nanzig, *3rd Virginia Cavalry,* 49; William B. Conway memoirs, 10, VHS; Stiles, *4th Virginia Cavalry,* 47.

5. McClellan, *Life and Campaigns of Stuart,* 410.

6. John H. Gafford memoirs, 1, VHS.

7. *OR,* I, 36, pt. 1: 790; 51, pt. 2: 911–14.

8. Andrew R. Venable to Fitzhugh Lee, June 7, 1888, Douglas Southall Freeman MSS.

9. Driver, *5th Virginia Cavalry,* 75; Longacre, *Mounted Raids of the Civil War,* 270.

10. Longacre, *Mounted Raids of the Civil War,* 271; Davis, *Last Cavalier,* 400–401.

11. McClellan, *Life and Campaigns of Stuart,* 412; Freeman, *Lee's Lieutenants,* 3: 421; Driver, *5th Virginia Cavalry,* 76–77. A variant account of the Stuart–Pate exchange is found in Trout, *Riding with Stuart,* 67.

12. *OR,* I, 36, pt. 1: 818.

13. Thaddeus Fitzhugh memoirs, 39–40.

14. Henry B. McClellan to Flora Cooke Stuart, Oct. 10, 1864, McClellan MSS, VHS; Hudgins, *Old Dominion Dragoon,* 89–90; Andrew R. Venable to Fitzhugh Lee, June 7, 1888, Douglas Southall Freeman MSS; Wise, *Long Arm of Lee,* 2: 796–97.

15. Thomas, *Bold Dragoon,* 293–96.

16. Charles R. Chewning diary, May 13, 1864; Neese, *Confederate Horse Artillery,* 282; Thaddeus Fitzhugh memoirs, 39.

17. Wade Hampton memoirs, 48; Lambert, *Grumble,* 122.

18. Blackford, *War Years with Jeb Stuart,* 253.

19. McCabe, *Andrew Reid Venable, Jr.,* 10.

20. *OR,* I, 36, pt. 2: 36, 41, 94, 113–14, 123, 127, 129, 131, 134, 139.

21. Fitzhugh Lee, Report of Lee's Division, [18]–[19].

22. Hartley, *Stuart's Tarheels,* 361–68; Robert T. Hubard memoirs, 94–95; "Brook Church Fight and Something about the Fifth North Carolina Cavalry . . . ," *SHSP* 29 (1901): 139–41.

23. *OR,* I, 51, pt. 1: 250; Fitzhugh Lee, Report of Lee's Division, [18]–[19].

24. *OR,* I, 36, pt. 2: 199–204.

25. Hampton memoirs, 51–52; Wells, *Hampton and His Cavalry,* 260–65.

26. *OR,* I, 36, pt. 1: 792; Fitzhugh Lee, Report of Lee's Division, [20]–[21].

27. Fitzhugh Lee, Report of Lee's Division, [21]–[22]; Robert T. Hubard memoirs, 95.

28. *OR,* I, 36, pt. 2: 269–72; St. George T. Brooke autobiography, 44–45; Beverly K. Whittle to "My Dear Sallie," May 30, 1864, Whittle MSS; "Brook Church Fight," 141.

29. Wade Hampton memoirs, 54–55; McDonald, *Laurel Brigade,* 243–44.

30. Beane, "Thomas Lafayette Rosser," 39–40; Rosser, *Riding with Rosser,* 25–26; Bushong and Bushong, *Fightin' Tom Rosser,* 93; Myers, *The Comanches,* 281–82.

31. Robert A. Williams, "Haw's Shop: A 'Storm of Shot and Shell'," *CWTI* 9 (Jan. 1971): 12–13.

32. *OR,* I, 36, pt. 2: 852–54; 1021–22; Hewett et al., *Supplement to the Official Records,* I, 6: 448–49; William Stokes, *Saddle Soldiers: The Civil War Correspondence of General William Stokes of the 4th South Carolina Cavalry,* ed. Lloyd Halliburton (Orangeburg, S.C., 1993), 135–36.

33. Fitzhugh Lee, Report of Lee's Division, [21], [23].

34. Williams, "Haw's Shop," 14.

35. Ibid., 14–15; Wade Hampton memoirs, 55; Fitzhugh Lee, Report of Lee's Division, [25]–[26]; John R. Haw, "The Battle of Haw's Shop, Va.," *CV* 33 (1925): 373–76.

36. Myers, *The Comanches,* 291.

37. Williams, "Haw's Shop," 15–19; Wade Hampton memoirs, 56–57; St. George T. Brooke autobiography, 41–42; Robert T. Hubard memoirs, 96–97.

38. Williams, "Haw's Shop," 18–19; Wade Hampton memoirs, 56.

39. Fitzhugh Lee, Report of Lee's Division, [26]; Samuel J. Martin, *Southern Hero: Matthew Calbraith Butler, Confederate General, Hampton Red Shirt, and U.S. Senator* (Mechanicsburg, Pa., 2001), 88.

40. *OR,* I, 51, pt. 2: 967–68; Fitzhugh Lee, Report of Lee's Division, [26]–[27]; Lewis T. Nunnelee memoirs, 135.

41. Fitzhugh Lee, Report of Lee's Division, [27].

42. *OR,* I, 36, pt. 2: 867; Wade Hampton memoirs, 58–61; Stokes, *Saddle Soldiers,* 141–42; Edward A. Green memoirs, 85–86.

43. Wade Hampton memoirs, 60–61; Robert T. Hubard memoirs, 97.

44. Wade Hampton memoirs, 62–63.

CHAPTER 21

1. Eric J. Wittenberg, *Glory Enough for All: Sheridan's Second Raid and the Battle of Trevilian Station* (Washington, D.C., 2001), 42–62.

2. *OR,* I, 36, pt. 1: 1095; Wade Hampton memoirs, 75–81.

3. *OR,* I, 36, pt. 1: 784, 807, 849, 1095; Sheridan, *Personal Memoirs,* 1: 420; Theophilus F. Rodenbough, "Sheridan's Trevilian Raid," *B&L* 4: 233; Lewis T. Nunnelee memoirs, 140; Edward A. Green memoirs, 87.

4. Wade Hampton to Edward L. Wells, Jan. 18, 1900, Wells MSS, Charleston Lib. Soc., Charleston, S.C.; Wells, *Hampton and His Cavalry,* 198–99; Rosser, *Riding with Rosser,* 38.

5. *OR,* I, 36, pt. 1: 784–85, 800–801, 823–24, 850; Sheridan, *Personal Memoirs,* 1: 420–21.

6. *OR,* I, 36, pt. 1: 808, 824, 841, 855, 858; Sheridan, *Personal Memoirs,* 1: 421–22; Fitzhugh Lee, Report of Lee's Division, [30]; Jay Monaghan, "Custer's 'Last Stand'—Trevilian Station, 1864," *Civil War History* 8 (1962): 249–55; Charles McVicar memoirs, 40; Robert T. Hubard memoirs, 99; J. W. Tayloe to Thomas T. Munford, Apr. 23, 1898, Tayloe MSS, UV.

7. Rosser, *Riding with Rosser,* 37–38; Beverly K. Whittle to his father, June 13, 1864, Whittle MSS.

8. Fitzhugh Lee, Report of Lee's Division, [29].

9. Sheridan, *Personal Memoirs,* 1: 422–23; Rodenbough, "Sheridan's Trevilian Raid," 234–35, 235n.

10. *OR,* I, 36, pt. 1: 784–85, 808–9, 824, 845–46, 850–51, 1096; 51, pt. 2: 1009; Sheridan, *Personal Memoirs,* 1: 425; Fitzhugh Lee, Report of Lee's Division, [31]; Rodenbough, "Sheridan's Trevilian Raid," 234; William S.

Ball memoirs, 37–38, VHS; Brooks, *Butler and His Cavalry,* 247–54; Charles McVicar memoirs, 44.

11. Wittenberg, *Glory Enough for All,* 337–45.

12. Fitzhugh Lee, Report of Lee's Division, [32]; Hewett et al., *Supplement to the Official Records,* I, 7: 337.

13. *OR,* I, 40, pt. 1: 747; pt. 2: 669–70; 51, pt. 2: 1081; Moore, *Stuart Horse Artillery,* 103; Milton B. Steele diary, June 20, 1864; Charles McVicar memoirs, 48–50; Hewett et al., *Supplement to the Official Records,* I, 7: 264, 338; Wise, *Long Arm of Lee,* 2: 843–44.

14. Robert T. Hubard memoirs, 102.

15. Noah Andre Trudeau, *The Last Citadel* (Boston, 1991), 29–55.

16. *OR,* I, 40, pt. 1: 209–10; pt. 2: 663; John W. Gordon diary, June 8–24, 1864, MC; W. A. Curtis memoirs, 32, in possession of Mr. Bryce Suderow, Washington, D.C.

17. *OR,* I, 40, pt. 1: 209, 645; pt. 2: 687.

18. Ibid., 687–88; Fitzhugh Lee, Report of Lee's Division, [33]–[34]; Edward A. Green memoirs, 88; Milton B. Steele diary, June 24, 1864.

19. Lee, *Lee's Dipatches,* 258.

20. Wade Hampton memoirs, 81.

21. *OR,* I, 40, p. 1: 808; Wilson, *Under the Old Flag,* 1: 465–66; John Z. H. Scott memoirs, 33; Robert T. Hubard memoirs, 103.

22. *OR,* I, 40, pt. 1: 210, 808; Fitzhugh Lee, Report of Lee's Division, [34]–[35]; Wilson, *Under the Old Flag,* 1: 466–69; W. A. Curtis memoirs, 43; Robert T. Hubard memoirs, 104–5.

23. Thomas Horne to "My dear Mollie," July 17, 24, 1864, Horne MSS, Ablah Lib., Wichita State Univ., Wichita, Kan.; Charles McVicar memoirs, 52–53.

24. Wade Hampton memoirs, 92; Krick, *9th Virginia Cavalry,* 39; L. R. Dalton to his mother, July 28, 1864, Dalton MSS, USAMHI.

25. Myers, *The Comanches,* 318.

26. *OR,* I, 37, pt. 1: 94–103, 160; Sheridan, *Personal Memoirs,* 1: 456–57.

27. Sheridan, *Personal Memoirs,* 1: 461–63; *OR,* I, 40, pt. 3: 640–41, 669; 43, pt. 1: 681, 719.

28. *OR,* I, 43, pt. 1: 799, 822, 990.

29. Ibid., 993, 1003–04.

30. Lee, *Lee's Dispatches,* 268–69; *OR,* I, 42, pt. 2: 1173.

31. *OR,* I, 40, pt. 2: 1170–72; 43, pt. 1: 995–96.

32. Ibid., 1024; Driver, *1st Virginia Cavalry,* 96; Wesley Merritt, "Sheridan in the Shenandoah Valley," *B&L* 4: 503.

33. Merritt, "Sheridan in the Shenandoah Valley," 500; Sheridan, *Personal Memoirs,* 1: 475.

34. *OR,* I, 43, pt. 1: 1025; Fitzhugh Lee, Report of Lee's Division, [41]; Robert T. Hubard memoirs, 109; Churchill Crittenden to his mother, Aug. 27, 1864, Crittenden MSS, Univ. of Washington Lib., Seattle.

35. Merritt, "Sheridan in the Shenandoah Vallcy," 505.

36. *OR,* I, 43, pt. 1: 46–47, 427, 443, 454, 481–82, 498, 518; Sheridan, *Personal Memoirs,* 2: 11–22.
37. Fitzhugh Lee, Report of Lee's Division, [42]–[51]; Hewett et al., *Supplement to the Official Records,* I, 7: 512–18; Jubal A. Early, "Winchester, Fisher's Hill, and Cedar Creek," *B&L* 4: 522–23.
38. Robert T. Hubard memoirs, 107.
39. Fitzhugh Lee, Report of Lee's Division, [50]; Thomas T. Munford, "Reminiscences of Cavalry Operations, Paper Number 2: Battle of Winchester, 19th September '64," *SHSP* 12 (1884): 447–50.
40. Robert T. Hubard memoirs, 107–8; Robert K. Krick, "'The Cause of All My Disasters': Jubal A. Early and the Undisciplined Valley Cavalry," in Gary A. Gallagher, ed., *Struggle for the Shenandoah: Essays on the 1864 Valley Campaign* (Kent, Ohio, 1991): 77–106.
41. *OR,* I, 43, pt. 1: 28–29, 554–55, 1028–29; Thaddeus Fitzhugh memoirs, 42–53; T. W. Grussell diary, Sept. 22–28, 1864; Milton B. Steele diary, Sept. 22–28, 1864; Munford, "Battle of Winchester," 451–56.
42. *OR,* I, 43, pt. 1: 650–61; pt. 2: 874; Rosser, *Riding with Rosser,* 43–44.
43. *OR,* I, 40, pt. 3: 1235–36.
44. Rosser, *Riding with Rosser,* 40–43; Richard W. Lykes, "The Great Civil War Beef Raid," *CWTI* 5 (Feb. 1967): 5–12, 47–49.
45. *OR,* I, 43, pt. 1: 612, 1028–29.
46. Ibid., 559, 612–13, 1030; pt. 2: 237; Robert T. Hubard memoirs, 114; Corson, *My Dear Jennie,* 130; Jubal A. Early to Thomas L. Rosser, Oct. 7, 1864, Rosser MSS, LC; Rosser, *Riding with Rosser,* 47–49; Lewis T. Nunnelee memoirs, 165.
47. *OR,* I, 43, pt. 1: 559.

CHAPTER 22
1. Early, "Winchester, Fisher's Hill, and Cedar Creek," 526.
2. *OR,* I, 43, pt. 1: 158–60, 561–62; pt. 2: 410; Benjamin W. Crowninshield, *The Battle of Cedar Creek, October 19, 1864* (Cambridge, Mass., 1879), 14–15; William J. Black diary, Oct. 19, 1864, Preston Lib., V.M.I.
3. Robert T. Hubard memoirs, 114.
4. Rosser, *Riding with Rosser,* 50–52; *OR,* I, 43, pt. 1: 433, 522–23; Crowninshield, *Cedar Creek,* 21; Rawleigh W. Downman to his wife, Oct. 20, 1864, Downman MSS.; Theodore C. Mahr, *Early's Valley Campaign: The Battle of Cedar Creek . . . October 1–30, 1864* (Lynchburg, Va., 1992), 270–76.
5. Mahr, *Early's Valley Campaign,* 337.
6. *OR,* I, 43, pt. 1: 38–39, 56, 667, 669–70; pt 2: 680, 684, 692; Musick, *6th Virginia Cavalry,* 70–71; Armstrong, *7th Virginia Cavalry,* 81–83; Sheridan, *Personal Memoirs,* 2: 102.
7. *OR,* I, 46, pt. 1: 126–27, 474–76; pt. 2: 792.

8. Sheridan, *Personal Memoirs,* 2: 116–19; *OR,* I, 46, pt. 1: 477–82, 486–88; pt. 2: 793.

9. *OR,* I, 46, pt. 2: 1296.

10. Nanzig, *3rd Virginia Cavalry,* 69.

11. *OR,* I, 46, pt. 1: 390; Balfour, *13th Virginia Cavalry,* 36; Beale, *Lieutenant of Cavalry,* 168.

12. Lee, *Lee's Dispatches,* 315.

13. Robert E. Lee to Wade Hampton, Aug. 1, 1865, copy in Edward L. Wells MSS, Charleston Lib. Soc.

14. *OR,* I, 42, pt. 1: 1178; 51, pt. 2: 1035; John W. Gordon diary, Aug. 14–18, 1864; W. A. Curtis memoirs, 44–45; Fitzhugh Lee, Report of Lee's Division, [95]–[96].

15. *OR,* I, 42, pt. 2: 375, 390, 393, 399, 407–8, 426, 428–30, 436, 441–42; Andrew H. Kay to his brother, Sept. 3, 1864, Kay MSS, VHS; Brooks, *Butler and His Cavalry,* 303–6.

16. Richard J. Sommers, *Richmond Redeemed: The Siege at Petersburg* (Garden City, N.Y., 1981), 196–97, 200–201, 204–5, 261, 267, 273–75, 285–87, 300, 309, 324, 351, 327–28, 339–40, 342–43, 534–51; *OR,* I, 42, pt. 1: 947–48.

17. *OR,* I, 42, pt 1: 949–50; Wellman, *Giant in Gray,* 60–61.

18. Trudeau, *Last Citadel,* 337–51; A. Wilson Greene, *Breaking the Backbone of the Rebellion: The Final Battles of the Petersburg Campaign* (Mason City, Iowa, 2000), 156–60.

19. Sheridan, *Personal Memoirs,* 2: 135–39; *OR,* I, 46, pt. 1: 1101; pt. 3: 234–35.

20. Ibid., pt. 1: 1299; Thomas T. Munford, "The Last Days of Fitz Lee's Division of Cavalry, Army of Northern Virginia," 4–10, VHS; Hiram W. Harding diary, Mar. 30, 1865, MC.

21. *OR,* I, 46, pt. 1: 1299; Hewett et al., *Supplement to the Official Records,* I, 7: 779; Rosser, *Riding with Rosser,* 63.

22. *OR,* I, 46, pt. 1: 1299; Hewett et al., *Supplement to the Official Records,* I, 7: 780–81; Chris M. Calkins, *The Appomattox Campaign, March 29–April 9, 1865* (Conshohocken, Pa., 1997), 22–24; Munford, "Last Days of Fitz Lee's Division," 10–11; Hiram W. Harding diary, Mar. 31, 1865; Francis W. Dawson, *Reminiscences of Confederate Service, 1861–1865,* ed. Bell Irvin Wiley (Baton Rouge, La., 1980), 142–43.

23. *OR,* I, 46, pt. 3: 259–60, 418; Sheridan, *Personal Memoirs,* 2: 160–61; Joshua L. Chamberlain, *The Passing of the Armies: An Account of the Final Campaign of the Army of the Potomac . . .* (New York, 1915), 103–7, 120–26.

24. *OR,* I, 46, pt. 1: 1299; Hewett et al., *Supplement to the Official Records,* I, 7: 781; Munford, "Last Days of Fitz Lee's Division," 30–33; Calkins, *Appomattox Campaign,* 28; Lee, *General Lee,* 376.

25. Rosser, *Riding with Rosser,* 64; Thomas T. Munford to Charles R. Irving, July 20, 1905, Munford MSS, LV.

26. Rosser, *Riding with Rosser,* 65; Trout, *In the Saddle with Stuart,* 105; Munford, "Last Days of Fitz Lee's Division," 34, 45; Hewett et al., *Supplement to the Official Records,* I, 7: 782–83, 829–31, 833–34; Thomas B. Keys, *Tarheel Cossack: W. P. Roberts, Youngest Confederate General* (Orlando, Fla., 1983), 64–65; James E. Tucker memoirs, 1–3, VHS.

27. Munford, "Last Days of Fitz Lee's Division," 39–40; Hiram W. Harding diary, Apr. 1, 1865; Keys, *Tarheel Cossack,* 64–65; James M. Scott memoirs, 14.

28. Calkins, *Appomattox Campaign,* 43–62; Edward M. Boykin, *The Falling Flag: Evacuation of Richmond, Retreat and Surrender at Appomattox, by an Officer of the Rear-Guard* (New York, 1874), 7–26; Cornelius H. Carlton diary, Apr. 3, 1865, VHS.

29. *OR,* I, 46, pt. 1: 1299; Trout, "Galloping Thunder," 82; Munford, "Last Days of Fitz Lee's Division," 58–59.

30. *OR,* I, 46, pt. 1: 1299–1300; Calkins, *Appomattox Campaign,* 54–55; Coltrane, *Memoirs,* 41; Garland H. Clarke diary, Apr. 2, 1865, VHS.

31. *OR,* I, 46, pt. 1: 1300–01; Rufus C. Barringer diary, Apr. 3, 1865, UNC; Clark, *Regiments and Battalions from North Carolina,* 1: 442; Calkins, *Appomattox Campaign,* 69–72, 82–83; Keys, *Tarheel Cossack,* 65–66; Coltrane, *Memoirs,* 41–42; Hiram W. Harding diary, Apr. 3, 1865; John B. Moseley diary, Apr. 3, 1865, VHS.

32. *OR,* I, 46, pt. 1: 1301; John B. Moseley diary, Apr. 4, 1865; Thomas G. Jones, *Last Days of the Army of Northern Virginia: An Address Delivered . . . before the Virginia Division of the Association of the Army of Northern Virginia . . .* (Richmond, Va., 1893), 23.

33. Rosser, *Riding with Rosser,* 66–68; Calkins, *Appomattox Campaign,* 85–88; Munford, "Last Days of Fitz Lee's Division," 75–77; John B. Moseley diary, Apr. 5, 1865; Milton B. Steele diary, Apr. 5, 1865; Wilson, *Borderland Confederate,* 96–97; William L. Wilson Memoir of Appomattox Campaign, 38–48, Gilder Lehrman Coll.

34. Ibid., 48–59; Wilson, *Borderland Confederate,* 98–99; Rosser, *Riding with Rosser,* 68–70; Rawleigh W. Downman to his wife, Apr. 6, 1865, Downman MSS; Munford, "Last Days of Fitz Lee's Division," 75–77; McDonald, *Laurel Brigade,* 377; Milton B. Steele diary, Apr. 6, 1865; James E. Tucker memoirs, 6; Calkins, *Appomattox Campaign,* 101–5; Noah Andre Trudeau, *Out of the Storm: The End of the Civil War, April–June 1865* (Boston, 1994), 102–6; Horace Porter, "Five Forks and the Pursuit of Lee," *B&L* 4: 720.

35. Cooke, *Wearing of the Gray,* 557–58; Calkins, *Appomattox Campaign,* 105–15; Trudeau, *Out of the Storm,* 106–16.

36. Munford, "Last Days of Fitz Lee's Division," 79; McDonald, *Laurel Brigade,* 379; Milton B. Steele diary, Apr. 7, 1865; Driver and Howard, *2nd Virginia Cavalry,* 162.

37. Calkins, *Appomattox Campaign,* 154–55; Henry C. Lee diary, Apr. 8, 1865, MC.

38. *OR,* I, 46, pt. 1: 1266; Hewett et al., *Supplement to the Official Records,* I, 7: 793; Munford, "Last Days of Fitz Lee's Division," 83–84; McDonald, *Laurel Brigade,* 380; Chris M. Calkins, *The Battles of Appomattox Station and Appomattox Court House, April 8–9, 1865* (Lynchburg, Va., 1987), 55–57; Trudeau, *Out of the Storm,* 131–32.

39. McDonald, *Laurel Brigade,* 381; Calkins, *Appomattox Campaign,* 159–62; Burleigh Cushing Rodick, *Appomattox, the Last Campaign* (New York, 1965), 93, 106–7.

40. Calkins, *Appomattox Campaign,* 162–63; Calkins, *Appomattox Station and Appomattox Court House,* 57–69; Robert T. Hubard memoirs, 114; Hiram W. Harding diary, Apr. 9, 1865; William L. Wilson memoir, 72–76; Peck, *Co. C, 2nd Va. Cavalry,* 71; Edwin E. Bouldin, "The Last Charge at Appomattox: The Fourteenth Virginia Cavalry," *SHSP* 28 (1900): 250–53.

41. Rosser, *Riding with Rosser,* 72; Driver, *1st Virginia Cavalry,* 117; Munford, "Last Days of Fitz Lee's Division," 93–94, 96; Calkins, *Appomattox Station and Appomattox Court House,* 123–24; Philip Van Doren Stern, *An End to Valor: The Last Days of the Civil War* (Boston, 1958), 247; Henry C. Lee diary, Apr. 9, 1865; Shoemaker, *Shoemaker's Battery,* 94–95; Wilson, *Borderland Confederate,* 104–6; William L. Wilson memoir, 76–78, 86–88.

42. McDonald, *Laurel Brigade,* 381; Thomas T. Munford to Ranald S. Mackenzie, Apr. 13, 17, 1865, Munford MSS, DU; John Gibbon to Thomas T. Munford, Apr. 21, 1865, ibid.; Rawleigh W. Downman to his wife, Apr. 25, 1865, Downman MSS; Armstrong, *11th Virginia Cavalry,* 98–99; Wert, "His Unhonored Service," 34.

43. Driver, *1st Virginia Cavalry,* 117; Samuel W. Melton to Thomas L. Rosser, Apr. 10, 1865, Rosser MSS, UV.

BIBLIOGRAPHY

MANUSCRIPTS

General Officers of Cavalry, Army of Northern Virginia

Barringer, Rufus. Correspondence and Diary, 1865. Wilson Library, University of North Carolina, Chapel Hill.

Beale, Richard L. T. History of 9th Virginia Cavalry. Alderman Library, University of Virginia, Charlottesville.

Butler, M. Calbraith. Correspondence. Historical Society of Pennsylvania, Philadelphia.

———. Correspondence. South Caroliniana Library, University of South Carolina, Columbia.

———. Correspondence. William R. Perkins Library, Duke University, Durham, N.C.

Dearing, James. Correspondence. Historical Society of Pennsylvania.

Gary, Martin W. Correspondence. South Caroliniana Library, University of South Carolina.

———. Correspondence. Virginia Historical Society, Richmond.

Gordon, James B. Correspondence. North Carolina State Department of Archives and History, Raleigh.

Hampton, Wade. Correspondence. Wilson Library, University of North Carolina.

———. Correspondence and Memoirs. South Caroliniana Library, University of South Carolina.

———. Letter of September 7, 1864. Gilder Lehrman Collection, New York.

Imboden, John D. Correspondence. Alderman Library, University of Virginia.

———. Correspondence. Wise Library, West Virginia University, Morgantown.

———. Letter of April 6, 1865. Gilder Lehrman Collection.

Johnson, Bradley T. Correspondence. Earl Gregg Swem Library, College of William and Mary, Williamsburg, Va.

———. Correspondence. William R. Perkins Library, Duke University.

———. Letter of May 9, 1865. Gilder Lehrman Collection.

Jones, William E. Correspondence. Historical Society of Pennsylvania.
———. Correspondence. Library of Virginia, Richmond.
Lee, Fitzhugh. Correspondence. Earl Gregg Swem Library, College of William and Mary.
———. Correspondence. U.S. Army Military History Institute, Carlisle Barracks, Pa.
———. Correspondence. Virginia Historical Society.
———. Report of Cavalry Operations, Army of Northern Virginia, March 28–April 9, 1865. Gilder Lehrman Collection.
———. Report of Lee's Division, Cavalry Corps, Army of Northern Virginia, May 1864. Eleanor S. Brockenbrough Library, Museum of the Confederacy, Richmond.
Lee, W. H. F. Correspondence. Alderman Library, University of Virginia.
———. Correspondence. Virginia Historical Society.
Logan, Thomas Muldrup. Papers. South Caroliniana Library, University of South Carolina.
Lomax, Lunsford L. Correspondence. Maryland Historical Society, Baltimore.
———. Correspondence. Virginia Historical Society.
———. Letter of April 16, 1865. Gilder Lehrman Collection.
Munford, Thomas T. Correspondence. Eleanor S. Brockenbrough Library, Museum of the Confederacy.
———. Correspondence. Library of Congress, Washington, D. C.
———. Correspondence. Library of Virginia.
———. Correspondence. Preston Library, Virginia Military Institute, Lexington.
———. Correspondence. William R. Perkins Library, Duke University.
———. "The Last Days of Fitz Lee's Division of Cavalry, Army of Northern Virginia, 1865." Virginia Historical Society.
Payne, William H. F. Correspondence. Virginia Historical Society.
———. Correspondence and Memoirs. Eleanor S. Brockenbrough Library, Museum of the Confederacy.
———. Papers. Library of Virginia.
Rosser, Thomas L. Correspondence. Alderman Library, University of Virginia.
———. Correspondence. Eleanor S. Brockenbrough Library, Museum of the Confederacy.
———. Correspondence. Library of Congress.
———. Correspondence. Virginia Historical Society.
Stuart, James Ewell Brown. Correspondence. Alderman Library, University of Virginia.
———. Correspondence. Gilder Lehrman Collection.
———. Correspondence. Henry E. Huntington Library, San Marino, California.
———. Correspondence. Library of Virginia.
———. Correspondence. Petersburg National Battlefield Park, Petersburg, Va.
———. Correspondence. Robert W. Woodruff Library, Emory University, Atlanta.

———. Correspondence. Virginia Historical Society.

———. Correspondence. William R. Perkins Library, Duke University.

———. Correspondence. Wilson Library, University of North Carolina.

Wickham, Williams C. Correspondence. Eleanor S. Brockenbrough Library, Museum of the Confederacy.

———. Correspondence. Library of Virginia.

———. Letter of December 6, 1862. Virginia Historical Society.

———. Letter of October 4, 1861. Gilder Lehrman Collection.

Young, Pierce M. B. Correspondence. Georgia Department of Archives and History, Atlanta.

Regimental and Staff Personnel, Cavalry and Horse Artillery Units, Army of Northern Virginia

Adams, Alfred (1st North Carolina). Correspondence. William R. Perkins Library, Duke University.

Adams, George F. (1st North Carolina). Correspondence. William R. Perkins Library, Duke University.

Aisquith, Hobart (1st Maryland Battalion). Correspondence and Memoirs. Virginia Historical Society.

Alexander, Charles G. (15th Virginia). Diaries, 1863–65. Alderman Library, University of Virginia.

Alexander, James H. (1st North Carolina). Correspondence. William R. Perkins Library, Duke University.

Alexander, Mark T. (3rd North Carolina). Correspondence. Earl Gregg Swem Library, College of William and Mary.

Allen, Edward (4th North Carolina). Letter of January 12, 1864. Eleanor S. Brockenbrough Library, Museum of the Confederacy.

Allen, John C. (7th Virginia). Diaries, 1864–65. Virginia Historical Society.

Allen, Richard P. (4th North Carolina). Correspondence. Eleanor S. Brockenbrough Library, Museum of the Confederacy.

Almond, C. H. (2nd Virginia). Correspondence. Alderman Library, University of Virginia.

Amiss, Thomas B. (6th Virginia). Correspondence. Eleanor S. Brockenbrough Library, Museum of the Confederacy.

Anderson, Edward C. (7th Georgia). Correspondence. Georgia Historical Society, Savannah.

Atkinson, Archibald, Jr. (10th Virginia). Memoirs. Carol M. Newman Library, Virginia Polytechnic Institute and State University, Blacksburg.

Baker, Samuel (35th Virginia Battalion). Letter of October 12, 1863. U.S. Army Military History Institute.

Ball, Mottrom D. (11th Virginia). Letter of May 25, 1863. Virginia Historical Society.

Ball, William S. (11th Virginia). Memoirs. Virginia Historical Society.

Barnes, Benjamin L. (13th Virginia). Letter of August 2, 1863. Virginia Historical Society.

Barnett, Joel C. (Cobb's Legion). Correspondence. Georgia Department of Archives and History.

Barry, John A. (Phillips Legion). Correspondence. Wilson Library, University of North Carolina.

Basham, William W. (2nd Virginia). Correspondence. Library of Virginia.

Baxter, Thornton R. (2nd Virginia). Correspondence. James Graham Leyburn Library, Washington and Lee University, Lexington, Va.

Baylor, Robert P. (9th Virginia). Letter of June 15, 1862. Virginia Historical Society.

Beale, John F. (13th Virginia). Letter of April 17, 1864. Virginia Historical Society.

Beale, William E. (5th Virginia). Letter of December 6, 1861. Virginia Historical Society.

Bennette, J. Kelly (8th Virginia). Correspondence and Diary, 1864. Wilson Library, University of North Carolina.

Betts, Luther R. (9th Virginia). Papers. Library of Virginia.

Biddle, J. W. (1st North Carolina). Correspondence. William R. Perkins Library, Duke University.

Biddle, Samuel S. (1st North Carolina). Correspondence. William R. Perkins Library, Duke University.

Black, William J. (Lynchburg Battery). Diaries, 1864–65. Preston Library, Virginia Military Institute.

Blackford, William W. (Staff Officer). Correspondence. Wilson Library, University of North Carolina.

———. "First and Last, or Battles in Virginia." Library of Virginia.

———. Letter of August 6, 1861. U.S. Army Military History Institute.

———. Papers. Alderman Library, University of Virginia.

Blaine, Randolph H. (Charlottesville Battery). Correspondence. James Graham Leyburn Library, Washington and Lee University.

Blakey, Angus R. (3rd Virginia). Correspondence. William R. Perkins Library, Duke University.

Blanton, J. A. (1st Virginia). Correspondence. Library of Virginia.

Bolling, John (3rd Virginia). Correspondence. U.S. Army Military History Institute.

———. Correspondence. Virginia Historical Society.

Bonney, U. P. (7th South Carolina). Correspondence. William R. Perkins Library, Duke University.

Boteler, Alexander R. (Staff Officer). Diary, 1864. Library of Congress.

Bouldin, Edwin E. (14th Virginia). Correspondence. Virginia Historical Society.

———. Memoirs. Alderman Library, University of Virginia.

Bowman, Ephraim (12th Virginia). Correspondence and Diaries, 1863–65. Alderman Library, University of Virginia.

Boykin, Alexander H. (2nd South Carolina). Papers. Wilson Library, University of North Carolina.

Boyle, William A. (Hampton Legion). Correspondence. Library of Congress.

Breckinridge, Cary (2nd Virginia). "The Second Virginia Cavalry Regt. from Five Forks to Appomattox." Virginia Historical Society.

Brice, Robert W. (2nd South Carolina). Correspondence. South Caroliniana Library, University of South Carolina.

Brooke, St. George T. (2nd Virginia). Autobiography. Virginia Historical Society.

Brooks, N. John (Cobb's Legion). Correspondence and Diary, 1864. Wilson Library, University of North Carolina.

————. Papers. Robert W. Woodruff Library, Emory University.

Brown, J. R. (7th Georgia). Correspondence. William R. Perkins Library, Duke University.

Browning, Hugh C. (2nd North Carolina). Correspondence. William R. Perkins Library, Duke University.

Brumback, Jacob H. (12th Virginia). Diary, 1863. Handley Regional Library, Winchester, Va.

Bryant, James F. (13th Virginia). Correspondence. Library of Virginia.

Burnley, William H. (2nd Virginia). Papers. Alderman Library, University of Virginia.

Byars, A. Henderson (1st Virginia). Correspondence. U.S. Army Military History Institute.

Cadwallader, James M. (1st Virginia). Diaries, 1864–65. Handley Regional Library.

Cameron, John H. (10th Virginia). Memoirs. Preston Library, Virginia Military Institute.

Camp, Thomas L. (Phillips Legion). Correspondence. Robert W. Woodruff Library, Emory University.

Capers, John S. (7th South Carolina). Correspondence. Earl Gregg Swem Library, College of William and Mary.

Caperton, George H. (2nd Virginia). Diaries, 1861–62. Virginia Historical Society.

Carlton, Cornelius H. (24th Virginia). Diaries, 1864–65. Library of Virginia.

————. Diary, 1865. Virginia Historical Society.

————. History of the 24th Virginia Cavalry. J. Y. Joyner Library, East Carolina University, Greenville, N.C.

Carneal, Lafayette J. (9th Virginia). Correspondence. Virginia Historical Society.

Carrington, James M. (Charlottesville Battery). Letter of October 15, 1864. Virginia Historical Society.

Carroll, Robert G. H. (1st Maryland Battalion). Correspondence. Maryland Historical Society.

Carter, Alfred B. (6th Virginia). Correspondence. Virginia Historical Society.

Carter, William R. (3rd Virginia). Correspondence and Diaries, 1862–64. Library of Virginia.
———. Letter of October 11, 1861. U.S. Army Military History Institute.
———. Memoirs. Handley Regional Library.
Cavin, Miles A. (2nd Virginia). Correspondence. North Carolina State Department of Archives and History.
Cawthorn, Joel T. (2nd Virginia). Letter of July 4, 1864. Appomattox National Historical Park Library, Appomattox, Va.
Chamberlayne, Francis W. (4th Virginia). Memoir of First Manassas Campaign. Virginia Historical Society.
Chandler, Norborne E. (1st Virginia). Correspondence. Virginia Historical Society.
Chappell, John T. (10th Virginia). Memoir of Yorktown-Williamsburg Operations. Virginia Historical Society.
Chew, Robert Preston (Ashby Battery). Correspondence. Preston Library, Virginia Military Institute.
Chewning, Charles R. (9th Virginia). Diaries, 1862–65. Handley Regional Library.
Chewning, John W. (9th Virginia). Diary, 1863. Mary Ball Library, Lancaster, Va.
Christian, Heath J. (3rd Virginia). Correspondence. Virginia Historical Society.
———. Letter of July 13, 1863. Library of Virginia.
Clark, Eutaw S. (7th Virginia). Letter of July 29, 1864. Eleanor S. Brockenbrough Library, Museum of the Confederacy.
Clarke, Garland H. (4th Virginia). Diary, 1865. Virginia Historical Society.
Clay, Calhoun G. (2nd Virginia). Letter of December 11, 1862. Virginia Historical Society.
Claybrook, Edwin C. (9th Virginia). Correspondence and Diaries, 1862–64. Eleanor S. Brockenbrough Library, Museum of the Confederacy.
Clement, Baxter (7th Confederate). Correspondence. Wilson Library, University of North Carolina.
Clement, W. Bailey (10th Virginia). Correspondence. North Carolina State Department of Archives and History.
Click, Jacob B. (5th Virginia). Letter of July 17, 1863. U.S. Army Military History Institute.
Cochran, Benjamin F. (1st Virginia). Correspondence. Carol M. Newman Library, Virginia Polytechnic Institute and State University.
Cole, J. W. (7th South Carolina). Correspondence. North Carolina State Department of Archives and History.
Colley, Thomas W. (1st Virginia). Diary, 1862. Eleanor S. Brockenbrough Library, Museum of the Confederacy.
Collins, John O. (10th Virginia). Correspondence. Virginia Historical Society.
Conrad, Holmes (1st and 11th Virginia). Correspondence. Virginia Historical Society.

Conway, William B. (4th Virginia). Memoirs. Virginia Historical Society.
Cooke, John Esten (Staff Officer). Correspondence. Library of Congress.
———. Correspondence. Virginia Historical Society.
———. Correspondence. William R. Perkins Library, Duke University.
———. Correspondence and Diaries, 1863–65. Alderman Library, University of Virginia.
Coons, Henry W. (4th Virginia). Correspondence. Virginia Historical Society.
Corson, William C. (3rd Virginia). Correspondence. Virginia Historical Society.
Cottrell, Edward D. (10th Virginia). Correspondence. Wilson Library, University of North Carolina.
———. Letter of October 16, 1862. Virginia Historical Society.
Cox, Leroy W. (Charlottesville Battery). Memoirs. Virginia Historical Society.
Crawford, David H. (Hampton Legion). Correspondence. South Caroliniana Library, University of South Carolina.
Creekmore, A. J. (Jeff Davis Legion). Diary, 1863. Mississippi Department of Archives and History, Jackson.
Crittenden, Churchill (1st Maryland Battalion). Correspondence. University of Washington Library, Seattle.
Crow, John T. (6th Virginia). Correspondence. Library of Virginia.
Cummings, John N. (5th South Carolina). Correspondence. William R. Perkins Library, Duke University.
Currie, Charles W. (12th Virginia). Correspondence. U.S. Army Military History Institute.
Curtis, Isaac S. (9th Virginia). Correspondence. Virginia Historical Society.
Curtis, W. A. (2nd North Carolina). Memoirs. In possession of Mr. Bryce Suderow, Washington, D.C.
Cushwa, Daniel G. (1st Virginia). Correspondence. Virginia Historical Society.
Dabney, Chiswell (Staff Officer). Correspondence. Virginia Historical Society.
Dailey, John (11th Virginia). Memoirs. University of West Virginia Library.
Dalton, L. R. (Hampton Legion). Correspondence. U.S. Army Military History Institute.
Darden, William H. (13th Virginia). Correspondence. Virginia Historical Society.
Davis, Eugene (2nd Virginia). Letter of August 29, 1863. Alderman Library, University of Virginia.
Davis, Thomas J. (5th Virginia). Diary, 1865. Maryland Historical Society.
Davis, Zimmerman (5th South Carolina). Correspondence. South Carolina Department of Archives and History, Columbia.
Decker, Marshall E. (9th Virginia). Correspondence. Library of Virginia.
Deloney, William G. (Cobb's Legion). Correspondence. Hargrett Library, University of Georgia, Athens.
Dendy, Daniel (7th South Carolina). Correspondence. Wilson Library, University of North Carolina.

Dewey, George L. (1st North Carolina). Letter of March 3, 1865. William R. Perkins Library, Duke University.

Dickinson, Henry C. (2nd Virginia). Diaries, 1864–65. Virginia Historical Society.

Dinwiddie, James (Charlottesville Battery). Correspondence. Library of Virginia.

Dobbins, John S. (Phillips Legion). Correspondence. Robert W. Woodruff Library, Emory University.

Donohoe, John C. (6th Virginia). Diaries, 1862–65. Library of Virginia.

Downman, John J. (4th Virginia). Correspondence. Virginia Historical Society.

Downman, Rawleigh W. (4th Virginia). Correspondence. Virginia Historical Society.

Drake, James H. (1st Virginia). Correspondence. Library of Congress.

Dulany, Richard H. (6th and 7th Virginia). Correspondence. Virginia Historical Society.

Dunaway, Raleigh W. (9th Virginia). Correspondence. Library of Virginia.

————. Correspondence. Randolph-Macon College Library, Lynchburg, Va.

Early, Samuel H. (2nd Virginia). Correspondence. Virginia Historical Society.

Edmundson, David (21st Virginia). Correspondence. Virginia Historical Society.

Edrington, John C., Jr. (9th Virginia). Correspondence. Virginia Historical Society.

Edwards, Julian T. (9th Virginia). Letter of October 15, 1862. Virginia Historical Society.

Edwards, Thomas W. B. (9th Virginia). Correspondence and Diaries, 1863–65. Library of Virginia.

Edwards, William H. (4th North Carolina). Correspondence. North Carolina State Department of Archives and History.

Eppes, Richard (5th Virginia). Correspondence and Diaries, 1861–62. Virginia Historical Society.

Ervine, John H. (1st Virginia). Letter of June 18, 1861. Preston Library, Virginia Military Institute.

Estill, John L. (1st Virginia). Correspondence. James Graham Leyburn Library, Washington and Lee University.

Evans, Maurice (4th Virginia). Correspondence. Virginia Historical Society.

Evans, Media (4th North Carolina). Memoirs. Wilson Library, University of North Carolina.

Feamster, Thomas L. (14th Virginia). Diaries, 1861–65. Library of Congress.

Ferguson, James D. (Staff Officer). Diary, 1864, and Papers. William R. Perkins Library, Duke University.

Fishburn, Elliott G. (1st Virginia). Papers. Alderman Library, University of Virginia.

Fisher, Jacob A. (1st North Carolina). Letter of December 8, 1861. U.S. Army Military History Institute.

Fitzhugh, Thaddeus (5th Virginia). Memoirs. Eleanor S. Brockenbrough Library, Museum of the Confederacy.

Foard, Frederick C. (1st North Carolina). Correspondence. North Carolina State Department of Archives and History.

Fontaine, Charles (5th Virginia). Letter of November 17, 1862. In possession of Mrs. Billie Satterfield, Hampton, Va.

Fontaine, John B. (4th Virginia). Correspondence. U.S. Army Military History Institute.

Forbes, Alfred T. (9th Virginia). Letter of July 10, 1863. U.S. Army Military History Institute.

Foster, John S. (Jeff Davis Legion). Correspondence. Hill Library, Louisiana State University, Baton Rouge.

Freaner, George (1st Virginia). Correspondence. Virginia Historical Society.

French, Marcellus (35th Virginia Battalion). Memoirs. Library of Virginia.

Funkhouser, Monroe (12th Virginia). Correspondence and Memoirs. Shenandoah County Library, Edinburg, Va.

Gafford, John H. (3rd Virginia). Memoirs. Virginia Historical Society.

Gallaher, DeWitt C. (1st Virginia). Correspondence. Wise Library, West Virginia University.

Gallaher, William B. (1st Virginia). Correspondence. Carol M. Newman Library, Virginia Polytechnic Institute and State University.

———. Correspondence. Library of Virginia.

Garber, Thomas M. (12th Virginia). Correspondence. Library of Virginia.

Gardner, William R. (4th Virginia). Letter of July 22, 1862. Eleanor S. Brockenbrough Library, Museum of the Confederacy.

Gatewood, Andrew C. L. (11th Virginia). Correspondence and Memoirs. Preston Library, Virginia Military Institute.

———. Diary, 1865. Wise Library, West Virginia University.

Gibson, John A. (14th Virginia). Diaries, 1864–65. Virginia Historical Society.

Gilchrist, Archibald E. (4th South Carolina). Correspondence. South Caroliniana Library, University of South Carolina.

Godsey, William A. (1st Virginia). Memoirs. Eleanor S. Brockenbrough Library, Museum of the Confederacy.

Gordon, Charles H. (4th Virginia). Correspondence. Virginia Historical Society.

Gordon, John W. (2nd North Carolina). Diaries, 1864–65. Eleanor S. Brockenbrough Library, Museum of the Confederacy.

Graham, William A., Jr. (2nd North Carolina). Correspondence. North Carolina State Department of Archives and History.

Grattan, Charles (Staff Officer). Letter of July 19, 1864. Wilson Library, University of North Carolina.

Grattan, Peter M. (1st Virginia). Correspondence. Wilson Library, University of North Carolina.

Grattan, Robert R. (1st Virginia). Correspondence. Wilson Library, University of North Carolina.

Gray, James W. (10th Virginia). Correspondence. Fredericksburg-Spotsylvania National Military Park Library, Fredericksburg, Va.

Grear, John C. (8th Virginia). Correspondence. Library of Virginia.

Green, Edward A. (12th Virginia). Memoirs. Eleanor S. Brockenbrough Library, Museum of the Confederacy.

Grimsley, Daniel A. (6th Virginia). Correspondence. Library of Virginia.

Grussell, T. W. (1st Virginia). Diaries, 1862–65. William R. Perkins Library, Duke University.

Gwathney, Llewellyn T. (5th Virginia). Letter of February 15, 1865. Virginia Historical Society.

Hairston, Peter W. (Staff Officer). Correspondence. Wilson Library, University of North Carolina.

Halsey, Edwin L. (Washington, South Carolina, Battery). Correspondence. Wilson Library, University of North Carolina.

Halsey, Joseph J. (6th Virginia). Papers. Alderman Library, University of Virginia.

Hammon, Reuben E. (7th Virginia). Correspondence. William R. Perkins Library, Duke University.

Hands, Washington (Baltimore Light Artillery). Memoirs. Maryland Historical Society.

Haney, Lucius C. (1st Virginia). Correspondence. William R. Perkins Library, Duke University.

Hansell, Charles P. (20th Georgia Battalion). Memoirs and Papers. Georgia Department of Archives and History.

Hardin, William D. (5th North Carolina). Letter of March 27, 1865. William R. Perkins Library, Duke University.

Harding, Hiram W. (9th Virginia). Diaries, 1864–65. Eleanor S. Brockenbrough Library, Museum of the Confederacy.

Harman, Asher W. (12th Virginia). Correspondence. Library of Virginia.

Hart, James F., L. C. Stephens, Louis Sherfesee, and Charles H. Schwing. "History of Hart's Battery." South Caroliniana Library, University of South Carolina.

Hawse, Jasper (7th and 11th Virginia). Diaries, 1863–64. Alderman Library, University of Virginia.

Haxall, Philip (4th Virginia). Correspondence. Virginia Historical Society.

Heath, Jesse H. (4th Virginia). Correspondence. Wilson Library, University of North Carolina.

Henninghausen, Charles A. (10th Virginia). Memoirs. Library of Virginia.

Hester, J. B. (6th South Carolina). Correspondence. South Caroliniana Library, University of South Carolina.

Hill, John L. (14th Virginia). Diary, 1861. Virginia Historical Society.

Hill, William P. (4th Virginia). Correspondence. Virginia Historical Society.

Hinton, William G. (7th South Carolina). Correspondence. Charleston Library, Charleston, S.C.

Holland, Mark (2nd Virginia). Correspondence. Alderman Library, University of Virginia.

Holley, Turner W. (1st South Carolina). Correspondence. William R. Perkins Library, Duke University.

Hooke, Robert W. (1st Virginia). Correspondence. William R. Perkins Library, Duke University.

Hopkins, George (10th Virginia). Correspondence. Library of Virginia.

Horne, Thomas (5th North Carolina). Correspondence. Ablah Library, Wichita State University, Wichita, Kans.

Hoxton, William H. (1st Stuart Horse Artillery). Correspondence. Virginia Historical Society.

Hubard, Robert T. (3rd Virginia). Letter of January 9, 1863. Alderman Library, University of Virginia.

———. Memoirs. William R. Perkins Library, Duke University.

Huddleston, Peter L. (2nd Virginia). Diaries, 1862–65. Fredericksburg-Spotsylvania National Military Park Library.

Hughes, Augustine S. (5th Virginia). Memoirs. Library of Virginia.

Humphreys, E. J. (Phillips Legion). Letter of July 22, 1861. U.S. Army Military History Institute.

Iredell, Cadwallader J. (1st North Carolina). Correspondence. Wilson Library, University of North Carolina.

———. Letter of July 9, 1863. U.S. Army Military History Institute.

Irving, Charles R. (1st Virginia). Correspondence. Virginia Historical Society.

Isbell, Robert B. (2nd Virginia). Correspondence. U.S. Army Military History Institute.

Jackson, Thomas C. (Cobb's Legion). Letter of July 11, 1864. William R. Perkins Library, Duke University.

Jeffress, Edward H. (3rd Virginia). Letter of June 22, 1862. Virginia Historical Society.

Jeter, James A. (9th Virginia). Correspondence. Virginia Historical Society.

Johnson, Elijah S. (15th Virginia). Diaries, 1864–65. Virginia Historical Society.

Jones, Abraham G. (5th North Carolina). Correspondence. J. Y. Joyner Library, East Carolina University.

Jones, Edmund (3rd North Carolina). Correspondence. Wilson Library, University of North Carolina.

Jones, George W. (2nd North Carolina). Memoirs. Eleanor S. Brockenbrough Library, Museum of the Confederacy.

Jones, Henry F. (Cobb's Legion). Correspondence. U.S. Army Military History Institute.

Jones, Jesse S. (3rd Virginia). Correspondence. William R. Perkins Library, Duke University.

Jones, Robert B. (5th Virginia). Correspondence. Virginia Historical Society.

Kay, Andrew H. (9th Virginia). Correspondence. Virginia Historical Society.

Keith, James (4th Virginia). Correspondence. Virginia Historical Society.

Kennon, Richard B. (4th, 8th, and 11th Virginia). Papers. Library of Virginia.

Kern, Joseph M. (13th Virginia). Memoirs. Wilson Library, University of North Carolina.

Kettlewell, Charles (1st Maryland Battalion). Correspondence. Maryland State Archives, Annapolis.

Keyser, William J. (1st Virginia). Correspondence. William R. Perkins Library, Duke University.

Lacy, B. (3rd Virginia). Correspondence. William R. Perkins Library, Duke University.

Landstreet, John (Staff Officer). Correspondence. Virginia Historical Society.

Langhorne, Jacob K. (2nd Virginia). Correspondence. Preston Library, Virginia Military Institute.

Larue, William A. M. (1st Virginia). Correspondence. Virginia Historical Society.

Latrobe, R. S. (1st Maryland Battalion). Memoirs. Maryland Historical Society.

Law, Hugh L. (6th South Carolina). Correspondence. South Caroliniana Library, University of South Carolina.

Law, Thomas C. (4th South Carolina). Correspondence. South Caroliniana Library, University of South Carolina.

Lee, Henry C. (Staff Officer). Diaries, 1864–65. Eleanor S. Brockenbrough Library, Museum of the Confederacy.

Lee, James I. (2nd Virginia). Correspondence. U.S. Army Military History Institute.

Leech, William B. F. (14th Virginia). Memoir of Appomattox Campaign. Virginia Historical Society.

Lemen, Thomas T. (1st Virginia). Correspondence. Wise Library, West Virginia University.

Lewis, William F. (10th Virginia). Diaries, 1864–65. Eleanor S. Brockenbrough Library, Museum of the Confederacy.

Ligon, James B. (Hampton Legion). Correspondence. South Caroliniana Library, University of South Carolina.

Lowther, Henry M. (10th Virginia). History of Company G, 10th Virginia Cavalry. Wise Library, West Virginia University.

Magruder, James W. (2nd Virginia). Letter of April 25, 1864. U.S. Army Military History Institute.

Manigault, Gabriel (4th South Carolina). Letter of June 30, 1864. Library of Congress.

Manigault, Lucius (4th South Carolina). Correspondence. Library of Congress.

Martin, Harmon (Cobb's Legion). Letter of August 25, 1863. U.S. Army Military History Institute.

Mason, St. George T. (13th Virginia). Diary, 1865, and Letter of January 6, 1864. Virginia Historical Society.

McBride, B. C. (1st South Carolina). Correspondence. William R. Perkins Library, Duke University.

McChesney, James Z. (11th and 14th Virginia). Correspondence. Wise Library, West Virginia University.

McClellan, Henry B. (Staff Officer). Correspondence. U.S. Army Military History Institute.

———. Correspondence. Virginia Historical Society.

McClellan, Robert M. (Jeff Davis Legion). Correspondence. In possession of Mr. David G. Evans, Pittstown, N.J.

McCutchan, James R. (5th Virginia). Correspondence. Rockbridge County Historical Society, Lexington, Va.

McDonald, Edward H. (11th Virginia). Memoirs. Wilson Library, University of North Carolina.

McGrorey, J. L. (4th South Carolina). Diary, 1864. South Caroliniana Library, University of South Carolina.

McIllwaine, Robert D. (13th Virginia). Letter of August 7, 1862. Virginia Historical Society.

McKnew, Mason E. (1st Maryland Battalion). Letter of November 28, 1864. Maryland Historical Society.

McLaurin, Daniel T. (4th North Carolina). Correspondence. Wilson Library, University of North Carolina.

McVicar, Charles W. (Ashby Battery). Memoirs. Library of Congress.

Mills, William H. (2nd North Carolina). Correspondence. J. Y. Joyner Library, East Carolina University.

Minor, Henry (5th South Carolina). Memoirs. South Caroliniana Library, University of South Carolina.

Mitteldorfer, Marx (1st Virginia). Correspondence. Library of Virginia.

Mobley, Benjamin L. (Cobb's Legion). Correspondence. Robert W. Woodruff Library, Emory University.

Moncure, Eustace C. (9th Virginia). Memoirs. Library of Virginia.

Moore, Fletcher B. (2nd Virginia). Correspondence. U.S. Army Military History Institute.

Moore, Thomas B. (2nd Virginia). Correspondence. U.S. Army Military History Institute.

Moorman, Marcellus N. (Lynchburg Battery). Letter of November 10, 1862. Eleanor S. Brockenbrough Library, Museum of the Confederacy.

Morgan, Robert S. (5th Virginia). Letter of October 26, 1863. Alderman Library, University of Virginia.

Morrissett, Lawson (4th Virginia). Diary, 1863. Eleanor S. Brockenbrough Library, Museum of the Confederacy.

Morton, William G. (3rd Virginia). Correspondence. Virginia Historical Society.

Mosby, John Singleton (1st Virginia). Papers. Alderman Library, University of Virginia.

———. Papers. Chicago Historical Society.

———. Papers. Library of Congress.

————. Papers. Missouri Historical Society, St. Louis.

————. Papers. New York Public Library, New York City.

————. Papers. U.S. Army Military History Institute.

————. Papers. Virginia Historical Society.

Moseley, John B. (14th Virginia). Diaries, 1864–65. Virginia Historical Society.

Munnerlyn, James K. (Jeff Davis Legion). Correspondence and Diary, 1864. Wilson Library, University of North Carolina.

Murray, John W. (4th Virginia). Correspondence. Library of Virginia.

Myers, Franklin M. (35th Virginia Battalion). Papers. Virginia Historical Society.

Neese, George M. (Ashby Battery). Correspondence. Jefferson County Museum, Charleston, W.Va.

————. Diaries, 1861–63. Library of Virginia.

Nelson, Hugh M. (6th Virginia). Letter of January 25, 1862. U.S. Army Military History Institute.

Nicholson, Edward A. T. (Staff Officer). Correspondence. Wilson Library, University of North Carolina.

Nunn, Jesse C. (Cobb's Legion). Correspondence. Georgia Department of Archives and History.

Nunnelee, Lewis T. (Lynchburg Battery). Memoirs. Eleanor S. Brockenbrough Library, Museum of the Confederacy.

Ogden, Dewees (Staff Officer). Correspondence. Library of Virginia.

Ord, Thomas J. (2nd North Carolina). Correspondence. William R. Perkins Library, Duke University.

Parker, Benjamin F. (2nd North Carolina). Letter of June 10, 1863. Fredericksburg-Spotsylvania National Military Park Library.

Parsons, William W. (13th Virginia). Correspondence. Library of Virginia.

Patrick, Henry M. (3rd North Carolina). Correspondence. North Carolina State Department of Archives and History.

Payne, Alexander D. (4th Virginia). Diaries, 1863–65. Virginia Historical Society.

Peek, William H. (2nd Virginia). Correspondence. Virginia Historical Society.

————. Correspondence. Wilson Library, University of North Carolina.

Pendleton, Charles K. (4th Virginia). Letter of March 27, 1862. Virginia Historical Society.

Pendleton, Philip H. (Charlottesville Battery). Correspondence. Virginia Historical Society.

Peoples, William J. (34th Virginia Battalion). Letter of May 25, 1864. Library of Virginia.

Perkins, Andrew J. (7th Georgia). Correspondence. Georgia Department of Archives and History.

Person, Jesse H. (1st North Carolina). Correspondence. William R. Perkins Library, Duke University.

Phelps, Charles R. (Lynchburg Battery). Correspondence. Alderman Library, University of Virginia.

Pierce, Hugh O. (11th Virginia). Autobiography. Handley Regional Library.

Pifer, Randolph (1st Virginia). Correspondence. Library of Virginia.

Powell, Charles H. (4th Virginia). Memoirs. Library of Virginia.

Powell, James L., Jr. (9th Virginia). Memoirs. Virginia Historical Society.

Powell, William L. (11th Virginia). Correspondence. Eleanor S. Brockenbrough Library, Museum of the Confederacy.

Powers, Philip H. (Staff Officer). Correspondence. Library of Virginia.

———. Correspondence. U.S. Army Military History Institute.

Preston, John (14th Virginia). Correspondence. Virginia Historical Society.

Price, R. Channing (Staff Officer). Correspondence. Virginia Historical Society.

———. Correspondence. Wilson Library, University of North Carolina.

Pritchett, Robert H. (6th Virginia). Correspondence. Eleanor S. Brockenbrough Library, Museum of the Confederacy.

Pugh, James T. (1st North Carolina). Correspondence. Wilson Library, University of North Carolina.

Randolph, Charles C. (6th Virginia). Letter of February 1, 1864. Virginia Historical Society.

Randolph, Robert (4th Virginia). Correspondence. Virginia Historical Society.

Reddick, M. A. (5th North Carolina). Correspondence. North Carolina State Department of Archives and History.

Rheney, John W. (Cobb's Legion). Correspondence. Georgia Department of Archives and History.

Riddick, D. Elbert (2nd North Carolina). Correspondence. U.S. Army Military History Institute.

Riddick, Samuel A. (13th Virginia). Letter of November 23, 1861. Eleanor S. Brockenbrough Library, Museum of the Confederacy.

Riddle, James C. (12th Virginia). Correspondence. Virginia Historical Society.

Robertson, Henry (3rd Virginia). Letter of October 20, 1861. Library of Virginia.

Robins, William A. (9th and 24th Virginia). Letter of March 18, 1865. Virginia Historical Society.

Robinson, Leiper M. (9th Virginia). Memoirs. Virginia Historical Society.

Rodman, William B. (1st North Carolina). Letter of December——, 1863. J. Y. Joyner Library, East Carolina University.

Roller, John E. (1st Virginia). Correspondence. Virginia Historical Society.

Rucker, Samuel B., Jr. (6th Virginia). Correspondence and Memoirs. Jones Memorial Library, Lynchburg, Va.

Ruffin, Edmund, Jr. (5th Virginia). Correspondence. Virginia Historical Society.

Ruffin, Thomas S. (5th and 13th Virginia). Correspondence. Virginia Historical Society.

———. Letter of July 9, 1864. Library of Virginia.

Scott, Alfred L. (10th Virginia). Memoirs. Virginia Historical Society.

Scott, James M. (5th and 10th Virginia). Memoirs. Virginia Historical Society.

Scott, John Z. H. (1st and 10th Virginia). Memoirs. Virginia Historical Society.

Scott, Richmond L. (5th Virginia). Memoirs. Virginia Historical Society.

Sedinger, James D. (8th Virginia). Memoirs. Wise Library, University of West Virginia.

Shaner, Jacob H. (14th Virginia). Correspondence. James Graham Leyburn Library, Washington and Lee University.

Shepherd, Lemuel C. (15th Virginia). Letter of February 10, 1863. Virginia Historical Society.

Sloan, Edwin R. (1st North Carolina). Correspondence. William R. Perkins Library, Duke University.

Smith, Addison A. (17th Virginia). Correspondence and Memoirs. Jackson County Historical Society, Ripley, W.Va.

Snider, John N. (14th Virginia). Letter of March 17, 1863. Carol M. Newman Library, Virginia Polytechnic Institute and State University.

Staples, Samuel G. (Staff Officer). Papers. Alderman Library, University of Virginia.

Steele, Milton B. (1st Virginia). Diaries, 1863–65. Eleanor S. Brockenbrough Library, Museum of the Confederacy.

Steptoe, William (2nd Virginia). Correspondence. William R. Perkins Library, Duke University.

Stone, James C. (6th Virginia). Letter of May 17, 1864. U.S. Army Military History Institute.

Strayhorn, W. H. (2nd North Carolina). Correspondence. William R. Perkins Library, Duke University.

Stringfellow, B. Franklin (4th Virginia). Correspondence. Virginia Historical Society.

Stuart, James Hardeman (Staff Officer). Correspondence and Diary, 1862. Mississippi Department of Archives and History.

Swann, John T. (Phillips Legion). Correspondence. Georgia Department of Archives and History.

Swann, Samuel A. (9th Virginia). Letter of July 3, 1864. Eleanor S. Brockenbrough Library, Museum of the Confederacy.

Swindler, Albert C. (12th Virginia). Correspondence. Earl Gregg Swem Library, College of William and Mary.

Sydnor, George B. (4th Virginia). Correspondence. Virginia Historical Society.

Talbott, Charles H. (2nd Virginia). Correspondence. William R. Perkins Library, Duke University.

Tate, William L., Jr. (10th Virginia). Correspondence. Library of Virginia.

Taurman, Henry E. (5th Virginia). Correspondence. William R. Perkins Library, Duke University.

Tayloe, J. W. (2nd Virginia). Correspondence. Alderman Library, University of Virginia.

Tayloe, Lomax (2nd Virginia). Correspondence. Historical Society of Southwestern Virginia, Roanoke.

Taylor, Charles E. (10th Virginia). Correspondence and Diary, 1863. Z. Smith Reynolds Library, Wake Forest University, Winston-Salem, N.C.

Taylor, William (6th Virginia). Letter of September 17, 1863. Virginia Historical Society.

Taylor, William (11th Virginia). Papers. Virginia Historical Society.

Thomson, William S. (12th Virginia). Correspondence. Robert W. Woodruff Library, Emory University.

Thornton, John T. (3rd Virginia). Correspondence. Alderman Library, University of Virginia.

Todd, Marius P. (5th Virginia). Papers. Library of Virginia.

Tompkins, James G. (5th Virginia). Correspondence. Alderman Library, University of Virginia.

Towles, John C. (9th Virginia). Diaries, 1862–63. Library of Virginia.

Towles, Robert C. (4th Virginia). Diary, 1863. Earl Gregg Swem Library, College of William and Mary.

Trowbridge, Alamin (Cobb's Legion). Correspondence. Georgia Department of Archives and History.

Trussell, Thomas W. (1st Virginia). Memoirs. Eleanor S. Brockenbrough Library, Museum of the Confederacy.

Tucker, James E. (2nd Virginia). Memoirs. Virginia Historical Society.

Turner, Charles B. (9th Virginia). Papers. Library of Virginia.

Turrentine, James A. (13th Virginia). Diary, 1865. Virginia Historical Society.

Tutwiler, Robert P. (15th Virginia). Letter of April 24, 1864. Wilson Library, University of North Carolina.

Tynes, Achilles J. (8th Virginia). Correspondence. Library of Virginia.

Unidentified Enlisted Man (5th Virginia). Letter of May 26, 1861. Virginia Historical Society.

Unidentified Enlisted Man (9th Virginia). Diary, 1865. Virginia Historical Society.

Upshaw, Thomas E. (13th Virginia). Letter of June 20, 1864. Virginia Historical Society.

Upshaw, William J. (3rd Virginia). Papers. Virginia Historical Society.

Vaiden, Melville (3rd Virginia). Letter of August 23, 1861. Eleanor S. Brockenbrough Library, Museum of the Confederacy.

Van Horn, James S. (10th Virginia). Correspondence. Virginia Historical Society.

Venable, Andrew R. (Staff Officer). Correspondence. Virginia Historical Society.

Venable, Charles S. (Staff Officer). Correspondence and Memoirs. Alderman Library, University of Virginia.

Wade, Horace M. (12th Virginia). Correspondence. U.S. Army Military History Institute.

Walker, Melville (5th Virginia). Letter of September 23, 1863. Library of Virginia.

Wall, Henry C. (4th North Carolina). Diary, 1862. North Carolina State Department of Archives and History.

Wallace, Charles I. (10th Virginia). Correspondence. Wise Library, West Virginia University.

Walters, Joseph (13th Virginia). Correspondence. Wilson Library, University of North Carolina.

Ward, F. B. (5th North Carolina). Letter of May 26, 1864. U.S. Army Military History Institute.

Ware, Cincinnatus J. (5th Virginia). Letter of September 29, 1864. Library of Virginia.

Ware, William H. (3rd Virginia). Memoirs. U.S. Army Military History Institute.

Ware, William S. (5th Virginia). Correspondence. Library of Virginia.

Waring, J. Frederick (Jeff Davis Legion). Correspondence. Georgia Historical Society.

————. Diaries, 1864–65, and Papers. Wilson Library, University of North Carolina.

Watkins, Richard H. (3rd Virginia). Correspondence. Earl Gregg Swem Library, College of William and Mary.

————. Correspondence. Virginia Historical Society.

Webb, Joseph P. (13th Virginia). Diaries, 1863–64. Alderman Library, University of Virginia.

Webb, William R. (2nd North Carolina). Correspondence. Wilson Library, University of North Carolina.

Weisiger, Samuel (1st Virginia). Correspondence. Library of Virginia.

Wells, Edward L. (4th South Carolina). Correspondence. Charleston Library Society.

————. Correspondence. South Caroliniana Library, University of South Carolina.

West, Van Buren (2nd Virginia). Correspondence. Library of Virginia.

White, Isaac (62nd Virginia Mounted Infantry). Correspondence. Carol M. Newman Library, Virginia Polytechnic Institute and State University.

Whittle, Beverly K. (2nd Virginia). Correspondence and Diaries, 1864–65. Alderman Library, University of Virginia.

Wigfall, Halsey (1st Stuart Horse Artillery). Correspondence. Library of Congress.

Wilkerson, Owen (2nd Virginia). Correspondence. Library of Virginia.

Williams, A. F. (1st North Carolina). Diary, 1862. J. Y. Joyner Library, East Carolina University.

Willis, Byrd C. (9th Virginia). Diaries, 1864–85, and Memoirs. Library of Virginia.

Wills, Henry A. (10th Virginia). Correspondence. Carol M. Newman Library, Virginia Polytechnic Institute and State University.

Wills, Irvin C. (13th Virginia). Correspondence. Virginia Historical Society.

Wilson, William B. (1st Maryland Battalion). Memoirs. Maryland Historical Society.

Wilson, William L. (12th Virginia). Memoir of Appomattox Campaign. Gilder Lehrman Collection.

Winfield, John Q. (7th Virginia). Memoirs. Wilson Library, University of North Carolina.

Wingfield, Chastain R. (4th Virginia). Correspondence. Virginia Historical Society.

Wise, John (11th Virginia). Correspondence. Alderman Library, University of Virginia.

Wood, James W. (7th Virginia). Diary, 1864. Library of Virginia.

Woods, Micajah (2nd Virginia and Charlottesville Battery). Correspondence and Diaries, 1861–64. Alderman Library, University of Virginia.

Woolwine, C. R. (14th Virginia). Correspondence. U.S. Army Military History Institute.

Workman, William (7th South Carolina). Correspondence. U.S. Army Military History Institute.

Worsley, H. G. (16th North Carolina Battalion). Memoirs. Wilson Library, University of North Carolina.

Wright, Gilbert J. (Cobb's Legion). Correspondence. Virginia Historical Society.

Wright, Joel (2nd Virginia). Correspondence. Library of Virginia.

Wynne, Richard H. (3rd Virginia). Correspondence. Eleanor S. Brockenbrough Library, Museum of the Confederacy.

Yancey, Benjamin C. (Cobb's Legion). Correspondence. Wilson Library, University of North Carolina.

Yates, Samuel B. (10th Virginia). Memoirs. William R. Perkins Library, Duke University.

Other Sources

Ashby, Turner. Correspondence. Chicago Historical Society.

Bachelder, John. Papers. New Hampshire Historical Society, Concord.

Baker, Isaac N. Memoir of the Gettysburg Campaign. Preston Library, Virginia Military Institute.

Cooke, John R. Papers. Virginia Historical Society.

Cowles, Calvin J. Correspondence. Wilson Library, University of North Carolina.

Daniel, John W. Papers. Alderman Library, University of Virginia.

Freeman, Douglas Southall. Papers. Library of Congress.

Gilmor, Harry. Papers. Maryland Historical Society.

Johnston, Bartlett S. Papers. Wilson Library, University of North Carolina.

Johnston, Joseph E. Letter of March 24, 1862. Gilder Lehrman Collection.
————. Papers. Earl Gregg Swem Library, College of William and Mary.
————. Papers. Virginia Historical Society.
Lee, Robert E. Papers. Chicago Historical Society.
————. Papers. Gilder Lehrman Collection.
————. Papers. Virginia Historical Society.
McCabe, W. Gordon. Papers. Virginia Historical Society.
Rawle, William Brooke. Papers. Historical Society of Pennsylvania.

UNPUBLISHED RECORDS
Battery Records, 1st Stuart Horse Artillery, Ashby Battery, and Charlottesville
    Battery. Jefferson County Museum.
Brigade Order Book, Hampton's Brigade, May–June 1863. U.S. Army Military
    History Institute.
Brigade Records, Hampton's Brigade, May–June 1862. U.S. Army Military
    History Institute.
Compiled Service Records, General and Staff Officers, Army of Northern Vir-
    ginia, 1861–65. Microcopy 331, National Archives, Washington, D.C.
Departmental Records, Cavalry, Army of the Peninsula, 1861–62. Eleanor S.
    Brockenbrough Library, Museum of the Confederacy.
Letters Received by the Adjutant General's Office. Record Group 393, National
    Archives.
Letters Received by the Confederate Secretary of War, 1861–65. Microcopy
    437, National Archives.
Unit Records, 1st Maryland Cavalry Battalion. Howard County Historical Soci-
    ety, Ellicott City, Md.
————. Maryland Historical Society.
————. Wise Library, West Virginia University.
Unit Records, 1st, 2nd, 3rd, 4th, 5th, 6th, 7th, 8th, 10th, 11th, 12th, 13th, 17th,
    and 24th Virginia Cavalries. Library of Virginia.
Unit Records, 1st, 4th, 5th, 6th, 9th, 10th, 11th, 12th, 14th, 15th, 21st, and 24th
    Virginia Cavalries. Eleanor S. Brockenbrough Library, Museum of the
    Confederacy.
Unit Records, 2nd Virginia Cavalry. Alderman Library, University of Virginia.
Unit Records, 3rd, 5th, 9th, 11th, 13th, 15th, 21st Virginia, and 35th Virginia
    Battalion Cavalries. Virginia Historical Society.
Unit Records, 5th South Carolina Cavalry. South Carolina Department of
    Archives and History.
————. South Caroliniana Library, University of South Carolina.
Unit Records, 6th South Carolina Cavalry. Charleston Library Society.
Unit Records, 6th Virginia Cavalry. William R. Perkins Library, Duke Univer-
    sity.
Unit Records, 6th and 10th Virginia Cavalries. Carol M. Newman Library, Vir-
    ginia Polytechnic Institute and State University.

Unit Records, 7th Virginia Cavalry. Preston Library, Virginia Military Institute.
Unit Records, 10th Virginia Cavalry. West Virginia Department of Archives and History, Charleston.
Unit Records, Jeff Davis Legion. Alabama Department of Archives and History, Montgomery.
War Department Collection of Confederate Records. Record Group 109, National Archives.

DISSERTATIONS, THESES, TYPESCRIPTS

Beane, Thomas O. "Thomas Lafayette Rosser: Soldier, Railroad Builder, Politician, Businessman (1836–1910)." Master's thesis, University of Virginia, 1957.
Bowmaster, Patrick A. "Brig. Gen. B. H. Robertson, C.S.A." Typescript in possession of the author.
————. "Confederate Brig. Gen. B. H. Robertson and the 1863 Gettysburg Campaign." Master's thesis, Virginia Polytechnic Institute and State University, 1995.
Fortier, John B. "Story of a Regiment: The Campaigns and Personnel of the Fifteenth Virginia Cavalry, 1862–1865." Master's thesis, College of William and Mary, 1968.
Readnor, Henry W. "General Fitzhugh Lee, 1835–1915." Ph.D. diss., University of Virginia, 1958.
Shriver, William H. "My Father Led J. E. B. Stuart to Gettysburg." Typescript in Gettysburg National Military Park Library, Gettysburg, Pa.
Storrick, W. C. "The Hunterstown Fight." Typescript in Gettysburg National Military Park Library.
Thomas, Robert N. "Brigadier General Thomas T. Munford and the Confederacy." Master's thesis, Duke University, 1958.
Tripp, Richard L. "Cavalry Reconnaissance in the Army of Northern Virginia: J. E. B. Stuart's Cavalry, 1861–64." Master's thesis, Duke University, 1967.
Turk, Toni R. "Thirty-fourth Battalion, Virginia Cavalry, Confederate States Army." Master's thesis, Midwestern State University, 1969.
Whitehead, Irving. "The Campaigns of Munford: History of the Second Virginia Cavalry." Typescript in Alderman Library, University of Virginia.

NEWSPAPERS

Army and Navy Journal (New York)
Charleston Daily Courier
Charleston Mercury
Charlotte Daily Observer
Daily Chronicle & Sentinel (Augusta, Ga.)
Daily Confederate (Raleigh, N.C.)
Daily Constitutionalist (Augusta, Ga.)
Daily Richmond Examiner

Daily South Carolinian (Columbia, S.C.)
Hillsborough (N.C.) *Recorder*
Lynchburg Virginian
Macon Daily Telegraph
New York Herald
New York Times
Petersburg Express
Petersburg Register
Richmond Daily Dispatch
Richmond Daily Enquirer
Richmond Sentinel
Richmond Whig
Savannah Daily Morning News
Savannah Republican

ARTICLES AND ESSAYS

Agnew, N. J. "With the Virginia Cavalry." *Confederate Veteran* 32 (1924): 344–45.

Allen, James H. "The James City Cavalry: Its Organization and Its First Service . . ." *Southern Historical Society Papers* 24 (1896): 353–58.

"An Appraisal of John S. Mosby." *Civil War Times Illustrated* 4 (November 1965): 4–7, 49–54.

Athearn, Robert G., ed. "The Civil War Diary of John Wilson Phillips." *Virginia Magazine of History and Biography* 62 (1954): 95–123.

Beale, George W. "A Soldier's Account of the Gettysburg Campaign: Letter from George W. Beale." *Southern Historical Society Papers* 11 (1883): 320–27.

Beale, R. L. T. "Part Taken by the Ninth Virginia Cavalry in Repelling the Dahlgren Raid." *Southern Historical Society Papers* 3 (1877): 219–21.

Bearss, Edwin C. "'. . . Into the very jaws of the enemy. . .': Jeb Stuart's Ride around McClellan." In *The Peninsula Campaign of 1862: Yorktown to the Seven Days,* edited by William J. Miller, vol. 1: 71–142. Campbell, Calif.: Savas Publishing Co., 1997.

Beauregard, P. G. T. "The First Battle of Bull Run." *Battles and Leaders of the Civil War* 1: 196–227.

———. "Four Days of Battle at Petersburg." *Battles and Leaders of the Civil War* 4: 540–44.

Bell, Harry, trans. "Cavalry Raids and the Lessons They Teach Us." *Journal of the U.S. Cavalry Association* 19 (1908-09): 142–52.

"The Black Horse Troop: The Members of the [Virginia] House of Delegates Who Served in the Famous Body . . ." *Southern Historical Society Papers* 24 (1896): 218–25.

Bliss, George N. "The Cavalry Affair at Waynesboro." *Southern Historical Society Papers* 13 (1885): 427–30.

Blow, William N. "Sussex Light Dragoons: A Roll of This Gallant Organization [and] Something of Its History." *Southern Historical Society Papers* 25 (1897): 273–75.

Bond, Frank A. "Fitz Lee in [the] Army of Northern Virginia." *Confederate Veteran* 6 (1898): 420–21.

Bouldin, Edwin E. "Charlotte Cavalry: A Brief History of the Gallant Command . . ." *Southern Historical Society Papers* 28 (1900): 71–81.

———. "The Last Charge at Appomattox: The Fourteenth Viginia Cavalry." *Southern Historical Society Papers* 28 (1900): 250–54.

Bowmaster, Patrick A., ed. "Confederate Brig. Gen. B. H. 'Bev' Robertson Interviewed on the Gettysburg Campaign." *Gettysburg Magazine* 20 (1998): 19–26.

Brennan, Patrick. "The Best Cavalry in the World." *North & South* 2 (January 1999): 11–27.

"Brook Church Fight and Something about the Fifth North Carolina Cavalry . . ." *Southern Historical Society Papers* 29 (1901): 139–44.

Brooksher, William R., and David K. Snider. "Stuart's Ride—The Great Circuit around McClellan." *Civil War Times Illustrated* 12 (April 1973): 5–10, 40–47.

Butler, M. C. "The Cavalry Fight at Trevilian Station." *Battles and Leaders of the Civil War* 4: 237–39.

Buxton, J. A. "One of Stuart's Couriers." *Confederate Veteran* 30 (1922): 343–44.

Campbell, William. "Stuart's Ride and Death of Latane . . ." *Southern Historical Society Papers* 39 (1914): 86–90.

Cardwell, David. "A Brilliant Cavalry Coup." *Confederate Veteran* 26 (1918): 474–76.

———. "A Soldier in Search of His Command." *Confederate Veteran* 26 (1918): 256–58.

Carpenter, Louis H. "Sheridan's Expedition around Richmond, May 9–25, 1864." *Journal of the United States Cavalry Association* 1 (1888): 300–324.

"The Cavalry at Fisher's Hill." *Confederate Veteran* 3 (1895): 51–52.

Clark, S. A. "Brandy Station, October, 1863." *Maine Bugle,* n.s. 3 (1896): 226–29.

———. "Buckland Mills." *Maine Bugle,* n.s. 4 (1897): 108–10.

"Col. John Logan Black of South Carolina." *Confederate Veteran* 35 (1927): 214.

Colley, Thomas W. "Brig. Gen. William E. Jones." *Confederate Veteran* 11 (1903): 266–67.

Collins, John L. "A Prisoner's March from Gettysburg to Staunton." *Battles and Leaders of the Civil War* 3: 429–33.

Colston, F. M. "Gettysburg as I Saw It." *Confederate Veteran* 5 (1897): 551–53.

"Company A, First Maryland Cavalry." *Confederate Veteran* 6 (1898): 78–80.

"Company C, Ninth Virginia Cavalry, C. S. A.: Its Roster and Gallant Record." *Southern Historical Society Papers* 23 (1895): 330–32.

Conrad, Holmes. "The Cavalry Corps of the Army of Northern Virginia." In *The Photographic History of the Civil War,* edited by Francis Trevelyan Miller, vol. 4: 76–114. New York: Review of Reviews Co., 1911.

Cooke, John Esten. "General Stuart in Camp and Field." *In The Annals of the War, Written by Leading Participants, North and South,* 665–76. Philadelphia: Times Publishing Co., 1879.

Copeland, J. E. "The Fighting at Brandy Station." *Confederate Veteran* 30 (1922): 451–52.

"Correspondence." *Confederate Veteran* 10 (1902): 261.

Coski, John, ed. "Forgotten Warrior: General William Henry Fitzhugh Payne." *North & South* 2 (September 1999): 76–89.

Couch, Darius N. "The Chancellorsville Campaign." *Battles and Leaders of the Civil War* 3: 154–71.

Cox, Thelma Wyche. "Jeb Stuart—Fighting Man." *Confederate Veteran* 40 (1932): 176–78.

Craige, Kerr. "Gen. James B. Gordon." *Confederate Veteran* 6 (1898): 216.

Curtis, William A. "A Journal of Reminiscences of the War: 1. Sketches of Company 'A,' 2nd Regiment of North Carolina Cavalry, from May 1st, 1861, to January 1st, 1862 . . . ." *Our Living and Our Dead* 2 (1875): 36–44.

Davis, George B. "The Antietam Campaign." *Papers of the Military Historical Society of Massachusetts* 3 (1903): 27–72.

———. "The Bristoe and Mine Run Campaigns." *Papers of the Military Historical Society of Massachusetts* 3 (1903): 470–502.

———. "The Cavalry Combat at Brandy Station, Va., on June 9, 1863." *Journal of the United States Cavalry Association* 25 (1914): 190–98.

———. "The Cavalry Combat at Kelly's Ford in 1863." *Journal of the United States Cavalry Association* 25 (1915): 390–402.

———. "From Gettysburg to Williamsport." *Papers of the Military Historical Society of Massachusetts* 3 (1903): 449–69.

———. "The Operations of the Cavalry in the Gettysburg Campaign." *Journal of the United States Cavalry Association* 1 (1888): 325–48.

———. "The Richmond Raid of 1864." *Journal of the United States Cavalry Association* 24 (1913–14): 702–22.

———. "The Stoneman Raid." *Journal of the United States Cavalry Association* 24 (1913–14): 533–52.

Davis, Leslie H. "Gen. T. L. Rosser in Rockbridge County, Va., in 1864." *Confederate Veteran* 23 (1915): 261–62.

Day, C. R. "Cavalry Raids—Their Value and How Made." *Journal of the United States Cavalry Association* 23 (1912–13): 227–38.

"The Death of General J. E. B. Stuart, by a Private of the Sixth Virginia Cavalry, C.S.A." *Battles and Leaders of the Civil War* 4: 194.

Dickman, L. T. "Services of a Maryland Confederate." *Confederate Veteran* 2 (1894): 165.

Douglas, Henry Kyd. "Stonewall Jackson in Maryland." *Battles and Leaders of the Civil War* 2: 620–29.

Doyle, W. E. "Seein' Things on Picket, 1864." *Confederate Veteran* 26 (1918): 391.

Early, Jubal A. "Early's March to Washington in 1864." *Battles and Leaders of the Civil War* 4: 492–99.

———. "Winchester, Fisher's Hill, and Cedar Creek." *Battles and Leaders of the Civil War* 4: 522–30.

Elmore, Albert R. "Incidents of Service with the Charleston Light Dragoons." *Confederate Veteran* 24 (1916): 538–43.

"The Famous Lee Rangers: The Organization, Service, and Roster of This Company." *Southern Historical Society Papers* 23 (1895): 290–92.

Fay, J. B. "Cavalry Fight at Second Manassas." *Confederate Veteran* 23 (1915): 263–64.

Ford, Noah P. "Wade Hampton's Strategy: An Attack on Richmond Foiled . . ." *Southern Historical Society Papers* 24 (1896): 278–84.

Fry, James B. "McDowell's Advance to Bull Run." *Battles and Leaders of the Civil War* 1: 167–93.

"Generals in the Confederate States Army from Virginia." *Southern Historical Society Papers* 36 (1908): 105–20.

"Gen. J. E. B. Stuart." *Confederate Veteran* 11 (1903): 390–92.

"Gen. M. C. Butler as a Confederate." *Confederate Veteran* 8 (1900): 110–11.

"Gen. Rufus Barringer." *Confederate Veteran* 9 (1901): 69–70.

Greene, A. Wilson. "Opportunity to the South: Meade versus Jackson at Fredericksburg." *Civil War History* 33 (1987): 295–314.

"'Grumble' Jones: A Personality Profile." *Civil War Times Illustrated* 7 (June 1968): 35–41.

Halstead, E. P. "Incidents of the First Day at Gettysburg." *Battles and Leaders of the Civil War* 3: 284–85.

Hanson, Joseph Mills. "A Stolen March: Cold Harbor to Petersburg." *Journal of the American Military History Foundation* 1 (1937–38): 139–50.

Harbord, J. G. "The History of the Cavalry of the Army of Northern Virginia." *Journal of the United States Cavalry Association* 14 (1904): 423–503.

Harden, B. J. "A Close Shave." *Confederate Veteran* 26 (1918): 390–91.

Hartley, Chris J. "Artillery Ambush at Willis Church." *America's Civil War* 14 (May 2001): 51–56.

Hartwig, D. Scott. "Robert E. Lee and the Maryland Campaign." In *Lee, the Soldier,* edited by Gary A. Gallagher, 331–55. Lincoln: University of Nebraska Press, 1996.

Hassler, William W. "The Battle of Yellow Tavern." *Civil War Times Illustrated* 5 (November 1966): 5–11, 46–48.

Hatfield, C. A. P. "The Evolution of Cavalry." *Journal of the Military Service Institution of the United States* 15 (1894): 89–103.

Havens, Edwin R. "How Mosby Destroyed Our Train." *Michigan History Magazine* 14 (1930): 294–98.

Haw, John R. "The Battle of Haw's Shop, Va." *Confederate Veteran* 33 (1925): 373–76.

Hay, W. H. "Cavalry Raids." *Journal of the United States Cavalry Association* 4 (1891): 362–76.

Hayden, Horace E. "The First Maryland Cavalry." *Southern Historical Society Papers* 5 (1878): 251–53.

"Heroic Capt. Francis Edgeworth Eve." *Confederate Veteran* 2 (1894): 342.

Hill, Daniel H. "The Battle of South Mountain, or Boonsboro'." *Battles and Leaders of the Civil War* 2: 559–81.

———. "Lee Attacks North of the Chickahominy." *Battles and Leaders of the Civil War* 2: 347–62.

———. "McClellan's Change of Base and Malvern Hill." *Battles and Leaders of the Civil War* 2: 383–95.

"History of Hart's Battery." *Confederate Veteran* 9 (1901): 500–501.

Hunt, Henry J. "The Third Day at Gettysburg." *Battles and Leaders of the Civil War* 3: 369–85.

Imboden, John D. "The Confederate Retreat from Gettysburg." *Battles and Leaders of the Civil War* 3: 420–29.

———. "Incidents of the First Bull Run." *Battles and Leaders of the Civil War* 1: 229–39.

———. "Jackson at Harper's Ferry in 1861." *Battles and Leaders of the Civil War* 1: 111–25.

James, C. F. "Battle of Sailor's Creek." *Southern Historical Society Papers* 24 (1896): 83–88.

"James G. Holmes of Charleston." *Confederate Veteran* 2 (1894): 178.

James, G. Watson. "Dahlgren's Raid." *Southern Historical Society Papers* 39 (1914): 63–72.

Johnston, Angus J. "Lee's Last Lifeline: The Richmond & Danville." *Civil War History* 7 (1961): 288–96.

Johnston, Joseph E. "Manassas to Seven Pines." *Battles and Leaders of the Civil War* 2: 202–18.

———. "Responsibilities of the First Bull Run." *Battles and Leaders of the Civil War* 1: 240–59.

Jones, J. William, comp. "Kilpatrick-Dahlgren Raid Against Richmond." *Southern Historical Society Papers* 13 (1885): 515–60.

Jones, Virgil Carrington. "The Story of the Kilpatrick-Dahlgren Raid." *Civil War Times Illustrated* 4 (April 1965): 12–21.

Kennedy, William V. "The Cavalry Battle at Brandy Station." *Armor* 65 (1956): 27–31.

Kerwood, John Richard. "His Daring Was Proverbial." *Civil War Times Illustrated* 7 (August 1968): 19–23, 28–30.

"Kilpatrick's and Dahlgren's Raid to Richmond." *Battles and Leaders of the Civil War* 4: 95–96.

Krick, Robert E. L. "Defending Lee's Flank: J. E. B. Stuart, John Pelham, and Confederate Artillery on Nicodemus Heights." In *The Antietam Campaign*, edited by Gary A. Gallagher, 192–222. Chapel Hill: University of North Carolina Press, 1999.

Krick, Robert K. "The Alriches of Spotsylvania." *Lincoln Herald* 82 (1980): 311–18.

———. "'The Cause of All My Disasters': Jubal A. Early and the Undisciplined Valley Cavalry." In *Struggle for the Shenandoah: Essays on the 1864 Valley Campaign*, edited by Gary A. Gallagher, 77–106. Kent, Ohio: Kent State University Press, 1991.

———. "Lee at Chancellorsville." In *Lee, the Soldier*, edited by Gary A. Gallagher. 357–80. Lincoln: University of Nebraska Press, 1996.

Kurtz, Henry I. "Five Forks—The South's Waterloo." *Civil War Times Illustrated* 3 (October 1964): 5–11, 28–31.

Lamb, John. "The Battle of Fredericksburg: Details of the Mighty Conflict." *Southern Historical Society Papers* 27 (1899): 231–40.

———. "The Confederate Cavalry, Its Wants, Trials, and Heroism: An Address by Hon. John Lamb, Late Captain of Cavalry, C.S. Army." *Southern Historical Society Papers* 26 (1898): 359–65.

———. "Malvern Hill—July 1, 1862: An Address . . ." *Southern Historical Society Papers* 25 (1897): 208–21.

Law, E. M. "From the Wilderness to Cold Harbor." *Battles and Leaders of the Civil War* 4: 118–44.

Lay, John F. "Reminiscences of the Powhatan Troop of Cavalry." *Southern Historical Society Papers* 8 (1880): 418–26.

Lee, Fitzhugh. "The Battle of Chancellorsville." *Southern Historical Society Papers* 7 (1879): 545–85.

———. "Letter from General Fitz. Lee." *Southern Historical Society Papers* 4 (1876): 69–76.

"Letters to Laura." *Civil War Times Illustrated* 32 (July-August 1992): 12, 58, 60–61.

"List of Officers and Men of the Cavalry Brigade of Brig.-Gen. R. L. T. Beale, C.S. Army, Surrendered at Appomattox C.H., Virginia, April 9th, 1865." *Collections of the Virginia Historical Society*, n.s. 6 (1887): 347–55.

Longacre, Edward G. "The Battle of Brandy Station: 'A Shock That Made the Earth Tremble.'" *Virginia Cavalcade* 25 (1976): 136–43.

———. "Boots and Saddles: Part I, The Eastern Theater." *Civil War Times Illustrated* 31 (March-April 1992): 35–40.

———. "Cavalry Clash at Todd's Tavern." *Civil War Times Illustrated* 16 (October 1977): 12–21.

————. "The Long Run for Trevilian Station." *Civil War Times Illustrated* 7 (November 1979): 28–39.

————. "Stuart's Dumfries Raid." *Civil War Times Illustrated* 15 (July 1976): 18–26.

Longstreet, James. "The Battle of Fredericksburg." *Battles and Leaders of the Civil War* 3: 70–85.

————. "The Invasion of Maryland." *Battles and Leaders of the Civil War* 2: 663–74.

————. "Lee's Invasion of Pennsylvania." *Battles and Leaders of the Civil War* 3: 244–51.

————. "Our March against Pope." *Battles and Leaders of the Civil War* 2: 512–26.

————. "'The Seven Days,' Including Frayser's Farm." *Battles and Leaders of the Civil War* 2: 396–405.

Lord, Francis A. "Confederate Cavalrymen Found Revolvers Better than Sabers or Rifles." *Civil War Times Illustrated* 1 (January 1963): 46–47.

Louthan, Henry T. "General Wade Hampton: Planter, Soldier, Statesman." *Confederate Veteran* 40 (1932): 65–69.

Luvaas, Jay. "Cavalry Lessons of the Civil War." *Civil War Times Illustrated* 6 (January 1968): 20–31.

Lykes, Richard W. "The Great Civil War Beef Raid." *Civil War Times Illustrated* 5 (February 1967): 5–12, 47–49.

Lynn, Bushrod W. "In the [First] Battle of Manassas." *Confederate Veteran* 26 (1918): 192.

Mackey, T. J. "Duel of General Wade Hampton on the Battle-Field at Gettysburg with a Federal Soldier." *Southern Historical Society Papers* 22 (1894): 122–26.

Mahone, William. "On the Road to Appomattox." *Civil War Times Illustrated* 9 (January 1971): 5–11, 42–47.

Malone, P. J. "Charge of Black's Cavalry Regiment at Gettysburg." *Southern Historical Society Papers* 16 (1888): 224–28.

"Maryland Campaign: The Cavalry Fight at Boonsboro' Graphically Described . . ." *Southern Historical Society Papers* 25 (1897): 276–80.

Matthews, H. H. "Major John Pelham, Confederate Hero." *Southern Historical Society Papers* 38 (1910): 379–84.

————. "A Maryland Confederate . . . Recollections of Major James Breathed." *Southern Historical Society Papers* 30 (1902): 346–48.

McCabe, W. Gordon. "Defence of Petersburg." *Southern Historical Society Papers* 2 (1874): 257–306.

McClellan, George B. "The Peninsular Campaign." *Battles and Leaders of the Civil War* 2: 160–87.

McClellan, Henry B. " . . . Address of Major H. B. McClellan on the Life, Campaigns, and Character of Gen'l J. E. B. Stuart." *Southern Historical Society Papers* 8 (1880): 433–56.

McClernand, Edward J. "Cavalry Operations: The Wilderness to the James River." *Journal of the Military Service Institution of the United States* 30 (1902): 321–43.

McDonald, Edward H. "Fighting under Ashby in the Shenandoah." *Civil War Times Illustrated* 5 (July 1966): 29–35.

———. "I Felt a Ball Strike Me, I Could Not Tell Where." *Civil War Times Illustrated* 7 (June 1968): 28–34.

———. "I Saw an Immense Column of Yankee Cavalry." *Civil War Times Illustrated* 6 (February 1968): 42–47.

———. "The Laurel Brigade Raid across Northern Virginia." *Civil War Times Illustrated* 5 (November 1966): 44–45.

———. "We Drove Them from the Field." *Civil War Times Illustrated* 6 (November 1967): 28–35.

McKim, Randolph H. "The Confederate Cavalry in the Gettysburg Campaign." *Journal of the Military Service Institution of the United States* 46 (1910): 414–27.

McLaws, Lafayette. "The Confederate Left at Fredericksburg." *Battles and Leaders of the Civil War* 3: 86–94.

McMahon, Martin T. "From Gettysburg to the Coming of Grant." *Battles and Leaders of the Civil War* 4: 81–94.

McWhiney, Grady. "Who Whipped Whom? Confederate Defeat Reexamined." *Civil War History* 11 (1965): 5–26.

Merritt, Wesley. "Sheridan in the Shenandoah Valley." *Battles and Leaders of the Civil War* 4: 500–21.

Mewborn, Horace. "The Operations of Mosby's Rangers." *Blue & Gray* 17 (August 2000): 6–21, 40–50.

Miller, Samuel H. "Yellow Tavern." *Civil War History* 2 (1956): 57–81.

———, ed. "Civil War Memoirs of the First Maryland Cavalry, C.S.A." *Maryland Historical Magazine* 58 (1963): 137–70.

Miller, William E. "The Cavalry Battle Near Gettysburg." *Battles and Leaders of the Civil War* 3: 397–406.

Mitchell, Frances Letcher. "A Georgia Henry of Navarre." *Confederate Veteran* 23 (1915): 363.

"A Model U.C.V. Camp." *Confederate Veteran* 7 (1899): 167–68.

Moffett, W. L. "The Last Charge of the 14th Virginia Cavalry at Appomattox C.H., Va., April 9, 1865." *Southern Historical Society Papers* 36 (1908): 13–16.

Monaghan, Jay. "Custer's 'Last Stand'—Trevilian Station, 1864." *Civil War History* 8 (1962): 245–58.

Moore, James O. "Custer's Raid into Albemarle County: The Skirmish at Rio Hill, February 29, 1864." *Virginia Magazine of History and Biography* 79 (1971): 338–48.

Moore, J. Scott. "Rockbridge Second Dragoons: A Short History of the Company . . ." *Southern Historical Society Papers* 25 (1897): 177–80.

————. "Unwritten History: A Southern Account of the Burning of Chambersburg . . ." *Southern Historical Society Papers* 26 (1898): 315–22.

Moore, J. Staunton. "The Battle of Five Forks." *Confederate Veteran* 16 (1908): 403–4.

Moore, Martin V. "The Crossing of the Potomac by the Confederate Cavalry." *Southern Historical Monthly* 1 (1876): 73–78.

————. "General Stuart in Pennsylvania: The Great Cavalry Expedition of 1862." *Transactions of the Southern Historical Society* 1 (1874): 121–34.

Morrison, James L. "The Struggle between Sectionalism and Nationalism at Ante-bellum West Point, 1830–1861." *Civil War History* 19 (1973): 138–48.

Mosby, John S. "A Bit of Partisan Service." *Battles and Leaders of the Civil War* 3: 148–51.

————. "The Confederate Cavalry in the Gettysburg Campaign." *Battles and Leaders of the Civil War* 3: 251–52.

Munford, Thomas T. "Reminiscences of Cavalry Operations: Paper No. 1." *Southern Historical Society Papers* 12 (1884): 342–50.

————. "Reminiscences of Cavalry Operations, Paper Number 2: Battle of Winchester, 19th September '64." *Southern Historical Society Papers* 12 (1884): 447–59.

————. "Reminiscences of Cavalry Operations, Paper No. 3: Operations under Rosser." *Southern Historical Society Papers* 13 (1886): 133–44.

Naisawald, L. VanLoan. "Stuart as a Cavalryman's Cavalryman." *Civil War Times Illustrated* 1 (February 1963): 7–9, 42–46.

Nolan, Alan T. "R. E. Lee and July 1 at Gettysburg." In *Lee, the Soldier,* edited by Gary A. Gallagher, 475–96. Lincoln: University of Nebraska Press, 1996.

Norvell, Guy S. "The Equipment and Tactics of Our Cavalry, 1861–1865, Compared with the Present." *Journal of the Military Service Institution of the United States* 49 (1911): 360–76.

Nye, Wilbur S. "The Affair at Hunterstown." *Civil War Times Illustrated* 9 (February 1971): 22–34.

————. "How Stuart Recrossed the Potomac." *Civil War Times Illustrated* 4 (January 1966): 45–48.

Parker, James. "Mounted and Dismounted Action of Cavalry." *Journal of the Military Service Institution of the United States* 39 (1906): 381–87.

Pearson, Everett I. "Stuart in Westminster." *Transactions of the Southern Historical Society* 2 (1875): 19–24.

Philpot, G. B. "A Maryland Boy in the Confederate Army." *Confederate Veteran* 24 (1916): 312–15.

Pleasonton, Alfred. "The Successes and Failures of Chancellorsville." *Battles and Leaders of the Civil War* 3: 172–82.

Pope, John. "The Second Battle of Bull Run." *Battles and Leaders of the Civil War* 2: 449–94.

Porter, Fitz-John. "The Battle of Malvern Hill." *Battles and Leaders of the Civil War* 2: 406–27.

———. "Hanover Court House and Gaines's Mill." *Battles and Leaders of the Civil War* 2 (1887–88): 319–43.

Porter, Horace. "Five Forks and the Pursuit of Lee." *Battles and Leaders of the Civil War* 4: 708–22.

———. "The Surrender at Appomattox Court House." *Battles and Leaders of the Civil War* 4: 729–46.

"Pouncing on Pickets: Bold Dash of a Detachment of the 9th Virginia Cavalry . . ." *Southern Historical Society Papers* 24 (1896): 213–18.

Powell, C. H. "Goochland Light Dragoons: Organization and First Outpost Experience." *Southern Historical Society Papers* 24 (1896): 359–61.

Power, J. Tracy. "The Confederate as Gallant Knight: The Life and Death of William Downs Farley." *Civil War History* 37 (1991): 247–55.

Price, R. Channing. "Stuart's Chambersburg Raid: An Eyewitness Account." *Civil War Times Illustrated* 4 (January 1966): 8–15, 42–48.

Purifoy, John. "Cavalry Action near Fairfield, Pa., July 3, 1863." *Confederate Veteran* 32 (1924): 345–46.

———. "Stuart's Cavalry Battle at Gettysburg, July 3, 1863." *Confederate Veteran* 32 (1924): 260–63.

———. "A Unique Battle." *Confederate Veteran* 33 (1925): 132–35.

Rawle, William Brooke. "Further Remarks on the Cavalry Fight on the Right Flank at Gettysburg." *Journal of the United States Cavalry Association* 4 (1891): 157–60.

———. "Gregg's Cavalry Fight at Gettysburg, July 3, 1863." *Journal of the United States Cavalry Association* 4 (1891): 257–75.

Rea, D. B. "Cavalry Incidents of the Maryland Campaign." *Maine Bugle* 2 (1895): 117–23.

"The Rebel Scout." *Confederate Veteran* 13 (1905): 220.

Redwood, Allen C. "Following Stuart's Feather." *Journal of the Military Service Institution of the United States* 49 (1911): 111–21.

———. "Jackson's 'Foot-Cavalry' at the Second Bull Run." *Battles and Leaders of the Civil War* 2: 530–38.

Rhea, Gordon C. "'The Hottest Place I Ever Was In': The Battle of Haw's Shop, May 28, 1864." *North & South* 4 (April 2001): 42–57.

Robertson, Beverly H. "The Confederate Cavalry in the Gettysburg Campaign." *Battles and Leaders of the Civil War* 3: 253.

Robins, W. T. "Stuart's Ride around McClellan." *Battles and Leaders of the Civil War* 1: 271–75.

Rodenbough, Theophilus F. "Cavalry War Lessons." *Journal of the United States Cavalry Association* 2 (1889): 103–23.

———. "Sheridan's Richmond Raid." *Battles and Leaders of the Civil War* 4: 188–93.

———. "Sheridan's Trevilian Raid." *Battles and Leaders of the Civil War* 4: 233–36.

"Roll and Roster of Pelham's, Afterwards Breathed's Famous Battery, Stuart Horse Artillery Battalion, Cavalry Corps, Army of Northern Virginia." *Southern Historical Society Papers* 30 (1902): 348–54.

"Roll of Company E, Thirteenth Virginia Cavalry, and as to the Role of the Flag of the Regiment." *Southern Historical Society Papers* 34 (1906): 210–11.

"Roster of the Amelia Troop, Which Constituted Company 'G,' First Regiment Virginia Cavalry . . ." *Southern Historical Society Papers* 38 (1910): 16–21.

Russell, Don. "Jeb Stuart on the Frontier." *Civil War Times Illustrated* 13 (April 1974): 13–17.

————. "Jeb Stuart's Other Indian Fight." *Civil War Times Illustrated* 12 (January 1974): 11–17.

Schuricht, Hermann. "Jenkins' Brigade in the Gettysburg Campaign: Extracts from the Diary of Lieutenant Hermann Schuricht, of the Fourteenth Virginia Cavalry." *Southern Historical Society Papers* 24 (1896): 339–50.

Scott, John. "The Black Horse Cavalry." In *The Annals of the War, Written by Leading Participants, North and South,* 590–613. Philadelphia: Times Publishing Co., 1879.

Scott, W. W., ed. "Two Confederate Items." *Bulletin of the Virginia State Library* 16 (July 1927): 5–76.

"The Second Virginia Regiment of Cavalry, C.S.A.: Tribute to its Discipline and Efficiency . . ." *Southern Historical Society Papers* 16 (1888): 354–56.

Shepard, James C. "'Miracles' and Leadership in Civil War Cavalry." *Military Review* 55 (1975): 49–55.

Shepherd, Joseph D. "Company D, Clarke Cavalry: History and Roster of This Command . . ." *Southern Historical Society Papers* 24 (1896): 145–51.

Smith, Everard H., ed., "Civil War Diary of Peter W. Hairston . . . 7 November–4 December 1863." *North Carolina Historical Review* 67 (1990): 59–86.

Smith, Gustavus W. "Two Days of Battle at Seven Pines (Fair Oaks)." *Battles and Leaders of the Civil War* 2: 220–63.

Steuart, Richard D. "Armories of the Confederacy." *Confederate Veteran* 35 (1927): 9–10.

————. "How Johnny Got His Gun." *Confederate Veteran* 32 (1924): 166–69.

————. "A Pair of Navy Sixes." *Confederate Veteran* 33 (1925): 92–95.

"Stoneman's Raid in the Chancellorsville Campaign." *Batles and Leaders of the Civil War* 3: 152–53.

"Strength of General Lee's Army in the Seven Days Battles around Richmond." *Southern Historical Society Papers* 1 (1876): 407–24.

Strickler, H. M. "My Experiences with the Cavalry." *Confederate Veteran* 32 (1924): 63.

"Stuart's Ride around McClellan." *Confederate Veteran* 5 (1897): 53–54.

Sulivane, Clement. "The Fall of Richmond." *Battles and Leaders of the Civil War* 4: 725–28.

Swift, Eben. "The Tactical Use of Cavalry." *Journal of the Military Service Institution of the United States* 44 (1909): 359–69.

Sword, Wiley. "Cavalry on Trial at Kelly's Ford." *Civil War Times Illustrated* 13 (April 1974): 32–40.

Taliaferro, W. B. "Jackson's Raid Around Pope." *Battles and Leaders of the Civil War* 2: 501–11.

Thompson, William Y. "Robert Toombs, Confederate General." *Civil War History* 7 (1961): 406–20.

Trout, Robert J. "Galloping Thunder: The Stuart Horse Artillery Battalion . . ." *North & South* 3 (September 2000): 75–84.

Turner, Charles W. "The Richmond, Fredericksburg and Potomac, 1861–1865." *Civil War History* 7 (1961): 255–63.

———, ed. "James B. Dorman's Civil War Letters." *Civil War History* 25 (1979): 262–78.

Venable, Charles S. "The Campaign from the Wilderness to Petersburg . . ." *Southern Historical Society Papers* 14 (1886): 522–42.

———. "General Lee in the Wilderness Campaign." *Battles and Leaders of the Civil War* 4: 240–46.

Walker, John G. "Jackson's Capture of Harper's Ferry." *Battles and Leaders of the Civil War* 2: 604–11.

———. "Sharpsburg." *Battles and Leaders of the Civil War* 2: 675–82.

Wallace, Lee A. "Sussex Light Dragoons, Virginia State Cavalry, 1861." *Military Collector & Historian* 7 (1955): 22.

Watson, Thomas J. "Was with 'Jeb' Stuart When He Was Shot." *Confederate Veteran* 11 (1903): 553.

Watson, Walter C. "The Fighting at Sailor's Creek." *Confederate Veteran* 25 (1917): 448–52.

Wert, Jeffry. "His Unhonored Service." *Civil War Times Illustrated* 24 (June 1985): 29–34.

Willcox, Orlando B. "Actions on the Weldon Railroad." *Battles and Leaders of the Civil War* 4: 568–73.

Williams, Albert F. "A. F. Williams Diary, 1862." *Lower Cape Fear Historical Society Bulletin* 17 (1974): 1–6.

Williams, Robert A. "Haw's Shop: A 'Storm of Shot and Shell'." *Civil War Times Illustrated* 9 (January 1971): 12–19.

Wilson, James Harrison. "The Cavalry of the Army of the Potomac." *Papers of the Military Histoical Society of Massachusetts* 13 (1880): 33–88.

Winschel, Terrence J. "The Jeff Davis Legion at Gettysburg." *Gettysburg Magazine* 12 (January 1995): 68–82.

Wooldridge, William B. "Itinerary of the Fourth Virginia Cavalry, March 27th–April 9th, 1865." *Southern Historical Society Papers* 17 (1889): 376–78.

Young, T. J. "Battle of Brandy Station." *Confederate Veteran* 23 (1915): 171–72.

BOOKS AND PAMPHLETS

Ackinclose, Timothy R. *Sabres and Pistols: The Civil War Career of Colonel Harry Gilmor, C.S.A.* Gettysburg, Pa.: Stan Clark Military Books, 1997.

Address Delivered Before R. E. Lee Camp, C.V. . . . in the Acceptance of the Portrait of General William H. Payne, by Leigh Robinson. Richmond: Wm. Ellis Jones, 1909.

Alexander, Edward Porter. *Fighting for the Confederacy: The Personal Recollections of General Edward Porter Alexander.* Edited by Gary A. Gallagher. Chapel Hill: University of North Carolina Press, 1989.

———. *Military Memoirs of a Confederate: A Critical Narrative.* New York: Charles Scribner's Sons, 1907.

Allardice, Bruce S. *More Generals in Gray.* Baton Rouge: Louisiana State University Press, 1995.

Anders, Curt. *Fighting Confederates.* New York: G. P. Putnam's Sons, 1968.

Anthony, William. *History of the Battle of Hanover . . . Tuesday, June 30, 1863.* Hanover, Pa.: Hanover Chamber of Commerce, 1945.

Armstrong, Richard L. *7th Virginia Cavalry.* Lynchburg, Va.: H. E. Howard, 1992.

———. *11th Virginia Cavalry.* Lynchburg, Va.: H. E. Howard, 1989.

Avirett, James B., et al. *The Memoirs of General Turner Ashby and His Compeers.* Baltimore: Selby & Dulany, 1867.

Balfour, Daniel T. *13th Virginia Cavalry.* Lynchburg, Va.: H. E. Howard, 1986.

Barnes, James H. *Recollections of a Confederate Soldier, James Henry Barnes, 1833–1909, as Told to His Daughter, Macon E. Barnes.* N.p.: privately issued, n.d.

Barringer, Rufus. *The First North Carolina—A Famous Cavalry Regiment.* N.p.: privately issued, ca. 1866.

Bartholomees, J. Boone, Jr. *Buff Facings and Gilt Buttons: Staff and Headquarters Operations in the Army of Northern Virginia, 1863–1865.* Columbia: University of South Carolina Press, 1998.

Bates, Louella H. *Confederate Cavalry: The Last Days of Chivalry.* Jacksonville, Fla.: privately issued, 1989.

Baylor, George. *Bull Run to Bull Run; or, Four Years in the Army of Northern Virginia . . .* Richmond: B. F. Johnson Publishing Co., 1900.

Beale, George W. *A Lieutenant of Cavalry in Lee's Army.* Boston: Gorham Press, 1918.

Beale, R. L. T. *History of the Ninth Virginia Cavalry, in the War Between the States.* Richmond: B. F. Johnson Co., 1899.

Bigelow, John, Jr. *The Campaign of Chancellorsville: A Strategic and Tactical Study.* New Haven, Conn.: Yale University Press, 1910.

Bilby, Joseph G. *Civil War Firearms: Their Historical Background, Tactical Use and Modern Collecting and Shooting.* Conshohocken, Pa.: Combined Books, 1996.

Black, John L. *Crumbling Defenses; or, Memoirs and Reminiscences of John Logan Black, Colonel, C.S.A.* Edited by Eleanor D. McSwain. Macon, Ga.: J. W. Burke Co., 1960.

Black, Robert C., III. *The Railroads of the Confederacy.* Chapel Hill: University of North Carolina Press, 1952.

Blackford, Charles M., and Susan Leigh Blackford. *Letters from Lee's Army . . .* Edited by Charles Minor Blackford, III. New York: Charles Scribner's Sons, 1947.

———. *Memoirs of Life in and out of the Army in Virginia during the War Between the States . . .* Edited by Charles Minor Blackford. 2 vols. Lynchburg, Va.: J. P. Bell Co., 1894–96.

Blackford, William W. *War Years with Jeb Stuart.* New York: Charles Scribner's Sons, 1945.

Blue, John. *Hanging Rock Rebel: Lt. John Blue's War in West Virginia and the Shenandoah Valley.* Edited by Dan Oates. Shippensburg, Pa.: Burd Street Press, 1994.

Boatner, Mark M., III. *The Civil War Dictionary.* New York: David McKay Co., 1959.

Booth, George Wilson. *Personal Reminiscences of a Maryland Soldier in the War Between the States, 1861–65.* Baltimore: Fleet, McGinley & Co., 1898.

Boykin, Edward. *Beefsteak Raid.* New York: Funk & Wagnalls Co., 1960.

Boykin, Edward M. *The Falling Flag: Evacuation of Richmond, Retreat and Surrender at Appomattox, by an Officer of the Rear-Guard.* New York: E. J. Hale & Son, 1874.

Boykin, Richard M. *Captain Alexander Hamilton Boykin, One of South Carolina's Distinguished Citizens.* New York: Pandick Press, 1942.

Brackett, Albert G. *History of the United States Cavalry . . . to the 1st of June, 1863.* New York: Harper & Brothers, 1865.

Brennan, Patrick. *"To Die Game": Major General Jeb Stuart.* Gettysburg, Pa.: Farnsworth House Military Impressions, 1998.

Brooks, U. R. *Butler and His Cavalry in the War of Secession, 1861–1865.* Columbia, S.C.: State Co., 1909.

Brooksher, William R., and David K. Snider. *Glory at a Gallop: Tales of the Confederate Cavalry.* Washington, D.C.: Brassey's, 1995.

Brown, R. Shepard. *Stringfellow of the Fourth.* New York: Crown Publishers, 1960.

Bushong, Millard K., and Dean M. Bushong. *Fightin' Tom Rosser, C.S.A.* Shippensburg, Pa.: Beidel Printing House, 1983.

Calkins, Chris M. *The Appomattox Campaign, March 29–April 9, 1865.* Conshohocken, Pa.: Combined Books, 1997.

———. *The Battles of Appomattox Station and Appomattox Court House, April 8–9, 1865.* Lynchburg, Va.: H. E. Howard, 1987.

Carmichael, Peter S. *Lee's Young Artillerist: William R. J. Pegram.* Charlottesville: University of Virginia Press, 1995.

Carter, Arthur B. *Tarnished Cavalier: Major General Earl Van Dorn, C.S.A.* Knoxville: University of Tennessee Press, 1999.

Carter, Samuel, III. *The Last Cavaliers: Confederate and Union Cavalry in the Civil War.* New York: St. Martin's Press, 1979.

Carter, William Harding. *Horses, Saddles and Bridles.* Baltimore: Lord Baltimore Press, 1902.

Carter, William R. *Sabres, Saddles, and Spurs: The Diary of Lt. Col. William R. Carter, 3rd Virginia Cavalry.* Edited by Walbrook D. Swank. Shippensburg, Pa.: Burd Street Press, 1998.

Cauthen, Charles E., ed. *Family Letters of the Three Wade Hamptons, 1782–1901.* Columbia, S.C.: University of South Carolina Press, 1953.

Cavalry Tactics. Philadelphia: J. B. Lippincott & Co., 1862.

Chalfant, William Y. *Cheyennes and Horse Soldiers: The 1857 Expedition and the Battle of Solomon's Fork.* Norman: University of Oklahoma Press, 1989.

Chamberlain, Joshua L. *The Passing of the Armies: An Account of the Final Campaign of the Army of the Potomac* . . . New York: G. P. Putnam's Sons, 1915.

Chewning, Charles A. *The Journal of Charles A. Chewning, Company E, 9th Virginia Cavalry, C.S.A.* Edited by Richard B. Armstrong. N.p.: privately issued, n.d.

Clark, Walter, ed. *Histories of the Several Regiments and Battalions from North Carolina in the Great War 1861–'65* . . . 5 vols. Goldsboro, N.C.: Nash Brothers; Raleigh, N.C.: E. M. Uzzell, 1901.

Coddington, Edwin B. *The Gettysburg Campaign: A Study in Command.* New York: Charles Scribner's Sons, 1968.

Coggins, Jack. *Arms and Equipment of the Civil War.* Garden City, N.Y.: Doubleday & Co., 1962.

Cole, Scott C. *34th Virginia Cavalry.* Lynchburg, Va.: H. E. Howard, 1993.

Coltrane, Daniel B. *The Memoirs of Daniel Branson Coltrane, Co. I, 63rd Reg., N.C. Cavalry, C.S.A.* Raleigh, N.C.: Edwards & Broughton Co., 1956.

Conrad, Thomas N. *The Rebel Scout: A Thrilling History of Scouting Life in the Southern Army.* N.p.: privately issued, 1904.

Cooke, Jacob B. *The Battle of Kelly's Ford, March 17, 1863.* Providence, R.I.: privately issued, 1887.

Cooke, Joel. *The Siege of Richmond: A Narrative of the Military Operations of Major-General George B. McClellan during May and June, 1862.* Philadelphia: G. W. Childs, 1862.

Cooke, John Esten. *Wearing of the Gray: Being Personal Portraits, Scenes and Adventures of the War.* Baton Rouge: Louisiana State University Press, 1997.

Cooke, Philip St. George. *Cavalry Tactics or Regulations for the Instruction, Formations, and Movements of the Cavalry of the Army and Volunteers of the United States*. Washington, D.C.: Government Printing Office, 1862.

Cooper, Samuel. *Cooper's Cavalry Tactics, for the Use of Volunteers*. New Orleans: H. P. Lathrop; Jackson, Miss.: Power & Cadwallader, 1861.

Cormier, Steven A. *The Siege of Suffolk: The Forgotten Campaign, April 11-May 4, 1863*. Lynchburg, Va.: H. E. Howard, 1989.

Corson, William Clark. *My Dear Jennie: A Collection of Love Letters from a Confederate Soldier to His Fiancée during the Period 1861–1865*. Edited by Blake W. Corson, Jr. Richmond: Dietz Press, 1982.

Couper, William. *One Hundred Years at V.M.I.* 4 vols. Richmond, Va.: Garrett & Massie, 1939–40.

Cowles, Calvin D., comp. *Atlas to Accompany the Official Records of the Union and Confederate Armies*. Washington, D.C.: Government Printing Office, 1891–95.

Crosland, Charles. *Reminiscences of the Sixties*. Columbia, S.C.: State Co., ca. 1910.

Crowninshield, Benjamin W. *The Battle of Cedar Creek, October 19, 1864*. Cambridge, Mass.: Riverside Press, 1879.

Cullen, Joseph P. *The Peninsula Campaign, 1862: McClellan & Lee Struggle for Richmond*. Harrisburg, Pa.: Stackpole Books, 1973.

Cullum, George W., comp. *Biographical Register of the Officers and Graduates of the U.S. Military Academy . . .* 2 vols. Boston: Houghton, Mifflin & Co., 1891.

Cunliffe, Marcus. *Soldiers & Civilians: The Martial Spirit in America, 1775–1865*. Boston: Little, Brown & Co., 1968.

Current, Richard N., ed. *Encyclopedia of the Confederacy*. 4 vols. New York: Simon & Schuster, 1993.

Dabney, Robert L. *A Memorial of Lieut. Colonel John C. Thornton, of the Third Virginia Cavalry, C.S.A.* Richmond: Presbyterian Committee of Publication, 1864.

Daly, Louise P. H. *Alexander Cheves Haskell: The Portrait of a Man*. Norwood, Mass.: Plimpton Press, 1934.

Davis, Burke. *Jeb Stuart, the Last Cavalier*. New York: Rinehart & Co., 1957.

———. *To Appomattox: Nine April Days, 1865*. New York: Rinehart & Co., 1959.

Davis, J. Lucius. *The Trooper's Manual; or, Tactics for Light Dragoons and Mounted Riflemen*. Richmond: A. Morris, 1861.

Davis, Julia. *Mount Up: A True Story Based on the Reminiscences of Major E. A. H. McDonald of the Confederate Cavalry*. New York: Harcourt, Brace & World, 1967.

Davis, William C. *Battle at Bull Run: A History of the First Major Campaign of the Civil War*. Garden City, N.Y.: Doubleday & Co., 1977.

Dawson, Francis W. *Reminiscences of Confederate Service, 1861–1865.* Edited by Bell Irvin Wiley. Baton Rouge: Louisiana State University Press, 1980.

Dawson, John Harper. *Wildcat Cavalry: A Synoptic History of the Seventeenth Virginia Cavalry . . .* Dayton, Ohio: Morningside House, 1982.

Denison, George T. *A History of Cavalry from the Earliest Times . . .* London: Macmillan Co., 1913.

Dickinson, Jack L. *8th Virginia Cavalry.* Lynchburg, Va.: H. E. Howard, 1986.

———. *16th Virginia Cavalry.* Lynchburg, Va.: H. E. Howard, 1989.

———. *Records of the 16th Virginia Cavalry.* Barboursville, W. Va.: privately issued, 1984.

Divine, John E. *35th Battalion Virginia Cavalry.* Lynchburg, Va.: H. E. Howard, 1985.

Dodge, Theodore A. *The Campaign of Chancellorsville.* Boston: James R. Osgood & Co., 1881.

Doster, William E. *Lincoln and Episodes of the Civil War.* New York: G. P. Putnam's Sons, 1915.

Doubleday, Abner. *Chancellorsville and Gettysburg.* New York: Charles Scribner's Sons, 1882.

Douglas, Henry Kyd. *I Rode with Stonewall: Being Chiefly the War Experiences of the Youngest Member of Jackson's Staff . . .* Chapel Hill: University of North Carolina Press, 1940.

Dowdey, Clifford. *Lee's Last Campaign: The Story of Lee and His Men against Grant—1864.* Boston: Little, Brown & Co., 1960.

Downey, Fairfax. *Clash of Cavalry: The Battle of Brandy Station, June 9, 1863.* New York: David McKay Co., 1959.

———. *The Guns at Gettysburg.* New York: David McKay Co., 1958.

Driver, Robert J., Jr. *First & Second Maryland Cavalry, C.S.A.* Charlottesville, Va.: Rockbridge Publishing, 1999.

———. *1st Virginia Cavalry.* Lynchburg, Va.: H. E. Howard, 1991.

———. *5th Virginia Cavalry.* Lynchburg, Va.: H. E. Howard, 1997.

———. *10th Virginia Cavalry.* Lynchburg, Va.: H. E. Howard, 1992.

———. *14th Virginia Cavalry.* Lynchburg, Va.: H. E. Howard, 1988.

———, and H. E. Howard. *2nd Virginia Cavalry.* Lynchburg, Va.: H. E. Howard, 1995.

Dufour, Charles L. *Nine Men in Gray.* Garden City, N.Y.: Doubleday & Co., 1963.

Dulany, Richard H., et al. *The Dulanys of Welbourne: A Family in Mosby's Confederacy.* Edited by Margaret Ann Vogtsberger. Berryville, Va.: Rockbridge Publishing Co., 1995.

Early, Jubal A. *War Memoirs: Autobiographical Sketch and Narrative of the War Between the States.* Edited by Frank E. Vandiver. Bloomington: Indiana University Press, 1960.

Eggleston, George Cary. *A Rebel's Recollections.* New York: G. P. Putnam's Sons, 1878.

Encounter at Hanover: Prelude to Gettysburg. Hanover, Pa.: Hanover Chamber of Commerce, 1963.

Evans, Clement A., ed. *Confederate Military History.* 13 vols. Atlanta: Confederate Publishing Co., 1899.

Faust, Patricia L., ed. *The Historical Times Illustrated Encyclopedia of the Civil War.* New York: Harper & Row, 1986.

Fortier, John. *15th Virginia Cavalry.* Lynchburg, Va.: H. E. Howard, 1993.

Freeman, Douglas Southall. *Lee's Lieutenants: A Study in Command.* 3 vols. New York: Charles Scribner's Sons, 1942–44.

———. *R. E. Lee: A Biography.* 4 vols. New York: Charles Scribner's Sons, 1934–35.

Fremantle, Arthur James Lyon. *Three Months in the Southern States, April–June, 1863.* New York: John Bradburn, 1864.

Frye, Dennis E. *12th Virginia Cavalry.* Lynchburg, Va.: H. E. Howard, 1988.

Furgurson, Ernest B. *Chancellorsville: The Souls of the Brave.* New York: Alfred A. Knopf, 1992.

Gallagher, Gary A. *Stephen Dodson Ramseur, Lee's Gallant General.* Chapel Hill: University of North Carolina Press, 1985.

Gallaher, DeWitt C. *A Diary Depicting the Experiences of DeWitt Clinton Gallaher in the War Between the States while Serving in the Confederate Army.* Charleston, S.C.: privately issued, 1945.

Garnett, Theodore S. *J. E. B. Stuart . . . An Address . . .* New York: Neale Publishing Co., 1907.

———. *Riding with Stuart: Reminiscences of an Aide-de-Camp.* Edited by Robert J. Trout. Shippensburg, Pa.: White Mane Publishing Co., 1991.

Garraty, John A., and Mark C. Carnes, eds. *American National Biography.* 24 vols. New York: Oxford University Press, 1999.

Gaston, John T. *Confederate War Diary of John Thomas Gaston.* Compiled by Alifaire Gaston Walden. Columbia, S.C.: Vogue Press, 1960.

Gill, John. *Reminiscences of Four Years as a Private Soldier in the Confederate Army, 1861–1865.* Baltimore: Sun Printing Office, 1904.

Gilmor, Harry. *Four Years in the Saddle.* New York: Harper & Brothers, 1866.

Glatthaar, Joseph T. *Partners in Command: The Relationships Between Leaders in the Civil War.* New York: Free Press, 1994.

Goff, Richard D. *Confederate Supply.* Durham, N.C.: Duke University Press, 1969.

Goldsborough, W. W. *The Maryland Line in the Confederate States Army.* Baltimore: Kelly, Piet & Co., 1869.

Grant, Ulysses S. *Personal Memoirs of U. S. Grant.* 2 vols. New York: Charles L. Webster & Co., 1885–86.

Green, Charles O. *An Incident in the Battle of Middleburg, Va., June 17, 1863.* Providence, R.I.: privately issued, 1911.

Greene, A. Wilson. *Breaking the Backbone of the Rebellion: The Final Battles of the Petersburg Campaign.* Mason City, Ia.: Savas Publishing Co., 2000.

Grimsley, Daniel A. *Battles in Culpeper County, Virginia, 1861–1865*. Culpeper, Va.: Raleigh-Travers-Green Co., 1900.

Hackley, Woodford B. *The Little Fork Rangers: A Sketch of Company "D," Fourth Virginia Cavalry*. Richmond: Dietz Printing Co., 1927.

Haden, B. J. *Reminiscences of J. E. B. Stuart's Cavalry* . . . Charlottesville, Va.: Progress Publishing Co., ca. 1890.

Hamlin, Augustus C. *The Battle of Chancellorsville* . . . Bangor, Maine: privately issued, 1896.

Harris, Nathaniel E. *Autobiography: The Story of an Old Man's Life, with Reminiscences of Seventy-five Years*. Macon, Ga.: J. W. Burke Co., 1925.

Harris, Nelson. *17th Virginia Cavalry*. Lynchburg, Va.: H. E. Howard, 1994.

Harsh, Joseph L. *Taken at the Flood: Robert E. Lee and Confederate Strategy in the Maryland Campaign of 1862*. Kent, Ohio: Kent State University Press, 1999.

Hartje, Robert G. *Van Dorn: The Life and Times of a Confederate General*. Nashville, Tenn.: Vanderbilt University Press, 1967.

Hartley, Chris J. *Stuart's Tarheels: James B. Gordon and His North Carolina Cavalry*. Baltimore: Butternut & Blue, 1996.

Haskell, John Cheves. *The Haskell Memoirs*. Edited by Gilbert E. Govan and James W. Livingood. New York: G. P. Putnam's Sons, 1960.

Hassler, William W. *Colonel John Pelham, Lee's Boy Artillerist*. Chapel Hill: University of North Carolina Press, 1965.

Heathcote, Charles W. *The Cavalry Struggle in the Battle of Gettysburg on July 3, 1863*. West Chester, Pa.: Horace Temple, 1959.

Heatwole, John L. *The Burning: Sheridan in the Shenandoah Valley*. Berryville, Va.: Rockbridge Publishing Co., 1999.

Hebert, Walter H. *Fighting Joe Hooker*. Indianapolis: Bobbs-Merrill Co., 1944.

Heitman, Francis B., comp. *Historical Register and Dictionary of the United States Army* . . . 2 vols. Washington, D.C.: Government Printing Office, 1903.

Henderson, E. Prioleau. *Autobiography of Arab*. Columbia, S.C.: R. L. Bryan Co., 1901.

Hendrickson, Robert. *The Road to Appomattox*. New York: John Wiley & Sons, 1998.

Hennessy, John J. *The First Battle of Manassas: An End to Innocence, July 18–21, 1861*. Lynchburg, Va.: H. E. Howard, 1989.

———. *Return to Bull Run: The Campaign and Battle of Second Manassas*. New York: Simon & Schuster, 1993.

Herr, John K., and Edward S. Wallace. *The Story of the U.S. Cavalry, 1775–1942*. Boston: Little, Brown & Co., 1953.

Heth, Henry. *The Memoirs of Henry Heth*. Edited by James L. Morrison, Jr. Westport, Conn.: Greenwood Press, 1974.

Hewett, Janet, et al., eds. *Supplement to the Official Records of the Union and Confederate Armies.* 3 pts., 95 vols. to date. Wilmington, N.C.: Broadfoot Publishing Co., 1994- .

Hoge, John M. *A Journal by John Milton Hoge, 1862–5 . . .* Cincinnati: M. H. Bruce, 1961.

Holland, Darryl. *24th Virginia Cavalry.* Lynchburg, Va.: H. E. Howard, 1997.

Holland, Lynwood M. *Pierce M. B. Young, the Warwick of the South.* Athens: University of Georgia Press, 1964.

Hopkins, Donald A. *Horsemen of the Jeff Davis Legion: The Expanded Roster of the Men and Officers of the Jeff Davis Legion, Cavalry, Army of Northern Virginia.* Shippensburg, Pa.: White Mane Publishing Co., 1999.

————. *The Little Jeff: The Jeff Davis Legion, Cavalry, Army of Northern Virginia.* Shippensburg, Pa.: White Mane Publishing Co., Inc., 1999.

Hopkins, Luther W. *From Bull Run to Appomattox: A Boy's View.* Baltimore: Fleet McGinley Co., 1908.

Horn, John. *The Petersburg Campaign, June 1864–April 1865.* Conshohocken, Pa.: Combined Books, 1993.

————. *The Petersburg Campaign: The Destruction of the Weldon Railroad, Deep Bottom, Globe Tavern, and Reams Station, August 14–25, 1864.* Lynchburg, Va.: H. E. Howard, 1991.

Howard, McHenry. *Recollections of a Maryland Confederate Soldier and Staff Officer under Johnston, Jackson and Lee.* Baltimore: Williams & Wilkins Co., 1914.

Howard, Wiley C. *Sketch of Cobb Legion Cavalry and Some Incidents and Scenes Remembered . . .* Atlanta: privately issued, 1901.

Hudgins, Robert S., II. *Recollections of an Old Dominion Dragoon: The Civil War Experiences of Sgt. Robert S. Hudgins II, Company B, 3rd Virginia Cavalry.* Edited by Garland C. Hudgins and Richard B. Kleese. Orange, Va.: Publisher's Press, 1993.

Hume, Edgar E. *Colonel Heros von Borcke, a Famous Prussian Volunteer in the Confederate States Army.* Edited by J. D. Eggleston. Charlottesville, Va.: Historical Publishing Co., 1935.

Humphreys, Andrew A. *Gettysburg to the Rapidan: The Army of the Potomac, July, 1863, to April, 1864.* New York: Charles Scribner's Sons, 1883.

————. *The Virginia Campaign of '64 and '65: The Army of the Potomac and the Army of the James.* New York: Charles Scribner's Sons, 1883.

Jacobs, Lee, comp. *The Gray Riders: Stories from the Confederate Cavalry.* Shippensburg, Pa.: Burd Street Press, 1999.

Johnson, Curt. *Cavalry Battles of the American Civil War.* Washington, D.C.: Brassey's, 1999.

Johnston, Angus James, II. *Virginia Railroads in the Civil War.* Chapel Hill: University of North Carolina Press, 1961.

Johnston, Joseph E. *Narrative of Military Operations during the Civil War.* New York: D. Appleton & Co., 1874.

Johnston, R. M. *Bull Run: Its Strategy and Tactics.* Boston: Houghton Mifflin Co., 1913.

Jomini, Henri. *Summary of the Art of War . . .* Edited by O. F. Winship and E. E. McLean. New York: Putnam, 1854.

Jones, J. B. *A Rebel War Clerk's Diary at the Confederate States Capital.* Edited by Howard Swiggett. 2 vols. New York: Old Hickory Bookshop, 1935.

Jones, J. William. *Personal Reminiscnces of General Robert E. Lee.* Baton Rouge: Louisiana State University Press, 1995.

Jones, Thomas G. *Last Days of the Army of Northern Virginia: An Address Delivered . . . before the Virginia Division of the Association of the Army of Northern Virginia . . .* Richmond: privately issued, 1893.

Jones, Virgil Carrington. *Eight Hours before Richmond.* New York: Henry Holt & Co., 1957.

———. *Gray Ghosts and Rebel Raiders.* New York: Henry Holt & Co., 1956.

———. *Ranger Mosby.* Chapel Hill: University of North Carolina Press, 1944.

Jones, Walter B. *The Great Cannoneer: An Address on the Life and Military Genius of Major John Pelham, C.S.A. . . .* Montgomery, Ala.: privately issued, ca. 1929.

Keen, Hugh C., and Horace Mewborn. *43rd Battalion Virginia Cavalry, Mosby's Command.* Lynchburg, Va.: H. E. Howard, 1993.

Kellogg, Sanford C. *The Shenandoah Valley and Virginia, 1861 to 1865: A War Study.* New York: Neale Publishing Co., 1903.

Keys, Thomas B. *Tarheel Cossack: W. P. Roberts, Youngest Confederate General.* Orlando, Fla.: privately issued, 1983.

King, Katherine Gray, comp. *The Seven Gray Brothers of the Confederate Cavalry.* Rochester, N.Y.: privately issued, 1983.

Kinsley, Ardyce, comp. *The Fitzhugh Lee Sampler.* Lively, Va.: Brandylane Publishers, 1992.

Knapp, David, Jr. *The Confederate Horsemen.* New York: Vantage Press, 1966.

Krick, Robert K. *9th Virginia Cavalry.* Lynchburg, Va.: H. E. Howard, 1982.

———. *Lee's Colonels: A Biographical Register of the Field Officers of the Army of Northern Virginia.* Dayton: Morningside Bookshop, 1979.

Ladd, David L., and Audrey J. Ladd, eds. *The Bachelder Papers: Gettysburg in Their Own Words . . .* Dayton: Morningside, 1994.

Lambert, Dobbie Edward. *Grumble: The W. E. Jones Brigade of 1863–1864.* Wahiawa, Hawaii: Lambert Enterprises, 1992.

Lee, Fitzhugh. *General Lee.* New York: D. Appleton & Co., 1894.

Lee, Robert E. *Lee's Dispatches: Unpublished Letters of General Robert E. Lee, C.S.A., to Jefferson Davis and the War Department of the Confederate States of America.* Edited by Douglas Southall Freeman and Grady McWhiney. New York: G. P. Putnam's Sons, 1957.

———. *The Wartime Papers of Robert E. Lee.* Edited by Clifford Dowdey and Louis H. Manarin. Boston: Little, Brown & Co., 1961.

Lewis, Thomas A. *The Guns of Cedar Creek.* New York: Harper & Row, 1988.

List of Staff Officers of the Confederate States Army, 1861–1865. Washington, D.C.: Government Printing Office, 1891.

Long, A. L. *Memoirs of Robert E. Lee: His Military and Personal History* . . . New York: J. M. Stoddart & Co., 1886.

Long, E. B., and Barbara Long. *The Civil War Day by Day: An Almanac, 1861–1865.* Garden City, N.Y.: Doubleday & Co., 1971.

Longacre, Edward G. *The Cavalry at Gettysburg: A Tactical Study of Mounted Operations during the Civil War's Pivotal Campaign, 9 June-14 July 1863.* Rutherford, N.J.: Fairleigh Dickinson University Press, 1986.

———. *Lincoln's Cavalrymen: A History of the Mounted Forces of the Army of the Potomac, 1861–1865.* Mechanicsburg, Pa.: Stackpole Books, 2000.

———. *Mounted Raids of the Civil War.* South Brunswick, N.J.: A. S. Barnes & Co., 1975.

———. *To Gettysburg and Beyond: The Twelfth New Jersey Volunteer Infantry, II Corps, Army of the Potomac, 1862–1865.* Hightstown, N.J.: Longstreet House, 1988.

Longstreet, James. *From Manassas to Appomattox: Memoirs of the Civil War in America.* Philadelphia: J. B. Lippincott Co., 1896.

Lonn, Ella. *Foreigners in the Confederacy.* Chapel Hill: University of North Carolina Press, 1940.

Mahan, Dennis Hart. *An Elementary Treatise on Advanced-Guard, Out-post, and Detached Service of Troops* . . . New York: John Wiley, 1853.

Mahon, Michael G. *The Shenandoah Valley, 1861–1865: The Destruction of the Granary of the Confederacy.* Mechanicsburg, Pa.: Stackpole Books, 1999.

Mahr, Theodore C. *Early's Valley Campaign: The Battle of Cedar Creek* . . . *October 1-30, 1864.* Lynchburg, Va.: H. E. Howard, 1992.

Mansfield, James R. *Robert Henry Jerrell (1843–1907) (Pvt. Co. E, 9th Virginia Cal [Cav.], C.S.A.)* . . . N.p.: privately issued, 1966.

Marks, J. J. *The Peninsular Campaign in Virginia* . . . Philadelphia: J. B. Lippincott & Co., 1864.

Marshall, Charles. *An Aide-de-Camp of Lee: Being the Papers of Colonel Charles Marshall* . . . Edited by Sir Frederick Maurice. Boston: Little, Brown & Co., 1927.

Marshall, Fielding L. *Recollections and Reflections of Fielding Lewis Marshall, a Virginian Gentleman of the Old School.* Compiled by Maria Newton Marshall. Orange, Va.: privately issued, 1911.

Martin, David G. *Gettysburg, July 1.* Conshohocken, Pa.: Combined Publishing, 1996.

Martin, Samuel J. *Kill-Cavalry: The Life of Union General Hugh Judson Kilpatrick.* Mechanicsburg, Pa.: Stackpole Books, 2000.

———. *Southern Hero: Matthew Calbraith Butler, Confederate General, Hampton Red Shirt, and U.S. Senator.* Mechanicsburg, Pa.: Stackpole Books, 2001.

Matter, William D. *If It Takes All Summer: The Battle of Spotsylvania*. Chapel Hill: University of North Carolina Press, 1988.

Maury, Dabney H. *Recollections of a Virginian in the Mexican, Indian, and Civil Wars*. New York: Charles Scribner's Sons, 1894.

Mays, Samuel E. *Genealogical Notes on the Family of Mays and Reminiscences of the War Between the States from Notes Written around the Campfires*. Plant City, Fla.: Plant City Enterprise, 1927.

McCabe, James D., Jr. *Life and Campaigns of General Robert E. Lee*. Atlanta: National Publishing Co., 1866.

McCabe, W. Gordon. *A Brief Sketch of Andrew Reid Venable, Jr., Formerly A.A. and Inspector General, Cavalry Corps, A.N.V.* Richmond: Wm. Ellis Jones, 1909.

————. *Theodore Stanford Garnett, Jr., 1844–1915*. Richmond: Virginia Historical Society, 1916.

McCarthy, Carlton. *Detailed Minutiae of Soldier Life in the Army of Northern Virginia, 1861-1865*. Richmond: Carlton McCarthy & Co., 1882.

McClellan, George B. *The Civil War Papers of George B. McClellan: Selected Correspondence, 1860–1865*. Edited by Stephen W. Sears. New York: Ticknor & Fields, 1989.

————. *McClellan's Own Story*. New York: Charles L. Webster & Co., 1887.

McClellan, Henry B. *The Life and Campaigns of Maj. Gen. J. E. B. Stuart, Commander of the Cavalry of the Army of Northern Virginia*. Boston: Houghton, Mifflin & Co., 1885.

McDonald, William N. *A History of the Laurel Brigade, Originally The Ashby Cavalry of the Army of Northern Virginia, and Chew's Battery*. Edited by Bushrod C. Washington. Baltimore: Sun Job Printing Office, 1907.

McKim, Randolph H. *A Soldier's Recollections: Leaves from the Diary of a Young Confederate . . .* New York: Longmans, Green, and Co., 1910.

McMurry, Richard M. *John Bell Hood and the War for Southern Independence*. Lexington: University Press of Kentucky, 1982.

————. *Two Great Rebel Armies: An Essay in Confederate Military History*. Chapel Hill: University of North Carolina Press, 1989.

McWhiney, Grady, and Perry D. Jamieson. *Attack and Die: Civil War Military Tactics and the Southern Heritage*. University, Ala.: University of Alabama Press, 1982.

Mercer, Philip. *The Life of the Gallant Pelham*. Macon, Ga.: J. W. Burke Co., 1929.

Merrill, James M. *Spurs to Glory: The Story of the United States Cavalry*. Chicago: Rand, McNally & Co., 1966.

Milham, Charles G. *Gallant Pelham, American Extraordinary*. Washington, D.C.: Public Affairs Press, 1959.

Miller, J. Michael. *The North Anna Campaign: "Even to Hell Itself," May 21–26, 1864*. Lynchburg, Va.: H. E. Howard, 1989.

Miller, Millard J. *My Grandpap Rode with Jeb Stuart: Experiences of James Knox Polk Ritchie, Company H, Twelfth Virginia Cavalry, Laurel Brigade, Army of Northern Virginia* . . . Westerville, Ohio: privately issued, 1974.

Montero, Aristides. *War Reminiscences by the Surgeon of Mosby's Command.* Richmond: privately issued, 1890.

Moore, Frank, ed. *The Rebellion Record: A Diary of American Events.* 12 vols. New York: various publishers, 1861–68.

Moore, Robert H., II. *Chew's Ashby, Shoemaker's Lynchburg, and the Newtown Artillery.* Lynchburg, Va.: H. E. Howard, 1995.

———. *The 1st and 2nd Stuart Horse Artillery.* Lynchburg, Va.: H. E. Howard, 1985.

———. *Graham's Petersburg, Jackson's Kanawha, and Lurty's Roanoke Horse Artillery.* Lynchburg, Va.: H. E. Howard, 1996.

Mosby, John Singleton. *The Letters of John S. Mosby.* Edited by Adele H. Mitchell. N.p.: Stuart-Mosby Historical Society, 1986.

———. *The Memoirs of Colonel John S. Mosby.* Edited by Charles Wells Russell. Boston: Little, Brown, & Co., 1917.

———. *Mosby's War Reminiscences and Stuart's Cavalry Campaigns.* Boston: G. A. Jones & Co., 1887.

———. *Stuart's Cavalry in the Gettysburg Campaign.* New York: Moffat, Yard & Co., 1908.

Mulligan, Abner B. *"My Dear Mother and Sisters": Civil War Letters of Capt. A. B. Mulligan, Co. B, 5th South Carolina Cavalry, Butler's Division, Hampton's Corps, 1861–1865.* Spartanburg, S.C.: Reprint Co., 1992.

Murfin, James V. *The Gleam of Bayonets: The Battle of Antietam and the Maryland Campaign of 1862.* New York: A. S. Barnes & Co., 1965.

Musick, Michael P. *6th Virginia Cavalry.* Lynchburg, Va.: H. E. Howard, 1990.

Myers, Franklin M. *The Comanches: A History of White's Battalion, Virginia Cavalry, Laurel Brig., Hampton['s] Div., A.N.V., C.S.A.* Baltimore: Kelly, Piet & Co., 1871.

Nanzig, Thomas P. *3rd Virginia Cavalry.* Lynchburg, Va.: H. E. Howard, 1989.

Neese, George M. *Three Years in the Confederate Horse Artillery.* New York: Neale Publishing Co., 1911.

Nelson, Horatio. *"If I am killed on this trip, I want my horse kept for my brother": The Diary of the Last Weeks in the Life of a Young Confederate Cavalryman.* Edited by Harold Howard. Manassas, Va.: Manassas Chapter, United Daughters of the Confederacy, 1980.

Nesbitt, Mark. *Saber and Scapegoat: J. E. B. Stuart and the Gettysburg Controversy.* Mechanicsburg, Pa.: Stackpole Books, 1994.

Newhall, F. C. *How Lee Lost the Use of His Cavalry before the Battle of Gettysburg.* Philadelphia: privately issued, 1878.

Nichols, James L. *General Fitzhugh Lee: A Biography.* Lynchburg, Va.: H. E. Howard, 1989.

Nye, Wilbur S. *Here Come the Rebels!* Baton Rouge: Louisiana State University Press, 1965.

O'Ferrall, Charles T. *Forty Years of Active Service . . . from Private to Lieutenant-Colonel and Acting Colonel in the Cavalry of the Army of Northern Virginia . . .* New York: Neale Publishing Co., 1904.

Olson, John E. *21st Virginia Cavalry.* Lynchburg, Va.: H. E. Howard, 1989.

O'Neill, Robert F. *The Cavalry Battles of Aldie, Middleburg and Upperville: "Small But Important Riots," June 10-27, 1863.* Lynchburg, Va.: H. E. Howard, 1993.

Opie, John N. *A Rebel Cavalryman with Lee, Stuart, and Jackson.* Chicago: W. B. Conkey Co., 1899.

Owen, William Miller. *In Camp and Battle with the Washington Artillery of New Orleans . . .* Boston: Ticknor & Co., 1885.

Parker, William L. *General James Dearing, C.S.A.* Lynchburg, Va.: H. E. Howard, 1990.

Peavey, James D. *Confederate Scout: Virginia's Frank Stringfellow.* Onancock, Va.: Eastern Shore Publishing Co., 1956.

Peck, Rufus H. *Reminiscences of a Confederate Soldier of Co. C, 2nd Va. Cavalry.* Fincastle, Va.: privately issued, 1913.

Pender, William Dorsey. *The General to His Lady: The Civil War Letters of William Dorsey Pender to Fanny Pender.* Edited by William W. Hassler. Chapel Hill: University of North Carolina Press, 1965.

Pennsylvania at Gettysburg. 2 vols. Harrisburg, Pa.: B. Singerly, 1893.

Pfanz, Donald C. *Richard S. Ewell: A Soldier's Life.* Chapel Hill: University of North Carolina Press, 1998.

Pollard, Henry R. *Memoirs and Sketches of the Life of Henry Robinson Pollard: An Autobiography.* Richmond: Lewis Printing Co., 1923.

Pond, George E. *The Shenandoah Valley in 1864.* New York: Charles Scribner's Sons, 1883.

Pope, John. *The Military Memoirs of General John Pope.* Edited by Peter Cozzens and Robert Girardi. Chapel Hill: University of North Carolina Press, 1998.

Power, J. Tracy. *Lee's Miserables: Life in the Army of Northern Virginia from the Wilderness to Appomattox.* Chapel Hill: University of North Carolina Press, 1998.

Price, William H. *The Battle of Brandy Station.* Vienna, Va.: Civil War Research Associates, 1963.

Proceedings of the General Court Martial, in the Case of Lieut. Col. H. Clay Pate, 5th Va. Cavalry. Richmond: privately issued, 1863.

Ramage, James A. *Gray Ghost: The Life of Col. John Singleton Mosby.* Lexington: University Press of Kentucky, 1999.

Rea, D. B. *Sketches from Hampton's Cavalry, Embracing the Principal Exploits of the Cavalry in the Campaigns of 1862 and 1863.* Columbia, S.C.: South Carolina Press, 1864.

Rhea, Gordon C. *The Battle of the Wilderness, May 5–6, 1864.* Baton Rouge: Louisiana State University Press, 1994.

———. *The Battles for Spotsylvania Court House and the Road to Yellow Tavern, May 7–12, 1864.* Baton Rouge: Louisiana State University Press, 1997.

———. *To the North Anna River: Grant and Lee, May 13–25, 1864.* Baton Rouge: Louisiana State University Press, 2000.

Rhodes, Charles D. *History of the Cavalry of the Army of the Potomac.* Kansas City, Mo.: Hudson-Kimberly Publishing Co., 1900.

Rich, Edward R. *Comrades Four.* New York: Neale Publishing Co., 1907.

Riley, Franklin L. *Grandfather's Journal: Company B, Sixteenth Mississippi Infantry Volunteers . . .* Edited by Austin C. Dobbins. Dayton: Morningside, 1988.

Ripley, Warren. *Artillery and Ammunition of the Civil War.* New York: Promontory Press, 1970.

Robertson, James I., Jr. *General A. P. Hill: The Story of a Confederate Warrior.* New York: Random House, 1987.

———. *The Stonewall Brigade.* Baton Rouge: Louisiana State University Press, 1963.

———. *Stonewall Jackson: The Man, the Soldier, the Legend.* New York: Macmillan Co., 1997.

Rodenbough, Theophilus F., and William L. Haskin, eds. *The Army of the United States: Historical Sketches of Staff and Line . . .* New York: Merrill & Co., 1896.

Rodick, Burleigh Cushing. *Appomattox, the Last Campaign.* New York: Philosophical Library, 1965.

Rogers, Ford H. *"Jeb" Stuart's Hat . . .* Detroit: privately issued, 1893.

The Roll of Officers and Members of the Georgia Hussars . . . Savannah, Ga.: Morning News Co., ca. 1906.

Roman, Alfred. *The Military Operations of General Beauregard in the War Between the States, 1861–1865.* 2 vols. New York: Harper & Brothers, 1884.

Ropes, John C. *The Army under Pope.* New York: Charles Scribner's Sons, 1882.

Ross, Fitzgerald. *Cities and Camps of the Confederate States.* Edited by Richard B. Harwell. Urbana: University of Illinois Press, 1958.

Rosser, Thomas L. *Addresses of Gen'l T. L. Rosser, at the Seventh Annual Reunion of the Association of the Maryland Line . . .* New York: L. A. Williams Printing Co., 1889.

———. *Riding with Rosser.* Edited by S. Roger Keller. Shippensburg, Pa.: White Mane Publishing Co., 1997.

Royall, William L. *Some Reminiscences.* New York: Neale Publishing Co., 1909.

Rummel, George A., III. *Cavalry on the Roads to Gettysburg: Kilpatrick at Hanover and Hunterstown.* Shippensburg, Pa.: White Mane Publishing Co., 2000.

Scales, Alfred M. *The Battle of Fredericksburg: An Address . . .* Washington, D.C.: R. O. Polkinhorn & Son, 1884.

Scheibert, Justus. *Seven Months in the Rebel States during the North American War, 1863.* Edited by William Stanley Hoole. Tuscaloosa, Ala.: Confederate Publishing Co., 1958.

Schildt, John W. *Roads from Gettysburg.* Shippensburg, Pa.: Burd Street Press, 1998.

———. *September Echoes: The Maryland Campaign of 1862 . .* Middletown, Md.: Valley Register, 1960.

Schultz, Duane. *The Dahlgren Affair: Terror and Conspiracy in the Civil War.* New York: W. W. Norton & Co., 1998.

Scott, J. L. *36th and 37th Battalions Virginia Cavalry.* Lynchburg, Va.: H. E. Howard, 1986.

Scott, John. *Partisan Life with Col. John S. Mosby.* New York: Harper & Brothers, 1867.

Sears, Stephen W. *Chancellorsville.* Boston: Houghton Mifflin Co., 1996.

———. *George B. McClellan: The Young Napoleon.* New York: Ticknor & Fields, 1988.

———. *Landscape Turned Red: The Battle of Antietam.* New Haven, Conn.: Ticknor & Fields, 1983.

———. *To the Gates of Richmond: The Peninsula Campaign.* New York: Ticknor & Fields, 1992.

Sheridan, Philip H. *Personal Memoirs of P. H. Sheridan.* 2 vols. New York: Charles L. Webster & Co., 1888.

Shoemaker, John J. *Shoemaker's Battery, Stuart's Horse Artillery, Pelham's Battalion . . .* Memphis: S.C. Toof & Co., 1908.

Sibley, F. Ray, Jr. *The Confederate Order of Battle: The Army of Northern Virginia.* Shippensburg, Pa.: White Mane Publishing Co., Inc., 1999.

Siepel, Kevin H. *Rebel: The Life and Times of John Singleton Mosby.* New York: Da Capo Press, 1997.

Simmons, Sampson S. *Memories of Sampson Sanders Simmons, a Confederate Veteran.* Edited by Naomi Sanders Klipstein. Pasadena, Calif.: Publications Press, 1954.

Smith, Gustavus W. *The Battle of Seven Pines.* New York: C. G. Crawford, 1891.

Smith, Hampden H. *J. E. B. Stuart: A Character Sketch.* Ashland, Va.: privately issued, n.d.

Sommers, Richard J. *Richmond Redeemed: The Siege at Petersburg.* Garden City, N.Y.: Doubleday & Co., 1981.

Sorrel, G. Moxley. *Recollections of a Confederate Staff Officer.* New York: Neale Publishing Co., 1905.

Stackpole, Edward J. *Chancellorsville, Lee's Greatest Battle*. Harrisburg, Pa.: Stackpole Co., 1958.

———. *Drama on the Rappahannock: The Fredericksburg Campaign*. Harrisburg, Pa.: Military Service Publishing Co., 1957.

———. *From Cedar Mountain to Antietam, August–September, 1862: Cedar Mountain—Second Manassas—Chantilly—Harpers Ferry—South Mountain—Antietam*. Harrisburg, Pa.: Stackpole Co., 1959.

———. *Sheridan in the Shenandoah: Jubal Early's Nemesis*. Harrisburg, Pa.: Stackpole Co., 1961.

———. *They Met at Gettysburg*. Harrisburg, Pa.: Eagle Books, 1956.

Starr, Stephen Z. *The Union Cavalry in the Civil War*. 3 vols. Baton Rouge: Louisiana State University Press, 1979–85.

Steere, Edward. *The Wilderness Campaign*. Harrisburg, Pa.: Stackpole Co., 1960.

Steffen, Randy. *The Horse Soldier, 1776–1943: The United States Cavalryman—His Uniforms, Arms, Accoutrements, and Equipments*. 4 vols. Norman: University of Oklahoma Press, 1977–80.

Stern, Philip Van Doren. *An End to Valor: The Last Days of the Civil War*. Boston: Houghton Mifflin Co., 1958.

Stiles, Kenneth L. *4th Virginia Cavalry*. Lynchburg, Va.: H. E. Howard, 1985.

Stiles, Robert. *Four Years under Marse Robert*. New York: Neale Publishing Co., 1903.

Stokes, William. *Saddle Soldiers: The Civil War Correspondence of General William Stokes of the 4th South Carolina Cavalry*. Edited by Lloyd Halliburton. Orangeburg, S.C.: Sandlapper Publishing Co., 1993.

Stonebraker, Joseph R. *A Rebel of '61* . . . New York: Wynkoop-Hallenbeck-Crawford Co., 1899.

Stribling, Robert M. *Gettysburg Campaign and Campaigns of 1864 and 1865 in Virginia*. Petersburg, Va.: Franklin Press Co., 1905.

Stringfellow, Frank. *War Reminiscences: The Life of a Confederate Scout Inside the Enemy's Line*. N.p.: privately issued, 1882.

Stuart, James Ewell Brown. *Letters of General J. E. B. Stuart to His Wife, 1861*. Edited by Bingham Duncan. Atlanta: Emory University Publications, 1943.

———. *The Letters of Major General James E. B. Stuart*. Edited by Adele H. Mitchell. N.p.: Stuart-Mosby Historical Society, 1990.

Sullivan, James W. *Boyhood Memories of the Civil War, 1861–'65: Invasion of Carlisle*. Carlisle, Pa.: privately issued, 1933.

Swank, Walbrook D. *Battle of Trevilian Station: The Civil War's Greatest and Bloodiest All-Cavalry Battle*. Shippensburg, Pa.: Burd Street Press, 1994.

———. *Clash of Sabres, Blue and Gray*. Columbus, Ohio: Avenelle Associates, 1981.

———, ed. *Confederate Letters and Diaries, 1861–1865*. Shippensburg, Pa.: White Mane Publishing Co., 2000.

Sword, Wiley. *Southern Invincibility: A History of the Confederate Heart.* New York: St. Martin's Press, 1999.

Symonds, Craig L. *Joseph E. Johnston: A Civil War Biography.* New York: W. W. Norton & Co., 1994.

Tagg, Larry. *The Generals of Gettysburg: An Appraisal of the Leaders of America's Greatest Battle.* Mason City, Ia.: Savas Publishing Co., 1998.

Tancig, W. J. *Confederate Military Land Units.* New York: Thomas Yoseloff, 1967.

Tanner, Robert G. *Stonewall in the Valley: Thomas J. "Stonewall" Jackson's Shenandoah Valley Campaign, Spring 1862.* Garden City, N.Y.: Doubleday & Co., 1976.

Taylor, Walter H. *Four Years with General Lee* . . . New York: D. Appleton & Co., 1877.

———. *General Lee: His Campaigns in Virginia, 1861–1865* . . . Norfolk, Va.: Nusbaum Book & News Co., 1906.

———. *Lee's Adjutant: The Wartime Letters of Colonel Walter Herron Taylor.* Edited by R. Lockwood Tower. Columbia: University of South Carolina Press, 1995.

Thomas, Clarence. *General Turner Ashby, the Centaur of the South.* Winchester, Va.: Eddy Press Corp., 1907.

Thomas, Emory M. *Bold Dragoon: The Life of J. E. B. Stuart.* New York: Harper & Row, 1986.

———. *Robert E. Lee: A Biography.* New York: W. W. Norton & Co., 1997.

Thomason, John W., Jr. *Jeb Stuart.* New York: Charles Scribner's Sons, 1930.

Trout, Robert J. *In the Saddle with Stuart.* Gettysburg, Pa.: Thomas Publications, 1998.

———. *They Followed the Plume: The Story of J. E. B. Stuart and His Staff.* Mechanicsburg, Pa.: Stackpole Books, 1993.

———, ed. *With Pen and Saber: The Letters and Diaries of J. E. B. Stuart's Staff Officers.* Mechanicsburg, Pa.: Stackpole Books, 1995.

Trowbridge, Luther S. *The Operations of the Cavalry in the Gettysburg Campaign.* Detroit: privately issued, 1888.

Trudeau, Noah Andre. *Bloody Roads South: The Wilderness to Cold Harbor, May–June 1864.* Boston: Little, Brown & Co., 1989.

———. *The Last Citadel.* Boston: Little, Brown & Co., 1991.

———. *Out of the Storm: The End of the Civil War, April–June 1865.* Boston: Little, Brown & Co., 1994.

Trueheart, Charles W., and Henry M. Trueheart. *Rebel Brothers: The Civil War Letters of the Truehearts.* Edited by Edward B. Williams. College Station: Texas A&M University Press, 1995.

Turner, George E. *Victory Rode the Rails: The Strategic Place of the Railroads in the Civil War.* Indianapolis: Bobbs-Merrill Co., 1953.

Utley, Robert M. *Frontiersmen in Blue: The United States Army and the Indian, 1848–1865.* New York: Macmillan Co., 1967.

Vandiver, Frank E. *Jubal's Raid: General Early's Famous Attack on Washington in 1864.* New York: McGraw-Hill Book Co., 1960.

———. *Ploughshares into Swords: Josiah Gorgas and Confederate Ordnance.* Austin: University of Texas Press, 1952.

Volunteer Cavalry—The Lessons of a Decade, by a Volunteer Cavalryman. New York: privately issued, 1871.

von Borcke, Heros. *Memoirs of the Confederate War for Independence.* 2 vols. New York: Peter Smith, 1938.

von Borcke, Heros, and Justus Scheibert. *Die Grosse Reiterschlacht bei Brandy Station, 9. Juni 1863.* Berlin: Paul Kittel, 1893.

Wagner, Arthur L., comp. *Cavalry Studies from Two Great Wars.* Kansas City, Mo.: Hudson-Kimberly Publishing Co., 1896.

Wainwright, Charles S. *A Diary of Battle: The Personal Journals of Colonel Charles S. Wainwright, 1861–1865.* Edited by Allan Nevins. New York: Harcourt, Brace & World, 1962.

Wallace, Lee A., Jr. *A Guide to Virginia Military Organizations, 1861–1865.* Richmond: Virginia Civil War Commission, 1964.

Ware, W. H. *The Battle of Kelly's Ford, Fought March 17, 1863.* Newport News, Va.: Warwick Printing Co., 1922.

Warner, Ezra J. *Generals in Blue: Lives of the Union Commanders.* Baton Rouge: Louisiana State University Press, 1964.

———. *Generals in Gray: Lives of the Confederate Commanders.* Baton Rouge: Louisiana State University Press, 1959.

War of the Rebellion: A Compilation of the Official Records of the Union and Confederate Armies. 4 series, 70 vols. in 128. Washington, D.C.: Government Printing Ofice, 1880–1901.

Watson, George W. *The Last Survivor: The Memoirs of George William Watson, a Horse Soldier in the 12th Virginia Cavalry (Confederate States Army).* Edited by Brian Stuart Kesterton. Washington, W.Va.: Night Hawk Press, 1993.

Weaver, Jeffrey C. *22nd Virginia Cavalry.* Lynchburg, Va.: H. E. Howard, 1991.

Webb, Alexander S. *The Peninsula: McClellan's Campaign of 1862.* New York: Charles Scribner's Sons, 1881.

Wellman, Manly Wade. *Giant in Gray: A Biography of Wade Hampton of South Carolina.* New York: Charles Scribner's Sons, 1949.

Wells, Edward L. *Hampton and His Cavalry.* Richmond: B. F. Johnson Publishing Co., 1899.

———. *A Sketch of the Charleston Light Dragoons, from the Earliest Formation of the Corps . . .* Charleston, S.C.: Lucas, Richardson & Co., 1888.

Wensyel, James W. *Appomattox: The Passing of the Armies.* Shippensburg, Pa.: White Mane Publishing Co., 2000.

Wert, Jeffry D. *From Winchester to Cedar Creek: The Shenandoah Campaign of 1864.* Carlisle, Pa.: South Mountain Press, 1987.

————. *General James Longstreet, the Confederacy's Most Controversial Soldier: A Biography.* New York: Simon & Schuster, 1993.

————. *Mosby's Rangers.* New York: Simon & Schuster, 1990.

Wheeler, Joseph. *A Revised System of Cavalry Tactics, for the Use of the Cavalry and Mounted Infantry, C.S.A.* 3 vols. Mobile, Ala.: S. H. Goetze & Co., 1863.

Wiley, Bell Irvin. *The Life of Johnny Reb: The Common Soldier of the Confederacy.* Indianapolis: Bobbs-Merrill Co., 1943.

Williams, T. Harry. *P. G. T. Beauregard, Napoleon in Gray.* Baton Rouge: Louisiana State University Press, 1954.

Williamson, James J. *Mosby's Rangers: A Record of the Operations of the Forty-third Battalion Virginia Cavalry.* New York: Ralph B. Kenyon, 1896.

Williamson, Mary L. *Life of J. E. B. Stuart.* Edited by E. O. Wiggins. Richmond: B. F. Johnson Publishing Co., 1914.

Wilson, James Harrison. *Captain Charles Corbit's Charge at Westminster . . . An Episode of the Gettysburg Campaign.* Wilmington, Del.: Delaware State Historical Society, 1913.

————. *Under the Old Flag: Recollections of Military Operations in the War for the Union, the Spanish War, the Boxer Rebellion, etc.* 2 vols. New York: D. Appleton & Co., 1912.

Wilson, William L. *A Borderland Confederate.* Edited by Festus P. Summers. Pittsburgh: University of Pittsburgh Press, 1962.

Wise, Jennings Cropper. *The Long Arm of Lee; or, The History of the Artillery of the Army of Northern Virginia . . .* 2 vols. Lynchburg, Va.: J. P. Bell, 1915.

Wise, John S. *The End of an Era.* Boston: Houghton, Mifflin Co., 1899.

Wittenberg, Eric J. *Gettysburg's Forgotten Cavalry Actions.* Gettysburg, Pa.: Thomas Publications, 1998.

————. *Glory Enough for All: Sheridan's Second Raid and the Battle of Trevilian Station.* Washington, D.C.: Brassey's, 2001.

Woodworth, Steven E. *Davis and Lee at War.* Lawrence: University Press of Kansas, 1995.

Wormser, Richard. *The Yellowlegs: The Story of the United States Cavalry.* Garden City, N.Y.: Doubleday & Co., 1966.

Wright, Marcus J. *General Officers of the Confederate Army . . .* New York: Neale Publishing Co., 1911.

Yates, Bernice-Marie. *Jeb Stuart Speaks: An Interview with Lee's Cavalryman.* Shippensburg, Pa.: White Mane Publishing Co., 1996.

Young, Bennett H. *Confederate Wizards of the Saddle: Being Reminiscences and Observations of One Who Rode with Morgan.* Boston: Chapple Publishing Co., Ltd., 1914.

INDEX